Public Spending and the Poor

Public Spending and the Poor

Theory and Evidence

Edited by
Dominique van de Walle
Kimberly Nead

Published for the World Bank
The Johns Hopkins University Press
Baltimore and London

© 1995 The International Bank for Reconstruction
and Development / THE WORLD BANK
1818 H Street, N.W.
Washington, D.C. 20433, U.S.A.

The Johns Hopkins University Press
Baltimore, Maryland 21211-2190, U.S.A.

MAIN

'⁰ 7160811

The findings, interpretations, and conclusions expressed in this study are entirely those of the authors and should not be attributed in any manner to the World Bank, to its affiliated organizations, or to members of its Board of Executive Directors or the countries they represent.

The material in this publication is copyrighted. Requests for permission to reproduce portions of it should be sent to the Office of the Publisher at the address shown in the copyright notice above. The World Bank encourages dissemination of its work and will normally give permission promptly and, when the reproduction is for noncommercial purposes, without asking a fee. Permission to copy portions for classroom use is granted through the Copyright Clearance Center, Inc., Suite 910, 222 Rosewood Drive, Danvers, Massachusetts 01923, U.S.A.

The complete backlist of publications from the World Bank is shown in the annual *Index of Publications*, which contains an alphabetical title list (with full ordering information) and indexes of subjects, authors, and countries and regions. The latest edition is available free of charge from the Distribution Unit, Office of the Publisher, The World Bank, 1818 H Street, N.W., Washington, D.C. 20433, U.S.A., or from Publications, The World Bank, 66, avenue d'Iéna, 75116 Paris, France.

Photographs on the cover, clockwise from upper left: a health clinic in Zaire, by Jennie I. Litvack; getting water at a public tap in Viet Nam, by Jennie I. Litvack; a health clinic in Rajasthan, India, by Curt Carnemark; children on their way to school in Sri Lanka, by Jennie I. Litvack; a public employment construction site in Benin, by Maurice Asseo.

Library of Congress Cataloging-in-Publication Data

Public spending and the poor : theory and evidence / edited by
    Dominique van de Walle, Kimberly Nead
        p. cm.
    "Published for the World Bank."
    Includes bibliographical references.
    ISBN 0-8018-5255-2
    1. Economic assistance, Domestic. 2. Expenditures, Public.
3. Government spending policy. 4. Transfer payments. 5. Income
distribution. 6. Welfare economics. I. van de Walle, Dominique.
II. Nead, Kimberly, 1960—   . III. International Bank for
Reconstruction and Development.
HC79.P63P83   1955
362.5'8—dc20   95-43787
                                                                    CIP

Contents

Foreword

Does public spending help the poor? Are there ways—such as finer targeting—to improve the impact of public spending on the poor? These are the questions at the heart of the research reported in this volume.

When deciding whether to read this volume, someone with an interest in public policy would want to know if these questions are important and if the volume sheds light on the answers. On the first, the reader can be assured that these are indeed important questions—public spending net of interest payments typically amounts to 20–25 percent of gross national product and therefore has the potential to influence poverty significantly; yet at the same time, demands on limited public resources are increasing, so getting more from less—as in targeting—becomes essential. On the second, the reader looking for definitive and universal policy conclusions may be disappointed. But the reader who recognizes the complexity of the issues, who is sensitive to the data limitations, and who wants to learn how to make better decisions in the future will reap enormous benefit from this volume.

Why is it so difficult to come to definitive conclusions? The answer lies in two sets of reasons. First, the analytical framework and empirical foundation for making decisions on the broad allocation of public spending are deficient. Yet, as this volume attests, whether to allocate public resources to, say, primary or tertiary education has a major impact on the well-being of the poor. Second, comprehensive evaluations of more targeted interventions—public works programs, for example—are sorely lacking. And yet again, as this volume shows, our assessment of such programs depends critically on what individuals forgo in order to participate in the scheme. The volume provides the best advice possible on how to approach these issues based on the latest available research.

Perhaps its main message, however, is to call attention to the weakness of the analytical and empirical base for making decisions that many would regard as fundamental to good governance, long-run development, and the eradication of poverty. Providing more guidance on how to allocate public spending to different categories to the greatest benefit of all and on how to design targeted interventions to greatest effect emerges from this study as a clear priority for future research.

Lyn Squire
Director, Policy Research Department
The World Bank

Acknowledgments

Much of the credit for instigating this project must go to Emmanuel Jimenez. For their leadership, advice and other forms of guidance and encouragement in the project we are grateful to Shankar Acharya, Nancy Birdsall, Shanta Devarajan, Emmanuel Jimenez, Johannes Linn, Lyn Squire, Lawrence Summers, and especially Martin Ravallion. We are enormously grateful to the authors for their contributions and their patience with the process of bringing a book to publication.

Preliminary drafts of the chapters in this book were presented and discussed at a World Bank conference in June of 1992. In addition to the authors, we would like to thank all conference participants and in particular, Shankar Acharya, Nicholas Barr, Timothy Besley, Nancy Birdsall, Edgar Chigudu, Stephen Coate, Anis Dani, Mark Gersovitz, Paul Gertler, Paul Glewwe, James Gordon, Lawrence Haddad, Ann Hamilton, Mahbub ul Haq, Gregory Ingram, Norman Ireland, Paul Isenman, Johannes Linn, Sarah Loza, Patricia Matte Larain, William McGreevey, Jonathan Morduch, Sanjay Pradhan, Rigoberto Quintero Torres, Mannete Ramaili, Smarajit Ray, Shlomo Reutlinger, Soekirman, Lyn Squire, Lawrence Summers, Suresh Tendulkar, Tesfaye Teklu, Vinod Thomas, Joachim von Braun, Michael Walton, and Patrick Webb.

The Ministry of Foreign Affairs of the Government of the Netherlands provided financial support without which the project would not have been possible. For their help in facilitating that support, we would like to thank the Minister for Development Cooperation, as well as Onno Ruhl and Eveline Herfkens. Financial help was also received from the World Bank's Research Support Budget and the Public Economics Division of the Policy Research Department.

We would also like to acknowledge the World Bank's Editorial Committee and three anonymous referees who provided useful comments and suggestions on the book manuscript.

Finally, special thanks go to Susheela Jonnakuty, Peggy Pender, Cynthia Bernardo, and Hedy Sladovich for their secretarial assistance and other support in preparing the manuscript, and to Ding Dizon, Elizabeth Forsyth, Audrey Heiligman, Alfred Imhoff, Donna Daniels Verdier, and others with the Bank's Office of the Publisher for bringing the book to its final form.

Contributors

Chapter authors and their affiliations as of late 1995:

Harold Alderman — Poverty and Human Resources Division, Policy Research Department, World Bank

Simon Appleton — Centre for the Study of African Economies, University of Oxford

Anthony B. Atkinson — Nuffield College, University of Oxford

Jere R. Behrman — Department of Economics, University of Pennsylvania

James A. Cercone — Consultant to the World Bank

Paul Collier — Centre for the Study of African Economies, University of Oxford and Kennedy School of Government, Harvard University.

Richard Cornes — Department of Economics, Keele University

Giovanni Andrea Cornia — UNICEF-International Child Development Center, Italy

Donald Cox — Department of Economics, Boston College

Gaurav Datt — Poverty and Human Resources Division, Policy Research Department, World Bank

Anil B. Deolalikar — Department of Economics, University of Washington

Donna M. Gibbons — Department of Economics, Carleton College

Margaret E. Grosh — Poverty and Human Resources Division, Policy Research Department, World Bank

Jeffrey S. Hammer — Public Economics Division, Policy Research Department, World Bank

Sarah J. Jarvis — Research Center on Micro-Social Change in Britain, University of Essex

Emmanuel Jimenez — Poverty and Human Resources Division, Policy Research Department, World Bank

Ravi Kanbur — Africa Regional Office, World Bank

Michael Keen — Department of Economics, University of Essex

Shahrukh Khan — Sustainable Policy Development Institute, Islamabad, Pakistan

John Micklewright — Department of Economics, European University Institute, Florence and Queen Mary and Westfield College, University of London

Branko Milanovic — Transition Economies Division, Policy Research Department, World Bank

Ijaz Nabi — East Asia and Pacific Region, World Bank

Kimberly Nead — Consultant to the World Bank

Mark M. Pitt — Department of Economics, Brown University

Martin Ravallion — Poverty and Human Resources Division, Policy Research Department, World Bank

Mark R. Rosenzweig — Department of Economics, University of Pennsylvania

David R. Ross — Department of Economics, Bryn Mawr College

Richard Sabot — Department of Economics, Williams College

David E. Sahn — Food and Nutrition Policy Program, Cornell University

Thomas M. Selden — Center for Intramural Research, Agency for Health Care Policy and Research, U.S. Department of Health and Human Services

Amartya Sen — Economics and Philosophy departments, Harvard University

Frances Stewart — Queen Elizabeth House, University of Oxford

Matti Tuomala — Department of Economics, University of Jyvaskyla, Finland

Dominique van de Walle — Public Economics Division, Policy Research Department, World Bank

Michael J. Wasylenko — Department of Economics, Syracuse University

1 Introduction

Dominique van de Walle

Public spending should promote efficiency (by correcting for various market failures) and equity (by improving the distribution of economic welfare). This book is concerned with the latter objective. It asks: Is the redistributive aim being met by current spending practices? What room is there for improvement? The book aims to bring together some of the best recent research on these questions.

The concern about the distributional outcomes of public spending stems from three sources:

(1) *Dissatisfaction with distributional outcomes in the absence of intervention.* Market failures—lack of access to credit, for example—may leave many households facing acute poverty. But even a well-functioning market economy can result in too much poverty and inequality according to prevailing social norms.

(2) *The lack of alternative policy instruments.* In high-income countries, the tax system provides an additional redistributive device to promote equity. In developing countries, where comprehensive income taxes are generally not a viable option, the tax system is much less useful in this task. Public spending's role in redistribution becomes that much more vital.

(3) *The need for fiscal restraint and the sharp tradeoffs this makes governments face.* Governments play a key role in the provision of certain public services, which are increasingly seen to be of critical importance to developing countries, notably inputs to human capital development such as basic schooling and health care. Provision is expensive, and so hard policy choices come to the fore. Information on distributional impacts—particularly the extent to which the poorest strata benefit—can help in making those choices. But getting the information can be expensive too.

How can research inform these issues? There has been a long-standing interest in the distribution of the benefits of public spending.

But it is only with the recent availability of high-quality household-level surveys that such studies have been able to achieve a level of disaggregation (across both benefit and beneficiary types) especially conducive to policy use. Nevertheless, the few incidence studies undertaken during the 1970s and the early 1980s (in an early flurry of interest in this question in the context of developing countries) have had considerable influence. The early empirical studies for developing countries often called for increased targeting and price discrimination, on the one hand, and cost recovery, on the other. Despite their tentative nature, these conclusions—based on extrapolation from a few country studies and using what most agree is less-than-ideal methodology—have often changed policies.

The recent literature has focused on some of the more worrying methodological drawbacks of the earlier studies and the need to allow for behavioral responses when measuring impacts. New approaches to measuring public spending impacts have used regression analysis on microdata sets to measure the consumer's willingness to pay for services or to quantify impacts on other measures of individual well-being. Improvements have also been made to the more traditional approaches. Previous conclusions have in some cases been reinforced or moderated and in others overturned. However, the lessons and insights from the latest investigations have not yet been properly digested or incorporated into policy discussions.

Meanwhile, many recent World Bank and other policy documents now call for increased targeting of government expenditures toward the poor. It is claimed that universal provision is too costly and fails to have much impact on poverty and that targeting can promote cost-effectiveness. So, in the context of pressures to reduce public expenditures, the view has become widespread that targeting allows governments to reduce poverty more effectively and at lower cost.

Such claims implicitly assume that incomes can be observed with little error and that the observed initial incomes are fixed, that is, unaffected by the policy. In reality, the policymaker has imperfect information and can incur (possibly high) administrative costs in attempting to identify the poor with precision. Furthermore, potential recipients often face an incentive to alter their behavior when facing a targeted (or untargeted) scheme. Potential losers from perfect targeting may also exercise greater political influence than gainers; political economy considerations may militate against the policy ideal of perfect targeting.

Although the literature recognizes that targeting imposes costs, we know very little about the actual costs associated with different forms of targeting. Without further research on its costs and benefits, we cannot operate on the presumption that targeting is an efficient instrument for fighting poverty in all circumstances. This is very much an area where received truths have led to policy prescriptions with little basis in knowledge about what really works and what does not.

This volume brings together recent policy-oriented research on public spending and poverty in developing and transition economies. The studies span the following specific questions: What is the incidence of existing public expenditures? What has been the trend? What can new data and methodological advances bring to the subject? Are past findings on the distribution of benefits upheld by the new studies? How can the distribution of benefits be improved? What are the arguments for and against targeting as a means of improving incidence? Is better targeting a more cost-effective means of reducing poverty than the policy alternatives, including universal provision? What are the arguments for and against alternative targeting mechanisms in terms of cost-effectiveness?

Recent innovations in theory, econometric techniques, and computing technology, and access to better household-level data sets, have allowed the subject to progress in many new and fruitful directions. Yet, I do not believe one could presently write an honest and nonmisleading treatise aimed at providing policymakers with tried and true answers to the above questions. A lot more analytical research, careful project evaluation work, and sensitivity analysis are necessary before that is the case. While this book points to policy directions, it also explores methodological questions of consequence to policy implications. Much of the included research is devoted to developing methodological tools for the analysis of poverty-reducing policy.

There are types of public spending that the book does not cover in any depth. The focus is primarily on the distribution of benefits from those categories of spending that have traditionally been perceived to be actually or potentially pro-poor. For example, this excludes outlays on physical infrastructure and many public goods, which have generally been assumed to benefit all equally. Studies have examined the distributional impacts of various infrastructural services—such as the provision of electricity or safe water—but in general, this has been a relatively neglected area of research and there are few new analyses to draw on.

Research on public spending and the poor has often illuminated the conceptual and methodological weaknesses in common methods of policy analysis. Part I consists of five chapters that examine some of the theoretical and methodological issues concerning public spending and poverty. How should we define the welfare objective? How should we measure the benefits and welfare effects of publicly provided goods? Chapter 2 by Amartya Sen examines how the chosen welfare objective, the quantifiable costs, and social and political conditions determine how finely to target. Grounding its arguments both in theory and in European and U.S. experience with social security benefits to families with children, chapter 3 by Anthony Atkinson then evaluates the scope for and limitations of targeting, given the range of policy instruments, objectives, and constraints. Richard Cornes focuses in chapter 4 on the conceptual and theoretical framework for attributing benefits from publicly provided public and private goods. In chapter 5, Ravi Kanbur, Michael Keen, and Matti Tuomala provide a theoretical exposition of the implications of variable labor supply for the design of poverty-alleviation schemes and targeting rules using both welfarist and non-welfarist frameworks. Finally, how to deal with the endogeneity of program placement in estimating the impact of public spending is the concern of Mark Pitt, Mark Rosenzweig, and Donna Gibbons in chapter 6, where they empirically investigate the issue for Indonesia.

Readers may find that the theoretical concerns of part I are not always reflected in the empirical studies that follow. This reflects a real tension between the empirical and theoretical ends of this field. Few people have tried to bring these ends together. By attempting to take this further and to mix theoretical and applied contributions to the subject, the book exposes a tension that is structural in the current state of the subject. Our hope is to move the understanding of how to bridge the gap further.

Among the various categories of public spending, the social sectors—education and health—have figured most prominently in concerns about impacts on poverty. In parts II and III, the book turns to empirical studies of spending in the education and health sectors, respectively. Each section consists of a chapter that uses the more conventional benefit incidence methodology and one that attempts to get at some of the same issues through econometric analysis. Both education studies examine policy options for improving the distribution of education spending. In chapter 7, Thomas Selden and Michael Wasylenko analyze the distributional implications of higher fees and reduced travel time to schools in Peru and compare methodologies. Chapter 8, by Harold Alderman, Jere Behrman, Shahrukh Khan, David Ross, and Richard Sabot, focuses on whether targeting schooling quantity and quality improvements to educationally disadvantaged groups in rural Pakistan implies an efficiency tradeoff. The two health sector studies, chapter 9 by myself and chapter 10 by Anil Deolalikar, share setting and time period: Indonesia during the 1970s and 1980s. However, their different analytical approaches enable them to investigate rather different aspects of government health spending.

Cash transfers have been an important instrument of poverty-alleviation policy in many countries, and they are the topic of the two chapters in part IV. A study of Hungary's family allowance scheme by Sarah Jarvis and John Micklewright investigates its historical development, incidence, and ways in which targeting could be improved (chapter 11). The overall impact, and policy and measurement implications, of introducing public transfer programs where private inter-household transfers are widespread are the focus of Donald Cox and Emmanuel Jimenez in chapter 12, using data for the Philippines.

Part V deals with another widely used set of potentially pro-poor spending policy instruments, namely food subsidy schemes. Policy discussion surrounding these schemes has focused on their high budgetary costs and how to improve targeting. In chapter 13, Giovanni Andrea Cornia and Frances Stewart make a plea for placing more emphasis on errors of exclusion and less on leakage in assessing food subsidy schemes. Labor supply responses of the beneficiaries of Sri Lanka's targeted rice subsidy scheme and their implications for net benefit levels are examined by David Sahn and Harold Alderman in chapter 14.

Public employment schemes have long been relied on as a means of reaching the poor through self-targeting. The evaluation of their cost-effectiveness in direct poverty alleviation is the focus of part VI's sole chapter, by Martin Ravallion and Gaurav Datt. In particular, chapter 15 estimates the costs of participation in the form of the forgone incomes of participants in an Indian public works scheme.

Part VII brings together a series of studies that share an emphasis on comparative techniques and cut across various issues and sectors. Focusing on Latin America, Margaret Grosh (chapter 16) reviews incidence outcomes and administrative costs across a number of cash and in-kind transfer programs classified according to targeting mechanism. In chapter 17, Branko Milanovic describes the distributional impact of social transfer systems in five Eastern European economies and in Russia around the beginning of transition to the market economy and compares their experience with that of Chile and selected countries in the Organization for Economic Cooperation and Development. The distributional incidence of health and education spending and the effects on health and education outcomes in Malaysia are investigated using various methodologies in chapter 18 by Jeffrey Hammer, Ijaz Nabi, and James Cercone. The justification for and feasibility of gender targeting using either generalized or in-kind transfers are examined at length by Simon Appleton and Paul Collier in chapter 19.

Much of the book argues for carefully testing the robustness of data-based policy recommendations to the assumptions underlying them. In terms of methodology and framework, some real disagreements exist in this field. This is to be expected given the ongoing nature of the subject and the different strands of welfare economics. The book's final chapter tries to weave the various methodological concerns, varying assumptions, and approaches into a whole and synthesizes the lessons from the book for both policy and future research on policy.

I Theory and Method

The five chapters composing part I examine some of the key theoretical and methodological issues that arise in analyzing public spending and poverty.

Policy debate on improving the incidence of public program benefits does not always reflect a full appreciation of how economic behavior as well as resources and administrative capabilities influence the performance of programs designed to reduce poverty. Chapters 2, 3, and 5 aim to advance understanding on these issues. The chapters by Sen (chapter 2) and Atkinson (chapter 3) are fairly expansive in scope, examining how a wide range of considerations influence the relative appeal of various degrees of targeting. Kanbur, Keen, and Tuomala (chapter 5) focus more narrowly on how alternative assumptions about labor incentive effects and the welfare objective influence optimal targeting rules.

Amartya Sen's essay, "The Political Economy of Targeting," examines the various costs associated with targeting and shows how they are closely tied to the behavioral responses of beneficiaries and other actors. The chapter describes how these costs limit the scope for, and desirability of, "perfect" targeting. Sen argues that approaches to poverty reduction have often faltered because of a general tendency to treat target groups as passive recipients and to focus almost exclusively on income deprivation. Viewing the subjects of targeting as active agents and treating poverty as a capability handicap rather than just low income can enhance efforts to alleviate poverty.

The chapter by Atkinson shows how the case for narrow targeting of social security programs hinges on certain views regarding policy objectives, the range of instruments available for achieving those objectives, and the constraints under which policy must operate. These issues are examined in the context of programs aimed at providing benefits to families with children in Western high-income countries. Atkinson carefully describes how choices concerning the specifics of the poverty line, the aggregate poverty index, and the indicator of welfare can mold perceptions of the relative efficiency of targeted versus universal transfers and even reverse policy recommendations.

Citing the considerable problems posed by means testing—relating to imperfect information, adverse effects on work incentives, and inadequate take-up of benefits—Atkinson makes a case in favor of universal programs. However, he is at pains to show that few transfers are in reality universally available, as some form of screening conditionality is generally present. A key message is that a rich array of possibilities that are not contingent on low income exist, and are used in practice, for influencing the incidence of programs. Transfers can be made conditional on a combination of characteristics, and benefits can be differentiated across households or incorporated into the tax base.

Taken together, the chapters by Sen and Atkinson encourage a healthy skepticism toward blanket calls for finer targeting. Their expositions clearly demonstrate that the comparative appeal of antipoverty measures can depend crucially on the precise welfare objective and dimension of poverty of concern. Little consensus exists on these matters. The authors differ in that Sen advocates a definition of poverty based on the adequacy of capabilities to perform certain functions, while Atkinson takes a more neutral position on which formulations are to be preferred, instead exploring their implications for the comparative efficiency of programs.

Chapter 5 also underscores the importance of choices regarding the definition of individual welfare and specification of the poverty index for policy decisions related to targeted schemes. Kanbur, Keen, and Tuomala examine how allowing for labor supply responses may require modification in the conception of programs to reduce poverty. The shadow price for labor, which is often implicit in the poverty index, is judged to be critical here. For example, the minimization of income poverty implies a shadow price for labor of zero. In part V, we will see just how important the valuation of leisure can be for evaluating the effectiveness of a transfer program with work disincentives (Sahn and Alderman, chapter 14).

Recent contributions to the literature on targeting have established a series of rules of thumb concerning optimal targeting by commodities, income, and other indicators. Kanbur, Keen, and Tuomala show how sensitive each rule is to assumptions about incentive effects on labor supply and the weight accorded to leisure. The issues addressed relate closely to the optimal tax literature. However, the approach differs in that the welfare objective is defined to be the minimization of a poverty measure within a nonwelfarist framework rather than the maximization of a social welfare function defined on individual utilities.

A frequently cited cost of targeting is that individuals adjust their supply of labor to ensure eligibility for benefits. Both Sen and Atkinson describe how the existence of work disincentives may influence the optimal degree and form of targeting in public programs. Kanbur, Keen, and Tuomala take this point a step further, formally showing just how incentive effects can affect policy recommendations related to targeting. Simulations of income-based targeting reveal that if minimization of income poverty is the policy goal, commonly held principles from the welfarist tradition are reversed. Instead of low marginal tax rates on the poor, simulations under the alternative framework suggest rates exceeding 60 percent. Losses from labor disincentives can dominate gains from targeting.

In chapter 4, Cornes takes a large step back from the fray of the policy debate on targeting and examines (within a welfarist framework) the economic theory relating to the measurement of the distributional impact of public spending in the presence of public goods. Cornes laments what he perceives to be a general neglect of this issue from either a theoretical or applied perspective. In his view, this has allowed an institutionalization of some makeshift techniques to apportion benefits. The chapter argues that such improvisations may be misleading, enough to identify wrongly the direction of a change in welfare in some cases.

Cornes critically reviews the development of the welfare measurement strand of the economics literature, and he suggests a measure related to index number theory that approximates "ideal" welfare measures (such as equivalent incomes) in the presence of public goods yet is not so informationally demanding. However, the measure is limited to providing an ordering of pre- and post-intervention welfare levels and to indicating whether real income has increased or decreased as a result of a policy change. The Cornes measure also requires prices so that the problem of nonmarket goods is not avoided.

Distributional analyses of public spending often use the value of the government subsidy to approximate the benefits of a public service; some of the book's chapters follow this approach. Chapter 4 underscores that the difference between the distribution of subsidies and that of utility gains may not be inconsequential. But while Cornes demonstrates the potential for error with the existing procedures for benefit apportionment, he provides less illumination on the likelihood or magnitude of such miscalculations.

Improvements in the quantity and quality of household-level data for developing countries, and in the sophistication of econometric techniques over the last decade, have permitted credible use of regression analyses to explore empirically various aspects of public spending in the social sectors. A number of the studies presented in this volume, including chapter 6, reflect this trend.

Chapter 6 is also concerned with introducing greater rigor to the measurement of public spending impacts. The focus here is on identifying an empirically valid methodology for estimating the impact of social sector programs on outcome measures such as school enrollment and child mortality rates. Pitt, Rosenzweig, and Gibbons discuss a now well-recognized difficulty in doing so, which has tended to undermine the results obtained from past methodologies used to estimate social sector program impacts in developing countries. They present a methodology that will provide more accurate estimates and demonstrate its use with data for Indonesia.

Pitt, Rosenzweig, and Gibbons argue that program investments are typically a function of political, social, and economic factors of which the researcher is often unaware. Yet, attempts to estimate program impacts have ignored this and treated the location of public programs as a random process. Thus common estimation techniques—comparing the variation across localities in program coverage (say, middle schools) with the variation among areas in program outcomes (say, attendance rates), using cross-sectional data for a single point in time—have tended to obscure real program impacts. The authors are also concerned with the biases that can result from failure to include information on access to other public programs. To obtain more accurate estimates, they recommend including information on a range of programs in the regression equations and using a fixed effects procedure that "sweeps out the unobservable."

Chapter 6 is particularly interesting on two counts. It reveals how the careful merging of separate data bases can substantially extend the possibilities for estimation-based research on public spending. The importance of such ingenuity is likely to continue for a long time, notwithstanding the significant improvements being made in household survey data for developing countries. In addition, its demonstration of the importance of accounting for the endogeneity of program placement when estimating program effects suggests that studies that do not do so risk serious misestimation. This is a point worth noting whether one is a researcher or a consumer of research results.

2 The Political Economy of Targeting

Amartya Sen

The use of the term "targeting" in eradicating poverty is based on an analogy—a target is something fired at. It is not altogether clear whether it is an appropriate analogy. The problem is not so much that the word "target" has combative association. This it does of course have, and the relationship it implies certainly seems more adversarial than supportive. But it is possible to change the association of ideas, and in fact, to some extent, the usage has already shifted in a permissive direction. The more serious problem lies elsewhere—in the fact that the analogy of a target does not at all suggest that the recipient is an active person, functioning on her own, acting and doing things. The image is one of a passive receiver rather than of an active agent.

To see the objects of targeting as *patients* rather than as *agents* can undermine the exercise of poverty removal in many different ways. The people affected by such policies can be very active agents indeed, rather than languid recipients waiting for their handouts. Not to focus on the fact that they think, choose, act, and respond is to miss something terribly crucial to the entire exercise. This is not just a terminological problem. The approach of what is called targeting often has this substantive feature of taking a passive view of the beneficiaries, and this can be a major source of allocational distortion.[1] There is something to be gained from taking, instead, a more activity-centered view of poverty removal.

Let us begin with the central case—the core argument—in favor of targeting. The theoretical point in favor of targeting in antipoverty policy is clear enough: the more accurate a subsidy in fact is in reaching the poor, the less the wastage, and the less it costs to achieve the desired objective. It is a matter of cost-effectiveness in securing a particular benefit. Or, to see it another way, it is one of maximizing the poverty-

The author is grateful to Dominique van de Walle and Kim Nead for their very helpful comments and suggestions.

removal benefits accruing from a given burden of cost. If antipoverty policy is to alleviate poverty most effectively, then—on this argument—it is reasonable to make sure that the subsidies reach the poor and *only* the poor. So, the argument concludes, be firm and aim at just that.

If the so-called targets were all identifiable and unreacting, that would be the end of the matter—we could converge on a fine strategy whose merit we would all accept. Some of the resonant appeals to the case for more targeting give one the haunting feeling that this is indeed the way the problem of poverty removal is seen by some advocates of no-nonsense targeting. The nature of the real problem of poverty removal differs from it precisely because the people involved act and react and fret and run in response to the policies aimed at poverty removal.

How so? We can begin with trying to distinguish between the different types of actions and reactions of which any poverty-removal policy has to take note.

Response and Social Costs

That targeting has many direct and indirect costs has been extensively recognized in the literature.[2] It is useful, however, to separate out—and distinguish between—the ways in which such costs can arise and to see how each of these distinct reasons relates to particular acts and responses of the people involved in poverty-alleviation programs.

Informational Distortion

If the subsidy is aimed at the poor who are identified by some specified criterion of being counted as poor, those who would not satisfy that criterion could nevertheless pretend that they do by providing inaccurate information. This is a practice hallowed by tradition and use, and I need not dwell on this well-understood phenomenon.

But it might be asked, how could targeting *even with* informational distortion possibly be worse than no targeting at all? Some would no doubt cheat and will not be caught, but others would not cheat, and surely this is still a better *overall* result—taking the rough with the smooth—than no targeting at all and providing the subsidy to everyone.

The picture is, however, more complex than that. Some would object—not without reason—to having a system that rewards cheating and penalizes honesty. No less important, any policing system that tries to catch the cheats would make mistakes, leave out some bona fide cases, and discourage some who do qualify from applying for the benefits to which they are entitled. Given the asymmetry of information, it is not possible to eliminate cheating without putting some of the honest beneficiaries at considerable risk (on the general problems underlying asymmetric information, see Akerlof 1984). In trying to prevent the type II error of including the nonpoor among the poor, some type I errors of not including some real poor among the listed poor would undoubtedly occur.[3]

Incentive Distortion

Informational distortion cooks the books but does not, on its own, change the underlying real economic situation. But targeted subsidies can also affect people's economic behavior. For example, the prospect of losing the subsidy if one were to earn too much can be a deterrent to economic activities. It could be open to question as to how substantial the incentive distortions are in any particular case, but it would be natural to expect that there would be *some* significant distorting shifts if the qualification for the subsidy is based on a variable (such as income) that is freely adjustable through changing one's economic behavior. The *social* costs of behavioral shifts would include inter alia the net loss of the fruits of economic activities forgone as well as the value of the changes in labor supply (some underlying issues in assessing changes in labor supply are discussed by Kanbur, Keen, and Tuomala in chapter 5 of this volume).

Disutility and Stigma

Any system of subsidy that requires people to be identified as poor and that is seen as a special benefaction for those who cannot fend for themselves would tend to have some effects on their self-respect as well as on the respect accorded them by others. These features do, of course, have their incentive effects as well, but quite aside from those indirect consequences, there are also direct costs and losses involved in feeling—and being—stigmatized. Since this kind of issue is often taken to be of rather marginal interest (a matter, allegedly, of fine detail), I would take the liberty of referring to John Rawls's argument that self-respect is "perhaps the most important primary good" on which a theory of justice as fairness has to concentrate (see Rawls 1971, pp. 440–46, where he discusses how institutional arrangements and public policies can influence "the social bases of self-respect").

Administrative and Invasive Losses

Any system of targeting—except targeting through self-selection—involves discriminating awards in which some people (typically government officials) judge the applications made by the would-be recipients. The procedure can involve substantial administrative costs, both in the form of resource expenditures and bureaucratic delays. No less important, losses of individual privacy and autonomy can be involved in the need for extensive disclosures.

The finer the targeting is meant to be, the more invasive would the investigations typically be. Means-tested awards would require detailed revelation of personal circumstances. When the targeting takes the form of giving priority to a large group (such as a relatively poor region of the country), the investigations need not be so invasive, but that is only because the targeting is less fine. In general, there is no way of targeting specific deprivations without a corresponding informational invasion. The problem here is not just the necessity of disclosure and the related loss of privacy but also the social costs of the associated programs of investigation and policing. Some of these investigations can be particularly nasty, treating each applicant as a potential criminal.

There are, furthermore, social costs of asymmetric power. Minor potentates can enjoy great authority over the suppliant applicants. There are plenty of actual examples of the exercise of official authoritarianism that frequently accompanies informational investigations. The possibility of corruption is, of course, also present whenever some officials have significant control over the process of dispensing favors in the form of targeted benefits.

Political Sustainability and Quality

The beneficiaries of thoroughly targeted poverty-alleviation programs are often quite weak politically and may lack the clout to sustain the programs and maintain the quality of the services offered. Benefits meant exclusively for the poor often end up being poor benefits. In the context of the richer countries, such as the United States, this consideration has been the basis of some well-known arguments for having "universal" programs rather than heavily targeted ones confined only to the poorest.[4] Something of this argument certainly does apply to the poorer countries as well.

These different considerations relate in different ways to actions, thoughts, choices, and feelings of the subjects of targeting. There is nothing necessarily complex about recognizing the legitimacy of these concerns, but it is important that they are brought into the policy choices in an explicit and scrutinized way. Seeing the people affected by targeting as agents rather than as patients does have far-reaching implications.

The Need for Selection

The immediate question is whether the questioning of the merits of targeting indicates a case for dropping it altogether. It would be amazing if that were so. Economic policies—those aimed at poverty removal as well as others—try to achieve some results. And any such attempt must involve *some* targeting. If the aim is to increase female literacy or to vaccinate children, surely the policies must somehow concentrate on the illiterate females or the unvaccinated kids. Like Monsieur Jourdain in Molière's *Le bourgeois gentilhomme,* who spoke prose "without knowing it," we are all targeting all the time if any selection of beneficiaries counts as that.

Coherence of poverty-relief policies would require some obvious selections—regions, classes, occupation groups, and so on. That is the "prose" we speak, and there is no question of doing without those selections. In most contexts, these elementary distinctions are well understood and can be fruitfully used in policymaking. Cogency of policy requires a concern with the identification of beneficiaries and some discrimination. The important issues lie elsewhere—to wit, in how far to push the discrimination and where to stop.

Poverty as Capability Deprivation

In answering these questions, there is a case for raising a fairly foundational issue about the nature of poverty: what is the shape of the beast we are trying to tackle with variable amounts of targeting? The policy literature on poverty removal has been deeply concerned with the perspective of income deprivation. I would even argue that it has been obsessed by this one, undoubtedly important but partial, aspect of deprivation.

Here too we may need to take a more activity-oriented view of human beings. I have tried to argue elsewhere for seeing poverty as the failure of some basic capabilities to function—a person lacking the opportunity to achieve some minimally acceptable levels of these functionings (Sen 1984, 1985, 1992; see also Hossain 1990). The functionings relevant to this analysis can vary from such elementary physical ones as being well nourished, being adequately clothed and sheltered, avoiding preventable morbidity, and so forth, to more complex social achievements such as taking part in the life of the community, being able to appear in public without shame, and so on. The opportunity of converting personal incomes into capabilities to function depends on a variety of personal circumstances (including age, gender, proneness to illness, disabilities, and so on) and social surroundings (including epidemiological characteristics, physical and social environments, public services of health and education, and so on).

If we insist on seeing poverty in the income space (rather than directly in terms of capability failure), the relevant concept of poverty has to be *inadequacy* (for generating minimally acceptable capabilities) rather than *lowness* (independent of personal and social characteristics; the extensive implications of this distinction are discussed in Sen 1992). Technically, this is "the inverse function" to that relating capabilities to incomes, but I shall not go into the formal representations here. The more general issue is that a concept of poverty that ignores the relevant variations in individual and social characteristics cannot do justice to our real concerns about poverty and deprivation, namely, inadequate capabilities.

It might be thought that to go beyond the low-income view of poverty must have the effect of making practical decisions much more complex than they already are. Even though the primary argument for seeking a better idea of poverty is not simplicity but cogency, I do not believe it does, in fact, make the practical problems *more* difficult. Indeed, in many ways, it does quite the contrary. The failure of some basic functionings (for example, having a disease or being illiterate) may be more directly observable than the actual income level of a person, so that the problem of informational distortions can be less acute.

Arguments for income-based targeting have tended to rely, typically implicitly, on two assumed advantages: (1) measurement opportunities and (2) relevance. Neither ground is very secure. Income estimates call for appropriate price and quantity data, and sometimes they are hard to get and easy to hide. Certainly, it is by no means clear that it is easier to get a firm view of personal income than to observe morbidity, disability, undernourishment, or illiteracy. And as far as relevance is concerned, since income is at best one of the means to other ends, there is some lack of directness in concentrating on incomes, rather than on the valued functionings that income promotes (along with other means).

Not all functioning achievements or failures are, of course, easy to observe. But some of the more basic and elementary ones are more amenable to direct observation and frequently enough provide useful informational bases for antideprivation policies. The informational bases for seeing the need for literacy campaigns, hospital service programs, and nutritional supplementation need not be particularly obscure.[5] To rely entirely on the income space would be, in such cases, quite counterproductive both on the grounds of relevance and that of observability.

This is not to deny that sometimes it will turn out that the functionings in question are really quite complex and are not so easily measurable, and there might well then be, in some cases, good pragmatic grounds for using income as the contingent criterion of discrimination (see Sen 1992). The measurement errors in assessing functionings can well be large enough in some cases to make it more sensible to rely on income information (despite the indirectness of its relevance and its own measurement problems). In practice, there is much to be said for using functioning information as well as income data after critically scrutinizing the appropriateness of each. The case for combining the two types of information is strong.

No matter which particular indicator is chosen in a specific case, the general approach of poverty removal has to take adequate note of the purely instrumental nature of the importance of income, in contrast with the more intrinsic relevance of functionings, in assessing deprivation (I have discussed the relationship between income and the capability to function in assessing deprivation in Sen 1992, chaps. 6 and 7). It is important to see human beings not merely as recipients of income but as people attempting to live satisfactory lives and to see poverty not simply as low income but as the lack of real opportunities to have minimally adequate lives. Even when income turns out to be a good enough indicator of capability deprivation, that connection with the capability perspective has to be brought out clearly.

Information and Incentive Compatibility

I turn now to a more specific discussion of the informational and incentive aspects of targeting. The informational aspect of targeting relates to the identifiability of the characteristics associated with deprivation. If the object of the exercise is to eliminate low incomes, then the income level of the person is the appropriate focal variable. If, however, the object is to eliminate, say, preventable morbidity or severe undernourishment or illiteracy, then those conditions, instead, must be the relevant focal variables.[6]

The main argument against taking income as the focal variable is that it is just a *means*—and only *one* of several means—to the type of life we have reasons to want to live. If, for example, we are talking about poverty in, say, Harlem in New York, the calculation of the lowness of income there is, I believe, a less telling indicator of poverty than the fact that a man born in Harlem has a lower expectation of living to any age above forty than the corresponding Bangladeshi has (and of course a much lower life expectancy than that enjoyed by the residents of China or Sri Lanka or the Indian state of Kerala).[7] In fact, the chances of surviving to higher age groups are systematically lower for the African American population as a whole (not just in Harlem) than for the Chinese or the Sri Lankan or the Keralan (even though the latter populations are immensely poorer, in terms of real income per person; see Sen 1993).

What about *incentives*? It is, in general, quite hopeless to look for some indicators that are both (1) relevant for identifying deprivation and (2) immune to incentive effects. This applies, I am afraid, to basic human functionings as well. But the picture is not entirely bleak for at least four distinct reasons.

First, people may typically be reluctant to refuse education, foster illnesses, or cultivate undernourishment on purely tactical grounds.

The priorities of reasoning and choice tend to militate against deliberately promoting these elementary deprivations. There are, of course, exceptions. Among the most distressing accounts of famine relief experiences are occasional reports of some parents keeping one child in the family thoroughly famished so that the family qualifies to get nutritional support (for example, in the form of take-home food rations)— treating the child, as it were, as a "meal ticket" (see the discussion of this issue in Drèze and Sen 1989, chap. 7, particularly pp. 109–13; the empirical observations come from Nash 1986 and Borton and Shoham 1989). But in general such incentive effects in keeping people undernourished or untreated or illiterate are relatively rare, for reasons that are not astonishing.

Second, the causal factors underlying some functional deprivations can go much deeper than income deprivation and may be very hard to adjust. For example, physical disabilities, old age, and gender characteristics are particularly serious sources of capability handicap because they are beyond the control of the persons involved. And for much the same reason, they are not open to incentive effects in the way the adjustable features are. This limits the incentive distortions of subsidies targeted on these features.

Third, there is a particular connection between the use of self-selection as a method of targeting and the valuational perspective to be used. If the selection can be left to the potential recipients themselves (for example, through offering employment at a basic wage to anyone who seeks such employment), the actual choices made will depend on all the values that influence the choices of the potential recipients. The result will not be based on income maximization only. A potential recipient may calculate the wage level associated with this employment offer, take note of any income forgone elsewhere, consider the levels of activity and toil involved in the respective alternatives, consider such nonwage benefits of employment as the promotion of self-respect and independence, and so on. Thus, through the choices made, the self-selecting potential recipient will tend to reflect a wider class of values than simply income maximization. Since the rationale of the capability perspective relates closely to this wider class of values, there is a clear connection between the move toward self-selection and the rationale of the capability perspective. Policymaking has to take note of the fact that the case for going beyond income considerations into the type of life led—including the various functionings performed— is relevant for the recipients themselves and will thus influence their decisions and choices (see Drèze and Sen 1989; Besley and Coate 1992; in addition, the chapters in this volume include enlightening explorations of the opportunities and costs of such programs—see, for example, Ravallion and Datt in chapter 15).

This type of self-selective targeting has been very successfully used in providing famine relief and can have a wider role in enhancing the economic opportunities of the able-bodied deprived population.[8] The argument for this approach takes note of the fact that the chosen activities of the potential recipients are governed by considerations that are broader than maximization of income earned. In critically scrutinizing the use of this approach, attention must be paid to the costs incurred by the participants in terms of extra work, in addition to the costs of income forgone and the expenses of operating these employment schemes. It might turn out, in many contexts, that judged purely as targeting of transfer payments, these schemes are not clearly better than untargeted transfers given to all in a particular region, and the overall assessment may thus be quite sensitive to the value of the assets actually created by the public works programs (see chapter 15 in this volume). But the important point to note here is that the use of self-selection through work has a tractable rationale that identifies a significant and incentive-compatible option that can be systematically assessed and discriminatingly used.

Fourth, the refocusing of attention from low personal incomes to capability handicaps also points directly to the case for greater emphasis on direct public provision of such facilities as medical services and educational programs (see Anand and Ravallion 1993; Griffin and Knight 1990). These services typically cannot be shifted nor sold, and are not of much use to a person unless he or she actually needs them. There is, thus, some built-in matching in such provisioning, which makes it more incentive-compatible than the transfer of generalized purchasing power in the form of income (see Sen 1973, pp. 78–79).

The redistributive impact of direct public provision is sometimes judged by examining its consequences on the distribution of per capita real income (or expenditure). It is appropriate that this be done, since income is a generalized means of commanding facilities and commodities. But it cannot be the only focus of distributive attention, since ultimately we must also be concerned with the disparities in actual functionings and capabilities (in chapter 9 in this volume, van de Walle assesses the health services in *both* perspectives; see also chapter 18 and the other country papers in this volume). Inequalities in health and education have a direct relevance to policy that is not parasitic on their roles in generating income inequalities as such. This is a consideration of some general pertinence in devising broad strategies of targeting over distinct groups, such as regions, classes, or genders.

To sum up, capability-oriented reasonings in dealing with targeting problems have some distinct merits with regard to incentive compatibility. These relate to (1) the frequently lower manipulability of observed functionings (such as illness or illiteracy), (2) the fixity of predispositional characteristics (such as disability or genetic proneness to illness), (3) the usefulness of self-selection (such as employment offers), and (4) the nontransferability of benefits tied to personal functionings (such as personal medical care).

Social and Political Feasibility

In this section, I discuss briefly a few social and political issues related to the general question of targeting. The social issue concerns the gap between the availability of public services and their actual use by deprived groups. The political question concerns the actual feasibility and acceptability of aiming public policy toward particular deprived groups.

To begin with the first problem, there is some evidence that even those services that are available, in principle, to all are nevertheless disproportionately used by some classes—usually the more affluent and better connected—than by others. This applies, for example, to urban medical services at free hospitals and even to institutions (such as the distinguished All India Institute of Medicine) that do not insist on a prior referral. The contrast is especially sharp in poor countries with large illiterate populations, and lack of education can certainly be an important constraint in the canny use of available public facilities on the part of the deprived.

In response, it is tempting to consider introducing forceful targeting to reserve free services only for the poor. It is very doubtful, however, that this can, in fact, be effectively done without being overwhelmed by the burden of costs of the different types discussed earlier. The need to examine this issue cannot be overlooked.

This question points to a related issue, the need to see the capability of making use of—and profiting from—untargeted public services as an important parameter that affects the consequences of public policy. That capability depends on a variety of considerations, but public education is certainly among the determining variables. It is, for example, arguable that one reason for the extensive and effective use of public health facilities in the state of Kerala in India (where the life expectancy at birth now exceeds 70 years—74 for women—despite the very low per capita income) is the high rate of literacy of the Kerala population (including women). Thus, a more comprehensive education policy can make the use of untargeted public services that much more effective in fighting poverty. Once again, the need to see the people involved as agents rather than as patients is central.

Turning to the second question—that of political feasibility—it is worth noting that there are some remarkable gaps in the focusing of public policy in many developing economies. For example, women in general and female children in particular are relatively deprived in terms of health care and basic education to an astonishing extent in many countries in the world, especially in Asia and North Africa. To do something about these inequalities would require policies more directed toward these deprived groups, including paying greater attention to female education and medical care in rural programs. Similarly, if there is clear evidence of so-called urban bias in the distribution of governmental support and attention, there will be a good argument for general reorientation of policies in the direction of supporting the rural population. That does point to the case for more targeting of that type, if it is politically feasible to do so.

The political feasibility of such differential use of public services depends to a considerable extent on what the more powerful groups in a poor country see as imperative. For example, easily infectious diseases receive much greater attention than other types of maladies do, and they tend to get eliminated with remarkable efficiency. It has happened to smallpox, has nearly happened to malaria, and is on the way to happening to cholera. Even the poor would tend to get a lot of attention partly for good humanitarian reasons but also because a poor person with an infectious disease is a source of infection for others. Ailments that are not so infectious, including regular undernourishment, do not get quite that comprehensive attention.

I sometimes wonder whether there is any way of making poverty terribly infectious. If that were to happen, its general elimination would be, I am certain, remarkably rapid. This, alas, will not happen, but that counterfactual consideration points to a relationship—on the nature of social divisiveness—that has some direct bearing on the problem of targeting and poverty removal. Infections break down social divisions. Anything else that can do so can be similarly positive in its results.

Even enlightened politics and informed public discussion can play that unifying role. This is, of course, a point that goes back to the concerns of the leading figures of the European enlightenment, including the Marquis de Condorcet and Adam Smith. As deprivations of particular groups get politicized, they acquire a level of support far beyond what obtained earlier. For example, in the United States the problem of the medically uninsured, which has existed for a very long time (without being a political embarrassment to any government in power), has now at last started to receive some of the attention (however inadequate) that it has always deserved. In India, famines are politicized in a way that would make it hard for any government to survive if it failed to prevent a famine. But the deprivation of many millions without effective medical attention does not receive much widespread attention. The political feasibility and priority of targeting the medically deprived sections of the Indian population would depend not a little on a change in this situation.

The political economy of targeting has to be concerned not just with the economic problems of selection, information, and incentives but also with the political support for, and feasibility of, aiming public policy specifically at removing the deprivation of particular groups. While the scope of this chapter will not permit me to go into this question further, it is obvious that there is a connection here with the political use of pressure groups and, more generally, with activist politics. The importance of agency, which was discussed earlier in the context of economic actions, extends to the political and social fields as well.

Concluding Remarks

First, the elementary case for targeting has to be qualified by taking adequate note of the various costs of targeting, including informational manipulation, incentive distortion, disutility and stigma, administrative and invasive losses, and problems of political sustainability. These diverse considerations, which can reinforce each other, limit the scope for no-nonsense targeting, tempting as it is.

Second, some types of selection are inescapable parts of cogency and coherence of economic policy, including that of poverty removal. The question is how far to push those requirements of discrimination and at what cost. There is not going to be any general formula here, and much would depend on particular circumstances. I do not doubt that some expert in modern economics would find it helpful to say that targeting should be pushed exactly to the point at which the marginal benefit from it equals its marginal cost. Anyone who is enlightened by that wonderful formula fully deserves that enlightenment.

Third, to treat poverty not just as low income but also as capability handicap makes the exercise of poverty removal both more cogent and, in some important ways, also less subject to targeting distortions. I must not overemphasize this connection, since there are many other factors to be considered in arriving at overall policy judgments, but the specific considerations discussed earlier in this chapter belong solidly among the relevant features of targeting policies.

Finally, one of the general themes of this chapter has been the necessity to see the people to be influenced by targeted benefits not just as patients for whom things have to be done but also as agents whose actions and choices are central to the operation—and distortion—of targeting arrangements. That agency-oriented view applies not only to the purely economic problems in targeting but also to problems in social and political fields; the challenging issues in targeting include economic arguments for and against particular proposals and also the specific problems of social usability and political feasibility. The importance of the agency view is one of the elementary aspects of the political economy of targeting.

Notes

1. The importance of recognizing the actions and reactions of recipients and other agents in devising policies to remove poverty is well brought out in a number of empirical studies included in this volume.

2. An account of some of the main problems, on the basis of the experiences of Western countries with targeting of family benefits, is provided in Atkinson's chapter in this volume (chapter 3). Various aspects of these problems, related primarily to developing countries, are discussed in Ahmad and others (1991).

3. Some of the underlying issues are discussed by Cornia and Stewart in chapter 13 of this volume, emphasizing the need to avoid what they call "F-mistakes" (F for the failure to cover all the genuine cases) in an attempt to prevent "E-mistakes" (E for excessive coverage). See also chapter 15.

4. See particularly Wilson (1987); Jencks and Peterson (1991); Skocpol (1991). I first saw the force of this argument in 1971 in a conversation with Terence (W. M.) Gorman at the London School of Economics, though I do not believe he ever wrote on this.

5. Undernourishment does, of course, have many complex aspects (see the papers included in Osmani 1992). Some aspects of nutritional deprivation are more easily observed than others.

6. The *capability* to achieve elementary levels of basic functionings is not directly measurable, but the actual fulfillment or the lack of it can tell us a great deal about whether the people in question had these elementary opportunities or not; indeed actual achievement is one of the possible ways of assessing capability itself. This connection is investigated from different perspectives in Sen (1992).

7. See McCord and Freeman (1990). The Harlem woman does better than her Bangladeshi counterpart, but only because of the extraordinarily high under-five mortality of females in Bangladesh, and indeed the life expectancy gap narrows radically as we consider later ages. See Sen (1993).

8. It will not help those who are too old or too disabled or too ill to work in that way, but such people can be easily identified in terms of these capability handicaps and supported through other, complementary schemes. The possibility and actual experiences of such complementary programs are discussed in Drèze and Sen (1989).

References

Ahmad, Ehtisham, Jean Drèze, John Hills, and Amartya Sen. 1991. *Social Security in Developing Countries*. Oxford, Eng.: Clarendon Press.

Akerlof, George A. 1984. *An Economic Theorist's Book of Tales*. Cambridge, Eng.: Cambridge University Press.

Anand, Sudhir, and Martin Ravallion. 1993. "Human Development in Poor Countries: On the Role of Private Incomes and Public Services." *Journal of Economic Perspectives* 7: 133–50.

Besley, Timothy, and Stephen Coate. 1992. "Workfare versus Welfare: Incentive Arguments for Work Requirements in Poverty Alleviation Programs." *American Economic Review* 82: 249–61.

Borton, James W., and Jeremy Shoham. 1989. "Experiences of Non-Governmental Organizations in Targeting of Emergency Food Aid." Report on a workshop held at the London School of Hygiene and Tropical Medicine.

Drèze, Jean, and Amartya Sen, eds. 1989. *Hunger and Public Action*. Oxford, Eng.: Clarendon Press.

Griffin, Keith, and John Knight, eds. 1990. *Human Development and the International Development Strategy for the 1990s*. London: MacMillan.

Hossain, Ifthekar. 1990. *Poverty as Capability Failure*. Helsinki: Swedish School of Economics.

Jencks, Christopher, and Paul E. Peterson, eds. 1991. *The Urban Underclass*. Washington, D.C.: Brookings Institution.

McCord, Colin, and Harold Freeman. 1990. "Excess Mortality in Harlem." *New England Journal of Medicine* 322 (3): 173–77.

Nash, Tony. 1986. "Report on Activities of the Child Feeding Center in Korem." Save the Children Fund, London.

Osmani, S. R., ed. 1992. *Nutrition and Poverty*. Oxford, Eng.: Clarendon Press.

Rawls, John. 1971. *A Theory of Justice*. Cambridge, Mass.: Harvard University Press.

Sen, Amartya. 1973. *On Economic Inequality*. Oxford, Eng.: Oxford University Press.

———. 1984. *Resources, Values, and Development*. Cambridge, Mass.: Harvard University Press.

———. 1985. *Commodities and Capabilities*. Amsterdam: North-Holland.

———. 1992. *Inequality Reexamined*. Cambridge, Mass.: Harvard University Press.

———. 1993. "The Economics of Life and Death." *Scientific American* 268 (May): 40–47.

Skocpol, Theda. 1991. *Protecting Soldiers and Mothers: The Politics of Social Provision in the United States, 1870–1920*. Cambridge, Mass.: Harvard University Press.

Wilson, William J. 1987. *The Truly Disadvantaged*. Chicago, Ill.: University of Chicago Press.

3 On Targeting Social Security: Theory and Western Experience with Family Benefits

Anthony B. Atkinson

Targeting is an attractive idea. The concentration of benefits on those in need is an objective that commands wide support. According to the *World Development Report 1990*, at a world level

> A comprehensive approach to poverty reduction ... calls for a program of well-targeted transfers and safety nets as an essential complement to the basic strategy. [World Bank 1990, p. 3]

At a national level, more efficient targeting has been seen as the key to reform of social security. According to the Green Paper outlining the approach of the United Kingdom government to social security reform,

> The Government believe that resources must be directed more effectively to the areas of greatest need.... We must target the resources we have more effectively. [Department of Health and Social Security 1985, p. 18]

In policy terms, this is taken to mean a shift toward income-related transfers and away from universal benefits paid without a test of means.

For policymakers, there is much appeal in the idea that the existing total of transfers can be reallocated to increase their effectiveness in combating poverty. Simple arithmetic appears to support this view. In the United States,

> In 1983 outlays on means-tested cash assistance totalled $31 billion.... In that same year, the poverty gap, measured before

This chapter is a development of a paper originally prepared for the World Bank and based on research carried out as part of the Welfare State Programme at STICERD, London School of Economics. I am grateful to Andrea Brandolini, Nicholas Barr, John Hills, John Micklewright, Dominique van de Walle, and the referees for their helpful comments on the earlier paper.

the receipt of any means-tested transfers, was $63 billion. If all of the money had been effectively targeted on the poor, it should have reduced the poverty gap to $32 billion, essentially cutting it in half. [Sawhill 1988, p. 1101]

But in fact, "The poverty gap measured after the receipt of transfers was still $47 billion, implying that only $16 billion actually reached the poor" (Sawhill 1988, p. 1101).[1]

Among the reasons for this apparent inefficiency are that transfers were more than sufficient to raise people to the poverty line and that transfers were made to people already above the poverty line. Seen in terms of poverty alleviation, there appears to be scope for better targeting, particularly in the field of family policy, which is the particular concern of this chapter.

However, although politically fashionable, calls for greater targeting need to be treated with caution. The argument in favor has to be made explicit and critically examined. Behind such policy recommendations lie views with regard to (a) the objectives of policy, (b) the range of instruments available to attain those objectives, and (c) the constraints under which policy has to operate (economic, political, and social).

All too often policy debate is based on implicit assumptions about the nature of objectives. It is tacitly assumed that the sole objective of policy is to reduce poverty, whereas the typical social security program in Western countries has a multiplicity of objectives. Even if the alleviation of poverty were the overriding concern, the relative efficiency of different policies would depend on the precise way in which poverty is measured and on the sharpness with which the poverty objective is defined.

The range of policy options may be wider than commonly supposed. Whereas the choice of policy is frequently represented in gladiatorial terms, with universal benefits opposed to targeted benefits, in reality most transfers involve a degree of conditionality. The choices to be made are more subtle. Conditional transfers can take a variety of forms and offer scope for fine-tuning. Consideration has to be given to the relation between social security and other areas of government policy, most obviously the personal income tax.

The case for greater targeting is typically based on the assumption of a fixed total budget for the social security ministry. The constraints on policy choice may be more complex, however. The capacity of the government to target benefits depends on the information available to it and the extent to which it can verify information supplied by others. The constraints may be administrative, an aspect all too often ignored by economists. Account has to be taken of changes in the behavior of recipients, and the limits to targeting may arise from the adverse incentives created. Targeting may affect the degree of political support for the program and hence the funds available for poverty alleviation.

One of the aims of this chapter is therefore to caution against drawing oversimplified conclusions. As such, its role is negative, and practical implementation has indeed suggested that targeting is less straightforward than may appear at first sight: "Experience since the 1970s shows ... that reaching the poor with targeted programs can be difficult" (World Bank 1990, p. 4).

But there are also positive conclusions to be drawn. Instead of viewing the issue as an either/or choice (uniform versus targeted), we can ask what are the appropriate conditions under which transfers should be made. The population is differentiated along many dimensions, and we have to ask which are the appropriate ones to take into account when determining benefit eligibility. How far can we allow for a range of objectives? How can we balance disincentive effects against effectiveness in meeting the redistributional goals? Taking account of the method of administration of benefits, we may be able to understand why certain policies are successful and others fail to reach their target. Two benefit systems with identical effects on the family budget constraint may have different implications, depending on whether the benefit administration identifies the recipient or whether the participants select themselves.

In evaluating the scope for targeting, and its limitations, the experience of Western high-income countries may be of value, and in this chapter the theoretical analysis is illustrated by reference to the targeting of social security benefits for families with dependent children. This review of Western experience makes no pretense of being comprehensive, either in terms of schemes within one country or in terms of the countries covered. The focus is on programs specifically directed at families with children, rather than on *general* programs of cash transfers that benefit families with children. A country may, for example, have a general social assistance scheme, where the amounts paid increase with the number of child dependents, but this is not explicitly considered. In terms of countries, the United Kingdom receives particular attention, with reference also being made to other members of the European Union and the United States. Nor does the review aim to be up-to-date in terms of describing the policies of different countries; when a particular scheme is cited, it should not be inferred that it is currently in operation.

This chapter is particularly concerned with the relation between targeting and the reduction of poverty. It is essential, however, to remember that social security has other important functions besides poverty alleviation. These include:

(a) Smoothing of income over the life cycle in relation to people's needs
(b) Provision of security against events such as sickness, disability, unemployment, or bereavement (where these involve a loss of income, but not necessarily poverty)

(c) Redistribution toward persons with dependents, such as children (where this may reflect pronatalist objectives)

(d) Redistribution according to gender and securing of individual independence.

These objectives are not discussed here but evidently must be taken into account in any assessment of the overall efficiency of the social security system. Expenditure that is considered poorly targeted when judged solely by the objective of alleviating poverty may well be directed at other objectives of the social security system. This might hardly seem worth saying, but much of recent debate seems to have lost sight of the fact that the relief of poverty is only one of the objectives of the transfer system. Indeed, historically in a number of Western countries, it was not even the most important motive for the introduction of transfers. For example, in France, "Social security was never primarily conceived as a tool to fight poverty. Security, in terms of protection against the risks and hazards of life, was its first, paramount objective" (Jallade 1988, p. 248). The objective was seen less in individualistic terms and more in terms of solidarity:

> When statutory social insurance and family allowances were first introduced in the 1930s, their purpose was not to combat poverty but to establish a form of mutual support, *solidarité*, first between wage-earners, then between wage-earners' families, and eventually among all categories of worker and family. [Ameline and Walker 1984, p. 193]

The existence of wider objectives of social security may in turn have implications for the ability of the government to finance transfer programs, the size of the poverty-alleviation budget being dependent on the form of the transfer. Some observers suggest that highly targeted benefits to a minority of the population lack political support. The International Labour Office report *Into the Twenty-First Century* commented that the argument that "more generous provision could be made for the poor on an income-tested basis seems at first sight to have a compelling logic," but went on to say that "people are more willing to contribute to a fund from which they derive benefits than to a fund going exclusively to the poor. The poor gain more from universal than from income-tested benefits" (International Labour Office 1984, p. 23). The political economy of targeting is not considered in this chapter but clearly is important.

Targeting and the Objectives of Social Security

The objective of alleviating poverty is taken for present purposes to mean raising people to a specified poverty line, expressed in terms of income per equivalent adult, using an appropriate equivalence scale. I refer to this poverty line as z and to the corresponding income variable as y, so that a person i with income y_i is in poverty where $y_i < z$.

Efficiency in Alleviating Income Poverty

The specification of the level and structure of the poverty line raises many difficult questions (some of which are considered below), but even when these issues of identifying the poverty population have been resolved, there remains the problem of arriving at an aggregate measure of poverty.[2] Among the aggregate measures in common use in the development literature are the proportion of families with incomes below z (referred to as the headcount ratio and denoted here by H) and the extent of the shortfall as measured by the poverty gap (denoted here by G), which is the total amount by which the incomes of the poor fall short of z, expressed per head of the total population.

The approach commonly taken to the measurement of efficiency may be illustrated by reference to figure 3-1, which is the inverse of the more usual cumulative distribution. All families are ranked in increasing order of income along the horizontal axis, and the solid line shows the income corresponding to a given percentile point in the distribution, so that for each proportion of the population, F, we can read off the highest income, y, found among the bottom F percent. The lowest observed income is denoted by y_{min}. The diagram is drawn for the special case where the density function is uniform for y greater than or equal to y_{min}, so that the cumulative distribution, shown by the solid line, is a linear function of y. The distance between the solid line and the dotted line where $y = z$ measures the extent of shortfall from the poverty line, or the individual family's poverty gap. The aggregate gap, G, is measured by the total area between these lines.[3]

Figure 3-1 is based on the diagram given by Beckerman (1979a, 1979b), who defines the poverty-reduction efficiency of transfers as the extent to which they reduce the poverty gap. Suppose that the solid line in figure 3-1 represents the situation before transfers and the dashed line represents the cumulative distribution after transfers. Everyone is better off up to the break-even level of income (no account is taken here of the financing of the transfers). The reduction in the poverty gap is then indicated by the area A, and the poverty-reduction efficiency of the transfers is measured by the ratio of the area A to the total transfer (A + B + C). The efficiency is less than 100 percent to the extent that there are payments to the nonpoor (C) and that there are "excess" payments to the poor (B).

In these terms, the figures quoted earlier for the United States indicate that only $16 billion of the $31 billion means-tested cash assistance contributed to reducing the poverty gap, or a poverty-reduction effi-

Figure 3-1. Measuring Target Efficiency: Hypothetical Example

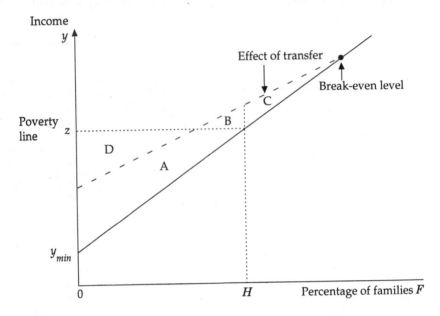

ciency of 52 percent. The estimates of Beckerman for four countries in the 1970s show the following results for total social security spending: Australia, 56 percent; Great Britain, 49 percent; Norway, 44 percent; and Belgium, 8 percent (Beckerman 1979b, table 19).

Vertical and Horizontal Efficiency

A program could score well on poverty-reduction efficiency but still leave a high level of poverty. The dashed line in figure 3-1 could be shifted vertically downward until the break-even point coincides with the poverty line, eliminating areas B and C, but the poverty gap would still remain substantial. Alternatively, a relief program could fill the poverty gap, but only for a fraction of the population below the poverty line.

This consideration led Weisbrod to introduce the distinction between *vertical* and *horizontal* efficiency: "Two issues are involved, having to do with the accuracy of the program in assisting *only* the 'target' group, and the comprehensiveness of the program in assisting *all* of that group" (Weisbrod 1970, p. 125). The former—vertical efficiency—is the efficiency that has already been discussed. The latter—horizontal efficiency—is "the ratio of benefits going to the target group to the total benefits 'needed' by that group" (Weisbrod 1970, p. 125). In terms of figure 3-1, horizontal efficiency is measured by the ratio of A to area A + D. For the four countries studied by Beckerman (1979b, table 19), the horizontal efficiency of the social security program was 74 percent in Australia, 92 percent in Norway, 96 percent in Great Britain, and 99 percent in Belgium. This gives a rather different picture, in part because of differences in the total level of spending, from the measures of vertical efficiency cited in the previous section, where Australia scored best and Belgium scored worst.

The vertical and horizontal efficiency indicators above are based on the poverty gap. Alternatively, they could be defined on the basis of the headcount measure of poverty. As Weisbrod noted, the indicator of horizontal efficiency is then "the ratio of the number of beneficiaries in the target group to the total number of persons in the target group" (1970, p. 125). This indicator will lead to different answers. The program represented by the dashed line in figure 3-1 achieves 100 percent horizontal efficiency measured in this way, since all those below the poverty line benefit, and the same would be true if the dashed line were shifted vertically downward until the break-even point coincides with the poverty line. Notions of "efficiency" are not independent of the way in which we choose to measure poverty.

Explicit Formulation of the Poverty-Alleviation Problem

Vertical and horizontal efficiency are therefore valuable indicators, but they are not on their own sufficient to guide policy formation. After all, a high level of horizontal efficiency may be achieved at great total cost; and we have seen that the value taken by the indicators depends on the choice of poverty measure. The indicators need to be related to the overall policy problem, with an explicit formulation of the objective and constraints. The statement that a particular program has x percent efficiency can only be interpreted in the context of such an explicit formulation.

Suppose that the government aims to maximize the poverty reduction achieved with a given budget, and that, initially, the degree of poverty is measured by the poverty gap, which is given algebraically by

(3-1) $$G/z = (1 / n) \Sigma_i [(z - y_i) / z],$$

where the sum is taken over those people with incomes below z, n denotes the total number of people, and the poverty gap has been normalized by dividing it by the poverty line (this problem has been studied by, among others, Bourguignon and Fields 1990; Kanbur 1987; Ravallion and Chao 1989).

The policy aim is to minimize G subject to a government budget constraint. In general, this constraint has to take account of changes in behavior by the recipients of transfers. Recipients may spend part of the transfer on taxed goods, generating additional indirect tax revenue, or on goods subsidized by the government, increasing public spending.

Figure 3-2. Three Special Cases of Transfer Programs

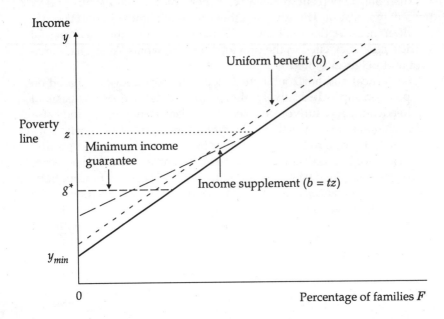

The beneficiaries may adjust their labor supply behavior, affecting the receipts from income and other taxation. For the present, these second-round effects are not taken into account, it being assumed that the cost of a transfer is measured simply by the difference between pre-transfer and post-transfer incomes. (Possible changes in labor supply are considered below.)

In this context, let us consider the class of transfer programs represented by the dashed line in figure 3-1. If y denotes pre-transfer income, then net income is equal to a guaranteed income, b, minus a tax rate, t, times the pre-transfer income, with a break-even level at b / t. The intercept on the vertical axis shows the net income received by a family with the lowest pre-transfer income (equal to y_{min}). Three special cases are shown in figure 3-2: (a) $t = 0$, (b) where the break-even level is set at the poverty line, so that $b = tz$, and (c) $t = 1$. The special case where $t = 0$ is often described as a uniform benefit, since it pays an equal amount, say b^*, to all families. Where t is positive, then the benefit may be said to be income targeted. The special case is where the break-even level is set at the poverty line, referred to as an income supplement, which eliminates the poverty-reduction inefficiency associated with the areas B and C in figure 3-1, since transfers are limited to those below the poverty line, and the transfer is less than the individual poverty gap. The same is true of the case where $t = 1$, which provides a minimum income guarantee, g^*, which concentrates the transfer on the poorest, with net income becoming g^* for all y less than or equal to g^*.

How do these transfer programs fare when compared according to the explicit poverty-alleviation problem? The answer obviously depends on whether the total budget is sufficient to eliminate all poverty. If the budget allows the poverty gap to be completely filled by a guaranteed income equal to z, then this policy could not be improved. In what follows, it is assumed that the available budget is less than the total poverty gap; this is certainly likely to be the case in the typical low-income country.

To illustrate the comparison, let us take a numerical example that is used at several points in this chapter. Although artificial, it provides a useful laboratory within which to explore the quantitative magnitudes. The example takes a poverty line of half the average family income. It assumes a uniform distribution of incomes over the relevant range upward from zero income (that is, $y_{min} = 0$). Taking the headcount as 30 percent, the poverty gap is then 7.5 percent of total income.[4] Suppose that the total budget is 2.5 percent of total income, allowing an income supplement of 33.3 percent, a uniform payment equal to 5 percent of the poverty line, and a minimum income guarantee of 57.7 percent of the poverty line.[5]

Where the poverty measure takes the form of the poverty gap, the income supplement, or any other transfer limited to persons below the poverty line, achieves the maximum reduction in poverty subject to the budget constraint. The value of the objective function is reduced to $1-t$ of its previous value, or by 33.3 percent with our numerical example. The reduction achieved by the uniform transfer is considerably less: the gap falls by a factor $[1 - b^* / (z - y_{min})]^2$. In our numerical example, the value of the objective function is reduced by some 10 percent (see figure 3-3, with $\alpha = 1$). Where the problem of poverty is that of a minority, the universal transfer does not score well on this measure of efficiency.

As has been brought out in the literature on poverty measurement, success in reaching the antipoverty objective may be measured in a variety of ways (see, for example, Foster 1984; Ravallion 1994; Sen 1976). There are not only the headcount and the poverty gap measures of poverty reduction but also objectives that give more weight to people who are a long way below the poverty line. A severe poverty gap may be of greater concern, dollar for dollar, than a smaller poverty gap. Following Foster, Greer, and Thorbecke (1984), we may introduce a parameter, α, that generates different forms:[6]

$$(3\text{-}2) \qquad P_\alpha = (1 \, / \, n) \, \Sigma_i \, [(z - y_i) \, / \, z]^\alpha,$$

where $\alpha \geq 1$ and where values of α above 1 give more weight to larger individual poverty gaps.

Figure 3-3. Effect of Variation in Poverty Objective on Relative Efficiency of Different Transfer Programs

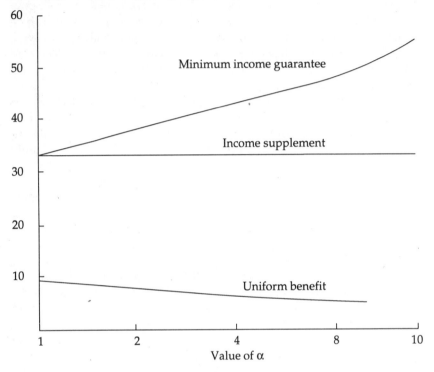

Percentage reduction in poverty objective

If the objective function attaches more weight to larger poverty gaps, then the relative advantage of the income supplement rises. The reduction in the objective function continues to be a factor of $1 - t$, but that from the uniform transfer is $[1 - b^* / (z - y_{min})]^{1 + 1/\alpha}$, which falls with α. The consequence in our numerical example is illustrated in figure 3-3. Where α equals 2, the reduction in poverty achieved by the uniform transfer falls to 7.5 percent. In the limit, as α approaches infinity, all weight is attached to the poverty gap of the poorest person, which is reduced by 33.3 percent in our numerical example, compared to a reduction of 5 percent with the uniform payment.

It is also clear that, where the government attaches more weight to larger poverty gaps, the targeted income subsidy is not the most effective means of poverty reduction. A greater reduction in the objective function can be achieved by the minimum income guarantee, as is illustrated in figure 3-3. As α rises toward infinity, approaching a Rawlsian concern with only the least advantaged, the remaining level of poverty reduction reaches 57.7 percent, compared with 33.3 percent with the income supplement.

The formulation used to date does not include the headcount measure of poverty. As is well known, the largest reduction in the headcount is attained by concentrating transfers on persons closest to the poverty line, since their poverty is the "cheapest" to alleviate. The same applies with forms of the objective (equation 3-2) with α positive but less than 1 (Bourguignon and Fields 1990). In our numerical example, it would mean raising to the poverty line all persons with incomes above $(1 - \sqrt{t})z$ but transferring nothing to those below this level. The headcount would be reduced by 57.7 percent. In contrast, the income supplement would fill only part of the poverty gap and hence would not reduce the headcount at all; in this respect, it would perform *less* well than the uniform payment, which in the numerical example reduces H by 5 percent. The ordering of the two policies is reversed. The same is true of the comparison of the uniform payment with the minimum income guarantee.

The headcount may continue to be popular in broad statistical analyses of the extent of poverty, but it seems of limited applicability in the present context. A policy calculated to reduce the poverty score by concentrating help on the *better off* of the poor, while denying it to those most in need, is not what most people appear to have in mind when they talk of targeting.

The Sharpness of Objectives

The crucial role played by the form of social objectives in this field may lead us to be more questioning about their formulation. The efficiency advantage of the income supplement arises because we are agreed that the poverty line is z. A marginal \$1 received by a person below z is valued in full, but a marginal \$1 to a person above z is valued at zero.

Such a sharp representation of social objectives may not, however, be universally accepted. There may well be disagreement about the location of the poverty line. What one person may see as wasteful expenditure on the nonpoor, another may regard as contributing to the reduction of poverty. We have then to consider a range of possible poverty lines (see Atkinson 1987a). Alternatively, there may be agreement about the location of z, but concern for the "near-poor," or the group above but close to the poverty line.

A wider distributional objective—while still concerned with poverty—may give some weight to transfers received within a range of the poverty line. Following the procedure of Ribich (1968), we may set a higher level so that transfers within a certain distance of the poverty line receive a positive weight (although less than that received below the poverty line). Another approach—that explored here—is to combine a "high" value of the poverty line with a form of the objective function (equation 3-2) with values of the parameter α greater than 1, "shading" the poverty objective, allowing differential weights to be attached to different poverty gaps.

With such a less sharp objective, the relative efficiency of the different transfer schemes is changed. We have seen that with the adoption of a value of the parameter α greater than 1, the minimum income guarantee (and the income supplement) becomes more efficient. The raising of the poverty line, in contrast, has the opposite impact. From figure 3-2, we may see that a rise in the poverty line brings with it a rise in the number of beneficiaries from the uniform transfer who are "deserving" according to the poverty criterion but that there is no increase in the case of the minimum income guarantee, which remains fixed at g^* (the total budget being held constant). In relative terms, the poverty reduction falls for both transfer programs, but the fall is much larger for the minimum income guarantee.

Suppose, for example, that we take α equal to 2, a value commonly used in empirical work. The minimum income remains at the same level as before in our example, which is 28.9 percent of average income; the uniform transfer is 2.5 percent of average income. With the poverty line set at 50 percent of average income, the efficiency of the minimum income guarantee is such that it reduces the poverty measure by 38 percent, compared with 7.5 percent for the uniform transfer, as shown in figure 3-3. However, if we take a high poverty line of 75 percent of average income, then the reduction achieved by the minimum income guarantee becomes 18 percent, compared with 5 percent with the uniform transfer. The relative superiority of the minimum income guarantee is less when we adopt this less sharp objective, as illustrated in figure 3-4 (the other points in figure 3-4 are discussed later).

Evaluation of Individual Welfare

Lack of sharpness in objectives does not simply affect the aggregate poverty measure; it may also apply to the assessment of individual welfare.

As a first example, we may refer to the relative poverty rates for families of different sizes, which are sensitive to the choice of equivalence scale used to put their incomes on a comparable basis. The potential room for disagreement may be illustrated if, following Buhmann and others (1988), we approximate the family equivalence scale by N^γ, where N is the number of members of the family.[7] Then, according to Buhmann and others, scales based on subjective evaluation of family needs tend to give relatively low values of γ (around 0.25), whereas those based on observed consumer spending behavior (and identifying restrictions) tend to be rather higher (say, 0.36), those based on expert

Figure 3-4. Relative Efficiency of Uniform Benefit and Minimum Income Guarantee in Different Situations (α = 2)

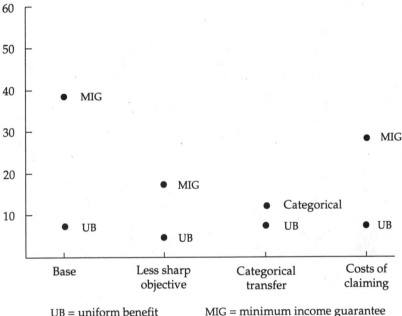

Percentage reduction in poverty objective

UB = uniform benefit   MIG = minimum income guarantee

assessment of consumption baskets tend to be higher still (around 0.55), and finally the scales applied in official statistics tend to be associated with values of around 0.72. Adopting a high value of γ, such as that applied in official statistical practice, would give a higher proportion in poverty among large families, whereas the low values of γ, such as those found in subjective evaluations, would give a smaller proportion.

The extent to which variation in the equivalence scales for different types of family can produce significantly different impressions is illustrated by figures 3-5 through 3-8, based on the results of Buhmann and others (1988). This shows the relative rates of poverty, defined as 50 percent of the median income, with the four equivalence scales identified above, for the overall population and for the subgroup of couples with two or more children (it also shows the position for single mothers, which is discussed below). In the United States, the overall poverty rate is much the same for all four scales, but that for couples with two or more children rises from less than half the overall rate to nearly the same level, as we move from the subjective scale to scales based on official statistical practice. A minimum income guarantee calculated on the basis of a subjective equivalence scale would provide less help,

Figure 3-5. Proportions in Poverty with Different Equivalence Scales, United States

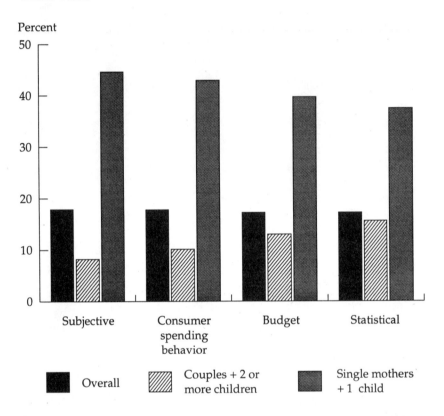

Percent

Source: Buhmann and others 1988, tables 10 and 12.

relatively, to families with children, and its performance in targeting help would appear to be less impressive when judged by the statistical scale. The same is true in Australia and Canada, where the poverty rate for couples with two or more children in fact rises above the overall average when we move to the scale based on official statistical practice. In the United Kingdom, the poverty rate for couples with two or more children is around a quarter of the overall rate with the subjective scale, suggesting that this group is less of a priority, but the rate rises to the national average with the statistical scale (in this case, the overall poverty rate falls as we move to the right).

A second example of potential disagreement about objectives concerns the treatment of earned incomes. As has been emphasized in the recent contributions of Kanbur, Keen, and Tuomala (1990; chapter 5 of this volume) and Besley and Coate (1992), there is a difference between evaluating the position of individuals in terms of their *con-*

Figure 3-6. Proportions in Poverty with Different Equivalence Scales, United Kingdom

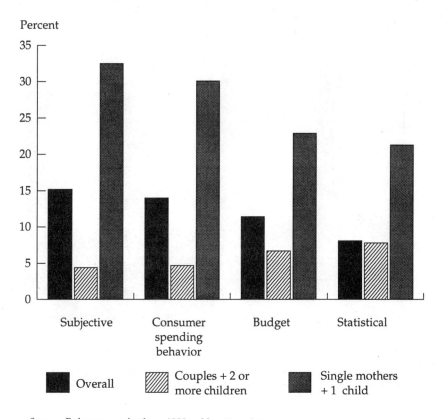

Percent

Source: Buhmann and others 1988, tables 10 and 12.

sumption and evaluating their *utility*, where the latter takes account of the disutility of work. To make the point, we may note that corresponding to a constant elasticity labor supply function with elasticity β (used later when the chapter examines work incentives):

$$(3\text{-}3) \qquad\qquad l = w^{\beta},$$

where w is the wage rate; the indirect utility function can be written as

$$(3\text{-}4) \qquad\qquad v = wl \,/\, (1 + \beta) + m,$$

where m denotes benefits and other (unearned) income. It is the level of indirect utility that would enter a welfarist measure of poverty, with labor income being discounted by a factor $(1 + \beta)$ that allows for the cost of working. In contrast, as Kanbur, Keen, and Tuomala point out, the policy debate gives no weight to the disutility of effort, and the individual situation is evaluated in terms of $wl + m$. The difference

Figure 3-7. Proportions in Poverty with Different Equivalence Scales, Australia

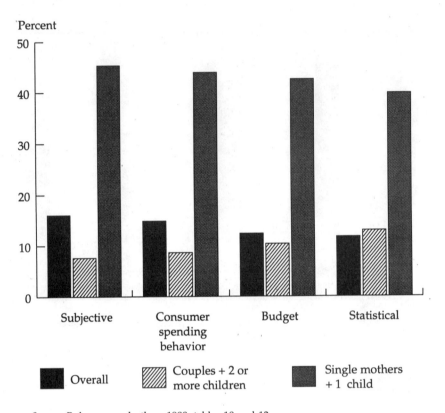

Percent

Source: Buhmann and others 1988, tables 10 and 12.

between these two valuations can affect the conclusions drawn regarding working families, in that the group identified as below a specified poverty line differs.

A third, related, example is that the claiming of benefits may involve costs for the recipient, either of time or money. There is then a question as to whether these costs should be deducted. Individuals may evaluate their welfare, and base their decision of whether or not to claim, on their net position, but the government may determine their poverty status according to their gross income, if only because the cost may be difficult to measure. Again, the policy definition excludes some people who consider their own welfare level to be below that attainable with a cash benefit of z.

Behind these examples lies the more general question of the dimension of poverty with which we are concerned. A move from income poverty to measures based on notions of utility is controversial, and

Figure 3-8. Proportions in Poverty with Different Equivalence Scales, Canada

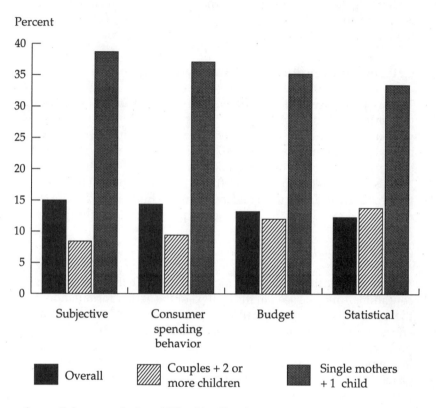

Source: Buhmann and others 1988, tables 10 and 12.

the evaluation of poverty may be based on nonutilitarian foundations, as in the capacity approach advocated by Sen (1985, 1992, chapter 2 of this volume). The adoption of such an approach may lead to significant changes in the recommendations regarding antipoverty policy (Sen, chapter 2 of this volume).

Conclusions

The aim of this section has been to set out the theoretical argument that is implicit in many of the calls for greater targeting and to show how the assessment of relative efficiency depends on the formulation of social objectives and the constraints under which they can be achieved. The statement that a particular program has x percent efficiency can only be interpreted in the context of such an explicit formulation of objectives and constraints. The attractiveness of targeting depends on how narrowly defined are the objectives of policy and on how much agreement there is about the form of those objectives. A highly targeted income guarantee may perform less well when judged according to less sharp criteria and according to objectives other than the alleviation of income poverty.

Categorical Conditions and Family Benefits

To this point, we have compared a targeted income supplement or minimum income guarantee with a completely universal benefit, whereas in practice all these benefits may be conditional on indicators other than income. As Barr (1987) brings out, the key distinction is between conditioning on income and conditioning on other variables. For instance, child allowances, often cited as an inefficient use of the transfer budget, are focused on families with children, and their relative efficiency depends on the incidence of poverty among this group.

Categorical Conditions in Principle

The use of indicators other than income, referred to here as "categorical conditions," may be seen in the context of the earlier formulation. With the poverty measure (equation 3-2), Kanbur (1987) shows that the effect of a marginal universal transfer to group i on the measure P_α is proportionate to the value of $P_{\alpha - 1}$ for group i. The marginal reduction in the poverty gap (α equal to 1) achieved by a universal payment to group i is proportionate to the proportion of that group in poverty. This provides justification for the policy that appears often to be implicitly adopted of giving priority to groups with a high poverty count. However, it depends on the choice of poverty measure. If we were to take a value of α equal to 2, then the marginal reduction would be indicated by the poverty gap for group i, rather than the headcount. This may well give a different order of priority for the allocation of a marginal increase in transfers.

In terms of an explicit minimization exercise, where the objective function takes the form of the poverty gap, the universal transfers would be allocated so as to equalize the poverty proportions. If there is a requirement that the transfers be non-negative, then this may involve no transfer to certain groups with a low poverty headcount. With α equal to 2, the first-order conditions for optimal allocation of a given budget require that the poverty gap be equalized across groups. An algorithm for this purpose is described by Ravallion and Chao (1989), who illustrate its application to a regional and rural/urban division.

The potential gain from the use of categorical conditions may be seen from the earlier illustrative example. Suppose that the overall poverty rate of 30 percent (with a poverty line of half the average income) is the average of that for two groups of equal size, with poverty rates of 10 and 50 percent, where the distribution is uniform over the range from zero to the poverty line (but the density is five times greater in the latter case). Where the transfers are constrained to be non-negative, the maximum reduction in poverty is obtained by concentrating the universal transfer on the group with the highest poverty rate for all values of α less than 15. The reduction in the poverty gap that can be achieved in this way is 16 percent, compared with some 10 percent with an unconditional universal transfer.

Policy toward Families with Children

In practice, one of the main groups singled out in antipoverty policy is that of families with children. Family poverty is an important issue on the agenda of many high-income countries. In the United States, it became evident during the 1980s that, while poverty among the elderly was declining, poverty among families with children was on the increase (Preston 1984; Palmer, Smeeding, and Torrey 1988). If the situation is less dramatic in other countries, there are nonetheless similar concerns about the growth of child poverty (see Smeeding, Torrey, and Rein 1988 and Cornia 1990 for an international comparison). In the United Kingdom, the Green Paper on the *Reform of Social Security* stated that

> In the 1930s working-age families were seen as the main group in poverty: the main causes being unemployment and low earnings among men with large families. By the 1950s and 1960s pensioners were the major cause for concern. Now the position has changed again and in 1985 it is families with children who face the most difficult problems. [Department of Health and Social Security 1985, p. 2]

At the same time, the identification of high-priority groups depends on the nature of social objectives. The choice of a poverty line of 40 percent of median income may lead to a quite different picture of the composition of the poverty population than would the choice of a 60 percent cutoff. Moreover, as emphasized above, the sharpness of the objective concerns not just the level of the poverty line but also its structure. As is apparent from figures 3-5 through 3-8, the poverty rate for couples with children, relative to that of the overall population, depends on the choice of equivalence scale.

This brings out how a lack of sharpness with regard to social objectives may limit the scope for targeting, not just by income testing but also by categorical criteria. There may be differences in view with regard to the treatment of different categories of the population and hence to the desirability of differentiating transfers on this basis. At the same time, the findings in figures 3-5 through 3-8 for single mothers with one child show that there may nevertheless be categorical conditions that allow priority groups to be unambiguously identified. The poverty rate for single mothers is considerably above the overall rate for all equivalence scales shown.

As the example of single mothers illustrates, there are in fact many possible dimensions along which transfers to families could be differentiated in addition to the number of children. The range of possibilities include:

(a) Payment of lump sums at birth, possibly with special provisions for multiple births (a further distinction is between payments during pregnancy and childbirth benefits)

(b) Cash payments, or paid leave, at birth that are related to labor market status, such as the provision to employees of maternity leave (a further distinction is between maternity and parental leave)

(c) In the case of continuing child benefits, amounts per child that vary with the number of children, for example, that rise less than proportionately with the family size (for example, where there is an additional family premium) or more than proportionately (for example, where no child benefits are paid for the first child)

(d) Child benefits that vary with the age of the child

(e) Child benefits that vary with the labor market status of the parents, including extra payments where there is a single wage earner or where one parent remains at home to take care of the child

(f) Payments for child care costs of persons who work

(g) Special payments for single-parent families

(h) Definitions of a child that are related to age, educational status, labor market status, residence, or other criteria

(i) Payments that vary geographically, as between rural and urban areas.

As this (incomplete) list indicates, there is considerable scope for the variation of transfers in order to achieve a greater reduction in poverty. Once again, this has to be qualified by the need to reach agreement about the nature of objectives. This is well illustrated by the approach of varying child benefits with the age of the child, where the direction of the differential with age is less than evident. The need for food and clothing increases with age and points to an allowance that increases with age; however, some analysts argue that the allowance for children below school age should be higher because child care costs are higher.

It should also be noted that benefits with respect to children may take the form of tax allowances rather than cash payments. Insofar as the amount of tax paid depends on variables such as the number of children, there are tax expenditures that have an effect equivalent to the provision of family benefits, and we may ask about the efficiency with which they are targeted just as we do for cash benefits.

Evolution of Child Benefits in the United Kingdom

How far in practice has targeting by categorical criteria been applied in family policy? The pattern of family benefits varies a great deal across countries—even among those at a similar level of development. This is demonstrated by the contrast between the United States, which has no universal child benefit, and almost all other major high-income countries, which do provide such a benefit. And among the latter group, there are large differences in the structure and operation of the benefit.

In this section, I describe the situation in the United Kingdom, taking this as a case study. After a long campaign before the Second World War, it was accepted that help for children should form part of the state social security system, and a crucial assumption underlying the Beveridge Plan for Social Security was that family allowances would be paid. Beveridge based the case for the introduction of family allowances on two main grounds. The first was that "Social surveys of Britain between the two wars show . . . that the want which remained was almost wholly due to two causes—interruption or loss of earning power and large families" (Beveridge 1942, p. 154). The second was a concern with maintaining a gap between incomes in and out of work. If adequate support was to be given to persons who were unemployed or sick, then this required "giving allowances for children in time of earning or not-earning alike" (Beveridge 1942, p. 154). (He also referred to pronatalist arguments.) The provision of child benefits in this way contributes to both incentive and antipoverty objectives. Family allowances, in the form of a cash payment to the mother, were introduced in 1944.

In the 1970s, family allowances were amalgamated with the (much older) income tax allowances for children. By eliminating the child income tax allowances, which increased in value with the marginal rate of income tax and hence with taxable income, the government was able to pay a more generous child benefit. This is an illustration of the government taking a wider view of policy instruments and planning social policy and fiscal policy in conjunction rather than in isolation.

The U.K. child benefit was designed as an equal universal payment per child. However, along with this apparent simplicity, there has in fact been considerable differentiation along the lines described earlier. To take the same lettering as above,

(a) Until it was abolished in 1987, a lump sum maternity grant per child was paid for all confinements.

Table 3-1. Variation of Child Benefits with Age of Child and Family Size in the European Community, 1990

| | Age of child | | |
Family size	Same benefit per child	Benefit increases with age	Benefit decreases with age
Same benefit per child	United Kingdom (before 1991) Spain Portugal		Denmark
Benefit increases with size	Germany Greece Ireland	Belgium France Luxembourg (up to three children) Netherlands	
Benefit decreases with size	United Kingdom (after 1991)		

(b) Maternity pay is provided for those in employment prior to the birth.

(c) When family allowances were introduced in 1944, they were paid for all children except the first in the family, the exclusion of the first child being justified by the assertion that even low wages were sufficient to support a family of this size. From 1956, the differentiation was taken further, with a higher rate being paid for the third and subsequent children. The introduction of child benefits led to uniformity of payments until 1991, when a higher rate was introduced for the first child.

(d) Child benefits have not varied with the age of the child, but the income tax allowances for children did vary with age.

(g) A uniform payment is made to all one-parent families (the One Parent Benefit).

Experience in a Range of Countries

The possibilities for a greater degree of targeting by a richer categorization are illustrated by the experience of other Western countries.

In many countries, child benefits are differentiated according to family size and age of the children. In table 3-1, the pattern of variation is summarized for countries in the European Union (except Italy). In two countries, the benefit is uniform; in three, it increases with family size; and in four, it increases both with family size and age. So that, in France, the analogous benefit to the U.K. child benefit, the *allocation familiale*, makes no payment for the first child and a smaller payment for the second child than for the third and subsequent children. There are age premia for older children. Whereas the amount for a two-child family is broadly similar in France and the United Kingdom, France strongly favors larger families and older children (Atkinson 1987b). The Dutch structure has three age bands (increasing with age up to sixteen, but with a lower rate above that age) and is graded more finely with the number of children, including benefit for the first child. The German benefit is paid for the first child and increases with the number of children, although not with age. In Denmark, in contrast to Benelux and France, a higher amount of child benefit is paid to younger children.

In Norway and Sweden the amount per child increases with the number of children: for example, in Sweden in 1990, the amount received by a family with six children was twelve times that received by a family with one child (NOSOSO 1993, p. 59). In Finland and Iceland, a higher rate is paid for younger children. In Canada, the federal family allowance is uniform per child, but the Family Allowance Act of 1973 allowed provincial governments to vary the allowance with the age of the child and the number in the family. Quebec and Alberta have availed themselves of this provision.

Any comparison of benefits has to take account of the relation with the tax system. The restructuring of child benefits in the Netherlands in 1980 was similar to that in the United Kingdom in that income tax allowances were abolished (Holmans 1987), and the same applies in Denmark. However, in Germany, tax allowances were reintroduced after their earlier abolition, and there is a supplement to the family benefits for those families whose income is too low to take advantage of the tax allowance (Commission of the European Communities 1990, p. 154). In France, the income tax offers significant benefits to taxpayers with children. Under the French *quotient familial*, the tax charged depends on income divided by the number of "parts." Each adult receives one part, and each child receives a half part, with a whole part for the third and subsequent children. This means that a couple with three children pay the same average tax rate as a single person earning a quarter of their income. Although there is an upper limit to the relief that may be given for children by the quotient system, for any given family size the system is of greatest benefit to those with the highest marginal tax rates (Atkinson, Bourguignon, and Chiappori 1988; Glaude 1991).

In addition to age and family size, a number of other dimensions may be varied within the universal child benefit program. For instance, the definition of an eligible child may differ. The normal age limit varies within the European Union from fourteen in Portugal, sixteen in the United Kingdom, Ireland, and Germany, and seventeen in France and the Netherlands to eighteen in Belgium, Denmark, Greece, Spain, Italy, and Luxembourg (Commission of the European Communities 1990). Above this normal age limit, there is further variation in qualifying conditions. In the United Kingdom, a child for the purposes of child benefits can be aged sixteen to eighteen if in full-time school education. Those studying in higher education, for professional qualifications, or taking an apprenticeship are excluded. In contrast, the German benefit is payable with respect to individuals aged sixteen to twenty-seven who are students or trainees with educational scholarships of less than a specified amount. In France, a benefit is payable with respect to children aged up to twenty who are apprentices, undergoing professional education, or students, providing that their income does not exceed 55 percent of the minimum wage.

A second example as to how the targeting of the benefit may be refined concerns the definition of the recipient. In the United Kingdom, the payment of the child benefit to the mother has played an important role and reflects concern with the distribution of income within the family. Even if the family or household is taken as the unit, the question as to *who* actually receives the transfer may affect the outcome.

Income Testing and Categorical Conditions

The use of categorical conditions may be an alternative to income testing, or it may be complementary. Almost all means-tested social security schemes are in practice conditional not just on income but also on satisfying criteria, and many are limited to subgroups of the population.

Various countries have attempted to target child benefits by relating them to family income, but this has taken different forms. First, the child benefit itself could be related to income. In Germany, the benefit for the second and subsequent children is reduced to approximately half its value if the parental annual income exceeds a specified figure. In Australia, the previously universal family allowance became subject to an income test in 1987; according to the estimates of Saunders (1991, fig. 4), in 1989 this reduced the expenditure by some 12 percent compared with the level without an income test. A more thoroughgoing income relation is to be found in Italy, where since 1988 the family allowance has been paid in inverse relation to the family income and in direct relation to the number of family members (Commission of the European Communities 1990). As a result, the benefit is scaled progressively down as income rises, until it is extinguished.

A second approach is to operate alongside child benefits a separate income-tested scheme for families with children. In the United Kingdom, in 1970, when the conservative government was elected with a pledge to "tackle the problem of family poverty," they rejected an across-the-board increase in family allowances and introduced an income-tested family income supplement (FIS). This benefit combined being both income tested and categorical, because it was limited to families with children and to families headed by a full-time worker. The amount paid fell progressively with family income and was extinguished at a relatively low level of income. Although benefiting only a small proportion of families, the scheme has since then formed a significant part of government policy, and in the 1988 social security reforms it was revised and extended as family credit. In 1990–91 there were on average 320,000 families in receipt, or some 5 percent of families receiving child benefits. A rather similar history has been followed in Australia, where a family income supplement scheme for working families with children was introduced in 1982–83 and then substantially extended in 1988, when the scheme was renamed family allowance supplement.

The French income-tested *complément familial* presents an interesting contrast to the U.K. family credit, in that it is not restricted to those in work but is restricted to families with three or more children, or with one child aged under three. Moreover, it is less sharply tapered with income, the ceiling for payment extending considerably farther up the income scale. This latter feature means that the proportion of all families in receipt is considerably higher in France. Despite the categorical restrictions, in 1988 the number of recipients was over 700,000 (Ministère des Affaires Sociales 1990, p. 159), or some 10 percent of all families, including those with one child. The transfers in France and the United Kingdom in 1987 are compared in figure 3-9 for a couple with three children (the amounts have been converted at an exchange rate of F9.5 to £1). Whereas FIS in the United Kingdom was tapered out at a relatively low level of earnings (at that time the average male earnings were about £225 a week), the *complément familial* continued to be paid until well above average earnings.

The experience of France and the United Kingdom shows the scope for choice between tapering at modest levels of income, confining the benefit to low-income families, and tapering at a relatively high level, excluding the upper-income groups. An upper taper can also be achieved by subjecting family benefits to income tax. In the latter case, the income tax operates like a test of means, reducing (although not eliminating) the value of the payment to families with higher incomes. The extent of tapering of the net benefit depends on the structure of marginal rates of tax. With a flat-rate tax, the only differentiation is between taxpayers and nontaxpayers; with a graduated rate structure, going up, say, by 5 percent steps, the net benefit can be quite finely tuned. There may in this regard be gains from the coordination of fiscal and transfer policy.

The taxation of benefits may, however, differ from an income test in the unit of assessment. Income tests are typically applied to the family unit or to a wider household definition. Income tax is more commonly applied to a narrow family unit or to the individual. Where

Figure 3-9. Income-related Benefits in France and the United Kingdom (for a Couple and Three Children Aged under Eleven)

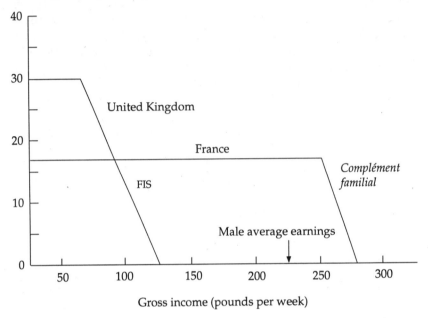

Benefit (pounds per week)

Gross income (pounds per week)

there is independent taxation of husbands and wives, the tapering achieved by taxation depends on whether the benefit is taxed in the hands of the husband or the wife.

Conclusions

The choice of family benefits is considerably richer than is suggested by a simple opposition of uniform and income-tested transfers. In principle, family benefits can be differentiated in a variety of ways, which may be combined in relation to income; income testing may take different forms. The experience of Western countries indicates that a wide variety of types of family benefits have been implemented.

Problems in Targeting: Imperfect Information and Administration

The scope for governments to target benefits effectively is limited not just by the budgetary cost, which was the sole constraint taken into account above, but also by administrative considerations and by the impact on economic incentives. In this section, I examine the problems of imperfect information and administration.

Imperfect Targeting

Imperfect targeting may arise on account of errors in administration. The conditions for receipt of a transfer such as child benefits may be perfectly aligned with social objectives, but the existence of the program may not be known to all those potentially eligible, or people may make false claims that are not detected. Imperfect targeting may also arise because the conditions of benefits are only imperfectly correlated with the objectives. A reduced rate of value added tax on clothes below a certain size, intended to benefit families with children, will exclude some families whose children are larger (and have to buy adult sizes) and falsely include some adults who are small enough to buy child-size clothes. Restriction of an income-related family benefit to those not in full-time work will mean that the families of low-paid workers may still be in poverty.

Where the correlation is less than perfect, or where there are errors in identification of the categories, this may lead to type I errors, or false negatives, where eligible families are not awarded benefits, and to type II errors, or false positives, where benefits are awarded to families who are not eligible.[8] The awarding of benefits to families who are not eligible (type II errors) reduces the vertical efficiency of the program; the exclusion of eligible families (type I errors) leads to horizontal inefficiency in that the program becomes less effective in covering the poor. Seen in terms of poverty minimization, type II errors add to the costs with no benefits (just as with the universal transfers paid to the nonpoverty population), and type I errors reduce both costs and benefits.

Administration of Benefits

This brings us to the question of the administration of benefits and the role of information. One of the most important advances in recent years in the theory of markets has been the exploration of the consequences of imperfect information. In many situations, there is an asymmetry, with one participant in the market being better informed than the other. The purchaser of life insurance, for example, may have information not available to the potential insurer. This recognition has radically changed the views held by economic theorists about the working and efficiency of competitive markets. The same considerations have, however, received less attention in the administration of government programs. In the operation of a transfer program, there is often an asymmetry of information in that the needs of the individual are known to him or her but not to the administering agency. There may also be third parties, like employers, who have the necessary information. There is, then, a principal-agent problem in the design of transfers, where the aim of the government is to induce all of those eligible to claim while ensuring that all of those who claim are in fact eligible.

If we begin with a purely categorical program, like child benefits, then it may be possible for the government to make use of information already available or collected for other purposes. If there are birth (and death) records, then these will provide a basis for establishing the eligible population for a child benefit and will allow payments to be made that vary with age. At the same time, birth records will not necessarily allow the present location of the family to be determined. To make the payment requires a file of current addresses. There may well be problems here in that those with low incomes are particularly mobile and may not want to publicize their whereabouts. For example, a battered wife who has left her husband may not register her new address, so as to reduce the risk that he will find her.

Even the simplest form of categorical benefits—a uniform child benefit—may therefore pose administrative problems. These are likely to become greater if the transfer payment is differentiated in the way described in the previous section. To take, in turn, some of the different dimensions (following the same lettering as before):

(b) (e) A payment related to labor market status requires that this status be identified and adjusted for changing circumstances, especially given that low-income families may exhibit higher rates of employment turnover.

(c) Birth records may not allow the benefit administration to identify the present composition of families, which is necessary to allow the payment to vary with the number of other children in the family or the position in the family.

(f) Payments for child care costs may be made at source, as with the free or subsidized provision of care, but this would not allow a transfer related to private child care expenditure.

(g) Birth records typically would not allow the administration to identify single-parent families; if a higher child benefit is to be paid to single parents, then it seems likely that they would have to initiate a claim.

(h) Where the definition of a child depends on the person's labor market or educational status, then this information would have to be collected.

There are limits, therefore, to the extent to which categorical benefits can be paid automatically. In many cases, the payment will require action on the part of the claimant. There are then two important stages:

(a) the decision by the potential beneficiary to make a claim and (b) the verification by the government of the claim.

The first of these may be considered purely as a problem of information, but in fact people may be aware of their entitlement but not make a claim, as where they regard the status of recipient as stigmatizing. This problem of incomplete take-up is particularly associated with income-tested benefits, and is discussed below, but may arise with categorical benefits such as those for single-parent families. Officially, take-up of the one-parent benefit in the United Kingdom for 1984 was estimated at 93 percent, and it was noted that "no significant increases in take-up are expected" (Her Majesty's Treasury 1988, p. 273).

The verification stage of the administrative process depends on the nature of the categorical distinction. Some criteria, such as age, may give rise to dispute but are intrinsically straightforward. Others, such as labor market status, are more complex. An example is provided by family credit in the United Kingdom, currently paid to those families where the head or partner is engaged in at least twenty-four hours of remunerative work per week. "Work" is defined to exclude training courses, or education, and charitable work for which the person is paid only expenses; it includes work paid in kind and self-employment (where the hours include preparation time). Hours may be aggregated for more than one job, and there are provisions for fluctuating weekly hours.

Administration of an Income-Tested Transfer

If we turn to a targeted income-related scheme, then it is possible to imagine circumstances in which there is no problem of information. *If* the government operates a personal income tax, *if* everyone files a tax return, and *if* this information is deemed sufficient to determine the payment, then in theory it would be possible for the agency to identify from the income tax records those people with low incomes, calculate the necessary benefit amount, and *if* the administrative machinery exists, mail a payment to the beneficiary. In the United States, the earned income tax credit for families with dependents operates by making payments to families whose income tax returns reveal that their earned income is below a certain level (and who satisfy a condition on total income). In this situation, one could operate an "automatic" income-related program.

However, these conditions are highly unlikely to be satisfied, even in high-income countries. The obligation to file a tax return may not be enforced among persons who are likely to have incomes below the tax threshold. In the case of the U.S. earned income credit, this means that a number of persons who are potentially eligible do not benefit (Seidman 1990, p. 92). As we have seen, the typical transfer program depends on categorical criteria as well as income eligibility. Information necessary to verify these categorical conditions may not be contained on the income tax return. For example, the income tax return in the United Kingdom does not include details of the number of children. Information on income in the past tax year, the basis for paying the U.S. earned income credit, does not allow urgent current needs to be met. The U.S. scheme does include provisions for the credit to be claimed in advance, but this has to be initiated by the recipient.

It seems likely, therefore, that any actual income-related transfer program will not be automatic, and we have again the two stages of claiming and verification. As far as verification is concerned, the problem faced by the government in the case of income testing is similar to that of tax evasion. As has been extensively discussed in the literature on evasion (see, for example, Cowell 1990), the government has to decide on an audit policy (the proportion of claims investigated, extent of the investigation, and so forth) and on the structure of penalties imposed in the event of income being understated. The factors limiting the enforcement activity will obviously include its cost but may also include the impact on the probability of claiming.

The problems of administration are illustrated by the U.K. family income supplement, whose introduction involved devising new administrative procedures to collect relatively current income information (and family credit requires in addition information on capital assets). The benefit must be claimed, and would-be recipients have to supply information on income in the past five weeks or two months. This imposes burdens on employers, and potential claimants may be deterred by the need to ask their employers for documentation. Special procedures are necessary for the self-employed. An important simplification is that, once the benefit has been assessed, no change in the payment is made for a specified period (which has been six months or one year). This means that the benefit paid is not necessarily appropriate to the current income but reduces the administrative costs. Nonetheless, the administrative costs are significantly higher than those for the universal child benefit. In 1991–92, the position was as follows (Department of Social Security 1993b, p. 20):

Cost	Child benefit / One-parent benefit	Family Credit
Administrative cost as a percentage of benefit expenditure	2.20	5.30
Average weekly administrative cost per family in receipt (pounds)	0.30	1.80

The figure for family credit includes increased capital investment for information technology and publicity costs, but the latter arises from the problem of securing take-up.

The calculation of benefits on the basis of past income is a device widely used in the administration of income-tested benefits. In France, certain benefits are based on net taxable income in the preceding tax year, so that applicants must make an annual declaration to the fiscal authorities, including persons below the tax threshold who can obtain a certificate that they are not liable for income taxation. This considerably simplifies the administrative procedure. It does, however, entail adopting the income tax definitions in assessing benefit eligibility, and these may not be considered appropriate. The use of a past earnings period also means that there are inevitably people currently in receipt who are not eligible on the basis of current circumstances. An interview study in the United Kingdom by the Department of Health and Social Security (1975) found that over half of FIS recipients would have been entitled to less benefit if eligibility had been assessed at the date of interview and that 20 percent would have had no entitlement. With an assessment based on income tax declarations, as in France, the problem is that receipt may be delayed far beyond the period of current need. A person whose income falls below the level of eligibility in tax year t may not be eligible in year $t + 1$, since the total annual income may exceed the ceiling, and may have to wait until well into year $t + 2$. In the case of the Australian family allowance supplement, payments are made for the calendar year on the basis of taxable income in the preceding tax year, ending 30 June.

The Problem of Take-Up

At the heart of the administrative problem is that the government has no machinery for identifying potential recipients, and operation of the system depends on claims being made. This may be purely a problem of information, as discussed above. People may be unaware of the existence of a benefit. They may be aware of its existence but not believe that they are entitled, as may happen where they have previously applied and have (correctly) been deemed ineligible but where a subsequent change in the program, or in their circumstances, makes them eligible. Informational deficiencies may apply to both categorical and income-tested programs, but the latter, with their inherently greater complexity, may be more difficult to communicate. In order to overcome these problems of information, substantial advertising and other costs may be entailed.

It is also possible that advertising alone is not sufficient. The potential beneficiaries may lack the necessary skills of literacy or numeracy required to assimilate the information provided. It may in such cases be possible to make use of third parties, such as social workers or employers. Employers may or may not have an incentive to convey information. If the employers believe that offering a package including government benefits allows labor costs to be reduced, then they may cooperate, but this may not happen if they believe that the effect on labor supply is unfavorable or if claiming the benefit involves them in additional paperwork.

People may not claim even where they are perfectly informed. Imperfect information is not the only reason for failure to take up. Nontake-up for other reasons is often regarded with suspicion by economists. Why should people pass up sizable amounts of money or valuable benefits in kind? This behavior scarcely accords with that assumed in other branches of public finance, such as the expected utility maximizing tax evader. But several explanations of the nontake-up of transfers are quite consistent with utility maximization. The simplest is the time required to file a claim. Where there is a time constraint as well as a budget constraint, nonclaiming may be a quite rational response. Where there is some degree of uncertainty about the answers to be given to certain questions on the application forms, and penalties are imposed on those making incorrect returns, then a potential applicant may consider it more prudent not to apply.

Nontake-up may be associated with preferences. People may be aware of their eligibility but not claim on the grounds that they regard receipt as demeaning or stigmatizing. They may be deterred by the way in which the benefit is administered and by the treatment they receive from officials. They may not wish to reveal information to their employer: for example, that they have a child. These kinds of considerations take us outside those usually discussed by economists, and we may need to draw on psychology and other disciplines (see, for example, the review of recipient reactions to aid, by Fisher, Nadler, and Whitcher-Alanga 1982).

The importance of the different reasons for nontake-up is likely to vary across groups of the population and across countries. Matters such as stigma clearly depend on the particular culture and are influenced by historical experience. For example, in the case of Australia, it is noted that

> Other countries are said to regard the means test as an abhorrent affront to social justice. It does not seem to be so regarded in Australia. . . . The means test as it is operated in Australia is not only fairly liberal, but also the "poor-house" and "work-house" connotations, which attach to the concept of the means test in some other countries, do not exist in Australia which had no experience of such institutions. [Henderson, Harcourt, and Harper 1970, pp. 10–11]

It is also the case that attitudes toward take-up depend on the *form* of the program. Taking again the case of Australia,

The wide coverage among the categorically eligible populations and the absence of a test on assets also mean that stigma does not appear to be a major problem and take-up is generally considered to be high. [McAlister, Ingles, and Tune 1981, p. 27]

However, the Australian experience with the family income supplement is less reassuring. According to Whiteford and Doyle (1991), the estimated take-up in 1986 among wage and salary earners was 24 percent, and on an expenditure basis it was 36 percent. Replacement by the new family allowance supplement, based on tax returns for the previous year, appears to have led to a substantial increase in receipt, but the extent of eligibility also increased.

There is indeed evidence from a range of countries that incomplete take-up is a serious problem and that it is not readily overcome. A recent survey of European experience, while stressing the limited knowledge about this subject in many countries, concluded that, "Research that has been carried out in Britain, West Germany, and the Netherlands invariably shows high to very high nontake-up of means-tested benefits" (van Oorschot 1991, p. 19). Much of the evidence relates to the United Kingdom. When the family income supplement was introduced in the United Kingdom, concern was expressed at the outset about the problem of incomplete take-up and the government set a target take-up rate of 85 percent. The early numbers submitting claims did not suggest that this had been attained, and examination of the time series of numbers in receipt indicated no trend toward improved take-up (Atkinson and Champion 1989). There is no evidence that advertising campaigns had any appreciable lasting effect on take-up. The official estimates for 1985–86 show that 48 percent of the persons eligible were submitting claims (Department of Social Security 1989, table 48.02); this corresponds to a headcount measure. Seen in terms of expenditure, which corresponds to the poverty gap, the take-up rate was rather higher, at 54 percent. Those with larger entitlements were more likely to claim.

One of the aims of family credit, which replaced FIS in the United Kingdom in 1988, was to improve take-up. At the same time, the new scheme widened the field of eligibility, so that nothing can be deduced from the rise in the number of families in receipt, which went from 220,000 families receiving a family income supplement in 1987–88 to 280,000 families receiving family credit in 1988–89 (Department of Social Security 1993a, p. 45). The official estimate of take-up of family credit in 1988–89 is that 57 percent of families were claiming a benefit and that the expenditure for the benefits claimed was 67 percent (Department of Social Security 1993a, p. 7). The same source quotes an estimate for 1991 by the Policy Studies Institute that 64 percent of families were claiming and that 70 percent of the benefit was claimed. It appears that nontake-up remains a serious problem with this means-tested benefit, whereas the government comments that for the main benefits that are not income tested "take-up is thought to be close to 100 percent" (Department of Social Security 1993b, p. 10).

The different reasons for the nontake-up of income-tested benefits have different implications for the design of programs. The natural policy response to lack of information is to seek to improve communication, through advertising and other campaigns, or to seek to identify potential beneficiaries through administrative records. However, the obstacles to claiming may be seen as a form of screening. Nichols and Zeckhauser (1982, pp. 376–77) argue that a role can be played by purely deadweight costs: "The demeaning qualification tests and tedious administrative procedures involved in many transfer programs *may* serve such a sorting function." It has similarly been argued that the time costs of claiming may be seen as a rationing device, limiting claims to those for whom time has a lower opportunity cost (Alderman 1987; Nichols, Smolensky, and Tideman 1971). However, the poor may also be poorly endowed with time, and they may also find interaction with benefit agencies more time-consuming (for example, where they have a low level of literacy) than the nonpoor.

These considerations are also relevant to the evaluation of individual welfare and to whether the value of a benefit is net of the cost of claiming or the gross amount. On the one hand, if the cost of claiming is forgoing an income-generating activity that is not observed by the benefit authorities, then the position of the individual may reasonably be assessed in terms of the gross transfer (the cost of claiming canceling with the unobserved income). On the other hand, where the cost is that of travel to the benefit office, stamps, and so forth, then there are good grounds for subtracting it from the gross transfer.

In the analysis of the implications of the cost of claiming for the comparison of a minimum income guarantee, g^*, and a universal benefit, Besley (1990) treats the cost as a fixed deduction from gross income, written here as cz. This cost deters from claiming those whose potential benefit, $g^* - y$, is less than cz; and, if we measure their net position, it leaves recipients below the poverty line by the amount cz. Making the same assumptions as in the numerical example of the chapter's second section, we can show how this affects the relative efficiency of the minimum income guarantee compared with the universal benefit.[9] With a cost of claiming equal to 10 percent of the poverty line, the gross guarantee that can be financed rises to 59 percent of the poverty line.[10] The take-up rate is 83 percent. Deducting the costs of claiming, the net guarantee is 49 percent of the poverty line, and the proportionate reduction in measured poverty is 24 percent with the poverty gap and 28 percent with a value of α equal to 2. The latter compares with 38 percent in the absence of claiming costs (figure 3-4). Although the higher costs of claiming may not, on their own, reverse the choice between a minimum income guarantee and a uniform benefit, they may materially reduce the attractiveness of the highly targeted benefit.

Conclusions

The problem of administration is often disregarded by economists, who concentrate solely on the benefit schedule. However, even purely categorical benefits may involve a decision by potential beneficiaries to make a claim and the verification by the government of their eligibility. In the case of income-tested transfers, it is very unlikely that the necessary information is available automatically to the government. Imperfect information may mean that some people receive benefits who are not entitled and that some of those who are entitled do not claim. Experience of Western countries suggests that the latter, take-up, problem can be serious for income-tested benefits, with a third or more of potential benefits going unclaimed. This reduces the effectiveness of the income-targeted transfer relative to a uniform benefit.

Problems in Targeting: Work Incentives

Income testing and categorical restrictions both raise important questions of work incentives. It is evident that the minimum income guarantee, involving a 100 percent marginal tax rate, is likely to affect work decisions. High rates of withdrawal of a targeted transfer may create a poverty trap, such that people have little inducement to increase their gross income. Similarly, the restriction of entitlement to people meeting certain conditions regarding family or labor market status may lead them to change their behavior in order to qualify. A system of family benefits payable, say, to single parents not in work may discourage them from seeking employment. We have to consider the trade-off between the efficiency of targeting and the possibly adverse effect on incentives.

Income Testing and Work Incentives

The conventional utility maximizing model of labor supply predicts that a minimum income guarantee of amount g, with 100 percent marginal tax rate, causes persons with incomes below g to cease to supply labor and also affects a range of families whose incomes were previously above g. The size of the pre-transfer poverty population is increased. As a result, the cost of the transfer rises above the earlier calculation (although it may still be considerably less than that of a universal benefit). This is illustrated by the indirect utility function (equation 3-4) considered earlier, according to which a person chooses not to work, but rather to live on the guaranteed income, g, where his previous income (assumed to be all earned) was less than $(1 + \beta)$ times g. Since β is the elasticity of labor supply, we can see that the recipient population increases, other things remaining equal, with the elasticity. A value of 0.5 means that the income-tested scheme brings in persons whose incomes would otherwise be up to 50 percent above the minimum income. In addition, the fact that recipients reduce their gross income to zero raises still further the cost of the transfer.

In order to see the implications of labor supply adjustments, let us take the earlier numerical example, but now assume that the wage rate (rather than income) is uniformly distributed over the relevant range upward from zero. The proportion considered to be in poverty in the absence of transfers depends on whether we evaluate the position of individuals according to gross income or utility, as discussed above. Suppose that we take gross income, so that persons with

$$(3\text{-}5) \qquad\qquad y = wl = w^{1 + \beta} \leq z$$

are in poverty. With the poverty line at 50 percent of average income, and $H = 30$ percent as before, the poverty gap where $\beta = 0.5$ is equal to 9 percent of total income.[11] If the available budget is a third of this gap, as before, then the transfer that can be financed is 32 percent of the poverty line.[12] The reduction in the poverty gap is 13 percent, compared with 10 percent with a uniform transfer costing the same amount. The targeting advantage of the minimum income relative to a universal benefit is much reduced when we take account of the work disincentive. Of course, the comparison depends on the value of β and on the particular labor supply function, but the calculation provides an indication of the possible importance.[13]

Concern about the poverty trap generated by high marginal tax rates has led governments to taper the withdrawal of benefits, the reduction being less than dollar for dollar. A typical formula would pay a benefit g to people with income less than or equal to y_e and then reduce the benefit by $\$t$ for each $\$1$ of income in excess of y_e. The universal benefit then emerges as the limiting case of $t = 0$. Choice of the withdrawal rate t subject to a budget constraint involves balancing the gains of increased concentration of benefit as t increases against the induced reductions in gross income (and welfare). The benefit may also be distinguished according to categorical conditions (see, for example, Akerlof 1978; Kanbur and Keen 1989; Stern 1982).

The Poverty Trap in Practice in the United Kingdom

In practice, the tapering of benefits with earnings is more complex. To begin with, many people on low income face the cumulation of several marginal tax rates. In the United Kingdom, a person increasing his or her gross earnings, for example by working additional hours, may pay higher income tax and national insurance contributions. In 1992–93, the marginal tax rate over the relevant earnings range was 34 percent, so that there remained in net terms a proportion $(1 - 0.34)$. For the low-paid family receiving family credit, there would in addition be the withdrawal of means-tested benefits when these are reassessed,[14] so that the net gain becomes: $(1 - 0.34)(1 - 0.7) = 0.20$, if family credit is received. But the person may also be eligible for a community charge benefit, which is also means tested, so that the net gain becomes $(1 - 0.34)(1 - 0.7)(1 - 0.15) = 0.17$, if family credit and community charge benefits are received. Finally, the person may be eligible for a housing benefit, so that the net gain is $(1 - 0.34)(1 - 0.7)(1 - 0.15 - 0.65) = 0.04$, if family credit, community charge benefits, and housing benefits are received. (The calculations have been rounded to two figures). This structure of means tests, applied to net income and taking into account benefits earlier in the chain, ensures that the overall marginal tax rate cannot exceed 100 percent, but it reaches 96 percent where all three benefits are received. As a result, the budget line relating net income to gross income is virtually flat for a wide band of earnings.

The position is further complicated by the aggregation of family earnings. The calculation in the previous paragraph assumes that there is only a single earner in the family, an assumption that does not apply in many cases and that fails to draw attention to the implications of means-tested benefits for family decisions. Since the test is applied to the joint earnings of husband and wife, they in effect face the same composite marginal tax rate as far as benefits are concerned. The situation is in this respect different from that which applies to income tax and national insurance contributions, which are essentially operated on an individual basis. Therefore, a married woman considering taking a part-time job that pays less than the income tax and contribution thresholds will face a marginal tax rate that depends on the family credit and other benefit withdrawal rates but can be between 70 and 91 percent. The poverty trap affects not just the main breadwinner, but also his or her partner.

How many people are, in fact, affected by high marginal tax rates depends on the joint distribution of earnings and family characteristics. The latter include, in the United Kingdom for example, the level of rent, which determines the range over which there is eligibility to housing benefit, and the level of family savings, which may disqualify them from benefits via the assets test. Estimates based on sample survey information suggest that the number of families facing marginal tax rates higher than 70 percent is some 0.5 million (Department of Social Security 1993b, p. 11). Overall, the numbers are small in relation to the total number of tax units in the United Kingdom of some 30 million. At the same time, it has to be remembered that people may have been led by the existence of the poverty trap to choose a level of work effort outside the range where the marginal rate is high.

Marginal Tax Rates and Work Incentives

Recent years have seen a great deal of research on the empirical magnitude of labor supply responses. In the reviews of this research there appears to be broad agreement that, to the extent to which disincentive effects exist, they are modest in size. Burtless summarized the evidence from the U.S. negative income tax (NIT) experiments as follows:

> On average, studies based on the NIT experiments suggest that means-tested transfers have a statistically significant, but quantitatively small, effect on the labor supply of low-income men and women who have children. [Burtless 1990, p. 73]

Similarly, Moffitt (1992, p. 56) concludes that there is unequivocal evidence of an effect of the U.S. welfare system on labor supply but that "the importance of these effects is limited in many respects."

In terms of hours of work, the value of 0.5 for the labor supply elasticity assumed in the numerical calculations is to the high end of the range typically estimated. The significance of labor supply adjustments may therefore be less than indicated. At the same time, labor supply has many dimensions. The main variations in annual hours may be attributable to periods out of the labor force (nonparticipation) or unemployment. While at work, people may be able to vary their effort, intensity of work, or the degree to which they are willing to take risks or responsibility. The working career has to be seen as a whole, with labor supply reductions taking the form of later entry or earlier retirement.

These dimensions of labor supply other than hours of work are important, because much less is known about how they are affected by transfer programs. Even in principle, the direction of the effect may be different. An income guarantee may give a positive incentive for people to make risky career decisions. Suppose that people are deciding whether to become self-employed, with all the attendant risks, rather than continue with a certain salary. The existence of an income supplement, payable in the event of low self-employment earnings, may induce them to take the plunge when they would not otherwise be willing to do so. This would be further reinforced if the benefit serves to finance an initial period of unprofitable operation before the business becomes successful.

The analysis of work incentives is further complicated by the fact that labor supply may not be purely the result of the decisions of individual workers. Choice of matters such as standard hours, or annual holiday, may be the result of collective bargaining. A transfer received by a minority of trade union members may have no impact on the collective choice. An individual worker is constrained by the labor market opportunities faced; the annual hours worked may be rationed where there is unemployment.

There are, therefore, grounds for being cautious about the conclusions that can be drawn regarding the relation between work incentives and the design of transfers. We have also to recognize that concern about incentives may arise less from the quantitative effect on labor supply as from a notion of just "deserts." It may not be regarded as "fair" that a person is unable to improve his or her position by working more. If this is the case, then "deserts," rather than an equity-efficiency trade-off, may determine the maximum rate of withdrawal and hence the acceptable level of targeting.

Categorical Conditions and Work Incentives

The discussion of work incentives to date has focused on the role of the benefit withdrawal rate under an income-tested scheme, but categorical conditions may also affect labor supply. Indeed, one important mechanism for reducing the possible disincentive effects of targeted transfers is through making the transfer conditional on a minimum level of work. Family credit in the United Kingdom is only available to families where the head is working for at least a specified number of hours per week.

An income-tested transfer with a minimum hours requirement has both positive and negative incentive effects. It may still cause people previously working more than the minimum to reduce their work effort or to take a less-demanding job, but it may also induce people to enter the labor force or increase their hours to the minimum.

The categorical restriction described above has a positive role as far as incentives are concerned, but these restrictions may also have adverse effects on incentives. The reverse restriction—where benefits are limited to persons not in work—is an obvious example. Categorical unemployment benefits may induce people to quit voluntarily or to delay their return to work, although in practice this is typically accompanied by sanctions on voluntary quitting—on the refusal of suitable job offers—and the benefits may be accompanied by job search or training requirements. These administrative elements of the benefit system may seriously moderate the disincentive that appears if one simply considers the budget constraint in isolation.

Categorical transfers may have other labor supply effects. Just to take one example, the provision of child benefits to those in full-time education may provide an incentive for young people to stay on at school; the extension of the definition of "child" to include those who are above the age of majority but attend higher education may influence the achievement of university-level qualifications.

Conclusions

Greater income testing of social security payments, as with a targeted minimum income guarantee, appears at first sight attractive, since it promises to concentrate benefits on individuals in need. The intention of this chapter, however, has been to caution against drawing oversimplified conclusions.

The first aim has been to set out the theoretical argument that is implicit in many of the calls for greater targeting and to show how the assessment of relative efficiency depends on the formulation of social objectives. The statement that a particular transfer scheme is more efficient than another can only be interpreted in the context of such an explicit formulation of objectives and constraints. The attractiveness of targeting depends on how narrowly defined are the objectives of policy and on how much agreement there is about the form of those objectives. Objectives may not be sharply defined, with differences of view about the weighting of different poverty gaps, about the location of the poverty line, and about the equivalence scale to be applied. A highly targeted income guarantee may perform less well when judged according to less sharp criteria and according to objectives other than poverty alleviation. The existence of wider objectives may, in turn, affect the level of benefits that can be financed.

The second main point of the chapter is that the choice of benefits is considerably richer than is suggested by a simple opposition of uniform and income-tested transfers, a point that has been illustrated with reference to family benefits. In principle, family benefits can be differentiated in many ways, which may be combined with income relation; income testing itself may take different forms. The experience of Western countries indicates that a wide variety of types of family benefits have been implemented in practice.

Third, the design of effective targeting faces the problems of imperfect information and of work incentives. These arise with both income testing and categorical conditions, but there are some reasons to suppose that they are more serious in the former case. Translating a scheme into practice in the face of imperfect information on the part of both administrators and potential recipients is particularly demanding for transfers that require evidence of current income. The experience of Western countries indicates that there is a major problem of securing adequate take-up of income-tested benefits. Concerns about work incentives, whether based on empirical findings or notions of deserts, may limit the acceptable degree of income targeting.

Notes

1. A billion is 1,000 million; all dollars are U.S. dollars.

2. Among the issues not examined here are the time period over which income is measured and the consequences of changing circumstances over time, together with the related choice between income and expenditure as indicators of resources.

3. The poverty deficit is found by integrating $F(y)$ between y_{min} and z (Atkinson 1987a).

4. With a uniform distribution, and a lowest income equal to zero, the poverty gap is $Hz / 2$.

5. The cost of the minimum income guarantee is $(H / z) (g^*)^2 / 2$, which is equal to $(g^* / z)^2$ times the poverty gap. With a budget equal to one-third of the poverty gap, the guarantee that can be financed is $\sqrt{(1 / 3)}z$.

6. This expression differs from that proposed by Foster, Greer, and Thorbecke (1984) and from that generally used, in that P is expressed to the power of α. This is to ensure that, as α tends to infinity, the measure converges to the Rawlsian form. It may be noted that, with a uniform continuous density h, the expression P is equal to

$$(hz / 1 + \alpha)^{1/\alpha} (1 - y_{min} / z)^{1 + 1/\alpha},$$

so that it converges to $(1 - y_{min} / z)$ as α tends to infinity.

7. This means that the equivalent income of a person in a family with total income Y and size N is calculated as Y / N^γ.

8. See Goodin 1985. Cornia and Stewart (chapter 13 of this volume) refer to F-mistakes (failure to reach the target population) and E-mistakes (excessive coverage).

9. The comparison differs from that of Besley (1990), who assumes that the government expenditure is determined by setting the minimum income guarantee equal to the poverty line. As a result, the introduction of claiming costs, which reduces take-up, reduces the total budget and hence the size of the uniform benefit. Here we follow the alternative approach suggested in Besley's footnote 5 of taking a fixed budget, assumed here to be less than that necessary to fill the poverty gap.

10. As a result of nonclaiming, the gross guarantee becomes $\sqrt{(t + c^2)}$.

11. The headcount is given by the density times w^*, where w^* is the level of w such that equation 3-5 holds with equality. The poverty gap is $(1 + \beta) / (2 + \beta)Hz$.

12. The transfer is received by all persons with w such that $w^{1 + \beta} \leq (1 + \beta)g$. If the budget is equal to t times the initial poverty gap, then the transfer that can be financed is

$$g / z = [t / (2 + \beta)]^{(1 + \beta) / (2 + \beta)} (1 + \beta)^{\beta / (2 + \beta)}.$$

13. The function assumed here does not allow for any income effect on labor supply, whereas both the minimum income and the universal benefit may have income effects.

14. As explained earlier, benefits may be assessed on past income, which means that a rise in earnings may have no immediate impact on benefit receipt.

References

Akerlof, George A. 1978. "The Economics of 'Tagging' as Applied to the Optimal Income Tax, Welfare Programs, and Manpower Planning." *American Economic Review* 68: 8–19.

Alderman, Harold. 1987. "Allocation of Goods through Non-price Mechanisms: Evidence on Distribution by Willingness to Wait." *Journal of Development Economics* 25: 105–24.

Ameline, Claude, and Robert Walker. 1984. "France: Poverty and the Family." In Robert Walker, Roger Lawson, and Peter Townsend, eds., *Responses to Poverty: Lessons from Europe*. London: Heinemann Educational Books.

Atkinson, Anthony B. 1987a. "On the Measurement of Poverty." *Econometrica* 55: 749–64.

———. 1987b. "Social Security Harmonisation in Europe: Evidence from Britain and France." In House of Lords, Select Committee on the European Communities, *Social Security in the European Community*. London: HMSO.

Atkinson, Anthony B., François Bourguignon, and P-A. Chiappori. 1988. "The French Tax System and a Comparison with the British System." In A. B. Atkinson and H. Sutherland, eds., *Tax-Benefit Models*. STICERD Occasional Paper 10. London: London School of Economics.

Atkinson, Anthony B., and Barbara Champion. 1989. "Family Income Supplement and Two-Parent Families, 1971–1980." In A. B. Atkinson, ed., *Poverty and Social Security*. Hemel Hempstead, Eng.: Harvester Press.

Barr, Nicholas A. 1987. "Strategies for Income Support." Welfare State Programme Research Note 3. STICERD, London School of Economics, London.

Beckerman, Wilfred. 1979a. "The Impact of Income Maintenance Payments on Poverty in Britain, 1975." *Economic Journal* 89: 261–79.

———. 1979b. *Poverty and the Impact of Income Maintenance Programs*. Geneva: International Labour Office.

Besley, Timothy. 1990. "Means Testing versus Universal Provision in Poverty Alleviation." *Economica* 57: 119–29.

Besley, Timothy, and Stephen Coate. 1992. "Workfare vs. Welfare: Incentive Arguments for Work Requirements in Poverty Alleviation Programs." *American Economic Review* 82: 249–61.

Beveridge, Sir William Henry. 1942. "Report on Social Insurance and Allied Services." HMSO Command 6404. London.

Bourguignon, François, and Gary S. Fields. 1990. "Poverty Measures and Anti-Poverty Policy." *Recherches Economiques de Louvain* 56: 409–27.

Buhmann, Brigitte, Lee Rainwater, Guenther Schmaus, and Timothy M. Smeeding. 1988. "Equivalence Scales, Well-being, Inequality, and Poverty." *Review of Income and Wealth* 34 (2): 115–42.

Burtless, Gary. 1990. "The Economist's Lament: Public Assistance in America." *Journal of Economic Perspectives* 4: 57–78.

Commission of the European Communities. 1990. "Social Protection in the Member States of the Community." MISSOC, Brussels.

Cornia, Giovanni A. 1990. "Child Poverty and Deprivation in Industrialized Countries: Recent Trends and Policy Options." Innocenti Occasional Paper 2. UNICEF, Florence.

Cowell, Frank A. 1990. *Cheating the Government*. Cambridge, Mass.: M.I.T. Press.

Department of Health and Social Security. 1975. "Two-Parent Families in Receipt of Family Income Supplement 1972." Statistical and Research Report Series 9. London.

———. 1985. "Reform of Social Security." HMSO Command 9517. London.

Department of Social Security. 1989. "Social Security Statistics." HMSO, London.

———. 1993a. "Income-Related Benefits: Estimates of Take-Up in 1989." London.

———. 1993b. "Social Security: The Government's Expenditure Plans, 1993–94 to 1995–96." HMSO, London.

Fisher, Jeffrey D., Arie Nadler, and S. Whitcher-Alanga. 1982. "Recipient Reactions to Aid: A Conceptual Review." *Psychological Bulletin* 91 (1): 27–54.

Foster, James E. 1984. "On Economic Poverty: A Survey of Aggregate Measures." *Advances in Econometrics* 3: 215–51.

Foster, James E., Joel Greer, and Eric Thorbecke. 1984. "A Class of Decomposable Poverty Measures." *Econometrica* 52: 761–66.

Glaude, Michel. 1991. "L'originalité du Système du Quotient Familial." *Economie et Statistique* 248: 51–67.

Goodin, R. E. 1985. "Erring on the Side of Kindness in Social Welfare." *Policy Sciences* 18: 141–56.

Henderson, Ronald F., Alison Harcourt, and R. J. A. Harper. 1970. *People in Poverty: A Melbourne Survey*. Melbourne, Australia: Cheshire.

Her Majesty's Treasury. 1988. "The Government's Expenditure Plans, 1988–89 to 1990–91." HMSO, London.

Holmans, S. K. 1987. *Social Security Systems in Selected Countries and their Integration with Tax Systems*. London: Her Majesty's Treasury.

International Labour Office. 1984. *Into the Twenty-First Century: The Development of Social Security*. Geneva.

Jallade, J-P. 1988. "Redistribution in the Welfare State: An Assessment of the French Performance." In J-P Jallade, ed., *The Crisis of Redistribution in European Welfare States*. Stoke-on-Trent, Eng.: Trentham Books.

Kanbur, Ravi. 1987. "Measurement and Alleviation of Poverty." *IMF Staff Papers* 34: 60–85.

Kanbur, Ravi, and M. J. Keen. 1989. "Poverty, Incentives, and Linear Income Taxation." In Andrew Dilnot and Ian Walker, eds., *The Economics of Social Security*, pp. 99–115. Oxford, Eng.: Oxford University Press.

Kanbur, Ravi, M. J. Keen, and M. Tuomala. 1990. "Optimal Non-linear Income Taxation for the Alleviation of Income Poverty." IFS Discussion Paper 91/2. Institute for Fiscal Studies, London.

McAlister, C., David Ingles, and D. Tune. 1981. "General Revenue Financing of Social Security: The Australian Minimum Income Support System." *Social Security Journal* (December): 24–38.

Ministère des Affaires Sociales. 1990. "Annuaire des statistiques sanitaires et sociales." SESI Documentation, Paris.

Moffitt, R. L. 1992. "Incentive Effects of the U.S. Welfare System." *Journal of Economic Literature* 30: 1–61.

Nichols, Albert L., and Richard J. Zeckhauser. 1982. "Targeting Transfers through Restrictions on Recipients." *American Economic Review Papers and Proceedings* 72: 373–77.

Nichols, Donald, Eugene Smolensky, and T. N. Tideman. 1971. "Discrimination by Waiting Time in Merit Goods." *American Economic Review* 16: 312–23.

NOSOSO (Nordic Social-Statistical Committee). 1993. *Social Security in the Nordic Countries*. Oslo.

Palmer, J. L., Timothy Smeeding, and B. B. Torrey, eds. 1988. *The Vulnerable*. Washington, D.C.: Urban Institute.

Preston, Samuel. 1984. "Children and the Elderly: Divergent Paths for America's Dependents." *Demography* 21: 435–57.

Ravallion, Martin. 1994. *Poverty Comparisons*. Fundamentals of Pure and Applied Economics, vol. 56. Chur, Switzerland: Harwood Academic Press.

Ravallion, Martin, and Kalvin Chao. 1989. "Targeted Policies for Poverty Alleviation under Imperfect Information: Algorithms and Applications." *Journal of Policy Modeling* 11: 213–24.

Ribich, T. I. 1968. *Education and Poverty*. Washington, D.C.: Brookings Institution.

Saunders, Peter. 1991. "Selectivity and Targeting in Income Support: The Australian Experience." *Journal of Social Policy* 20: 299–326.

Sawhill, Isabel V. 1988. "Poverty in the U.S.: Why Is It So Persistent?" *Journal of Economic Literature* 26: 1073–1119.

Seidman, L. S. 1990. *Saving for America's Economic Future*. Armonk, N.Y.: Sharpe.

Sen, Amartya K. 1976. "Poverty: An Ordinal Approach to Measurement." *Econometrica* 44: 219–31.

———. 1985. *Commodities and Capabilities*. Amsterdam: North-Holland.

———. 1992. *Inequality Reexamined*. Cambridge, Mass.: Harvard University Press.

Smeeding, Timothy, Barbara B. Torrey, and Martin Rein. 1988. "Patterns of Income and Poverty: The Economic Status of Children and the Elderly in Eight Countries." In J. L. Palmer, Timothy Smeeding, and B. B. Torrey, eds., *The Vulnerable*. Washington, D.C.: Urban Institute.

Stern, Nicholas H. 1982. "Optimum Taxation with Errors in Administration." *Journal of Public Economics* 17: 181–211.

van Oorschot, Wim. 1991. "Non-Take-Up of Social Security Benefits in Europe." *Journal of European Social Policy* 1: 15–30.

Weisbrod, Burton A. 1970. "Collective Action and the Distribution of Income: A Conceptual Approach." In R. H. Haveman and J. Margolis, eds., *Public Expenditure and Policy Analysis*. Chicago, Ill.: Markham.

Whiteford, Peter, and J. Doyle. 1991. "The Take-Up of FIS in 1986." SPRC Discussion Paper 29. University of New South Wales.

World Bank. 1990. *World Development Report 1990: Poverty*. New York: Oxford University Press.

4 Measuring the Distributional Impact of Public Goods

Richard Cornes

When you know, to know that you know,
And when you do not know, to know that you do not know,
That is knowledge.
    Confucius, *Analects* (c. 500 B.C., book 2, chap. 17)

For when I dinna clearly see,
I always own I dinna ken,
An' that's the way o' wisest men.
    Allan Ramsay, *The Clock and Dial* (1721, p. 28)

To be conscious that you are ignorant is a great step to knowledge.
    Benjamin Disraeli, *Sybil* (1845, p. 40)

Knowledge is the knowing that we cannot know.
[Orig.: He knows most that knows he knows little.]
    Ralph Waldo Emerson, *Representative Men: Montaigne* (1850, p. 174)

Whatever the focus of one's particular interest in the issues involved in targeting public expenditures toward the poor, sooner or later one has to confront difficult measurement problems. This chapter concentrates on two important issues that arise in assessing the distribution of the benefits of expenditure policies in an economy. These concern (a) what we need to measure and (b) how we should use the information we have. On the first of these questions, my concern is with the link that needs to be established, certainly if the conceptual framework is that of the welfarist approach, between the goods or services made available to individuals, on the one hand, and their effect on individual welfare, on the other. Even if one rejects this tradition in favor of the capability approach advocated by Amartya Sen, similar issues arise in terms of the productivity of, say, health or education policies as enhancers of individual capabilities. It is one thing to measure the extent to which health care or education, as measured by objective indexes of their services, reach their intended recipients. Within the welfarist tradition, to which I shall confine this discussion, to provide a proper evaluation of such services, we ideally need to go at least one step further and consider their marginal valuation by recipients as measuring, however crudely, their impact on individual welfare. I shall have little to say about how to obtain such information, though a clear implication of my arguments is that its present paucity is a major obstacle to policy evaluation in this context.

I shall be more concerned with identifying the kind of information regarding individuals' valuations of publicly provided goods and services that is required for informed appraisal of their distributional consequences and in providing a review, somewhat critical, of some suggested procedures for using such information in defining individuals' real incomes in situations where a substantial proportion of consumption is of commodities that are not provided through markets and whose prices, as a consequence, convey little information about the recipients' valuations. The bottom line of this review is that these procedures, which have been approvingly cited in treatments of benefit incidence, may perform rather worse than the intelligent application of fairly standard index number theory.

How should one apportion, or attribute, the benefits generated by government expenditure on goods and services? Such expenditures are far from negligible. For example, in one of the more substantial studies of government expenditure and income distribution in a developing country, Meerman (1979, p. 26) points out that federal expenditures in Malaysia in 1972 accounted for more than 30 percent of gross national product (GNP). Moreover, he specifically identifies 13.5 percent of GNP as representing outlays "possibly of high value to the poor." Certainly the policy objectives of many developing countries place great weight on the redistributive potential of such expenditures. Whether or not these objectives are realized remains a moot point. There can be little doubt, however, that government expenditures do have profound distributional consequences. Anyone with a concern for income or welfare distribution must therefore, sooner or later, be confronted with the need to incorporate them into the analysis.

What are the relevant characteristics of such expenditures that are responsible for the peculiar difficulties that they raise for welfare analysis? An examination of such sources as Meerman (1979), a companion study of Colombia by Selowsky (1979), and the large literature on transfers in kind (see, for example, Moon 1984, especially the papers by Olsen and York and by Smeeding) suggests a number of situations that are commonly encountered.

First, the government may simply produce a good and supply it at a subsidized price to consumers, while allowing them to act as price-takers. This is the framework adopted in Selowsky's study of Colombia. If the implied budget constraint and the chosen allocation can be observed, the pursuit of price-taking utility maximization by the consumers allows us to infer at least their marginal valuation of, or marginal benefit derived from, the subsidized good. Possible complications arise from nonlinear subsidies—for example, if the first measure of rice is free to the consumer, the second costs x rupees, and subsequent measures must be bought at the ruling market price—and from the possibility that different individuals, for whatever reason, face different subsidy schedules. Informationally, however, this situation is less problematic than some of the others to be considered. Subject to the qualification that an individual may be at a corner, or kink, of the budget constraint, marginal valuations are directly revealed to us by consumer behavior.

A more complicated situation arises when the subsidized commodity is allocated in a way that involves nonprice rationing. Indeed, in some cases, if the good is made available at zero direct cost to the consumer, such a constraint is necessary. This was the situation with respect to "free" school milk in pre-Thatcherite Britain. Not only may the price vary across individuals, perhaps being subject to some form of means test, but so too may the rationed quantity. This is the typical characteristic of in-kind subsidies (see Moon 1984).

Finally, there is the case of the pure nonexcludable public good. Here, each individual has access to the same quantity of the good at zero price. Whatever one may feel about the empirical relevance of such goods, this case is of great interest if only because of the frequency with which empirical studies cite it as providing an appropriate conceptual and theoretical framework. For present purposes, it can be thought of as being essentially like a subsidy accompanied by quantity rationing, in which the price of a publicly provided good is zero for all consumers and the rationed quantity is the same for all.

There are obviously many differences among the various situations outlined above. For example, into the public good category one might wish to place a whole group of general expenditures concerned with defense, internal security, general administration, and diplomacy whose benefits are so diffuse and intangible, though significant and real, that it is difficult even to imagine allocating their benefits among individuals, let alone accomplish the task empirically. With this view, which is espoused by Meerman (1979, p. 68), one can only have sympathy. I shall, however, argue that for present purposes it is useful—indeed important—to see all these situations as being united by two simply stated characteristics. The first is that, even if all persons are able to act as price-takers, those prices may differ across individuals. Consequently, even when comparing incomes across individuals at a single allocation, we have to be aware of and, if possible, allow for the implications of different prices when comparing individuals' real incomes. Second, if quantity constraints are present or, more generally, if there are significant kinks in individuals' budget constraints, information about preferences, even in the less ambitious form of local estimates of marginal willingness to pay, is not readily yielded up by observation of market transactions.

Understandably, analyses of distributional issues typically concentrate on models in which individuals are seen simply as competitive price-takers in the markets for those private goods that they demand. Even in this simple setting, there are enough thorny problems to exercise the mind. However, there is also a literature that seeks to accommodate the existence of goods that, for one reason or another, are not provided to individuals at prices that reflect their marginal valuations. These may include goods that are commonly thought of as possessing "intrinsic publicness," along with those that happen to be provided by the public sector and for which use of the price mechanism to assist their allocation is deliberately eschewed. As so often happens, impatient empirical workers had been asking questions about the possible regressive or progressive implications of public good provision, and developing ad hoc ways to tackle them, long before theorists got interested in analyzing the conceptual and theoretical questions raised by these issues.

Existing Literature

Existing studies of the distributional consequences of public good provision typically make scant appeal to economic or welfare theory. Indeed, it seems that attempts before 1970 to distribute the benefits of public good provision made no use of demand theory, but instead used various ad hoc procedures for allocating the cost of provision across individuals in proportion to money income, disposable income, and capital income, equally across families, and so on. Aaron and McGuire (1970) appear to have been the first to consider explicitly how, if at all, measures of the benefits accruing to individuals from public goods could be linked to and justified by the standard model of consumer behavior and welfare that is found in textbooks.

The initial Aaron-McGuire paper generated a flurry of literature. In particular, their suggested alternative measure of the impact of a public good on the distribution of "total income" provoked a sharp criticism from Brennan (1976a). There was a brief exchange of views (see Aaron and McGuire 1976; Brennan 1976b) followed by a summary and restatement by Brennan (1981) of his position. Independent of this exchange, the Aaron-McGuire piece prompted a contribution from Maital (1973, 1975). However, Maital did not question their procedure, but rather concentrated on experimenting with parameter values within the framework offered by Aaron and McGuire. Since that time, there has been little activity on this front. In spite of Aaron and McGuire's contribution, the ensuing debate remains curiously, it seems almost willfully, uninfluenced by developments elsewhere in economics. Later empirical work (for example, Meerman 1979; Smolensky and others 1977; Gillespie and LaBelle 1978) generally refers to Aaron-McGuire approvingly. It appears that, although empirical workers remain skeptical about the operational usefulness of the procedures—and this is an understandable reaction on the part of those facing the task of deriving empirical results from meager data sets—the Aaron-McGuire procedure nevertheless is seen as providing a theoretically attractive framework for benefit and income measurement in the presence of government expenditure. Indeed, Gillespie and LaBelle (1978, p. 188) refer to the Aaron-McGuire methodology as "based on a rigorous theoretical foundation." Textbooks on public economics are generally uninformative on this topic. Tresch (1981, pp. 420–23), Atkinson and Stiglitz (1980), and Brown and Jackson (1986, pp. 162–67) have brief discussions, but all are based on acceptance of the Aaron-McGuire procedure. Most textbooks and surveys, such as Auerbach and Feldstein (1985, 1987), ignore the topic entirely. It seems as though, while some may feel uneasy with the standard procedures for attributing the shares of benefits from public goods to individual consumers, it is generally thought that there is no more that can usefully be said concerning the conceptual or theoretical framework for such an endeavor.

I do not take this view. I believe that, even though we may not now, or in the foreseeable future, possess the information required to compute "ideal" measures of total income in contexts where part of that income appears in the form of public or publicly provided goods, there are substantial returns to be gained by considering what would constitute such ideal measures and how one might use them. Indeed, I would go further and suggest that informational constraints, whether real or imaginary, may have tempted researchers to fall back on simple ad hoc measures that may be worse than useless, insofar as they encourage the belief that we have answered questions when in fact we have not. My own reading of the theoretical literature, particularly of Brennan's last word, suggests that failure to keep the mind firmly focused on the original motive for this line of inquiry has led to a preoccupation with concerns that are, at times, of questionable relevance. In particular, it has led to the suggestion of various properties considered desirable for operational measures of income that have little bearing on their suitability or accuracy as measures of full real income.

"Ideal" Measures of Individual Income

Any measure of an individual's full "real" income should ideally have certain elementary properties. First, suppose we are considering a situation in which each individual can consume the same quantity of a public, or publicly provided private, good. Suppose further that we are prepared to regard individuals as identical in every respect except that their money incomes differ. In particular, we are prepared to say that, of any two individuals, the one with the higher money income is the better off of the two. Then, since we are trying to obtain an index of welfare, or real income, we would want our measure to impute a higher full income to the individual with higher money income. Second, suppose that we are comparing an initial situation with another in which, say, the provision of the publicly provided good has risen and the level of money income has fallen, perhaps because the individual is compelled to pay a share of the cost of the extra provision. We would want our measure to increase, remain the same, or fall, depending on whether the individual is made better off, left unaffected, or made worse off by the change. In short, we want to define an index that labels an individual's indifference map in such a way that it takes on higher values for more preferred bundles of goods. There are many ways of doing this, but a few recommend themselves by virtue of being easy to interpret in a straightforward way. These are measures that express a welfare change in terms of the equivalent change in an individual's income at a given set of prices under well-defined conditions.

If we seek an exact money measure of the welfare of an individual, it is natural to turn to the idea of equivalent income based on some form of the income compensation function, introduced by McKenzie (1957), analyzed systematically by Hurwicz and Uzawa (1971), and since developed by a number of writers (for example, McKenzie and Pearce 1976; Vartia 1983; McKenzie 1983) as a tool of applied welfare economics. My exposition will consider, in turn, two situations: those involving private goods and those involving public or publicly provided private goods provided at zero or positive direct cost, but in rationed quantities. It transpires that, when there are quantity constraints in addition to the standard budget constraint, there are alternative natural welfare measures, no one of which commands attention as inherently superior. A longer and more thorough discussion of much of the material in this section can be found in Cornes (1992, chap. 9).

Price-taking Situations

The first case to be considered is the standard "pure price-taking" situation, in which the individual faces a set of exogenous prices and, subject to the implied single linear budget constraint, chooses the most preferred bundle. I assume that the individual's preferences are representable by a utility function that is everywhere differentiable and strictly quasi-concave and that this function can be taken as providing

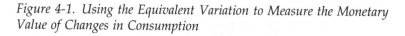

Figure 4-1. Using the Equivalent Variation to Measure the Monetary Value of Changes in Consumption

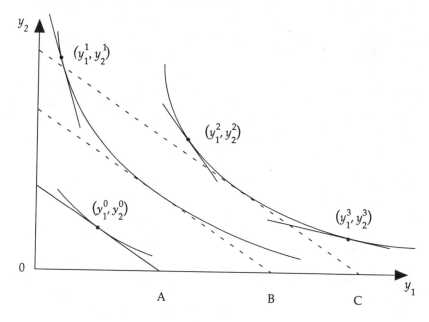

an ordinal representation of individual welfare. That is, I wish to give it normative as well as positive significance.

Let p be the vector of competitive prices, m the exogenous income, and y the vector of quantities chosen. Situation j is completely described by the vector of exogenous variables (p^j, m^j) and the individual's choice y^j. I shall denote the utility level associated with y^j by u^j. Suppose that, starting from a status quo situation, (p^0, m^0), we want to evaluate the consequences of adopting any one of a number of alternative situations, (p^j, m^j), where $j = 1, 2, \ldots, n$. A natural money measure of the level of welfare in situation j is the minimum expenditure required by the individual, if facing the price vector p^0, to be just as well off as in situation j. Symbolically, we can write this as $E[p^0, V(p^j, m^j)]$. The equivalent variation (EV, as suggested in Hicks 1943) is simply the change in this magnitude associated with the move from situation 0 to situation j:

(4-1) $$EV^{0j} = E[p^0, V(p^j, m^j)] - E[p^0, V(p^0, m^0)].$$

It is shown in figure 4-1. Suppose that the individual's initial budget constraint is represented by the continuous straight line through point A. In terms of commodity 1, initial income is OA. With prices held constant at their initial levels, the move from situation 0 to situation 1, in which the individual chooses the bundle (y_1^1, y_2^1) and attains the utility level u^1, is equivalent to a change in income that moves the budget constraint in a parallel fashion until it passes through point B, so that the individual can just attain the utility level u^1. In terms of commodity 1, the required change in income is $OB - OA = AB$. The figure also shows two further alternative situations between which the individual is indifferent. This allows us to see very clearly that the equivalent variation takes the same value for each of these situations: $EV^{02} = EV^{03} = OC - OA = AC$. Equally clearly, $EV^{02} > EV^{01}$. The equivalent variation satisfies our requirement that it should take on higher values for more preferred alternatives. Had we considered an alternative that was less attractive than the initial situation, the associated EV would have taken a negative value.

Before moving on to the second situation, let me draw attention to the following points.

(a) The reference price vector at which the minimum expenditure is evaluated need not be the vector associated with the status quo. It could be any arbitrary reference price vector. What is important is that the same price vector be used for all comparisons. The EV is simply a natural special case.

(b) Contingent on a particular choice of p^r, the expenditure function is a perfectly good ordinal utility function. Consequently, for a given initial situation (p^0, m^0) and, therefore, the associated reference price vector, EV^{0j}, $j = 1, \ldots, n$ provides a correct welfare ranking of the alternative situations.

(c) However, without further assumptions, we are not justified in conferring any cardinal significance on the expenditure function. The fact that $EV^{0i} = 2EV^{0j}$, for example, does not justify the statement that the welfare improvement in moving to situation i is twice that implied by the move to situation j.

(d) The EV is identical with the notion of willingness to accept. Although most discussions of the equivalent income concept concentrate on comparing a given individual's welfare in two or more alternative situations, the emphasis of this chapter is on distributional concerns. We are therefore also interested in comparing welfare levels across individuals in a given allocation. In general, of course, this raises informational problems of measurability and interpersonal comparability for which there are no clear answers. The literature on public good benefit attribution has typically assumed that individuals have identical preference maps and that we can rank the individual welfare levels implied by a given allocation. We are therefore assuming a certain degree of interpersonal comparability, without committing ourselves to any notion of cardinal measurability of individual welfare. This can be summarized in the final observation:

(e) Let individuals A and B have identical preferences over the vector of goods y. Then if $E[p^r; V(p, m^A)] > E[p^r; V(p, m^B)]$, we can say that A is better off at (p, m^A) than B is at (p, m^B).

Figure 4-2. *Measuring Welfare with a Public Good*

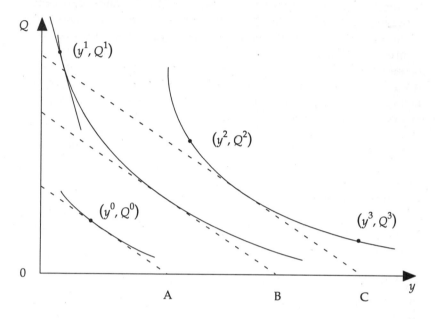

Situations Involving Publicly Provided Goods

Retain the assumption that the individual can freely choose the vector of private goods y subject to the standard linear budget constraint. However, now introduce a public, or publicly provided private, good about which the individual cares and which is made available at zero price to that individual in a quantity taken as exogenous. (It is easy to generalize the argument to situations involving more than one type of public good.) If we denote this level by Q, the utility function is now $U(y, Q)$. There are two natural ways of adapting the notion of equivalent income. The figures are restricted to a single private good, which may be thought of as a Hicksian composite good, and a single public good. This restriction has a geometric implication that I should emphasize in order to avoid potential misunderstanding. This is that the price vector p nowhere appears in those figures, such as figure 4-2, that depict this situation. The assumption is that, in the background, the individual is choosing the various private goods optimally. The figures do not show this but simply show the individual as faced with an endowment of money income m, which is equivalent to an endowment of the composite private commodity y, together with an endowment of the single public good, Q. I shall normalize the composite good so that a unit of it costs a unit of money. This enables me to equate distances along the private good axis with money income.

One alternative is to mimic the analysis of the price-taking situation. The most obvious difference, of course, is that we cannot observe the individual's marginal rate of substitution, or relative demand price (v^0), for the public good at the initial situation. Suppose, however, that we are able to obtain an estimate of it. The initial situation is equivalent to one in which the individual is facing a budget line that passes through the initial bundle and has slope equal to the value of the demand price at that point. We wish to evaluate the move to an alternative economic environment (p^j, Q^j, m^j) in which the individual is observed consuming the bundle (y^j, Q^j), thereby achieving utility level u^j. Now imagine the individual instead facing the set of initial prices (p^0, v^0) for both private and public goods, and able to act as a price-taker for every commodity, and consider the question: What additional income would just enable the individual, when facing the price vector (p^0, v^0), to attain an allocation that is as attractive as the observed situation? This again defines the equivalent variation,

(4-2) $$EV^{0j} = E(p^0, v^0, u^j) - E(p^0, v^0, u^0).$$

This is shown in figure 4-2. The slope of the dashed line that touches the indifference curve at (y^0, Q^0) reflects the value of v^0. The dashed line is the hypothetical budget line that would lead a price-taker to choose the initially observed bundle. If the individual is imagined to act as a price-taker facing the prices (p^0, v^0), then the distance OB represents the amount of income required to attain the level of utility associated with situation 1. The distance OB − OA = AB is the equivalent variation associated with the move from 0 to 1. The figure is in fact the same as figure 4-1 except that there is no directly observed demand price for the rationed good Q. Hence the initial "budget" line, which is hypothetical, is dashed instead of continuous. The basic argument, however, is essentially identical with that for the price-taking situation. The current thought experiment answers the question: If the individual were able to act as a price-taker and were to face the prices (p^0, v^0), what minimum income would be required for him to be as well off as in the constrained situation (p^j, Q^j, m^j)? In making interpersonal comparisons, we have to be careful. Since both face the same initial prices for private goods, we can choose the common reference price vector $p^r = p^0$. However, it is important to observe that, in general, individuals' demand prices at their initial situations will differ. Consequently, if we wish to use initial magnitudes as reference prices, we need to choose one or the other individual's initial demand price— or, indeed, some other common price—as the reference price for the public good.

Although the measure that I have just defined is a perfectly acceptable ordinal welfare measure, some writers feel that if the situations that are under evaluation involve quantity constraints, then it is preferable

Figure 4-3. Introducing Rationing of a Public Good

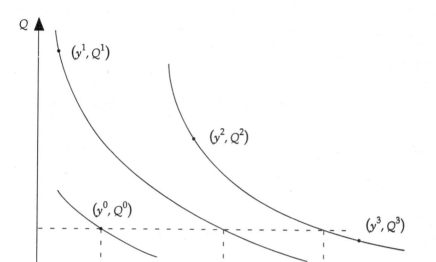

to use welfare measures that themselves incorporate such constraints. It is easy to construct such measures. Consider the following question: If an individual were confronted with the private goods price vector p^0 and were also constrained to consume the quantity Q^0 of a public good, what level of expenditure on private goods would just enable him to be as well off as in the constrained situation (p^i, Q^i, m^i)? This defines a quantity-constrained expenditure function, $E[p^0, Q^0, V(p^i, Q^i, m^i)]$. Figure 4-3 shows the resulting measure for the two-good example. Given the reference quantity Q^0, each indifference curve is indexed by the quantity of the (composite) private good required to attain that curve.

Imagine a government agency making units of some commodity z available to a consumer at some positive price π, while at the same time restricting the level of consumption of the subsidized commodity. I shall assume that the restriction forces consumption to be below some level, although the analysis goes through if the individual is, instead, compelled to consume at least a certain minimum level. Also, the price π that is actually paid for units of z could, if desired, be zero. This takes us back to the setting that we have just analyzed. Even with a positive price, however, the same principles apply. If we can estimate the preference map, then we can calculate either equivalent variations or equivalent surpluses associated with moves from a given initial situation. We may use these measures both to rank the initial welfare levels of individuals and also to identify whether a given change makes an individual better or worse off.

The Aaron-McGuire and Brennan Measures

Aaron and McGuire (1970) suggest that the benefit to an individual of consuming the quantity Q of a public good should be evaluated at that individual's demand price—or, in the language of rationing theory, the virtual price—for that good. The resulting value should then be added to money income to obtain the value of full income. For example, suppose an individual receives a money income of $30 and can consume twelve units of a publicly provided good. Suppose we know that at the margin they regard one unit of the publicly provided good as having the same value as one unit of money income. Then Aaron and McGuire would calculate the value of the publicly provided good as $12 and full income as $30 + 12 = \$42$. Algebraically, their suggested measure of benefit is

$$(4\text{-}3) \qquad\qquad B^{AM}(p, Q, m) = v^*(p, Q, m)Q,$$

where the marginal valuation $v^*(p, Q, m)$, or marginal rate of substitution between public and private goods, is evaluated at the observed allocation. It is asterisked to emphasize the fact that it is a restricted or rationed function, since one of its arguments is the quantity Q. Aaron and McGuire's suggested measure of full income is then

$$(4\text{-}4) \quad I^{AM}(p, Q, m) = m + B^{AM}(p, Q, m) = m + v^*(p, Q, m)Q.$$

It can be seen that the Aaron-McGuire measures use information about individual preferences. One other significant characteristic, to which I shall return later, is that the price used for evaluating the public good generally varies across individuals.

By contrast with Aaron-McGuire, the procedure suggested by Brennan essentially ignores individual preferences. Brennan (1976a, p. 396; 1981, p. 355) suggests that the benefit to an individual of the services provided by the quantity Q of a public good be computed by valuing each unit of the public good at its per capita marginal cost. Let the constant unit cost of the public good be C. Then, if there are n individual consumers, the per capita unit cost is $c = C / n$. Brennan's measure of the benefit to the individual is then

$$(4\text{-}5) \qquad\qquad B^B(c, Q) = cQ,$$

and the individual's full income is

$$(4\text{-}6) \qquad\qquad I^B(c, Q, m) = m + cQ.$$

Brennan points out that if public goods are optimally supplied, in the sense that Samuelson's optimality condition is satisfied, then under his assumptions this procedure is equivalent to valuing the public good at the arithmetic mean of all the individual marginal valuations. In a sense, then, Brennan would claim that his procedure uses demand information. However, this seems no more than an arbitrary, if tidy, normalization. It seems fair to characterize Brennan's measure of benefit and of full income as differing from those of Aaron and McGuire in two respects. First, the former ignores information about preferences, basing valuation instead on cost considerations. Second, it uses a common valuation across individuals of the benefits associated with Q.

An Assessment of the Aaron-McGuire–Brennan Debate

Whatever one may feel about the operational usefulness of the "ideal" measures of income defined in the third part of this chapter, the analysis there provides one with a helpful perspective from which to assess the Aaron-McGuire and Brennan contributions. As I mentioned in the introduction, prior to Aaron-McGuire the attribution of benefits from public goods—and indeed from government expenditures in general— was determined somewhat arbitrarily by dividing them equally among families or in proportion to individual incomes (variously defined) or asset holdings, or on some other equally ad hoc basis. Aaron and McGuire should take credit for arguing, more persuasively in my view than in Brennan's view, that individual preferences—more specifically, individual marginal valuations of the good in question—are important ingredients of any exercise that attempts to say something about the benefits of public and publicly provided private goods.

There are two legitimate worries about their analysis. The first is best appreciated by considering figure 4-4. Suppose that we interpret the two axes as representing the quantities of two private goods and that allocations A and B are thought of as the allocations chosen by a price-taking individual with given stable preferences before and after an exogenous change in economic circumstances. If it were suggested that we might use the horizontal distances 0C and 0D to represent the individual's income in the two states, an obvious objection would occur—I hope!—to the intelligent reader of any undergraduate microeconomics text. Although B is preferred to A, it can be seen that 0D < 0C, indicating that the move from A to B results in a fall in income. 0C and 0D should not be used as indicators of real income, or welfare, because their values are influenced by the use of different prices for valuing the two allocations. From this sort of observation has developed a large part of the literature on the economic theory of index numbers. The same figure, however, can be interpreted as showing the allocations enjoyed by two individuals, A and B, who have identical preference maps, both of whom consume the same quantity of the good measured along the horizontal axis (the "public good"), but one of whom—

Figure 4-4. Illustrating an Objection to the Aaron-McGuire Measure

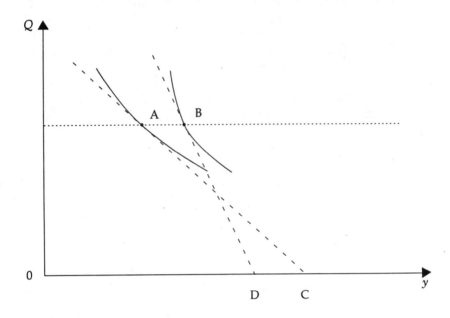

individual B—enjoys a higher level of consumption of the other good
(the "private good"). Brennan (1981) uses this observation to poke fun
at the Aaron-McGuire measure, since it shows A as having higher full
income even though tastes are identical and A consumes an unambiguously smaller bundle of goods. Although, as Aaron and McGuire correctly point out, information about the individual's preferences is
important, their suggested procedure contaminates the measure by
evaluating expenditures for different individuals at different prices.

   Brennan's own measure passes this particular "test by thought experiment" without difficulty. His use of a common valuation across individuals overcomes the possibility of the sort of anomaly that may result
from the Aaron-McGuire procedure. Using Brennan's approach, if *n*
individuals with identical preference maps, and each consuming the
same quantity of the public good, differ only in terms of exogenous
money income, then the ranking of "full" income is the same as the
ranking of utility levels; indeed, both will correspond to the ranking of
money income. But this is true whatever (positive) common valuation is
placed on the public good. So long as Q is fixed, and we want to
rank welfare levels for individuals with identical preference maps, any
common non-negative valuation of Q will do the trick. If we want an
ordering of welfare levels for a given value of Q, we may equally well
use money income as Brennan's measure of full income.

Figure 4-5. Illustrating an Objection to the Brennan Measure

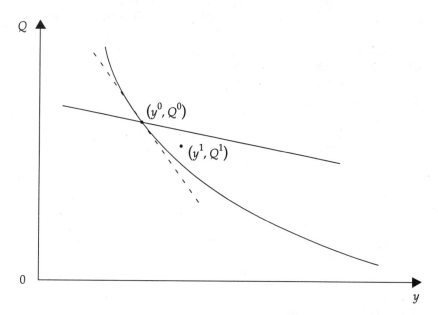

Brennan's measure, however, does not use information about the individual's preferences, and this makes it also prone to error, as the following simple thought experiment shows. Imagine a given individual in the one private good, one public good world. We wish to consider the change in real income implied by the move from allocation 0 to allocation 1 in figure 4-5. If the Aaron-McGuire measure is applied to measure the value of the change in consumption bundle *at the initial demand prices*, as seems natural in this context, then for small (strictly speaking, infinitesimal) changes it will correctly indicate whether an individual's real income has risen or fallen as a result of the move. This follows simply from the observation that the marginal valuation at the observed observation is the slope of the indifference curve at that point. By contrast, since Brennan's measure is not related to an individual's marginal rate of substitution, it can, even for small changes, indicate an increase in income when welfare has fallen and a fall in income when welfare has risen. Suppose that, using Brennan's measure, the continuous line through (y^0, Q^0) in figure 4-5 indicates situations of the same value. Then Brennan's measure would suggest that the move from (y^0, Q^0) to (y^1, Q^1) makes the individual worse off, even though in fact she is better off. Whatever the problems with the Aaron-McGuire procedure, at least it provides a locally valid approximation of an individual's indifference curve. For the same reason, if we were to imagine an economy in which there are two public goods, and consider the consequences of diverting expenditure away from one and toward the other, while keeping individual money incomes net of tax constant, Brennan's measure would bear no relationship to the direction of changes in individual welfare levels to such a reallocation. It cannot capture the fact that a sick individual with no children may benefit from a diversion of public expenditure from education to health, while a healthy family with children may lose out.

Whether this method of applying Aaron and McGuire's procedure is in the spirit of their initial contribution is for them, not for me, to say. However, this example makes clear the need to follow them in using information about individual demand prices once both Q and y differ across the situations being compared. Information about demand prices, or marginal rates of substitution, is necessary if we are to avoid generating measures with anomalous—indeed, downright perverse— properties. The following section of this chapter sets out the current received wisdom on the definition of conceptually exact measures of "real income." The resulting measures followed Aaron and McGuire in using information about individual preferences while at the same time avoiding the problems associated with using different prices for evaluating different individuals' full incomes.

An Alternative Operational Procedure

There is no doubt that the "ideal" measures presented earlier are informationally very demanding. They require the estimation of systems of demand and inverse demand functions in a setting in which relevant data are especially hard to come by. However, they provided, in the last section, a convenient vantage point from which to examine the Aaron-McGuire and Brennan procedures. I now want to exploit the insights gained to suggest a procedure that is less informationally demanding than the construction of an "ideal" measure but that does, subject to the availability of reliable data, allow us to make at least some interesting and valid inferences about the distributional impact of government expenditures. The suggestion involves little more than a simple application of index number theory, of which Pollak (1989) provides a useful discussion, to situations of the kind considered in this chapter. Its simplicity makes it easy to see what can, and what cannot, be inferred from given observations. The reader who feels that even this procedure makes unrealistic demands on sparse data sets should wait until after my description of the procedure for further remarks on this matter.

Suppose we wish to compare two situations, identified by the superscripts 0 and 1. In the notation of this chapter, household h faces an economic environment described by the vector (p^0, Q^0, m^{h0}) in the initial situation and (p^1, Q^1, m^{h1}) in the final situation. These vectors are observable, as are the actual consumption bundles chosen in each situation.

In the initial situation, if preferences are identical across individuals, we have already seen that either the Brennan measure or, indeed, nominal income provides the correct ranking of welfare *levels*. Similarly, we can obtain the correct ordering of welfare levels in the final situation.

If not only income levels but also levels of Q differ across individuals within each situation, then we will need estimates of their demand prices in the neighborhood of their observed bundles in order to have any chance of ranking their welfare levels correctly. Consider, for example, the welfare ranking of two individuals at the initial situation. Four possibilities arise, exactly analogous to the reasoning provided by, for example, Samuelson (1950) in his comparison of a single individual in two situations:

(a) If A's bundle, (y^{A0}, Q^{A0}), costs more than B's bundle, (y^{B0}, Q^{B0}), whether valued at A's reference prices, (p^0, v^{A0}), or B's, (p^0, v^{B0}), then A has a higher real income than B.

(b) If B's bundle, (y^{B0}, Q^{B0}), costs more than A's bundle, (y^{A0}, Q^{A0}), whether valued at A's reference prices, (p^0, v^{A0}), or B's, (p^0, v^{B0}), then B has a higher real income than A.

(c) If B's bundle costs more at A's references prices, and A's bundle costs more at B's reference prices, then our observations are consistent with A and B having the same preference map, but their real incomes cannot be ranked on the basis of the information available.

(d) If A's bundle costs more at A's reference prices, and B's bundle costs more at B's reference prices, then our observations are inconsistent with A and B having the same preference map.

To compare situations 0 and 1—specifically, to identify the direction of welfare *changes* for a representative individual—we can calculate the standard Paasche and Laspeyres quantity index numbers. To calculate the Laspeyres index, we need to estimate the status quo valuations, (p^0, v^{h0}), and the Paasche index requires an estimate of the final period valuations, (p^1, v^{h1}). Again, there are four possible outcomes, and we can appeal again to standard results (Samuelson 1950). If both QI_L and QI_P exceed unity, then the individual is made better off by the move from situation 0 to situation 1. If both fall short of unity, the individual is made worse off. If $QI_L > 1$ and $QI_P < 1$, behavior is consistent with the model of utility maximizing behavior, but we cannot say whether the individual is made better or worse off—we may, in short, be in the "zone of ignorance." Finally, if $QI_L < 1$ and $QI_P > 1$, then observed or predicted behavior is inconsistent with that model, and we have no coherent basis whatever for welfare statements.

By following these procedures, we may be able to obtain (a) an ordering of the individual's initial and final welfare levels and (b) a reliable indicator of whether a given individual's "real" income has risen or fallen in the move from situation 0 to 1. This is, indeed, as far as we can go without making stronger assumptions about measurability and interpersonal comparability of welfare.

It may be objected that even the local information requirements of this procedure are unrealistically demanding. If this view is accepted, the analysis of the present chapter suggests that it may be very misleading to resort to alternative ad hoc procedures of benefit apportionment according to income levels, or whatever, without some rationale along the lines offered above. If such procedures for apportionment have any attraction, it must be because they provide us with our best estimate of demand prices. If we use weights that depart significantly from those valuations, then we run the risk of wrongly identifying even the direction of change in an individual's welfare. It is surely preferable, if we can do no better, to admit the fact rather than to devise ingenious procedures that may provide us with answers, but not to the questions that initially motivated the enquiry.

Concluding Comments

The twin aspects of economics, as both an intellectual discipline concerned with understanding and as an input into policy prescriptions, create peculiar tensions. On the one hand, economic problems cry out for urgent action to enhance individual well-being and alleviate the misery of poverty and deprivation. On the other, the complexity of economic systems challenges our ability to understand how best to set about such tasks. This tension is clear in the literature on public expenditure benefit attribution. On the one hand, the policy-minded economist is impatient to measure and to draw policy conclusions, while on the other hand, the theorist worries about the slender foundation on which such endeavors necessarily rest. Two sorts of informational constraints limit what we can legitimately conclude about the likely consequences of government expenditure policies for the distribution of well-being. The difficulty of obtaining information about demand prices for specific goods, or bads, is a particular feature in this area. While difficult to resolve, it is essentially a technical problem for which increasingly attractive solutions have been developed. In addition, though, there are the informational problems, of a rather deeper nature, that have to do with the measurability of individual welfare and our ability to make interpersonal welfare comparisons. How far we are able or willing to go in this direction inherently limits our ability to evaluate income distributions, however satisfactorily we solve the first problem.

When Aaron and McGuire's initial contribution to this topic appeared in 1970, very little attention had been given to the empirical problem of deriving estimates of demand prices of nonmarketed goods. One can understand, without necessarily agreeing with, those who may have felt that even the estimation of a locally valid value for a demand price, let alone a more general preference map, should be put in the "too hard" basket and that Aaron and McGuire's procedure, whatever its potential theoretical merits, required too much unobtainable information to be operationally useful. However, we now know more than we once did about the possibility of obtaining such information. The two decades that have passed since the Aaron-McGuire contribution have witnessed an enormous amount of research on methods of obtaining estimates of individual valuations on nonmarketed goods. In the space available I can do little more than cite a few of the more significant contributions, but the existence of excellent surveys and expository treatments of the current state of the art make it an easy matter for the interested reader to go further.

The literature on environmental economics has been especially productive of suggested methods of valuing nonmarketed goods. This is hardly surprising, since environmental goods such as clean air, clean water, climate, open-access recreational facilities, and other environmental amenities are obvious and significant examples of such goods. The difficulties of obtaining valuations have provoked a good deal of ingenuity in suggested alternative methods and a good deal of controversy over their usefulness. I can do no more than draw attention to two bodies of literature, sometimes seen as competing alternatives, but more helpfully thought of, in my view, as complementary. These are (a) indirect market techniques and (b) the contingent valuation approach.

Given that demands for, or valuations of, public and publicly provided private goods are not directly observed, it is natural to consider whether observed behavior in private goods markets may indirectly reveal information. For example, it has long been recognized that expenditures of money and time that individuals are willing to incur to travel to and from a national park should tell us something about their valuation of the park's services. Techniques pioneered by Mäler (1971), Bradford and Hildebrandt (1977), and Willig (1978) allow us, in somewhat more general settings, to make inferences about the valuation of nonmarketed goods from information concerning market transactions together with data on the quantities consumed of the nonmarketed goods.

This indirect market approach has the great advantage of being cheap to undertake. However, it requires assuming a rather particular structure for preferences, and in some situations it may simply not work. Because of this, more expensive techniques involving surveys and questionnaires have received a good deal of attention. Such exercises attempt to elicit directly from respondents information about their valuation of a particular good. There are now several good surveys of this important body of literature, and one that I have found particularly helpful is Mitchell and Carson (1989).

The analysis of this chapter provides no ready comfort to individuals required to evaluate the distributional incidence of expenditure policies. The main message is that, if we wish to base such evaluations on the sort of considerations deemed significant in the literature on welfare economics, we need, at the very least, hard-to-get estimates of marginal valuations of the goods being provided. On a more positive note, I have suggested that given such estimates, at least locally, we can do a lot worse than apply the insights of plain old-fashioned index number theory. If such estimates are not available, we should heed the quotations that head this chapter and not delude ourselves into thinking that ingenious technical procedures can conjure empirical conclusions out of a dataless void. In particular situations, it is of course possible that the rankings of individual welfare levels and the signing of welfare responses to given expenditure changes are not very sensitive to the estimates of demand prices. Sensitivity tests may be done to confirm this. Alternatively, it may be useful to turn the analysis around and ask what has to be assumed about marginal valuations in order for a given expenditure policy to change distribution in a direction considered desirable.

One last comment may be made that is, perhaps, of particular relevance to this book. All the literature discussed in this chapter has assumed identical preferences across consumers. This is always a limiting and worrying assumption. However, it may be particularly so in the present context. There is an important strand of literature on targeting that stresses the problems governments have in identifying the appropriate recipients of transfers, and there has been growing interest in the suggestion that the prevalence of in-kind transfers and of public provision of goods may be positively explained, and normatively justified, by their ability to exploit self-selection processes in a way that is not possible with cash transfers. To the extent that this is so, the mechanism relies crucially on preference differences across individuals. If a government announces that it will give cash benefits to all sufferers from disease x, and if it is difficult to diagnose that disease with confidence—as appears to have been the case in Australia, with repetitive stress injury—this announcement will do much to spread the disease. However, if the transfer is in a form that greatly benefits genuine sufferers but not others, it is easier to target resources at the genuine sufferers. Perhaps heterogeneous preferences lie at the heart of many instances of in-kind transfers. If so, we still have a long way to go in order to be able to appraise the distributional consequences of such policies.

References

Aaron, Henry, and Martin C. McGuire. 1970. "Public Goods and Income Distribution." *Econometrica* 38 (6): 907–20.

————. 1976. "The Distributional Implications of Public Goods: Comment." *Econometrica* 44: 400–04.

Atkinson, A. B., and J. E. Stiglitz. 1980. *Lectures on Public Economics*. New York: McGraw-Hill.

Auerbach, Alan J., and Martin S. Feldstein. 1985. *Handbook of Public Economics*, vol. 1. Amsterdam: North-Holland.

————. 1987. *Handbook of Public Economics*, vol. 2. Amsterdam: North-Holland.

Boadway, R. W., and Neil Bruce. 1984. *Welfare Economics*. Oxford, Eng.: Blackwell.

Bradford, David F., and Gregory G. Hildebrandt. 1977. "Observable Preferences for Public Goods." *Journal of Public Economics* 8 (2): 111–31.

Brennan, Goeffrey. 1976a. "The Distributional Implications of Public Goods." *Econometrica* 44: 391–99.

————. 1976b. "A Reply to Aaron and McGuire." *Econometrica* 44: 405–08.

————. 1981. "The Attribution of Public Goods Benefits." *Public Finance / Finances Publiques* 36: 347–73.

Brown, C. V., and P. M. Jackson. 1986. *Public Sector Economics*, 3d ed. London: Martin Robertson.

Confucius. c. 500 B.C. *Analects*. In A. Waley, trans., *The Analects of Confucius*, book 2, chap. 17. London: Allen and Unwin, 1938.

Cornes, Richard C. 1992. *Duality and Modern Economics*. New York: Cambridge University Press.

Disraeli, Benjamin. 1845. *Sybil*. In *The Bradenham Edition*. Vol. 9: *Novels and Tales*. London: Peter Davies, 1927.

Emerson, Ralph Waldo. 1850. *Representative Men: Montaigne*. In *The Complete Works of Ralph Waldo Emerson*. Vol. 4: *Representative Men*. Boston: Houghton Mifflin and Company, 1903.

Gillespie, W. I., and J. B. LaBelle. 1978. "A Pro-Poor or Pro-Rich Redistribution of Income?" *National Tax Journal* 31: 185–89.

Hicks, J. R. 1943. "The Four Consumers' Surpluses." *Review of Economic Studies* 11: 31–41.

Hurwicz, Leonid, and Hirofumi Uzawa. 1971. "On the Integrability of Demand Functions." In J. S. Chipman, Leonid Hurwicz, M. K. Richter, and H. F. Sonnenschein, eds., *Preferences, Utility, and Demand*. New York: Harcourt Brace Jovanovich.

McKenzie, G. W. 1983. *Measuring Economic Welfare: New Methods*. Cambridge, Eng.: Cambridge University Press.

McKenzie, G. W., and I. F. Pearce. 1976. "Exact Measures of Welfare and the Cost of Living." *Review of Economic Studies* 43: 465–68.

McKenzie, L. W. 1957. "Demand Theory without a Utility Index." *Review of Economic Studies* 24: 185–89.

Maital, Shlomo. 1973. "Public Goods and Income Distribution: Some Further Results." *Econometrica* 41: 561–68.

————. 1975. "Apportionment of Public Goods Benefits to Individuals." *Public Finance* 30: 397–416.

Mäler, Karl-Göran. 1971. "A Method for Estimating Social Benefits from Pollution Control." *Swedish Journal of Economics* 73: 121–33.

Meerman, Jacob. 1979. *Public Expenditure in Malaysia: Who Benefits and Why.* New York: Oxford University Press.

Mitchell, R. C., and R. T. Carson. 1989. *Using Surveys to Value Public Goods: The Contingent Valuation Method.* Washington, D.C.: Resources for the Future.

Moon, Marilyn, ed. 1984. *Economic Transfers in the United States: Studies in Income and Wealth,* vol. 49. Chicago, Ill.: University of Chicago Press for the National Bureau of Economic Research.

Olsen, E. O., and K. A. York. 1984. "The Effect of Different Measures of Benefit on Estimates of the Distributive Consequences of Government Programs." In Marilyn Moon, ed., *Economic Transfers in the United States: Studies in Income and Wealth,* vol. 49. Chicago, Ill.: University of Chicago Press for the National Bureau of Economic Research.

Pollak, Robert A. 1989. *The Theory of the Cost-of-Living Index.* New York: Oxford University Press.

Ramsay, Allan. 1721. *The Clock and Dial.* In B. Martin and J. W. Oliver, eds., *The Works of Allan Ramsay,* vol. 3. Edinburgh: William Blackwood and Sons, 1953.

Samuelson, P. A. 1950. "Evaluation of Real National Income." *Oxford Economic Papers* 2: 1–29.

Selowsky, Marcello. 1979. *Who Benefits from Government Expenditures? A Case Study of Colombia.* New York: Oxford University Press.

Smeeding, T. M. 1984. "Approaches to Measuring and Valuing In-Kind Subsidies and the Distribution of Their Benefits." In Marilyn Moon, ed., *Economic Transfers in the United States: Studies in Income and Wealth,* vol. 49. Chicago, Ill.: University of Chicago Press for the National Bureau of Economic Research.

Smolensky, Eugene, Leanna Stiefel, Maria Schmundt, and Robert D. Plotnick. 1977. "Adding In-Kind Transfers to the Personal Income and Outlay Account: Implications for the Size Distribution of Income." In F. T. Juster, ed., *The Distribution of Economic Well-Being.* Cambridge, Mass.: Ballinger.

Tresch, Richard W. 1981. *Public Finance: A Normative Theory.* Plano, Texas: Business Publications.

Vartia, Y. O. 1983. "Efficient Methods for Measuring Welfare Change and Compensated Income in Terms of Ordinary Demand Functions." *Econometrica* 51: 79–98.

Willig, Robert D. 1978. "Incremental Consumer's Surplus and Hedonic Price Adjustment." *Journal of Economic Theory* 17: 227–53.

5 Labor Supply and Targeting in Poverty-Alleviation Programs

Ravi Kanbur, Michael Keen, and Matti Tuomala

For many governments of developing countries, finer targeting of poverty-alleviation programs appears an attractive option in an era of greatly constrained expenditure budgets. It seems as though policy-makers could achieve greater poverty reduction with fewer resources, if only they would resort to the magic of targeting. But fine targeting is not without its costs. It is now appreciated that the administrative costs of ensuring that benefits from a program reach the target group can be high (see Besley and Kanbur 1993). One response is to target by subsidizing commodities largely consumed by the poor or on the basis of other observable indicators—such as age, gender, region, or crop group—that are correlated with deprivation. There is now a litera-ture on how such indicators might be used for optimal targeting (see, for instance, Akerlof 1978; Atkinson in chapter 3 of this volume; Besley and Kanbur 1988; Kanbur 1987).

An aspect of the costs of fine targeting that has not been as well appreciated in the development literature as it should be is the effect on incentives. Consider, for example, the moves in Sri Lanka, in the wake of the economic reforms of the late 1970s, to target the rice ration subsidy (see Anand and Kanbur 1991). The system was transformed from one with a universal benefit to one in which the benefit was restricted (in principle) to persons with incomes below a critical level (although in practice, as discussed by Sahn and Alderman in chapter 14 of this volume, enforcement of the income test was highly imperfect). Such income testing targets benefits on the poor, but it is administra-tively costly and, in particular, has incentive effects that diminish its appeal.

The authors are very grateful to Steve Coate, Jonathan Morduch, Kim Nead, and Dominique van de Walle for helpful comments. Errors and views are the authors'. This chapter appeared in slightly different form in *World Bank Economic Review,* vol. 8 (May 1994), pp. 191–211.

Consider the position of a household that increases its income, through its own efforts, to such an extent that it crosses the critical threshold and so (with perfect enforcement) loses eligibility for the benefit. The income relation of the benefit clearly reduces the incentive of the household to increase its income. Such effects are a familiar part of the policy debate in high-income countries (a representative example being Dilnot and Stark 1989) but have not been prominent in the developing countries. The potential practical significance of incentive effects is emphasized, however, by the empirical work of Sahn and Alderman (chapter 14). They find that the Sri Lankan rice subsidy was associated with a substantial reduction in the labor supply of recipients, with potentially important implications for the evaluation of the scheme.

The purpose of this chapter is therefore to take up the broad issue of targeting and incentives in developing countries and, in particular, to explore the implications of variable labor supply for the design of poverty-alleviation programs. It will be seen that once the potential incentive effects of such programs are recognized, previous discussions of optimal targeting require revision. Simple rules of thumb—for example, "spend more on the group with greater measured poverty"—have to be modified to take into account such features as differing labor supply elasticities. Similarly, commodity-based targeting rules need to be modified.

The general issues here have been extensively addressed in the optimal tax literature, with tools and results that can be borrowed for the analysis of the incentive effects of targeting in developing countries. The approach pursued here, however, departs from the usual optimal tax tradition in two ways. First, we take the object of policy to be the minimization of a poverty index rather than the maximization of a social welfare function. This approach is not without its critics (see, for instance, Stern 1987), but in a technical sense at least it is relatively straightforward. Loosely speaking, a poverty index defined on utility—attaching zero weight to all households above some threshold—is merely a special form of social welfare function.

Our second point of departure is more fundamental. The motivation for this begins with the observation that the poverty indexes on which much policy discussion focuses are, in practice, almost invariably defined in terms not of utility but of income. In the presence of incentive effects, these are very different things (and can move in different directions). Indexes that focus on income attach no significance to the effort put into earning income or, to put it the other way around, attach no weight to the leisure of the poor. And indeed it is clear that much policy debate is cast in precisely these terms: the focus is on the income of the poor, not on how hard they work to get it. This is not to deny that, from the Factory Acts to the Maastricht Treaty, policymakers have sought to avoid excessive work hours. In 1904, for instance, Churchill was arguing eloquently that working people "demand time to look about them, time to see their homes by daylight, time to see their children, time to think and read and cultivate their gardens—time, in short, to live" (quoted in Gilbert 1991, p. 196). The point is rather one of emphasis.

A large part of our purpose here is to explore the implications of a nonwelfarist approach to policy analysis. We do not advocate the evaluation of policy by its effects on some income-based poverty index, but there are two reasons why it may nevertheless be useful to explore the implications of doing so. First, to the extent that—right or wrong—policy is often evaluated, at least in part, by the use of such indexes, it is helpful to know what kind of policy would be implied by the explicit pursuit of such a minimand (or minimization of a poverty index). Second, following the work of Sen (1985), there has been growing interest in nonwelfarist approaches to policy analysis. Yet there has been relatively little formal work along these lines (an exception is Ulph 1991). The work reported here may contribute to the development of this research agenda. It should immediately be stressed, however, that we do not set out to capture the richness of Sen's capabilities approach. For although there is only one kind of welfarism, there are potentially many kinds of nonwelfarism. Here we report on, and extend, recent work on one perhaps crude form of nonwelfarism, one that has the merits of capturing the common preoccupation with income-based measures of poverty and, moreover, of being readily tractable.

The next section tackles the underlying conceptual problem: the measurement of poverty when the labor supply is variable. The rest of the chapter then applies this nonwelfarist approach to three aspects of targeting, focusing in each case on the role played by labor supply responses. We consider, in turn, commodity-based targeting, income-based targeting, and the use of other observable characteristics for indicator targeting. The final section presents conclusions.

Labor Supply and the Measurement of Poverty

The measurement of poverty is of course a vast topic in itself, and we make no attempt to survey it here (see, for instance, Atkinson 1987; Ravallion 1994). But before addressing the implications of variable labor supply for the design of poverty-alleviation programs, we need to specify the way in which labor supply affects the perceived extent of poverty, this being the presumed minimand for the policy exercises in subsequent sections. The first task is thus to consider the ways in which variable labor supply might be incorporated into the measurement of poverty. These issues have been little discussed and, as will be seen, remain somewhat perplexing.

The standard approach to the measurement of poverty proceeds by comparing the income some individual h has available to spend, y^h say, to a poverty line z.[1] Because h is poor if $y^h \leq z$, aggregate poverty might be measured by an index of the form

$$(5\text{-}1) \qquad\qquad P = \int_0^\infty D(z,y)f(y)dy,$$

where $D(z,y)$ can be thought of as the deprivation of an individual with income y, and $f(y)$ denotes the density of y. This is a fairly general form of poverty index, encompassing a range of widely used measures as special cases. (The only substantive restriction is additive separability, which precludes Gini-based indexes such as that of Sen 1976.) If $D(z,y) = \max [z - y, 0]$, for example, then P is the aggregate poverty gap. For present purposes, we need not assume any particular form for $D(\cdot)$ beyond making the natural assumptions that deprivation is positive only for the poor, so that $D(z,y)$ is strictly positive if $y < z$ and zero otherwise—and decreases as income rises toward the poverty line, so that $D_y < 0$ for $y < z$, with subscripts indicating differentiation.

In the absence of labor supply responses, and assuming there to be only a single consumption good, this approach to measuring poverty might be justified in two very different ways. The first is welfarist in the sense that the primitive concern in identifying and quantifying poverty is with individuals' realized levels of welfare. In this view, a household is poor if and only if it fails to achieve some poverty line utility level, u_z. With only a single consumption good, h's utility is simply $u(x^h)$, where $u(\cdot)$ is the direct utility function and x denotes consumption of the single good. Because $x^h = y^h$ from h's budget constraint, the condition $u(x^h) \leq u_z$ is equivalent to $y^h \leq z$, where $z = u^{-1}(u_z)$. The poverty index P simply puts a metric on the shortfall of utilities from u_z.

The second justification of equation 5-1 makes no appeal to notions of utility and is in that sense nonwelfarist. It views poverty as the inability to acquire an amount z of the consumption good. The primitive concern is with the potential to consume rather than the well-being derived from doing so.

In the simplest case—which is implicitly assumed in much of the literature—the welfarist and nonwelfarist approaches are thus indistinguishable in terms of poverty measurement. The equivalence collapses, however, when labor supply responses are admitted because the assumption of one good is relaxed. Households acquire the consumption good, at least in part, by forgoing another good: leisure. Some way must then be found to compare deprivation across alternative bundles of consumption x (now thought of as an N-vector) and labor supply L. The welfarist will use individuals' own preferences to make the comparison; a nonwelfarist may not.

In a sense, there is nothing special about labor supply here. The same issue—that of deciding how to evaluate the deprivation associated with distinct bundles—would arise if labor supply were fixed but there were two consumption goods. Rather the point is that labor supply makes the issue unavoidable and has a distinctive feature that adds a further layer of complexity. Although it is usually reasonable to assume that consumer and producer prices for consumption goods do not vary across households, wage rates clearly do. Indeed the tradition of the optimal income tax literature is to view variation in the wage rate—ability, broadly interpreted—as essentially the only way in which households differ.

To bring out these points concretely, consider first a welfarist approach to the measurement of poverty in the presence of labor supply responses. Starting with a poverty line utility level u_z, define the indirect utility function $V(q,w,B)$, giving the maximum utility that can be attained at consumer prices $q = (q_i)$ for the N goods at wage rate w and with lump-sum income B. We define the lump-sum income to be exclusive of the value of the individual's endowment of time and, perhaps, goods. Assuming that consumer prices are common across households, the utility achieved by h is thus $V(q,w^h,B^h)$; so h is poor if

$$(5\text{-}2) \qquad\qquad V(q,w^h,B^h) \le u_z.$$

To move from utility to income space, follow King (1983) in defining the equivalent income function $y_E(q,q^R\ w^h\ w^R,B^h)$ by

$$(5\text{-}3) \qquad\qquad V(q^R,w^R,y_E) = V(q,w^h,B^h).$$

That is, y_E is the lump-sum income at which h would be as well off when facing reference consumer prices q^R and a reference wage w^R as in the situation being evaluated (the latter being described by the consumer prices q, wage rate w^h, and lump-sum income B^h that h actually faces).[2] The condition of equation 5-2 for h to be poor is then equivalent to $y_E \le z$, where z is now defined by $V(q^R,w^Rz) = u_z$, and poverty is naturally measured by

$$(5\text{-}4) \qquad\qquad P = \int_0^{\hat{w}} D(z,y_E)g(w)dw,$$

where $\hat{w}$ is the poverty wage defined by $z = y_E(q,q^R,\hat{w},w^R,O)$; $g(w)$ is the density of wages; and (to avoid a double integral) we assume, here and henceforth, that $B^h = O,\ \forall h$. In principle, there is thus no difficulty in developing welfarist measures of poverty in the presence of labor supply responses and household-specific wage rates. Note, though, the element of arbitrariness in the choice of reference prices and, in particular, the reference wage for the evaluation of equivalent incomes.[3]

Different choices of reference prices may lead to different rankings of poverty-alleviation strategies.

An alternative to developing a welfarist measure of poverty would be to generalize the nonwelfarist approach. As noted in the introduction, there are many conceivable kinds of nonwelfarism. One example is focusing on the income that could be earned by working an acceptable number of hours. The implications of this for the empirical measurement of poverty have indeed been explored by Garfinkel and Haveman (1977) and by Haveman and Buron (1993). It may well be that their approach—perhaps closer to the capabilities notion—yields qualitatively very different conclusions from that pursued here. Kanbur and Keen (1989) show that the two approaches—of what they call standard and received income—do indeed have distinct implications for the design of a linear income tax. We pursue only one kind of nonwelfarism here, not because we advocate it, but for brevity and because it seems to capture much of the common tone of policy discussion.

In generalizing the nonwelfarist approach, one starting point is the specification of a particular bundle of consumption and labor supply to act as the reference for evaluating actual bundles. This target (N + 1)-vector (x^*, L^*) is generated not by any reference to utility, but by prior views as to the consumption standards that households need to attain. To avert deprivation, for instance, households ought to be able to attain a reasonable nutritional intake without an excessive amount of work effort. The task then becomes that of measuring the distance between an individual's actual consumption vector (x, L) and the target vector. There are an infinite number of possible metrics.

For simplicity, we consider here only deprivation measures of the form $D[z, y(q,w)]$, where

$$(5\text{-}5) \qquad\qquad z^h = s_x x^* - s_L^h L^*$$

and

$$(5\text{-}6) \qquad\qquad y(q,w^h) = s_x x(q,w^h) - s_L^h L(q,w^h),$$

where $x(\cdot)$ and $L(\cdot)$ denote the Marshallian commodity demand and labor supply functions. In equation 5-5, z^h is a poverty line defined as the value, at some shadow prices $S^h = (s_x, s_L^h) > 0$, of the resources needed to attain the target vector. In equation 5-6, $y(q,w^h)$ is the shadow value of the net resources actually enjoyed by h. Assuming that y is strictly increasing in w, and that z^h does not increase too rapidly with w^h (typically it would fall), there exists a unique poverty line wage w^* at which $y(q,w^*) = z$, and poverty can be measured as:

$$(5\text{-}7) \qquad\qquad P = \int_0^{w^*} D[z,y(q,w)]g(w)dw.$$

Consider, for concreteness, the case in which $D(\cdot)$ depends on the poverty gap $z - y(w)$. Deprivation, and hence poverty, can then be assessed by asking the question: By how much do the resources that h needs to attain the target vector (x^*, L^*) exceed those actually made available to h?

The question, then, is how to value these resources—the specification, that is, of the shadow prices S^h. There are an infinite number of possible choices and few natural axioms to invoke. Technological and ethical considerations both arise. Emphasizing the former, a natural approach is to value resources at producer prices. This can be done by taking $s_x = p = q - t$, where p denotes producer prices, t denotes the vector of commodity taxes, and (assuming that earned income is untaxed) $s_L^h = w^h$. The value judgments underlying the nonwelfarist approach, however, may point toward other shadow prices. It may be, for instance, that some goods are felt to be irrelevant to the achievement of minimal living standards, in which case their appropriate shadow price is zero.

Of more particular importance to our concerns here is that policy-makers often seem to attach positive weight to the capacity to consume but zero weight to the enjoyment of leisure. Put crudely, policymakers may not care how hard people have to work so long as they are able to sustain a decent level of consumption. Taken to the extreme, such a view corresponds to $s_L^h = 0$. An alternative and very different ethical position is that work effort in excess of the target L^*—or, underenjoyment of leisure relative to some target—should not only be valued positively, but, at least for the least able, be valued at a shadow wage in excess of the actual wage w^h. Taking $s_L^h = w^h$ implies that a given shortfall in leisure hours relative to the target translates into less deprivation for a low-paid individual than for a high-paid one.

These issues will not be resolved here, but we focus on their implications for the incorporation of labor supply responses into the analysis of poverty alleviation. We simply assume, when defining poverty as in equation 5-7, that $s_x = p$. That is, we assume that consumption goods are valued at producer prices, but for the moment the value placed on leisure, s_L^h, is unrestricted. We assume, however, that s_L^h is independent of consumer prices, q. This seems a reasonable simplification for present purposes, there being no instantly compelling reason to suppose that the extent of deprivation in excessively hard work depends on the prices of the goods it buys.

Targeting by Commodities

Which kinds of goods should be subsidized by a government seeking to alleviate poverty, and which should be taxed? Specifically, suppose there are two commodities, 1 and 2, which the government can subsidize or tax as it pleases, subject only to an overall budget constraint.

Labor supply is variable—the implications of this being our central concern—but labor income cannot be taxed. Starting from a position in which neither good is subsidized (or taxed), what is the effect on aggregate poverty, P, of introducing a small subsidy on good 2 financed by a tax on good 1?

Besley and Kanbur (1988) address this question in a welfarist context. They effectively assume labor supply responses to be zero, but it is straightforward to show that relaxing this assumption does not affect their central result. Defining poverty in terms of equivalent income (taking the reference wage for each household to be its actual wage), the effect on P of introducing a small tax on good 1 (and hence a small subsidy on good 2) can be shown to be

$$(5\text{-}8) \qquad \frac{\partial P}{\partial t_1} = (\bar{x}_1) \int_0^{\bar{w}} \left(\frac{x_2}{\bar{x}_2} - \frac{x_1}{\bar{x}_1} \right) D_y[z, y_E(q, p, w, w)] g(w) dw,$$

where x_i denotes consumption of good i and $\bar{x}_i$ its mean in the population.[4] Recalling that $D_y < 0$, the interpretation of equation 5-8 is straightforward: good 2 should be subsidized by a tax on good 1 if and only if the consumption of good 2 is more heavily concentrated among the poor than is consumption of good 1 (weighted, by the terms D_y, to attach most importance to the most deprived households). (Note that the convenient absence of price elasticities reflects the assumption that the starting point is one with no taxes or subsidies. When considering large reforms, excess burden considerations will also arise, bringing into play elasticities of demand for consumer goods and, hence, labor supply responses.)

Condition 5-8 is essentially the same form as the result of Besley and Kanbur (1988, equation 26). The only difference is that they work with the poverty index of Foster, Greer, and Thorbecke (1984) rather than with the more general form used here. Variable labor supply thus makes no difference to the welfarist analysis. The impact on a household's welfare of a change in the consumer price of good i is simply proportional to its consumption of i. The induced effect on the pattern of consumption—and, by the same token, on labor supply—drops out by the envelope property. That is, because the initial level of labor supply is chosen by the individual so as to maximize utility, a small change in that level—as might be induced by the commodity price change associated with the tax/subsidy scheme—will have no (first-order) effect on welfare and, hence, also no effect on poverty defined in welfarist terms.

Consider now the same problem from the nonwelfarist perspective. The revenue-neutral introduction of a small subsidy on good 2, but now evaluated in terms of a poverty index of the form in equation 5-7 (see appendix 5-1):

(5-9) $$\frac{\partial P}{\partial t_1} = (\bar{x}_1) \int_0^{w^*} (A_2 - A_1) D_y[z^*, y(q, w)] g(w) dw,$$

where

(5-10) $$A_i = \frac{x_i + (s_L^h - w^h) \frac{\partial L}{\partial q_i}}{\bar{x}_i}.$$

Comparing equations 5-9 and 5-10 with equation 5-8 shows that the sole consequence of adopting the nonwelfarist approach to the targeting of subsidies is thus to introduce labor supply considerations in the form of the terms $(s_L^h - w^h) \partial L / \partial q_i$.[5]

There are two cases of interest in which these terms vanish. The first, trivially, is that in which labor supply decisions are unaffected by the consumer prices of the goods being studied $(\partial L / \partial q_i = 0)$. In practice, it may often be tempting to assume that this is indeed the case. As an antidote to routinely doing so, however, it is worth recalling that (in the absence of lump-sum income) to assume labor supply to be independent of all consumer prices is to assume it also to be independent of the wage rate. This follows from homogeneity of degree zero of the labor supply function $L(q, w)$. The second case in which these labor supply terms disappear is that in which the leisure component of an individual's deprivation is valued at the individual's wage rate ($s_L^h = w^h$). The intuition for this is that with $s_x = q$ and $s_L^h = w^h$, the impact on deprivation of behavioral responses to the tax reform is being evaluated at the prices actually faced by the consumer; just as those responses can have no effect on the consumer's budget constraint, so they can have no effect on measured deprivation.

But there are, of course, other possible choices of s_L^h. One is to attach no weight at all to labor supply ($s_L^h = 0$). Then equation 5-10 becomes

(5-11) $$A_i = \frac{b_i - \epsilon_{Li}}{\bar{b}_i},$$

where $b_i = q_i x_i / wL$ denotes the budget share of good i, $\bar{b}_i$ its mean, and $\epsilon_{Li} (= \partial \ln L / \partial \ln q_i)$ the elasticity of labor supply with respect to q_i. Other things being equal, the case for subsidizing good i is thus weaker the more positive is ϵ_{Li}; weaker, that is, the more such a subsidy tends to reduce labor supply. This is reminiscent of optimal tax arguments— pointing to relatively heavy taxation of relatively strong complements with leisure—but the underlying reasoning is very different.[6]

With $s_L^h > 0$, the sole object of policy is to push poor individuals' consumption as far toward the target consumption vector (x_1^*, x_2^*) as possible. There are broadly two ways of doing this. The first is to deploy subsidies that enable households to afford greater quantities at any given income. The other is to encourage them to increase their earnings and so purchase more at any given price. It is on this second front that complementarities between goods and leisure enter the picture. Expanding the consumption of (relative) complements with leisure may be more expensive than expanding that of substitutes. The effects of subsidizing the former are liable to be at least partly offset by an induced reduction in disposable income, whereas subsidizing the latter generates a reinforcing expansion of income.

For reasons discussed above, however, it might be preferable to attach a large positive weight to leisure in measuring deprivation. The implications of doing so are not merely qualitative; it can turn the conclusions of the previous paragraph on their head. Suppose, for instance, that s_L^h is at or above the poverty line wage $\hat{w}$. Other things being equal, the goods that ideally should be subsidized to alleviate poverty are thus precisely those for which $\partial L/\partial q_i > 0$. Instincts honed on the optimal tax literature are confounded because complements with leisure should be subsidized rather than taxed. The reason, however, is straightforward. With $s_L^h > 0$, one way of reducing deprivation is by reducing the work effort of the poor. Against this, less effort means less consumption and so a greater shortfall from x^*; but with s_x equal to the prices faced by the consumer and $s_L^h > w^h$, the deprivation measure attaches more weight to the hour of leisure gained than it does to the consumption consequently forgone.

Consider, for instance, the appropriate treatment of food. In the developing-country context, it could plausibly be argued that greater food intake may enhance the capacity to work. Food and leisure would then be thought of as substitutes: a reduction in the consumer price of food will tend to increase labor supply (so that $\epsilon_{L,food} < 0$). With $s_L^h = 0$, the implication of the analysis above is thus that (other things being equal) food should be subsidized, reflecting the secondary benefit of expanded income that such a subsidy induces. If, however, s_L^h is above the poverty line wage, the implication is that food should be taxed. This may at first seem strange but has a straightforward explanation. Although taxing food in itself increases deprivation, this may be more than offset by the expanded consumption of both leisure and the second commodity in the background, the latter now being subsidized by receipts from the food tax.

Pursuing the nonwelfarist approach, rules of thumb for commodity targeting are thus highly sensitive to the weight attached to deprivation of leisure. The issue is a troublesome one. Having raised it, however, we now put it aside by assuming in the next two sections that $s_L^h = 0$. Because there will also be only one consumption good—commodity subsidies not being at issue—the nonwelfarist deprivation measure in what follows is simply the shortfall of aggregate consumption (equivalently, of net income) from some poverty line.

Targeting by Income

In the absence of incentive effects (and with sufficient resources available for poverty relief), the design of income-based targeting is a trivial exercise. After the poverty line is established, everyone who is initially below it is given exactly that transfer needed to bring them just above it.[7] Such a scheme involves no leakages. If there are no labor supply or other effects in transferring or raising these resources, and if the informational and administrative requirements can be met costlessly, this method gives perfect targeting. But once incentive effects are admitted, the difficulties noted in the introduction arise. Because perfect targeting implies an effective marginal tax rate of 100 percent on those below the poverty line, the poor have no incentive to earn income. Their rational labor supply decisions would then be liable to increase greatly the revenue costs of alleviating their poverty. Incentive effects thus rule out marginal rates on the poor of 100 percent. The questions of precisely how high or low those rates should be, and of how they should vary with income, then become considerably more complex.

A large literature, initiated by Mirrlees (1971), addresses the optimal design of nonlinear income taxes in a welfarist setting. In this work, the issue of incentives to supply labor is tackled directly by modeling individuals as choosing between work and leisure, given the tax-transfer schedule they face. There are assumed to be a large number of individuals, differing only in the pretax wage they can earn. (We relax this homogeneity assumption in the next section.) The government then chooses a schedule that maximizes a social welfare function defined on individuals' welfare; that is, on the utility they derive from their consumption-leisure bundles. As noted in the introduction, however, there is a striking and fundamental dissonance between this welfarist approach and the tone of much policy debate. It is the consequence of reform for the incomes of the poor—the money in their pockets, not something akin to money metric measures of their welfare—that is commonly discussed and analyzed. Kanbur, Keen, and Tuomala (1994) therefore examine the implications of an alternative approach to the design of nonlinear income tax schemes. Besley and Coate (1992) adopt a similar approach in analyzing the case for workfare schemes. In Kanbur, Keen, and Tuomala's approach, the objective of policy is to minimize an income-based poverty index rather than to maximize social welfare. This section reviews their conclusions.

We begin by recalling the main lessons from the welfarist literature on optimal nonlinear income taxation (as reviewed, for instance, in Tuomala 1990). Three general qualitative conclusions emerge:

- The marginal rate of tax should everywhere be non-negative.
- The marginal rate of tax on the lowest earner should be zero, so long as everyone supplies some labor at the optimum.
- The marginal rate of tax on the highest earner should be zero, so long as wages in the population are bounded above.

The first result is more striking than is commonly recognized. Although it may well be optimal for the average rate of tax on the least well-off to be negative, it cannot be desirable to subsidize their earnings at the margin. The second and third results, the limitations of the end points, are well known. Simulations suggest that zero may be a bad approximation to optimal marginal tax rates in the tails of the distribution. The simulations also show that if it is optimal for some not to work, the optimal marginal tax rate at the bottom of the income distribution can be shown to be strictly positive (Tuomala 1990). Nevertheless, these results continue to color professional thinking on issues of rate structure. The lower end-point result, in particular, has been taken as suggestive in arguing against very high effective marginal rates on the poor (as, for instance, by Kay and King 1986).

Do these conclusions continue to apply when the objective of policy is not the maximization of social welfare but the minimization of income poverty? The third result certainly does (see Kanbur, Keen, and Tuomala 1994 for proofs of this and the claims below). As expected, the third result applies because in the context of poverty alleviation the only reason to care about the highest earner—indeed about any of the nonpoor—is as a source of revenue. It is well known that in these circumstances the marginal rate of tax on the highest earner should be zero; if it were strictly positive, additional revenue could be extracted by slightly lowering it and thereby inducing the highest earner to earn additional taxed income.

The first and second results, in contrast, are overturned if the objective is to minimize income poverty. If it is optimal for the lowest-ability earner to work, then the marginal rate of tax at the lower end of the distribution should be strictly negative. That is, a marginal earnings subsidy should be paid to the very poorest. This may be optimal from the nonwelfarist perspective even though it cannot possibly be optimal from a welfarist one. To see why, consider an initial position in which the lowest-ability individual works and faces a strictly negative marginal tax rate. Imagine now increasing the marginal tax rate faced by this individual while leaving the average rate at the individual's initial gross income unchanged. The effects of this rotation of the poorest worker's budget constraint through the initial consumption/leisure bundle are that the individual's welfare rises (because with the initial consumption/leisure bundle remaining feasible, any change in the individual's behavior must signify an increase in welfare), the individual's net income falls (because the only incentive effect is a substitution toward leisure induced by the higher marginal tax rate), and the government's revenue increases (because the subsidy is paid at a lower rate on a narrower base). From the welfarist perspective, the combination of the utility gain to the individual and the revenue gain to the government make this reform unambiguously desirable. From the nonwelfarist perspective, however, opposing effects are at work. The revenue gain is desirable, but the net income loss to the poorest worker is not. Minimization of an income-based poverty index will require striking a balance between the two effects, which will make a marginal subsidy on the very poorest optimal.

This possibility of an optimally negative marginal tax rate is confined, however, to the poorest of the poor. For those who find themselves exactly at the poverty line, the optimal marginal rate can be shown to be strictly positive.

These qualitative implications of the nonwelfarist approach thus point to a pattern of marginal tax rates below the poverty line that is both complex and potentially of a kind very different from that suggested by the welfarist tradition. But how far do low or even negative marginal tax rates on the very poorest individuals extend into the range of incomes? And how is the poverty-minimizing rate structure affected by the precise location of the poverty line z and by the form of the deprivation function $D(\cdot)$?

Table 5-1 reports simulation results intended to address these concerns. These assume Cobb-Douglas preferences:

$$(5\text{-}12) \qquad u(x,L) = (1-\delta)\ln(x) + \delta\ln(1-L) \qquad \delta\epsilon[0,1]$$

(the time endowment being normalized at unity); with $\delta = 1/2$, ln (w) is normally distributed (with mean -1 and standard deviation 0.39), and the revenue requirement is about 10 percent of gross income. These are the standard assumptions in simulations of this sort. The novelty is in the form of the objective function. For this we take a poverty index of the form developed by Foster, Greer, and Thorbecke (1984):

$$(5\text{-}13) \qquad P^\alpha = \int_0^{w^*} \left(\frac{x(w)-z}{z}\right)^\alpha g(w)dw \qquad \alpha>1,$$

where $x(w)$ denotes the consumption of an individual with wage w. The parameter α in equation 5-13 provides a convenient parameterization of alternative degrees of aversion to inequality among the poor.

One immediate implication of this specification should be noted. With Cobb-Douglas preferences (so that the marginal rate of substitution between consumption and work is strictly positive at zero hours) and a lognormal wage distribution (so that the lower bound of w is zero), there are some who will work only if the marginal tax rate at

Table 5-1. *Simulation Results for Optimal Average and Marginal Tax Rates at Various Percentiles of the Wage Distribution*

Poverty line	Percentile of the wage distribution	Average tax rate	Marginal tax rate
(a) Low poverty line			
Low[a]	0.06	−100	69
Poverty line	0.31	−3	62
	0.50	12	53
	0.90	29	35
High	0.99	29	23
(b) Middle poverty line			
Low[a]	0.02	−100	63
Poverty line	0.43	0	54
	0.50	9	53
	0.90	27	34
High	0.99	27	17
(c) High poverty line			
Low[a]	0.003	−87	56
	0.50	8	54
Poverty line	0.56	16	48
	0.90	26	34
High	0.99	26	17
(d) Maximin[b]			
Low[a]	0.16	−100	73
	0.50	17	53
	0.90	32	35
High	0.99	32	26

Note: In all four groups, the ratio of aggregate consumption to aggregate output is 0.9. In groups a, b, and c, the parameter for aversion to inequality among the poor, α, is 2. In groups a, b, and c, the minimum level of consumption, $x(n_0)$, is 0.06; in group d, it is 0.07.

a. The percentile of the wage distribution below which individuals choose not to work.

b. Assumes infinite aversion to inequality among the poor ($\alpha = \infty$).

Source: Authors' calculations.

the bottom of the distribution is infinitely negative. In both the welfarist context and that of income poverty minimization, it would be optimal to have some of the population idle. As noted above, in the welfarist case the optimal marginal rate at the bottom of the income distribution is then strictly positive. For the case in which the objective is to minimize income poverty and some households are idle at the optimum, however, we have been unable to sign the optimal marginal rate at the lower end point. The simulations can thus provide some indication of the extent to which the argument for nonpositive marginal rates at the lower end when the poorest work continues to exert some force when instead the wage distribution is not bounded away from zero. Table 5-1 gives optimal average and marginal tax rates at various percentiles of the wage distribution, starting at the bottom and including the point at which the assumed poverty line is to be found. Panels a, b, and c all take $\alpha = 2$ and differ in taking successively higher poverty lines. Panel d looks at the maximin case, which corresponds to $\alpha = \infty$.

Several features stand out in the table. First, the marginal rate on the lowest gross income—which, as just noted, we are unable to sign in principle—emerges as very strongly positive: not only is it not negative, it is not even low. Second, marginal tax rates decline monotonically from the poorest to the richest individual. This is striking in two respects. It implies that the dictates of effective targeting can run exactly counter to the popular notion that equity concerns require the marginal tax rate to increase with income. And it runs counter to the conclusion sometimes drawn from the welfarist literature that the administrative advantages of linear taxation can be bought at relatively little loss in terms of policy effectiveness.

The third feature of the table is that, comparing panels a and c, increases in the poverty line reduce optimal marginal rates at and below the poverty line. The intuition for this seems to be that the case for low marginal rates in order to encourage those at or near the poverty line to move over it becomes stronger as the poverty line moves into denser parts of the distribution. Fourth, comparing panel d with the rest, increases in the extent of aversion to inequality among the poor tend to increase the marginal rates that they optimally face. Other simulations (not reported here) suggest that moderate variation in the revenue requirement affects the general level of marginal tax rates (which tend to increase with the revenue required), but not the qualitative pattern of their variation with income. The increase in the marginal rates is perhaps as would be expected, because the greater the concern with poverty alleviation, the more attractive are schemes approaching minimum income guarantees likely to be. The emphasis is then on raising the consumption of the very poorest. Financing the transfer this requires calls for relatively high marginal tax rates in the lower part of the distribution in order to impose sufficiently high average tax rates further up the distribution.

But perhaps the most important feature of the results is the finding of marginal tax rates on the poor that are invariably rather high (bearing in mind the fairly minimal revenue requirement). In most cases marginal rates on the bulk of the poor exceed 60 percent, and in all cases they exceed 50 percent. The case for low marginal tax rates to encourage the poor to help themselves thus is less discernible in the simulations than expected. Even with the relatively elastic labor supply responses implicit in Cobb-Douglas preferences (the elasticity of substitution between consumption and leisure being unity), a stronger mark is left by the case for high marginal rates associated with the unattainable ideal of perfect targeting described at the start of this section. Simulations for the case in which the elasticity of substitution is 0.5 (reported in Kanbur, Keen, and Tuomala 1994) confirm this impression.

The optimal marginal tax rates that emerge from these simulations are not necessarily higher in the nonwelfarist case than in the welfarist one. Indeed it is not clear that a coherent comparison between the two approaches can be made, because the latter, but not the former, depends on the cardinal representation of preferences. The safest conclusion—albeit a provisional one, because our simulations are inevitably only special cases—seems to be that a concern with income poverty does not in itself provide a strong case for marginal tax rates on the bulk of the poor that are substantially lower than expected from the perspective of the welfarist tradition. The reason for this, it seems, is that shifting from the welfarist to the nonwelfarist perspective introduces two considerations that point in opposite directions. First, the case for lower marginal tax rates on the poor is strengthened by the prospect of inducing them to raise their own incomes. The nonwelfarist view attaches no weight to the leisure that the poor forgo; this underlies the result that a marginal earnings subsidy on the very poorest is optimal when that individual works. Second, the case for lower marginal tax rates on the poor is weakened by the need to support the incomes of the poor, rather than their welfare, which could be "bought" by allowing them a relatively high amount of leisure. Supporting the incomes of the poor calls for relatively high marginal tax rates in the lower part of the income distribution; the revenue needed for this support requires imposing sufficiently high average tax rates on higher incomes. The simulations suggest that these two opposing effects broadly offset one another.

Targeting by Indicators

In the analysis so far, individuals have been assumed to differ only in their unobserved ability. It is now widely recognized, however, that there are potentially severe incentive and other costs of administering income-related transfers. One way of overcoming these costs, particularly in developing countries, is to differentiate the population by easily observable indicators that are correlated with the unobservable characteristic of interest. An individual's labor market status or demographic attributes, for instance, may convey information on underlying ability. Transfers can usefully be made contingent on such characteristics. The theory of the optimal use of such information was first considered by Akerlof (1978), and developed by, among others, Kanbur (1987), Besley and Kanbur (1988), and Ravallion (1987). But most of the simple rules of thumb for targeting that have been developed simply assume away labor supply effects. An exception is Kanbur and Keen (1989), who develop a relatively simple framework that gives some feel for the optimal use of nonincome information in the presence of incentive effects. This section reports on that work.

Suppose the population can be divided into two mutually exclusive and exhaustive groups, A and B. The underlying contingencies are assumed to be absolute, so that households are unable to switch between groups. The contingency is costlessly verifiable, but we assume—to keep matters simple—that only linear income taxation is feasible. What makes the problem interesting is that distinct schedules may be applied to the two groups: They may be faced, that is, with different poll subsidies G_K and with different marginal tax rates t_K (for $K = A,B$). This ability to treat the two groups differently is only valuable, of course, if they differ in some way that is relevant for poverty alleviation. We allow them to differ in two respects. First, the within-group wage distributions $g_K(w)$ may differ. Thus one group may, for instance, be systematically poorer than the other. Second, they may differ in the responsiveness of their labor supply behavior.

Specifically, we assume that while all individuals have Cobb-Douglas preferences, as in equation 5-12, the parameter δ may differ across the two groups. Imposing the further restriction, for definiteness, that poverty is to be assessed in terms of the Foster-Greer-Thorbecke index, the objective of policy is thus taken to be the minimization (subject to the government's budget constraint) of

$$(5\text{-}14) \qquad P^\alpha = \theta P_A^\alpha + (1-\theta)P_B^\alpha,$$

where P_K^α is defined as in equation 5-13, θ is the proportion of the population in group A, and the net income of a type K household with pretax wage w is

$$(5\text{-}15) \qquad x(w;K) = (1-\delta_K)[(1-t_K)w + G_K].$$

The two groups are assumed to have the same poverty line, z. This precludes a range of (troubling) issues concerning the relationship between needs and optimally targeted benefits. Depending on the form of the deprivation function $D(\cdot)$, it may be, for example, that the level of support optimally targeted to a group varies inversely with its neediness, as measured by z. The intuition is that the very needy may simply be too expensive to help (see Keen 1992).

Taking the tax rates t_K as given, under what circumstances would aggregate poverty P^α be reduced by cutting the poll subsidy given to one group in order to finance an increase in that paid to the other? A retargeting of support of this kind away from group B and toward group A can be shown to reduce aggregate poverty if and only if[8]

$$(5\text{-}16) \qquad \sigma(\delta_A,t_A)P_A^{\alpha-1} > \sigma(\delta_B,t_B)P_B^{\alpha-1},$$

where

$$(5\text{-}17) \qquad\qquad \sigma(\delta,t) = \frac{(1-\delta)(1-t)}{1-t(1-\delta)}.$$

To develop the intuition behind inequality 5-16, consider first the role of the $P_K^{\alpha-1}$ terms. These emphasize the simple but important point that the reduction of aggregate poverty measured in some particular way is typically not best pursued by redirecting resources toward whichever group is poorest in terms of that same measure. What matters is the marginal effect on the measure of interest. The structure of the P^α index happens to be such that the implied rule takes an especially simple form. Assuming away incentive effects for the moment, so that $\delta_A = \delta_B = 0$, minimization of the aggregate index for some specific choice of α requires looking first at the within-group indexes for $\alpha - 1$. Suppose, for instance, that we have chosen $\alpha = 1$. This means that our objective is simply to minimize the aggregate poverty gap or, equivalently, to maximize the net income of the poor. Imagine now that we have some fixed sum to spend on increasing the poll subsidy G_K to one group or the other (and assume for simplicity that $\theta = 1/2$). Which group should we favor? The disadvantage of having to spend this money as a poll subsidy is that some of it will be wasted on the nonpoor; giving it to group K, the proportion of our fixed sum that will reach the poor is just the proportion of that group which is in poverty. To achieve the largest possible increase in the total income of the poor, we should therefore allocate the funds to whichever group has the larger number of poor individuals; that is, to whichever group has the higher P_K^0.

Incentive effects enter the story through the $\sigma(\cdot)$ terms in inequality 5-16, with retargeting toward group A more likely to be desirable, other things being equal, the higher is $\sigma(\delta_A, t_A)$ and the lower is $\sigma(\delta_B, t_B)$. It is easily seen from equation 5-17 that $\sigma(\delta,t)$ is decreasing in both δ and t. Thus group A is more likely to be favored the less responsive is its labor supply behavior and the lower is the marginal tax rate it initially faces. The intuition is straightforward. When δ_A is relatively low, the income effect of increasing the poll subsidy to group A—which points toward a reduction in hours and hence in net income, dampening the beneficial impact on poverty—is relatively weak. Conversely, a high δ_B indicates a relatively powerful income effect acting to mitigate the impact of reducing the poll subsidy to group B. And when t_A is relatively low, so too is the revenue cost of the reduction in hours worked—and hence taxes paid—by members of group A as a result of their higher lump-sum income. Conversely, a high t_B is helpful in recouping revenue from the increased labor supply of group B.

The tension to which inequality 5-16 points emerges especially clearly if the initial position is one in which $t_A = t_B = 0$. Retargeting toward group A is then desirable if and only if

(5-18) $$(1-\delta_A)P_A^{\alpha-1} > (1-\delta_B)P_B^{\alpha-1}.$$

On the one hand, there is the intuition that suggests favoring the group with the higher incidence of poverty. We have already discussed why this has to be modified to the group with higher $P^{\alpha-1}$. But incentive effects can more than offset this consideration. It may be optimal to cut the poll subsidy paid to the group with the higher $P^{\alpha-1}$ if its labor supply behavior is sufficiently more sensitive (that is, if δ for that group is sufficiently high).

The targeting rule 5-16 is valid for arbitrary marginal tax rates t_K. When these too can be chosen by the government, from the associated first-order conditions,[9] poverty minimization requires

(5-19) $$\frac{P_A^{\alpha-1}-P_A^{\alpha}}{P_B^{\alpha-1}-P_B^{\alpha}} = \frac{\bar{x}_A}{\bar{x}_B},$$

where $\bar{x}_K$ denotes the mean net income of group K. The difference between the P^{α} and $P^{\alpha-1}$ indexes must thus stand in the same ratio across groups as do their mean net incomes. For the case in which $\alpha = 1$, this reduces to the simple condition that

(5-20) $$\Gamma_A = \Gamma_B,$$

where Γ_K denotes the share of the poor in group K of the total net income of that group. The significance of rules 5-19 and 5-20 is less in the additional insight they convey—which adds little to what has gone before—than in their applicability. They show how simplifying assumptions can be used to incorporate labor supply responses, in a relatively straightforward way, into the use of indicators for targeting.

Conclusions

Labor supply introduces some new considerations into the design of poverty-alleviation programs. First and foremost, it forces us to reconsider the standard objective function according to which these programs are evaluated: the minimization of poverty as measured by the shortfall of income or expenditure from a critical value. This objective leaves out of consideration the effort that individuals make in earning their incomes. How is this effort, or rather the leisure that is lost in making it, to be valued? Valuing it at the market wage—which is the welfarist approach, because this is how individuals would value it themselves—has the unappealing feature that the effort of less able individuals is valued less. Many poor men and women perform back-breaking labor to earn a meager living, and that surely should be given emphasis. The conceptual issues are not easily resolved, and here we have done no more than make a start. We feel that nonwelfarist perspectives have special interest where labor supply is concerned, but in this chapter we have restricted ourselves to examining the consequences of just one particular—and particularly convenient—approach within this broad class.

A good example of how the new perspective can alter basic results in the targeting literature is provided in the section on targeting by commodities. Besley and Kanbur (1988) establish, under certain conditions, the validity of the simple rule of thumb that commodity subsidies should focus on those commodities whose consumption by the poor is a large fraction of total consumption. This is done in a welfaristic framework. However, if labor supply is elastic, then, under the nonwelfarist approach considered here, the rule is modified depending on the weight given to disutility of effort in evaluating poverty. If no weight is given at all, then the case for subsidizing good i is weaker the more such a subsidy would tend to reduce labor supply, that is, the greater the complementarity between i and leisure. But this result is reversed by attaching a sufficiently high weight to the disutility of effort. It is then no longer acceptable to provide poverty line consumption by inducing individuals to work excessively, and complements with leisure should therefore be subsidized rather than taxed.

The rest of the chapter followed through the consequences of assuming that no weight is given to leisure in the social welfare function. For income-based targeting (and for conventional parameter values), the optimal marginal withdrawal of benefits as income increases is around 60–70 percent. This should provide a benchmark for the evaluation of income-tested schemes. Marginal withdrawal rates far above this may look good from the simplest targeting perspective, but the incentive effects are liable to dominate any targeting gains. Finally, we considered modifications to rules of thumb in nonincome-based targeting. We showed that, for any indicator that divides the population into mutually exclusive groups for targeting purposes, positive correlation between labor supply elasticity and poverty incidence across the groups reduces the usefulness of the indicator. Thus, relying only on poverty incidence can give a false sense of the value of an indicator for targeting purposes.

This chapter is only a start in the direction of introducing labor supply considerations into the targeting of poverty-alleviation programs in developing countries. We end by noting that the issues raised here extend well beyond the specific case of labor supply and income poverty. They apply to any measure of the standard of living (such as nutrition) when individuals have choices to make between alternative forms of consumption and differ in their ability to transform one type of consumption into another.

Appendix 5-1: The Derivation of Equation 5-9

We describe here the derivation of equation 5-9. Using the government's budget constraint

(5A-1) $\qquad R = t_1 \displaystyle\int_0^{\infty} x_1(q,w)g(w)dw + t_2 \int_0^{\infty} x_2(q,w)g(w)dw$

to define t_2 as a function of t_1 (for fixed R), the effect on poverty—defined as in equation 5-7—of slightly increasing the tax on good 1 in order to lower that on good 2 is given by

(5A-2) $\qquad \dfrac{dP}{dt_1} = \dfrac{\partial P}{\partial t_1} + \dfrac{\partial P}{\partial t_2}\dfrac{dt_2}{dt_1} \,|R.$

Differentiating equation 5A-1 at $t_1 = t_2 = 0$ gives:

(5A-3) $\qquad \dfrac{dt_2}{dt_1}\,|\,R = -\dfrac{\bar{x}_1}{\bar{x}_2},$

while from equation 5-7, and assuming that $D(z,z) = 0$,

(5A-4) $\qquad \dfrac{\partial P}{\partial t_i} = D_y\dfrac{\partial y}{\partial q_i}g(w)dw.$

Assuming constant producer prices, p, equation 5-6 implies that

(5A-5) $\qquad \dfrac{\partial y}{\partial q_i} = s_x \cdot \dfrac{\partial x}{\partial q_i} - s_L^h\dfrac{\partial L}{\partial q_i}$

(5A-6) $\qquad = -\left(x_i + (s_L^h - w)\dfrac{\partial L}{\partial q_i}\right),$

the second equality following from the choice $s_x = p$, the assumption that both taxes are initially zero (so that $p = q$), and differentiation of the individual's budget constraint, $q.x - wL = 0$. Substituting equations 5A-3 through 5A-6 in equation 5A-1 gives equation 5-9.

Notes

1. The terms "individual" and "household" are used synonymously in what follows, the issues raised by the distinction between the two being somewhat removed from the central concerns here.

2. Use of the equivalent income function is not unproblematic: Blackorby and Donaldson (1988) show that it is not in general concave (in the underlying consumption bundle). In the present context, this is liable to mean, for instance, that transferring commodities from one poor person to another but richer one could actually reduce the aggregate poverty gap measured in terms of y_E.

3. To be precise, what really matters is the vector of relative reference prices, q^R / w^R. Because indirect utility is homogeneous of degree zero in prices and income, it follows from equation 5-3 that equivalent income measured in units of leisure (that is, y_E / w^R) depends on reference prices only through q^R / w^R.

4. In equation 5-8, $\tilde{w}$ is a poverty line wage defined by $y_E(q,q^R,\tilde{w},\tilde{w}) = z$. For brevity, the derivation of equation 5-8 is omitted. It is similar to that of equation 5-9, which is sketched in the appendix. The critical step is to note (in place of equations 5A-5 and 5A-6) that $\partial y_E / \partial q_i = -x_i$ at $q^R = q$ and $w^R = w^h$. The

simplicity of equation 5-8 would not be obtained if the reference were specified to be other than w^h.

5. Here and elsewhere, by "the" nonwelfarist approach is meant the particular variant of nonwelfarism described in the last section.

6. Some emphasis should be put on the word "relatively." It is not necessary for the arguments here that there exist any good j that is complementary with leisure in the sense that the compensated demand for j falls as w rises; indeed, there may exist no such good. It is the degree of complementarity that is important. It is convenient, for clarity, to speak of taxing/subsidizing complements with leisure. The more delicate and exact formulation of the argument is straightforward, but cumbersome.

7. Bourguignon and Fields (1990) examine the optimal poverty-alleviation strategy (in the absence of behavioral responses) when the available budget is insufficient to eliminate poverty.

8. Proofs of the claims that follow are in Kanbur and Keen (1989).

9. Details of the proof can again be found in Kanbur and Keen (1989).

References

Akerlof, George A. 1978. "The Economics of 'Tagging' as Applied to the Optimal Income Tax, Welfare Programs, and Manpower Planning." *American Economic Review* 68: 8–19.

Anand, Sudhir, and Ravi Kanbur. 1991. "Public Policy and Basic Needs Provision: Intervention and Achievement in Sri Lanka." In Jean Drèze and Amartya Sen, eds., *The Political Economy of Hunger*, vol. 3. Oxford, Eng.: Clarendon Press.

Atkinson, Anthony B. 1987. "On the Measurement of Poverty." *Econometrica* 55: 749–64.

Besley, Timothy, and Stephen Coate. 1992. "Workfare vs. Welfare: Incentive Arguments for Work Requirements in Poverty Alleviation Programs." *American Economic Review* 82: 249–61.

Besley, Timothy, and Ravi Kanbur. 1988. "Food Subsidies and Poverty Alleviation." *Economic Journal* 92: 701–19.

———. 1993. "The Principles of Targeting." In Michael Lipton and Jacques van der Gaag, eds., *Including the Poor*. Washington, D.C.: World Bank.

Blackorby, Charles, and David Donaldson. 1988. "Money Metric Utility: A Harmless Normalization?" *Journal of Economic Theory* 46: 120–29.

Bourguignon, François, and Gary S. Fields. 1990. "Poverty Measures and Anti-Poverty Policy." *Recherches Economiques de Louvain* 56: 409–27.

Dilnot, Andrew, and Graham Stark. 1989. "The Poverty Trap, Tax Cuts, and the Reform of Social Security." In Andrew Dilnot and Ian Walker, eds., *The Economics of Social Security*. Oxford, Eng.: Clarendon Press.

Foster, James E., Joel Greer, and Erik Thorbecke. 1984. "A Class of Decomposable Poverty Measures." *Econometrica* 52: 761–66.

Garfinkel, Irvin, and Robert Haveman. 1977. "Earnings Capacity, Economic Status, and Poverty." *Journal of Human Resources* 12: 49–70.

Gilbert, Martin. 1991. *Churchill: A Life*. London: Minerva.

Haveman, Robert, and L. F. Buron. 1993. "Escaping Poverty through Work—The Problem of Low Earnings in the United States, 1981–90." *Review of Income and Wealth* 39: 141–57.

Kanbur, Ravi. 1987. "Transfers, Targeting, and Poverty." *Economic Policy* 4: 112–36, 141–47.

Kanbur, Ravi, and M. J. Keen. 1989. "Poverty, Incentives, and Linear Income Taxation." In Andrew Dilnot and Ian Walker, eds., *The Economics of Social Security*. Oxford, Eng.: Clarendon Press.

Kanbur, Ravi, M. J. Keen, and Matti Tuomala. 1994. "Optimal Non-linear Income Taxation for the Alleviation of Income Poverty." *European Economic Review* 38: 1613–32.

Kay, J. A., and M. A. King. 1986. *The British Tax System,* 4th ed. Oxford, Eng.: Oxford University Press.

Keen, M. J. 1992. "Needs and Targeting." *Economic Journal* 102: 67–79.

King, M. A. 1983. "Welfare Analysis of Tax Reforms Using Household Data." *Journal of Public Economics* 21: 183–215.

Mirrlees, J. A. 1971. "An Exploration in the Theory of Optimum Income Taxation." *Review of Economic Studies* 38: 175–208.

Ravallion, Martin. 1987. "Land-Contingent Poverty Alleviation Schemes." *World Development* 17: 1223–33.

———. 1994. *Poverty Comparisons.* Fundamentals of Pure and Applied Economics, vol. 56. Chur, Switzerland: Harwood Academic Press.

Sen, Amartya K. 1976. "Poverty: An Ordinal Approach to Measurement." *Econometrica* 44: 219–31.

———. 1985. *Commodities and Capabilities.* Amsterdam: North-Holland.

Stern, N. H. 1987. " 'Comment' on Kanbur (1987)." *Economic Policy* 4: 136–41.

Tuomala, Matti. 1990. *Optimal Income Tax and Redistribution.* Oxford, Eng.: Clarendon Press.

Ulph, David. 1991. "Optimal Income Taxation: Resourcism vs. Welfarism." University of Bristol.

6 The Determinants and Consequences of the Placement of Government Programs in Indonesia

Mark M. Pitt, Mark R. Rosenzweig, and Donna M. Gibbons

Developing countries invest heavily in a wide variety of social sector programs, with health, fertility control, and schooling being central among them. Much literature in the social sciences is devoted to evaluating these programs. Most such studies have essentially compared the intensity of program efforts across localities with the corresponding variation among areas in program outcomes. A fundamental problem in program evaluation is that the coverage of programs and the timing of program initiatives—program placement—are not likely to be random. This is true to the extent that governmental decision rules are responsive to attributes of the targeted populations that are not measured in the data. Simple measured associations between programs and program outcomes, anticipated or unanticipated, will therefore not provide correct estimates of program effects. A research methodology and data base that can accommodate the existence of unobserved, location-specific attributes that influence both program placement and program outcomes are needed. This chapter uses Indonesia's uniquely rich data base to employ methods of analysis that reveal both the patterns of public program placement and the consequences of the programs, even if the programs are endogenously allocated.

In any country, at a point in time, program efforts vary widely across areas, even if the programs are funded and controlled by the central government. Given the limited resource capacities of the central public agency, program allocations must be rationed. The placement of programs is thus likely to depend on the expected location-specific returns from the program, which will vary across areas according to, among other attributes, their physical and demographic characteristics or endowments. If program placement is attentive to locational endowments and such endowments also influence outcomes of interest to

This chapter appeared in slightly different form in *World Bank Economic Review*, vol. 7 (September 1994), pp. 319–48.

policymakers, it is important in evaluating policies or programs to have information on endowments. It is inevitable, however, that not all exogenous locational characteristics are measured or are measurable.

Data on the spatial distribution of programs and population characteristics at more than one point in time can be used to identify program effects and the "rules" by which programs are allocated. When program placement depends on unmeasured time-persistent characteristics of locations but varies as a function of aggregate economywide trends or shocks (economic or political), cross-sectional data cannot readily be used to identify either program allocation rules or their consequences, unless the strong assumption is made that some area-specific characteristics affect program placement and not, net of the programs, program outcomes. However, estimates of program effects that are free from the contamination of area heterogeneity bias can be obtained from estimates of how changes in local programs affect changes in local population characteristics (fixed effects).

The placement of any particular type of program is likely to be sensitive not only to the demographic characteristics of regions but also to the regional distribution of programs that are already in place. A primary goal of the placement of a program in a specific locality is to enhance access to the program. Because fees charged by government programs are nominal or zero, "access" represents the cost of traveling to a program—its distance from a spatially defined population. Gertler and van der Gaag (1990) have shown that in Côte d'Ivoire the market for medical care is rationed by the time costs involved in obtaining care from providers. If similar or identical programs are located nearby, the initiation of a new program of the same type has a lower return compared with placing it where no programs of a similar type are located nearby. Where medical providers are more densely distributed over a fixed area, the incremental reduction in the average time cost falls. Thus, the effectiveness of a local program depends on its proximity to other programs.

The returns from a particular program may also be enhanced by the attributes of affected households. For example, the payoff to programs providing medical care may be enhanced by higher levels of education. Comprehensive information on programs is thus required, or the estimated average effects of any specific program will be biased because of omitted, correlated (program) variables. If, for example, the researcher omits variables reflecting the availability or levels of schooling when evaluating the effects of a health program whose payoff depends on the education levels of its clients, the evaluation will tend to overstate the effectiveness of the health program if its placement is positively correlated with schooling availability. Thus, useful studies of the impact of programs must take into account the endogenous placement of programs and must use information on the proximity of as many programs as possible to the relevant individuals and households. And, of course, appropriate data on outcomes of interest to policymakers must also be used.

Existing studies and data bases have several deficiencies. Only one study (Rosenzweig and Wolpin 1986) has examined the problem of the endogeneity of program placement. That study, which used longitudinal data on nutritional status, found that inattention to this problem led to severe biases in the estimates of the effectiveness of the two programs studied (health and family planning programs). In particular, because the government evidently placed these programs first in less healthy areas, standard (cross-sectional) estimation procedures led to the erroneous inference that exposure to the programs reduced nutritional status. In fact, their estimation results indicated that the programs enhanced nutritional status once the endogeneity of the placement was "controlled." The Rosenzweig-Wolpin study thus demonstrates empirically the importance of the nonrandomness of the spatial distribution of government programs. However, the study used information on households in only twenty barrios in the Philippines and did not have comprehensive data on programs and exogenous population characteristics. Whether generalizations can be made from the study is not clear.

Existing micro data bases are not well suited for program analysis. Although many contain the necessary detail on outcomes (such as health, productivity, and education) and on relevant demographic and socioeconomic variables, they rarely have information on access to programs. And they rarely cover a sufficient number of localities to support reliable estimates of program effects. In recent years, economists have merged area-specific information on programs with large household-level data sets providing location-of-residence information. In all of these cases, however, the program data are highly aggregated, so that the proximity of the households to the programs is poorly measured. For example, household data have been combined with district-level information on programs in Colombia by Rosenzweig and Schultz (1982), in Indonesia by Pitt and Rosenzweig (1985), and in Côte d'Ivoire by Strauss (1990).

In recent years, new data collection initiatives (including the Living Standards Measurement Surveys) have included information on program proximity in survey instruments. Although initial surveys of this type collected data only on the distance to programs actually used by the sample respondents, the newer efforts have collected data on program proximity independent of use. However, the cross-sectional or closely spaced panel data that result from these surveys cannot be used to correct for the problem of endogenous program placement.[1]

This chapter reports on research based on data consisting of newly merged Indonesian household-level, cross-sectional census data and comprehensive *kecamatan* (subdistrict)-level information on programs from two time periods. These data are used to assess the effects of a variety of programs on the schooling of children by gender, child mortality, and fertility.

This first section sets out a framework to estimate both the effects of programs when program placement is nonrandom and the determinants of program placement. The next describes the creation of the data set used in the estimation. The existing data base on Indonesia, when appropriately assembled, aggregated, and merged, offers a unique opportunity to study the determinants and consequences of program placement at a highly disaggregated spatial level by using fixed effects methods. It also allows exploration of nonlinearities in program effects. The third section presents estimates of the effects of programs and parental schooling on six outcome measures: attendance rates, by gender, of children ten to fourteen and fifteen to eighteen years of age; the children ever born to all women ages twenty-five to twenty-nine; and the cumulative mortality rates of children of women ages twenty-five to twenty-nine.

The analysis indicates that the proximity of grade schools, middle schools, and health programs significantly affects the school attendance of teenagers. And there is some evidence that the grade school effects are stronger among households in which mothers are less educated. There is no evidence, however, that family planning programs significantly affect any of the outcomes studied. In addition, the contrast between the cross-sectional effects and results obtained using fixed effects is quite marked. The cross-sectional estimates underestimate by 100 percent the effect of grade school proximity on the schooling attendance of both boys and girls ages ten to fourteen. The cross-sectional estimates also suggest that family planning programs increase fertility, the result being significant at the 0.05 level, whereas the results based on the fixed effects method suggest that family planning clinics reduce fertility (although the coefficient is imprecisely measured). Estimates of the determinants of program placement confirm that they are not random with respect to unobserved factors determining outcome and behaviors and that, during 1980–86, program coverage across subdistricts was being equalized for all programs considered except one.

The Analytic Framework

This section presents the analytic framework for estimating endogenous program effects and government placement rules.

Estimating Endogenous Program Effects

Equation 6-1 is a representation of a set of program evaluation equations based on data describing programs, population characteristics, and outcomes across geographic regions that is typical in program evaluation studies that do not focus solely on one program.

$$(6\text{-}1) \qquad H_{rit} = \Sigma_k \beta_{rk} P_{kit} + \Sigma_m \theta_{rm} Z_{mit} + \Sigma_n \Phi_m E_{ni} + \mu_{ri} + \epsilon_{rit},$$
$$r = 1,...,R,$$

where H_{rit} is policy outcome r in geographic region i at time period t (for example, the fraction of children of a specific age and sex who are in school); P_{kit} are the set of N programs in the regions at time t; Z_{mit} are the relevant socioeconomic characteristics (age, sex, level of education, and so on) of the individuals or households in the region; E_{ni} are measured environmental characteristics of the region (for example, altitude, propensity to drought and flood); μ_{ri} is a time-invariant, outcome-specific, unmeasured attribute (latent policy outcome) of the region; and ϵ_{rit} is a random, time-varying error. The β_{rk}, θ_{rm}, and Φ_m are parameters to be estimated; β_{rk}, in particular, are the estimates of the program effects on the outcomes.

Program effects may differ across households and individuals; for example, the more educated may benefit more or less from particular programs, or there may be different effects for males and females. Allowing program effects in the program evaluation equation to differ with the household attributes, Z_{mit}, results in the specification

$$(6\text{-}2) \quad H_{rit} = \Sigma_k \beta_{rk} P_{kit} + \Sigma_m \theta_{rm} Z_{mit} + \Sigma_n \Phi_m E_{ni} + \Sigma_k \Sigma_m \delta_{rkm} P_{kit} Z_{mit}$$
$$+ \mu_{ri} + \epsilon_{rit}; \quad r = 1,...,R,$$

where δ_{rkm} are the parameters describing the attribute-specific program effects. These terms provide estimates of how the effectiveness or effects of each of the programs on each outcome, H_r, depend on observable attributes of households. For example, are health clinics more effective at reducing child mortality for mothers who are better schooled? Are the returns on increasing the coverage of schools higher if the schools are located in areas in which schooling of parents is low? The answers to these questions are useful for allocating programs efficiently and for designing and evaluating patterns of program allocation that are intended to target benefits to certain classes of households defined by their characteristics, Z_{mit}.

The principal problem in obtaining estimates of the matrix of program effects described in equations 6-1 and 6-2 is that the programs may not be orthogonal to the unmeasured attributes of the localities, μ_{ri}. If, for example, the government, because of financial constraints, cannot provide program support across all areas at one time, it may implement a plan for a phased distribution of programs to be allocated to the regions over time. The existence of a program in a region at any point in time is likely to be a function of the permanent latent outcomes of the region that are unobserved by the researcher (μ_{ri}). Thus, for program P_{kit},

(6-3) $P_{kit} = \Sigma_n \gamma_{1kn} E_{ni} + \Sigma_r \gamma_{2kr} \mu_{ri} + u_{kit}, \ k = 1,...,N,$

where γ_{1kn} and γ_{2kr} are unknown estimable parameters characterizing the government program placement rule and u_{kit} is a random time-varying error. A more dynamic representation of the governmental decision rule is one in which the coverage of programs in a locality at time t influences the subsequent growth of program coverage across areas. Thus,

(6-4) $P_{kit+1} - P_{kit} = \Sigma_n \alpha_{1kn} E_{ni} + \Sigma_o \alpha_{2ko} P_{oit} + \Sigma_r \alpha_{3kr} \mu_{ri} + e_{kit},$
$$k = 1,...,N,$$

where P_{oit} are the existing set of programs in region i at time t including P_{kit}; the α_{1kn}, α_{2ko}, and α_{3kr} are estimable parameters; and e_{kit} is a random time-varying error.

Equations 6-3 and 6-4 indicate that as long as $\gamma_{2kr} \neq 0$ and $\alpha_{3kr} \neq 0$—that is, program placement is attentive to area attributes not measured in the data—use of least squares applied to cross-sectional data to estimate program effects, from equations 6-1 or 6-2, will be biased. That is, both the region-specific outcomes and the programs are correlated with μ_{ri}. One method of eliminating the bias is to eliminate the μ's from the equations, because they are the source of the correlation between the least squares residual and the regressors. With information on program placement and outcomes at two points in time for the same region, for example, a fixed effects procedure can be implemented that sweeps out the unobservable, as in equation 6-5:

(6-5) $H_{rit+1} - H_{rit} = \Sigma_k \beta_{rk}(P_{kit+1} - P_{kit}) + \Sigma_m \theta_{rm}(Z_{mit+1} - Z_{mit})$
$$+ \ \epsilon_{rit+1} - \epsilon_{rit}, \ r = 1,...,R.$$

Thus, by relating the changes over time in outcome variables to changes over time in program placement, the biases resulting from the endogeneity of program placement are eliminated as long as the region-specific, time-varying shocks affecting program placement in equations 6-3 or 6-4 are uncorrelated with the region-specific, time-varying disturbances in the outcome equations.

The outcome equations (6-1 and 6-2) assume that programs affect outcomes only contemporaneously. They assume that the history of programs in an area does not matter for current-period program outcomes. This assumption may be reasonable for some outcomes, such as period-specific birth rates for young women, infant mortality rates, or school enrollment rates for children of primary-school age.[2] However, the assumption that the existence of programs in the past does not influence such contemporaneous outcomes as the schooling of older children, the cumulative fertility of older women, or the health of older children is not realistic. Whether primary schools were present in an area in the past, for example, clearly affects whether or not children currently of secondary-school age will attend secondary schools, as will the existence of secondary schools in the area in the current period. And whether or not family planning programs were present in the past clearly affects the current birth decisions of older women, because it will have affected their cumulative fertility.

Thus, for some outcomes, a more appropriate specification of the set of outcome equations, ignoring, for simplicity, differences in program effects across socioeconomic groups, is

$$(6\text{-}6) \quad H_{rit} = \Sigma_j \Sigma_k \beta_{rkj} P_{kit-j} + \Sigma_m \theta_{rm} Z_{mit} + \Sigma_n \Phi_{rn} E_{ni} + \mu_{ri} + \epsilon_{rit};$$
$$r = 1,...,R, \, j = 0,...,J,$$

where, for simplicity as well, we assume that there are no lagged effects of socioeconomic variables. Equation 6-6 differentiates program effects, β_{rkj}, by their lags of length, j. Estimation of equation 6-6 using least squares also results in biased estimates of all of these program effects, for the same reason as it does for equations 6-1 and 6-2, because the programs are correlated with the latent outcome variables, as in equation 6-3.

With only two (N) time-specific observations on outcomes and programs and no retrospective information on the history of programs by region, it is obvious that not all of the lagged program effects can be estimated without bias or even at all. Indeed, no lagged program effects for lags greater than two (N) can be estimated at all in that case. However, if the program allocation rule is described by equation 6-3, differencing across the two periods can yield unbiased estimates of the contemporaneous program effects, β_{rk0}, even if such programs are endogenous and even if there is no information on lagged programs. To see this, substitute equation 6-3 for all of the relevant lagged programs in equation 6-6 so that the outcomes are functions only of the contemporaneous programs, the time-invariant latent variables, and the lagged program shocks:

$$(6\text{-}7) \quad H_{rit} = \Sigma_k \beta_{rk} P_{kit} + \Sigma_k \Sigma_j \beta_{rkj} \Sigma_n \gamma_{2kn} \mu_{ni} + \Sigma_k \Sigma_j \beta_{rkj} u_{kit-j}$$
$$+ \Sigma_m \theta_{rm} Z_{mit} + \Sigma_n \Phi_{rn} E_{ni} + \mu_{ri} + \epsilon_{rit}; \, r = 1,...,R, \text{ and } j = 1,...,J$$

so that

$$(6\text{-}8) \quad H_{rit} = \Sigma_k \beta_{rk0} P_{kit} + \Sigma_m \theta_{rm} Z_{mit} + \Sigma_n \Phi_{rn} E_{ni} + \mu^*_{ri} + \epsilon^*_{rit};$$
$$r = 1,...,R.$$

Equation 6-8 is similar to equation 6-1 except that the fixed effect μ^*_{ri} contains the lagged program effects and program responses to the set of area outcome-specific endowments as well as the endowment specific to the outcome r.

Differencing equation 6-7 across two periods thus yields

$$(6\text{-}9) \quad H_{rit+1} - H_{rit} = \Sigma_k \beta_{rk0}(P_{kit+1} - P_{kit}) + \Sigma_k \Sigma_j \beta_{rkj}(u_{kit+1-j} - u_{kit-j})$$
$$+ \Sigma_m \theta_{rm}(Z_{mit+1} - Z_{mit}) + \epsilon_{rit+1} - \epsilon_{rit}; \, r = 1,...,R,$$

which provides an unbiased estimate of β_{rk0} as long as program changes do not respond to lagged program shocks. Thus, no matter how many lags there are in the program effects (equation 6-6), it is still possible to obtain unbiased estimates of the contemporaneous effects of the programs with only two sets of period-specific observations. However, these contemporaneous effects are not the full effects of the programs if there are lags, because the current programs will have effects on future outcomes that cannot be estimated. Moreover, from equation 6-8, if the program allocation rules conform to equation 6-4 and are dynamic, then differencing across the two periods does not yield unbiased estimates of even contemporaneous program effects when there are important lagged program effects, because the history of program shocks influences the current program allocations.

Estimating Government Placement Rules

The effects of endogenously placed programs on outcomes of policy interest can be estimated under a plausible set of assumptions even with two sets of cross-sectional data by using fixed effects techniques to estimate the sets of equations described by equations 6-1 and 6-2 or equation 6-6. Because such estimates can also be used to obtain estimates of the fixed effects themselves (for each outcome), the program placement rules described by equations 6-3 and 6-4 can also be estimated. That is, the analysis can be used to assess whether the spatial distribution of programs tends to equalize spatial differences in outcomes (such as health) or to exacerbate them. For example, it can be ascertained whether localities tending to exhibit high child mortality rates, net of programs, are more likely to have received health programs or whether areas of high fertility are more likely to have received family planning programs.

Theory does provide much guidance in predicting how public programs are allocated across population groups. Altruism theories of public behavior suggest that the government would allocate more programs to those areas in which latent outcomes (such as health and schooling) are least. Thus, areas with high fertility would receive the greatest coverage of family planning clinics, and areas with high child mortality would receive the greatest coverage of health clinics. In this model, the government allocates programs to compensate populations that are poorly endowed with latent outcomes. Alternatively, pressure-group theories suggest that the government may respond to populations who have high demands for these outcomes by providing them with a disproportionate share of program resources. Households having the highest latent outcomes would derive the greatest private benefit from these programs and may be willing to lobby hardest for these resources. Efficiency criteria and externalities such as the transmission of disease, as in the model of Rosenzweig and Wolpin (1986), may also influence the allocation of programs. Program allocations may respond to differentials in gross returns on programs across population groups—defined by parental schooling, for example—resulting from nonlinearities in the program effects function (as in equation 6-2).

An econometric problem in estimating the program placement equations is that the estimates of the fixed effects contain errors, which will lead to biases (Pitt, Rosenzweig, and Hassan 1990). However, with two estimates of each latent outcome based on two matched cross sections, the set of estimated endowments from one cross section can be used as instruments for the set of estimated endowments from the other as long as the time-varying or transitory errors (ϵ_{rit}) are independent and identically distributed, as is necessary to assume if there are lagged program effects. Thus, the parameters of equations 6-3 and 6-4 can be estimated by using instrumental variable methods to correct for "errors in variables" in the measurement of μ_{ri}, with noncontemporaneous estimates of fixed effects as identifying instruments.

The dynamic program allocation equation (6-4) has the coverage of programs, P_{kit}, on both sides of the equation, suggesting an additional errors-in-variables problem in its estimation. If P_{kit} is measured with error, own-program coverage will have a possibly spurious negative effect on program growth, and the estimated effects of other programs, P_{mit} ($m \neq k$), on the growth of coverage of program k will be biased toward zero. Program coverage in a period before year t can be used as instruments for the set of (level) program coverage in period t.[3]

The Data Set

To create a data set that provides answers to questions about the effects of programs, the influence of nonrandom program placement on program assessments based on cross-sectional data, and the relation between area endowments and program allocations, information is needed at, minimally, two points in time on programs, outcomes of program effects, and characteristics of geographical areas that may have influenced program placement. The data used in the empirical research combine the 1986 and 1980 Potensi Desa of Indonesia (PODES), the 1976–77 Fasilitas Desa of Indonesia (FASDES), the 1985 Intercensal Population Survey of Indonesia (SUPAS), and the 1980 Population Census of Indonesia. All the surveys were carried out by the Central Bureau of Statistics of Indonesia (Biro Pusat Statistik [BPS]).

The 1986 and 1980 PODES and the 1976–77 FASDES provide information at the village level on government programs such as schools, family planning clinics, health centers, and sources of water for drinking and bathing. The surveys also include data on population; on other infrastructure, such as marketplaces, banks, factories, types of roads, recreation facilities, communication facilities, and electricity; and on area-specific geophysical characteristics, including altitude, land type, proximity to coastline, and the history of natural disasters. Approximately 67,000, 62,000, and 58,000 villages were surveyed in the 1986 PODES, the 1980 PODES, and the 1976–77 FASDES, respectively.

The 1980 Population Census of Indonesia and the 1985 SUPAS provide information, including census block information that can be mapped into village of residence, for a stratified random sample of households throughout Indonesia on individual schooling, labor force participation, marriage, fertility, birth control, and child mortality. They also provide data on selected household assets, structure, land area, and cooking and bathing facilities. The detailed questionnaire for the 1980 census was used for a stratified random sample of 1,502,075 households containing 7,234,634 individuals, approximately 5 percent of the total population of Indonesia. The 1985 SUPAS surveyed 126,370 households across Indonesia containing 602,885 individuals. An important shortcoming of the survey data is that information on income, expenditures, and the total value of household assets is not available.[4]

To obtain a data set that combines the program and household information at two points in time (1980 and 1985), it is necessary to link all of the data sets by geographical area. Indeed, the assumption that program placement rules depend on regional-level characteristics means that data over time must be linked at that level. Thus, it is not necessary to have household-level longitudinal data to estimate program effects appropriately.[5] Because the data on individual Indonesian households are not longitudinal, the successive cross sections are aggregated to the *kecamatan* level and matched at that level. Because the underlying data are individual, however, the specification need not be restricted to linear forms with respect to individual or household characteristics. Thus, for example, logarithmic specifications can be tried, aggregating up from log transforms of the micro variables.

Because information at the village level provides the most accurate information on households' proximity to programs, it would have been desirable to link the data at that level. Unfortunately, this was not possible because there were administrative changes in the boundaries and names of villages throughout 1976–86. Also, the BPS updated geographical location codes at the village (*desa*), subdistrict (*kecamatan*), district (*kabupaten*), and province (*provinsi*) levels three times from 1976 through 1986: in 1980 coinciding with the population census (*Sensus Penduduk*), in 1983 coinciding with the agricultural census (*Sensus Pertanian*), and in 1986 coinciding with the economic census (*Sensus Ekonomi*). In each of these years a PODES survey was also conducted as part of the corresponding census. Thus, all of the original data sets used in this research have different location codes. The BPS does not comprehensively document location code changes over time. However, for

*Table 6-1. Institutional and Program Coverage in Indonesia,
1980 and 1986*
(percentage of households residing in a village with a program or institution)

Institution or program	1980	1986	Growth (percent)
Grade school	74.4	93.0	25.0
Middle school	26.7	39.0	46.1
High school	10.3	17.7	71.8
Family planning clinic	45.9	76.5	66.7
Health clinic (*puskesmas*)	24.4	42.4	73.8

Note: Data are based on 3,302 matched *kecamatans*.
Source: The 1980 and 1986 PODES data sets are from the government of Indonesia.

1980–86 the BPS provides a master list with names and codes of all villages, subdistricts, districts, and provinces for the years of the updating. These lists, called "master files," do not enable data sets to be matched accurately and consistently at the village level but do enable the codes to be tracked over time at the *kecamatan* level. The appendix provides details on the matching procedures that were used.

This study examines the effects of, and placement rules for, three types of programs: schooling institutions by level (grade, middle, and high schools); health clinics, especially the *puskesmas* program; and family planning. Table 6-1 provides information on the coverage of these programs in Indonesia based on the aggregated and matched PODES data for 1980 and 1986. The proportion of households living in a village with each of the programs increased considerably during that period. For example, 93 percent of households resided in a village with a grade school in 1986, up from 74 percent in 1980. In 1986, 42 percent of households resided in a village with a government health clinic, compared with 24 percent in 1980. Given that the methodology exploits the change in program coverage over time, this evident substantial change is a useful feature of the constructed data set.

The spatial correlations among the program variables indicate that *kecamatans* that have a high degree of exposure to one type of program are likely also to have relatively high coverage of the other programs— all spatial correlations of program variables are positive and statistically significant. For example, in 1980 the correlation between the coverage of middle schools and high schools is 0.72 and that between grade schools and family planning programs is 0.48. Thus, to the extent that each program has cross-effects—that is, each program affects outcomes in addition to those it is intended to influence—it may be important in the Indonesia context to estimate program effects jointly to evaluate appropriately the effects of any one type of program on any particular outcome (Rosenzweig and Wolpin 1982). For example, family planning programs may reduce not only births but also child mortality rates. If the effects of health clinics on child mortality are estimated without considering the presence of family planning clinics, given that both tend to be in the same areas, the effects of the health clinics may be overestimated. We present estimates below of the extent to which the changes in program coverage during 1980–86 reduced or increased the spatial correlation in programs.

The 1985 SUPAS and 1980 population census include sample weighting factors (frequency weights) for both individuals and households. In both data sets separate records describe the household characteristics and each individual's characteristics. The weighted variables are summed to aggregate these individual and household data at the sub-district level. (A weighted variable is the original sample variable multiplied by the appropriate sample weight.) The resulting aggregated data thus are representative of the population of Indonesia in both 1980 and 1985. There were 3,179 aggregated *kecamatan* "observations" for the 1985 SUPAS and 3,253 for the 1980 population census.

There are two principal advantages to aggregating from micro data of the type available in the census and SUPAS samples. First, there can be an appropriate matching of dependent and independent variables. For example, if the dependent variable characterizes children of a given age, then it is possible to obtain information on the parents of those children. Second, as noted, the appropriate aggregation of any micro functional form can be obtained. Any nonlinearities hypothesized about relations between independent and dependent variables at the household or individual level can be appropriately aggregated.

We create three types of outcome variables characterizing the schooling of children, fertility, and child mortality. For schooling, there are four attendance rates for female and male children ages ten to fourteen and fifteen to eighteen. Fertility is measured by the number of children ever born to all women ages twenty-five to twenty-nine. And child mortality is measured by the cumulative child death rates for all women ages twenty-five to twenty-nine. Selecting the vital rates of relatively young women minimizes the potential influence of lagged program effects; however, such lagged effects may be important for the estimates of attendance rates of children ages fifteen to eighteen.

The independent variables for the school attendance outcomes are the mean schooling attainment and age for mothers of children ages ten to fourteen and fifteen to eighteen and the mean schooling attainment for heads of the households in which children ages ten to fourteen and fifteen to eighteen reside. The independent variable for the fertility and child mortality outcomes is the average schooling attainment for women ages twenty-five to twenty-nine. Table 6-2 provides the means of the outcome and independent variables for 1980 and 1985 and the number of matched *kecamatans* for each variable. These figures indicate that, just as program exposure for the basic schooling, health, and fertility programs increased significantly from 1980 through 1986, the

Table 6-2. Policy Outcomes and Independent Variables for Matched Kecamatans in Indonesia, 1980 and 1985

Variable	Mean		Number of matched kecamatans
	1980	1985	
Policy outcome			
School attendance (percentage of total in age group)			
Females ages 10–14	76.9	88.1	3,043
	(14.08)	(16.3)	
Males ages 10–14	81.6	90.2	3,048
	(12.5)	(14.8)	
Females ages 15–18	29.2	44.8	2,887
	(19.7)	(33.8)	
Males ages 15–18	39.2	52.9	2,548
	(20.3)	(33.0)	
Number of children ever born to women ages 25–29	2.60	2.45	3,014
	(0.69)	(0.79)	
Cumulative mortality rate[a] of children of women ages 25–29	14.2	8.0	3,005
	(8.6)	(10.3)	
Independent variable			
Schooling attainment (years)			
Mothers of children ages 10–14	2.65	3.54	3,043
	(1.52)	(2.05)	
Household heads in households with children ages 10–14	3.61	4.53	3,043
	(1.62)	(2.62)	
Mothers of children ages 15–18	2.08	3.06	2,887
	(1.46)	(2.21)	
Household heads in households with children ages 15–18	3.11	4.17	2,887
	(1.53)	(2.46)	
Women ages 25–29	4.20	4.78	3,014
	(1.86)	(2.16)	

Note: Standard deviations are in parentheses.
a. Percentage of total live births that died.
Source: The 1980 census and the 1985 SUPAS.

basic human capital outcome indicators—school attendance (particularly for females) and child survival—also increased substantially during the period, although fertility dropped only marginally. Of course, the correlation in the overall trends in program exposure and the outcomes cannot be used to infer much about the effectiveness of the programs. For example, it is clear from table 6-2 that the average schooling levels of parents (and potential parents) also increased during the period. Here the basic methodology for discerning the impact of programs essentially tests whether the changes in outcomes were greater in areas in which there were greater changes in program population (village) coverage net of changes in the schooling levels of parents.

To test whether program effects on school attendance, child mortality, and fertility outcomes differ by the schooling level of women, the micro sample is split into three education groups—women (for the relevant school-age children or in the relevant age group) with no schooling, women with one to five years of schooling, and women with six or more years of schooling.[6] The *kecamatan* aggregation was performed for each of these three groups.

Estimates of Program Effects

Tables 6-3, 6-4, and 6-5 report the estimates of program and parental schooling effects on six outcome measures. In each table, three sets of estimates are reported. All the regression estimates reported here provide *t*-ratios based on Huber's method for calculating the parameter covariance matrix (Huber 1967; see also White 1980). The estimates of the *t*-ratios are generally consistent even if there is heteroskedasticity or clustered sampling or weighting not correctly accounted for in the aggregation of the micro data or in the weighting of the least squares estimates. The first set is obtained using weighted least squares, where the weights are the sample number of households, based on the 1980 merged cross-sectional, *kecamatan* data. The first set includes in the specification only the program variables directly relevant to the outcome.[7] Thus, for the school attendance measures, the health and family planning clinics are excluded. For the fertility outcome, the three school types and the health clinic are excluded. For the child mortality outcome, the family planning clinic and school programs are excluded. This first specification corresponds to that which is prevalent in the evaluation research literature, where estimates of program effects are based on cross-sectional data and tend to focus on a narrow set of programs that are assumed to be relevant to the outcome being studied. The second set of estimates differs from the first only in that all of the program measures are included. The third specification implements the fixed effects methodology, using both the 1985 and 1980 data sets and including all of the program measures.[8]

All of the specifications also include the amount of land owned by each household and the proportion of households residing in urban areas. The fixed effects estimates also allow for a time trend in all dependent variables. Thus, those estimates of program effects are net of aggregate trends in the outcomes that are visible in table 6-2. Although the fixed effects estimates are net of the influence of both locality-specific fixed effects and of aggregate time trends, such estimates based on only two points in time cannot control for the potential influence of area-specific time trends. This may be particularly important for the estimates, given the absence of information on incomes.

Table 6-3. Estimates of the Determinants of School Attendance for Females and Males, Ages 10–14

Variable	Females			Males		
	Weighted least squares		Fixed-effects methodology	Weighted least squares		Fixed-effects methodology
	Excluding health and family planning clinics	Including health and family planning clinics		Excluding health and family planning clinics	Including health and family planning clinics	
Schooling attainment						
Mothers	0.035 (10.5)	0.035 (10.7)	0.034 (3.51)	0.0017 (0.62)	0.0033 (1.20)	0.010 (3.65)
Household heads	0.024 (6.37)	0.023 (6.17)	0.0075 (2.19)	0.039 (12.8)	0.037 (12.3)	0.0078 (3.05)
Age of mother	0.010 (8.31)	0.0094 (7.35)	−0.0030 (2.36)	0.0071 (6.59)	0.0059 (5.43)	−0.0013 (1.37)
Owned land per household (0.01 hectares $\times$ 10^{-4})	0.19 (0.34)	−0.20 (0.35)	1.6 (2.12)	−1.1 (2.25)	−1.2 (2.50)	1.4 (2.20)
Proportion of households in urban areas	−0.065 (7.15)	−0.062 (6.81)	−0.029 (0.57)	−0.042 (5.62)	−0.040 (5.15)	0.012 (0.25)
Proportion of households in villages						
With grade school	0.039 (3.81)	0.048 (4.68)	0.11 (5.90)	0.052 (2.97)	0.041 (4.79)	0.088 (5.61)
With middle school	0.067 (5.82)	0.085 (6.88)	0.085 (3.87)	0.050 (5.45)	0.073 (7.45)	0.054 (3.02)

128

With high school	0.011 (0.88)	−0.14 (1.13)	−0.035 (1.57)	0.0010 (0.09)	0.0003 (0.03)	−0.011 (0.55)
With health clinic (*puskesmas*)	n.a.	−0.028 (3.19)	0.033 (2.01)	n.a.	−0.031 (3.92)	0.001 (0.07)
With family planning clinic	n.a.	−0.015 (2.25)	0.0076 (0.85)	n.a.	−0.029 (5.59)	0.010 (1.26)
Time trend	n.a.	n.a.	0.052 (9.43)	n.a.	n.a.	0.037 (7.49)
Constant	0.15 (3.01)	0.19 (3.68)	n.a.	0.38 (8.54)	0.43 (9.58)	n.a.
R^2	0.53	0.53	n.a.	0.48	0.49	n.a.
Number of *kecamatans*	2,904	2,904	2,874	2,904	2,904	2,881

n.a. Not applicable.

Note: Weights are the sample number of households. The least squares estimates are based on the 1980 merged cross-sectional subdistrict data. The fixed effects methodology uses the 1980 and 1985 data sets. *Kecamatans* with fewer than ten survey households were excluded from the analysis. Absolute values of asymptotic *t*-ratios are in parentheses.

Table 6-4. *Estimates of the Determinants of School Attendance for Females and Males, Ages 15–18*

Variable	Females			Males		
	Weighted least squares		Fixed effects methodology	Weighted least squares		Fixed effects methodology
	Excluding health and family planning clinics	Including health and family planning clinics		Excluding health and family planning clinics	Including health and family planning clinics	
Schooling attainment						
Mothers	0.011	0.011	0.026	0.040	0.038	0.022
	(2.47)	(2.53)	(5.14)	(8.44)	(8.09)	(4.69)
Household heads	0.058	0.057	0.039	0.090	0.088	0.036
	(13.8)	(13.6)	(9.02)	(19.5)	(19.1)	(9.28)
Age of mother	0.015	0.014	0.0049	0.016	0.014	0.0010
	(12.4)	(11.2)	(3.61)	(11.2)	(9.85)	(0.75)
Owned land per household (0.01 hectares $\times$ 10^{-4})	−3.10	−2.90	0.570	−0.510	−0.500	−1.000
	(5.39)	(5.03)	(0.48)	(7.31)	(7.19)	(0.98)
Proportion of households in urban areas	0.280	0.031	−0.110	0.046	0.051	0.016
	(2.15)	(2.31)	(1.34)	(3.34)	(3.58)	(0.20)
Proportion of households in villages						
With grade school	−0.080	−0.067	0.045	−0.069	−0.042	0.054
	(8.28)	(6.64)	(1.76)	(5.84)	(3.45)	(2.07)
With middle school	0.086	0.110	0.011	0.110	0.160	0.049
	(6.07)	(7.54)	(0.34)	(7.24)	(9.41)	(1.53)

With high school	0.130 (6.69)	0.130 (6.65)	0.0086 (0.26)	0.120 (6.12)	0.120 (6.15)	0.0058 (0.18)
With health clinic (*puskesmas*)	n.a.	−0.057 (5.10)	0.078 (3.26)	n.a.	0.078 (5.96)	0.034 (1.51)
With family planning clinic	n.a.	−0.012 (1.69)	−0.010 (0.69)	n.a.	−0.037 (4.46)	0.0034 (0.31)
Time trend	n.a.	n.a.	0.066 (7.48)	n.a.	n.a.	0.062 (7.08)
Constant	−0.53 (10.2)	−0.48 (8.99)	n.a.	−0.47 (7.50)	−0.38 (6.07)	n.a.
R^2	0.73	0.74	n.a.	0.65	0.66	n.a.
Number of *kecamatans*	2,899	2,899	2,753	2,903	2,903	2,805

n.a. Not applicable.

Note: Weights are the sample number of households. The least squares estimates are based on the 1980 merged cross-sectional subdistrict data. The fixed-effects methodology uses the 1980 and 1985 data sets. *Kecamatans* with less than ten survey households were excluded from the analysis. Absolute values of asymptotic *t*-ratios are in parentheses.

Table 6-5. Estimates of the Determinants of Fertility and Child Mortality for Women and Mothers, Ages 25–29

	Children ever born			Child mortality		
	Weighted least squares			Weighted least squares		
Variable	Excluding health clinics and schools	Including health clinics and schools	Fixed-effects methodology	Excluding family planning clinics and schools	Including family planning clinics and schools	Fixed-effects methodology
Schooling attainment Women ages 25–29	−0.015 (1.61)	−0.0023 (0.28)	−0.083 (8.03)	−0.011 (10.00)	−0.010 (9.49)	−0.0095 (6.17)
Age Women, ages 25–29	−0.100 (2.20)	−0.082 (1.78)	0.270 (13.6)	−0.027 (4.03)	−0.022 (3.89)	0.0073 (1.98)
Owned land per household (0.01 hectares × 10⁻²)	0.100 (3.72)	0.120 (3.62)	−0.021 (0.76)	−0.015 (4.81)	−0.010 (2.97)	−0.0088 (2.30)
Proportion of households in urban areas	−0.290 (6.01)	−0.087 (1.31)	−0.250 (0.78)	−0.014 (2.26)	−0.0027 (0.31)	−0.027 (0.62)
Proportion of households in villages With grade school	n.a.	0.060 (1.03)	0.260 (3.72)	n.a.	−0.0095 (1.41)	−0.0016 (0.13)
With middle school	n.a.	−0.190 (2.26)	0.017 (0.19)	n.a.	−0.036 (3.92)	−0.0078 (0.54)
With high school	n.a.	−0.330 (3.49)	0.140 (1.33)	n.a.	0.00031 (0.03)	0.019 (1.21)

	(1)	(2)	(3)	(4)	(5)	(6)
With health clinic (*puskesmas*)	n.a.	0.200 (3.22)	0.230 (3.37)	0.011 (1.57)	0.012 (1.56)	0.011 (0.97)
With family planning clinic	0.075 (1.99)	0.071 (1.77)	−0.018 (0.05)	n.a.	0.034 (6.82)	−0.0035 (0.55)
Time trend	n.a.	n.a.	0.25 (10.6)	n.a.	n.a.	−0.056 (14.9)
Constant	5.28 (4.40)	4.70 (3.88)	n.a.	0.90 (5.97)	0.77 (5.20)	n.a.
R^2	0.062	0.074	n.a.	0.13	0.14	n.a.
Number of *kecamatans*	2,904	2,904	2,862	2,904	2,904	2,856

n.a. Not applicable.

Note: Weights are the sample number of households. The least squares estimates are based on the 1980 merged cross-sectional subdistrict data. The fixed-effects methodology uses the 1980 and 1985 data sets. *Kecamatans* with fewer than ten survey households were excluded from the analysis. Absolute values of asymptotic *t*-ratios are in parentheses.

Thus, significant variation in economic growth rates across areas might cause bias in the fixed effects estimates.[9]

Table 6-3 reports the estimates of the determinants of school attendance for females and males ages ten through fourteen. From these, we can draw two conclusions, which are applicable to both gender groups. First, in the cross section, exclusion of the evidently relevant health and family planning clinics from the specification results in underestimates by up to 50 percent of the impacts of the presence of both grade schools and middle schools on the school attendance of ten through fourteen year olds. Second, use of the cross-sectional data, not taking into account the possibly nonrandom spatial location of programs, results in an underestimate by 100 percent of the effect of being proximate to a grade school on the school attendance of both males and females ages ten through fourteen.

The cross-sectional estimates indicate that an increase in the coverage of villages with grade schools to 100 percent, from, say, the 1980 figure of 74 percent, would increase school attendance by 1.0 to 1.2 percentage points, whereas the fixed effects estimates indicate that the increase would be by 2.2 to 2.8 percentage points. The fixed effects estimates indicate that an increase to universal coverage of grade schools would have raised the school attendance rates, based on the 1980 census figures in table 6-2, to 79.7 and 83.7 percent for females and males, respectively. The estimates also indicate that a similar increase by about 25 percentage points in the coverage of middle schools would have raised school attendance rates by an additional 2.1 percentage points for females and by an additional 1.4 percentage points for males. This is substantially less than the growth in the rates that occurred during 1980–85, when coverage of grade schools increased to 93 percent and coverage of middle schools increased by only 19 percentage points (a substantial relative increase). The best estimates thus indicate that the growth in the spatial coverage of grade schools and middle schools played a relatively small, but not insignificant, part in the growth in school attendance of females and males in the ten through fourteen age group during this period.

The cross-sectional estimates of the effects of the health and family planning clinics on school attendance are not credible, being both negative and statistically significant, whereas the fixed effects estimates indicate that both programs may have a positive impact on school attendance. The positive effect of the health clinic on the school attendance of females is statistically significant, just as it is for the fifteen to eighteen age group. The cross-sectional estimates of the effects of the schooling attainment of household heads, almost all of whom are male, on school attendance rates are also considerably higher than the fixed effects estimates, whereas the estimates of the effects of maternal schooling are relatively robust to estimation procedure. The preferred fixed effects estimates indicate that, for both males and females, the effect of the mother's schooling attainment on school attendance is greater than that of the male head's schooling. The differences are statistically significant for both gender groups. The fixed effects point estimates indicate that for each one-year increase in the number of years of schooling of mothers, the school attendance rate of their female children rises by 3 percentage points and that of their male children by 1 percentage point. For each one-year increase in the schooling attainment of household heads, school attendance rises by three-fourths of a percentage point for both males and females. The increase in schooling attainment (by less than one year) for mothers and household heads between 1980 and 1985 thus accounts for only a small part of the actual increase in school attendance of almost 19 percentage points during that period.

The contrast between the set of cross-sectional program effects estimates and those obtained using fixed effects is even more marked for the school attendance rates of the fifteen through eighteen year olds, as reported in table 6-4. The cross-sectional estimates indicate that in *kecamatans* in which higher proportions of the population are located in villages with middle and high schools, attendance rates for this age group are significantly higher; however, the rates are significantly lower where there is a greater coverage of grade schools, health clinics, and family planning clinics. In contrast, the fixed effects estimates indicate that grade schools are significantly positively related to the school attendance of fifteen through eighteen year olds (only at the 10 percent level for females), as are the health clinics for females, but there are no effects of the coverage of either of the other school types or of the family planning clinics. The difference between the effects of the schooling attainment of the mother and household head on school attendance is also substantially reduced when the fixed effects procedure is compared with the cross-sectional estimates. The point estimates of the grade school effects and the parental schooling variables are relatively small and indicate that the growth in grade school coverage and in the schooling of parents in Indonesia between 1980 and 1986 cannot alone account for the 53 percent increase in school attendance among female teenagers ages fifteen through eighteen or the 35 percent increase among males over that period, as exhibited in table 6-2.

Similar dramatic differences in inferences about program effects by estimation procedure and noncredible results from cross-sectional estimates are seen in table 6-5, which presents the estimates of the determinants of fertility and child mortality. For fertility, the estimates that are based on the cross-sectional association between program coverage and outcomes, and that exclude the effects of alternative programs, indicate that family planning programs increase fertility, with the result significant at the 0.05 level! The point estimate of the effect is not influenced very much by the inclusion of other programs in the specification, although the significance level drops. The fixed effects estimate, however, indicates that the increased coverage of family planning clinics does reduce fertility, although the coefficient is imprecisely measured and the impact is very small.

The cross-sectional fertility results indicate that the presence of middle and high schools significantly reduces fertility, but this result also appears to be due to the nonrandomness of school placement, because these effects disappear when the fixed effects procedure is used to obtain estimates. The latter estimates, however, indicate that the presence of grade schools positively affects fertility, but by only a small amount. Both the cross-sectional and the fixed effects estimates indicate that the health clinics also positively affect fertility, although the effects are also small. An increase in the number of grade schools to attain universal coverage across villages would increase fertility by only 0.07 children. A doubling of the coverage of health clinics from 1980 levels would increase fertility by a similar amount. Finally, the cross-sectional method, based on the full specification, substantially underestimates (by a factor of 36, compared with the fixed effects method) the negative effect of maternal schooling on fertility. The negative effect is statistically significant when the fixed effects are taken into account.

The cross-sectional estimates of the determinants of child mortality based on the more complete specification of programs indicate that family planning clinics lower child survival, whereas middle schools increase survival. In contrast, the fixed effects estimates indicate that program coverage of schools, health clinics, or family planning clinics does not have a significant impact on child mortality; only the schooling attainment of women appears to affect child survival, a result that is robust to the estimation method. The point estimates indicate that for each year of schooling acquired by women ages twenty-five through twenty-nine, child mortality declines 7 percent. The small (just over a half year) increase in the schooling attainment of women ages twenty-five through twenty-nine between 1980 and 1985 cannot account for the 43 percent decline in child mortality among women in this age group during this period.

Thus, estimated program effects are often small or insignificant even when the influence of unmeasured area endowments on outcomes and program placement are taken into account. One reason is that the effects may not be linear, as in equation 6-2. To test whether program effects differ by the schooling level of women, the model is reestimated using fixed effects based on the data divided into the three schooling groups of women—no schooling, one through five years of schooling, and six or more years of schooling. Using the pooled data set of all three schooling groups, all coefficients were allowed to differ by group, and three tests were performed: a test of whether the program coefficients

Table 6-6. *Tests of Differences in Program Effects by Schooling*
Class of Women
(test statistic for differences in coefficients)

Outcome variable	All three schooling groups	Lowest and middle schooling groups	Lowest and highest schooling groups
School attendance (percentage of total in age group)			
Females ages 10–14	1.60[a]	1.00	2.47[b]
	(12, 3460)	(6, 3460)	(6, 3460)
Males ages 10–14	2.30[b]	0.92	2.82[b]
	(12, 3489)	(6, 3488)	(6, 3489)
Females ages 15–18	1.16	0.76	1.42
	(12, 3155)	(6, 3155)	(6, 3155)
Males ages 15–18	1.15	0.80	1.53
	(12, 3263)	(6, 3263)	(6, 3263)
Number of children ever born	1.10	0.92	1.12
to women ages 25–29	(12, 3327)	(6, 3327)	(6, 3327)
Cumulative mortality rate[c] of	1.51	1.57	2.54[b]
children of women ages 25–29	(12, 3368)	(6, 3268)	(6, 3268)

Note: Test statistics are F-statistics from weighted fixed-effects estimates of program effects. The null hypothesis for each test is that there is no difference in the coefficients. The three schooling groups are for women ages twenty through forty. The groups are no schooling (19 percent), one through five years of schooling (35 percent), and six or more years of schooling (46 percent). Degrees of freedom are in parentheses.
a. Significance level is at least 0.10.
b. Significance level is at least 0.05.
c. Percentage of total births that died.

differed across all three groups and tests of whether the program effects of the lowest (zero years) and the highest (six or more years) female schooling groups differed.

The test statistics are reported for each of the dependent variables in table 6-6. Of the six outcomes, in only two (school attendance for both males and females ages ten through fourteen) were there differences in program effects across the three schooling groups of women; this difference arose between the lowest and highest schooling groups for both females and males. Inspection of these estimates indicates that the only significant difference in program effects was in the influence of the coverage of grade schools on attendance. The stratified estimates indicate that grade school coverage has a significantly higher positive effect on school attendance for teens ages ten through fourteen among the lowest educational strata of women (mothers) compared with the highest. In particular, the point estimates indicate that grade school proximity has no effect on school attendance of males ages ten through fourteen whose mothers have more than five years of schooling. The coefficient is just slightly above that estimated from the whole sampled population reported in table 6-3 (0.11 for the two lowest education groups of women compared with 0.09 in table 6-3). The grade school effect on school attendance of females ages ten through fourteen whose mothers have no schooling is twice that among the women with one or more years of schooling. The coefficient for the lowest schooling group is 0.14, compared with the overall estimate of 0.11 in table 6-3, and it is 0.07 for the two highest schooling groups. No other program effects differed across the schooling groups with respect to these school attendance variables.

These results suggest that the linear specification, with respect to female schooling, is a reasonable approximation for the Indonesian population. The results also indicate that the average returns on increasing the number of grade schools may be higher if they are located in populations in which schooling levels of women are low. No other basis for targeting programs is discernible from these results with respect to the criterion of different gross program returns.

How Are Programs in Indonesia Targeted?

The marked differences between the cross-sectional and fixed effects estimates of program effects suggest that the cross-area placement of programs is significantly correlated with time-persistent unmeasured factors influencing the policy outcomes. In this section, estimates are presented of the determinants of program placement, including these latent effects. Specifically, the cross-*kecamatan* variation in program coverage for each program in 1980 is related to the cross-subdistrict variation in the latent or fixed outcome factors that are net of program effects, obtained from the fixed effects estimates; measures of *kecamatan* endowments, such as altitude, disaster history, and geographical location; and measured characteristics of the *kecamatan* population, such as schooling levels.

The Determinants of the Cross-Kecamatan Variation in Program Coverage

To estimate the latent outcome variables, the analysis uses the fixed effects coefficient estimates of tables 6-3, 6-4, and 6-5 and applies them to the 1980 and 1985–86 data sets. There are thus two measures of each of the six time-invariant factors for each *kecamatan* corresponding to the six outcome variables. Because each estimated factor contains measurement error, use of either set as regressors in the specification that determines program placement would result in bias. Instead, one set of the measures of the fixed factors (those from the 1985–86 data set) is used as instruments for the other set of factors (1980) that are used in the program placement equation in a two-stage estimation procedure, as in Rosenzweig and Wolpin (1986) and Pitt, Rosenzweig, and Hassan (1990). Because the latent factors for the four age- and gender-specific school attendance groups are highly correlated, no precise estimation of the individual school attendance factors was possible. Statistical tests indicate that the set of four can be reduced to any two. Accordingly, results are reported using two schooling factors and those for fertility and child mortality.

Table 6-7 reports the weighted two-stage least squares estimates for each of the program variables of the effects of the *kecamatan* characteristics on *kecamatan* program coverage as of 1980. For brevity, the five locational and physical characteristics variables describing each *kecamatan* are omitted from the table. Tests of the joint significance of the effects of the four fixed latent factors on the placement of programs are reported at the bottom of the table. These statistics indicate that the placement of each of the five programs as of 1980 was significantly related to the unmeasured fixed factors relating to the six policy outcomes. Evidently, the distribution across *kecamatans* in the coverage of programs is not random with respect to the unmeasured factors determining outcomes and behaviors.

The estimates of the latent factor effects indicate that, in particular, *kecamatans* in which fertility is high, net of program and parental schooling effects, receive a lower level of program coverage with respect to all of the five programs or institutions. Most notably, *kecamatans* with a propensity to have higher fertility receive less family planning support, suggesting that such support is provided where it is most desired. It is less obvious why, net of the latent factors determining school attendance, the villages in high-fertility *kecamatans* are less likely to have schools. Because of the evident collinearity between the latent school attendance factors (which are jointly significant), it is not possible to discern the effects of those factors. The latent factors determining child mortality, however, do not appear to influence the coverage of any of the programs.

The results obtained by stratification of the population into women's schooling groups suggest that the targeting of grade schools to areas in which women (mothers) have lower levels of schooling would be more effective in raising average attendance rates for ten through fourteen year olds than a random allocation would. The estimates in table 6-7 suggest that grade school coverage is lower, net of the influence of the latent school attendance factors, in *kecamatans* in which mothers of teens ages ten through fourteen have higher levels of schooling, consistent with efficiency criteria. Such areas, however, are also less likely to receive middle and high schools, for which no nonlinear effects were found. The negative relation between school placement and the

Table 6-7. *Weighted Two-Stage Least Squares Estimates of the Determinants of Spatial Program Placement, 1980*

Variable	Grade school	Middle school	High school	Health clinic	Family planning clinic
Latent fertility[a]	-0.120 (5.13)	-0.082 (3.69)	-0.060 (3.66)	-0.048 (1.93)	-0.120 (3.40)
Latent mortality[a]	-0.0061 (0.02)	-0.197 (0.53)	0.099 (0.36)	-0.390 (0.95)	0.950 (1.57)
Latent schooling Females ages 10–14[a]	-0.428 (0.51)	0.790 (1.02)	0.457 (0.79)	-1.90 (2.18)	1.70 (1.36)
Males ages 10–14[a]	-0.618 (0.82)	-0.620 (0.89)	-0.200 (0.40)	0.930 (1.18)	-2.30 (2.07)
Schooling Women ages 25–29	0.072 (7.20)	0.033 (3.61)	0.011 (1.63)	0.048 (4.59)	0.022 (1.49)
Mothers of children ages 10–14	-0.10 (3.76)	-0.083 (3.30)	-0.033 (1.76)	-0.018 (0.63)	-0.093 (2.30)
Heads of households with children ages 10–14	0.037 (1.84)	0.067 (3.61)	0.046 (3.33)	0.009 (0.44)	0.071 (2.34)
Proportion of households in urban areas	-0.063 (2.32)	0.410 (16.2)	0.430 (22.9)	0.220 (7.70)	0.170 (4.11)
Land owned by household (0.01 hectares $\times 10^{-2}$)	-0.210 (14.7)	0.017 (1.29)	0.0031 (0.31)	0.010 (0.68)	-0.160 (7.13)
Test statistics: latent variable significance, $F_{(4, 2537)}$	29.8	10.2	7.65	11.1	12.2

Note: Specification also includes three altitude variables; indicators of history of earthquakes, drought, floods, and other natural disasters; and proximity of *kecamatan* to coast. Absolute values of asymptotic *t*-ratios are in parentheses. Instruments include 1985 latent variable measures.

a. Variable potentially measured with error.

schooling attainment of women may reflect equity concerns, although *kecamatans* characterized by (male) heads of household who have higher levels of schooling are more likely to receive each of the three levels of schools.

Is There Convergence in Program Coverage?

As noted, in 1980 the six types of programs tended to be clustered, in that the programs were spatially positively intercorrelated. In this section, we report estimates of the dynamic version of the placement "rules," equation 6-4, which assess how the change in program coverage across *kecamatans* between 1980 and 1986 is related to the latent outcome effects, the measured time-invariant characteristics of subdistricts, the 1980 population characteristics, and the 1980 program coverage. Estimates of the effects of the 1980 program distribution on the growth in program coverage across *kecamatans* permit an assessment of whether between 1980 and 1986 program placement became more or less evenly distributed, that is, whether there was convergence or divergence in program coverage across *kecamatans*. If the coverage of a particular program grew less in *kecamatans* in which the coverage was already relatively high, then convergence is indicated.

The regression of a change in a variable on its initial level, required to test for convergence or equalization, is problematic because if the variable is measured with error, then it is easy to show that the coefficient of the program-level effect will be biased negatively. Thus one may falsely accept the convergence hypothesis. To eliminate this problem, the program coverage information from the 1976–77 FASDES was used to construct instruments for the 1980 program coverage. As discussed in the appendix, we were able to match at the *kecamatan*-level data from this source, which provides similar program coverage information for the same variables, with the 1980 PODES data. If the measurement errors in the programs are independent across the two data sources, then the instrumented estimates are consistent.

Table 6-8 reports the weighted, two-stage, least squares estimates of the program coverage growth equation. Two sets of estimates are reported for each program. The first set was obtained without using the 1976–77 instruments to correct for measurement error in the 1980 program variables; the second set was obtained using the instruments and treating the 1980 programs as potentially error-ridden. On the basis of Hausman-Wu type tests, the hypothesis that the programs are measured without error is rejected in all cases except for the family planning growth equation.[10] The existence of the measurement-error problem is evident in the difference in the "own" effects of programs on their growth—for each program, there is an increase in the own effect when the instruments are employed. Indeed, for middle schools,

Table 6-8. *Weighted Two-Stage Least Squares Estimates of Growth in Program Coverage without and with Correction for Measurement Error in Programs, 1980–86*

Variable	Grade school		Middle school		High school		Health clinic		Family planning clinic	
	Without	With	Without	With	Without	With	Without	With	Without	With
Grade schools (1980)[a]	-0.790 (44.80)	-0.520 (13.20)	-0.031 (0.84)	0.016 (1.91)	-0.032 (1.06)	0.0065 (0.10)	-0.016 (0.35)	0.024 (0.22)	0.043 (0.74)	0.061 (0.69)
Middle schools (1980)[a]	0.034 (2.60)	0.075 (1.54)	-0.250 (9.17)	0.170 (1.62)	0.250 (11.40)	0.540 (6.91)	0.330 (9.86)	0.710 (5.35)	0.070 (1.65)	-0.020 (0.17)
High schools (1980)[a]	0.049 (2.91)	0.023 (0.43)	0.094 (2.69)	0.070 (0.34)	-0.460 (16.20)	-0.350 (4.13)	0.065 (1.51)	0.0054 (0.04)	0.031 (0.57)	0.120 (0.94)
Health clinics (1980)[a]	-0.036 (1.86)	-0.034 (0.77)	0.077 (1.90)	0.014 (0.15)	0.052 (1.57)	0.020 (0.27)	-0.590 (11.90)	-0.300 (2.41)	0.027 (0.43)	-0.097 (0.89)
Family planning clinics (1980)[a]	-0.003 (0.22)	-0.220 (2.26)	0.033 (1.32)	-0.450 (2.70)	0.0095 (0.47)	-0.370 (2.83)	0.089 (2.89)	-0.700 (3.19)	-0.860 (21.70)	-0.670 (3.37)
Latent fertility[b]	-0.013 (1.24)	-0.0083 (0.58)	0.061 (2.75)	0.044 (1.46)	0.033 (1.85)	-0.0060 (0.26)	-0.078 (0.25)	-0.092 (2.34)	-0.009 (0.25)	-0.013 (0.38)
Latent mortality[b]	-0.120 (0.68)	0.350 (1.47)	-0.210 (0.57)	0.630 (1.26)	-0.460 (1.53)	0.350 (0.89)	-0.610 (1.30)	1.000 (1.53)	0.550 (0.94)	0.850 (1.45)
Latent schooling										
Females ages 10–14[b]	-0.630 (1.50)	-0.730 (1.26)	-0.570 (0.65)	-0.810 (0.67)	-0.048 (0.07)	-0.410 (0.43)	-0.900 (0.83)	-0.790 (0.50)	0.840 (0.61)	-0.660 (0.46)
Males ages 10–14[b]	0.250 (0.71)	0.410 (0.83)	0.600 (0.80)	0.520 (0.50)	0.035 (0.06)	0.150 (0.19)	0.680 (0.74)	0.170 (0.12)	-0.820 (0.70)	0.620 (0.51)

Note: Specification also includes three altitude variables; indicators of history of earthquakes, drought, floods, and other natural disasters; and proximity of *kecamatan* to the coast. Correction for measurement error uses the 1976–77 program coverage information to construct instruments for the 1980 program coverage. Absolute values of asymptotic *t*-ratios are in parentheses.

a. To correct for measurement error, instruments include program distribution variables in 1977.

b. In the specifications with and without correction for measurement error, this variable is treated as measured with error. Instruments include 1985 latent variable measures.

the use of the instruments changes the sign of the effect of the 1980 coverage of middle schools on the 1980–86 growth rate of middle school coverage from negative (with an asymptotic t-ratio of more than 9) to positive (but not statistically significant). All of the other instrumented own-coefficient estimates, however, retain their negative sign and are statistically significant when the instruments are employed.[11] Thus, the results indicate that during 1980–86, program coverage across *kecamatans* was being equalized. Except for the middle schools, the coverage of a program grew less in areas that were better endowed with respect to that program.

The fixed effects estimates of program effects indicate that health clinics had a positive impact on school attendance, net of the presence of schools, for females in both the ten through fourteen and fifteen through eighteen age groups. To the extent that these programs augment school attendance, fewer schools are needed to achieve the same attendance rates. Equalization would thus imply that grade schools and middle schools would grow less in *kecamatans* with a greater presence of health clinics. However, the estimates in table 6-8 indicate that the growth in the coverage of both school types was not responsive to the level of health clinic coverage in 1980. Moreover, the coverage of health clinics grew more in areas with a greater number of middle schools, as did the growth in coverage of high schools. One puzzling result in table 6-8 is that the coverage of each of the programs grew less in *kecamatans* with a higher coverage of family planning clinics in 1980; yet, there is no evidence of this program having any effects on the outcome variables.

Conclusions

In this chapter, we have reported estimates of the effects of several important public programs associated with human resource investments (in schools, health clinics, and family planning clinics) on basic human capital indicators (school attendance, fertility, and child mortality). The estimates were based on a "new" data set constructed from a pool of *kecamatan*-level observations on human capital outcomes, socioeconomic variables, and program coverage based on the successive sets of cross-sectional household and administrative data describing Indonesia in 1976–86. This data set also enabled the investigation of the biases in conventional cross-sectional estimates of program effects arising from two sources: the lack of comprehensive information on programs and the nonrandom placement of governmental programs across areas. The data were also used to examine how the spatial allocation of programs in Indonesia in 1980 and the growth in program coverage by area were related to area-specific endowments in the 1980s and contributed to the efficiency of program effects and spatial and socioeconomic equity.

The empirical results, based on matched 1980 and 1985–86 information on more than 3,000 *kecamatans*, indicated that the presence of grade schools and, to a lesser extent, middle schools in villages has a significant effect on the school attendance rates of teenagers. The results also indicated that the presence of health clinics in villages positively affects the schooling of females ages ten through eighteen. Estimates based on the data stratified by the educational attainment of adult women also indicated that the effects of grade school proximity on the school attendance rates of teens ages ten through fourteen is significantly greater in households in which mothers have little or no schooling compared with households in which mothers have more than a grade school education. However, no other program effects appeared to differ across educational classes of women. Moreover, based on the statistically preferred models, there was no evidence of any significant effects of the presence of family planning and health programs on either the survival rates of children or cumulative fertility.

The estimates also suggested that the use of cross-sectional data, which does not take into account the possibly nonrandom spatial location of programs, results in substantial biases in the estimates of program effects because of the evident nonrandom spatial allocation of public programs. For example, cross-sectional estimates from the 1980 data resulted in an underestimate by 100 percent of the effect of being proximate to a grade school on the school attendance of both males and females ages ten through fourteen, compared with estimates based on the pooled 1980 and 1985–86 data, which allowed for nonrandom program placement. The cross-sectional estimates also indicated clearly counterintuitive results, for example, that family planning clinics significantly raise fertility and reduce schooling investments. These results were not apparent when the nonrandomness of program placement was taken into account.

The estimates pertaining to the spatial and intertemporal allocation of programs in Indonesia indicated that the 1980 spatial distribution of each of the five programs examined here is significantly related to the unmeasured fixed factors relating to the six policy outcomes; the placement across *kecamatans* in the coverage of programs is not random with respect to the unmeasured factors determining outcomes and behaviors. Most notably, *kecamatans* with a propensity to have higher fertility receive less family planning support, suggesting that such support is provided where it is most desired. The coverage of programs also tends to be lower in areas in which the educational level of mothers is high, an allocation consistent with an efficiency criterion, given the finding that the effect of grade school proximity on school attendance is greater in households with less-educated mothers. However, this relation was also true for all of the programs studied for which there was no evidence of nonlinearities with respect to the schooling attainment of adult women. Finally, examination of the change in the spatial allocation of programs between 1980 and 1986 indicated that the spatial program distribution became more equal; there was clear evidence of area-specific convergence in program coverage.

Although there was some evidence of significant program effects, particularly of school proximity on school attendance, it was apparent from exploiting the constructed longitudinal data that the quantitative estimates of these effects cannot account for a large part of the actual growth in human capital outcomes in Indonesia in the 1980s. In part this may be the result of measurement error in the program variables, for which there is some evidence, which would bias the program estimates toward zero. Some of the improvements in the human resource outcomes examined may reflect economic growth, which the data do not measure. Even with income information, however, the endogeneity of income must be considered as well as the possibility that human capital programs contribute to economic growth. Controlling for incomes could thus result in a misleading inference about the long-term consequences of public investments in human resource investments.

In future work we will explore the issue of the longer-term effects of these programs by extending the data set across time. Additional data will enable us to utilize the methods used here and to include the effects of lagged program distributions in the specification of program effects, to assess the role of area-specific income growth rates, and to investigate the effects of human resource programs on income growth.

Appendix 6-1: Construction of the Data Set

To obtain a geographically consistent set of intertemporal observations, we matched the data set–specific geographic codes in two stages: the 1986 codes were matched to the 1980 codes, and the 1976 codes were matched to the 1980 codes. The 1980 and 1986 codes were matched using their respective master files. The province and district codes between two consecutive master files were matched, and then the subdistricts were matched by name. However, many names had changed or new subdistricts emerged because there were different abbreviations between periods or because some subdistricts split. The nonmatched subdistricts were then visually matched, but still the matching was not complete.

The subdistricts that were not matched based on names were brought to the attention of the Mapping Department at the BPS. From internal documents we tried to find the origin of the nonmatched subdistricts. However, the Mapping Department updated their maps in 1980 and 1986 only, not in 1983, and their documents listing code changes were not complete. For the remainder of the subdistricts that we could not match, we used various issues of the *Lembaran-Negara Republik Indonesia*, the annual, official government gazette that publishes decrees and contains official documents recording villages that are changing subdistricts, new villages, new subdistricts, and boundary changes. This publication does not contain location codes, just names. To obtain the origin of the villages in the nonmatched subdistricts, we matched the village names from the gazette with village names from the master files. We changed the subdistrict codes according to the origin of most of the villages of the subdistricts in the master file. There were 103 location code changes between 1983 and 1986 and 217 location code changes at the subdistrict level from 1980 through 1983. Once we completed the master file changes, we converted the 1986 PODES into 1983 codes and then into 1980 codes.[12]

The 1976–77 FASDES contains just one code for the province and district combined, ranging from 1 to 287, whereas subsequently provinces and districts were identified with separate two-digit codes. To convert the FASDES geographic codes into 1980 codes, documentation on the three-digit location codes for the provinces and districts combined was used to update to the 1980 scheme of two-digit province codes and two-digit district codes. However, conversion of the FASDES codes to 1980 codes at the subdistrict level was made difficult by the fact that the FASDES subdistrict codes and names were not available. Thus, we had to match the village names from the FASDES master file along with their subdistrict codes with the village names and subdistrict codes on the 1980 master file. If five or more villages matched, we took the subdistrict codes from the 1980 master file. Village naming was sufficiently stable over time to permit us to match all of the subdistrict codes between 1976 and 1980.

To convert the 1985 SUPAS into 1980 codes necessitated use of the 1985 Sample List (*Daftar Sampel*), which contains the sample code numbers along with the province, district, subdistrict, and village codes. The raw data for SUPAS include only the province and district codes, along with the sample code number. The three codes combined—for the province, the district, and the sample number—were used to obtain the subdistrict and village codes from the sample list. We converted the SUPAS into subdistrict codes using the sample list. These codes were based on the 1983 master file, so we then converted them from 1983 codes into 1980 codes.

Once the geographic codes of all of the data sets were made comparable, we aggregated the data at the common subdistrict level. With the PODES and FASDES, we calculated for each subdistrict the proportion of households whose village of residence contained each program, type of infrastructure, or environmental variable.[13]

Because the 1986 PODES was converted to 1980 codes, there were some duplicate location codes as villages and *kecamatans* split between

1980 and 1986. In 1986 there were 66,922 villages. Knowing which *kecamatans* and villages split between 1980 and 1986 allowed us to reaggregate 1986 administrative units back to their 1980 form. If areas were combined, we were unable, of course, to disaggregate program coverage into 1980 codes. There were 65,924 villages in 1986 with the 1980 codes. The FASDES did not contain any duplicate location codes after the conversion to 1980 codes. The total number of *kecamatans* in the 1980 PODES was 3,318. Of these, we were able to match all but 16 in the 1986 PODES.[14]

Notes

1. The problem with closely spaced panel data is that program change is likely to be small for periods shorter than two or three years. As a result, it is difficult to identify program effects statistically with any precision.

2. This assumes that households or individuals do not use the history of program placement to form expectations about future program placements.

3. If program coverage is measured with error, classical errors-in-variables bias will contaminate the estimates of the program effects from equation 6-1. Parameters will be biased toward zero. Unfortunately, it is difficult to find instruments that can be used to correct for this potential bias. To our knowledge, no other study of program effects has addressed the issue of measurement error in the program coverage variables.

4. The implications of the absence of this information are discussed below.

5. This assumes that program placement rules are attentive only to fixed geographic characteristics.

6. The 1985 SUPAS indicates that 19 percent of women ages twenty to forty had received no schooling; 35 percent had one to five years of schooling.

7. *Kecamatans* with fewer than ten survey households were excluded from the analysis.

8. We have also estimated, using random effects methods, the same specifications based on the pooled 1980 and 1985 data. The results from these estimates are not very different from those obtained from the cross-sectional 1980 data. We show the cross-sectional 1980 estimates as these correspond to those obtained in the literature. If data analysts had pooled time-series, cross-sectional data of the type we have constructed, with both program proximity information and relevant outcomes, fixed effects methods would very likely be employed.

9. For example, high-growth areas may have sharply increasing demands for additional schooling for their children and for additional schools, to which the government may respond.

10. The F-statistics $(5, 2098)$ for the grade school, middle school, high school, health clinic, and family planning clinic growth equations are, respectively: 95.4, 16.33, 8.82, 16.7, and 1.58.

11. The existence of measurement error in the programs, as indicated in the growth equations, implies that some of the estimates of program effects may be biased toward zero. It is not clear, however, what instruments are available to resolve this problem in estimating program effects. Models of dynamic decisionmaking imply that current decisions, such as the distribution of programs, depend on the values of current state variables (the 1980 program distribution in this case) and not on past state values (unless they predict

the future), so that past program distributions are valid instruments for 1980 programs in the post-1980 program growth equations. However, as discussed, the distribution of programs in the past may have a direct influence on cumulative human capital outcomes, given current programs.

12. We also tracked the location code changes from 1990 to 1986, as we had expected to be using data with 1990 location codes. From 1986 to 1990, we found 1,927 location code changes at the subdistrict level.

13. Although the PODES data are unique in the developing world for their detailed and comprehensive spatial information on program availability in 67,000 locales, they lack information on the "quality" dimension of public program provision. If quality is an important dimension of program effectiveness and if it is correlated with quantity measures of program availability, then estimation of a policy outcome equation will result in biased estimates of program effects. Even if quality and quantity are correlated, unbiased estimates of program effects can be obtained as long as variation in quality takes the form of a subdistrict-specific fixed effect or varies only with time. Again, this highlights the importance of data on program placement and outcomes at more than two points in time for the same village in eliminating bias.

14. Because the newly acquired province of East Timor was not included in the 1980 PODES, the 1986 PODES contains sixty-eight more subdistricts.

References

Gertler, Paul, and Jacques van der Gaag. 1990. *The Willingness to Pay for Medical Care: Evidence for Two Developing Countries*. Baltimore, Md.: Johns Hopkins University Press.

Huber, P. J. 1967. "The Behavior of Maximum Likelihood Estimates under Non-Standard Conditions." In *Proceedings of the Fifth Berkeley Symposium on Mathematical Statistics and Probability*, vol. 1. Berkeley: University of California at Berkeley.

Indonesia, Government of. Annual. *Lembaran-Negara Republik Indonesia*. Jakarta, Indonesia.

Pitt, Mark M., and Mark R. Rosenzweig. 1985. "Health and Nutrient Consumption across and within Farm Households." *Review of Economics and Statistics* 67 (2): 212–23.

Pitt, Mark M., Mark R. Rosenzweig, and M. N. Hassan. 1990. "Productivity, Health, and Inequality in the Intrahousehold Distribution of Food in Low-Income Countries." *American Economic Review* 80: 1139–56.

Rosenzweig, Mark R., and Paul Schultz. 1982. "Child Mortality and Fertility in Colombia: Individual and Community Effects." In *Health Policy and Education*, vol. 2. Amsterdam: Elsevier Scientific Publishing Co.

Rosenzweig, Mark R., and Kenneth I. Wolpin. 1982. "Governmental Interventions and Household Behavior in a Developing Country." *Journal of Development Economics* 10: 209–25.

———. 1986. "Evaluating the Effects of Optimally Distributed Public Programs: Child Health and Family Planning Interventions." *American Economic Review* 76: 470–82.

Strauss, John. 1990. "Households, Communities, and Preschool Children's Nutrition Outcomes: Evidence from Rural Côte d'Ivoire." *Economic Development and Cultural Change* 38 (2): 231–62.

White, Halbert. 1980. "A Heteroskedasticity-Consistent Covariance Matrix Estimator and a Direct Test for Heteroskedasticity." *Econometrica* 48: 817–38.

Spending on
Education

II

Part II presents recent empirical research on the benefits derived from government spending on education in Peru (chapter 7) and in rural Pakistan (chapter 8). Both country case studies explore and present evidence relating to specific policy options for improving distributional impacts within the education sector. Yet, they do so within distinct strands of the current research on equity and education outlays in developing countries, focusing on different sets of questions and basing their analyses on different methodologies.

In their study of Peru, Selden and Wasylenko focus on what they term nonestimation-based analytical techniques that assume away behavioral responses and contrast them with estimation-based methods. They examine the distributional allocation of government education subsidies across households using the conventional benefit incidence approach. As we will see throughout the book, this is a popular tool for analyzing distributional aspects of public programs.

Consistent with a number of other studies for developing countries, Selden and Wasylenko's analysis finds that girls generally receive fewer benefits than boys because of their lower enrollment rates. Per capita spending on primary schooling is pro-poor, though less so than is often indicated for other countries. Per capita spending on secondary education first rises and then falls with household per capita consumption, while spending on higher education is pro-rich. The chapter's findings that intrasectoral allocations, in particular, matter for distributional outcomes echo those of many past studies.

The relationship between the availability of private sector alternatives and the distribution of the benefits of public spending is highlighted: urban areas exhibit a more propoor distribution than rural areas in Peru because better-off urban children have access to private schools that they are more likely to attend. Other chapters (notably chapter 18) also focus on the private-public sector connection and its potential impact on incidence. Selden and Wasylenko also illustrate how incidence outcomes vary according to whether subsidies are calculated on a per child or per capita basis. Which set of calculations is more relevant depends on the policy question of interest: Are education subsidies equitably distributed across children in different income classes? Or, does education spending provide a good means for redistributing income toward the poor?

The authors are careful to clarify what can and cannot be inferred from their analysis, emphasizing, for example, the distinction between the incidence of current educational spending and that which would result from marginal changes in spending. This issue is further taken up in part III.

Although it is useful to know the incidence of an existing pattern of public spending, policymakers also care about the distributional impacts of proposed policy changes. Selden and Wasylenko describe an easy nonbehavioral approach to examine potential reforms, as an alternative to more data-heavy willingness-to-pay or compensating variation methods. Simple, but relatively crude, first-order approximations are calculated to examine the distributional implications of (a) increasing school fees and (b) building closer secondary schools financed (at least partially) through fee increases. The results suggest that higher school fees would be regressive particularly as applied to primary schooling, while benefits from closer secondary schools appear to be far outweighed by average secondary schooling costs. The authors argue that although benefit measures derived from demand behavior are more theoretically consistent and therefore appealing to economists, they also have important drawbacks. Ultimately, choice of methodology depends on the research questions of interest, the availability of data and computational techniques, and the adopted theoretical framework.

In contrast to Selden and Wasylenko, in chapter 8 Alderman, Behrman, Khan, Ross, and Sabot adopt a behavioral approach to measure precisely the benefits of public education with household- and school-level data for rural Pakistan.

Using econometric techniques and several unusually rich and complementary micro data sets, Alderman and others estimate the effects of schooling attainment and school quality on cognitive achievement and (via cognitive achievement) on future earnings, for four separate groups: girls, boys, all children in a better-off region, and all children in a backward region. With cost estimates for providing primary and middle schooling of varying levels of quality, they are able to calculate the private and social rates of return to various schooling investments targeted alternatively to the subgroups. The chapter examines the following questions: Should education expenditures be targeted to disadvantaged groups? To what degree should intervention focus on supply-side factors and on which ones—for example, quality or quantity aspects of schooling—in trying to correct for unequal gender and regional education outcomes? And last, do investments targeted at disadvantaged groups result in an equity/efficiency tradeoff?

A number of studies have investigated the relative returns to improvements in the quality and quantity of schooling in developing countries. This study is unique in that it tracks the entire sequence of relationships between level of schooling attained, school quality, cognitive outputs and labor productivity. It also controls for preschool ability and family background and uses highly disaggregated measures of schooling quality.

Supply-side factors clearly account for a considerable amount of the disparities in educational outcomes that are found in Pakistan. Benefits from schooling investments are measured in terms of incremental gains in lifetime earnings. Other benefits accruing to the students, to members of their households, or to society as a whole are not taken into account. The chapter's main findings are that even excluding such additional benefits, the rates of return to primary-level schooling investments are generally high across all groups and that targeting disadvantaged groups does not entail a significant tradeoff in terms of efficiency.

The study does not specifically calculate the willingness to pay for various levels of schooling quantity and quality, but it does provide information on what households should rationally be willing to pay at a minimum, assuming that parents are perfectly informed and altruistic. Relative to government unit costs, benefit estimates obtained using this approach could perhaps provide the foundation for a rigorous distributional assessment.

While chapter 8 focuses on gender and regional targeting of education benefits, its basic methodology could be adapted to a number of contexts and to various important issues in public spending and targeting. However, Alderman and others have had access to an unusually detailed data set. In practice, data constraints still often prevent such a data-intensive methodology.

7 Measuring the Distributional Effects of Public Education in Peru

Thomas M. Selden and
Michael J. Wasylenko

It has become widely recognized that education can play an important role in the development process and in the alleviation of poverty. However, in many countries, including Peru, important educational policy issues remain unresolved. For example, how effectively has public education spending been targeted to the poor? Is it more effective to expand enrollment through increased government expenditure on education, or should educational spending be targeted more specifically on a subset of the school-age population? Should greater emphasis be placed on primary education at the expense of secondary or higher education? Do males receive a larger share of public educational expenditure than females? Should school fees be increased—and if so, should the increased revenues be used to defray existing government expenditures or to finance further improvements in the quality of education? Even without fee increases, do substantial commuting, textbook, and uniform costs represent barriers to enrollment in primary school for children in the poorest households?

To help policymakers address these and similar questions, economists have strived for decades to provide improved measures of the benefits from education. Because it aligns with economic theory, the most natural approach for economists is to focus on benefit measures that involve areas underneath estimates of individual compensated demand curves. Using estimation-based approaches, behavioral changes induced by policy changes can be analyzed, and the private willingness to pay for such changes can be measured. This approach is best illustrated by recent research based on the World Bank's Living

We thank Emmanuel Jimenez for his help in shaping our topic. We thank Paul Gertler, Paul Glewwe, James Gordon, Barbara Grosh, Margaret Grosh, Kim Nead, and Dominique van de Walle for useful comments. Kalpana Mehra provided the Peru household data, and Gillette Hall and Dean Jolliffe provided advice and documentation on how to use the data. Marco Terrones of GRADE in Lima helped us to obtain data on education spending in Peru.

Standards Measurement Surveys, including Gertler and Glewwe's (1990, 1992) studies of Peruvian education.[1] However, although estimation-based approaches are generally preferred by economists, they have conceptual and practical limitations. For example, despite the increasing availability of household-level data, even the most detailed data frequently impose important constraints on the questions that estimation-based analyses can address.

In this chapter, we examine several alternative, nonestimation-based approaches to analyzing education and employ these measures in an empirical study of Peru. One well-known nonestimation-based approach is the benefit-incidence methodology applied in developing countries by Meerman (1979) and Selowsky (1979), among others.[2] By allocating government education outlays to households in proportion to enrollment in public schools, standard benefit-incidence analysis seeks to answer questions concerning the targeting of public expenditures.[3] Although the methodology is well understood, it is not well known that nonestimation-based methods can be used to examine a range of policy-relevant questions. In particular, we use alternative nonestimation-based methods to examine the incidence in Peru of (a) higher public school fees and (b) reduced travel time to public secondary schools.

Thus, the objective of this chapter is both methodological and empirical. First we present the theory underlying both the estimation-based and nonestimation-based approaches to measuring willingness to pay, examining not only standard benefit-incidence measures but also several alternative nonestimation-based measures. In particular, we focus on the strengths and weaknesses of both estimation- and nonestimation-based approaches within a discrete-choice context. We then employ the 1985–86 Peru Living Standards Survey (PLSS) data used by Gertler and Glewwe (1990, 1992) to analyze Peru's public education system with the presented nonestimation-based methods.

Theoretical Considerations

To clarify the theoretical issues involved in measuring the distributional effects of education, it is useful to begin with a highly simplified formal model, building on the work of Gertler and van der Gaag (1988) and Gertler and Glewwe (1990, 1992). For simplicity of exposition, we focus on the case in which the household faces a simple, binary decision of whether to send a child to public school or not send a child to school. However, the analysis can readily be expanded to include private schooling as a third option.

The household decisionmaker is assumed to have a utility function defined over the enrollment choice, $s \in \{0, 1\}$, school quality, q, and other household consumption, $c \geq 0$: $U = U(sq, c)$. The decisionmaker's maximization problem, assuming no rationing, is

(7-1) $$\max_{s} U\ [sq,\ c_0 - (p + wt)s],$$

where c_0 is household consumption without schooling, p is the household's total schooling expense (including school fees, uniform expenses, educational material expenses, and transportation expenses, all of which are assumed to be exogenous to the household), t is the amount of employment time forgone when attending school, and w is the child wage rate. For simplicity, we assume that schooling requires classroom time, t_S, and travel time, t_T, both of which are exogenous to the household.[4] Assuming that total schooling hours equal forgone employment, we have $t = t_S + t_T$.[5]

Solving the household problem yields the following *unconditional* indirect utility function:

(7-2) $$V(p + wt, q, c_0) \equiv \max\ [U(0, c_0), U(q, c_0 - p - wt)].$$

To derive compensating variation (CV) measures of benefit, it is also useful to derive the (unconditional) expenditure function:

(7-3) $$e(p + wt, q, U) \equiv \min\ [c_0 \mid V(p + wt, q, c_0) \geq U]$$

and the compensated (or Hicksian) demand:

(7-4) $$s^c(p + wt, q, U) = \frac{\partial e(p + wt, q, U)}{\partial(p + wt)}.$$

Because enrollment is a discrete choice, the compensated demand curve is a step function with values 0 and 1, for which one can define the compensated crossover price, $(p + wt)^*$, to be the highest level of $p + wt$ at which the child is enrolled in school (holding U constant).

Given these definitions and results, it is straightforward to expand the household's choice set to include both public and private schooling options (or some other policy-relevant set of choices), enabling one to pose the following three incidence questions. First, what is the incidence of benefits from public education (both on a per capita and a per child basis), by household expenditure decile, region, and gender, and what would be the incidence of a marginal reallocation of public funds from secondary and higher education to primary education? Second, what would be the incidence of an increase in schooling fees? Third, what would be the incidence of using higher school fees to finance the construction of additional, closer schools?

Measuring the Incidence of Benefits from Public Education

Within the context of the schooling decision model presented above, the household decisionmaker's net benefit from the public schooling option can be measured by the following compensating variation (CV_1):

$$(7\text{-}5) \qquad\qquad CV_1 = \int_{p+wt}^{\infty} s^c(z, q, U) \, dz,$$

where U is the status quo level of utility and z is a variable for integration. Intuitively, CV_1 measures the disbenefit of eliminating the public schooling option from the household decisionmaker's choice set.[6] To assess the incidence of benefits, one might compute CV_1 for each eligible child in the sample and allocate benefits to households in proportion to their eligible children. Average benefits might then be compared among households grouped by income or other relevant socioeconomic characteristics.

AN ESTIMATION-BASED MEASURE OF BENEFIT. Following Small and Rosen (1981), Gertler and Glewwe (1990, 1992) use estimated discrete-choice probabilities to compute the expected value of CV_1 across the distribution of unobserved factors affecting schooling. The advantage of their approach is that it links well-known discrete-choice estimation methods with the computation of widely accepted benefit measures. Nevertheless, one may encounter difficulties in implementing this approach. For instance, the researcher must specify a functional form for utility and a distribution for the error terms in the model. These assumptions are typically difficult to justify a priori. In addition, this approach can be costly to implement.

Perhaps more important, demand estimation requires information on school fees (and other expenses) for all choices that a given individual faces (regardless of the individual's actual schooling decision). Such information is rarely available. For instance, this data requirement leads Gertler and Glewwe to analyze only the rural regions of Peru, because the PLSS urban data do not provide information on key components of the prices of alternative schooling choices, such as travel times and school fees. Similarly, they examine local versus faraway schooling, rather than public versus private schooling, because the data do not reveal private school prices unless the private schooling option is actually chosen.[7] Since they are unable to distinguish between public and private schooling, their analyses of fee increases and travel time reductions should be interpreted with caution.

BENEFIT-INCIDENCE ANALYSIS. An alternative, nonestimation-based approach to assessing the incidence of education benefits is to examine average government outlays per capita among households grouped by income or other relevant socioeconomic characteristics, as in standard benefit-incidence analysis. Although this approach is perhaps best interpreted as providing a perspective on the use of government funds, it is also possible to make a more formal comparison with CV_1. Let $AC = g + p + wt$ be the full economic cost (both government and

Figure 7-1. Potential Approximation Error from Standard Incidence Calculations

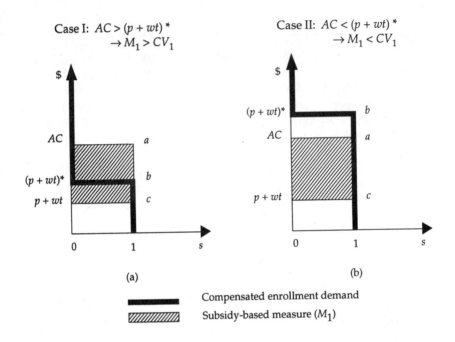

private) of the public schooling option, where g is the government's per pupil expenditure (plus any public scholarships received). The benefit-incidence measure for a given individual can be written as:

$$(7\text{-}6) \qquad\qquad M_1 \equiv gs = [AC - (p + wt)]\, s,$$

where s is observed public school enrollment. If AC happens to equal the compensated crossover price at which households reject the public school option, then this nonestimation-based measure and the estimation-based measure discussed above coincide. Figure 7-1 illustrates the more likely cases in which M_1 either overestimates or underestimates CV_1. In graph a, AC exceeds the crossover price, so that M_1, the shaded region, exceeds CV_1, which is given by the rectangle $(p + wt)^*bc(p + wt)$. In graph b, AC is less than the crossover price, so that M_1 understates CV_1, which is again given by $(p + wt)^*bc(p + wt)$.

Crossover prices may vary among households, and M_1 may approximate CV_1 more closely for some households than for others. For example, one might expect that M_1 would tend to understate the willingness to pay of higher-income relative to lower-income households, because the compensated crossover prices are likely to be an increasing function of income. As a result, education benefits measured using M_1 would appear more pro-poor than they are in reality.

Another related problem with this standard approximation concerns quality differences among schools. Presumably, schools with higher quality will lead to greater net benefit, because the crossover price at which students no longer enroll will be higher. Quality can be explicitly incorporated into CV_1 to the extent that the researcher has access to data on differences in school quality for each of the options facing each household. In contrast, quality differences among schools are only indirectly incorporated in M_1 to the extent that such differences are captured by per pupil expenditure data. If, as is typically the case, the researcher only has access to national totals for government expenditures on primary, secondary, and higher education, then differences in quality will be ignored. Insofar as quality is positively related to per capita income, education benefits measured by M_1 would therefore appear to be more pro-poor than they are in reality.[8]

SOME CAVEATS REGARDING WILLINGNESS TO PAY. There is a long list of reasons why the private willingness to pay of household decisionmakers, either CV_1 or its approximation M_1, may be an overly restrictive measure of benefit. First, it is partial equilibrium (that is, other prices and incomes are held constant). Second, this measure ignores education externalities and the shifting of benefits to unintended parties.[9] Third, the incidence of education benefits is measured at a single point in time, rather than over the lifetimes of the individuals involved. Of course, the present value of the future stream of benefits may be partially captured in the current willingness to pay. However, this correspondence need not be exact due to imperfect information and credit constraints, particularly among the poor. Also, note that parents with children in school tend not to have reached their peak earnings. Transfers to such households from better-off households (some of which might simply be similar households in a later stage of life) may thus appear more progressive from a cross-sectional perspective than if viewed over the life cycle.[10] Fourth, parental willingness to pay may not adequately reflect the benefits children receive from education. At a more fundamental level, Sen (1987a, 1987b) argues for a "capabilities"-oriented approach, which might suggest in the present context a reduced emphasis on the willingness to pay for schooling and a greater emphasis on the abilities of individuals to pursue their education (see also Anand and Ravallion 1993). Although nonestimation-based approaches may not always provide accurate measures of willingness to pay, they are in some cases better suited than estimation-based methods for researchers whose interests extend beyond analyses based on willingness to pay. For instance, from a capabilities perspective, benefit-incidence analysis can be interpreted as offering evidence on the incidence of the government's contribution to participation in the education process—as distinct from valuing such participation according to the household decisionmaker's willingness to pay.

PER CAPITA VERSUS PER CHILD MEASURES OF INCIDENCE. Whether one uses CV_1 or M_1 to measure the incidence of schooling benefit, an important issue is whether to examine benefits on a per capita or a per child basis. The benefit-incidence approach typically adopts a per capita focus, which is appropriate insofar as benefits from subsidized public schooling are at least partially shared by all household members. However, it is also true that household composition may vary substantially across the income distribution, with the highest concentrations of children typically being in the poorest household deciles (as is the case in Peru; see below). For this reason, public education may appear pro-poor in per capita analyses of spending even though poor children receive lower educational spending per child. It may therefore be useful to compute incidence on a per child basis, as well as on a per capita basis, in order to see how education outlays received by children depend on income. The per child analytical lens may be especially important if one adopts a capabilities approach that focuses on actual enrollment by children.

MARGINAL VERSUS TOTAL MEASURES OF INCIDENCE. Finally, note that both the estimation and nonestimation-based approaches presented above measure *total* rather than *marginal* benefits. The incidence of total benefits can provide insights into the government's overall contribution toward the reduction of inequality and poverty through educational spending. Strictly speaking, the aggregate analysis contributes to an understanding of the total expenditure on education and the implications of eliminating government expenditure. However, the elimination of public schooling is rarely the relevant policy alternative. More often, the debate surrounds a *marginal* reallocation of resources, either within the education sector (say, from higher to primary education) or between the education sector and the rest of the government budget (see, for instance, Psacharopoulos 1977; Mingat and Tan 1985, 1986, among others).

Of course, the total benefit measures may well offer useful insights for policymakers. A finding that primary education benefits have a more pro-poor incidence than other forms of education, for example, suggests that a shift in resources from secondary to primary education would have a positive distributional impact (if only because the poor have more children enrolled at the primary levels). Nevertheless, the marginal incidence of this change may differ greatly from what one might expect based on total incidence calculations.[11] If the goal were to increase coverage and retention, the distribution of marginal benefits would likely be more pro-poor than that of average benefits. An important consideration in this regard is whether the marginal expenditures help to remove barriers to enrollment and attendance facing the poor, such as high out-of-pocket costs and forgone earnings (especially at the secondary level). In contrast, if the aim were to increase quality, that process might well begin in the big cities and in the better-off school districts, causing the marginal incidence to be less pro-poor than on average. This would be particularly true if improvements in quality prompted nonpoor students in private schools to shift into public schools. Because a gap can often exist between marginal and average incidence, the most policy-relevant incidence analyses focus on narrowly defined policy changes, such as those examined below.

Measuring the Benefit from a Change in School Fees

An important policy question concerns the incidence of increased fees for public schools (these issues are discussed in Jimenez 1986, 1987, 1989, as well as in the introduction to Gertler and Glewwe 1990). Within the binary choice model presented above, the cv for an increase in public school fees, Δf, is

$$(7\text{-}7) \qquad CV_2 = -\int_{P_0 + wt_0}^{P_0 + wt_0 + \Delta f} s^c(z, q, U) dz.$$

An alternative measure that does not require demand-curve estimation is simply

$$(7\text{-}8) \qquad M_2 = -s\Delta f.$$

Indeed, for a small enough change in fees, Small and Rosen's 1981 discrete-choice analog of Roy's Identity demonstrates that M_2 is exact. Intuitively, enrollment frequencies can be interpreted as first-order approximations of the loss in benefit from a \$1 increase in school fees. Of course, for larger changes in fees, this first-order approximation *overstates* the loss in benefit from an increase in school fees, because it ignores the possibility that the child would withdraw from school as a result of the price change (thereby avoiding any further losses from higher fees).

Figure 7-2 illustrates this potential bias. In graph a, the increase in fees would not induce the child to drop out, so the fee increase would, in essence, be a lump-sum tax equal to the welfare loss. In graph b, the increase in fees *would* induce the child to drop out, so that only a portion of the fee increase would constitute a welfare loss. Nevertheless, note that while M_2 may tend to overstate the private losses per child, CV_2 may understate the social losses associated with fee increases. External benefits, short planning horizons, and intrahousehold inequity are among the many reasons why there may be positive social net

Figure 7-2. Potential Approximation Error in the Case of a Discrete Fee Increase

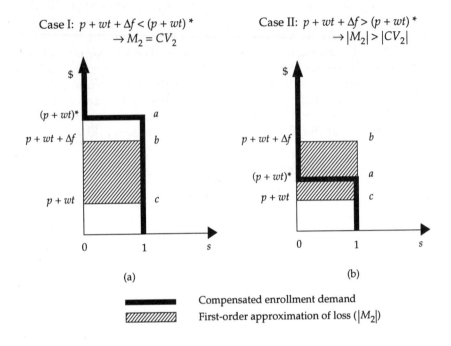

Case I: $p + wt + \Delta f < (p + wt)$ *
$\rightarrow M_2 = CV_2$

Case II: $p + wt + \Delta f > (p + wt)$ *
$\rightarrow |M_2| > |CV_2|$

Compensated enrollment demand

First-order approximation of loss ($|M_2|$)

benefits from enrollment that are not reflected in CV_2. If so, it is an open question whether CV_2 or M_2 provides the more accurate measure of welfare loss.

Measuring the Benefit from Reduced Travel Time

An important policy issue concerns building new schools to reduce travel costs for communities located far from existing schools, with expenditures being financed with higher school fees. Closer schools would reduce the magnitude of both forgone labor earnings and out-of-pocket travel expenses. Closer schools may increase the quality of the schooling option (Gertler and Glewwe 1990), through reductions in both student fatigue and any risks associated with extensive travel. Closer schools also enable parents to play a more active role in the education process. For all of these reasons, closer schooling would benefit households that currently enroll their children and may increase enrollment. At the same time, increased school fees would work in the opposite direction, reducing enrollment and the benefit derived therefrom.

Gertler and Glewwe (1990) address the willingness to pay for closer secondary schooling by examining the fee change that would make households indifferent between the status quo and a policy of closer, but more expensive, secondary schooling. Letting q be a function of t, they compute the following CV for reduced distance to school:

$$(7\text{-}9) \qquad CV_3 = e[p_0 + wt_0, q(t_0), U_0] - e[p_1 + wt_1, q(t_1), U_0],$$

where $t_0 - t_1$ is the reduction in travel time, and where $p_1 - p_0$ measures only the difference in out-of-pocket travel costs (fees are held constant). Using this measure, they compute the average willingness to pay within each quartile (as a function of distance), which they then compare with the average cost of secondary schooling.

Several conceptual issues surround Gertler and Glewwe's compensating variation approach. First, even if average willingness to pay for closer schooling is substantial, it may be impractical to reduce travel times for widely dispersed students living in low-density rural areas. Policy conclusions are therefore best made in a community- and location-specific context, rather than on an aggregate basis. Second, their approach ignores any reductions in government expenditures associated with the decline in enrollment at more distant schools when students switch to the new, more proximate schools. Third, CV_3 measures the maximum payment a given household would be willing to make for closer schools, rather than simulating an actual fee increase. If the maximum willingness to pay varies and if schools are constrained to charge flat fees in order to avoid the stigma and administrative cost of charging differentiated fees, then the total revenue obtained by fee imposition would fall short of the community's aggregate willingness to pay. A more policy-relevant approach, for example, might be to compute CV_3 using a fee increase that holds net government outlays constant and then to examine the distribution of net benefits by income level.

In any event, calculating CV_3 entails estimation of household enrollment demands. It may also be possible to gain some insight into the willingness to pay higher fees without doing so. Consider the following statistic computed for children currently enrolled in school:

$$(7\text{-}10) \qquad\qquad M_3 = \Delta p + w\Delta t,$$

where Δp is the change in out-of-pocket transportation costs and Δt is the change in travel time. Intuitively, M_3 is a lower bound on the maximum fee increase that would make a household indifferent between the status quo and closer, but higher-priced, schooling. Indeed, for children currently enrolled in school, M_3 offers an exact answer to the question posed by Gertler and Glewwe so long as school proximity affects welfare only through its effect on forgone earnings and out-of-pocket travel expense. Of course, as in the case of CV_3, average levels of M_3 computed for a given community must be interpreted with caution if schools are constrained to charge flat fees. Moreover, some children who are not currently in school may enroll (if the actual fee increase is small enough). Nevertheless, we believe that M_3, combined with information for each decile about enrollment rates and distance from school, can offer a useful perspective on the incidence of closer, but more expensive, schooling.

Empirical Results for Peruvian Education

In this section, we use the Peruvian Living Standards Survey data to construct the nonestimation-based incidence measures presented in the last section. Ideally, one would in each instance use the PLSS to construct the corresponding estimation-based measure, enabling a direct comparison of the two approaches. Our initial objective was to build on the estimation-based analysis of the PLSS in Gertler and Glewwe (1990). Unfortunately, this proved infeasible for a number of reasons. Chief among these is that the data did not enable Gertler and Glewwe to distinguish between public and private schooling nor to include the urban areas of Peru. As discussed, the PLSS does not contain sufficient price information to support such analyses.[12] Therefore, we primarily focus our analysis in this section on the nonestimation-based approaches presented above, though we compare our results with theirs whenever possible (for an analysis that directly compares estimation and nonestimation-based measures using a common data set, see Schwabe 1994).

The PLSS Data

The 1985–86 PLSS household survey data on education used in this chapter are from Peru's Instituto Nacional de Estadística (INE), as compiled by the World Bank's Living Standards Measurement Unit.[13] World Bank economists have also compiled a file with total real expenditures by household for 1985. The sample is self-weighting (nationally representative), including households from the metropolitan area of Lima, as well as from the rural and urban areas of the coast (*costa*), the mountains (*sierra*), and the jungle (*selva*).[14]

We use total real per capita expenditures as a measure of the living standard (thereby giving equal weight to each person in the household).[15] We then rank households into deciles (and the top 5 percent) based on their per capita real total expenditure. One problem in this regard is that nearly 15 percent of the school-age children in the PLSS data are recorded as residing in households other than those of their parents.[16] For such children, we know the household information for only their current (and presumably temporary) residences. We examine the ramifications of this issue in greater detail below.

Table 7-1 presents the mean household expenditure per capita, mean household size, and mean number of children in age categories six and under, seven to twelve, and thirteen to seventeen, for each decile. The highest two deciles account for about 52 percent of total expenditure. Both household size and the number of children in each age category decline as household per capita expenditure increases.

Our analysis utilizes data for 1980 through 1986 on current government spending for primary, secondary, nonuniversity, and university higher education from Peru's Ministry of Education. These data enable the computation of real current government expenditure per pupil, averaged over 1985 and 1986, by level of education. The data also report total capital spending (although not by education level). Capital spending is a relatively small part of Peru's education budget, averaging 5.48 percent of total current educational spending during the 1980 to 1986 period, although the percentage fluctuates during these years. Accordingly, we increase the current spending figure for each education level by 5.48 percent as a proxy for the benefits derived from the flow of services from capital.[17] The expenditure figures by level of education are presented in table 7-2.

Benefit-Incidence Analysis

To derive the incidence of public outlays on education by decile and region, we multiply the per pupil outlays in table 7-2 by the number of public pupils in each household at each level of education.[18] We then add scholarships awarded to students in the household to the outlay measures.[19] Next, we group the households by decile and region. Total outlays in each decile are then divided by the number of persons in the decile in each region. These are presented in table 7-3. Per capita outlays as a percentage of per capita household expenditure are presented in table 7-4.

On average, the fraction of the population enrolled in primary education is higher in rural than in urban areas. This is because (a) there are more children per household (at every age level) in rural areas, and (b) rural teenagers are far more likely than their urban peers to be enrolled in primary, as opposed to secondary, school. These demographic and enrollment patterns cause per capita primary education benefits to be higher in rural areas than urban areas. The reverse is true for both secondary and higher levels (in part because of lower enrollment rates, and in part because rural teenagers, when enrolled in school, are more likely than their urban counterparts to be enrolled in primary school). Of course, these results should be interpreted with care, because they are computed using national average expenditures. Insofar as per pupil expenditures are higher in urban than in rural areas, our conclusions regarding secondary and higher education hold

Table 7-1. Real Total Expenditure Distribution and Average Number of Children in Each Age Group, by Decile, Peru, 1985

Decile	Mean household per capita expenditure (1985 intis)	Household expenditure as a percentage of total	Mean household size	Mean number of children per household, by age group		
				0–6	7–12	13–17
1	932	1.7	6.5	1.6	1.2	0.9
2	1,609	2.9	6.1	1.4	1.2	0.8
3	2,161	3.9	6.1	1.3	1.2	0.7
4	2,693	5.0	5.9	1.1	1.0	0.8
5	3,335	6.0	5.8	1.1	0.9	0.7
6	4,113	7.5	5.2	0.9	0.8	0.6
7	5,049	9.0	4.9	0.8	0.8	0.6
8	6,430	11.7	4.7	0.7	0.7	0.5
9	8,857	16.2	4.5	0.6	0.5	0.5
10	19,645	35.6	4.0	0.4	0.4	0.4
Top 5 percent	26,646	24.1	4.1	0.4	0.4	0.4

Note: Households are ranked into deciles by household per capita expenditures.
Sources: Peru, Instituto Nacional de Estadística (INE), Household Questionnaire, and the World Bank, Living Standards Measurement Unit.

166

Table 7-2. Average per Pupil Current and Capital Government Spending, Peru, 1985–86
(1985 intis)

Level of education	Average
Primary education	661.5
Secondary education	999.0
Tertiary education	
Nonuniversity	2,363.5
University	3,756.5

Note: The estimates reported are pupil-weighted averages of real current spending in 1985 and 1986 (the two years of the household survey), plus 5.48 percent of current spending as a proxy for capital expenditure.

Source: Ministry of Education, Government of Peru, made available to us through GRADE, a private research institute in Lima, Peru.

a fortiori, whereas primary education would be less "pro-rural" than our analysis suggests.

Given our concerns regarding the use of average per pupil expenditures, it is perhaps best to focus on incidence patterns within regions. Per capita expenditures on primary education are about the same for the first seven rural deciles and somewhat lower for the three richest deciles. In contrast, in urban areas of Peru per capita expenditures on primary education are a steadily declining function of household per capita expenditure. This is due in part to greater enrollment in private schools in higher-income households and in part to differences in age composition and educational attainment, as discussed below. In particular, as in our urban/rural comparisons, there are important differences across deciles in the proportion of teenagers attending primary, rather than secondary, school. For example, figure 7-3 demonstrates that approximately half of the fifteen year olds in the lowest income decile who are in public school are enrolled at the primary level, while this percentage falls to zero in the highest decile.

Per capita government expenditures on secondary education present a somewhat different picture. In both the urban and rural areas of Peru, they first rise and then fall with income (an inverted-U shape). While secondary school enrollment in both public and private schools increases monotonically with income, pupils in the highest deciles are more likely to opt for private school and thereby forgo the benefits of public outlays. Finally, the benefits of higher education are pro-rich in both urban and rural areas.

When per capita public outlays are divided by per capita household expenditure, the resulting incidence patterns for primary and secondary education are pro-poor, while higher education is neither pro-rich nor pro-poor.

The findings of the above analysis are broadly similar to those found elsewhere in the literature, although education spending in Peru does

Table 7-3. Amount of Public Education Outlays per Capita by Decile, Region, and Level of Education, Peru, 1985
(1985 intis)

Region and level of education	1	2	3	4	5	6	7	8	9	10	Top 5	Average
Rural												
Primary	85.2	91.0	86.0	83.6	83.1	83.7	84.1	60.4	43.0	69.6	71.5	84.4
Secondary	29.6	38.4	48.6	57.5	51.7	56.4	85.6	70.0	61.7	28.9	32.8	48.1
Higher	6.8	16.6	3.6	9.4	29.0	25.1	44.3	26.0	37.8	37.8	24.7	16.8
Urban												
Primary	105.9	89.4	87.0	86.1	81.1	60.8	68.3	59.0	36.8	23.4	21.8	65.2
Secondary	98.9	115.0	121.5	148.0	106.2	110.9	102.3	90.9	71.7	70.7	67.8	104.1
Higher	36.5	50.9	96.4	132.8	116.4	183.9	182.8	182.5	197.0	174.3	174.2	160.6
All Peru												
Primary	88.9	90.6	86.5	85.0	81.9	69.4	73.1	59.2	37.7	28.8	27.3	73.6
Secondary	41.9	59.5	80.6	107.9	84.2	90.4	97.2	86.7	70.3	65.6	63.6	79.4
Higher	12.1	26.1	44.2	78.1	81.1	124.4	140.4	151.1	173.8	157.6	155.7	97.2

Note: Average government outlays per student (not including fees), plus scholarships, divided by total population in each cell.
Sources: Peru, Instituto Nacional de Estadística (INE), Household Questionnaire, and the World Bank, Living Standards Measurement Unit.

Table 7-4. *Per Capita Public Education Outlays as a Percentage of Household per Capita Expenditure, by Decile, Region, and Level of Education, Peru, 1985*

Region and level of education	1	2	3	4	5	6	7	8	9	10	Top 5	Average
Rural												
Primary	9.4	5.7	4.0	3.1	2.5	2.0	1.7	0.9	0.5	0.4	0.3	2.8
Secondary	3.3	2.4	2.2	2.1	1.6	1.4	1.7	1.1	0.7	0.2	0.1	1.6
Higher	0.8	1.0	0.2	0.4	0.9	0.6	0.9	0.4	0.4	0.2	0.1	0.6
Urban												
Primary	10.1	5.6	4.0	3.2	2.4	1.5	1.4	0.9	0.4	0.1	0.1	1.0
Secondary	9.4	7.1	5.6	5.5	3.2	2.7	2.0	1.4	0.8	0.4	0.3	1.7
Higher	3.5	3.2	4.5	4.9	3.5	4.5	3.6	2.8	2.2	0.9	0.7	2.6
All Peru												
Primary	9.6	5.6	4.0	3.2	2.5	1.7	1.4	0.9	0.4	0.2	0.1	1.5
Secondary	4.5	3.7	3.7	4.0	2.5	2.2	1.9	1.4	0.8	0.3	0.2	1.7
Higher	1.3	1.6	2.0	2.9	2.4	3.0	2.8	2.4	2.0	0.8	0.6	2.0

Sources: Peru, Instituto Nacional de Estadística (INE), Household Questionnaire, and the World Bank, Living Standards Measurement Unit.

Figure 7-3. Enrollment in Public Primary Schools as a Percentage of Total Public Enrollment, by Age and Decile, Peru, 1985

Percentage at primary level

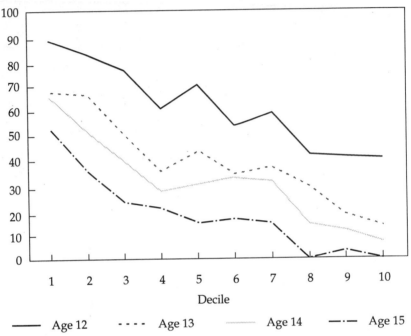

not appear to be as pro-poor as in other countries.[20] Indeed, education would be substantially less pro-poor were it not for the large variation in age composition of the population (see figure 7-4). In particular, seven through twelve year olds constitute a differentially large fraction of the population in the lowest deciles, whereas eighteen through twenty-five year olds constitute a larger fraction in the upper deciles. (Percentages of thirteen through seventeen year olds are roughly equal among income groups.) Thus, age composition at least partially drives our finding that primary education is more pro-poor on a per capita basis than higher education.[21] As discussed in the preceding section, this may at least partially arise because households with young children tend to be headed by adults who have not yet reached their peak earnings. If viewed from a life cycle perspective, the progressivity of education spending may therefore be somewhat lower. Nevertheless, this approach offers useful insights into the success of the public education system in targeting resources at children who are in poverty at a given point in time. The next subsection illustrates that it can also be

Figure 7-4. Student-Age Population as a Percentage of Total Population, by Age and Decile, Peru, 1985

Percentage of population

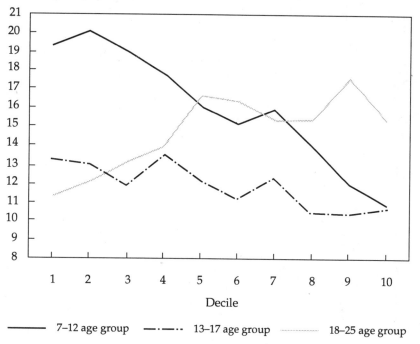

| | 7–12 age group | 13–17 age group | 18–25 age group |

useful to compute benefits on a per child basis in addition to the per capita basis used to this point.

Incidence on a per Child Basis

In tables 7-5 and 7-6, we proceed as above to assign public outlays at each level of education (plus any scholarships received), except that we separate the population by age groups seven through twelve, thirteen through seventeen, and eighteen through twenty-one and divide the total outlays for primary, secondary, and higher education flowing to each cohort in each decile and region by the total number of children in the corresponding group. We also examine incidence by gender. This measure gives a better sense of the benefits accruing per child, because it controls for the effects of household size and educational attainment. Also, by focusing on children, it is possible to restrict the sample to those children who are recorded as residents of their parents' households (thereby ensuring correct expenditure imputations).[22]

Table 7-5. Amount of Public Education Outlays per Child, by Region, Age Group, Gender, and Decile, Peru, 1985
(1985 intis)

Region, age group, and gender		1	2	3	4	5	6	7	8	9	10	Top 5
Rural												
7–12	Male	340.6	347.9	417.9	372.8	486.2	429.7	421.6	369.7	428.0	375.9	319.5
	Female	278.4	345.3	409.4	364.2	390.3	321.8	464.6	355.8	438.5	368.6	538.6
13–17	Male	307.0	305.2	408.7	386.4	399.3	409.9	511.0	520.1	454.5	615.3	649.7
	Female	199.9	232.2	341.2	307.0	323.6	282.6	420.7	340.7	295.4	228.9	215.6
18–21	Male	106.1	154.1	162.5	132.2	309.2	291.4	199.3	22.6	92.9	186.4	194.8
	Female	44.7	140.5	32.6	134.2	82.9	106.8	131.7	246.9	288.5	279.8	467.8
Urban												
7–12	Male	437.1	470.3	478.0	486.5	490.3	468.5	398.3	452.5	379.9	337.4	409.2
	Female	425.3	395.2	418.9	481.8	487.9	436.0	425.7	447.0	339.6	328.0	306.6
13–17	Male	461.7	406.6	519.2	540.5	547.6	530.8	510.3	483.3	461.6	404.6	400.6
	Female	544.3	477.4	452.6	539.0	465.2	528.9	472.8	438.9	276.7	305.3	203.2
18–21	Male	304.2	212.5	359.7	508.9	349.9	587.4	597.8	675.0	556.8	621.8	776.6
	Female	107.6	344.9	263.1	594.9	364.0	354.6	449.6	414.4	512.7	439.4	433.6
All Peru												
7–12	Male	358.2	376.5	445.1	434.4	488.5	451.4	405.1	437.0	386.0	343.5	390.7
	Female	309.7	357.8	413.8	429.7	450.0	392.4	437.6	429.8	352.2	336.7	340.4
13–17	Male	334.3	333.1	467.4	483.6	490.5	489.7	510.6	492.8	460.6	413.4	416.5
	Female	249.1	321.7	391.2	454.2	411.5	437.5	456.9	415.9	279.5	297.0	204.8
18–21	Male	143.3	177.5	266.3	364.3	334.3	500.6	497.8	561.1	511.0	586.6	750.5
	Female	55.2	214.5	164.3	413.7	271.1	287.5	366.4	387.7	486.8	425.5	436.8

Note: For rural areas, the number of observations in the eighth, ninth, and tenth deciles becomes small for certain age groups, and grouping observations across these cells might provide a more accurate picture. Nonetheless, the general pattern of propoor benefit holds.
Sources: Peru, Instituto Nacional de Estadística (INE), Household Questionnaire, and the World Bank, Living Standards Measurement Unit.

172

Table 7-6. *Subsidy as a Percentage of Household per Capita Expenditures, by Decile, Region, Age Group, and Gender, Peru, 1985*

Region, age group, and gender		1	2	3	4	5	6	7	8	9	10	Top 5
Rural												
7–12	Male	36.5	21.6	19.3	13.8	14.6	10.4	8.3	5.7	4.8	1.9	1.2
	Female	29.9	21.5	18.9	13.5	11.7	7.8	9.2	5.5	5.0	1.9	2.0
13–17	Male	32.9	19.0	18.9	14.3	12.0	10.0	10.1	8.1	5.1	3.2	2.4
	Female	21.4	14.4	15.8	11.4	9.7	6.9	8.3	5.3	3.3	1.2	0.8
18–21	Male	11.4	9.6	7.5	4.9	9.3	7.1	3.9	0.4	1.0	1.0	0.7
	Female	4.8	8.7	1.5	5.0	2.5	2.6	2.6	3.8	3.3	1.4	1.8
Urban												
7–12	Male	46.9	29.2	22.1	18.1	14.7	11.4	7.9	7.0	4.3	1.7	1.5
	Female	45.6	24.6	19.4	17.9	14.6	10.6	8.4	7.0	3.8	1.7	1.2
13–17	Male	49.5	25.3	24.0	20.1	16.4	12.9	10.1	7.5	5.2	2.1	1.5
	Female	58.4	29.7	20.9	20.0	14.0	12.9	9.4	6.8	3.1	1.6	0.8
18–21	Male	32.6	13.2	16.6	18.9	10.5	14.3	11.8	10.5	6.3	3.2	2.9
	Female	11.5	21.4	12.2	22.1	10.9	8.6	8.9	6.4	5.8	2.3	1.6
All Peru												
7–12	Male	38.4	23.4	20.6	16.1	14.6	11.0	8.0	6.8	4.4	1.8	1.5
	Female	33.2	22.2	19.1	16.0	13.5	9.5	8.7	6.7	4.0	1.7	1.3
13–17	Male	35.9	20.7	21.6	18.0	14.7	11.9	10.1	7.7	5.2	2.1	1.6
	Female	26.7	20.0	18.1	16.9	12.3	10.6	9.0	6.5	3.2	1.5	0.8
18–21	Male	15.4	11.0	12.3	13.5	10.0	12.2	9.9	8.7	5.8	3.0	2.8
	Female	5.9	13.3	7.6	15.4	8.1	7.0	7.3	6.0	5.5	2.2	1.6

Sources: Peru, Instituto Nacional de Estadística (INE), Household Questionnaire, and the World Bank, Living Standards Measurement Unit.

173

In the seven through twelve age group, males receive more benefits than females in almost every decile and region (though the differences are not always large). In the thirteen through seventeen age category, this gender gap is even more pronounced.[23] A similar pattern between genders emerges in the eighteen through twenty-five age cohort, although females in the three highest deciles in rural areas receive more education benefits than their male peers.

Outlays for the seven through twelve age group appear substantially less pro-poor when viewed on a per child rather than on a per capita basis. Indeed, public outlays received by children in this age group are neither pro-poor nor pro-rich. For the thirteen through seventeen age group, the incidence of outlays is pro-rich in rural areas, in part because many poor rural children in this age group continue to be enrolled in primary, rather than secondary, school. Incidence for this age group in the urban areas of Peru first rises and then falls with income (an inverted U-shape). This is because poor children have low enrollment rates at the secondary level, whereas the highest-income children, while typically enrolled in school, are more likely than their poorer peers to be enrolled in private schools. Finally, outlays per child in the eighteen through twenty-one age cohort tend to be pro-rich.[24] Overall, the incidence of education outlays per child is less pro-poor than the incidence of education outlays per capita. However, when outlays per child are expressed as a proportion of average per capita expenditures, the pattern is still basically pro-poor.

Private Costs of School Attendance

Based on the weight of the results reported so far and on the assumption that the benefit distribution of marginal public outlays will be similar to the benefit distribution of average public outlays, one might conclude that spending more at the primary level, while spending less at the secondary and higher levels, would better target educational benefits toward the poor. As discussed above, although the thrust of this argument is probably correct, it gives little guidance on how to target marginal public outlays to the poor. More spending will not necessarily mean better school attendance among poor children if there are barriers such as high out-of-pocket expenditures.

In an effort to examine such barriers to school attendance in Malaysia, Meerman (1979) computes out-of-pocket expenses for books, uniforms, transportation, forgone labor earnings, and other expenses that are likely to deter school attendance for lower-income children. He finds that such costs exceed 13 percent of per capita expenditures for the poorest 10 percent of Malaysia's households. Using regression analysis, Chernichovsky and Meesook (1985) find similar results in Indonesia. Moreover, they report evidence suggesting that long travel times may hinder attendance. Both results may have important implications for efforts to target marginal schooling expenditures to children in the lowest deciles.

In table 7-7, we examine the PLSS reported annual out-of-pocket costs for fees paid to schools (net of scholarships received), transportation costs (excluding time costs), uniforms, books and supplies, and others. Especially in the poorest deciles, per pupil, these can amount to a substantial fraction of the household's per capita expenditure. These results suggest that the private costs of public school enrollment may be a formidable barrier for many poor children, highlighting the need for careful consideration of the marginal incidence of any policies intended to channel benefits to this segment of the population.

The Incidence of Higher School Fees

As discussed above, an important policy debate concerns increases in school fees. Advocates of increased fees argue that the additional revenues generated could secure enrollment expansion and quality increases that would generate positive net benefits. Opponents express concern that fee increases will be disproportionately borne by the poor.

As noted earlier, one can interpret enrollment rates as providing a first-order approximation of the incidence of a small change in fees. Table 7-8 presents enrollment rates, by age group, education level, and decile. These numbers are of interest in and of themselves as measures of the performance of the educational system. From this perspective, perhaps the most striking result to emerge is the high primary school enrollments in the thirteen through seventeen year old age group at all levels of income.

Moreover, when interpreted as first-order approximations of the welfare loss from an increase in school fees, the figures in table 7-8 suggest that a fee increase at the primary level would be roughly proportional on a per child basis and therefore regressive on a per capita basis (because poor households tend to have more young children than higher-income households). A fee increase at the secondary level would be less regressive, in part because poor thirteen through seventeen year olds are far more likely than their wealthier counterparts to be either enrolled in primary school or simply not enrolled in school.

Of course, numerous caveats can be raised concerning this approximation. On the one hand, approximation error due to the implicit assumption of inelastic demand may make fee increases appear more regressive than they in fact are. This would be the case if higher enrollment elasticities among the poor cause differentially higher dropout rates (so that welfare losses due to fee increases would be avoided to some extent). On the other hand, differentially large enrollment declines among the poor may themselves be of concern.

Table 7-7. Annual Out-of-Pocket School Expenditures per Pupil, by Decile, Region, and Level of Education, Peru, 1985
(1985 intis)

Region and level of education	1	2	3	4	5	6	7	8	9	10
Rural										
Primary education										
Fees	0.8	1.4	-42.8	-4.4	-25.7	1.9	-37.6	1.6	3.6	3.2
Transportation	9.2	1.0	4.4	5.6	2.9	0.7	18.3	0.0	24.1	9.4
Uniforms	30.3	76.3	97.9	107.5	160.0	103.8	157.7	157.2	84.9	149.6
Books and supplies	55.5	56.8	60.5	76.0	78.9	89.7	104.4	77.6	154.3	121.1
Other	5.2	7.5	11.1	10.3	29.1	11.4	8.6	7.4	12.4	133.6
Secondary education										
Fees	5.0	3.6	-42.4	21.0	-14.9	5.8	-15.6	5.0	3.5	8.1
Transportation	28.6	6.6	30.2	129.5	52.6	18.4	50.6	0.0	44.7	53.4
Uniforms	144.8	142.6	236.6	232.2	358.1	312.8	387.1	309.2	297.1	187.2
Books and supplies	96.0	98.0	115.4	234.2	188.7	103.0	242.5	168.9	270.3	194.0
Other	10.7	19.0	16.4	42.3	15.4	25.0	22.6	12.7	41.3	28.1
Urban										
Primary education										
Fees	2.9	-2.2	4.7	4.5	5.3	13.0	11.2	8.5	29.0	-12.7
Transportation	3.0	8.5	15.2	16.5	16.7	14.7	10.1	62.2	37.7	86.1
Uniforms	60.7	143.5	155.1	166.7	216.5	221.6	239.4	415.4	285.8	294.1
Books and supplies	52.3	131.6	122.0	147.6	147.6	144.1	149.2	157.8	256.0	198.1
Other	4.7	7.9	9.6	10.6	28.0	25.7	40.6	29.2	48.6	25.9
Secondary education										
Fees	6.3	10.7	15.4	18.3	22.5	25.7	17.6	13.2	57.6	117.7
Transportation	22.0	33.4	23.6	29.5	54.2	35.9	40.5	48.2	48.4	38.2
Uniforms	94.2	142.6	215.1	238.0	268.6	250.7	297.2	412.2	473.8	516.5
Books and supplies	102.6	161.4	155.0	198.3	209.4	204.4	214.1	250.3	252.3	285.7
Other	11.7	19.9	22.1	20.5	33.6	23.6	38.7	40.0	49.5	65.4

Sources: Peru, Instituto Nacional de Estadística (INE), Household Questionnaire, and the World Bank, Living Standards Measurement Unit.

Table 7-8. *Percentage of School-Age Population in Each Decile Enrolled in Public School, by Age and Level of Education, Peru, 1985*

Age and level of education	1	2	3	4	5	6	7	8	9	10
Primary education										
6–12	73.8	76.0	83.3	79.9	86.7	80.7	82.5	82.2	82.9	81.4
13–17	31.5	27.7	19.4	18.5	17.0	18.0	19.0	9.0	6.2	4.3
6–17	57.2	57.3	59.6	53.6	58.3	55.2	55.8	52.1	50.2	46.8
Secondary education										
13–17	24.1	32.6	51.2	58.8	59.7	61.4	563.9	71.7	79.8	79.6
18–21	12.0	15.6	22.6	27.7	15.7	18.8	21.5	14.0	13.9	14.8
13–21	20.5	27.1	41.4	48.8	41.7	44.7	48.5	51.5	53.0	54.8

Sources: Peru, Instituto Nacional de Estadística (INE), Household Questionnaire, and the World Bank, Living Standards Measurement Unit.

Table 7-9. Nonestimation-Based Evidence on Willingness to Pay Higher Fees to Reduce Travel Time to Secondary School, by Quartile, Peru, 1985
(percentage of eligible children)

Eligible children and travel time to nearest secondary school[a]	Quartile by household expenditure				Total school enrollment rate
	1	2	3	4	
Eligible children[b]					
0–30 minutes	19.2	38.0	47.2	51.8	37.7
31–90 minutes	33.4	26.3	21.2	22.7	26.4
91–150 minutes	19.9	12.5	13.0	15.6	15.6
Over 150 minutes	27.4	23.1	18.6	9.8	20.6
Eligible children who commute daily to local public secondary school[a]					
0–30 minutes	64.3	59.6	63.5	65.4	63.3
31–90 minutes	46.5	50.0	51.4	52.0	49.5
91–150 minutes[c]	14.3	29.2	29.4	35.5	28.2
Over 150 minutes[c]	0.0	12.0	0.0	25.0	5.6

a. Travel time to the nearest secondary school is reported for the community in which child is a resident.

b. Eligible children must be between ten and eighteen years old and have completed primary school (but not yet completed secondary school).

c. Calculations are based on fewer than forty children per cell, and should therefore be interpreted with caution.

Sources: Peru, Instituto Nacional de Estadística (INE), Household Questionnaire, and the World Bank, Living Standards Measurement Unit.

Willingness to Pay Higher School Fees for Reduced Travel Time

As discussed above, preliminary evidence concerning the desirability of closer but more expensive schooling can be gained from readily calculated indicators of whether households are currently incurring substantial transportation expenses to send their children to school.

Using the quartile definitions employed by Gertler and Glewwe (1990), table 7-9 presents the distribution, by household expenditure quartile and distance to secondary school, of children aged ten through eighteen who live in rural communities and are eligible to enroll in secondary school.[25] As these results show, a substantial fraction of Peru's eligible children, especially among the poor, live more than 90 minutes from the nearest secondary school. Table 7-9 also presents current enrollment rates for each of these groupings. Not surprisingly, travel time appears to have an important negative effect on school enrollment (as was found by Gertler and Glewwe). For example, for the poorest quartile, 64 percent of eligible children who live 0–30 minutes away from a secondary school commute daily to that school; in contrast, only 14 percent of eligible children who live 90–150 minutes away from the nearest secondary school do so. Thus, one might well

expect shorter travel times to result in a substantial increase in enrollment (holding school fees constant).

Although these measures raise the possibility that closer but more
expensive schooling would be welfare-improving in at least some communities, our estimates of M_3 do not reveal a substantial willingness
to pay. Multiplying the reduction in travel time by the mean rural child
wage rate and adding the average out-of-pocket travel costs reported
by pupils traveling the corresponding distance, our estimate of willingness to pay for a one-hour reduction in travel time is only 77 intis per
child per year (Peru's currency is the inti). For a two-hour reduction,
the corresponding figure is only 110 intis per year. Children who are
not currently enrolled in school would presumably exhibit lower willingness to pay for closer schooling. Clearly, these amounts fall far short
of the average per pupil expenditure for secondary education of 999
intis (see table 7-2).[26]

Of course, as we note above, there may be quality- and learning-
related benefits to school proximity that our crude measure ignores.
Indeed, Gertler and Glewwe's estimates suggest that school proximity
has a positive effect on enrollment in local schools independent of the
effect of distance on expenditures. This may be one reason our estimates
fall short of those presented by Gertler and Glewwe for reduced travel
time to the local secondary school. Moreover, as noted above, a complete benefit-cost analysis must account for reduced spending associated with lower enrollment at the more distant schools, in addition to
accounting for the increase in spending associated with the provision of
more proximate schooling. Higher fees need only cover the differential
outlays incurred by the government. For both of these reasons, we
view our computations as a very first step in the development of
nonestimation-based methods for assessing the demand for closer, but
more expensive, schooling.

Conclusions

This chapter presents both a theoretical comparison of alternative benefit measures and an empirical application of nonestimation-based methods to issues surrounding public education expenditures in Peru. On
the first point, we distinguish between benefit measures that involve
the estimation of demand functions and those that do not. The latter
include standard benefit-incidence analysis (which allocates government outlays in proportion to household use), as well as a number of
other nonestimation-based methods that may be more appropriate for
analyzing marginal changes in public policy.

Because estimation-based methods enable the researcher to construct
estimates of compensating variation, such methods are generally
viewed as being more firmly grounded in economic theory than the

nonestimation-based methods. However, we argue in this chapter that each of the methods has its own strengths and weaknesses. On the one hand, while the nonestimation-based approaches are less costly to implement and impose fewer data requirements, they clearly offer only approximations to the true willingness to pay. In particular, because these measures ignore any behavioral responses, they are especially inaccurate whenever elasticities are significantly large. However, this would only appear to be a serious omission to the extent that behavioral responses are known to be distributionally differentiated.

On the other hand, while the estimation-based approaches are more rigorously linked to an explicit model of consumer behavior, they typically have large informational demands and require strong assumptions about the functional form for household decisionmaking and about the distribution of the error term. Similarly, the private willingness to pay of the household decisionmaker may not be a good indicator of the social benefit derived from a child's education in the presence of externalities or intrahousehold inequity. Moreover, from the standpoint of analyzing capabilities rather than utilities, some of the nonestimation-based measures, such as government outlays per child, enrollment rates, and distance to school, may provide a more useful representation of the social value of education.

In its conception, our chapter would have compared the incidence results that others obtain using the compensating variation approach with those we obtain using standard incidence analysis and our other nonestimation-based measures. In its implementation, however, we have discovered that as extensive as the PLSS data are, important data limitations still face researchers seeking to implement demand-curve estimates. For instance, the data do not contain sufficient price information to distinguish between public and private schooling options in the rural areas of Peru, and price information is even more limited for Peru's urban areas. Similar problems are likely to confront researchers using other household data, so that it will rarely be possible to rely exclusively on compensating variation measures derived from demand-curve estimates, however desirable such measures are from the standpoint of economic theory.

In our empirical analysis, several results stand out. Using the benefit-incidence approach, we find that educational benefits are mildly pro-poor in Peru. A much lower proportion of poor children aged 6 through 12 are enrolled in primary schools compared to middle- and higher-income children. We also find that females of school age as a group receive fewer expenditures than their male counterparts as a result of differential enrollment rates.

Our analysis of the out-of-pocket expenses of attending school reveals that private costs represent a substantial barrier to participation for children in low-income households. These results parallel the findings of several earlier studies and suggest that policies designed to increase enrollment rates among the poor should focus not only on reducing school fees but also on defraying the out-of-pocket expenses of sending children to school.

Our nonestimation-based analysis of the welfare effects associated with increasing school fees suggests that the incidence of losses would be regressive as a percentage of household income, although the largest absolute losses would fall on middle-income households. A similar analysis to gauge the willingness to pay for better proximity to schools suggests that a substantial fraction of households in rural Peru live far from the nearest secondary school. This is especially true for the poor (although the data reveal that households have overcome this barrier to enrollment with surprising frequency). Despite this, our results suggest that the potential reduction in travel expenses from more proximate secondary schools falls well short of the average cost of secondary schooling. However, our nonestimation-based approach neglects many potential benefits, such as reduced travel fatigue and an associated increase in learning. Moreover, one must factor in cost savings at the more distant schools as children switch to the local facilities.

Our empirical analysis leads to several strategies that Peruvian policymakers might employ to improve the targeting of public education expenditures in Peru. At the most basic level, because primary education is more pro-poor than secondary or higher education, reallocating government resources toward primary education is likely to be pro-poor. In particular, the pro-poor pattern reflects the fact that a substantial fraction of poor children are enrolled in primary school up to the age of fifteen or sixteen years old (an issue that itself deserves additional analysis).

However, even at the primary level, the incidence of government outlays on a per child basis is approximately proportional. Because of this, and because out-of-pocket expenses and the opportunity cost of forgone labor pose important barriers to enrollment by poor children, policies to reduce schooling costs for the poor would probably have a more progressive incidence than a general increase in expenditures at the primary level.

With regard to the incidence of closer but more expensive secondary schooling, our results are mixed. Closer schools would probably be pro-poor, simply because the poor tend to live farther from the nearest secondary school. However, the welfare effects of closer schooling should be examined carefully on a community-by-community basis, especially in light of our finding that potential savings in travel costs are unlikely to justify large increases in school fees.

Notes

1. A partial list of other references includes Dor, Gertler, and van der Gaag (1987); Gertler and van der Gaag (1988); Gertler, Locay, and Sanderson (1987); and Ellis and Mwabu (1991).

2. Early studies of high-income countries include Gillespie (1965); Tax Foundation (1967); Maital (1975); Musgrave, Case, and Leonard (1974); and Reynolds and Smolensky (1977). A partial list of other developing-country studies includes the early studies by Foxley (1979) and Sahota (1977), as well as more recent studies by Bahl, Kim, and Park (1986); Meesook (1984); Petrei (1987); Riboud (1990); and van de Walle (1992).

3. Selden and Wasylenko (1992) review the recent literature on standard benefit incidence. For reviews of the earlier benefit-incidence literature, see De Wulf (1975, 1981).

4. The model therefore ignores issues surrounding attendance.

5. It is unlikely, however, that the entire time devoted to schooling would have been spent in employment at wage rate w, especially for younger children. To the extent $t < t_s + t_T$, the willingness to pay computed from demand-curve estimates would be overstated. Lower opportunity costs from forgone labor would also result in lower willingness-to-pay estimates for reduced travel time (see below).

6. An alternative measure, the equivalent variation (EV), replaces the status quo utility with the utility level if no public schooling option is available. Both are valid money metric measures of utility; however, the EV is preferable when multiple policy changes are being considered (L. W. McKenzie 1957; G. W. McKenzie 1983; King 1983).

7. In this regard, although most faraway schools are indeed private, the local schooling option includes both public and private schools.

8. Data permitting, an alternative way to address quality differences without estimating demand curves is to examine the incidence of qualified teachers, free textbooks, travel time, and other quality-related variables. This requires data on school quality only for the option actually chosen.

9. For instance, public expenditures on education may crowd out private transfers that would have helped to finance education in the absence of such expenditures. Developing-country studies of public and private transfers include Cox and Jimenez (1990) and Rempel and Lobdell (1978). Also, see Lampman and Smeeding (1983).

10. Choosing between a current versus a lifetime perspective is the subject of a well-known debate on the California education system between Hansen and Weisbrod (1969) and Pechman (1972). For an excellent example of a lifetime incidence analysis of *social security* benefits in a developing-country context, see Burkhauser (1986).

11. Selden and Wasylenko (1992) discuss this in greater detail. Also, Piggott and Whalley (1987) provide simulation results demonstrating that marginal and average calculations of benefit can yield very different conclusions about incidence even in the case of a pure public good.

12. Moreover, an unresolved issue is whether the coefficient estimates published in Gertler and Glewwe (1990) imply a negative marginal utility of income for at least some deciles. The marginal utility of income in their quadratic specification is $\lambda \equiv \alpha_1 + 2\alpha_2 c$, where c denotes per capita consumption. The authors have clarified that α_2 in table 6 of their paper should be -0.031 rather than -0.31. However, this does not, by itself, eliminate the problem of λ being negative.

13. We are grateful to the government of Peru for their permission to use their data for our project. We also thank Kalpana Mehra of the World Bank for supplying the data to us on tape.

14. However, certain politically unstable portions of the *sierra* are not represented in the PLSS.

15. Note in this regard that the price indexes attached to the PLSS are region specific. One might ideally use adult equivalency scales to deflate total expenditures. However, there is no accepted equivalency scale measure. Deflating by the number of persons in the household also maintains comparability of our results with those obtained in other studies, which do not in general use equivalency scales. For an excellent discussion of equivalency scales, see Deaton and Muellbauer (1980, chap. 8).

16. One reason may be that the children have moved into a relative's household for education purposes. The residency requirement for the PLSS is three months.

17. Meerman (1979) shows that omitting the flow of capital services from benefit measures can seriously misrepresent the benefits of public spending. Although we were unable to obtain an accurate measure, capital spending was only a small part of total education spending in Peru during this period.

18. This is straightforward for primary and secondary education. However, the PLSS does not enable one to distinguish between current enrollment in university and nonuniversity forms of higher education. For our calculations, we simply use an (unweighted) average of the per pupil costs of the two forms of schooling. This may slightly understate the magnitude of the higher education benefits (because the higher-cost universities serve more students than the nonuniversity alternatives). More significantly, the fraction of pupils completing at least one year of university education (as opposed to nonuniversity education) is an increasing function of income, so that the incidence of higher education benefits may be more pro-rich than our measures suggest.

19. Most scholarships are public. In any event, this does not qualitatively affect our results.

20. Among the better-known studies are Meerman (1979) for Malaysia and Selowsky (1979) for Colombia. Other studies include Bahl, Kim, and Park (1986) for the Republic of Korea; Foxley (1979) and Castañeda (1989) for Chile; Jallade (1974) for Colombia; Das Gupta and Tilak (1983) for the West Godavari District of the Indian state of Andhra Pradesh; Meesook (1984) and van de Walle (chapter 9 of this volume) for Indonesia; and Petrei (1987) for five countries in Central and South America. Though conducted at different times and in different countries, the results of these studies are largely congruent. In all cases, primary education is at least weakly pro-poor in absolute terms—and strongly pro-poor as a percentage of income. Secondary education presents a more mixed picture. All studies find secondary education to be less pro-poor than primary education. However, although most studies find secondary outlays to be pro-poor, Meerman finds a proportional distribution of secondary outlays in Malaysia (in absolute terms), while Meesook finds a pro-rich distribution in Indonesia (in absolute terms, but not as a percentage of income). Higher education is typically found to be pro-rich (this is often true even when outlays are calculated as a percentage of income).

21. For example, a household with four adults and one school-age child would have outlays for the child in school imputed to the household, but the expenditure would be deflated by the number of persons in the household.

22. This procedure is also followed by Gertler and Glewwe (1990 and 1992). Many children who attend faraway schools are still included (so long as they are listed as residents of their parents' households). Nevertheless, children who reside with relatives for education purposes may be underrepresented in the sample as a result of this procedure. Although this might be especially

problematic in the context of an education analysis, in practice our calculations using the full sample of children yield similar results to those presented here.

23. Gertler and Glewwe (1992), using the same data that we use, find that the willingness to pay for reduced travel time to secondary school is lower for females than for males.

24. For this age group, the most reliable calculations are those for all of Peru, because some of the cells in tables 7-5 and 7-6 have fewer than forty observations.

25. Our sample differs from theirs, however, insofar as theirs excludes a large number of observations for which parental education data are missing. Such data are not required for our calculations, so we do not exclude these observations.

26. Note that this is more than twice the per pupil cost used by Gertler and Glewwe. Their cost estimate has the advantage of being specific to rural Peru (ours is a nationwide average). However, to obtain this estimate, they simply divide the average teacher salary by an assumed class size of thirty.

References

Anand, Sudhir, and Martin Ravallion. 1993. "Human Development in Poor Countries: On the Role of Private Incomes and Public Services." *Journal of Economic Perspectives* 7: 133–50.

Bahl, Roy, Chuk Kyo Kim, and Chong Lee Park. 1986. *Public Finances during the Korean Modernization Process.* Cambridge, Mass.: Harvard University Press.

Burkhauser, Richard V. 1986. "Social Security in Panama: A Multiperiod Analysis of Income Distribution." *Journal of Development Economics* 21: 53–64.

Castañeda, Tarsicio. 1989. "Innovative Social Policies for Reducing Poverty: Chile in the 1980s." Washington, D.C.

Chernichovsky, Dov, and Oey A. Meesook. 1985. *School Enrollment in Indonesia.* World Bank Staff Working Paper 746. Washington, D.C.

Cox, Donald, and Emmanuel Jimenez. 1990. "Private Transfers and Public Transfers in Developing Countries: A Case of Peru." Policy, Planning, and Research Working Paper 345. World Bank, Washington, D.C.

Das Gupta, Ajit K., and Janhyala B. G. Tilak. 1983. "Distribution among Income Groups: An Empirical Analysis." *Economic and Political Weekly* 18: 1442–47.

Deaton, Angus, and John Muellbauer. 1980. *Economics and Consumer Behavior.* Cambridge, Eng.: Cambridge University Press.

De Wulf, Luc. 1975. "Fiscal Incidence Studies in Developing Countries." *International Monetary Fund Staff Papers* 22: 61–131.

———. 1981. "Incidence of Budgetary Outlays: Where Do We Go from Here?" *Public Finance* 36: 55–76.

Dor, Avi, Paul Gertler, and Jacques van der Gaag. 1987. "Non-Price Rationing and the Choice of Medical Care Providers in Rural Côte d'Ivoire." *Journal of Health Economics* 6: 291–304.

Ellis, Randall P., and Germano M. Mwabu. 1991. "The Demand for Outpatient Medical Care in Rural Kenya." Institute for Economic Development Discussion Paper Series 15. Boston University, Boston, Mass.

Foxley, Alejandro. 1979. *Redistributive Effects of Government Programmes: The Chilean Case*. In collaboration with Eduardo Aninat and J. P. Arellano. Oxford: Pergamon Press.

Gertler, Paul, and Paul Glewwe. 1990. "The Willingness to Pay for Education in Developing Countries: Evidence from Rural Peru." *Journal of Public Economics* 42: 251–75.

――――. 1992. "The Willingness to Pay for Daughters in Contrast to Sons: Evidence from Rural Peru." *World Bank Economic Review* 6: 171–88

Gertler, Paul, Luis Locay, and Warren Sanderson. 1987. "Are User Fees Regressive? The Welfare Implications of Health Care Financing Proposals in Peru." *Journal of Econometrics* 36: 67–80.

Gertler, Paul, and Jacques van der Gaag. 1988. "Measuring the Willingness to Pay for Social Services in Developing Countries." Living Standards Measurement Study Working Paper 45. World Bank, Washington, D.C.

Gillespie, W. Irwin. 1965. "Effect of Public Expenditures on the Distribution of Income." In Richard Musgrave, ed., *Essays in Fiscal Federalism*. Washington, D.C.: Brookings Institution.

Hansen, W. Lee, and Burton A. Weisbrod. 1969. *Benefits, Costs, and Finance of Public Higher Education*. Chicago, Ill.: Markham.

Jallade, Jean-Pierre. 1974. "Public Expenditures on Education and Income Distribution in Colombia." Occasional Paper 18. World Bank, Washington D.C.

Jimenez, Emmanuel. 1986. "The Public Subsidization of Education and Health in Developing Countries: A Review of Equity and Efficiency." *World Bank Research Observer* 1 (1): 111–29.

――――. 1987. *Pricing Policy in the Social Sectors*. Baltimore, Md.: Johns Hopkins University Press.

――――. 1989. "Social Sector Policy Revisited: A Survey of Some Recent Controversies." *Proceedings of the World Bank Annual Conference on Development Economics 1989*, pp. 109–38. World Bank, Washington, D.C.

King, M. A. 1983. "Welfare Analysis of Tax Reforms Using Household Data." *Journal of Public Economics* 21: 183–214.

Lampman, Robert J., and Timothy M. Smeeding. 1983. "Interfamily Transfers as Alternatives to Government Transfers to Persons." *Review of Income and Wealth* (March): 45–66.

Maital, Shlomo. 1975. "Apportionment of Public Goods Benefits to Individuals." *Public Finance* 30: 397–416.

McKenzie, G. W. 1983. *Measuring Economic Welfare: New Methods*. Cambridge, Eng.: Cambridge University Press.

McKenzie, L. W. 1957. "Demand Theory without a Utility Index." *Review of Economic Studies* 24: 185–89.

Meerman, Jacob. 1979. *Public Expenditure in Malaysia: Who Benefits and Why*. New York: Oxford University Press.

Meesook, Oey A. 1984. *Financing and Equity in the Social Sectors in Indonesia*. Staff Working Paper 703. Washington, D.C.: World Bank.

Mingat, Alain, and Jee-Peng Tan. 1985. "Subsidization of Higher Education versus Expansion of Primary Enrollments: What Can a Shift in Resources

Achieve in Sub-Saharan Africa?" *International Journal of Educational Development* 5: 259–68.

———. 1986. "Who Profits from the Public Funding of Education? A Comparison of World Regions." *Comparative Education Review* 30: 260–70.

Musgrave, Richard A., Karl E. Case, and Herman Leonard. 1974. "The Distribution of Fiscal Burdens and Benefits." *Public Finance Quarterly* 2: 259–311.

Pechman, Joseph A. 1972. "Note on the Intergenerational Transfer of Public Higher Education Benefits." *Journal of Political Economy* 80: 256–59.

Petrei, A. Humberto. 1987. "El gasto público social y sus efectos distributivos." Programa ECIEL, Rio de Janeiro.

Piggott, John, and John Whalley. 1987. "Interpreting Net Fiscal Incidence Calculations." *Review of Economics and Statistics* 69: 685–94.

Psacharopoulos, George. 1977. "The Perverse Effects of Public Subsidization of Education or How Equitable Is Free Education?" *Comparative Education Review* 25 (2): 69–90.

Rempel, Henry, and Richard A. Lobdell. 1978. "The Role of Urban-to-Rural Remittances in Developing Countries." *Journal of Development Studies* 14: 324–41.

Reynolds, Morgan, and Eugene Smolensky. 1977. *Public Expenditures, Taxes, and the Distribution of Income: The United States, 1950, 1961, and 1970.* New York: Academic Press.

Riboud, Michelle. 1990. "Costa Rica: Public Sector Social Spending." World Bank, Washington, D.C.

Sahota, Gian S. 1977. "The Distribution of the Benefits of Public Expenditure in Panama." *Public Finance Quarterly* 5: 203–30.

Schwabe, Christopher. 1994. "Assessing the Distributive Equity Implications of Health Sector Pricing Policies in Juba, Sudan." Ph.D. diss., Syracuse University, Syracuse, N.Y.

Selden, Thomas M., and Michael J. Wasylenko. 1992. "Benefit Incidence Analysis in Developing Countries." Policy Research Working Paper WPS 1015. World Bank, Washington, D.C.

Selowsky, Marcelo. 1979. *Who Benefits from Government Expenditures? A Case Study of Colombia.* New York: Oxford University Press.

Sen, Amartya K. 1987a. *On Ethics and Economics.* The Royer Lectures at the University of California at Berkeley. Oxford, Eng.: Basil Blackwell, Ltd.

———. 1987b. *The Standard of Living.* The Tanner Lectures. Cambridge, Eng.: Cambridge University Press.

Small, Kenneth A., and Harvey S. Rosen. 1981. "Applied Welfare Economics with Discrete Choice Models." *Econometrica* 49: 105–30.

Tax Foundation, Inc. 1967. *Tax Burdens and Benefits of Government Expenditures by Income Class, 1961 and 1965.* New York.

van de Walle, Dominique. 1992. "The Distribution of the Benefits from Social Services in Indonesia, 1978–87." Policy Research Working Paper 871. World Bank, Washington, D.C.

8

Public Schooling Expenditures in Rural Pakistan: Efficiently Targeting Girls and a Lagging Region

Harold Alderman, Jere R. Behrman, Shahrukh Khan, David R. Ross, and Richard Sabot

Estimated private and social returns on education are generally high in developing countries.[1] Likewise, output accounting exercises indicate that differences in the educational attainment and cognitive skills of the labor force explain a substantial proportion of differences among countries in average labor productivity (Knight and Sabot 1987; Krueger 1968). In addition to raising their productivity, schooling tends to augment the income, wealth, nutrition, and health of the educated and to decrease the quantity, and improve the "quality," of their children.

In no society is the distribution of schooling equal. Instead, there are systematic, group-based differences in the probability of going to school. In particular, in many developing countries there are large differences between genders and among regions in educational opportunities and in the quality of schooling. Recent surveys indicate that the gaps favoring boys over girls in schooling enrollment and attainment vary considerably across countries but tend to be relatively large in South Asia, in the Middle East, and in North Africa (Behrman 1993; King 1990; King and Hill 1993). Country case studies indicate substantial regional gaps in schooling, with particularly low levels of attainment in such regions as the Northeast in Brazil, northern Nigeria, northeastern Thailand, and the Sind in Pakistan.

In this chapter, we focus on rural Pakistan, where the gender and regional gaps are large.[2] Our survey evidence for 1989 indicates sub-

This chapter builds on results generated by the Human Capital Accumulation in Post Green Revolution Pakistan Project of the International Food Policy Research Institute (IFPRI). We are grateful to the World Bank and United States Agency for International Development (USAID) for financial support; to Mary Bailey, Meg Ewing, Emily Mellott, and Matthew Tropp for able research assistance; and to Dominique van de Walle and Kim Nead for helpful comments. The views presented here are those of the authors and should not be interpreted as reflecting the views of IFPRI, USAID, or the World Bank.

Table 8-1. Gender and Regional Gaps in Selected Schooling Indexes

Gender or region	Primary school enrollment rate (10–18 cohort, percentage)[a]	Cognitive achievement (20–24 cohort, percentage)[b]	Availability of primary school (10–18 cohort, percentage)[c]
Boys	74.6	15.7	98.2
Girls	38.0	3.8	60.1
Faisalabad	73.8	11.5	93.0
Badin	34.8	3.2	57.3

a. The primary school rate gives the percentage of individuals in the ten to eighteen year old cohort of the gender or in the region indicated who ever have enrolled in primary school.

b. Cognitive achievement is measured by reading and mathematics tests that are described in some detail in the text.

c. The availability of a primary school refers to whether a primary school was available locally at the time that an individual in the sample was of primary school age.

stantial gaps in schooling enrollments and cognitive achievement between boys and girls and between a relatively prosperous district, Faisalabad in the Punjab, and a relatively poor district, Badin in the Sind (see table 8-1).[3] Boys are twice as likely as girls to start school in our sample. This contributes to a gender gap in cognitive skills of 76 percent. That is, for persons aged twenty to twenty-four, the mean score for women on a test of literacy and numeracy (3.8 points out of a maximum of 72) is 76 percent of the male score (15.7 points). Comparing the regions, nearly three-fourths of children in Faisalabad start school, while barely a third start school in Badin. The gap in mean cognitive achievement scores between these regions is 72 percent.

These gender and regional divergences in schooling in rural Pakistan, and those elsewhere in the developing world, raise an important issue. When allocating education expenditures, should the disadvantaged groups—including girls and children in lagging regions—be targeted in order to assure more equitable gains from schooling? This in turn raises three related questions.

First, how important is the supply side relative to the demand side in the determination of gender and regional gaps in schooling attainment and achievement? The supply of public schools can be controlled directly by governments, whereas the demand for schooling cannot. If the conventional wisdom is correct and gender and regional gaps are largely due to gaps in demand, then, in Pakistan, targeting more schooling resources toward schooling for girls and children in Badin would not have much of an effect.

Second, if supply-side factors indeed are important, on which dimensions of supply should interventions focus? To attain the desired targeted reduction in cognitive achievement gaps, would it be more cost-effective, for example, to increase the number of primary schools of a given quality, to increase the number of middle schools of a given quality, to increase the quality of existing primary schools, or to increase the quality of existing middle schools? If it is worth attempting to target schooling investments, it is desirable to do so in the most cost-effective way.

Third, does targeting force a trade-off between greater equity and reduced productivity, or might both equity and productivity be enhanced by effective targeting? How do the rates of return on targeted investments compare with those to other potential uses of the same resources?

In this chapter, we attempt to answer these questions using a special data set for rural Pakistan designed and generated, in part, with these questions in mind. The first section summarizes the evidence that has led us to conclude that differences in the supply of schools are strongly associated with the gender and regional schooling gaps. Next, we present the simple schooling demand/supply analytic framework we use to assess the relative rates of return on improving the quality and increasing the quantity of schooling. The following section describes the data used in the analysis. Our survey permits us to go beyond previous analyses of the relative returns on changes in the quality and quantity of schooling. It links households with the schools attended by household members. One questionnaire and a set of tests were administered in surveyed households. Another questionnaire and the same set of tests were administered to teachers in surveyed schools. The data set contains, inter alia, measures of preschool ability; a wide range of school "quality" characteristics, some of which—for example, the preschool ability and cognitive achievement of teachers—have not previously been available; other inputs into the education production process; cognitive outputs (literacy and numeracy) of the education production process; and the earnings of employed members of the household.[4] The next section presents estimates of the impact of schooling quality and quantity on cognitive achievement and—through cognitive achievement—on daily earnings in labor markets. This section also presents the implied rates of return on investments in school quality versus quantity for girls and for children in Badin. These estimates permit us to answer the second and third questions posed above. The final section presents our conclusions.

Most studies that have investigated the impact of schooling quality in developing countries focus on its influence on grades or test scores, not on postschool outcomes, and have limited controls for preschool ability and for family and community background. These estimates have yielded mixed results with regard to the magnitude, significance, and even signs of the effects of some variables (for example, teacher/student ratios), but they do fairly consistently find evidence of an impact on achievement of variation in some school inputs such as textbooks and materials.[5] The few studies that consider the impact of school quality on postschooling productivity, proxied primarily by wages, suggest that the impact of schooling quality may be considerable, with rates of return at least as high as those for investing in school quantity.[6] However, none of these studies traces the links from school quality to cognitive outputs and thence to labor productivity. Nor do they control for preschool ability or for family background, so the estimated returns on school quality and quantity may reflect omitted variable and selectivity biases. A further limitation of most of these studies is that the quality indicators used are highly aggregated and crude, depending on variations across large (regional) groupings of schools in such characteristics as number of teachers per student or average teacher schooling.

In contrast, the data that we use in this study permit investigation of the whole chain that links family background and preschool ability through the quality and quantity of schooling to labor market outcomes, not just part of this chain as in previous studies. Through estimates of education production functions that incorporate measures of school quality as well as years of schooling, ability, and family background variables, we are able to assess the relative impacts on learning outcomes of targeted improvements in schooling quality versus targeted improvements in school quantity for girls and for children in Badin. Estimated earnings functions that incorporate measures of cognitive skill permit us to put a value on these learning outcomes by translating them into earnings gains. By linking these gains to estimates of the costs of additional years of schooling and of improvements in quality, we are able to compare rates of return on alternative targeted investments among four groups of children: boys, girls, children in Faisalabad, and children in Badin. For each group, we calculate the rates of return on (a) enabling a child to complete a low-quality primary school, where previously no school was available, (b) raising the quality of a primary school from low to high, and (c) enabling the graduate of a low-quality primary school to complete middle school. Our principal finding is that targeting the relatively educationally disadvantaged groups (girls in general and children in Badin) involves little, if any, sacrifice in aggregate returns to society in Pakistan.

Importance of School Supply

The gaps in primary school enrollment rates documented in column 1 of table 8-1 are associated in large part with differences in school availability among the four groups of children.[7] The third column of table 8-1 reveals the substantial gender and regional gaps in the availability of a local primary school in rural Pakistan. Limiting the

Table 8-2. Decomposing Gaps in Cognitive Skills for the 20–24 Cohort
(percentage)

Indicator	Gender gap[a]	Regional gap[b]
Net predicted gap[c]	68	72
Equating supply of primary school	36	41
Equating demand and supply for some schooling	5	22

a. (Boys − Girls) / Boys.

b. (Faisalabad − Badin) / Faisalabad.

c. The predicted net gap differs from the observed gap because of nonlinearities in the underlying models being estimated.

sample to children for whom a primary school was available narrows the enrollment gap substantially. Conditional on availability, we find that 76 percent of boys and 63 percent of girls start school.[8] For Faisalabad and Badin, the comparable percentages are 80 and 60. Alderman and others (forthcoming, 1995) and Khan, Ross, and Sabot (1992) conclude that these differences in school availability account for a substantial portion of the observed gender and regional gaps in cognitive skills in rural Pakistan.

Table 8-2 summarizes the results of two counterfactual exercises in these studies to decompose the gender and regional gaps into supply and demand components.[9] Had girls and boys had equal access (at the boys' access level) to primary school, and children in Badin the same access to primary school as children in Faisalabad (at the Faisalabad access level), then the gender and regional gaps would have been reduced by more than 40 percent in both cases (from 68 to 36 percent for gender and from 72 to 41 percent for region). Equating demand for some schooling (at least one year of primary school) for girls and boys virtually eliminates the remaining gender gap in cognitive skills, reducing it from 36 to 5 percent. In contrast, equating demand for schooling in Faisalabad and Badin does not eliminate so much of the remaining regional gap in cognitive skills; a gap of 22 percent still remains. In part, this remaining gap reflects differences between regions in parental inputs into the education process and regional differences in how far children who begin school progress in the schooling system. However, a substantial portion of this gap is likely to reflect differences between these two regions in school quality.

Conceptual Framework

In our framework, both the quantity and the quality of schooling received are presumed to be determinants of a child's cognitive achievement, which in turn is presumed to be a determinant of that child's subsequent productivity and earnings, as proxied by annual earnings in paid labor markets.[10] Thus our system of relations includes a cognitive achievement production function (equation 8-1) conditional on the quality of local schools and schooling attainment (equation 8-2); an earnings function dependent in part on cognitive achievement, rather than, as in a conventional Mincerian earnings function, on years of schooling (equation 8-3); and an incremental schooling cost function (equation 8-4). Each of these relations explicitly includes gender and region since we focus on these characteristics in this study and the relations may vary with gender or region.

(8-1) $CA = CA(G, PSA, F, A, QS, SA, R)$,

(8-2) $SA = SA(G, PSA, F, A, P, QS, R, SAV)$,

(8-3) $E = E(G, CA, EX, R)$,

(8-4) $SC = SC(G, SA, QS, R)$

where

A = age

E = earnings

EX = earnings experience (that is, time spent in the paid labor force or time since finishing school)

F = a vector of family background characteristics including parental education and household income

CA = cognitive achievement

G = gender

P = a vector of prices including school fees, transportation costs, and costs of books and other supplies for schooling

PSA = preschool ability

QS = a vector of quality characteristics of schools attended

SA = schooling attainment

SC = school costs

SAV = school availability in the local area

R = region.

To isolate the independent effects of quality and quantity (attainment) on cognitive achievement and to avoid omitted variable bias, the production function 8-1 includes indicators of both, as well as such other determinants of achievement as preschool ability and, as a proxy for out-of-school investments in human capital, family background.

Because schooling attainment and cognitive achievement are simultaneously determined, relations 8-1 and 8-2 must be estimated simultaneously. Estimates of relations 8-1 and 8-2 permit an assessment of the importance of school supply-side factors in determining schooling success, with school quality working through both of these relations and local school availability working directly through the latter.

Using estimates of relations 8-1 and 8-3, we also can trace the effects on boys and girls and on children from different regions of, alternatively, improvements in quality and increases in quantity (attainment) on cognitive achievement and thence earnings.[11] Relation 8-4 provides a measure of the incremental costs of these improvements. We are therefore able to calculate and to compare the rates of return for these alternatives. All of these estimates may reflect differences by gender and by region, either with regard to the parameters or with regard to the levels of right-side variables.

For the relevant time period in rural Pakistan, almost all schools were public. Primary school (generally kindergarten plus five grades) is followed by middle school (grades six to eight), and our analysis below focuses on these two school levels since relatively few individuals continue beyond them.[12] Virtually all students attend primary and middle school in their village or in a nearby village or town. The availability and quality of local schools appear to be determined by district and higher-level decisions, perhaps in response to the wishes of politically powerful individuals such as landlords and military officers, but not in direct response to household demand, though village population and proximity to towns and cities both are positively related to schooling quality and quantity. Therefore, we consider the availability and the quality of locally available schools to be given from the point of view of individual households.[13] Our estimation of the cognitive achievement production function in relation 8-1 is thus conditional on the quality of schools attended by respondents.[14]

The rate of return on a given investment in education is defined as that rate of interest that equalizes the present value of the benefits and the costs of that investment. Figure 8-1 illustrates how we calculate the rates of return (a) on investing in middle schooling for a graduate of an average-quality primary school and (b) on augmenting the quality of primary schooling. $O-U$, $O-P_{LQ}$, $O-P$, $O-P_{HQ}$, and $O-M$ represent the lifetime earnings profiles of, respectively, uneducated workers, graduates from low-, average-, and high-quality primary schools, and graduates from middle schools.[15]

Comparing these profiles during the period in which all these groups are economically active, $O-P$ lies above $O-U$ because workers with five years of primary schooling are presumed to have more productivity-augmenting cognitive skills than uneducated workers. Similarly workers with middle schooling are presumed to have more cognitive skills

Figure 8-1. Social Returns on High-Quality Primary Schooling Compared with Returns on Middle Schooling

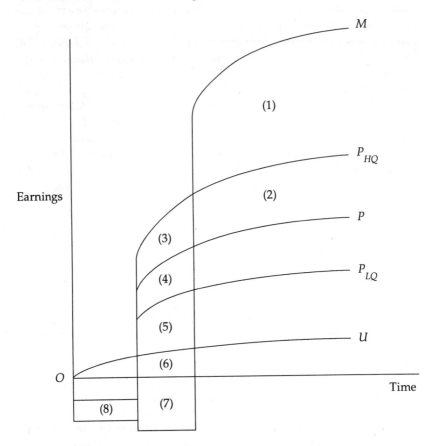

than workers with only average-quality primary schooling, and so $O-M$ lies above $O-P$. Likewise, $O-P_{HQ}$ lies above $O-P$ because workers who attended high-quality primary schools are presumed to have greater cognitive skills than workers who attended average-quality primary schools. The area $1 + 2$ thus signifies the gross returns on middle school for the graduate of an average-quality primary school who otherwise would enter the labor market, and the area $2 + 3$ signifies the gross returns on high-quality primary school for a student who otherwise would attend an average-quality primary school.

The area $4 + 5 + 6$ signifies the opportunity cost of attending middle school, while area 7 represents the direct costs. Since our concern is with policy choices between increasing quantity and improving quality for girls and for children in Badin, our focus is on social and not on private rates of return. Therefore, the direct costs include both those borne by the household and those borne by the government. Area 8 represents the incremental expenditures necessary to transform an average-quality primary school into a high-quality primary school. To estimate rates of return on improving quality and to increasing quantity, we require measures of each of these various components of benefits and costs.

Our presumption is that a student who attends an improved quality primary school would not have been in the labor market but rather would have attended an average-quality primary school, so there is no opportunity cost associated with investing in quality improvement for such students.[16] The opportunity costs of investment in education are often a substantial proportion of total costs, so their absence (or limited role) in this case is likely to have an important influence on the rate of return on improving quality relative to the rate of return on increasing quantity.

Data

Since 1986, the International Food Policy Research Institute (IFPRI), under the auspices of the Pakistan Ministry of Food and Agriculture, has been administering a multipurpose survey to a panel of 800 + rural households containing more than 7,000 individuals drawn from villages in three relatively poor districts—Attock in the Punjab, Dir in the North West Frontier Province, and Badin in the Sind—and one relatively prosperous district—Faisalabad in the Punjab (the only province not represented, Baluchistan, has a small proportion of the rural population). The households have been interviewed approximately four times each year. Human capital modules, on which we draw heavily for this study, were administered in the spring of 1989, the tenth round of the survey. These modules contain, inter alia, measures for individual respondents of the variables needed to estimate our model: that is, family background, school availability, educational attainment, preschool reasoning ability, and postschooling cognitive achievement. A questionnaire designed to yield indicators of school quality also was administered to teachers in the schools attended by sample members.

Our analysis focuses on the 637 respondents between ages ten and twenty-five who had an opportunity to attend one of our sample schools and for whom all variable values were available.[17] Of these, 244 respondents completed at least four years and had nonmissing values for the variables needed to estimate cognitive skills production functions. Descriptive statistics for the measures of particular importance in this study appear in table 8-3 and are discussed below. The greater representation of boys than girls and of respondents from

Table 8-3. Sample Means and Standard Deviations for Cognitive Achievement Production Functions

Characteristic	Selectivity estimation					Production function				
	Full	Boys	Girls	Faisalabad	Badin	Full	Boys	Girls	Faisalabad	Badin
Individual, family, and other characteristics										
Reading score						13.29	13.02	14.05	14.34	11.86
						(7.02)	(6.94)	(7.27)	(7.44)	(7.31)
Math score						11.62	12.29	9.70	14.08	7.24
						(6.70)	(6.67)	(6.47)	(7.01)	(5.10)
Schooling attainment	4.08	4.60	3.06	4.67	2.03	7.28	7.61	6.33	7.61	6.29
	(3.51)	(3.66)	(2.94)	(3.39)	(2.91)	(2.32)	(2.33)	(2.01)	(2.38)	(1.71)
Preschool ability	19.41	20.88	16.56	19.23	18.29	22.70	24.03	18.87	22.82	22.05
	(6.85)	(6.98)	(5.59)	(6.70)	(6.97)	(7.17)	(6.86)	(6.72)	(6.91)	(8.75)
Family income	24.19	24.39	23.80	23.23	21.75	25.52	26.06	23.96	25.08	25.54
	(8.71)	(9.39)	(7.24)	(7.82)	(10.79)	(8.95)	(9.41)	(7.34)	(9.18)	(11.30)
Mother primary or more (percentage)	5.8	5.7	6.0	9.3	0.0	10.7	9.9	12.7	16.8	0.0
Father middle or more (percentage)	20.3	15.2	30.0	26.2	4.5	30.7	23.2	52.4	35.2	4.8
Primary book cost proxy	55.45	55.83	54.71	64.61	56.99	53.37	54.16	51.09	64.51	55.82
	(19.54)	(18.42)	(21.56)	(16.67)	(11.94)	(19.41)	(19.01)	(20.52)	(13.55)	(10.50)
Middle book cost proxy	215.60	217.12	212.68	253.38	169.05	215.62	222.62	195.51	237.32	189.53
	(74.44)	(67.89)	(85.81)	(46.52)	(97.83)	(68.90)	(57.52)	(91.89)	(64.00)	(81.39)
Middle school available (percentage)	92.0	93.1	88.0	98.3	75.3	94.7	97.8	85.7	97.8	85.7

School characteristics

	(1)	(2)	(3)	(4)	(5)	(6)	(7)	(8)	(9)	(10)
Student/teacher ratio	56.27	64.78	39.79	52.82	65.40	57.60	63.08	41.86	53.19	75.70
	(36.74)	(41.41)	(15.28)	(21.62)	(20.76)	(37.90)	(41.77)	(14.99)	(22.58)	(24.76)
Average teacher reading score	19.38	18.86	20.39	20.11	21.75	19.66	19.32	20.65	20.21	23.24
	(4.89)	(5.64)	(2.67)	(3.81)	(3.06)	(5.20)	(5.69)	(3.27)	(4.04)	(2.39)
Average teacher math score	17.39	18.41	15.42	18.52	17.39	18.00	19.63	13.34	20.11	18.64
	(7.48)	(6.74)	(8.41)	(7.28)	(2.77)	(7.94)	(7.32)	(7.83)	(7.52)	(2.66)
Average teacher experience	9.98	10.78	8.42	9.53	9.70	10.21	10.69	8.84	10.67	8.85
	(4.36)	(4.62)	(3.32)	(5.21)	(2.04)	(4.51)	(4.81)	(3.14)	(5.36)	(2.33)
Average teacher schooling	3.30	3.24	3.42	3.28	4.10	3.26	3.24	3.34	3.33	4.35
	(0.69)	(0.74)	(0.57)	(0.38)	(0.62)	(0.60)	(0.64)	(0.48)	(0.40)	(0.60)
Teacher reading quality index						2.70	2.70	2.71	2.90	3.30
						(0.84)	(0.92)	(0.56)	(0.97)	(0.51)
Teacher math quality index						1.69	1.80	1.46	1.81	1.63
						(0.67)	(0.71)	(0.47)	(0.81)	(0.30)
N	637	420	217	301	89	244	181	63	125	21

Note: Standard deviations are in parentheses.

197

Faisalabad than from Badin reflects in part the differences in school availability described above.

Cognitive Achievement

Our measure of cognitive skills was generated by administering (in the regional language) to every person in our sample more than ten years old, and with at least four years of schooling, tests of literacy and numeracy especially designed by the Educational Testing Service.[18] The distribution of the cognitive skills test scores is not truncated, exhibits substantial variance, and appears to be normally distributed, all of which suggests that the tests were appropriate for the population sampled. Because school quality affects scores on our literacy and numeracy tests differently, we report separate production function estimates using the reading and mathematics scores. The sample means suggest that when girls are permitted to progress through the school system, their cognitive achievement compares well with that of boys who have greater access. Girls completing at least four years of schooling score significantly below boys in mathematics but exceed boys on the literacy test. In contrast, children from Badin who progressed through the school system still lag in cognitive achievement in mathematics. Respondents from Faisalabad score nearly twice as high on the mathematics test as do respondents from Badin; however, Badin respondents lag only slightly on the reading test.

School Attainment

We report the mean level of schooling completed (no adjustment is made for repetition) for all respondents for whom a school was available (the selectivity estimation columns of table 8-3) and who completed at least four years of school (the production function columns). As the sample sizes suggest, fewer primary schools are available for girls than for boys. Virtually all of the difference in schooling attainment for respondents who started school is associated with differences in the availability of middle school.[19]

Preschool Ability

To obtain a measure of preschool reasoning ability, we administered Raven's (1956) Coloured Progressive Matrices (CPM), a test of reasoning ability that involves the matching of patterns, to everybody in the sample ten years of age or older.[20] The test is designed so that formal schooling does not influence performance, though performance may reflect early childhood environment as well as innate capacity. The distribution of the CPM test scores is not truncated at either tail; it exhibits substantial variance and appears to be normally distributed. The disaggregated distributions for Dir, the Punjab, and Badin are very similar. Since educational levels differ substantially across regions, this similarity is consistent with the presumption that educational attainment does not influence performance on Raven's CPM test.[21]

Family Background

We summarize family characteristics by indicators of parental schooling and by income (in thousands of rupees). The low level of schooling attainment for parents (in our sample, none of the mothers from Badin had completed primary school) in comparison with the schooling for their children suggests the progress that Pakistan has made in expanding the rural educational system. We use predicted rather than observed household income in relation 8-2. In much of agriculture in developing countries, transitory income fluctuations may be considerable because of weather shocks and limited mechanisms to buffer such shocks. If longer-run income measures determine investments such as schooling, the extent of income variance in the annual data may be misleading regarding the effective income spreads for the analysis of the determinants of cognitive achievement. Similarly, if current income at the time of the survey is influenced by the productivity of respondents who earlier completed schooling, then it will be a positively biased proxy for income at the time schooling decisions were made. Therefore for our sample we use parents' assets and other characteristics to yield an unbiased measure of permanent family income at the time the respondent was of school age.[22]

Price of Schooling

To explain schooling attainment for students for whom a primary school was available, we require cost indicators. Virtually all boys in all regions and all children in Faisalabad who had a primary school available also had access to a middle school. Girls in all other regions and all children in Badin were less fortunate. Expenditures on books and school supplies are dependent not only on the school system, but also on the household's preferences and income. Consequently, they have endogenous components. To obtain an instrumental variable or proxy for the exogenous cost component, we estimate educational expenditure functions including a vector of household characteristics, dummy variables for district, level of schooling, gender, and whether the school was located in the village or a nearby town. The household variables are then held constant to predict exogenous costs, that is, prices. Because of the high correlation among costs for books, clothing, and other fees, we include only textbook costs in our estimates.

School Characteristics

As noted above, the school survey permits us to identify which schools respondents attended. It also provides measures of a rich array of school characteristics—too many to include individually in the cognitive skills production function. Instead, we use the measures to create indexes summarizing the important dimensions of school quality. The teacher quality in reading index is a linear function of teacher literacy, schooling attainment, teaching experience, and experience squared; the teacher quality in mathematics replaces teacher literacy with teacher numeracy. Coefficients for the variables in the index are estimated jointly with the cognitive skills production function. The ratio of students to teachers serves as an index of student-teacher contact. Attempts to create an index of physical characteristics of schools—using linear functions incorporating, for example, measures of the year in which the school was constructed, textbook availability, the number of classrooms with blackboards and chalk, and desk availability—did not add significant explanatory power to the production function. Weights for the component measures are estimated as part of the cognitive skills production function.

The teacher quality index for reading does not differ significantly by gender (in our sample, girls are taught exclusively by women, boys by men). Teachers in Badin actually have a higher reading index than teachers in Faisalabad. Although there is no significant difference in the teacher quality index for mathematics by region, female teachers have a mathematics index well below that of male instructors. There is much greater variation in student/teacher ratios. The student/teacher ratio for girls (42) is not quite two-thirds that for boys (64).[23]

Estimates

Relations 8-1 (cognitive achievement) and 8-2 (schooling attainment conditional on availability) are estimated simultaneously in Behrman and others (1993) by maximizing the joint likelihood functions for educational attainment and the production of cognitive skills, controlling for the sample truncation resulting from the fact that cognitive achievement at each level is observed only for respondents who did not remain in school beyond that level. Schooling attainment—measured as no schooling, less than fourth grade, fourth or fifth grades, and postprimary—is a linear function of the explanatory variables. The selectivity thresholds indicate movements in the latent schooling attainment variable among levels.[24] Because the level of schooling, the quality of schooling, and the ability of the individual all interact with one another,[25] a multiplicative (Cobb-Douglas) functional form is used for the production function—with gender and regional dummies serving as shifters for the constant. Parameter estimates appear in table 8-4. Counting the exponent, more coefficients than variables are associated with the teacher quality indexes. We arbitrarily normalize the coefficient on the average teacher reading (mathematics) test score to 1. Sigma is the standard error of the production function; rho is the correlation coefficient for the production and attainment function error terms. The Wald statistics allow one to reject the null hypothesis that all but the intercept coefficients are zero at the 1 percent significance level for the entire model and for the production functions.

As the results presented in table 8-4 show, assuming all else is equal, a 10 percent increase in schooling attainment raises reading and mathematics scores by just over 4 percent. A 10 percent increase in the teacher quality indexes raises the predicted reading test score by 3 percent and the mathematics score by 1 percent. Lowering the student/teacher ratio by 10 percent raises the predicted mathematics score by 2 percent. Within the production function, the gender and regional dummies allow for quality differences captured by neither the teacher quality index nor the student/teacher ratio. Thus, even though the *t*-ratio on the student/teacher ratio in the reading production function is insignificant and the regional dummy variables are jointly insignificant (Wald statistic = 3.67), the relevant Wald statistic rejects the null hypothesis that the student/teacher ratio and the regional dummies are jointly insignificant determinants of reading. Apparently, the student/teacher ratio is correlated with school quality characteristics not captured by our model.

Holding all other factors constant, there is no evidence that girls or children from Badin are at a disadvantage in mastering reading skills. The coefficients on the regional dichotomous variables suggest that children from Badin are at a significant disadvantage relative to children from Faisalabad in mastering numeracy, even after controlling for all the other variables in our model. There may also be uncaptured factors that place girls at a disadvantage when mastering mathematics skills, although the coefficient on the 0/1 female dummy variable is insignificantly different from zero.

Of course, the other explanatory variables in these relations vary by region and gender. These variations must be taken into account in decomposing variations in cognitive achievement. Based on our cognitive achievement production function estimates (table 8-4)[26] and the sample means (from table 8-3), we derive the predicted cognitive achievement scores for boys and girls and for children of both sexes from Faisalabad and from Badin for our three schooling investment alternatives (holding all other characteristics at their sample means).

Thus, we predict (in table 8-5) cognitive skills after five years (completed primary) of low-quality primary school, five years of high-quality primary, and eight years of schooling (completed middle

Table 8-4. Cognitive Achievement Production Function Estimates

Indicator	Reading		Mathematics	
	Production	Selection	Production	Selection
Female	0.41	−0.72	−0.26	−0.76
	(2.09)	(4.96)	(1.08)	(5.42)
Faisalabad	0.19	1.69	0.92	1.67
	(1.36)	(4.60)	(3.68)	(5.00)
Dir	−0.27	−2.54	0.065	−2.51
	(0.78)	(5.66)	(0.18)	(3.88)
Badin	0.079	−1.23	−0.50	−1.31
	(0.27)	(5.68)	(1.24)	(5.19)
Preschool ability	0.34	0.051	0.42	0.052
	(3.18)	(5.92)	(2.43)	(5.86)
Schooling level	0.42	n.a.	0.41	n.a.
	(4.07)		(3.65)	
Student/teacher ratio	−0.058	−0.0001	−0.16	−0.0001
	(0.80)	(0.06)	(2.71)	(0.09)
Teacher quality	0.29	n.a.	0.10	n.a.
	(2.12)		(2.99)	
Reading/math score	1.00	0.015	1.00	−0.012
			(1.12)	(1.36)
Schooling level	2.36	0.029	1.66	0.14
	(1.04)	(0.28)	(0.45)	(1.11)
Experience	−0.16	0.014	0.01	0.011
	(0.41)	(1.01)	(0.21)	(0.63)
Experience squared	0.024	n.a.	0.15	n.a.
	(0.58)		(1.56)	
Father middle or more	n.a.	0.54	n.a.	0.49
		(3.20)		(3.36)
Family income	n.a.	0.030	n.a.	0.030
		(4.64)		(3.64)
Primary book cost proxy	n.a.	−0.012	n.a.	−0.013
		(4.12)		(3.08)
Middle book cost proxy	n.a.	−0.036	n.a.	-0.034
		(3.92)		(3.65)
Middle school available	n.a.	−8.09	n.a.	−7.76
		(4.03)		(3.49)
Production function constant	1.90	n.a.	2.19	n.a.
Selectivity threshold 1	n.a.	−7.67	n.a.	−7.56
Selectivity threshold 2	n.a.	−7.40	n.a.	−7.30
Selectivity threshold 3	n.a.	−6.58	n.a.	−6.48
Sigma	n.a.	5.44	n.a.	5.56
		(18.37)		(21.27)
Rho	n.a.	−0.008	n.a.	0.182
		(0.05)		(1.04)
Wald statistic (df)	53.02 (11)	257.78 (25)	62.52 (11)	247.31 (25)
N	244	637	244	637

n.a. Not applicable.

Note: Numbers in parentheses are *t*-ratios.

Table 8-5. *Predicted Cognitive Skills at Sample Means*

Skill	Boys	Girls	Faisalabad	Badin
Reading				
Low-quality primary	10.6	12.5	11.9	11.4
High-quality primary	12.2	13.5	12.9	12.1
Average middle	12.9	15.2	14.5	13.8
Mathematics				
Low-quality primary	9.4	8.2	11.0	5.7
High-quality primary	10.9	9.0	11.5	6.1
Average middle	11.4	10.0	13.4	6.9
Cognitive skills				
Low-quality primary	20.0	20.7	22.9	19.8
High-quality primary	23.1	22.5	24.4	21.2
Average middle	24.3	25.1	27.8	24.1

school), including five years at a low-quality primary school. A low-quality primary school is defined to be one with all quality measures set to one-half standard deviation below the mean for each group.[27] Under all three scenarios, girls perform better than boys in reading. This is consistent with the superior performance of women on the reading test reported in table 8-3 and suggests that the gender gap in literacy in rural Pakistan is a function of lower schooling attainment by women—not quality differences in schools. There is no significant regional difference in predicted reading scores. However, the model predicts lower levels of numeracy for girls and for all children from Badin.

The impact of quality differences on cognitive achievement is substantial relative to the effect of increasing schooling attainment. Raising the quality of primary schools in Badin raises cognitive skills by 1.4 points $(21.2 - 19.8)$, or 32 percent of the gain a student from a low-quality primary school would realize from completing middle school. For girls, the gain in cognitive skills from raising primary school quality is 41 percent of the gain from completing middle school.

To measure the value of these variations in cognitive skills, we rely on estimates of the monthly wage labor earnings function provided by Alderman and others (forthcoming, 1996). We summarize their results briefly here. The wage labor market is still quite small in rural Pakistan.[28] Of 2,285 respondents for whom nonmissing values of all relevant variables were available, 207 were engaged in wage labor (table 8-6 provides descriptive statistics). These workers move back and forth between wage employment and (primarily) own-farm agricultural work. As a result, current wage workers have spent just over half of their working careers in wage jobs.

Table 8-7 provides maximum likelihood parameter estimates of the earnings function with controls for self-selection into wage employ-

Table 8-6. Sample Means and Standard Deviations for Earnings Function

Characteristic	All adults	Wage workers
Individual characteristics		
Wage worker	0.09	n.a.
Log (wage)	n.a.	6.74
		(0.64)
Female	0.53	0.06
Attock	0.20	0.32
Faisalabad	0.19	0.22
Dir	0.22	0.18
Badin	0.39	0.28
Total experience	19.77	19.11
	(17.25)	(13.85)
Wage labor experience proxy	0.32	11.85
	(1.61)	(3.63)
Cognitive skills proxy	4.06	12.29
	(10.18)	(14.23)
Body-mass index proxy	0.19	0.21
	(0.01)	(0.01)
Father was a wage worker	0.14	0.18
Household characteristics		
Distance to work proxy	19.68	16.97
	(10.80)	(20.72)
Males over 16	3.25	3.07
	(1.79)	(1.55)
Net transfers	5,180.48	4,146.06
	(15,456.56)	(14,618.69)
Rain-fed acres	2.72	2.94
	(9.49)	(10.98)
Irrigated acres	6.09	2.27
	(15.07)	(6.16)
N	2,285	207

n.a. Not applicable.
Note: Standard deviations are in parentheses.

ment.[29] All else remaining equal, women are much less likely to enter wage employment than men; however, the estimates suggest no significant regional variation in the probability of wage employment, controlling for other determinants.[30] Respondents are more likely to have wage employment if they are younger,[31] have higher cognitive skills, live closer to the location of wage jobs, or live in households farming smaller plots.

For those employed, the log of monthly earnings is regressed on cognitive skills, health status, wage labor market experience, as well as gender and regional dummies. Because cognitive skills, health status (body mass index, BMI), and years of wage labor experience are likely to be correlated with unobserved determinants of wages, Alderman and others (forthcoming, 1996) derive proxy instrumental variables.[32]

Table 8-7. Wage Function Estimates, Controlling for Selectivity

Characteristic	Log (wage) function	Selectivity controls
Female	−0.248	−0.952
	(0.68)	(3.93)
Faisalabad	−0.394	−0.129
	(2.47)	(0.60)
Dir	−0.304	−0.303
	(1.79)	(1.36)
Badin	0.072	−0.144
	(0.52)	(0.85)
Cognitive skills proxy	0.012	0.019
	(7.07)	(2.45)
Wage proxy for educated labor experience	0.035	−0.006
	(1.70)	(0.24)
BMI proxy	18.15	28.27
	(1.20)	(2.86)
Years of schooling proxy		0.027
		(1.25)
Preschool ability		0.015
		(1.51)
Total experience		−0.011
		(2.32)
Father was a wage worker		0.420
		(2.88)
Distance to work proxy		−0.011
		(3.99)
Males over 16		−0.075
		(2.52)
Net transfers		0.000
		(1.43)
Rain-fed acres		
Attock		−0.012
		(1.91)
Dir		−0.083
		(1.71)
Irrigated acres		
Attock		−0.054
		(0.26)
Faisalabad		−0.125
		(3.34)
Dir		−0.078
		(0.91)
Badin		−0.013
		(1.39)
Constant	2.64	−6.20
Sigma		0.602
		(11.50)
Rho		0.369
		(1.27)
Wald statistic (df)	44.9 (7)	157.7 (27)
N	207	2,285

Note: Numbers in parentheses are *t*-ratios.

Table 8-8. Selected School Costs as a Function of School Quality

Characteristic	Public expenditures		Distance to school (time)	
	(1)	(2)	Boys	Girls
Teacher reading quality index	8.62	3.71	-8.22	-1.31
	(2.40)	(1.92)	(5.95)	(0.76)
Teacher math quality index	-0.75	0.14	0.18	-0.48
	(1.32)	(0.47)	(2.85)	(2.26)
Student/teacher ratio	-0.59	-0.036	-0.10	-0.061
	(5.75)	(0.66)	(2.75)	(2.27)
Female	1.08	-3.40	n.a.	n.a.
	(0.11)	(0.62)		
Attock	n.a.	14.95	-2.45	-11.72
		(1.42)	(0.42)	(2.42)
Faisalabad	1.69	-2.22	-4.61	-14.09
	(0.16)	(0.40)	(0.79)	(3.19)
Dir	21.96	-0.42	10.87	-18.31
	(2.43)	(0.09)	(1.33)	(3.16)
Constant	44.64	-7.80	35.91	41.63
Adjusted R^2	0.394	0.026	0.249	0.097
F (probability)	7.86	1.28	8.62	3.46
	(0.001)	(0.27)	(0.001)	(0.003)
N	75	75	139	200

n.a. Not applicable.
Note: Numbers in parentheses are t-ratios. Figures in column (1) refer to monthly teacher salaries per pupil; column (2) figures are for the annual recurring nonsalary expenses per pupil.

They found no evidence that years of schooling or preschool ability has any effect on wages independent of cognitive achievement; that is, they found no evidence of credentialism or screening effects. Wage labor experience affects wages only for respondents who have completed primary school. The coefficients on the female dummy variable and the body mass index instrumental variable are jointly significant (Wald statistic = 9.27), suggesting that, all else remaining equal, the logarithm of the monthly wage for women is −0.42 less than that for men.[33] Wages in Faisalabad are significantly lower than wages in Badin (the finding of lower wages in Faisalabad is consistent with results reported by Kozel and Alderman 1990 for an urban sample). Alderman and others (forthcoming, 1996) find that the regional variations are a function of differences in the occupational composition of the work force. Highly paid supervisory positions are relatively more common among respondents from Badin, lower-paying semiskilled positions are relatively more common among respondents from Faisalabad. Occupational status is in part a function of cognitive skills. To the extent that regional dummy variables and cognitive skills are each correlated with occupational status, the coefficients on the regional dummy variables are capturing some of the effect of cognitive skills on wages. This has the effect of biasing the coefficient on cognitive skills down somewhat.

The last component required for a rate-of-return comparison is the calculation of school costs. Behrman and others (1993) found that per student teacher pay varies with measures of school quality, but that nonsalary recurring expenditure does not. Their results appear as columns 1 and 2 in table 8-8.[34] Using these results, we calculate the public expenditures per pupil at each school quality level (columns 1 and 2 of table 8-9; expenditure estimates not based on table 8-8 are sample means). Note that the provision of even low-quality primary education for girls is relatively expensive—largely because of the high level of student-teacher contact that prevails at girls' schools.

We found no evidence that private out-of-pocket expenditures on books, clothing, and school fees vary with our quality measures. However, we did find that the distance students travel to school does vary with quality and in a different fashion for boys and girls (we found no evidence that out-of-pocket expenditures vary by gender). The last two columns of table 8-8 provide those regression estimates. Students who travel a longer distance tend to have smaller classes. A longer commute gives boys higher-quality mathematics instruction, but lower-quality reading instruction. The longer commute gives girls *lower-*quality mathematics instruction. To translate variations in commuting time into dollar costs, we use estimates of the determinants of the demand for schooling in Alderman, Ross, and Sabot (1991).[35]

The final dimension needed to calculate the costs of alternative schooling options is the opportunity cost of schooling. We do not have

Table 8-9. *Schooling Costs, by Gender and Region*
(rupees per year)

Gender and region	Teacher salary per pupil	Recurring nonsalary expense per pupil	Private out-of-pocket expenses	Opportunity cost of schooling at age 15
Boys				
No school	0.0	0.0	0.0	6,589.8
Low-quality primary	198.1	2.8	282.1	8,376.2
High-quality primary	444.7	2.8	280.9	8,693.9
Average middle	516.1	34.0	631.6	n.a.
Girls				
No school	0.0	0.0	0.0	3,346.9
Low-quality primary	508.5	7.5	310.6	4,289.9
High-quality primary	583.5	7.5	303.7	4,385.2
Average middle	1,073.2	56.6	634.9	n.a.
Faisalabad				
No school	0.0	0.0	0.0	5,784.3
Low-quality primary	190.2	3.3	282.2	7,616.6
High-quality primary	356.8	3.3	280.4	7,753.3
Average middle	999.5	34.2	929.4	n.a.
Badin				
No school	0.0	0.0	0.0	6,997.3
Low-quality primary	213.2	0.16	279.8	8,583.8
High-quality primary	367.4	0.16	279.2	8,705.1
Average middle	604.1	14.4	351.2	n.a.

n.a. Not applicable.

estimates of the value of production within the household or on the family farm, and our wage labor sample includes few observations for school-age children. On the assumption that rural Pakistanis not in school typically enter the wage labor market at age fifteen, we use the estimated wage of a respondent with no experience as a measure of the opportunity cost of schooling for a fifteen year old.[36] To bracket the opportunity cost of younger children in our subsequent calculations, we use two extreme bounds. First, we assume zero opportunity cost for children fourteen and younger. Second, we assume that there is zero opportunity cost to attending the first grade, but that the opportunity cost rises linearly until it reaches the market wage at age fifteen.

The bracketing is important because, as table 8-9 indicates, opportunity costs are potentially the dominant cost of schooling. Column 1 presents estimates of the annual teacher salaries per pupil in rupees. The higher costs for girls reflect a lower student/teacher ratio and the lower variance in that ratio between high- and low-quality primary schools. Column 2 reports the much lower charge for recurring nonsalary expenses per pupil. Column 3 presents out-of-pocket annual household expenditures per student. There is little variation in these expenditures by region and gender. The variation in private expenditures between high- and low-quality primary schools reflects the small savings from the shorter commute (on average) to high-quality schools observed in our sample. Column 4 reports the opportunity cost of attending a year of school at age fifteen for a child with no previous schooling, with five years of low-quality primary school, and with five years of high-quality primary school. Gender and regional differences reflect the impact of the gender and regional dummy variables in the wage equation, which as noted above reflect differences in the occupational composition of our sample.[37] Within each gender and region category, the opportunity cost reflects the impact on the logarithm of monthly wage earnings of the cognitive skills obtained in low- and high-quality primary schools.

We turn now to the calculation of the private and social rates of return on various schooling investments. The benefits of improving the quality and quantity of schooling are represented by the discounted present values of the resulting increases in postschooling lifetime (four decades) earnings. We perform the following simulation exercise. A student enters primary school at age eight and attends school for five years. The student achieves a particular level of cognitive skills at a particular annual cost depending on whether the student (a) attended an average low-quality primary school or (b) an average high-quality primary school. If the student leaves after primary school (at age thirteen), the student enters productive work at age fifteen and works until age sixty.[38] As a third option, we explore what happens if a student attends three years of an average-quality middle school after attending

Table 8-10. *Rates of Return on Alternative Schooling Investments*
(percent)

Gender, region, and level of schooling	Social		Private	
	(1)	*(2)*	*(1)*	*(2)*
Boys				
Low-quality primary vs. no school	33.0	19.2	40.7	20.3
Middle school after low-quality primary	5.7	2.2	6.6	2.4
High- vs. low-quality primary	16.8	19.1	n.a.	n.a.
Girls				
Low-quality primary vs. no school	20.0	15.4	30.3	18.8
Middle school after low-quality primary	3.6	1.4	5.8	2.3
High- vs. low-quality primary	17.5	20.0	n.a.	n.a.
Faisalabad				
Low-quality primary vs. no school	33.0	20.0	40.5	21.3
Middle school after low-quality primary	5.2	2.3	6.7	2.8
High- vs. low-quality primary	13.1	14.5	n.a.	n.a.
Badin				
Low-quality primary vs. no school	31.9	18.1	39.7	18.4
Middle school after low-quality primary	5.2	1.7	6.2	2.0
High- vs. low-quality primary	12.7	14.0	n.a.	n.a.

n.a. Not applicable.

Note: (1) Assuming the opportunity cost of attending school is limited to age fifteen; (2) assuming a linear extrapolation of the age fifteen opportunity cost for younger children.

an average low-quality primary school. That student starts productive work at age sixteen and works for forty-four years.

Table 8-10 reports social and private returns for the three targeting alternatives for boys, girls, children in Faisalabad, and children in Badin under our two bounding opportunity cost assumptions.[39] The rates of return on the provision of middle- and low-quality primary school do not incorporate capital costs. The rates of return on improving quality are understated to the extent that improvements in quality reduce repetition rates and hence recurrent costs.[40] All rates of return are understated to the extent that social benefits exceed private benefits or to the extent that there are private benefits (for example, better health and nutrition, better information processing capacities for purchases, and greater efficiency in household production) that are not included in these calculations. The only benefits to education included in the analysis are increased earnings, which are assumed to reflect directly economic productivity, narrowly defined.

The social rates of return on the provision of even a low-quality primary school for all four groups are high—between 15 and 33 percent, depending on the treatment of opportunity costs. The high returns on improving quality reflect the absence of any opportunity cost to the students and the absence of higher capital costs for students already enrolled in school. For the purposes of this chapter, the key finding is that rates of return from targeting the educationally disadvantaged groups are high. The return on improving the quality of a low-quality primary school in Badin is comparable to that in Faisalabad for each of the four calculations. The return on improving the quality of primary schools is slightly higher for girls than for boys, reflecting the lower cost of a smaller adjustment in class size for girls. Although the returns on investing in a low-quality primary school for girls are lower than those for boys, they are high relative to those in noneducational marginal investments.[41] Expanding the number of middle schools has the lowest return of the three alternatives. The implication is that targeting girls in all regions or all children in Badin would not involve a substantial efficiency trade-off relative to investing in middle schools for boys or children in Faisalabad.

Conclusions

Schooling is distributed unequally by gender and by region in many developing countries. As a result, the gains from schooling also are distributed unequally. In this chapter, we investigate the consequences of targeting to improve the schooling attainment of two disadvantaged groups, defined by gender (girls) and by region (Badin), in rural Pakistan using an unusually rich micro data set. We address three major points.

First, supply-side factors appear to be important in determining the level and the distribution of schooling performance in rural Pakistan. Our results suggest that, in addition to household demand considerations, both the availability of local schooling and the quality of those schools are significant factors in understanding the observed patterns, including the gender and regional gaps: 40 percent or more of gender and regional gaps in cognitive achievement are associated with gender and regional gaps in local school availability. Thus it would appear that there is leverage for targeted policies to operate through school supply to improve the distribution of the benefits of schooling.

Second, the rates of return on investments in school quantity and quality for all girls and for all children in Badin are high and, for the most part, comparable to the returns on corresponding investments for boys and children in Faisalabad. Making even low-quality primary schools available has the highest return for all groups except girls under our high-bound estimates of opportunity costs. In all cases, raising the quality of primary schools has a substantially higher rate of return than expanding the availability of middle schools.

Third, the estimated social rates of return on targeted schooling investments that expand the quantity of even low-quality primary schools and that improve the quality of primary schools are fairly high regardless of gender and region in rural Pakistan. Therefore targeting investments in schooling in rural Pakistan in order to reduce educational inequities would not have high opportunity costs in terms of forgoing other much more productive investments. Thus equity can be increased without sacrificing much in the way of productivity.

Computational Appendix 8-1

The equations in table 8-8 are ordinary least squares regressions estimated using the SAS computer package REGRESSION procedure. The equations in tables 8-4 and 8-7 use the MAXLIK applications module to the GAUSS computer package.

The production function estimated in columns 1 and 3 of table 8-4 regresses the mathematics or reading score on

$(\alpha_0 + \alpha_1 \text{Female} + \alpha_2 \text{Faisalabad} + \alpha_3 \text{Dir} + \alpha_4 \text{Badin}) \times (\text{Preschool Ability})^{\beta_1} \times (\text{Schooling Attainment})^{\beta_2} \times (\text{Student/Teacher Ratio})^{\beta_3} \times (\text{Teacher Quality})^{\beta_4} + \epsilon$; Teacher Quality $= (\gamma_0 \text{Mathematics/Reading} + \gamma_1 \text{Schooling Attainment} + \gamma_2 \text{Experience} + \gamma_3 \text{Experience}^2)$,

where the αs, βs, and γs are parameters to be estimated and ϵ is an error term.[42] Counting the exponent, more coefficients than variables are associated with the teacher quality indexes. We normalize the equation arbitrarily by setting $\gamma_0 = 1$.

To control for the simultaneous determination of schooling attainment, we start by assuming that a latent continuous schooling attainment index is a linear function of the variables in columns 2 and 4 of table 8-4 and a normally distributed error term v. Schooling attainment is observed as no schooling, less than fourth grade, fourth or fifth grades, and postprimary.[43] Let τ_1 be the threshold parameter for the transition from no schooling to less than fourth grade; τ_2 be the parameter for the transition from less than fourth grade to grades four or five; and τ_3 be the parameter for the transition from fourth or fifth grades to postprimary schooling. The probability that a particular respondent who has completed his or her schooling will be observed as completing grades four or five is the probability that the predicted value of the latent schooling attainment function plus v lies between τ_2 and τ_3. This is the standard ordered probit model. However, our sample contains a number of students still in school, for whom we do not observe final schooling attainment. The probability that a particular respondent who is still in school will be observed in grades four or five is the probability that the predicted value of the latent schooling attainment function plus v exceeds τ_2.

We obtain estimates of the coefficients of the cognitive skills and schooling attainment functions by maximizing the bivariate normal likelihood functions for ϵ and v. Sigma is the standard error of the production function; rho is the correlation coefficient for the production and attainment function error terms.

The earnings function presented in table 8-7 defines the logarithm of monthly earnings to be a linear function of the variables listed in column 1 and an error term. The sample is truncated, in that we observe wages only for respondents currently engaged in wage work. To control for the resulting sample selection bias, we start by assuming there is some latent index of the value of wage work to the respondent, which is a linear function of the variables in column 2 plus an error term. The probability that a respondent is engaged in wage work is the probability that the expected value of the latent value index plus the error term exceeds a threshold parameter, arbitrarily set to zero.

Notes

1. See, for example, Behrman (1990a, 1990b, 1990c); Birdsall and Sabot (1993); Colclough (1982); Eisemon (1988); Haddad and others (1990); King (1990); King and Hill (1993); Knight and Sabot (1990); Psacharopoulos (1985, 1988); Schultz (1988, 1993); UNDP (1990); and World Bank (1980, 1981, 1990, 1991).

2. The gender distinction is easier to measure in Pakistan than in many countries because of the prevalence of single-sex schools.

3. The schooling enrollment and availability data are taken from Alderman, Ross, and Sabot (1991); the cognitive achievement data by gender from Alderman and others (forthcoming, 1995); the data by region from Khan, Ross, and Sabot (1992). The gender gaps in enrollment rates and primary school availability are consistent with data drawn from the Pakistan Integrated Household Survey, a nationally representative sample for 1990–91 (Sather and Lloyd 1993). Large gender gaps in schooling and other human resources in Pakistan on an aggregate level in comparison with other countries with more or less the same real gross domestic product per capita are reported in Behrman and Schneider (1993). Other characteristics, such as low income, also may be of interest for targeting. As is often the case, and is certainly true for rural Pakistan, however, regional differences are correlated with a large fraction of variations in income. Therefore we concentrate on gender and region in this study and leave questions about possible targeting by income to other analyses.

4. In human capital models, it is the output of schooling—cognitive and other skills—not such inputs to educational production as years of schooling, that is presumed to affect subsequent productivity. The variance in cognitive skills among children with the same number of years of schooling is generally high. Some of the variance is due to differences among children in such other inputs to educational production as ability and out-of-school investments in human capital made by parents, which are not directly influenced by government policy. Some of the variation, however, is due to differences in the quality of schooling, a policy variable. This implies that improving the quality of schooling is an alternative to increasing the quantity as a means of raising the skill level and productivity of the labor force. Most data sets are limited to measures of schooling attainment (grades, years, or levels of schooling) that preclude investigating the impact of quality differentials on cognitive achievement. For example, the only other data set of which we are aware that contains data on cognitive achievement of both students and teachers together with other socioeconomic information is that for Northeast Brazil, analyzed by Hanushek,

Gomes-Neto, and Harbison (1992) and by Harbison and Hanushek (1992). But this data set includes neither preschool ability measures nor information with which to assess the impact of cognitive achievement on postschooling outcomes.

5. See the recent surveys in Fuller (1986); Haddad and others (1990); Hanushek (1986, 1989); Hanushek, Gomes-Neto, and Harbison (1992); Harbison and Hanushek (1992).

6. See Behrman and Birdsall (1983, 1985); Behrman, Birdsall, and Kaplan (1994); Behrman and Sussangkarn (1989); and King and Bellew (1988).

7. We consider a school to have been available if, when that individual was of the appropriate age for that school level, there was a school (for that person's gender) at that level in the same village or in a village sufficiently nearby that costs of travel did not preclude attendance by students from the same village in the same age cohort and of the same gender. Our school survey indicated whether a school was available in the village at the time the respondent was of school age. If a respondent was from a village not included in the school survey, we proxied school availability by determining the earliest date a respondent from the village attended school in or near the village. We verified, in villages in which we administered the school survey, that the proxy was an accurate indicator of the year the school was first available. For the ten to eighteen age cohort, just under 30 percent of those with some schooling attended primary school outside of their home village. Of course, the travel time to a school defined as available in this manner may be sufficiently great to discourage some students. For that reason, we include distance to school variables in the schooling attainment relation estimated below.

8. Where distance is not a factor, that is, when the school is located in the child's village, the conditional probability of attending school rises to over 90 percent for both boys and girls.

9. These decompositions are conditional on the assumption that school supplies are not determined importantly by local household demands, an assumption that is discussed further in the next section.

10. Increased cognitive achievement generally is thought to be a major product of schooling. There may be other products as well (such as increased discipline), but we do not have measures of them, so we proceed as if cognitive achievement is the key output of schooling (or is highly correlated with other products).

11. There are relatively few data sets for developing countries that include both earnings and cognitive achievement test scores. Those that do suggest that earnings are affected significantly by cognitive achievement (see, for example, Boissiere, Knight, and Sabot 1985; Glewwe 1990, 1992; Knight and Sabot 1990).

12. Students continuing in school usually complete two more grades (nine and ten) before sitting for the matric exam, then possibly two more grades (eleven and twelve) before taking the F.A. or F.Sc. exam, and possibly two more grades (thirteen and fourteen) before taking the B.A. or B.Sc. exam.

13. Of course, households may have some indirect effect on the availability and the characteristics of governmental schools through the political process. We do not have longitudinal data that would permit the investigation of whether unobserved community characteristics determine the availability and quality of local schooling (see Rosenzweig and Wolpin 1986; Pitt, Rosenzweig, and Gibbons in chapter 6 of this volume).

14. In our sample districts, there are no private schools. In principle, location (hence, availability of schooling) can be changed by migration. But migration

is very limited within rural Pakistan (though there is more emigration from rural to urban areas). Fewer than 2 percent of respondents in our sample attended primary school away from the immediate vicinity of their village. Therefore we basically avoid the analytic problems due to migration that are discussed in Rosenzweig and Wolpin (1988).

15. We include in our analysis only the returns that are captured in earnings, not other effects of schooling such as those on health, nutrition, fertility, and enjoyment of leisure time. If such effects are positive, our procedure underestimates the returns on schooling. If they are more positive for females than for males as usually is assumed, this underestimation is greater for females than for males.

16. There are two cases where opportunity cost is relevant to investment in quality improvements. In the first case, the improved quality induces some increase in primary school enrollment; in the second, students are induced to extend their postprimary schooling because of higher-quality primary schools. In both cases, the private returns for such students must outweigh the private costs (including the opportunity costs) for them to be induced to attend school. Our estimate of the private rate of return on improving quality for students already in primary school underestimates the total returns on quality improvements by failing to incorporate these incremental gains (though it is possible that the incremental social costs of any additional publicly provided inputs outweigh the incremental private gains).

17. As noted below, our test of preschool ability was administered only to respondents ten years of age and older. Current measures of school quality are less likely to be valid for older respondents. The cutoff at age twenty-five balances the desire for more observations against the validity of our quality measures.

18. Since tests were administered only to persons with at least four years of schooling, scores had to be imputed for those with less schooling. Those with no education were assigned zero scores. (The scores of a subsample of the uneducated who were given the tests confirmed the appropriateness of this assignment.) Respondents with one to three years of schooling and qualified respondents who failed to take the test are kept in the sample for the estimates of the schooling attainment relations. Both tests have been used successfully in research on human capital accumulation and labor markets in East and West Africa (see Knight and Sabot 1990; Glewwe 1990, 1992; Behrman and Lavy 1994). We assume that cognitive skills so measured, perhaps several years after the completion of school, reflect the cognitive skills at the time of termination of school. That is, there is not subsequent investment or depreciation in cognitive skills. Estimates in Behrman, Ross, and Sabot (1991) indicate that time and experience subsequent to schooling do not affect cognitive achievement in our data. For this reason, we do not include age in the estimates that are presented below in table 8-4.

19. For example, 98 percent of boys completing four years of schooling had a middle school available, while fewer than 86 percent of girls had the option of continuing in school. Alderman and others (forthcoming, 1995) found no significant difference in the probability that boys and girls would go on to middle school were one available.

20. Since the tests were administered to people ten years and older, rather than preschool ability, it might be more accurate to refer to these tests as measuring ability that is independent of schooling. But such phraseology is cumbersome, so, with this caveat, we continue to refer to these test results as measuring preschool ability.

21. The average score on the Raven's CPM test, however, is roughly 6 points (out of a possible 35) lower for women than for men even though this test was designed to be gender neutral (Raven 1956). Court (1983) surveys forty-five studies in dozens of countries and concludes that observed gender differences in a minority of studies "do not justify the production of separate norms for the two sexes." But none of the studies of the CPM test that Court surveys was conducted in Pakistan or in other Islamic societies. The exploration of this phenomenon, which is reported in Alderman and others (forthcoming, 1995), tentatively suggests that this result is due to early childhood acculturation that is not otherwise related to the variables in the present analysis.

22. To obtain predicted income, we first regress current household income on parental characteristics, including education, employment, and acreage farmed, if any. We then use the parameters of this equation together with measures of the corresponding variables for each respondent's parents to obtain a measure of the parents' permanent income in 1989 rupees. Our regression explains 23 percent of the variation in household income. Seventeen of the twenty-four explanatory variables have statistically significant coefficients of the expected sign. Among the 846 households in our sample for which permanent income data could be calculated in this procedure, average household income is just over Rs23,000, with a standard deviation of Rs13,500.

23. Student/teacher ratios in our sample are higher than those published by Pakistan's Ministry of Education, which reports ratios of 34 and 36 for boys and girls, respectively, in rural Punjab and 36 and 34, respectively, in rural Sind in 1990. The gender difference in our sample can be explained by the tendency for girls' schools to draw mainly from the immediate village, while boys' schools often draw students from nearby villages as well.

24. When the latent schooling attainment variable exceeds threshold 1, we model the respondent as having attended at least some school. Threshold 2 corresponds to the completion of grade four, hence, eligibility to take the cognitive skills tests. Threshold 3 corresponds to completion of primary school.

25. A family background index was found to be insignificant for this sample and, hence, is dropped from the estimates reported here. The school infrastructure index also proved insignificant. The coefficients on the teacher quality indexes and student/teacher ratio variable are not affected substantially by dropping these other indexes. Adding other measures—for example, whether instruction is in the language spoken at home—to the teacher quality index alters the value of coefficients on the index components but does not alter the impact of the index on student cognitive skills. See Behrman and others (1993) for more details and for explorations of alternative specifications.

26. In our simulations, we use even insignificant coefficients as "best point estimates." Setting these coefficient values to zero does not alter the major implications of the simulations.

27. For example, for girls, teaching quality in reading at a low-quality primary school is represented by subtracting half the standard deviation (0.51/2) from the mean of the teacher reading quality index, 3.30, to yield 3.04.

28. No direct estimates of the contribution of cognitive skills to productivity in agriculture are currently available. Also, as we note above, we do not incorporate possible schooling effects on household production. The impact of education on wage earnings captures the impact of education on the shadow price of labor if factor markets are competitive or if segmentation of factor markets neither raises nor lowers the return on education in wage labor relative to the return on other activities. Alderman and others (forthcoming, 1996) find

no evidence of credentialist or screening biases in the educational structure of wages.

29. This procedure yields consistent estimates of the parameters. The corresponding ordinary least squares estimates explain 22 percent of the variation in log earnings.

30. Regional variations in distance to wage work and acreage farmed explain most of the regional variation in the probability of wage employment.

31. The total labor market experience variable is age minus fifteen or age minus the age that the respondent completed school, whichever is smaller.

32. BMI is defined as an individual's weight in kilograms/height^2 and has been widely used as an index for identifying obesity or malnutrition—and related health status—in adults in various societies in the epidemiological literature and increasingly in the economics literature. Cole (1991, p. 106) surveys the epidemiological literature and concludes that BMI "is the best weight-stature index" for such purposes. Fogel (1991a, p. 31) states that "Extensive clinical and epidemiological studies over the past two decades have shown that height at given ages, weight at given ages, and weight-for-height (body mass index) are effective predictors of the risk of morbidity and mortality." Behrman and Lavy (1994); Behrman and Wolfe (1987); and Fogel (1989, 1991b) are examples in the recent economics literature that use BMI extensively, with references therein to a number of studies that also use BMI.

33. The average body mass index for women is 0.091 points below that for men, implying a gender effect of $-0.248 - (18.15 \times 0.0094) = -0.419$.

34. The F-test on the latter equation provides no evidence that nonsalary recurring expenditures vary with any of our quality measures. However, teacher pay per student rises with teacher quality for reading and as student/teacher contact improves. Separate estimates indicate that teacher pay is positively related to teacher quality in mathematics. Apparently schools with high-quality mathematics teachers tend to have low rates of student-teacher contact.

35. Probit estimates find the probability of starting school as a function of distance (significantly different for boys and girls) and the cost of books, among other factors. By dividing the probit coefficients for the cost of books variable by the coefficient for distance to school, we obtain a rupee price for the impact of a minute of daily commuting time on the decision to go to school—1.74 rupees for girls, 0.38 rupees for boys.

36. Our sample includes a thirteen year old and a fifteen year old with no experience. Their wages do not differ substantially from the predicted wage. Our opportunity cost estimates are also consistent with the wages of other teenagers in our wage sample adjusted for years of experience.

37. Thus, the reported opportunity costs overstate the regional and gender differences a new entrant to the wage labor force would expect to face. In estimating rates of return below, it is the variation in the opportunity cost across alternative schooling investments rather than the opportunity cost itself that matters.

38. The choice of age of retirement has no effect on the relative ranking of returns. The value of work before age fifteen in the simulation is bracketed by the alternative opportunity cost assumptions.

39. The private returns estimates subtract public expenditures. The calculated private rate of return on improving quality would be infinite since the out-of-pocket cost is actually (marginally) smaller for the high-quality school.

40. Hanushek, Gomes-Neto, and Harbison (1992) argue that the rates of return on changes in schools that reduce repetition in Brazil would be very high.

41. In our sample, virtually all of the youngest boys have access to a primary school, so that this investment option is not likely to be very important.

42. We estimated preliminary versions of this regression using additive and multiplicative error terms with little qualitative difference in the results reported. As noted above, the variables in the teacher quality index are averages for all teachers at the school. The average teacher mathematics score is used to explain student mathematics scores; the average teacher reading score is used to explain student reading scores.

43. Our raw data indicate the actual number of years of schooling completed. However, because so few respondents completed certain intermediate years, we collapsed the number of schooling transitions to obtain reliable estimates of the thresholds.

References

Alderman, Harold, Jere R. Behrman, David R. Ross, and Richard Sabot. Forthcoming, 1995. "Decomposing the Gap in Cognitive Skills in a Poor Rural Economy." *Journal of Human Resources.*

_____ . Forthcoming, 1996. "The Returns to Endogenous Human Capital in Pakistan's Rural Wage Labor Market." *Oxford Bulletin* 58(1).

Alderman, Harold, David R. Ross, and Richard Sabot. 1991. "Who Goes to School in Rural Pakistan?" International Food Policy Research Institute, Washington, D.C.; Williams College, Williamstown, Mass.

Behrman, Jere R. 1990a. *The Action of Human Resources and Poverty on One Another: What We Have Yet to Learn.* Washington, D.C.: Population and Human Resources Department, World Bank.

_____ . 1990b. *Human Resource Led Development?* ARTEP/International Labour Organisation, New Delhi, India.

_____ . 1990c. "Women's Schooling and Nonmarket Productivity: A Survey and A Reappraisal." Prepared for the Women in Development Division, Population and Human Resources Department, World Bank. University of Pennsylvania, Philadelphia, Penn.

_____ . 1993. "Investing in Female Education for Development." *Journal of Educational Planning and Administration* 7: 393–412.

Behrman, Jere R., and Nancy Birdsall. 1983. "The Quality of Schooling: Quantity Alone is Misleading." *American Economic Review* 73: 928–46.

_____ . 1985. "The Quality of Schooling: Reply." *American Economic Review* 75: 1202–05.

Behrman, Jere R., Nancy Birdsall, and Robert Kaplan. 1994. "The Quality of Schooling and Labor Market Outcomes in Brazil: Some Further Explorations." Williams College, Williamstown, Mass.; World Bank, Washington, D.C.

Behrman, Jere R., Shahrukh Khan, David Ross, and Richard Sabot. 1993. "School Quality and Cognitive Achievement Production: A Case Study for Rural Pakistan." Bryn Mawr College, Bryn Mawr, Penn.

Behrman, Jere R., and Victor Lavy. 1994. "Child Health and Schooling Achievement: Association, Causality, and Intrahousehold Allocations." World Bank, Population and Human Resources Department, Washington, D.C.

Behrman, Jere R., David Ross, and Richard Sabot. 1991. "Production of Cognitive Skills in Rural Pakistan." Williams College, Williamstown, Mass.

Behrman, Jere R., David R. Ross, Richard Sabot, and Matthew Tropp. 1993. "Improving the Quality versus Increasing the Quantity of Schooling." Bryn Mawr College, Bryn Mawr, Penn.

Behrman, Jere R., and Ryan Schneider. 1993. "An International Perspective on Pakistani Human Capital Investments in the Last Quarter Century." *Pakistan Development Review* 32: 1–68.

Behrman, Jere R., and Chalongphob Sussangkarn. 1989. "Parental Schooling and Child Outcomes: Mother versus Father, Schooling Quality, and Interactions." University of Pennsylvania, Philadelphia, Penn.

Behrman, Jere R., and Barbara L. Wolfe. 1987. "How Does Mother's Schooling Affect the Family's Health, Nutrition, Medical Care Usage, and Household Sanitation?" *Journal of Econometrics* 36: 185–204.

Birdsall, Nancy, and Richard H. Sabot. 1993. "Virtuous Circles: Human Capital, Growth, and Equity in East Asia." World Bank, Policy Research Department, Washington, D.C.

Boissiere, Maurice, J. B. Knight, and Richard H. Sabot. 1985. "Earnings, Schooling, Ability, and Cognitive Skills." *American Economic Review* 75: 1016–30.

Colclough, Christopher. 1982. "The Impact of Primary Schooling on Economic Development: A Review of the Evidence." *World Development* 10: 167–85.

Cole, T. J. 1991. "Weight-Stature Indices to Measure Underweight, Overweight, and Obesity." In John Hines, ed., *Anthropometric Assessment of Nutritional Status*, pp. 83–111. New York: Wiley-Liss, Inc.

Court, John H. 1983. "Sex Differences in Performance on Raven's Progressive Matrices: A Review." *Alberta Journal of Educational Research* 29: 54–74.

Eisemon, Thomas Owen. 1988. "The Consequences of Schooling: A Review of Research on the Outcomes of Primary Schooling in Developing Countries." Harvard University, Cambridge, Mass.

Fogel, Robert W. 1989. "Second Thoughts on the European Escape from Hunger: Famines, Price Elasticities, Entitlements, Chronic Malnutrition, and Mortality Rates." Development of the American Economy Working Paper 1. National Bureau of Economic Research, Cambridge, Mass.

———. 1991a. "New Findings on Secular Trends in Nutrition and Mortality: Some Implications for Population Theory." University of Chicago, Chicago, Ill.

———. 1991b. "New Sources and New Techniques for the Study of Secular Trends in Nutritional Status, Health, Mortality, and the Process of Aging." National Bureau of Economic Research, Cambridge, Mass.

Fuller, Bruce. 1986. *Raising School Quality in Developing Countries: What Investments Boost Learning?* Washington, D.C.: World Bank.

Glewwe, Paul. 1990. "Schooling, Skills, and the Returns to Education: An Econometric Exploration Using Data from Ghana." World Bank, Policy Research Department, Washington, D.C.

———. 1992. "Are Rates of Return to Schooling Estimated from Wage Data Relevant Guides for Government Investments in Education? Evidence from a Developing Country." LSMS Working Paper 76. World Bank, Washington, D.C.

Haddad, Wadi D., Martin Carnoy, Rosemary Rinaldi, and Omporn Regel. 1990. *Education and Development: Evidence for New Priorities.* World Bank Discussion Paper 95. Washington, D.C.

Hanushek, Eric. 1986. "The Economics of Schooling." *Journal of Economic Literature* 24: 1141–77.

———. 1989. "The Impact of Differential Expenditures on School Performance." *Educational Researcher* (May): 45–62.

Hanushek, Eric A., João Batista Gomes-Neto, and Ralph W. Harbison. 1992. "Self-financing Educational Investments: The Quality Imperative in Developing Countries." University of Rochester, Rochester, N.Y.

Harbison, Ralph W., and Eric A. Hanushek. 1992. *Educational Performance of the Poor: Lessons from Rural Northeast Brazil.* New York: Oxford University Press.

Khan, Shahrukh, David R. Ross, and Richard Sabot. 1992. "The Regional Gap in Cognitive Achievement in Rural Pakistan." Vassar College, Poughkeepsie, N.Y.

King, Elizabeth M. 1990. *Educating Girls and Women: Investing in Development.* Washington, D.C.: World Bank.

King, Elizabeth M., and Rosemary Bellew. 1988. *Education Policy and Schooling Levels in Peru.* Washington, D.C.: World Bank.

King, Elizabeth M., and M. Anne Hill, eds. 1993. *Women's Education in Developing Countries: Barriers, Benefits, and Policies.* Baltimore, Md.: Johns Hopkins University Press.

Knight, J. B., and Richard H. Sabot. 1990. *Education, Productivity, and Inequality: The East African Natural Experiment.* New York: Oxford University Press.

———. 1987. "Educational Policy and Labor Productivity: An Output Accounting Exercise." *Economic Journal* 385: 199–214.

Kozel, Valerie, and Harold Alderman. 1990. "Factors Determining Work Participation and Labor Supply Decisions in Pakistan's Urban Areas." *Pakistan Development Review* 29 (spring): 1–18.

Krueger, Anne O. 1968. "Factor Endowments and per Capita Income Differences among Countries." *Economic Journal* 78: 641–59.

Psacharopoulos, George. 1985. "Returns to Education: A Further International Update and Implications." *Journal of Human Resources* 20: 583–97.

———. 1988. "Education and Development: A Review." *World Bank Research Observer* 3 (1): 99–116.

Raven, John C. 1956. *Guide to the Coloured Progressive Matrices (Sets A, Ab, B).* London: Lewis.

Rosenzweig, Mark R., and Kenneth J. Wolpin. 1986. "Evaluating the Effects of Optimally Distributed Public Programs." *American Economic Review* 76 (3): 470–87.

———. 1988. "Migration Selectivity and the Effects of Public Programs." *Journal of Public Economics* 37 (2): 265–89.

Sather, Zeba A., and Cynthia B. Lloyd. 1993. "Who Gets Schooled in Pakistan: Is High Fertility a Constraint?" Pakistan Institute of Development Economics.

Schultz, T. Paul. 1988. "Education Investments and Returns." In Hollis B. Chenery and T. N. Srinivasan, eds., *Handbook of Development Economics*. Amsterdam: North-Holland.

———. 1993. "Returns to Women's Education." In Elizabeth M. King and M. Ann Hill, eds., *Women's Education in Developing Countries: Barriers, Benefits, and Policies*. Baltimore, Md.: Johns Hopkins University Press.

UNDP (United Nations Development Programme). 1990. *Human Development Report*. New York.

World Bank. 1980. *World Development Report 1980*. New York: Oxford University Press.

———. 1981. *World Development Report 1981*. New York: Oxford University Press.

———. 1990. *World Development Report 1990: Poverty*. New York: Oxford University Press.

———. 1991. *World Development Report 1991: The Challenge of Development*. New York: Oxford University Press.

III *Spending on Health*

Part III consists of two empirical studies on government health spending and its impact on the poor in Indonesia. Both studies attempt to shed light on how the benefits that households receive from the public provision of health care services vary with living standards. A motivating concern is how effectively health sector spending is used as a redistributive policy instrument in Indonesia.

Like the education studies in part II, the work presented here is neatly split along methodological lines between a more traditional benefit-incidence approach and econometric modeling of behavioral relationships. Van de Walle (chapter 9) uses the former to examine the distribution of government health subsidies in 1987 and to show how that distribution altered between 1978 and 1987; Deolalikar (chapter 10) uses econometric techniques to estimate the effects of health spending in a child's province of residence on children's use of health facilities and their health outcomes, conditional on household socioeconomic characteristics and, in particular, living standards. Both studies use Indonesia's 1987 SUSENAS household consumption survey. Their juxtaposition thus provides a unique opportunity to compare and contrast the two methodologies both from the point of view of which questions each allows us to answer and from that of the results obtained from each approach.

Disaggregating across household expenditure groups, sector, area of residence, and type of health facility, chapter 9 draws a profile of the use of health facilities and of the incidence of health sector subsidies

223

in 1987. Van de Walle examines how the factors that determine inci-dence—the number of reported illnesses, the proportion of reported illnesses that are treated, and the type of treatment received—vary across expenditure groups. Final incidence outcomes are due not to differences in the number of illnesses reported but to the fact that the poor are less likely to seek treatment for an illness and more likely to use less expensive treatment options when they do (for example, public health centers rather than hospitals). The research demonstrates the usefulness of highly disaggregated analysis. The results clearly indicate that, among existing health facilities, subsidies to primary health care centers provide the best way of reaching the poor. Still, primary health care is not particularly well targeted—at least in rural areas, the rich appear to share equally in the benefits.

In addition to providing a detailed static picture of the situation in 1987, van de Walle introduces a dynamic element. Using the 1987 survey to replicate previous incidence work done using the 1978 SUSENAS, she is able to examine changes over time—how marginal spending changes are distributed across households. Her analysis sug-gests that use of health services has risen among all groups since the late 1970s and that changes in use patterns and in subsidy incidence have been pro-poor. However, despite a marked decline in use dispari-ties, the poor continue to receive a smaller share than the nonpoor of the subsidies devoted to the health sector. Moreover, pro-poor changes have benefited the urban poor more than the rural poor.

In chapter 10, Deolalikar merges individual- and household-level data with provincial-level information on per capita government health expenditures. Reduced-form regression models are used to estimate relationships between provincial spending levels, children's use of health services (the probability of being immunized, of receiving treat-ment if sick, and of receiving "modern" treatment), their health out-comes (the probability of reporting an illness in the last week, the length of that illness, and weight-for-age), and the impact of household per capita expenditure on these relationships.

Deolalikar's approach, which controls for various individual- and household-specific factors, gets at the marginal impact of public spend-ing on the dependent variables (health use or outcome measures). It can be termed incremental-benefit incidence in contrast to the traditional incidence approach typified by chapter 9, which examines how infra-marginal spending is distributed. The comparisons of incidence profiles at two dates included in this book aside (chapters 9 and 18), the analysis of marginal benefits has and continues to be a fundamental lacuna of the benefit-incidence approach. Deolalikar's chosen approach can add an important complementary dimension to our understanding of public spending impacts. Pointing out that, in terms of policy decisionmaking (where other things are not held constant), the more relevant issue is how higher spending affects the poor regardless of their characteristics, he also estimates a model in which the explanatory variables are confined to log per capita government health expenditure and its interaction with household expenditure.

The incremental impact of Indonesia's public health spending is estimated to raise the use of health services and to improve health outcomes. Yet—with the exception of reported morbidity—children from richer households appear to benefit more from government health outlays than children from poorer households. A possible explanation, backed up by van de Walle's incidence work, is that a smaller incremental health benefit is derived by poor children from an additional rupiah of health spending because of their limited access to facilities.

In sum, the two studies are consistent in indicating that the benefits from public health spending in Indonesia are still disproportionately captured by richer households. This is true despite the pro-poor changes in incidence that have undoubtedly occurred since 1978.

On a final note, both these studies use highly aggregated measures of government spending. For example, available budget data do not allow use of facility-specific unit costs. This was the case for the education sector analysis in chapter 7 and tends to be common in benefit-incidence analysis. As van de Walle emphasizes, this limitation can introduce biases in the incidence picture if, for example, the quality and unit costs of the health facilities that poorer households tend to frequent are systematically lower. Similarly, the provincial-level spending data used in Deolalikar's study do not capture potential variations in spending at the district and subdistrict levels or differences among provinces in intrasectoral allocations. This could hinder his attempt to clarify the relationships between government health spending, health services use and outcomes, and how these vary depending on the household's socioeconomic status. The fact that data inadequacies impede distributional analyses for Indonesia—widely viewed as having unusually good data—underscores their omnipresence in research of this sort.

9 The Distribution of Subsidies through Public Health Services in Indonesia, 1978–87

Dominique van de Walle

There is an emerging consensus that poverty reduction and human development call for expanding access to certain publicly provided social services such as basic education and health care.[1] Both privately and publicly provided goods matter for well-being. But increasing concern about this role of the public sector raises the issue of how the benefits of public spending are distributed.

Many public services are publicly provided private goods, and for them use is the key determinant of benefits derived. Measuring use clearly requires going beyond aggregate social indicators such as infant mortality rates. Household-level data sets reveal how the use of, for example, public health services varies with other aspects of living standards, such as consumption of private goods, and other relevant household characteristics, including urban/rural location and region of residence.

Use incidence patterns are the outcome of the interlinkage of both public sector inputs and household behavioral responses. At the household level, decisions are influenced by household endowments, prices faced, and various exogenous characteristics of households and individuals. The key determinants of health facility choice are the full cost of using the facility (comprising the price charged, transport costs, and forgone income), the quality of medical care, and any disutility incurred. Use and distributional outcomes are thus influenced by public

The author gratefully acknowledges support from RPO 67642 as well as help from Indonesia country operations. The author thanks Anupa Bhaumik for her research assistance; Anil Deolalikar for providing tabulations of data from the 1987 SUSENAS and 1986–87 Potensi Desa; Benu Bidani for providing tabulated numbers from the 1990 SUSENAS health module; and Shankar Acharya, Emmanuel Jimenez, Paul Gertler, Sandy Lieberman, Kim Nead, Nicholas Prescott, Martin Ravallion, and the *World Bank Economic Review*'s editor and referees for helpful comments. This chapter appeared in slightly different form in *World Bank Economic Review*, vol. 8 (May 1994), pp. 279–309.

sector decisions affecting these variables, including the aggregate resource levels spent on the sector, allocation within the sector, degree of private financing, pricing policies, and organization of sector inputs.

This chapter looks at three specific empirical questions related to the public health care system in Indonesia. First, how does the use of different services vary by household living standards? A key question here is whether there is evidence of self-selection. Do the nonpoor opt out of the public health care system? Second, what is the combined effect of use and pricing policy in determining the incidence of public health care subsidies? Third, how have the answers to the first and second questions changed over time?

These questions are particularly pertinent for Indonesia. The country made great progress in alleviating income poverty during the 1980s. The incidence of poverty is estimated to have declined from 40 percent in 1980 to 22 percent in 1987 (Ravallion and Huppi 1991; World Bank 1990a). But there has been some concern that improvements in certain social indicators (such as infant mortality rates and life expectancy) have not kept pace with improvements in poverty measures. In particular, there is concern about whether increases in the incomes of the poor have been commensurately matched by higher access to and use of health and education services (World Bank 1991).

The period from the late 1970s through the 1980s in Indonesia is particularly interesting because it coincides, first, with substantial declines in income poverty and, second, with considerable emphasis by the government on primary health care (World Bank 1990a, 1991; Yahya and Roesin 1990). Large investments were made and substantial initiatives begun in the primary health care system, including the integrated family planning and health post (*posyandu*) system. Progress in these areas was threatened in the mid-1980s when Indonesia sustained various external shocks. The shocks resulted in substantial deterioration in the external terms of trade and a subsequent macroeconomic adjustment program involving, among other things, cuts in public expenditures, though (relative to other sectors) spending on social services appears to have been somewhat protected (see World Bank 1992).

A limited set of policy instruments is typically available for alleviating poverty in developing countries. A long-standing concern in Indonesia is the effectiveness of health sector expenditures in reaching the poor. Of special interest is identifying which of the intrasector services and facilities can best be used to target in-kind transfers to the poor.

The next section discusses Indonesia's health care system and summarizes key policy issues of relevance for the study. The main methodological issues are addressed in the following section. The third section looks at the use of health care facilities across various groups in 1987 and how it changed after 1978. Next, the chapter examines the incidence of public expenditures in the health sector, again starting with an analysis of the situation in 1987 and then turning to how it changed after 1978. Finally, some conclusions are offered.

The Setting

Indonesia's health care problems are dominated by communicable diseases (such as malaria and tuberculosis), respiratory and diarrheal diseases, and injuries. Maternal and perinatal morbidity is high, as are anemia and vitamin and micronutrient deficiencies. Indonesia's health profile is widely seen to require a significant, continuing role for public intervention.

Overall, public spending in Indonesia is very low in the health sector (Griffin 1990; World Bank 1991). Although it has risen considerably from its level in 1975 of about 0.2 percent of gross national product (GNP), in 1985 it still remained under 1 percent of GNP, below the Asian mean of 1.3 percent of GNP (Griffin 1990). In addition, government per capita spending on health declined by about 25 percent between 1982–83 and 1987–88, though it has increased again since then (Ministry of Health 1991a). At least half of total public outlays are disbursed to hospitals. Private spending accounts for more than half of total expenditures on health.

District, provincial, and central governments all contribute to the funding of Indonesia's public health care system. However, the center is by far the main source of funding through its routine and development budgets and various grants and subsidies. The political economy of health sector budget allocations to the regions is unclear. Most of the allocations seem to be dictated by an underlying view of egalitarianism with respect to *inputs*. But the result is not necessarily an equitable interregional distribution of *outcomes*. For example, INPRES grants— central transfers to the regions intended for primary health care—are based on one of three criteria: population size, number of villages, or equal absolute amounts to each region (World Bank 1992). The distribution of funding can also be partly explained by past investment decisions. Large, specialized hospitals, built at a time when development dogma championed such investments, engender important future recurrent expenditure commitments.

Whatever the political economy dynamics, resource allocation outcomes across geographical areas are generally inequitable. On a per capita basis, allocations from the center exhibit high variance across provinces. And the individual components of the funding (excluding spending on salaries) tend to be positively correlated with provincial per capita incomes and local revenue capacity (World Bank 1991). Griffin (1990) finds the distribution of central government health resources to the provinces to be inversely correlated with need as revealed by infant mortality rates.

Public treatment options include hospitals and the various facilities that make up the primary health care system: health centers (in Indonesia these are called *puskesmas*), subcenters (*puskesmas pembantu*), and integrated health and family planning posts (*posyandus*). The health centers are intended to provide preventive and curative care and to have a doctor in charge and paramedics, nurses, and a midwife in attendance. Health centers average fifteen staff in Java, but a fraction of that in the Outer Islands (World Bank 1991). A handful of health centers provide inpatient services. Subcenters are headed by a nurse or midwife, have few staff, and offer curative and maternal and child care. The integrated health and family planning posts are makeshift clinics set up on a monthly basis in villages with support from the health centers and village health volunteers. The health and family planning clinics aim to provide preventive services to children under five and pregnant and nursing women. Although the health system is designed to function on the basis of referrals from the lowest service up, the sick tend to go directly to the highest accessible tier, where better quality of both staff and equipment can be expected.

Medical care is also available from the private sector, consisting of traditional medicine and modern health care services delivered by private doctors and paramedics (both are often public sector employees who set up private practice after hours), polyclinics (which are private outpatient clinics; in some cases, the outpatient units of public hospitals are also termed polyclinics), and private hospitals. In 1985, 255 private hospitals provided 34 percent of all inpatient days. Many private hospitals are maternity or industrial hospitals that only cater to company employees and their families.

Access to facilities is likely to be an important determinant of the cost of usage. In terms of health infrastructure, Indonesia had six hospital beds per 10,000 population in 1987. There were 5,639 public health centers, 17,382 subcenters, and 23,084 doctors for a population estimated at 172 million in 1987 (BPS 1990).

The availability of health facilities has considerably improved since the late 1970s. Though the number of hospitals (private and public) increased from 602 in 1978 to 703 in 1987, the number of beds just kept pace with population growth. A better measure of progress is at the level of community and primary health care, where development began in earnest in 1978. By 1987, the number of health centers had increased by 30 percent (from 4,353 in 1978–79), subcenters by 162 percent, and physicians by 121 percent. The implementation of the system of health and family planning posts was just getting under way in 1978. In 1987–88 there were 13,754 government-trained paramedical graduates, compared to 2,789 in 1979–80. During the same period, the number of new government health posts increased from 5,651 to 11,907, and Indonesia's population grew by 17 percent (BPS 1983).

Despite these improvements, the availability of health services continues to vary significantly across geographical regions and to be inequitable. In general, all medical facilities are more readily accessible in urban areas. Though a majority of villages now have access to the integrated health and family planning posts, other facilities remain sparse in rural Indonesia. The national figure for hospital beds quoted above masks large regional disparities, illustrated by a comparison between Jakarta (the wealthiest region) and Lampung (one of the poorest provinces) with, respectively, 1.24 and 0.18 beds per 1,000 population. The average distance to a health center varies widely across provinces from 0.8 kilometers in Jakarta to 33 kilometers in Irian Jaya. Those same health centers average 1.8 and 0.35 doctors per center, respectively. Subcenters and health and family planning posts tend to be more accessible, but average distances depend on location: the average patient must travel 0.2 kilometer to reach a health and family planning post in Jakarta and 14 kilometers in Irian Jaya (World Bank 1991).

The evidence suggests that travel time and costs in seeking medical care may still be prohibitive for households in many of Indonesia's rural areas. One reason is that population densities are uneven and extremely low in some parts of the country. Such areas also tend to have low per capita incomes. Of course, these circumstances are unlikely to attract private providers of health care.

The quality of medical facilities also varies markedly. Quality is often lower in poorer, more isolated regions, taking the form of inadequate and unreliable drug supplies, a lower range of services, and fewer and less qualified staff. For example, public health centers in poor remote areas often find it difficult to attract and keep a trained doctor and so function without one.

Many observers have remarked on the low use rates of hospitals and health centers (see World Bank 1991). Distances appear to be an important part of the explanation. Low use rates are also found to be correlated with low levels of regional per capita expenditure. And there is evidence linking low quality with low use as well. For example, the presence of surgical services and of specialist doctors in a facility has been shown to have a high positive effect on use rates (World Bank 1991).

In addition to the private time and transport costs entailed in traveling to public facilities, Indonesians must pay for health care. A set fee of Rp300 per health center visit covers consultation and three days worth of drugs (Indonesia's currency is the rupiah). Visits to health and family planning posts are free. Hospitals charge a series of fees differentiated according to whether inpatient or outpatient care is provided and the class of room in the case of inpatient care. Additional charges are imposed for a range of special services. In general, private facilities charge much higher fees. Many public sector doctors and paramedics successfully charge significantly higher rates in after-hours private practices. Their availability at more convenient times appears to explain, in part, the demand for their services.

Quality and travel times vary across expenditure groups. To what extent do prices vary across groups? The government has made some attempts at protecting the poor from health care fees. The health center fixed fee is considered within the reach of most households. Provision of low-cost beds is required of all public and private hospitals. The government has also promoted the *surat kataranaan lurah*, an affidavit of indigence that poor individuals who are sick can obtain from the village head. The *surat* exempts the recipient from paying the fees associated with one medical treatment. However, anecdotal evidence suggests that the *surat* is used very little.

There is also limited health insurance coverage under PHB (Perum Umum Husada Bhakti, formerly ASKES). This government-run insurance scheme covers active and retired public servants and their dependents for treatment in public facilities. Estimates of the number of people covered vary from around 10.5 million to 14 million for 1986 (World Bank 1991). The scheme is financed through a 2 percent levy on the base salaries of all government workers and the pension payments of retired government workers. The persons covered are rarely poor (World Bank 1991).

How important are private expenditures on health care? Table 9-1 presents monthly per capita expenditures on health according to deciles of total consumption per capita as recorded in the 1987 SUSENAS household survey. Absolute magnitudes are low. The bottom decile spent most on nondoctor-prescribed drugs, paramedics, and, in urban areas only, private doctors. In contrast, the highest-expenditure components for the top decile were doctor-prescribed medicines and private doctors. Generally, the amounts increase with overall living standards. And they also increase more than proportionately with consumption in that the elasticity of expenditures in each category with respect to total consumption expenditures tends to exceed 1. As a simple summary measure, the least squares elasticities are recorded in the last column.

The above observations suggest the following characterization of the process determining public health care use in Indonesia. Potential patients choose between subsidized public health care, where choice is limited in terms of quantity and quality, and unsubsidized private care, where individuals can choose more freely but at a higher price (assumed here to include the full cost). Under certain conditions, there will then be an equilibrium in which the rich (whose perceived net benefits from attending public facilities are assumed to be lower than they are for others) opt out of the public health sector.[2] However, access to private care may entail prohibitively high prices such that

Table 9-1. *Monthly Household per Capita Expenditure on Health Care, by Decile, Indonesia, 1987*
(rupiah)

Expenditure and region	1	2	3	4	5	6	7	8	9	10	Expenditure elasticity	t-ratio
Doctors												
All Indonesia	1.90	5.06	6.13	8.03	8.23	10.73	19.44	25.49	39.64	86.04	1.85	(17.4)
Urban	7.27	10.13	15.47	26.72	33.65	25.95	37.34	47.11	73.27	116.62	1.40	(12.6)
Rural	1.53	2.94	5.29	7.10	8.22	8.06	8.80	16.08	20.81	63.29	2.05	(17.1)
Inpatient care												
All Indonesia	0.75	1.53	7.39	1.79	2.93	3.76	4.23	11.03	14.35	63.41	2.01	(6.9)
Urban	4.31	1.27	5.74	4.21	7.12	13.33	7.85	21.60	89.29	97.48	2.05	(5.6)
Rural	0.95	0.34	2.58	8.23	1.88	3.67	3.26	3.10	10.72	23.54	1.99	(4.0)
Nurses/midwives												
All Indonesia	0.25	0.77	0.75	1.53	2.21	1.90	3.35	7.47	9.45	10.03	1.93	(7.7)
Urban	1.95	2.02	1.96	6.72	10.47	7.29	11.04	7.92	8.84	6.81	0.82	(2.6)
Rural	0.15	0.97	0.38	0.29	1.62	2.60	2.14	1.99	5.96	11.38	2.47	(6.1)
Paramedics												
All Indonesia	4.68	7.29	7.07	9.21	8.65	9.57	8.52	9.27	8.74	6.27	0.10	(0.8)
Urban	5.55	4.93	3.77	4.03	3.56	2.93	5.08	2.47	1.58	2.12	−0.56	(3.7)
Rural	4.16	7.51	6.79	8.13	9.38	10.11	10.72	10.45	13.05	15.18	0.69	(7.4)
Birth control												
All Indonesia	0.06	0.15	0.29	0.44	0.46	0.25	1.17	1.20	1.02	2.09	1.67	(6.0)
Urban	0.02	0.36	0.43	1.60	2.07	1.81	1.29	0.90	2.37	3.70	1.98	(3.5)
Rural	0.04	0.21	0.06	0.43	0.54	0.47	0.28	0.52	1.08	0.71	1.65	(3.4)

	1	2	3	4	5	6	7	8	9	10		(%)
Traditional healers												
All Indonesia	2.79	2.58	3.05	4.89	4.68	3.99	4.58	3.88	3.38	5.50	0.28	(2.4)
Urban	2.25	7.98	3.68	4.36	1.96	1.51	3.32	3.06	5.84	2.16	−0.14	(0.5)
Rural	3.08	2.75	2.79	2.88	5.11	3.66	4.35	4.80	4.75	6.36	0.51	(4.6)
Doctor-prescribed drugs												
All Indonesia	1.09	1.76	3.35	3.23	5.74	7.41	16.91	24.34	40.27	98.42	2.40	(16.3)
Urban	5.95	8.17	14.76	38.80	36.43	35.19	42.59	68.48	82.50	161.97	1.66	(9.6)
Rural	1.13	0.97	2.66	2.50	2.08	5.34	4.72	9.40	14.26	49.85	2.37	(11.4)
Non-prescribed drugs												
All Indonesia	3.98	5.53	6.98	8.50	8.52	12.21	12.96	13.77	16.56	24.95	0.90	(12.8)
Urban	9.66	8.94	15.73	12.48	14.46	15.32	16.96	18.11	26.02	30.68	0.61	(8.1)
Rural	3.38	5.10	5.95	7.41	7.72	8.59	10.87	12.68	12.95	18.90	1.00	(12.9)
Other health goods and services												
All Indonesia	1.47	2.04	2.31	3.22	3.55	3.79	5.16	6.66	5.90	13.02	1.07	(15.2)
Urban	3.61	4.16	4.97	8.11	8.41	5.63	7.09	5.00	9.77	26.36	0.81	(4.5)
Rural	1.61	1.38	2.14	2.74	2.95	2.69	4.27	3.70	5.45	6.70	0.96	(8.3)
Total												
All Indonesia	16.95	26.71	37.32	40.85	44.96	53.61	76.33	103.11	139.31	309.74	1.43	(34.9)
Urban	40.57	47.95	66.50	107.03	118.14	108.95	132.57	174.66	299.48	447.90	1.25	(14.7)
Rural	16.03	22.17	28.64	39.72	39.50	45.18	49.41	62.71	89.03	195.90	1.43	(27.3)

Note: Deciles are ranked by total household consumption per capita.

Source: 1987 SUSENAS data tapes.

the demand for private health care becomes zero. For example, in many rural areas, rich and poor individuals would have to travel very long distances—with a high opportunity cost of time—to reach private facilities. In these circumstances, everyone opts out of the private sector.

A similar situation arises in choosing between different public services. The highest levels—hospitals—dispense higher-quality care but are also more expensive, both because of higher user fees and because they are scarcer and, hence, entail greater traveling costs for most patients. Some self-selection across expenditure groups can be expected. Finally, the low quality of services and significant distances in some regions are likely to deter even the poor and result in continued reliance on traditional medicine or self-treatment, neglect of preventive care, and delays in seeking treatment except in emergencies. Increased availability of facilities as well as higher living standards can be expected to relax some of these constraints and to improve access to health care.

In the following sections, we will see how closely the data conform to this characterization of the determinants of health care use in Indonesia and what the outcomes are in terms of the incidence of subsidies to public health care.

The Methodology

A household's standard of living depends on its command over both private goods and the benefits derived from publicly provided goods such as education and health care. Thus an assessment of the interhousehold distribution of the benefits of public expenditures should compare the distribution of living standards without government spending to the one that attains with publicly provided services.

Commonly used indicators of living standards, such as household per capita expenditures, exclude the monetary value derived from publicly provided goods. However, for several reasons, they provide only a rough approximation of the distribution that would be obtained prior to government intervention. Household expenditures on private goods are influenced by what governments spend on public services. Public services may displace private spending: for example, when outpatient care in a public hospital is provided at a subsidized rate, people will spend less on private doctors. Public services may also augment private spending: for example, subsidized schooling may encourage households (who might not otherwise send their children to a private school) to spend income on their children's clothing. Furthermore, the distribution of living standards is influenced by the outcomes (such as good health) of past public spending. These are very difficult effects to quantify. Here, I follow common practice in assuming that total household consumption expenditure on privately supplied goods (consumption for short) is an adequate proxy for living standards in the absence of publicly provided goods. Thus, the distribution of the benefits of publicly provided goods across households ranked by consumption is the basis of an assessment of the impact of public provisioning on living standards.

It should be pointed out that the study makes a risk-neutral valuation of the subsidies. That is, it examines the transfer benefits, not the risk benefits, of public health care provision. The risk benefits will depend on the availability of risk markets (including insurance), and on how well these perform. It could be argued that risk markets work less well for the poor, so that there are potentially large risk benefits from public health care subsidies for them and for many of the nonpoor in rural areas. But there is no way of measuring this.

Benefit-Incidence Analysis

Use is measured as the proportion of an eligible subgroup who makes use of a health facility. Estimated government unit costs are then attributed across households according to use patterns. This approach is usually referred to as benefit-incidence analysis.[3] It became popular in the late 1970s, spurred in part by increased availability and improvements in household-level surveys. The best-known applications for developing countries are the studies of Malaysia by Meerman (1979) and of Colombia by Selowsky (1979).

It is notoriously difficult to measure the benefits from publicly provided goods and services (see Cornes, chapter 4 of this volume). The problems associated with the benefit-incidence approach are well documented (for example, see Selden and Wasylenko 1992). Here, it may be useful to point out what are likely to be some of the more important concerns in the present context. A key question has always been how well the standard methodology approximates the distribution of the *value* of the benefits. Use need not fully reflect the actual benefits derived from a health facility. "Need," as measured by reported illness, is often juxtaposed with treatments received to judge equity of access and value of benefits. Yet, when medical need is based on whether the household reports a member being sick in the prior week, there is no information about the severity of the illness. It may be reasonable to assume that poor households tend to ignore illnesses (out of necessity) more than rich ones. Chernichovsky and Meesook (1986) also speculate that access to health services influences illness reporting because the likelihood of being treated encourages recognition of a poor health condition. In either case, a biased assessment of the degree of need impairs the ability to assess the distribution of health spending. The probable direction of the bias in recall will be to underestimate the need of the poor.

Another weakness of the methodology relates to the fact that all facilities dispensing a certain type of service are treated identically. Yet, differential service quality is an important characteristic of the provision of health care in Indonesia. This is relevant in allocating subsidies in that the per unit cost of a low-quality service generally does not equal that of a high-quality one.[4] The methodology tends to underestimate the disparities in how benefits are distributed. Policy implications may also be affected. Finally, the approach does not allow for the private costs of participation. These are likely to be correlated with living standards and so could be important in assessing the results and the implications of incidence estimates.

In estimating unit costs, this study (like most such studies) concentrates on variable and semivariable or "recurrent" costs. It does not account for capital costs. This may lead to biases in the qualitative results. Meerman (1979) found that failure to account for public capital in Malaysia leads to serious underestimation of the total community resources used to provide medical care. For example, accounting for imputed capital service costs for the Malaysia data increased total costs per inpatient day by 78 percent. Capital costs may also matter to policy decisions. Higher-level services necessitate more costly capital inputs and are likely to be used relatively more by wealthier groups. Ignoring capital, then, results in an underestimation of the inequality in the distribution of public expenditures. In addition, in allocating spending between sectors in the most cost-effective way, *total* public costs are often more relevant than recurrent expenditures on their own. It is important to keep these points in mind when drawing conclusions from the incidence estimates.

Implementation for Indonesia

The data used here are from Indonesia's 1978 and 1987 National Socio-Economic Surveys (SUSENAS), which are large, nationally representative samples. The SUSENAS are detailed consumption surveys that provide the best source of household-level data for Indonesia (for a description of total household expenditures in the SUSENAS surveys and of the data generally, see van de Walle 1988). It is therefore natural to use consumption expenditures as the welfare indicator.

The analysis is carried out along two separate dimensions. At one level, an attempt is made to provide a broad profile of use and of the incidence of subsidies for 1987. Incidence analysis at one point in time attempts to estimate how average benefits are distributed. It says nothing about whether increments to public expenditures are well distributed or pro-poor. For example, the rich may receive a large share of the inframarginal subsidies, while the poor benefit most from the marginal spending. One way to get at this is by comparing incidence at two points in time. At a second level, the chapter attempts to characterize the changes in incidence since the late 1970s. A study by Meesook and Chernichovsky used the 1978 SUSENAS to examine the incidence of public health expenditures using the benefit-incidence methodology (Meesook 1984; Chernichovsky and Meesook 1986). This provides a benchmark for comparing use incidence across income groups between the two dates.

The work by Meesook and Chernichovsky is based on the May subround of the 1978 SUSENAS covering 6,000 households. In 1987, the entire survey comprising 55,000 households was held during January. Overall, survey methodologies and questionnaires are generally comparable across the two surveys. Any dissimilarities are discussed in the text when they arise.

There is a worry that the timing of the surveys may affect the results of the comparison over time. For instance, the incidence of illnesses may vary across the seasons, as may the opportunity cost of seeking treatment. And this variability may differ across expenditure groups. Little is known about seasonality in sickness, in health facility use, or in employment in Indonesia. Nor is much known about the link between seasonality in work and seasonality in agriculture. Indonesia is in an equatorial region with no real dry season (Walsh 1981). There appears to be some seasonality in agriculture, but it varies significantly between and within islands. In addition, Indonesia has a well-diversified rural economy, so that seasonality in work is less likely to be closely linked with crop seasonality than in many rural settings. Statistics on average maximum and minimum temperatures, wind velocity, and relative humidity across provinces and months indicate negligible differences between January and May (BPS 1990). Average rainfall tends to be lower in May, but this is not systematic across regions. It seems unlikely that there is any significant seasonal difference between May of 1978 and January of 1987, at least in the aggregate.

The analysis of health costs and budgets in Indonesia is not straightforward for several reasons. There are numerous budgetary sources for the sector, and numerous ministries, as well as foreign funds, contribute to overall expenditure levels. But there is no central accounting system keeping track of total spending, and the composition of expenditures is not clear from outlay accounting classifications. Calculating total recurrent spending, let alone the per visit subsidies, is therefore a complex task (see World Bank 1991). With these difficulties in mind, the chapter tries to follow the methodology detailed in Meesook (1984) as closely as the available data permit.

Implementation of the approach requires calculation of the per visit costs for the various public health facilities. Government expenditures on health care are for hospitals and the primary health care system as well as for training and communicable disease control. The study

Table 9-2. *Use of Public Hospitals, by Decile, Indonesia, 1990*
(public hospital visits as a proportion of total hospital visits)

Region and type of visit	1	2	3	4	5	6	7	8	9	10	All
All Indonesia											
All visits	68.72	76.60	61.76	69.70	64.41	55.17	62.20	64.57	63.99	53.65	61.16
Inpatient visits	57.87	78.80	67.22	82.92	77.74	73.94	66.57	71.91	67.00	52.82	65.83
Urban											
All visits	62.45	49.20	56.10	50.54	59.98	62.58	49.79	64.16	56.74	39.47	54.38
Inpatient visits	75.48	83.40	79.93	63.74	64.78	69.25	55.59	60.80	52.31	45.61	59.36
Rural											
All visits	56.99	80.69	68.94	72.88	69.35	75.59	67.39	57.16	77.22	68.06	69.58
Inpatient visits	68.47	53.48	75.04	65.32	82.51	82.37	71.90	67.38	74.80	68.88	71.67

Note: Deciles are ranked by total household consumption per capita.
Source: 1990 SUSENAS data tapes.

focuses on the apportionment of the benefits of expenditures on hospitals and public health centers (including subcenters) for which use is identifiable from the household-level data.

The requisite health financing data are taken from a careful compilation of recurrent expenditures on public hospitals and health centers (World Bank 1991). The same source estimated cost recovery to be 3 percent of total recurrent expenditures on the health center system and 20 percent of recurrent expenditures on hospitals. These amounts are subtracted from recurrent expenditures to get the net government subsidy. Finally, the number of yearly visits to hospitals and to primary health centers is derived directly from the SUSENAS and, together with the recurrent expenditure levels, used to calculate per visit subsidies.

The earlier study (Meesook 1984) added up the 1980–81 routine budgets from all government levels, assumed that about two-thirds went to health care as an estimate of recurrent expenditures, and apportioned that amount between hospitals and public health centers. Fees collected from users and ASKES insurance were then subtracted to get the total yearly subsidy. Total annual visits to different health facilities were assessed from the 1980 census.

One difficulty arises because hospital care is also provided by private facilities in Indonesia. Public hospitals accounted for 66 percent of total inpatient days and 72 percent of all outpatient visits in 1985 (72 percent of total hospital visits).[5] The subsidy for each hospital visit is calculated to be Rp5,200 when no distinction is made between public and private hospitals. This appears to be what was done in Meesook (1984) and thus provides the only basis for comparison with her study's results.

A different approach is adopted in presenting subsidy-incidence estimates for 1987. Although it is not possible to identify visits to public as opposed to private facilities from the 1987 SUSENAS, this information is available from the special health module included in the 1990 SUSENAS. Public as a proportion of total hospital visits derived from the 1990 data are given in table 9-2 and underlie the 1987 distribution of subsidies across consumption expenditure deciles presented later. This is the first time that such information has been available at the household level for Indonesia. Although the rich are widely believed to self-select away from public facilities, table 9-2 provides little evidence for this in rural areas. Indeed, the absence of any pattern across consumption deciles in the rural distribution of total public hospital outpatient or inpatient visits is striking. In urban Indonesia, there is some evidence of a negative correlation between the share of public visits and consumption levels. The rural numbers no doubt reflect lower rural densities and the consequent lack of a feasible public/private choice.

It is also important to allow for the fact that hospital visits include both inpatient and outpatient care and that different subsidy magnitudes are associated with each. In addition, as a proportion of total hospital visits, inpatient visits tend to increase with consumption. The level of each subsidy can be obtained by solving for x_i in the identity $H = x_O N_O + x_I N_I$, where H denotes the hospital budget net of user fees, x_O is the average subsidy to a hospital outpatient visit, x_I is the average subsidy to one inpatient day, N_O stands for the number of public outpatient visits, and N_I stands for the number of public inpatient visits. N_I and N_O are known from the SUSENAS, and H is also known, as discussed earlier. An estimate of the ratio of the outpatient to inpatient rate of subsidy (x_O / x_I) is needed.

Several studies have evaluated unit costs for individual health facilities in Indonesia.[6] Unit costs are consistently found to vary widely across facilities. This study is unable to take this variation into consideration and must therefore average over various estimates. One study of a sample of forty hospitals calculated average unit costs in 1986–87 to be Rp3,593 for an outpatient visit and Rp12,803 for one inpatient day (Djuhari Wirakartakusumah and others 1988).[7] Data on tariffs charged by a number of facilities for specific hospital treatments indicate an average fee of Rp300 for outpatient and Rp2,089 for inpatient care (Ministry of Health 1991b). This establishes a subsidy ratio of 0.307. Based on this information, the hospital outpatient subsidy is estimated to be Rp4,500 and the inpatient subsidy to be Rp14,600.

Finally, another factor that tends to influence the distribution of health subsidies is government health insurance coverage under PHB. Coverage is thought to boost use of both primary health care centers and government hospitals where free care is accorded to cardholders. It can be presumed that PHB subscribers use facilities relatively more than others, ceteris paribus. However, there is some controversy about what this implies for subsidy incidence. From existing evidence, it is probable that PHB contributions do not cover costs; what is less clear is whether the costs that are covered are subsidized more or less than others. It has been claimed that PHB reimburses health facilities at the official tariff rates (and perhaps at even lower rates; World Bank 1991). This would imply higher subsidy rates to PHB patients (because tariffs are lower than average prices) and an underestimation of the regressivity of the health care subsidy distribution. However, others claim that PHB reimbursements are actually higher than what other patients pay in user fees, making the subsidies to civil servants lower than to others. This would, in turn, tend to imply a more progressive distribution of overall subsidies. It is unfortunately not clear how to take account of this without data that identify PHB recipients. For lack of any better evidence, I shall assume that the rate of subsidy for persons covered by PHB is the same as for those not covered.

The average subsidy from recurrent expenditures for a visit to a health center is calculated to be Rp500. A study based on a survey of forty-two rural health centers in five provinces in 1986–87 found average unit costs for curative care to average around Rp900 per visit, varying from a low of Rp526 for mother and child health care to a high of Rp1,337 for family planning consultations (Gani, Najib, and Wangsaraharja 1988). Although the official (recommended by the Ministry of Health) fee in 1986–87 was Rp150, it seems that many local governments actually charged fees somewhere between Rp300 and Rp1,000 (World Bank 1991). Based on a fee of Rp300, the average unit cost estimate points to a subsidy of Rp600 per visit, not too far off from the estimate here for primary health centers. Some patients pay less, while some are treated gratis if they are in possession of a letter of indigence from the village headman. Total visits from the SUSENAS data set include consultations at health and family planning posts, whose unit costs are low and that were not considered in the Gani, Najib, and Wangsaraharja study. Although estimates of the per unit subsidies must be viewed as rough, they do permit an idea of the relative orders of magnitude at stake.

The Use of Health Services

This section examines the profile of the use of health care services across consumption expenditure groups in urban and rural areas in 1987. It then compares that use profile to one drawn up for 1978.

The Picture in 1987

According to the 1987 SUSENAS, 65 percent of all persons reporting ill during the preceding week also reported seeking treatment outside the family. Of all persons seeking outside treatments in 1987, the greatest numbers consulted a primary health center (43 percent), followed by paramedics (22 percent), private doctors (17 percent), hospitals (8 percent), traditional healers (6 percent), and polyclinics (4.5 percent). (Note that the surveys only recorded one treatment option per reported illness.) The 1978 SUSENAS implied that 23 percent of visits were to public health centers, 19 percent to hospitals, and 14 percent to private doctors (Meesook 1984). Thus there has been a sizable increase in the relative importance of public health centers.

For a variety of reasons, including both the availability of and the demand for services, the use of health facilities often differs between expenditure groups. Table 9-3 provides evidence from the 1987 SUSENAS of how individuals ranked into deciles of per capita household expenditures (with decile one being the poorest and ten being the wealthiest) responded to sickness. This information is presented for the total, urban, and rural distributions. It is clear that area of residence also has bearing on the use of facilities.

The percentage of reported illnesses treated by private doctors was an increasing function of per capita expenditures, ranging from just

Table 9-3. Treatment of Illness, by Decile, Indonesia, 1987
(percent)

Region and treatment	1	2	3	4	5	6	7	8	9	10
All Indonesia										
Last week's illness treated by										
Private doctor	2.15	2.54	3.43	5.28	6.82	8.62	12.21	14.18	20.43	31.65
Hospital	1.99	2.25	2.42	4.01	4.49	4.33	6.59	6.43	7.32	11.42
Primary health center	26.75	29.35	28.05	29.10	27.21	29.47	29.49	32.15	27.72	19.48
Polyclinic	3.44	2.73	2.02	3.82	3.56	2.16	2.26	3.14	3.42	2.85
Paramedic	14.93	16.20	16.92	14.64	15.01	16.51	15.57	12.32	11.60	8.73
Traditional healer	4.39	4.45	4.34	4.64	4.83	3.80	3.55	3.24	3.88	2.39
Self or family	35.72	34.60	33.26	31.12	32.67	30.33	25.79	23.97	21.60	20.74
No medication	10.63	7.87	9.57	7.41	5.42	4.78	4.55	4.59	4.04	2.75
Percentage of above receiving inpatient treatment	1.92	1.95	1.99	1.77	2.12	2.20	2.75	2.97	3.03	6.41
Inpatient at										
Primary health center	36.84	44.95	53.83	29.31	21.30	34.31	14.70	36.95	23.92	20.28
Hospital	26.17	34.51	31.35	40.98	53.29	54.08	75.00	57.28	66.04	74.43
Paramedic	32.59	7.80	6.09	14.87	9.82	6.82	6.98	2.18	3.66	4.67
Traditional healer	4.39	12.74	8.72	14.83	15.59	4.79	3.31	3.60	6.39	0.63
Urban Indonesia										
Last week's illness treated by										
Private doctor	7.59	10.61	19.03	21.53	18.76	22.15	32.69	31.54	36.60	46.77
Hospital	7.14	5.65	8.67	12.28	13.72	9.28	8.83	13.10	15.77	15.72
Primary health center	26.98	27.64	29.31	28.76	29.90	33.04	24.75	21.22	16.46	11.00
Polyclinic	1.06	5.41	1.56	0.51	3.03	3.66	5.50	0.65	1.09	3.48
Paramedic	13.38	14.11	10.28	11.02	4.86	3.17	3.84	6.91	3.19	3.32
Traditional healer	2.94	2.28	0.89	2.08	0.67	1.05	1.34	2.58	1.44	1.44
Self or family	33.40	30.08	25.91	20.73	26.40	22.55	19.45	20.42	23.17	18.01
No medication	7.51	4.22	4.35	3.10	2.64	5.10	3.61	3.59	2.28	0.28

Percentage of above receiving inpatient treatment	2.36	0.44	2.96	3.25	2.54	2.81	3.07	4.47	5.04	9.44
Inpatient at										
Primary health center	39.25	0.00	3.10	5.20	21.77	6.46	15.51	19.39	12.47	1.64
Hospital	45.37	100.00	96.50	94.80	78.23	89.72	64.33	78.07	84.84	92.46
Paramedic	0.00	0.00	0.39	0.00	0.00	3.39	3.16	2.54	0.55	5.90
Traditional healer	15.38	0.00	0.00	0.00	0.00	0.43	17.00	0.00	2.15	0.00
Rural Indonesia										
Last week's illness treated by										
Private doctor	1.81	1.73	2.28	3.42	4.51	6.09	5.84	8.01	11.52	15.94
Hospital	1.56	2.21	1.66	2.66	3.54	3.83	3.06	4.42	3.87	5.60
Primary health center	26.80	28.67	29.21	29.00	28.61	27.85	29.76	29.29	32.13	27.05
Polyclinic	3.64	2.65	3.14	2.13	4.08	2.94	1.82	2.81	3.43	3.57
Paramedic	15.49	15.23	17.29	17.17	14.59	15.69	16.73	17.91	15.93	17.13
Traditional healer	4.85	5.23	3.32	5.18	4.31	5.15	5.23	4.15	4.52	4.72
Self or family	34.21	36.35	33.04	33.22	31.36	32.66	32.89	28.21	23.81	21.64
No medication	11.64	7.92	10.06	7.24	9.01	5.81	4.68	5.20	4.78	4.36
Percentage of above receiving inpatient treatment	1.81	1.50	2.08	2.18	2.11	2.78	1.85	2.46	2.86	4.25
Inpatient at										
Primary health center	26.81	55.49	43.97	54.32	28.58	23.06	36.74	29.51	40.95	37.95
Hospital	34.81	7.43	43.03	25.57	44.92	51.60	42.21	60.02	48.89	54.05
Paramedic	33.07	21.44	6.40	11.21	13.80	10.63	10.62	6.18	5.15	5.54
Traditional healer	5.32	15.64	6.60	8.90	12.70	14.72	10.43	4.29	5.01	2.46

Note: Deciles are ranked by total household consumption per capita.
Source: 1987 SUSENAS data tapes.

under 2 percent for the poorest 20 percent in rural areas to 47 percent for the richest 10 percent in urban areas. Visits to private doctors exceeded those to hospitals for all groups and also increased much more steeply across household expenditure deciles. Both options were more common in urban than in rural areas. Conversely, the share of individuals who either took no medication or were treated exclusively by themselves or their families fell across the deciles: 46 percent of total reported illnesses for the poorest decile and 23 percent for the wealthiest. The disparity was even more pronounced for those who did not seek any medication: 12 percent did not do so among the poorest decile in rural areas compared with 0.3 percent for the richest urban decile.

Recourse to primary health centers dropped systematically for the sixth through tenth deciles in urban areas. Use does not appear to have been linked to consumption levels in rural areas, where the proportion of total illnesses treated in primary health centers ranged from around 27 to 32 percent. The use of polyclinics was consistently low and appears to have been unrelated to household living standards. Use of paramedics declined with expenditures in urban areas as well as at the national level. In rural areas, in contrast, their use was maintained around 15 to 18 percent across the deciles. The percentage of illnesses attended to by traditional healers was generally low and was lowest for urban individuals. However, it does not seem to have been significantly influenced by household expenditure levels, though this is less true for urban areas.

Table 9-3 also shows the proportion of persons reporting an illness who received inpatient care and where they received it. Again, the evidence suggests that the incidence of inpatient care is correlated with living standards. A larger proportion of the sick went on to be treated as inpatients in urban than in rural areas. Across deciles, a majority of these persons were admitted to hospitals. In rural areas, primary health centers and hospitals shared the burden of inpatient care. The homes of paramedics were a popular option for the bottom deciles and less so for the middle ones. Lastly, traditional healers also played a role in rural areas.

Table 9-4 presents additional detail on annual absolute use rates per person for modern health care providers. This reveals how yearly per capita, total, and provider-specific visits differ across consumption deciles and sectors. It is clear from table 9-4 that the rate at which morbidity is treated varied across deciles and rose with consumption. The latter effect is more pronounced in rural areas where individuals in the poorest decile visited one of the modern facilities an average of 1.4 times a year, while individuals in the wealthiest decile did so 3 times. In urban Indonesia, the variability was lower, ranging from 1.8 to 2.2 visits per person per year.

Table 9-4. *Use of Modern Health Care Providers, by Decile, Indonesia, 1987*
(annual rates per capita)

Region and type of provider	1	2	3	4	5	6	7	8	9	10	All
All Indonesia											
Total visits	1.44	1.71	1.66	1.88	1.91	2.19	2.45	2.51	2.61	2.30	2.07
Doctor	0.06	0.08	0.11	0.17	0.23	0.31	0.45	0.52	0.76	0.98	0.37
Hospital	0.06	0.07	0.08	0.13	0.15	0.16	0.24	0.24	0.27	0.35	0.18
Primary health center	0.78	0.94	0.88	0.96	0.91	1.06	1.09	1.18	1.03	0.60	0.94
Polyclinic	0.10	0.09	0.06	0.13	0.12	0.08	0.08	0.12	0.13	0.09	0.10
Paramedic	0.44	0.52	0.53	0.48	0.50	0.59	0.58	0.45	0.43	0.27	0.48
Urban											
Total visits	1.76	2.50	2.16	2.39	2.06	2.16	2.25	2.10	1.95	2.17	2.15
Doctor	0.24	0.42	0.60	0.69	0.55	0.67	0.97	0.90	0.98	1.26	0.73
Hospital	0.22	0.22	0.27	0.40	0.40	0.28	0.26	0.37	0.42	0.42	0.33
Primary health center	0.85	1.09	0.92	0.93	0.88	1.00	0.74	0.61	0.44	0.30	0.77
Polyclinic	0.03	0.21	0.05	0.02	0.09	0.11	0.16	0.02	0.03	0.09	0.08
Paramedic	0.42	0.56	0.32	0.35	0.14	0.10	0.11	0.20	0.08	0.09	0.24
Rural											
Total visits	1.41	1.70	1.56	1.75	1.78	1.83	2.12	2.38	2.82	3.00	2.03
Doctor	0.05	0.06	0.07	0.11	0.14	0.20	0.22	0.30	0.49	0.69	0.23
Hospital	0.04	0.07	0.05	0.09	0.11	0.12	0.11	0.17	0.16	0.24	0.12
Primary health center	0.77	0.96	0.85	0.93	0.92	0.90	1.10	1.11	1.35	1.17	1.01
Polyclinic	0.10	0.09	0.09	0.07	0.13	0.10	0.07	0.11	0.14	0.15	0.11
Paramedic	0.44	0.51	0.50	0.55	0.47	0.51	0.62	0.68	0.67	0.74	0.57

Note: Deciles are ranked by total household consumption per capita.
Source: 1987 SUSENAS data tapes.

Changes in Incidence of the Use of Health Services between 1978 and 1987

Table 9-5 presents statistics on individuals reporting illnesses and where they were treated as recorded in both the 1978 and 1987 surveys. The table provides insights into how the type of treatment sought by different subgroups altered between 1978 and 1987. For example, of all persons reporting ill in urban Java in the lower 40 percent of the per capita expenditure distribution, 32 percent did not seek treatment outside the home in 1987. The 1978 results, taken from Chernichovsky and Meesook (1986), are also given in the table. In 1978, 58 percent of urban Javanese in the poorest expenditure group who claimed to have been ill did not seek treatment.

The following observations can be made about each treatment option.

SELF, FAMILY, OR NO TREATMENT. At both dates, the lowest-income groups were least likely to seek treatment outside the home. Indeed, self, family, or no treatment was consistently their most common course of action. But the use of facilities outside the home by the poorest 40 percent clearly increased after 1978. For example, in urban Java, self, family, or no treatment declined from 58 to 32 percent. Urban residents were also more likely to pursue outside treatment than rural residents at any given consumption level.

PRIMARY HEALTH CENTERS. The 1978 results indicate that, for rural areas, primary health centers were predominantly used by middle-expenditure households. The poor used these facilities relatively little (many went without treatment), while the rich tended to use other facilities more intensively (such as private doctors). In urban areas, the pattern differed between Java, where use was also highest for the middle-expenditure group (22 percent), and the Outer Islands, where use was highest among the poorest (27 percent) and lowest among the middle-expenditure group (10 percent). By 1987, the use of primary health centers increased for most subgroups. There were two exceptions. It dropped for the wealthiest groups in the urban areas of both Java and the Outer Islands and for the middle-expenditure group in rural areas.

In the urban areas of both Java and the Outer Islands, the use of health centers declined with consumption expenditures, though only mildly between the bottom and middle groups. In marked contrast, use of *rural* primary health centers appears to have been relatively equal across expenditure groups. The upper 20 percent were just as likely (if not slightly more likely) to use them as the lower 40 percent. Based on these data for 1987, and tables 9-2 and 9-3, one could not conclude now that subsidizing primary health care in rural areas is

Table 9-5. Treatment of Illness, by Region and Household Expenditure Quantile, Indonesia, 1978 and 1987
(percent)

Treatment of last week's illness and year	Java						Outer Islands					
	Urban			Rural			Urban			Rural		
	Lower 40	Middle 40	Upper 20	Lower 40	Middle 40	Upper 20	Lower 40	Middle 40	Upper 20	Lower 40	Middle 40	Upper 20
Self, family, or no treatment												
1978	58	27	12	53	41	40	33	52	26	43	39	33
1987	31.8	26.4	19.6	45.7	37.6	27.6	34.7	23.7	27.9	41.2	35.6	28.0
Primary health center												
1978	19	22	15	17	37	21	27	10	22	11	35	23
1987	26.9	26.3	14.4	30.5	31.5	31.0	31.2	30.1	14.5	25.5	25.8	28.0
Private doctor												
1978	13	34	58	22	12	29	17	27	38	15	9	25
1987	29.3	33.0	46.2	19.0	23.0	32.7	19.1	26.5	39.4	17.9	22.3	26.8
Hospital												
1978	0	14	5	1	1	7	7	5	11	1	2	6
1987	8.21	9.63	16.5	1.11	3.31	3.69	9.01	14.9	14.1	3.07	4.56	5.73
Private clinics												
1978	0	0	9	1	2	0	0	3	2	8	5	3
1987	2.41	3.43	2.58	1.55	2.31	1.64	2.06	2.61	1.89	4.51	3.97	5.15
Traditional healer												
1978	10	3	1	6	7	3	13	4	1	22	10	10
1987	1.46	1.19	0.88	2.12	2.31	3.35	3.92	2.19	2.23	7.78	7.68	6.37

Note: Each number indicates the proportion of all persons reporting ill in each expenditure quantile, by geographical area, who seek each type of treatment. Individuals are ranked by per capita household expenditures. Private clinics include maternity hospitals and clinics from the 1978 SUSENAS and polyclinics from the 1987 SUSENAS. Paramedics are included in private doctors in both surveys.

Source: 1987 SUSENAS data tapes; Chernichovsky and Meesook 1986.

inherently pro-poor; the benefits are quite uniformly distributed. However, the benefits of subsidized primary health care will tend to be more pro-poor in urban areas.

PRIVATE DOCTORS. Unlike public health centers, visits to doctors increased markedly with expenditure levels in both rural and urban areas. Use was also higher in urban areas at any consumption level. The rate of use of private doctors increased for five out of six subgroups in the Outer Islands. In Java the use of private doctors increased for only half of all subgroups. This may reflect the relatively lower availability of cheaper yet acceptable alternatives in the Outer Islands.

HOSPITALS. Hospital treatment also increased with urban residence and household per capita expenditures. The rich used hospitals less in rural and more in urban areas in 1987 than in 1978. Other groups mostly increased their rate of use of hospitals.

PRIVATE CLINICS. The categories listed in the 1978 and 1987 surveys do not correspond exactly for private clinics. The 1978 SUSENAS asked about maternity hospitals and clinics, while the 1987 survey listed polyclinics. Both categories cover private facilities, which often offer better quality than the available public facilities and charge more for it. Therefore, the two are compared here. The proportion of individuals using these facilities in 1987 tended to be highest for the middle-expenditure group. The exception was the rural Outer Islands where both the lower- and upper-expenditure groups exhibited higher use. By contrast, in 1978 there was very uneven use of private clinics, and a pattern is difficult to discern. After 1978, use generally decreased in the Outer Islands and increased in Java.

TRADITIONAL HEALERS. The importance of traditional healers declined almost consistently over the decade, though this form of treatment retained many followers in the rural areas of the Outer Islands. But there was on the whole much less differentiation in use across expenditure classes in 1987 than evidenced for 1978. It seems that where health centers exist, the local poor use them in preference to traditional medical practitioners.[8]

Public Expenditures in the Health Sector

This section estimates the distribution of public subsidies in the health sector in 1987. Changes in the distribution of subsidies after 1978 are also examined.

The Incidence of Government Health Subsidies in 1987

Tables 9-6 and 9-7 present data on health subsidies in 1987 for the urban, rural, and total population distributions. Monetary units are expressed in monthly rupiahs per person. Table 9-6 characterizes the decile-specific distribution of public subsidies to hospitals and primary health centers. The hospital subsidies are calculated by differentiating between inpatient and outpatient visits as described above and assuming that the decile distribution of public hospital visits in 1987 was as indicated by the 1990 SUSENAS health module (see table 9-2).

The overall subsidy is found to have been mildly progressive in that the subsidy as a percentage of household consumption tended to be higher for the poor. Absolute subsidy levels tended to increase with per capita expenditure levels but to decline as a proportion of them. Hence, they reduced inequality. However, the programs were not particularly well targeted. Indeed, uniform (untargeted) provision of lump sum transfers to the whole population would have been much more progressive. The magnitude of the hospital subsidy tended to increase much more with per capita expenditures than that of the health center benefits. The latter were generally flatter across deciles, though they tended to increase for the top three rural deciles and to decrease for the top three urban ones. This result is in line with the earlier findings that, in rural areas, all groups used health centers, but that the poor used them relatively more than others in urban Indonesia.

Table 9-7 summarizes Indonesia's "household health account" for 1987. Outlays on health care by both the government and the household (table 9-1) are juxtaposed across consumption expenditure deciles. Total per capita health spending is found to have generally increased (with some ups and downs) the higher the decile. Both public and private expenditures followed a similar upward trend, though public exceeded private outlays for most deciles. The exceptions occurred for the top deciles in all groups and for the seventh through tenth deciles in urban Indonesia. Again, for the poor, public provisioning was relatively more important than private provisioning.

Variations in household per capita expenditures across consumption expenditure groups result from various factors. Specifically, spending per individual can be interpreted as the product of the number of illnesses reported per person, the proportion of total reported illnesses that are treated, and the level of expenditures per treatment. Table 9-8 presents the results of this decomposition. Private per capita outlays followed an upward trend, because of the way in which expenditures per treatment rose and because there was an increase in the share of reported illnesses that were treated, as total household per capita consumption increased. By contrast, reported illnesses appear not to have varied much with total expenditures, though there was a tendency

Table 9-6. *Incidence of Public Subsidies to Hospitals and Primary Health Centers, by Decile, Indonesia*
(rupiah per capita per month)

Region and type of subsidy	1	2	3	4	5	6	7	8	9	10	Average
All Indonesia											
Hospital subsidy	21.79	34.67	28.30	50.57	60.20	57.98	98.58	93.86	105.48	135.33	68.68
Public health center subsidy	32.06	38.77	36.20	39.46	37.38	43.48	44.96	48.61	42.26	24.86	38.80
Total per capita subsidy	53.85	73.44	64.50	90.03	97.58	101.46	143.54	142.47	147.73	160.19	107.48
Subsidy as a percentage of household per capita expenditures	0.67	0.69	0.52	0.63	0.60	0.55	0.67	0.55	0.45	0.26	0.49
Urban											
Hospital subsidy	72.89	52.31	116.02	126.49	120.61	109.02	75.58	139.36	137.86	151.27	110.14
Public health center subsidy	34.84	44.70	37.82	38.07	36.02	41.14	30.31	24.96	18.04	12.21	31.81
Total per capita subsidy	107.73	97.02	153.84	164.56	156.63	150.16	105.89	164.33	155.90	163.48	141.95
Subsidy as a percentage of household per capita expenditures	0.95	0.63	0.82	0.75	0.62	0.52	0.32	0.42	0.32	0.19	0.43
Rural											
Hospital subsidy	19.61	23.84	28.71	32.73	50.01	66.53	45.52	67.00	83.16	117.99	53.51
Public health center subsidy	31.46	39.61	35.05	38.29	37.77	37.11	45.36	45.82	55.64	48.16	41.43
Total per capita subsidy	51.08	63.45	63.75	71.01	87.78	103.64	90.88	112.82	138.80	166.15	94.94
Subsidy as a percentage of household per capita expenditures	0.67	0.64	0.56	0.55	0.61	0.65	0.50	0.54	0.55	0.39	0.53

Note: Deciles are ranked by total household consumption per capita.
Source: Author's calculations from 1987 and 1990 SUSENAS data tapes.

Table 9-7. *Household Health Account, by Decile, Indonesia, 1987*
(rupiah per capita per month)

Region and type of expenditure	1	2	3	4	5	6	7	8	9	10	Average
All Indonesia											
Total per capita expenditure on health care	70.81	100.15	101.82	130.88	142.54	155.07	219.87	245.58	287.04	469.93	192.37
Spent by household directly	16.96	26.71	37.32	40.85	44.96	53.61	76.33	103.11	139.31	309.74	84.89
Subsidized by the government	53.85	73.44	64.50	90.03	97.58	101.46	143.54	142.47	147.73	160.19	107.48
Mean total consumption per capita	8,007	10,621	12,421	14,212	16,160	18,501	21,460	25,764	32,997	60,757	22,090
Urban											
Total per capita expenditure on health care	148.30	144.97	220.34	271.59	274.77	259.11	238.46	338.99	455.38	611.39	296.33
Spent by household directly	40.57	47.95	66.50	107.03	118.14	108.95	132.57	174.66	299.48	447.90	154.38
Subsidized by the government	107.73	97.02	153.84	164.56	156.63	150.16	105.89	164.33	155.90	163.48	141.95
Mean total consumption per capita	11,372	15,503	18,785	21,903	25,194	28,803	33,383	39,522	49,378	88,144	33,199
Rural											
Total per capita expenditure on health care	67.12	85.62	92.39	110.73	127.28	148.82	140.29	175.53	227.83	362.05	153.77
Spent by household directly	16.04	22.17	28.64	39.72	39.5	45.18	49.41	62.71	89.03	195.90	58.83
Subsidized by the government	51.08	63.45	63.75	71.01	87.78	103.64	90.88	112.82	138.80	166.15	94.94
Mean total consumption per capita	7,595	9,909	11,432	12,860	14,373	6,065	18,123	20,841	25,429	42,614	17,924

Note: Deciles are ranked by total household consumption per capita.
Source: Author's calculations from 1987 and 1990 SUSENAS data tapes.

251

Table 9-8. *Monthly Household per Capita Expenditure on Health Care, by Decile, Indonesia, 1987*
(rupiah)

Region and expenditure	1	2	3	4	5	6	7	8	9	10
All Indonesia										
Expenditure per treatment	130.05	173.29	249.41	241.61	260.65	276.09	354.35	470.73	605.99	1,564.38
Treatment per illness	0.54	0.58	0.57	0.62	0.62	0.65	0.70	0.71	0.74	0.77
Illness per person	0.24	0.27	0.26	0.28	0.28	0.30	0.31	0.31	0.31	0.26
Expenditure per person	16.96	26.71	37.32	40.85	44.96	53.61	76.33	103.11	139.31	309.74
Urban										
Expenditure per treatment	262.11	222.59	364.37	523.51	681.62	596.51	693.90	963.45	1,807.02	2,434.39
Treatment per illness	0.59	0.66	0.70	0.76	0.71	0.72	0.77	0.76	0.75	0.82
Illness per person	0.26	0.33	0.26	0.27	0.24	0.25	0.25	0.24	0.22	0.23
Expenditure per person	40.57	47.95	66.50	107.03	118.14	108.95	132.57	174.66	299.48	447.90
Rural										
Expenditure per treatment	124.37	141.98	206.85	249.12	247.35	271.73	256.06	296.87	355.09	733.28
Treatment per illness	0.54	0.56	0.57	0.60	0.60	0.62	0.62	0.67	0.71	0.74
Illness per person	0.24	0.28	0.24	0.27	0.27	0.27	0.31	0.32	0.35	0.36
Expenditure per person	16.04	22.17	28.64	39.72	39.50	45.18	49.41	62.71	89.03	195.90

Note: Deciles are ranked by total household consumption per capita.
Source: 1987 SUSENAS data tapes.

for reported illnesses to diminish in urban Indonesia and to increase (more markedly) in rural areas.

Changes in the Distribution of Health Subsidies between 1978 and 1987

Table 9-9 compares data for 1978 and 1987 on the distribution of the percentage shares of subsidies to hospitals and public health centers across consumption and geographical groups (this comparison is made under the same assumptions as Meesook 1984). It should be noted that the underlying population distribution is likely to have altered between the two dates, particularly due to urbanization. The regional population shares given in the last rows of table 9-9 can help in judging the equity of subsidy shares in rural compared with urban areas and in Java compared with the Outer Islands. The necessary data are not available to enable the comparison across consumption groups in specific regions. The last column gives the shares for the total Indonesian population. It clearly shows that at the national level the distribution of health subsidies became more equitable. The lower 40 percent expenditure group gained substantially. This result appears to have been driven by gains to the urban poor.

Yet, the distribution does not suggest that public health care expenditures are well targeted. Geographically, urban areas appropriated much more on a per capita basis. If anything, this appears to have become more pronounced after 1978 and was particularly so in the Outer Islands. Conversely, the overall share going to rural areas dwindled, most dramatically in rural Java.

The distribution of health sector subsidies became decidedly more equitable after 1978. To make this point more forcefully, it is useful to contrast the results here, based on 1987 patterns of use, with the results of an exercise aimed at making a rough estimate of the distribution of health spending in 1985–86 using the 1978 pattern of use (Griffin 1990). Griffin combined the 1978 use incidence with 1985–86 public health expenditures on hospitals and health centers, using essentially the same budget data as used here.[9] Griffin's approximation produced an extremely skewed distribution in which the poorest 40 percent of the population captured about 17 percent, the middle 30 percent captured 31 percent, and the wealthiest 30 percent captured some 52 percent of total health care outlays. By contrast, the percentage shares here in table 9-9 are 31, 30, and 39 percent, respectively. The bias in Griffin's results was caused by his assumption that the pattern of use was static.

Conclusions

The last fifteen years have witnessed concerted government effort to increase the aggregate provision of basic health care services in Indone-

Table 9-9. *Percentage Shares of Government Health Subsidies, by Household Expenditure Quantile, Area, and Region, Indonesia, 1978 and 1987*

Household economic quantile and year	Java			Outer Islands			Indonesia		
	Urban	Rural	Total	Urban	Rural	Total	Urban	Rural	Total
Lower 40 percent									
1978	1	14	15	0	4	4	1	18	19
1987	11	7	18	4	9	13	15	16	31
Middle 30 percent									
1978	3	21	25	2	9	11	5	31	36
1987	8	9	17	4	8	12	12	17	30
Upper 30 percent									
1978	12	15	27	4	14	18	16	29	45
1987	9	14	23	4	12	16	14	25	39
Total									
1978	16	50	67	6	27	33	23	77	100
1987	29	30	59	13	29	41	41	59	100
Percentage share of population									
1978	12	52	64	7	29	36	19	81	100
1987	20	42	62	8	30	38	27	73	100

Note: Data are ranked in deciles by per capita household expenditure. Lower 40 percent is the first four deciles taken together, the middle 30 three deciles, and the upper 30 percent comprise the three highest deciles.

Source: 1987 SUSENAS data tapes; Meesook 1984.

sia. Little is known, however, about differences in access to and use of these publicly provided services and, hence, about how the benefits of health expenditures are distributed across socioeconomic groups. This chapter has characterized the profile of the use of health facilities and the incidence of health sector subsidies using household-level data for 1987. It has also examined how the use and subsidy incidence profiles have altered since the late 1970s, a period that has seen a steady fall in absolute income poverty in Indonesia.

The health sector has undergone significant changes. Public policy efforts at achieving widespread provision of primary health care in rural Indonesia are reflected in the use data. The study finds that there has been increased recourse to medical service by all persons who report being ill—whether poor or otherwise—together with a drop in the use of traditional medicine. The changes since 1978 are most striking for the poorest groups. Nonetheless, in 1987 it remained true that, whether or not an illness resulted in outpatient or inpatient care was highly correlated with living standards; the likelihood of visiting a private doctor or a hospital was still lower for the poor than for the non-poor.

The use of primary health centers in rural areas spread and equalized over the consumption groups. The poorer groups used these services much more in 1987 than they did in 1978. In rural areas in 1987, rich and poor appeared to be equally likely to seek treatment in these facilities. This result suggests that public subsidies to primary health care centers in rural Indonesia are not as pro-poor as seems to be widely believed. It also suggests that a more pro-poor distribution of benefits would require price discrimination in the absence of increased private sector provision, though it is unclear how feasible that would be in rural areas. In 1987 the use of health centers in urban areas contrasted with that in rural areas in that it declined much more with rising living standards, suggesting self-selection. Subsidized primary health care was therefore more pro-poor in the urban sector.

The overall health subsidy is found to be progressive (in that it tends to represent a larger *relative* share of consumption expenditure by the poor), but only mildly so. Subsidies are not particularly well targeted in that the *absolute* subsidy received tends to be higher for the nonpoor. As expected, the incidence of subsidies to hospitals increased with consumption, while that to primary health centers was generally constant across deciles. For all but the highest consumption groups, public exceeded private spending on health care.

All in all, patterns of use altered enough to make the distribution of public subsidies to the health sector more equitable in 1987 than in 1978. The lowest 40 percent of the consumption distribution experienced considerable gains, driven primarily by gains to the urban poor. Although the aggregate distribution of the subsidies improved after

1978, benefits in 1987 were still far from being focused on the poor. Urban areas continued to be relatively favored and rural ones to be shortchanged, and this tendency appears to have increased.

From the point of view of using health sector spending as an instrument for poverty alleviation in Indonesia, the study findings indicate that, within the health sector, subsidies to basic primary health care provide the best option for reaching the poor. Based on the recent patterns of use reviewed in this chapter, however, even subsidies on primary health care are still far from an ideal instrument.

Notes

1. This view has been recently articulated in World Bank (1990b), UNDP (1990), and Drèze and Sen (1989). On the relative importance of income poverty reduction and public services in promoting human development, see Anand and Ravallion (1993).

2. For example, with additively separable utility between health care and other goods, declining marginal utility of consumption, common preferences, and a competitive private sector, there will exist a unique expenditure switch point below which people use only public facilities and above which they opt for private care.

3. In contrast, expenditure-incidence studies examine the question of who receives government expenditures through, for example, being employed by the public sector (for example, doctors, nurses, teachers). For a detailed review of the past and present state of benefit-incidence analysis, see Selden and Wasylenko (1992).

4. The per unit cost of a low-quality service may in fact be higher than that of a high-quality service if, for example, low quality is the result of the costs of reaching the area in which the service is located. But the costs of reaching the area may be the result of low public spending in the past. What time horizon to use and how to treat the incidence of capital expenditures are problematic. In any case, the benefits of health care subsidies will not be equal across regions.

5. Public visits as a percentage of total hospital visits are calculated from Ministry of Health data reported in World Bank (1991, table 2.4). The calculation is based on the total number of discharges and the total number of outpatient visits and the proportion of those that were private.

6. In these studies, unit costs are derived by adding up the individual cost components for a specific service output. This method represents a very different approach to the one pursued here, but it shares some of the same difficulties, including those encountered in collecting the data.

7. These are averages for class D and C hospitals. Note also that the SUSENAS does not contain details on the length of hospitalization episodes. Here I assume that each inpatient visit is worth one subsidy amount.

8. The term traditional healers encompasses various types of practitioners of "traditional" medicine as opposed to "modern" medicine. The SUSENAS include bonesetters but probably exclude traditional midwives. There appears to be declining demand for some types of traditional healers. For example, from casual observation, *dukuns* (a broad category of traditional healer), who are trained by the government, seem to be in steady decline, whereas bonesetters maintain high popularity in many areas of Indonesia.

9. The budget data used by Griffin have not been updated to 1986–87 as done here, and it is not clear whether cost recovery has been withheld from the budget totals to get net subsidy amounts.

References

Anand, Sudhir, and Martin Ravallion. 1993. "Human Development in Poor Countries: On the Role of Private Incomes and Public Services." *Journal of Economic Perspectives* 7 (1): 133–50.

BPS (Biro Pusat Statistik). 1983. *Statistik Indonesia: 1982.* Jakarta. February.

——. 1990. *Statistik Indonesia: 1989.* Jakarta. January.

Chernichovsky, Dov, and Oey A. Meesook. 1986. "Utilization of Health Services in Indonesia." *Social Science and Medicine* 23 (6): 611–20.

Drèze, Jean, and Amartya K. Sen. 1989. *Hunger and Public Action.* Oxford, Eng.: Oxford University Press.

Gani, Ascobat, Mardiati Najib, and Mary Wangsaraharja. 1988. "Indonesia Rural Health Services Cost Study. Final Report." Development Studies Project, Faculty of Public Health, University of Indonesia; Johns Hopkins University School of Public Health, Baltimore, Md.

Griffin, Charles. 1990. "Health Sector Financing in Asia." Internal Discussion Paper, Asia Regional Series, Report IDP 68. World Bank, Washington D.C.

Meerman, Jacob. 1979. *Public Expenditure in Malaysia: Who Benefits and Why?* New York: Oxford University Press.

Meesook, Oey A. 1984. *Financing and Equity in the Social Sectors in Indonesia: Some Policy Options.* World Bank Staff Working Paper 703. Washington, D.C.

Ministry of Health. 1991a. "Analysis of Health Financing in Indonesia 1982–83–1986–89 (Data Updating)." Health Sector Financing Monograph Series 10. Bureau of Planning, HE/PAU, Jakarta.

——. 1991b. "Study on Operational and Maintenance Cost of Government Hospitals, Fiscal Year 1988–1989." Health Sector Financing Project Monograph Series 8. Bureau of Planning, HE/PAU, Jakarta.

Ravallion, Martin, and Monika Huppi. 1991. "Measuring Changes in Poverty: A Methodological Case Study of Indonesia during an Adjustment Period." *World Bank Economic Review* 5 (1): 57–82.

Selden, Thomas M., and Michael J. Wasylenko. 1992. "Benefit Incidence Analysis in Developing Countries." Policy Research Working Paper WPS 1015. World Bank, Washington, D.C.

Selowsky, Marcelo. 1979. *Who Benefits from Government Expenditures? A Case Study of Colombia.* New York: Oxford University Press.

UNDP (United Nations Development Programme). 1990. *Human Development Report.* New York: Oxford University Press.

van de Walle, Dominique. 1988. "On the Use of the SUSENAS for Modelling Consumer Behavior." *Bulletin of Indonesian Economic Studies* 24: 107–22.

Walsh, R. P. D. 1981. "The Nature of Climatic Seasonality." In Robert Chambers, Richard Longhurst, and Arnold Pacey, eds., *Seasonal Dimensions to Rural Poverty.* London: Frances Pinter, Ltd.

Wirakartakusumah, Djuhari M., Prijono Tjiptoherijanto, Azwini Kartoyo, Ricardi W. Alibasjah, Darwis Hartono, Eko Ganiarto, and Erinos Muslim Tanjung. 1988. "Phase II Evaluation and Analysis of Hospital Costs." Bureau of Planning, Department of Health; Demographic Institute, School of Economics, University of Indonesia.

World Bank. 1990a. *Indonesia: A Strategy for a Sustained Reduction in Poverty.* World Bank Country Study. Washington, D.C.

———. 1990b. *World Development Report 1990: Poverty.* New York: Oxford University Press.

———. 1991. *Indonesia: Health Planning and Budgeting.* World Bank Country Study. Washington, D.C.

———. 1992. "Indonesia: Public Expenditures, Prices, and the Poor." Report 11293-IND. Washington, D.C.

Yahya, Suyono, and Runizar Roesin. 1990. "Indonesia: Implementation of the Health for All Strategy." In E. Tarimo and Andrew Creese, eds., *Achieving Health for All by the Year 2000: Midway Reports of Country Experiences.* Geneva: International Labour Office.

10 Government Health Spending in Indonesia: Impacts on Children in Different Economic Groups

Anil B. Deolalikar

Although the distribution of access to and use of social services, such as education and health, among households has been a long-standing concern among economists, relatively few studies have looked at the incidence of public expenditure on social services. Important exceptions are the studies by Meerman (1979) for Malaysia and Selowsky (1979) for Colombia, which adopted the benefit-incidence methodology to calculate the benefits of social sector spending. In the benefit-incidence approach, estimated government unit subsidies for specific social services (for example, education and health facilities) are attributed to households depending on their rates of use of these facilities.

There are a number of drawbacks to measuring the benefits of public expenditure with the benefit-incidence approach (Selden and Wasylenko 1992 and chapter 7 of this volume; van de Walle, chapter 9). First, in most such studies, the *value* of consumer benefits is assumed to be reflected by the subsidy or cost to government of the use of services. Although this assumption is virtually required given the framework of the benefit-incidence approach, it is overly restrictive. Since individuals and households obtain utility from their health status—and not from their use of health services per se—the welfare impacts of public expenditure can ultimately be discerned only by analyzing health outcomes. The link between health status and the use of health services is likely to be complex, since the latter is only one of several (possibly substitutable) inputs in the determination and maintenance of health status. For example, individuals may adjust to an inadequate supply of health services by substituting non–health care inputs, such as nutrition and hygiene, for health care inputs. As a result, the use of health services may not accurately reflect the consumer benefits derived from public expenditure.[1]

I am grateful to Dominique van de Walle, Kim Nead, Jere Behrman, and an anonymous referee for useful suggestions on an earlier draft. Support from the World Bank Research Committee is gratefully acknowledged.

A second weakness of the traditional approach is that it tends to ignore quality differences and to allocate government subsidies equally to all facilities providing a particular service. This is not inherent to the approach but has been the case in most empirical studies of benefit incidence. In most countries, but particularly in developing countries, there are wide differences in service quality in the provision of health services. Since high-income households typically choose higher-quality care than low-income households, the neglect of quality variations implies that the disparity in the distribution of benefits will be underestimated.

Third, the traditional approach ignores the role of private health services. To the extent that there are complementarities between public and private health services, government health expenditure might stimulate the provision of private health services and thereby indirectly improve access to health care. However, if public and private health services are substitutes, government health expenditure could reduce the supply of private health services and possibly worsen access to health care.

Finally, in the benefit-incidence approach, there is typically no control for household and individual factors influencing the use of social services. Since health status and health care inputs are normal goods, higher-income individuals are likely to use more health care inputs and enjoy better health than low-income individuals. Likewise, individuals with more schooling are likely to make greater use of health care facilities than individuals with less schooling. It is of interest to know how government health expenditure and infrastructure affect the use of health services and health outcomes after controlling for income and other effects.

This chapter attempts to estimate the distributional benefits of government health expenditure in Indonesia using a reduced-form demand approach. Government health expenditure is treated as a fixed factor that influences household health behavior, conditional on such factors as household income, education, and family size. The following questions are addressed. Is per capita government health expenditure associated with measures of use as well as with direct measures of health outcomes and status, after controlling for the socioeconomic factors that normally influence use and outcomes? Does the impact of government health expenditure on health services use and health outcomes differ significantly across economic groups?

The reduced-form regression strategy avoids many of the weaknesses of the benefit-incidence approach discussed earlier. First, the reduced-form approach lets us work with direct measures of health status, such as weight-for-age or incidence of morbidity, which arguably are better indicators of consumer welfare and benefits than the use of health services. Second, since per capita government health expenditure reflects both the quantity as well as the quality of health services, the reduced-form approach permits variations in service quality to have an impact on health services use and on health outcomes. Third, the reduced-form approach allows for a private sector response to public health expenditure. Since the provision of private health services is not included as an explanatory variable in the individual behavioral equations, the estimated government expenditure effects include the indirect effect that social spending has on health outcomes and service use via stimulating the supply of private health services in an area. Finally, the approach adopted here allows us to control for household socioeconomic variables that are important determinants of health use and health status.

However, the reduced-form approach employed here has its own shortcomings. First, it treats the provincial distribution of government health expenditure as being exogenous with respect to individual health behavior and outcomes. If governments allocate health spending across spatial units on the basis of health indicators, the estimated effect of government health expenditure on health outcomes and services use could be spurious. This may be a real possibility in the Indonesian context. The chapter by Pitt, Rosenzweig, and Gibbons in this volume (chapter 6) specifically addresses this issue for Indonesia and finds that the spatial placement of health clinics (and other social infrastructure) is not random with respect to unobserved factors determining household behavior.

A second limitation of the reduced-form approach adopted here is that it focuses inordinately on marginal effects, thereby ignoring some average effects that might be important. Indeed, the approach employed here could be regarded as "incremental benefit incidence," whereas the traditional incidence approach (as illustrated by van de Walle in chapter 9 of this volume) attempts to estimate the "average" benefit. In many cases, it is important to identify both. For instance, the reduced-form approach tells us nothing about the distribution of government health spending. On its basis, one cannot conclude anything about how equitable the distribution of spending is or whether government health expenditure is well targeted. Indeed, it is possible for low-income households to receive a disproportionately small share of (inframarginal) subsidies and yet benefit the most from these subsidies at the margin.

Asking which of the two methodologies—the benefit-incidence or the reduced-form approach—is more appropriate to analyze the impact of public expenditure may be the wrong question. Indeed, for the reasons discussed above, the two approaches complement each other well because they answer different questions. The benefit-incidence approach answers the question, On average, how equitably or inequitably is government health expenditure distributed across expenditure groups? The reduced-form approach indicates how the last dollar of the health budget affects the health outcomes of different expenditure groups. Together, the two approaches can be useful in guiding spending policy changes.

Analytical Issues

This chapter focuses on the reduced-form demand relations for health inputs and outcomes as dependent on prices, income, and various individual and household characteristics. Such relations are consistent with constrained maximization of a unified preference function or with the bargaining framework emphasized by Folbre (1984a, 1984b, 1986), Manser and Brown (1980), and McElroy and Horney (1981).[2] In either case, preferences are defined over the health status of individuals, and the constraints typically include a budget or income constraint and biological health production functions for each individual that characterize the "production" of health from food, nutrition, and health care inputs, conditional on the health endowments of that individual, on the state of health technology (embodied in, say, the education of the health care provider at home—typically, the mother), and on various environmental influences (such as the availability of clean drinking water; see Behrman and Deolalikar 1988 for a generic household model of health determination in a developing-country context).

The intrahousehold allocation process results in a system of reduced-form individual demand equations for health status, as well as derived demand equations for medical care and other health-related inputs. These reduced-form equations have as their arguments all prices (including the prices of food and medical care), household income, personal characteristics of household members, and relevant family- and community-specific variables.

Within this very general framework, the public provision of medical care and other health goods (for example, clean drinking water and sanitation), as reflected in government health expenditure, can have important reduced-form effects on the health outcomes of individuals and on their demand for medical care. Such effects may operate through a number of mechanisms. First, higher per capita government health expenditure in a region may be associated with greater availability of health facilities and health services per capita. If the demand for health care is constrained by an inadequate supply of health facilities and services (both curative and preventive), supply improvements could promote demand and thereby improve health outcomes. Second, better government health infrastructure in a region may draw private health providers into that region, thereby increasing the aggregate supply of private health services. Given competitive markets for health care, this would lower the price for private care, which in turn would raise the demand for private and public health services (depending on the own- and cross-price elasticities of demand for such services) and improve health outcomes.[3] Third, higher levels of government health expenditure might reflect better quality of government health services. If the quality of health services is an important determinant of their use, improvements in quality could lead to greater use and better health outcomes. Fourth, the association between government health expenditure and health outcomes may have nothing to do with the provision of health services, but have everything to do with environmental hygiene. In many countries, the health budget includes expenditure on the supply of drinking water and sanitation. To the extent that better environmental hygiene promotes health, higher levels of government health expenditure could be associated with improved health outcomes and greater derived demand for medical care.

Unfortunately, the reduced-form framework does not permit separate identification of the various mechanisms discussed above. Instead, it merely indicates the ultimate effects of public health spending on individuals' use of health services and health outcomes.

So far the discussion has adopted a "representative consumer" approach, making the assumption that government health expenditure affects health services use and health status identically across all individuals. This may be an overly restrictive assumption for a number of reasons. First, access to government health facilities may be unequal across economic groups. For example, urban dwellers may have disproportionately greater access to better-quality health care than rural households. To the extent that urban households are typically more affluent than rural households, the urban bias in government health expenditure could translate into larger health benefits for richer relative to poorer households. Second, there could be behavioral differences among individuals belonging to different income groups that might lead them to respond differently to identical levels of availability, quality, and price of health services. For instance, there is growing evidence to suggest that the price elasticity of demand for medical care is larger for the poor than for the nonpoor (Gertler and van der Gaag 1990). If this is indeed the case, an equivalent reduction in the price of medical care (induced, say, by an improved supply of public and private health services) would increase the poor's use of health services more than the nonpoor's. Third, identical use of health services (of the same quality) could be associated with different health outcomes due to biological differences across individuals. For instance, a diminishing marginal product of health care and other health inputs would imply that innately healthier individuals would benefit proportionately less from the same amount and quality of health care than would less healthy individuals. If health outcomes and incomes were positively associated with each other, one would then observe larger health gains for the poor from identical provision of health services.

To illustrate these effects, assume that individual health outcomes (*H*) are "produced" with only two inputs, government health services (*M*) and private health services (*P*):

(10-1) $H = H(M,P); H' > 0$ and $H'' < 0.$

The impact of aggregate government health spending (*G*) on the health outcomes of the *i*th economic group is then given by:

(10-2) $$\partial H_i/\partial G = [(\partial H_i/\partial M_i)(\partial M_i/\partial G)]$$
$$+ [(\partial H_i/\partial P_i)(\partial P_i/\partial G)].$$

A priori, both $\partial H_i/\partial M_i$ and $\partial H_i/\partial P_i$ (the marginal product of public and private medical care) are likely to be greater for low-income than for high-income groups, since the former typically consume lower quantities of medical care. However, the total impact of aggregate government spending on the health outcomes of the *i*th economic group also depends on how aggregate government spending influences the supply of public and private medical services. If an additional dollar of government health spending increases access to medical care for the nonpoor much more than for the poor, $\partial H_i/\partial G$ could be greater for the nonpoor than for the poor even though the latter have higher values of $\partial H_i/\partial M_i$ and $\partial H_i/\partial P_i$.

Background and Data

With a total population estimated at 175 million in mid-1988, Indonesia is the fifth most populous country in the world (World Bank 1990). Although the World Bank ranks Indonesia as a low-income economy with a per capita income of $440 in 1988, the Indonesian economy enjoyed rapid economic growth during the last two decades. For example, between 1965 and 1988, Indonesia achieved an annual growth rate of per capita gross national product (GNP) of 4.3 percent, a rate that few developing countries could match. Available estimates also suggest an impressive reduction in infant mortality during the same period— from 128 infant deaths per 1,000 live births in 1965 to 61 in 1990 (World Bank 1992). Despite this performance, Indonesia has one of the highest infant and maternal mortality rates among Southeast Asian countries. For example, in 1988 Indonesia had much higher infant and maternal mortality levels than the Philippines, Thailand, or even Viet Nam. Anemia is the major cause of maternal mortality (Gopalan 1988), while immunizable diseases (particularly, tetanus), diarrhea, and acute respiratory infections are thought to be the leading causes of infant and child mortality (Government of Indonesia and UNICEF 1989).

Indonesia has been successful in expanding access to health care for its population. The number of primary health services in rural areas has increased dramatically. The proportion of households seeking curative and preventive treatment for their children is relatively high across all expenditure classes. The changes between 1978 and 1987 are most striking. In chapter 9 of this volume, van de Walle compares use data for 1978 and 1987 and finds that during this period the use of primary health centers in rural areas spread and equalized considerably across expenditure quantiles. The poorer groups used health services much more in 1987 than they did in 1978.

The data for this study come from the 1987 round of the National Socioeconomic Survey (SUSENAS), which is a nationally representative survey of Indonesia that is undertaken periodically. The 1987 round, conducted in January, covered roughly 250,000 individuals residing in 50,000 households. While focusing on the health status of individuals and the choice of health providers for curative care, the 1987 SUSENAS survey obtained detailed information on household consumption expenditure and income as well. Using both one-week and three-month recall techniques, the health module collected data on perceived illnesses (occurrence, type, and length) and the choice of provider for any treatment obtained. In addition, data on weight and immunization history were collected for all children under five years of age.

The major problem with the health module of the 1987 SUSENAS survey is that no clinical diagnosis was performed in assessing morbidity. All measures of morbidity were reported by the respondents and, as such, are subject to measurement error and respondent biases in illness perception. Not much can be done about this problem, except to recognize the potential biases it may cause in the empirical estimates. It is usually possible to speculate on the direction of such biases, since we know that certain variables such as mother's education and household income are associated with increased perception and early recognition of illness.

Since three months is generally too long a period to recall an illness with any degree of accuracy, the one-week recall data are likely to be more reliable and are therefore the data on morbidity reported in this chapter.[4] In addition to the probability of reporting an illness episode during the one-week reference period, I also use the reported length (in days) of the illness episode as an alternative indicator of health status. Finally, the weight data collected by the SUSENAS for children under five provides a third, much more objective and reliable, indicator of health status.

The other data used in this study are recurrent government health expenditure data that were compiled for Indonesia's twenty-seven provinces. There are three major problems in compiling and reporting data on public health spending in Indonesia. First, expenditure on health originates in a multiplicity of budgets and at several levels of government (central, provincial, and district). There are at least ten different budgetary sources of funds for the public health system in the country (APBN-DIP, APBN-DIK, INPRES, SDO, BLN, and so forth). Second, no comprehensive data source aggregates these budgetary outlays into a single, consolidated account of actual or budgeted expenditure on health. Third, as there is no suitable spatial price index for Indonesia, it is difficult to adjust government—or, for that matter, household— expenditures for provincial price differences.[5] Despite these problems, data collected by the Bureau of Planning in the Department of Health through a special survey of central, provincial, and district government accounts were compiled for each of the twenty-seven provinces for the fiscal year 1986–87. These were merged with the SUSENAS health data at the province level.

Table 10-1, which provides the details on government health expenditure for each of the twenty-seven provinces, shows wide interprovincial variations in government recurrent health expenditure per capita (the terms government health expenditure or public health spending refer to recurrent government health expenditure per capita in the remainder of this chapter). Government health expenditure per capita was lowest in Nusa Tenggara Barat (Rp644) and highest in DKI Jakarta (Rp15,321; Indonesia's currency is the rupiah). If the city of Jakarta is excluded, the highest level of government health spending per capita was in the province of Timor Timur (Rp4,182). The extraordinarily high level of government health expenditure in DKI Jakarta, especially in relation to other provinces, implies either that public health spending is really skewed in favor of Indonesia's capital city or that a (large) portion of the public health spending reported for Jakarta is on administrative items relating to the country as a whole (in principle, expenses for administrative items are supposed to be allocated across provinces on the basis of a formula). Although the latter possibility cannot be completely ruled out, other data on the availability and quality of health infrastructure across provinces suggest that, as the primary city in Indonesia, Jakarta is exceptionally favored in terms of health and other social infrastructure.

Empirical Model

The study focuses on the demand for health status and the derived demand for health-related inputs for children under five years of age. I thus assume implicitly that the health demand relations differ by age groups (although the demand relations for older children and adults are not estimated here).[6] Since differences across economic groups are an important concern of the chapter, the parameters of the demand relations are allowed to depend (log-linearly) on household expenditure per capita.[7] The equations to be estimated are:

$$(10\text{-}3) \qquad \mathbf{H}_{ij} = a_1(Y) + a_2(Y)\mathbf{X}_{ij} + a_3(Y)\mathbf{Z}_{ij} + a_4(Y)G_j + \mu_{ij};$$

$$a_k = a_{k1} + a_{k2}Y, \qquad k=1,\ldots,4,$$

where

i = indexes the individual child;
j = indexes the province of residence;
H = vector of health care inputs and health outcomes;
Y = log household monthly expenditure per capita;
X = vector of individual characteristics (age and sex);
Z = vector of household characteristics, including Y;
G = log government health expenditure per capita; and
μ = stochastic disturbance term.

It is important to note that, since the relations in equation 10-3 are of the reduced form, all dependent variables—whether health inputs or health outcomes—have the same set of explanatory variables. Also, since an individual's health status is a cumulative outcome of health care and other (nutritional) inputs over a number of years, the analysis implicitly assumes that the explanatory variables reflect medium- or long-run living standards of households and communities—and not just living standards in the year of the survey. This in turn implies that the explanatory variables, including provincial government health expenditures per capita, have been stable over time.[8] The vector of *health care inputs* (H) includes both curative care (whether any treatment and whether treatment from a modern health care provider—physician, paramedic, or nurse—was sought for an illness during the week preceding the interview) and preventive care (whether the child has been immunized against DPT, cholera, measles, or polio). Since all of these variables are dichotomous in nature, the corresponding equations are estimated by the maximum likelihood logit method.

Health outcomes (H) are proxied by the occurrence of an illness episode during the reference period and the duration of any such illness episode. In addition, the age- and sex-standardized weight of a child is included as an indicator of health (or, more appropriately, nutritional) status. Child weight is standardized by the median weight of a well-nourished child of the same age and sex in the United States (NCHS 1977).[9] The probability of an illness episode during the reference period is estimated by the maximum likelihood logit method, while the illness length and standardized weight equations are estimated by ordinary least squares.

The individual child characteristics (X) that are included in the health demand relations are sex, age (in months), and age squared. The vector of household characteristics (Z) includes household size, urban/rural status of residence, age of the household head, schooling of the child's mother and of the household head, and the natural log of household per capita monthly expenditure.

The coefficient $a_4(Y)$ in relation 10-3 represents the marginal effect of log government health expenditure on health services use and on health outcomes, controlling for observed household and individual characteristics such as age, education, and household per capita expen-

Table 10-1. *Government Health Expenditures in Twenty-seven Indonesian Provinces, 1986–87* (rupiah)

Province	Recurrent expenditures				Government recurrent health expenditure	
	Capital expenditure[a]	Salary	INPRES drug supply	Others[b]	Total	Per capita
Dista Aceh	351,884	901,152	1,009,759	1,163,422	3,074,333	1,109
Sumatra Utara	1,027,051	3,959,021	3,202,148	2,011,260	9,172,429	1,044
Sumatra Barat	1,090,849	2,946,166	1,332,164	3,142,169	7,420,498	2,245
Riau	228,985	769,124	849,479	907,578	2,526,181	1,029
Jambi	909,025	643,384	—	700,597	1,343,981	1,220
Sumatra Selatan	486,356	4,050,335	1,771,224	4,260,488	10,082,048	1,882
Bengkulu	151,497	487,795	117,070	577,132	1,181,997	1,329
Lampung	624,590	991,522	1,994,764	841,097	3,827,383	700
DKI Jakarta	50,781,543	29,763,854	2,737,081	44,882,055	77,382,990	15,321
Jawa Barat	1,640,525	10,793,007	10,206,933	9,955,386	30,955,326	1,021
Jawa Tengah	2,238,485	9,897,536	8,924,518	10,312,885	29,134,939	1,143
DI Yogyakarta	795,559	3,191,979	943,386	2,992,238	7,127,603	2,653
Jawa Timur	1,760,177	8,648,904	10,234,162	5,039,996	23,923,062	805
Bali	605,268	3,094,027	876,974	2,811,183	6,782,184	2,730
Nusa Tenggara Barat	314,417	629,540	565,529	473,498	1,668,567	644

Nusa Tenggara Timur	861,466	809,047	1,084,967	901,717	2,795,731	1,155
Timor Timur	162,468	1,164,735	341,330	1,072,185	2,578,250	4,182
Kalimantan Barat	531,167	854,895	902,436	1,250,177	3,007,508	1,208
Kalimantan Tengah	119,733	522,628	406,902	732,477	1,662,006	1,520
Kalimantan Selatan	951,714	853,921	755,149	1,140,937	2,750,007	1,582
Kalimantan Timur	132,718	709,969	563,978	861,040	2,134,987	1,404
Sulawesi Utara	881,741	1,072,703	972,244	1,154,540	3,199,487	1,718
Sulawesi Tengah	171,587	653,154	510,042	709,641	1,872,838	1,289
Sulawesi Selatan	1,005,472	2,385,632	2,185,354	2,655,861	7,226,846	1,213
Sulawesi Tenggara	264,048	543,043	368,482	583,017	1,494,541	1,491
Maluku	423,531	718,450	583,259	813,648	2,115,357	1,517
Irian Jaya	519,864	886,591	515,436	878,550	2,280,577	1,915

—Not available.

Note: Includes DIP, INPRES, and routine budgets.

a. Includes DIP (land, machinery and equipment, and construction) and INPRES (investment in new *puskesmas, puskesmas pembantus*, and doctors' living quarters, clean water, and sanitation).

b. Includes DIP (materials, transportation, and other costs), routine budget (material expenditure, maintenance, and transportation), and INPRES budget (operational costs, *puskesmas keliling*, vehicle maintenance, program expenditure, staff distribution, medical equipment and supply, and nonallocation budget).

Source: Pusat Pengolahan Data dan Informasi Anggaran, Bandung, Dirjen Anggaran, Departemen Keuangan.

diture. In practice, however, when governments increase social spending, there is typically no control for other effects. For policy purposes, it may be useful to know how increased social spending affects poor households, whatever their characteristics. For this reason, I also estimate an ultimate reduced-form version of relation 10-3 in which the only regressors are log per capita government health expenditure and the interaction of log per capita government health expenditure and log per capita household expenditure (to distinguish this model from the full model in equation 10-1, the abridged model will be referred to as the reduced-form model and the complete model as the full model in the remainder of this chapter). The coefficients of this model indicate the impact of government health expenditure without controlling for any household or individual characteristics.

Differences in Health Inputs and Health Outcomes across Expenditure Classes

Table 10-2 reports the mean levels of health care inputs and health outcomes for the entire sample as well as for three expenditure classes (low, middle, and high) separately. The low-expenditure class includes children whose household per capita expenditure falls below Rp12,000 in the rural areas and Rp14,000 in the urban areas. These cutoff points correspond closely to commonly used poverty lines for Indonesia. The middle-expenditure group includes children having household per capita expenditure between Rp12,000 and Rp25,000 in rural areas and between Rp14,000 and Rp30,000 in urban areas. All other observations fall in the high-expenditure class.

The 1987 susenas data yielded data on 28,194 children under the age of five years. A total of 3,046 episodes of illness were reported with the one-week recall method, giving a period prevalence rate of 10.8 percent. This is a fairly high prevalence rate, since it implies, on extrapolation to an annual rate, that each child experienced an average of 5.6 episodes of illness per year.[10] Relatively few (5.5 percent) of the reported illnesses were not treated at all; about 25 percent were treated at home by the family, and 4.2 percent were treated by traditional healers. The remaining two-thirds were treated in the modern sector, with public health centers (*puskesmas*) being the most common health providers (34.7 percent). The average duration of an illness experienced during the reference period was 4.2 days.

Neither the incidence nor the duration of illness differs significantly across the three expenditure classes. However, the pattern of treatment is very different across the expenditure classes. For example, only 59 percent of children in the low-expenditure class experiencing an illness episode received any treatment, compared with 80 percent of ill children in the high-expenditure class. Likewise, a much larger proportion

of children in the high-expenditure class were immunized (71 percent) relative to those in the low-expenditure class (45 percent). The higher levels of curative and preventive care appear to translate into higher levels of age- and sex-standardized weights for children belonging to the high-expenditure class.

Empirical Results

The concern of the analysis is not so much with the differences in levels of health care inputs and health outcomes across expenditure classes as with the *varying impact* of government health expenditure on child health inputs and outcomes across economic groups. These can be obtained from the estimates of the demand functions for health care and health outcomes, which are reported in tables 10-3 and 10-4. The top panel in each table shows the linear portion of the relevant coefficient (a_{k1}), while the lower panel indicates the coefficient on the interaction between the relevant independent variable and log household expenditure per capita (a_{k2}). The marginal effect of an independent variable—say, government health expenditure—on health use and outcomes is obtained by:

$$(10\text{-}4) \qquad \partial H_i \ / \ \partial G \ = \ a_{K1} \ + \ a_{K2} \ (Y_i).$$

Demand for Curative Care

Table 10-3 shows logit estimates of both the probability of seeking *any* treatment for an illness episode reported during the reference period (one week preceding the survey) and the probability of seeking treatment from a modern (as opposed to a traditional) provider. Since Wald tests could not reject the hypothesis of coefficients being independent of household expenditure per capita for both equations, the estimated coefficients are not allowed to vary by per capita expenditure. Indeed, government health expenditure per capita in the province of residence does not have a significant effect on the probability of seeking treatment of either type. However, a number of other variables do influence treatment probabilities. These include mother's schooling, log household expenditure per capita, urban residence (all positive effects), and household size (negative effect). The household expenditure elasticity of treatment is estimated to be 0.12, while the elasticity of treatment from a modern provider is 0.14. Controlling for other factors, urban residence increases the probability of treatment for an illness episode by about 0.05 and the probability of a modern treatment by 0.08. Surprisingly, boys have a significantly lower (by about 0.04) probability of receiving treatment for an illness than girls, while health insurance coverage does not have a significant association with treatment probabilities. The latter result may simply reflect the fact that too few children

Table 10-2. Descriptive Statistics for Sample of Children under Five Years, Indonesia, 1987

	Total sample		Low expenditure		Middle expenditure		High expenditure	
Independent variable	Mean	Standard deviation	Mean	Standard deviation	Mean	Standard deviation	Mean	Standard deviation
Whether ill during previous week	0.108	0.310	0.108	0.310	0.106	0.307	0.115	0.319
If ill, length of illness (days)	4.151	1.997	4.213	2.038	4.136	1.960	4.114	2.039
Whether illness treated by/at								
Private physician	0.082	0.275	0.021	0.145	0.066	0.249	0.199	0.400
Hospital	0.062	0.241	0.031	0.175	0.064	0.246	0.094	0.292
Primary health care center	0.347	0.476	0.303	0.460	0.370	0.483	0.343	0.475
Polyclinic	0.048	0.214	0.064	0.245	0.042	0.200	0.044	0.205
Paramedic	0.115	0.319	0.122	0.328	0.117	0.322	0.099	0.299
Traditional healer	0.042	0.201	0.048	0.213	0.048	0.213	0.020	0.141
Self-treated or not treated	0.304	0.833	0.410	0.768	0.292	0.729	0.202	0.779
Whether illness treated other than by self	0.696	0.460	0.590	0.492	0.707	0.455	0.799	0.401
Whether illness treated by modern provider	0.654	0.476	0.542	0.499	0.660	0.474	0.779	0.415
Standardized weight (percent)	81.736	12.440	79.566	11.669	81.495	12.166	85.291	13.385
Whether child vaccinated for								
DPT	0.442	0.497	0.340	0.474	0.429	0.495	0.612	0.487
Cholera	0.075	0.263	0.033	0.179	0.068	0.253	0.148	0.355
Polio	0.409	0.492	0.284	0.451	0.402	0.490	0.592	0.492
Measles	0.140	0.347	0.087	0.282	0.130	0.337	0.239	0.426
Any of the above	0.552	0.497	0.451	0.498	0.542	0.498	0.714	0.452
Age of child (months)	28.548	16.152	28.626	16.080	28.832	16.168	27.661	16.176

Log of household per capita monthly expenditure	9.774	0.536	9.153	0.212	9.787	0.231	10.567	0.338
Household size	5.835	2.172	6.391	2.148	5.795	2.150	5.203	2.074
Age of household head	36.992	10.768	39.041	11.289	36.531	10.576	35.534	10.184
Schooling years of household head	5.575	3.781	3.645	2.805	5.453	3.445	8.482	4.015
Schooling years of mother	4.821	3.452	3.209	2.599	4.657	3.099	7.419	3.860
Whether household insured	0.013	0.113	0.004	0.060	0.009	0.095	0.035	0.184
Whether urban resident	0.297	0.457	0.130	0.336	0.289	0.453	0.544	0.498
Per capita recurrent government health expenditure in province of residence (rupiah)	1,768	2,547	1,260	651	1,611	2,072	2,876	4,357
Total number of observations	28,194	7,377		15,279			5,538	
Number of children reporting ill during reference period	3,046	795		1,613			638	

Note: Low-expenditure households are those whose total consumption expenditure per capita falls below Rp12,000 in rural areas and Rp14,000 in urban areas. The per capita expenditure range for the middle group is Rp12,000–Rp25,000 in rural areas and Rp14,000–Rp30,000 in urban areas. All other households are regarded as high-expenditure households.

Table 10-3. Determinants of Health Care Use, Children under Five Years, Indonesia, 1987

Variable	Probability of seeking any treatment for illness (logit)		Probability of seeking "modern" treatment for illness (logit)		Probability of having received any immunization (logit)	
	Parameter	t-ratio	Parameter	t-ratio	Parameter	t-ratio
Independent variable						
Intercept	-3.669	-3.3	-4.025	-3.8	-4.779	-13.5
	0.39	0.6	0.264	0.4	-0.725	-3.9
Age	-0.003	-0.3	0.006	0.6	0.082	24.8
Age squared	0.000	-0.1	0.000	-0.7	-0.001	-21.0
Whether male	-0.186	-2.2	-0.159	-2.0	-0.021	-0.8
Age of household head	0.003	0.8	0.006	1.3	0.015	9.8
Schooling years of household head	0.009	0.6	-0.001	-0.1	0.052	10.0
Schooling years of mother	0.049	2.9	0.064	3.9	0.079	14.4
Log household per capita expenditure	0.412	4.2	0.414	4.3	0.221	6.6
Whether insured	-0.493	-1.4	-0.372	-1.0	0.778	4.9
Household size	-0.049	-2.1	-0.056	-2.5	-0.076	-10.5
Whether urban	0.227	2.1	0.345	3.2	0.618	17.7
Log recurrent government health expenditure per capita in province of residence	0.074	0.8	0.063	0.7	0.122	4.5
	-0.850	-5	-0.919	-6.1	-0.986	-19.8

Independent variable interacted with log household per capita expenditure	(1)		(2)		(3)		(4)		(5)		(6)	(7)	
Age									0.031	4.7			
Age squared									0.000	−4.0			
Whether male									0.079	1.4			
Age of household head									0.001	0.3			
Schooling years of household head									0.050	4.8			
Schooling years of mother									−0.005	−0.4			
Log household per capita expenditure									0.020	0.4			
Whether insured									0.150	0.5			
Household size									0.028	1.9			
Whether urban									0.120	1.6			
Log recurrent government health expenditure per capita in province of residence	−1,710	8.3			−1,782		0.100	9.1	0.163	3.1	−15,755	0.115	31.1
	0.09						−1,803					−16,710	
Log likelihood ratio	−1,725								−15,706				
Number of observations	2,901		2,901		2,901		2,901		25,323		25,323	25,323	
Wald test for no ln per capita expenditure interaction effects	12.37		11.61						93.60				
Significance level for Wald test	0.34		0.39						0.00				
Mean of dependent variable	0.70		0.70		0.66		0.66		0.56		0.56	0.56	

Table 10-4. Determinants of Health Outcomes, Children under Five Years, Indonesia, 1987

Variable	Probability of reported illness episode (logit)				Duration of illness (ordinary least squares)				Standardized weight (ordinary least squares)					
	Param-eter	t-ratio	Param-eter	t-ratio	Param-eter	t-ratio	Param-eter	t-ratio	Param-eter	t-ratio	Param-eter	t-ratio	Param-eter	t-ratio
Independent variable														
Intercept	-1.314	-2.6	-0.768	-2.7	4.891	5.2	5.598	10.4	62.604	2.3	64.333	34.7	83.895	82.0
Age	0.021	4.3			-0.001	-0.1			-0.536	-1.7	-0.717	-40.3		
Age squared	0.000	-5.8			0.000	-0.9			0.012	2.2	0.010	34.1		
Whether male	0.037	0.9			-0.173	-2.3			-3.764	-1.4	-2.826	-19.3		
Age of household head	-0.007	-3.2			0.002	0.5			-0.133	-0.9	0.037	4.7		
Schooling years of household head	-0.020	-2.6			-0.038	-2.7			-1.528	-3.0	0.096	3.5		
Schooling years of mother	-0.005	-0.6			-0.001	-0.1			-0.527	-1.0	0.183	6.3		
Log household per capita expenditure	0.109	2.3			0.106	1.2			1.121	0.2	2.760	15.5		
Whether insured	0.234	1.4			0.427	1.3			24.159	2.2	2.513	3.8		
Household size	-0.051	-4.6			0.014	0.7			0.502	0.7	-0.065	-1.7		
Whether urban	-0.024	-0.5			-0.078	-0.8			-0.802	-0.2	1.228	6.6		
Log recurrent government health expenditures per capita in province of residence	-0.166	-4.2	-0.285	-3.9	-0.199	-2.7	-0.162	-1.2	3.919	1.7	-0.201	-1.5	-6.030	-21.5

Independent variable interacted with log household per capita expenditure

Age								−0.018	−0.6			
Age squared								0.000	−0.3			
Whether male								0.097	0.4			
Age of household head								0.017	1.1			
Schooling years of household head								0.164	3.2			
Schooling years of mother								0.070	1.3			
Log household per capita expenditure								0.179	0.7			
Whether insured								−2.122	−2.0			
Household size								−0.057	−0.8			
Whether urban								0.203	0.5			
Log recurrent government health expenditures per capita in province of residence	0.011	2.1			−0.004	−0.4		−0.412	−1.8		0.587	28.6
Log likelihood ratio	−8,929											
	−9,003											
Number of observations	25,323	25,323		2,901		2,901		25,323		25,323	25,323	
R-squared				0.02		0.00		0.13		0.12	0.03	
F-test				4.35		4.29		166.06		325.72	438.64	
Wald/F test for no ln per capita expenditure interaction effects	11.43			1.43				5.72				
Significance level for Wald test	0.41											
Mean of dependent variable	0.11	0.11		4.16		4.16		81.85		81.85	81.85	

277

in the sample—only 1.3 percent—have health insurance coverage. In addition, since health insurance coverage in Indonesia is typically limited to government employees and salaried individuals working in the formal sector, insurance coverage is correlated strongly with both log household expenditure per capita and schooling of the household head. Indeed, a joint test of significance indicates that the three variables are jointly significant at the 5 percent level.

The reduced-form estimates of the curative care equations differ substantially from the estimates of the full model. In particular, per capita government health expenditure in the province of residence is observed to have a strong negative effect—but one that becomes positive at higher levels of household expenditure per capita—on treatment probabilities. What this means is that government health spending is associated with the use of curative health services primarily via other control variables. When evaluated at the sample mean level of household expenditure per capita, the elasticity of curative care with respect to per capita government health expenditure is estimated to be only 0.020 (see table 10-5). However, it varies from −0.015 at a household per capita monthly expenditure level of Rp5,000 to 0.115 at a per capita monthly expenditure of Rp500,000 in the case of any treatment (and from −0.023 to 0.134 for treatment from a modern provider).

Demand for Preventive Care

Table 10-3 also shows the logit estimates of the probability of a child being immunized against DPT, cholera, measles, or polio. In this case, a Wald test solidly rejected the hypothesis of coefficients being independent of log household expenditure per capita. The association between per capita government health expenditure and the probability of child immunization is observed to depend significantly (and positively) on household expenditure per capita. The estimated elasticity of child immunization with respect to government health expenditure is positive (0.030) at the sample mean but varies enormously with household expenditure per capita. Indeed, the estimated elasticity is slightly negative (although not significantly different from zero) for households having per capita monthly expenditures under Rp10,000 but is as large as 0.270 for households spending Rp500,000 per capita per month. The association between use of preventive health services (child immunization) and government health spending is generally stronger than that between use of curative services and government health spending, presumably because preventive health services, unlike curative services, are typically provided free of charge. However, the finding that the positive association between child immunization rates and government health expenditure is stronger for affluent than for poor house-

Table 10-5. *Elasticity of Health Care Use and Health Outcome Variables with Respect to Government Recurrent Health Expenditure per Capita, Children under Five Years, Indonesia, 1987*

Dependent variable and model	At sample mean	At household per capita expenditure (rupiah) of							
		5,000	10,000	15,000	25,000	50,000	100,000	250,000	500,000
Probability of illness episode									
Full	−0.148	−0.148	−0.148	−0.148	−0.148	−0.148	−0.148	−0.148	−0.148
Reduced form	−0.158	−0.170	−0.163	−0.160	−0.155	−0.148	−0.141	−0.132	−0.125
Probability of any treatment for illness									
Full	n.s.	n.s.	n.s.	n.s.	n.s.	n.s.	n.s.	n.s.	n.s.
Reduced form	0.020	−0.015	0.004	0.016	0.030	0.050	0.069	0.095	0.115
Probability of "modern" treatment for illness									
Full	n.s.	n.s.	n.s.	n.s.	n.s.	n.s.	n.s.	n.s.	n.s.
Reduced form	0.020	−0.023	0.001	0.014	0.032	0.055	0.079	0.110	0.134
Probability of any immunization									
Full	0.030	−0.061	−0.011	0.018	0.055	0.105	0.154	0.220	0.270
Reduced form	0.061	−0.003	0.032	0.053	0.079	0.114	0.149	0.195	0.230
Weight-for-age									
Full	−0.109	0.410	0.124	−0.043	−0.253	−0.539	−0.824	−1.202	−1.487
Reduced form	−0.291	−1.030	−0.624	−0.386	−0.086	0.321	0.728	1.266	1.673
Illness duration									
Full	−0.048	−0.048	−0.048	−0.048	−0.048	−0.048	−0.048	−0.048	−0.048
Reduced form	n.s.	n.s.	n.s.	n.s.	n.s.	n.s.	n.s.	n.s.	n.s.
Percentage of sample observations falling below this expenditure per capita level	n.a.	0.2	13.8	41.2	75.8	96.3	99.6	99.9	100.0

n.a. Not applicable.
n.s. Coefficient not significant at the 5 percent level. Underlying coefficients are reported in tables 10-3 and 10-4.

holds suggests that public preventive health programs in Indonesia are poorly targeted to the poor.

Although the interactions with log household expenditure per capita are jointly significant in the child immunization equation, the interactions reduce the number of significant coefficients obtained in the model. For example, on the one hand, in the model without any log expenditure interactions, all estimated coefficients except the one on gender are significant at the 5 percent level. Further, all the estimated coefficients have the "correct" signs. On the other hand, in the model with log expenditure interactions, a number of variables, including mother's schooling, household head's age, and insurance coverage, no longer have significant coefficients.

The ultimate reduced-form estimates, also shown in table 10-3, are similar in sign, although not in magnitude, to the estimates discussed above. The elasticity of child immunization with respect to per capita government health expenditure is estimated to be 0.061 (table 10-5) in the reduced-form model (as opposed to 0.030 in the full model). This elasticity ranges from −0.003 for children whose families earn Rp5,000 per capita per month to 0.230 for those whose families earn Rp500,000 per capita per month.

Child Health Outcomes

As noted earlier, an important advantage of the reduced-form estimation strategy adopted here is that it is possible to estimate directly the marginal benefits of government spending in terms of health outcomes of different economic groups. Three variables in the SUSENAS survey can be used as proxies for child health outcomes: the probability of an illness episode during the week preceding the survey, the duration of an illness, and the weight of a child. Unfortunately, the morbidity measures are self-reported. The analysis of self-reported morbidity measures confounds the effects of exogenous variables on *true* morbidity with those on *reporting* of morbidity. However, it is often the case that reporting bias is systematically related to variables such as parental education and household expenditure. Although there is control for these variables in the health outcome equations, the bias in the estimated effect of government health expenditure on reported health status is unlikely to be completely eliminated, since individuals living in areas well served by health facilities and well endowed with health infrastructure may recognize ill health more accurately, and respond to it with more prompt treatment, than individuals residing in poorly served areas. Little can be done about this bias.

However, as discussed earlier, although the perception of an illness is likely to vary among persons of different educational and expenditure backgrounds and among persons residing in areas differentially served by health services, the reported duration of an illness, conditional on an illness already being reported, is likely to be less contaminated by respondent bias. Therefore, the reported length of an illness is a useful additional measure of health status to analyze.

Since an illness episode in the relevant reference period is a dichotomous variable (assuming a value of 1 if the child was ill and zero otherwise), I estimate the relations for the probability of an illness episode during the week preceding the survey by the maximum likelihood logit method. Illness duration, conditional on an illness episode being reported, is estimated by ordinary least squares.

Since a Wald test could not reject the hypothesis that the coefficients of the illness equation were independent of log household expenditure per capita, the illness episode equation is estimated without any expenditure interactions (table 10-4). The estimates indicate that government health expenditure has a significant negative association with reported morbidity (with an elasticity of morbidity with respect to government health spending of -0.16). Surprisingly, however, household expenditure per capita is associated with an increase in reported morbidity, most likely reflecting the fact that the reporting of child morbidity is greater in more affluent than in poor households. Other surprising and counterintuitive results in the illness episode equation include the nonsignificance of mother's schooling, urban residence, and health insurance coverage and a negative effect of household size on reported morbidity. The nonsignificance of the insurance variable is most likely due to the fact that households having health insurance coverage have a greater propensity to report minor illnesses of their children. But since these households, which typically tend to be more affluent and educated than households not covered by insurance, are likely to experience lower levels of *actual* morbidity among their children, the net effect of insurance coverage on *reported* illness incidence is not significantly different from zero. Likewise, the negative effect of household size probably reflects the fact that there is less reporting of child illness episodes in large households (or households that have a large number of children).

The reduced-form model of illness incidence yields a significant interaction effect between government health expenditure and household expenditure per capita (table 10-4). However, the estimated elasticity of government health expenditure does not vary much by household expenditure per capita. At a monthly expenditure per capita of Rp5,000, the elasticity is estimated to be -0.170, while it is -0.125 at a per capita expenditure level of Rp500,000.

An F-test also failed to reject the hypothesis that the coefficients of the illness duration equation are independent of household per capita expenditure (table 10-4). Government health expenditure per capita has a strong negative association with illness duration, such that a 5 percent increase in government health spending is associated with a reduction in illness duration of a day. Children in households with better educated heads tend to have illness episodes of shorter duration, as do boys (relative to girls). The reduced-form model yields no significant effects of government health spending, either by itself or interacted with household expenditure.

Child Nutritional Outcomes

Weight-for-age provides another, more objective measure of nutritional or health outcomes. I analyze the determinants of child weight, standardizing it by the median weight of a well-nourished child of the same age and sex in the United States (NCHS 1977). The standardized weight-for-age equation, estimated by ordinary least squares, is reported in table 10-4. An F-test rejected the hypothesis of coefficients being independent of household expenditure per capita. Per capita government health expenditure in the province of residence has a strong positive association with child weight, but one that declines (significantly) with household expenditure per capita. The estimated elasticity of child weights with respect to government health expenditure varies from a high of 0.410 for households spending Rp5,000 per person per month to a low of -1.487 for households spending Rp500,000 per person per month.

An interesting finding is the strong positive association, albeit decreasing in household expenditure per capita, of insurance coverage with child weights. At the sample mean level of household expenditure per capita, children with health insurance coverage weigh, other things being equal, 3.4 percentage points (on a 100-point standardized weight scale) more than children with no insurance coverage. At an expenditure per capita level of Rp5,000 per month, the weight premium associated with insurance coverage is much larger—6.1 percentage points. However, the weight advantage of children with insurance coverage disappears by the time household expenditure per capita reaches Rp88,000 per month.[11]

Unlike insurance coverage, schooling of the household head has a strong negative effect on child weight, albeit one that becomes increasingly positive as household expenditure per capita rises. Surprisingly, however, mother's schooling has no significant effect on child weight in the fully interacted model.

As in the immunization equation, although the interactions with log household expenditure per capita are jointly significant in the weight equation, the interactions reduce the number of significant coefficients. For example, on the one hand, in the model without any log expenditure interactions, all estimated coefficients except the one on per capita government health expenditure are significant at the 10 percent level.

In addition, all the estimated coefficients have the a priori expected signs. On the other hand, in the model with log expenditure interactions, a number of variables, including mother's schooling, log expenditure per capita, household size, and urban residence, are rendered insignificant.

The association of government health expenditure with child weights in the reduced-form model is completely opposite in sign to that obtained from the full model. In the reduced-form weight model, government health expenditure per capita has a very significant *negative* association with child weight, although the association is positive at higher levels of household expenditure per capita. The elasticity of child weights with respect to government health expenditure is − 1.030 at a monthly expenditure per capita level of Rp5,000 and increases to 1.673 at the highest expenditure (Rp500,000) level.

The complete switch in signs between the reduced-form and the full model is troubling. However, it is probably due to the fact that government health expenditure per capita is inversely correlated with adult schooling in the sample. Since population densities are much lower in the Outer Islands than in Java, government health expenditure on a per capita basis is higher in the Outer Islands. But schooling levels in the Outer Islands tend to be lower than in Java. As a result, when there is no control for the schooling of the household head in the reduced-form model, the coefficient on government health expenditure per capita is much smaller and that on government health expenditure interacted with household expenditure per capita is much larger.

Discussion and Concluding Remarks

There are two major findings in this chapter, one robust and the other not. First, the evidence clearly suggests that, at the margin, government health expenditures are associated with higher use of both preventive and curative health services by children (the estimates of the reduced-form (as opposed to the full) models are the ones used in the policy discussion here). However, only households with per capita monthly expenditures of Rp15,000 and above appear to realize the beneficial marginal effect of government health expenditure on the health services use of their children (table 10-5). Although these households constitute a majority of the sample, the findings imply that the poor in Indonesia do not benefit from government health expenditures. Indeed, the evidence indicates that increased government expenditure is actually associated with lower use of health services by the children of the poor, although this negative association is generally weak.

Second, the findings with respect to the marginal effect of government health spending on health outcomes are less clear. Government health spending is associated with a reduction in both the incidence and duration of reported morbidity. Since households residing in communities where government health spending is greater and public health infrastructure is better are more likely to report their children's morbidity, the association between government expenditure and true (as opposed to self-reported) child morbidity is likely to be even more negative. In addition, unlike the case with use of health services, the evidence points to government expenditure benefiting (in terms of lowering child morbidity) the poor more than the nonpoor. However, the difference between the marginal effects of spending on the poor and the nonpoor is relatively small.

The only case in which the empirical results are somewhat ambiguous is with respect to child weight. The full model indicates a positive association of government health spending with child weight, but one that declines with household expenditure per capita. These results are similar to the reduced-form estimates of the illness-incidence equation and imply that the association between government expenditure and improved health is stronger for children of the poor than for children from affluent households. However, the reduced-form estimates of the child weight equation suggest exactly the opposite conclusion; that is, the association between government health expenditure and child weight becomes stronger with a household's standard of living. As indicated earlier, the complete switch in signs is probably due to the inverse correlation between adult schooling and government health expenditure per capita. From a policy perspective, the reduced-form estimates are more relevant, since parental schooling cannot be held constant in practice when government spending is increased.

Thus, with the sole exception of reported morbidity, all the evidence points to the children of high-expenditure households benefiting more (in terms of the marginal effects on both health use and health outcomes) from government health spending than the children of low-expenditure households. Even in the case of reported morbidity, the greater benefit derived by the poor relative to the nonpoor from government health spending is quite small. What could account for the poor benefiting less from government health expenditure than the nonpoor? The earlier discussion of analytical issues suggests that the marginal effect of government spending on the health outcomes of the poor depends on four factors: (a) the extent to which government spending improves access to publicly provided health services for the poor ($\partial M_i / \partial G$ in relation 10-2), (b) the effect of increased spending on access to private health services for the poor ($\partial P_i / \partial G$), (c) the marginal product of government health services for the poor ($\partial H_i / \partial M_i$), and (d) the marginal product of private health services for the poor ($\partial H_i / \partial P_i$). Since the poor consume less of both public and private medical care than the nonpoor, a priori one would expect public and private health inputs to have larger marginal effects on their health outcomes. However, if increased government spending improves health care opportunities for the nonpoor more than for the poor, the total effect of government spending on the health outcomes of the poor could be smaller even though they have a higher marginal product of health care inputs.

Van de Walle's results (chapter 9), based on the same 1987 SUSENAS data but using a different methodology, provide further evidence on this issue. She finds that the amount of per capita health subsidy in Indonesia increases as household per capita expenditure increases. For example, 31 percent of government health subsidies in Indonesia accrue to the poorest 40 percent of households, while 39 percent of the subsidies benefit the richest 30 percent of households. The fact that van de Walle's approach and the methodology adopted here yield similar results is reassuring and suggests that the distribution of government health subsidies across expenditure classes is unequal enough to offset the intrinsic health advantage that the poor should have over the nonpoor in terms of benefiting from equal amounts of government health spending.

The discussion of the four mechanisms through which government spending influences health outcomes is also useful in understanding why government health spending is associated with lower levels of health status at some expenditure levels. If government health spending largely improves publicly provided health care opportunities for the nonpoor but also crowds out private providers (say, traditional healers) that are used typically by the poor, it could reduce the total amount of medical care opportunities available to the poor. If the health outcomes of the poor are highly responsive to medical care inputs, this could have a detrimental effect on their health.

An important caveat is that the methodology employed here implicitly assumes that the interprovincial distribution of per capita government health expenditure is exogenous to household health decision-making. If public health spending is allocated across provinces on the basis of unobserved health conditions, the estimated effects of government health expenditure on individual health behavior and health outcomes may be spurious. The chapter by Pitt, Rosenzweig, and Gibbons in this volume (chapter 6) suggests that the spatial placement of social infrastructure and public programs in Indonesia is not random with respect to unobserved factors determining household behavior. However, this problem is not likely to be important in the current context for three reasons. First, while the study by Pitt, Rosenzweig, and Gibbons found that the placement of health clinics (*puskesmas*) across subdistricts (*kecamatans*) was significantly influenced by "latent" fertility and "latent" child schooling in the subdistrict, it explicitly rejected the hypothesis that health clinic placement responded to "latent" health or mortality outcomes. This means that cross-sectionally estimated child health equations having health programs (or health expenditure) as independent variables are less likely to be contaminated with simultaneity bias than, say, similarly estimated child schooling equations. Second, the primary focus of this chapter is on how the marginal impact of government health spending varies across children of different economic backgrounds. In order for the differential effects of government health spending by household expenditure level to be biased, it would not be sufficient to show that provincial differences in government health expenditure respond to provincial differences in average (unobserved) health status. Instead, government health expenditure would have to respond to provincial differences in the *distribution* of (unobserved) health status across economic groups, which is a considerably different proposition. Third, if governments indeed allocated more resources to provinces having worse health conditions, a regression of health outcomes on government health spending would show a positive association between the two variables. But most of the empirical results obtained in this chapter show exactly the opposite association, which suggests that the endogeneity of public health spending is not a serious problem in this context.

Together, chapter 9 and this chapter suggest that government health spending in Indonesia is not well targeted to the poor. In fact, owing to the diminishing marginal product (in terms of improved health outcomes) of health care, one would expect the children of the poor, who typically consume less medical care than the children of the nonpoor, to obtain larger marginal health benefits from equivalent quantities (and qualities) of health care. But because of the unequal distribution of government health subsidies, the incremental health benefit derived from an additional rupiah of government health spending is significantly smaller for children belonging to poor households than for children from nonpoor households.

Notes

1. Of course, health outcomes do not accurately represent the value of consumer benefits derived from public interventions either. However, there is likely to be greater correlation between health outcomes and individual utility than between individual utility and use of health services.

2. Available data generally do not permit testing a bargaining model with a fixed structure against the maximization of common preferences. Rosenzweig and Schultz (1982, 1984), McElroy and Horney (1981), Schultz (1990), and Thomas (1990), among others, have argued that differential effects on human capital outcomes of unearned income accruing to husbands and to wives provide support for the bargaining model. However, the conditions under which this is likely to be true are quite restrictive (Chiappori 1988a, 1988b). At any rate, since unearned income data are not available separately for males and females in the Indonesian SUSENAS survey, the distinction between a bargaining and common-preferences approach is not relevant here.

3. Of course, as noted earlier, it is entirely possible that the government may "crowd out" the private sector, in which case an increase in government health expenditure could reduce the supply of private health services.

4. All of the analysis undertaken with the one-week recall data (reported in this chapter) was done with the three-month recall data as well. The broad pattern of results obtained were similar, although there were minor differences in the magnitude and statistical significance of estimated coefficients. The analysis with the three-month recall data are neither reported nor discussed here owing to space considerations.

5. Arndt and Sundrum's (1975) estimates of regional price differentials in Indonesia are now nearly twenty years out of date. More recently, Ravallion and van de Walle (1991) have estimated a behavioral cost-of-living index based on an empirical demand model, but this is available only for Java. Bidani and Ravallion (1993) have constructed provincial poverty lines, but these take into consideration only spatial variations in food prices, not spatial variations in the prices of nonfood items.

6. It might be argued that the demand for curative health care depends importantly on the severity of an illness episode, in which case the demand equations should be stratified by this variable. However, like most household surveys, the SUSENAS lists only respondent-reported "symptoms," not diagnosis by a medically qualified individual. In fact, the list of symptoms among which respondents had to choose is so short and so vague as to be of no use for any serious analysis—that is, tuberculosis/hemoptysis, diarrhea, malaria, "internal disease," measles/morbilli, and others.

7. As in most empirical studies, household expenditure per capita is used as a proxy for per capita income, both because expenditure is a better indicator of a household's permanent income and because expenditure data tend to be more reliable than data on income in a developing country.

8. Unfortunately, in the absence of panel data, these assumptions are impossible to test. However, most, if not all, cross-sectional data analysis suffers from this shortcoming. An examination of government health expenditure data for a time period (1979–80) earlier than the one considered here suggests that the pattern of government recurrent health expenditure per capita across provinces was broadly similar in 1979–80 as in 1986–87.

9. Sample-based standardizations are not appropriate for studying gender discrimination, since the standards themselves may reflect the long-term consequences of gender discrimination in a society.

10. In a survey in West Java in 1985, Berman, Ormond, and Gani (1987, p. 290) obtained a two-week prevalence rate of 9.47 percent, which translates into an annual rate of 2.46 episodes per person per year. However, rates were not computed separately for children and adults in that study.

11. More than 99 percent of sample observations fall below this expenditure per capita level, so health insurance coverage is associated with healthier children for virtually the entire sample.

References

Arndt, H. W., and R. M. Sundrum. 1975. "Regional Price Disparities." *Bulletin of Indonesian Economic Studies* 11 (2): 30–68.

Behrman, Jere R., and Anil B. Deolalikar. 1988. "Health and Nutrition." In Hollis B. Chenery and T. N. Srinivasan, eds., *Handbook of Development Economics*. Amsterdam: North-Holland.

Berman, Peter, Barbara A. Ormond, and Ascobat Gani. 1987. "Treatment Use and Expenditure on Curative Care in Rural Indonesia." *Health Policy and Planning* 2 (4): 289–300.

Bidani, Benu, and Martin Ravallion. 1993. "A Regional Poverty Profile for Indonesia." *Bulletin of Indonesian Economic Studies* 29 (3): 37–68.

Chiappori, D. A. 1988a. "Rational Household Labor Supply." *Econometrica* 56 (1): 63–89.

_____. 1988b. "Nash-Bargained Household Decisions." *International Economic Review* 29 (4): 791–96.

Folbre, Nancy. 1984a. "Comment on 'Market Opportunities, Genetic Endowments, and Intrafamily Resource Distribution.'" *American Economic Review* 74 (June): 518–20.

_____. 1984b. "Household Production in the Philippines: A Non-Neoclassical Approach." *Economic Development and Cultural Change* 32 (2): 303–30.

_____. 1986. "Cleaning House: New Perspectives on Households and Economic Development." *Journal of Development Economics* 22 (1): 5–40.

Gertler, Paul, and Jacques van der Gaag. 1990. *The Willingness to Pay for Medical Care: Evidence from Two Developing Countries*. Baltimore, Md.: Johns Hopkins University Press.

Gopalan, C. 1988. *Nutrition: Problems and Programmes in Southeast Asia*. SEARO Regional Health Paper 15. Regional Office for Southeast Asia of the World Health Organization, New Delhi.

Government of Indonesia and UNICEF. 1989. *Situation Analysis of Children and Women in Indonesia*. Jakarta.

Manser, Marilyn, and Murray Brown. 1980. "Marriage and Household Decision-Making: A Bargaining Analysis." *International Economic Review* 21 (1): 31–44.

McElroy, M. B., and M. J. Horney. 1981. "Nash-Bargained Household Decisions: Toward a Generalization of the Theory of Demand." *International Economic Review* 22 (2): 333–50.

Meerman, Jacob. 1979. *Public Expenditure in Malaysia: Who Benefits and Why*. New York: Oxford University Press.

NCHS (National Center for Health Statistics). 1977. "NCHS Growth Curves for Children Birth–18 Years: United States." *Vital and Health Statistics* 11 (165). U.S. Department of Health, Education, and Welfare, Washington, D.C.

Ravallion, Martin, and Dominique van de Walle. 1991. "Urban-Rural Cost-of-Living Differentials in a Developing Country." *Journal of Urban Economics* 19: 113–27.

Rosenzweig, M. R., and T. Paul Schultz. 1982. "Market Opportunities, Genetic Endowments, and Intrafamily Resource Distribution: Child Survival in Rural India." *American Economic Review* 72 (4): 803–15.

_____. 1984. "Market Opportunities, Genetic Endowments, and Intrafamily Resource Distribution: Reply." *American Economic Review* 74 (June): 521–22.

Schultz, T. Paul. 1990. "Testing the Neoclassical Model of Family Labor Supply and Fertility." *Journal of Human Resources* 25 (4): 599–634.

Selden, Thomas M., and Michael J. Wasylenko. 1992. "Benefit Incidence Analysis in Developing Countries." Policy Research Working Paper 1015. World Bank, Washington, D.C.

Selowsky, Marcelo. 1979. *Who Benefits from Government Expenditures? A Case Study of Colombia*. New York: Oxford University Press.

Thomas, Duncan. 1990. "Intrahousehold Resource Allocation: An Inferential Approach." *Journal of Human Resources* 25 (4): 635–64.

World Bank. 1990. *World Development Report 1990: Poverty*. New York: Oxford University Press.

———. 1992. "Indonesia: Public Expenditures, Prices, and the Poor." Report 11293-IND. Washington, D.C.

IV Cash Transfers

In contrast to the in-kind nature of government health and education subsidies, the programs we now turn to redistribute income directly by making cash payments to recipients. Poverty reduction is typically the main objective, but there may be others (Atkinson, chapter 3 of this volume).

Generous, universal cash transfer programs can be of particular concern when budget constraints bite—as in Eastern Europe, where such programs have become a heavy fiscal burden. These considerations motivate the analysis in chapter 11, which investigates the distributional impact of payments to families with children in Hungary and the issue of whether to target them more finely. Jarvis and Micklewright describe the evolution of the family allowances program in terms of both benefit levels and breadth of coverage and examine its incidence using household data from the 1988 Income Survey. The authors are concerned with achieving a greater concentration of benefits to poorer households and limiting the net cost to the government, while maintaining the program's universal nature. They reject calls for making receipts conditional on income tests, citing problems with take-up, administrative costs, and political economy considerations. Jarvis and Micklewright argue that universal schemes have a number of advantages over income-tested programs and highlight the potential for improving benefit incidence without tying eligibility to low income.

In particular, a careful consideration is given to making family allowances liable to the personal income tax. Introducing the family allowance into the tax base would seem to resolve some of the scheme's current shortcomings. Benefits received by the less needy could be "clawed back" and the program's universal character maintained. However, a close examination of the design of Hungary's personal income tax persuades Jarvis and Micklewright to recommend against this as a way to improve targeting. Instead, the authors propose a number of other options worth exploring, including modifications to how the scheme is administered and greater differentiation of payments by family size and composition. In providing insight on a specific policy, Jarvis and Micklewright show more generally how systematically to evaluate options for improving targeting in universal programs. A key message is the importance of considering suggested policy reforms from a variety of angles, including administrative capabilities, a program's history and design, the wider political environment, and consistency with other policies already in place. The chapter also demonstrates that while conventional benefit incidence analysis can provide perspective on the need for improved targeting, distributional results can depend crucially on the equivalence scale chosen to compensate for variations in the needs of households. This choice is far from obvious, yet it has strong policy implications.

Whereas Jarvis and Micklewright contemplate ways to scale down the costs and enhance the pro-poor focus of an existing social security program, Cox and Jimenez consider the expansion of social security and how private transfer responses might intervene to alter a program's intended incidence and success in raising the incomes of the target group.

Using household survey data for the Philippines, Cox and Jimenez empirically investigate the determinants of income transfers between households. The authors argue that if such transfers are a function of the same household characteristics that ascertain eligibility to public redistributive programs, then introduction of the latter may have consequences for the former. For example, a well-off relative may reduce cash grants to his poor unemployed relation in response to expanded unemployment benefits. The government program's net impact on poverty for a given budget, and its incidence, will be affected as some of the benefits slide to unintended beneficiaries.

Cox and Jimenez's research is part of the rising tide of interest in the implications of behavioral responses for the evaluation of poverty-reduction strategies. Indeed many chapters in this volume touch on these issues. However, Cox and Jimenez's perspective differs in that their concern is with the behavioral responses of nonbeneficiary households as opposed to those of the direct recipients of public intervention.

Private transfers are found to be widespread in the Philippines as well as responsive to household characteristics that can be influenced by government policy. Their net effect is to reduce both income inequality and poverty rates. Cox and Jimenez express net transfer receipts as a function of household pre-transfer income and other socioeconomic characteristics. Their estimates suggest that unemployment of the household head prompts large private transfers, holding all else constant; increases in income for households in the lowest quartile result in cutbacks in interhousehold transfers; and the receipt of retirement income tends to greatly reduce transfer amounts, above and beyond the impact it has in boosting household income.

The transfer function estimates are used to simulate the consequences of three policy reforms: creation of an unemployment insurance program, elimination of retirement benefits, and introduction of a minimum income guarantee scheme. These indicate that the receipt of unemployment benefits would be accompanied by large declines in cash transfers from other households. While interhousehold transfers appear somewhat less sensitive to retirement income, the analysis suggests that retirement coverage results in lower private transfers. Finally, a program giving all poor households sufficient cash to raise them to the poverty line would be undermined by cutbacks in interhousehold transfers. Of course, in interpreting these findings, it is important to note that these are simulations of policy changes, not the observed effects of actual changes in social security.

Empirical studies on the connection between private and public transfers have tended to report smaller crowding out effects than those found by Cox and Jimenez; however, most such studies are for the United States, where the pre-intervention counterfactual is much more difficult to obtain. Based on their results, Cox and Jimenez argue that due to private transfer responses, public transfers may be less effective than expected. If such programs are to deliver net benefits to the poor, policymakers must carefully design income redistribution programs to take such behavioral responses into consideration.

11 The Targeting of Family Allowances in Hungary

Sarah J. Jarvis and John Micklewright

Family allowances, in the form of cash payments made by the state to families with children, are a common feature of social policy in high-income countries. In Europe, this has applied both to the market economies of the West and the former command economies of the East. The level of family allowance, in relation to wages, has been in general more generous in the latter (although the pre-reform picture in Eastern Europe is more complicated than this suggests; see Atkinson and Micklewright 1992, chap. 8; table 11-1).

The transition of the Eastern European economies toward a market system has resulted in attention being paid to the role of family allowance in the countries concerned. One view sees generous family allowance as a natural feature of a command economy, but not of a market economy. It is argued that governments in command economies could, and did, hold down wages but returned some of the proceeds in the form of price subsidies and "social income" in cash and in kind, including generous family benefits. Within this view, transition to the market economy implies a reduction in the ratio of family allowance to wages. A second view takes a more neutral position on the place of family allowance within an economic system. The lower family benefits in Western Europe may result from political choice rather than the natural

We are grateful to Gaspar Fajth, Judit Salamin, and Peter Szivos of the Hungarian CSO and to Endre Sik, Ildiko Merkl, and Janos Szantos of TARKI for help with the Income Survey microdata. We also thank the director of TARKI, Tamas Kolosi, for aiding our access to these data and Judit Salamin again for advice on the history of the family allowance in Hungary. Marina Varga and Antal Szantay kindly translated Hungarian sources. Helpful discussions with Tony Atkinson, Zsuzsa Ferge, and Sándor Sipos on the topic of the chapter are acknowledged. We thank Dominique van de Walle, Kim Nead, Nick Barr, John Hills, and seminar participants at Eötvös Lórand University, Budapest, for comments on earlier versions. We alone are responsible for the views in the chapter and our use and interpretation of Hungarian data.

Table 11-1. Family Allowances for Two Children as a Percentage of Average Earnings in Select Countries, 1980

Region and country	Percentage
Eastern Europe	
Hungary	24.9
Bulgaria	22.2
Czechoslovakia	20.0
Poland	19.6
Romania	17.0
German Democratic Rep.	3.9
Western Europe	
Austria	16.9
Belgium	10.7
Netherlands	9.0
Sweden	8.7
United Kingdom	8.2
Switzerland	6.9
Germany, Federal Rep. of	6.6
France	6.5
Norway	6.4
Italy	5.4
Denmark	3.0

Note: The figures for Denmark, Federal Republic of Germany, Norway, and Sweden refer to 1981; the figure for Poland refers to 1984.

Source: International Labour Office 1989, table 8, p. 55.

features of a market economy. Reasoned arguments for substantially higher family allowances (coupled with other changes) have been put forward in the United Kingdom (Johnson, Stark, and Webb 1989; Parker and Sutherland 1991). The maintenance of generous family allowance in Eastern Europe may be seen as desirable, but it is argued that macroeconomic stabilization in the face of stagnant or negative growth requires a reduction in government expenditure and a focus of cash support on those persons most in need. Within this view, the debate is about *targeting*.

In this chapter, we consider the targeting of the family allowance in Hungary. Hungary stands out in table 11-1 as having the most generous family allowance in 1980 among the six Eastern European countries illustrated. In 1989, expenditure on family allowance amounted to 20 percent of government expenditure on social income in cash (and half of nonpension expenditure), the total representing 3 percent of gross domestic product (World Bank 1992, table 2.2, p. 10). The family allowance scheme inherited by the incoming, democratically elected government in May 1990 is a *universal* scheme. By this we mean that allocation, and hence "targeting," is determined by the demographic characteristics of the household with no explicit reference to income or employment status. Family allowance in Hungary is paid to all families with

Table 11-2. Family Allowance Rates, Hungary, 1987 and 1990
(August rate, forints per month per child)

Family allowance	1987	1990
Both parents present, more than one child		
First child	520	1,870
Second child	820	2,470
Third child	850	2,560
Fourth plus child	950	2,300
Both parents present, one child[a]	820	2,170
Single parent		
First child	820	2,170
Second child	1,080	2,430
Third child	850	2,300

Note: All allowances are Ft100 per month higher, up to the age of three.

a. Previously the family contained two or more qualifying children. In 1987, this rate applied only if the child was under six years old; in 1990, this rate also applied if the child was over six.

Source: *Statistical Yearbook 1989*, table 20.5; World Bank 1992, p. 169.

children under the age of sixteen (and up until the age of twenty for persons in full-time education).[1] The rate per child varies with family size, and higher rates are paid to single parents (the rates in August 1990 are shown in table 11-2).

In considering the situation in Hungary, we are not necessarily advocating either of the views expressed above of family allowance in transition economies. Rather, we are concerned that debate about the future of family support in Hungary should take account of a range of issues relevant to any discussion of targeting. There is a naive view that the targeting of a benefit paid without explicit reference to income must be inefficient by definition. But if the categorical criterion for receipt, in this case children, is correlated with low income, then the targeting of a universal benefit may be much better than is presumed. The *degree* of targeting achieved is a matter for empirical research. We also believe that the debate should take place in the knowledge of what the *pre-1990* system did or did not achieve. Discussion of reform of social security in any country is influenced by its history, not least since the past may condition the attitudes of those persons responsible for reform. In the case of Eastern Europe, the historical context may be particularly important if negative feelings exist toward everything associated with the communist period.

The pre-reform situation is the subject of the first two sections of the chapter. First, we consider the evolution of the pre-1990 system of family allowance, using aggregate statistics on coverage and benefit levels. We show that coverage of all children by the allowance scheme in Hungary, in the practical as well as the formal sense, is a comparatively recent phenomenon. The level of the allowance in relation to wages was notably higher in 1990 than in 1980, which was in turn substantially above levels existing earlier in the postwar period. These trends can be expected to have influenced attitudes toward family support in Hungary and therefore the political economy of family policy.

Next we analyze the incidence of pre-reform family allowance using household microdata from the 1988 Income Survey conducted by the Hungarian Central Statistical Office (CSO). We consider the share of family allowance going to each decile of the pre-allowance distribution of income (this of course is only one of several possible measures of incidence). The picture of pre-reform targeting varies with the equivalence scale that is chosen to allow for differences in family size, a choice that we emphasize is open to genuine debate and that may be affected by economic transition. The results could be used as ammunition by persons with a variety of views about the need for changes in targeting.

In the following section, we consider a policy change that might improve the targeting of family allowance by introducing an explicit link between receipt and income level, namely the inclusion of the allowance in the base for personal income taxation. This possibility has been discussed in Hungary since the introduction of a progressive personal income tax in 1988. It may seem an attractive option since it would claw back allowance from persons with higher incomes while retaining the benefits of a universal allowance free of the well-known problems associated with means testing. We discuss the unit of assessment for the personal income tax, the issue of existing child tax allowances, the administrative problems of taxing family allowance, and the degree of progression in the system. Taxation appears a much less attractive option than it might first seem and has become increasingly less attractive over time.

In the concluding section, we remind the reader of those aspects relevant to the debate on targeting that we have not been able to consider and that would be worthy of more attention. In part, this returns us to the theme of the first part of the chapter, since we note that payments of family allowance in Hungary in the past were much more differentiated by family size and composition than at present. This may have lessons for the present government, which appears to be moving toward family support through the tax system in a manner that is regressive and is therefore inconsistent with any view that family support in Hungary needs better targeting.

The Development of Family Allowances

The law making family allowance in Hungary a universal benefit, independent of employment status, was one of the last pieces of legislation passed by the outgoing communist government in April 1990 (there were concerns that the law might be repealed by the new democratically

Table 11-3. Changes in Rules on Entitlement to Family Allowance, Hungary, 1946–90

Year	Change
1946	Allowance given only to state sector employees; members of agricultural cooperatives excluded from receipt; no restriction according to number of children
1953 (March)	Coverage extended to families of members of agricultural cooperatives with three or more children but at lower benefit rate than for families of state sector employees; coverage of state sector employees restricted to families with two or more children
1959 (April)	Coverage extended to all single mothers with one or two children
1966 (July)	Coverage extended to all agricultural cooperative families with two or more children
1972 (January)	Coverage extended to all families with one child qualifying for the allowance where there were previously two or more qualifying
1975 (July)	Benefit rates for agricultural cooperative families raised to the level of that for families of state sector employees
1983 (July)	Coverage extended to families with only one child if aged under six
1990 (April)	Universal allowance, independent of employment status, and coverage extended to families with only one child over six

Source: Nepszava lap es konyvkiado 1986, 1987.

elected coalition even before it could come into effect; see Adamik 1991). This recent change should not obscure the fact that family allowance in Hungary has a long history. It was introduced in 1938, and Hungary was the first Eastern European country to give cash benefits to families with children (Ferge 1991b, table 3.3) and among the first in Europe as a whole (Gordon 1988, p. 283). The benefit has never been subject to a means test, but up until April 1990 receipt of family allowance was conditional on a satisfactory employment record (and was funded out of the social insurance fund rather than the state budget). Ferge (1991a, p. 20) reports that payments were made only to parents with twenty-one days of employment in a given month.

The payment of family allowance conditional on an employment record is an example of the underlying principle of much of social security provision in pre-reform Eastern Europe. Benefits were often restricted to those who could demonstrate current or past employment in the socialized sector (Ferge 1991b; Atkinson and Micklewright 1992, chap. 8). Prior to 1990 family allowance in Hungary was restricted to the children of those persons working in the state sector or in agricultural cooperatives. Table 11-3 summarizes the changes during the postwar period in the rules relating to the type of employment and family size. The table gives a general picture of increasing coverage over time.[2]

Figure 11-1. Number of Children for Whom Family Allowance is Paid as a Percentage of All Children through Age 14, Hungary, 1950–90

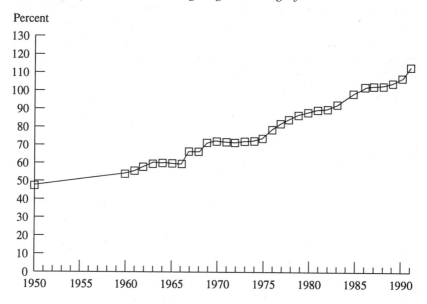

Sources: (i) Number of children for whom family allowance paid, for 1950: Ferge 1991a, p. 22; for 1959–83: Nepszava lap es konyvkiado 1986, 1987; for 1986, 1987: *Statistical Yearbook 1987*, table 20.7, p. 334; for 1985, 1988, 1989: *Statistical Yearbook 1989*, table 20.6, p. 318; for 1990: *Statistical Yearbook 1990*, table 15.9, p. 239. (ii) Number of children aged 0–14 (1 January), for 1949, 1960, 1970, 1980, 1985–89: *Statistical Yearbook 1988*, table 3.2, p. 38; for 1990: *Statistical Yearbook 1990*, table 2.2, p. 25. All other years were interpolated linearly from data for the above years.

Two features may be noted. First, the 1990 changes not only removed the employment rules on eligibility but also extended the allowance to all children in the family, something that had existed previously only in 1946–53 and then only for families of state sector employees. Second, prior to 1975, agricultural cooperative families received less favorable treatment with lower rates of benefit and, until 1966, a restricted coverage of smaller families.

How did the rule changes in table 11-3 translate into changes in the number of children for whom family allowance was paid? In figure 11-1 we show for 1950 to 1990 the number of children for whom any family allowance was paid in each year as a proportion of the number of children in the population in that year aged under fifteen. The denominator in this calculation is not ideal because it excludes some older children who are eligible, but the calculation provides a reasonable indication of changing coverage in the postwar period.

From 1985 onward, the number of children covered by family allowance exceeded the total number of children aged under fifteen. That coverage was not in fact complete is shown by the sharp rise in the proportion between 1989 and 1990, from 107 to 117 percent. This reflects both the extension to the children of unemployed parents and the payment in respect of all children under the age of sixteen irrespective of family size or age of the child. Prior to the mid-1980s, coverage was significantly lower. In 1975, the proportion illustrated in figure 11-1 was 79 percent, and if we go back to 1950 we find a figure of less than 50 percent. Between 1965 and 1985, we see a fairly steady increase in the proportion of children covered by family allowance.

In addition to coverage, we need to consider the development of the *level of payments* of family allowance. Has the relationship between family allowance and average earnings in Hungary always been that shown for 1980 in table 11-1? Figure 11-2 sheds some light on this. In view of the changes that have occurred during the postwar period in the relative rates for different family sizes, we provide three series, taking in each case the same average earnings denominator. The numerators are (1) the two-child rate of family allowance (both parents present, state sector employee), (2) the average payment per family receiving family allowance, and (3) the average payment per child covered by family allowance. For the first two series, we have figures from 1949. The series for the average payment per child is shown from 1959. Looking first at 1980, the year that was the subject of the international comparison of table 11-1, we see that the average payment per family was the same as the two-child rate in 1980 shown in that table—25 percent of the average wage—while the average payment per child was 15 percent of the average wage.

The 1980 figures were notably higher than those for earlier years in the postwar period. The series for the average payment per family displays a sequence since 1950 of sharp increases followed by gradual and smaller declines. The movement of this series reflects both changes in coverage and changes in benefit rates. As regards the latter, the two-child rate was unchanged between 1951 and 1965, thus declining relative to average wages, and then was fixed again from 1966 to 1973. The average payment per family in 1950 was only 6 percent of the average wage, about a quarter of its 1980 level, and the average payment per child (not shown on the diagram) was only 3 percent of the average wage. It was not until 1975 that the average payment per child reached 10 percent of the average wage.

Turning to the period after 1980, it can be seen that in 1987 the average payment per child and the payment for two children were about the same as in 1980, relative to the average wage, while the series for the average payment per family declined somewhat, reflecting the extension of coverage to certain single-child families in 1983 (table 11-3). In 1988, all three series displayed a sharp increase that was repeated in 1989. The slight fall in the two average payments series in 1990,

Figure 11-2. Level of Family Allowance Payments as a Percentage of Average Earnings, Hungary, 1949–90

Percentage of average wage

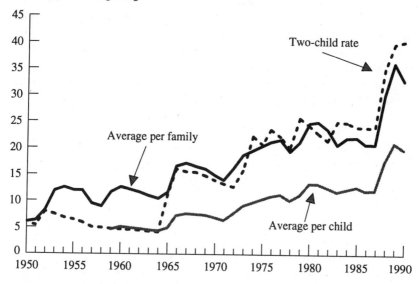

Note: Average family allowance per family and per child has been calculated from information on annual total expenditures and on number of families and of children in receipt. The two-child rate is for a family where both parents are present and, prior to 1975, is the rate for workers in the state sector; in each year, we take for this series the rate applying in August, except in 1984–85 when (because of lack of information on the August rate) we take the rate applying earlier in the year.

Sources: (i) Annual expenditure on family allowance, for 1949–52: *Statistical Yearbook 1961,* p. 271; for 1953–64: *Statistical Yearbook 1964,* p. 282; for 1965: *Statistical Yearbook 1965,* p. 292; for 1966–73: *Statistical Yearbook 1973,* p. 391; for 1975–85: World Bank 1992, table 2.2, p. 10; for 1986–90: *Statistical Yearbook 1990,* table 14.4, p. 216. (ii) Number of families receiving family allowance, for 1950–1989: *Statistical Yearbook 1989,* table 1.17, p. 22; for 1990: *Statistical Yearbook 1990,* table 1.16, p. 21. (iii) Number of children for whom family allowance paid, see sources for figure 11-1. (iv) Rate of family allowance for a two-child family, for 1950–83: Nepszava lap es konyvkiado 1986, 1987; for 1984–85: *Statistical Yearbook 1987* (Hungarian edition), table 20.6, p. 253; for 1987: *Statistical Yearbook 1988,* table 20.6, p. 334; for 1988–89: *Statistical Yearbook 1989,* table 20.5, p. 318; for 1990: *Statistical Yearbook 1990,* table 15.9, p. 239. (v) Average monthly wage, for 1950–87: *Statistical Yearbook 1989,* table 1.14, p. 19; for 1988–90: 1987 figure adjusted by net earnings index given in *Statistical Yearbook 1989,* p. vi (implied figure for 1990), and table 19.2, p. 300 (explicit figures for 1988–89).

in contrast to the two-child/two-parent series, probably reflected the extension of coverage to all single-child families in that year.

By 1989, the average payment per family represented 36 percent of the average wage and the average payment per child represented 21 percent. What were the reasons for the policy change in 1988–89 that led to these figures being some 70 percent higher than those for 1987? One reason was the phasing out of consumer price subsidies, which led the government to increase the family allowance to compensate for the change in real incomes. A second reason was the introduction of a progressive personal income tax in Hungary in January 1988. Wages in the main jobs of persons employed in the state and cooperative sectors were increased so as to ensure that net wages remained the same. (This has no impact on the denominator of the series in figure 11-2, since we have calculated average earnings in 1988–90 by adjusting the 1987 figure using a net earnings index.) However, incomes from a second job—a widespread phenomenon of the Hungarian labor market—were subjected to the new tax. Thus, as a result,

> In the case of those having incomes from several sources, the summarized (after-tax) real income may decline. . . . The surplus of state revenues deriving therefrom [the tax] has to be used—by increasing family allowance—to ease the situation of families with children. [Ministry of Finance 1987, p. 7]

In effect, higher family allowance was used to legitimize the introduction of taxation, or at least to legitimize its treatment of the family, a subject we return to below.

The family allowance scheme in Hungary has a long history that can be expected to exert an important influence on the expectations of the electorate and the decisions of policymakers. Taking the postwar period as a whole, there have been large increases in the number of children covered by the scheme and in the level of payments relative to average wages. The extension of the scheme to full universal coverage in 1990 and the increase in benefit rates in 1988–89 should be seen in the context of the earlier history.

Pre-1990 Targeting of Family Allowances

In this section, we try to shed some light on the targeting of the family allowance in the pre-reform period using household survey microdata. The definition we take of "targeting" is important to spell out. We look at the proportion of total family allowance expenditure going to each decile of the pre–family allowance income distribution. This means that targeting, on this measure, is improved by any reform of family allowance that cuts the share of expenditure going to the upper parts of the distribution. This could be achieved by either a reduction in payments to higher-income households or an increase in expenditure on lower-income households (or both). The distinction is an important one. If our criterion of targeting were to be the reduction of poverty, then merely cutting expenditure to high-income households would do nothing to improve targeting.

Family Allowance and the 1988 Income Survey

The data source we use is the 1988 Income Survey conducted by the Hungarian CSO, which collected information on annual incomes in 1987.[3] This survey was the sixth in a line of quinquennial surveys begun in 1963 (we draw here on the description of the survey given in Atkinson and Micklewright 1992, sources and methods). The survey aims to sample all private households of Hungarian citizens resident in the country in the reference year. Response to the Income Survey was quite high: the 1988 survey had a response rate of 83 percent, with refusal accounting for less than a third of nonresponse. The achieved sample size of 19,856 households was also quite large by international standards. As the name indicates, the principal purpose of the survey was to collect information on individual and household incomes. Detailed information was sought on annual income from all sources, including second jobs, agricultural income in kind, tips, and social security benefits. Reported earnings in the first job were checked with employers, taking into account any changes of employment during the year. The assessment of this source by Atkinson and Micklewright (1992, chap. 3) is that it compares favorably with household income data available in Western countries, taking the sources in the United Kingdom as a yardstick.

The amounts of family allowance recorded in the survey are calculations made by the CSO based on a combination of information provided by the responding households and tables of benefit rates. If a household indicated that it received family allowance during the year, the CSO calculated the annual figure on the basis of the number, age, and educational activity of the children, taking into account whether one or two parents were present. This clearly may be expected to result in a higher degree of accuracy than annual figures based solely on respondent recall. There are 7,863 households in the 1988 survey with recorded family allowance.[4]

The grossed-up aggregate amount of family allowance recorded in the Income Survey may be compared with that in administrative statistics. We multiply the sum of annual family allowance recorded in the (unweighted) data by the ratio of the Hungarian population on January 1, 1988 (10,464,000) to the number of individuals in the survey (56,439). The resulting figure is 106 percent of the total family allowance expenditure in 1987 recorded in administrative sources (population and family allowance expenditure totals are from *Statistical Yearbook* 1990, tables 1.1 and 14.4). We suspect that the small overstatement of allowance in the Income Survey is the result of greater-than-average response by households with children.

The CSO calculates weighting factors for the survey that adjust for some nonproportional elements in the sampling procedure (which has

Table 11-4. *Distribution of Share of Family Allowance in Total Net Household Income among Households Receiving the Allowance, Hungary, 1987*

Percentage of households receiving family allowance	Percentage of net income
Share ≤ 10	2.5
20	3.7
30	4.8
40	6.1
50	7.6
60	9.0
70	10.5
80	12.8
90	17.6
100	81.4

Note: We take all households in the income survey who received family allowance during 1987 and calculate the share of their total annual net income accounted for by their allowance payments (taking no account of differences in household size). We then rank the households by the value of this share; the results of this exercise are shown above in terms of the deciles of the distribution of the share. There are twenty-five households in the top decile with shares in excess of 50 percent; the figure of 81.4 percent is for the household with the highest recorded share.

Source: 1988 Income Survey microdata; calculations based on 7,863 households.

a stratified random design). We use these weights in the rest of the chapter. (These weights do not take into account any differential nonresponse.)

The Income Survey data allow us to see how important in practice family allowance payments were in total household incomes in 1987. The figures given in the previous section for the average payments as a percentage of average earnings provide an indication of changes in the generosity of the benefit over time, but they do not show the importance of the allowance for individual families. On the one hand, a family receiving the allowance may have two earners; in fact, this is the normal pattern for married couples in Eastern European countries. In addition, there may be other sources of income, notably, in the case of Hungary, the second economy. On the other hand, there may be households who rely heavily on the family allowance as a major source of income (for example, single-parent households).

To shed light on this issue we take all households in the Income Survey who received family allowance during 1987 and calculate the share of their total annual net income accounted for by their allowance payments (taking no account of differences in household size). We then rank the households by the value of this share and summarize the distribution in table 11-4. The table shows that for 60 percent of the households receiving family allowance, the payments they received made up less than 10 percent of their net income; for nearly a third of the households, the share was less than 5 percent. Family allowance constituted more than 20 percent of income for less than a tenth of the households receiving the benefit. While this is a significant minority, it suggests that the relationship between the average payment per family in 1987 and the average wage, shown earlier in figure 11-2, is not a good indicator of the importance of family allowance in household incomes at that time.

Measuring the Incidence of the Family Allowance

We now examine the targeting of Hungary's family allowance system in 1987. As explained earlier, we look at the share of total family allowance expenditure received by each decile of the distribution of net household income. We include *all* households in the Income Survey for the purpose of these calculations, not just those who have children or who actually received family allowance. Our purpose is to consider the incidence of family allowance in the population as a whole.

In doing so, a number of methodological issues need to be made clear. First, our unit of analysis is the *household*, defined in the Hungarian data as a group of persons living in the same dwelling who partly or entirely share expenses. An alternative, which might give rather different results, would be to look at the incidence of family allowance across the distribution of *families*, defined as persons or couples plus any dependent children.

Second, in view of the size of the family allowance payments, we look at the incidence of family allowance across the *pre-allowance* distribution of income. That is, we subtract any recorded allowance from each household before ranking it in the distribution on the basis of household income (adjusting for size and composition of the household as explained below). It is important to note, however, that the distribution of incomes minus the allowance does not necessarily represent the distribution that would have existed in the absence of the family allowance system. The changes in labor supply and other aspects of household behavior that might have occurred in the absence of the allowance need to be taken into account. The same applies to increased entitlement to means-tested benefits that can be expected to have resulted. In common with other Eastern European countries, means-tested social assistance benefits in pre-reform Hungary were less developed than in Western countries (Ferge 1991b; Atkinson and Micklewright 1992, chap. 8). Nevertheless, it is still the case that in 1987, the year covered by the Income Survey data we use, there were more than half a million "one-off" emergency social assistance payments to adults and, in addition, a separate scheme providing coverage for children (World Bank 1992, p. 177; Zám 1991).

The third issue is the treatment of household size and composition in our calculations. What equivalence scale should be applied to the income of each household in the distribution? This can be expected to have a major impact on the results obtained. We wish to look at the incidence of a benefit related to the number of children, and, via the equivalence scale adjusting for household size and composition, the number of children will in part determine a household's rank in the income distribution and hence the picture of family allowance incidence.

It has been a common practice in Eastern European statistics on the distribution of income to consider household per capita income (Atkinson and Micklewright 1992, chap. 3). In the case of Hungary, this was the practice adopted by the World Bank–funded study on the incidence in 1989 of social income in cash and kind and of price subsidies (Kupa and Fajth 1990; World Bank 1992). Such an equivalence scale could be expected to result in more large families being nearer to the bottom of the income distribution than would be the case with an alternative scale, with obvious consequences for the picture of the incidence of family allowance.

The choice of equivalence scale reflects judgments about technical issues such as economies of scale in consumption, as well as value judgments about the priority assigned to the needs of different groups, such as children and the elderly. The use of a per capita scale in Hungary, less commonly applied in Western countries, might be considered appropriate in the pre-reform period due to low housing costs (a "fixed cost") or the oft-expressed position that children were "put first." But in our view, it is important to recognize the diversity of opinion as to the appropriate equivalence scale. Hence, we present results on a number of different bases.

The differences between equivalence scales have been summarized by Buhmann and others (1988), who suggest that the measure of income entering the distribution may be written as:

(11-1) $$E = Y / H^{\alpha},$$

where E is equivalized income, Y is total household income, H is household size, and α is the elasticity of household needs with respect to household size. For example, the OECD equivalence scale of 1 for the first adult, 0.7 for other adults, and 0.5 for each child corresponds broadly to a value of α equal to 0.7. A 10 percent increase in household size leads, with this value of α, to a 7 percent increase in household needs. We show the effect of taking four different equivalence scales. We consider the distribution of:

(1) *Household per capita income,* which corresponds to setting the parameter α equal to 1 in the Buhmann and others (1988) formula;

(2) *Total household income,* which corresponds to setting α equal to 0;

(3) CSO equivalized income, in which total household income is divided by the equivalence scale used by the Hungarian CSO for the 1988 Income Survey. This is given in the notes to figure 11-3. For a household with a couple and two children in which at least one adult works, it corresponds to a value of α in the range 0.66–0.89, depending on the age of the children and whether the second adult works[5]; and

(4) OECD equivalized income, in which total household income is divided by the OECD equivalence scale described above and, as noted, corresponds approximately to setting α equal to 0.7.

The adjustments in the first two distributions represent the extreme values of α. The per capita scale ($\alpha = 1$), on the one hand, implies maximum adjustment with no account taken of any economies of scale with increasing household size; the total household income distribution ($\alpha = 0$), on the other hand, implies that there is no change in household needs as size increases. The third and fourth distributions are based on intermediate values. The CSO scale takes more account of household composition than does the OECD scale; in the former, household needs vary with activity status and age in addition to adult/child status.

Some readers may feel this discussion of equivalence scales in terms of needs ignores any argument that household size in a high-income country is a matter of choice and that children may generate private benefits as well as costs. This choice might in part be affected by the existence of family policy such as generous family allowance payments.[6] This is a well-known problem with the equivalence scale literature. For example, scales that are derived from econometric estimates are conditional on choice of household size; they reflect the costs of children to the family, but not the benefits. However, it is important to remember that the choice of household size is made by the parents rather than the children, and the welfare of both must be taken into account. Household size has a significant impact on household costs, and hence on the children's welfare; this provides a rationale for the use of econometric estimates of equivalence scales that condition on the choice of size.[7]

This leads us to the final methodological issue. What weight should each household receive in calculating the distribution of income? Should we look at the distribution of *household* income equivalized by the different scales we have discussed, or should we consider the distribution of equivalized household income of the *individuals* who make up those households? Here we feel that the choice is clear and that the distribution of individuals is the one to be considered, implying that each household receives a weight equal to household size, H, in our calculations. Having adjusted for differences in needs between households with an equivalence scale, each member of every household

Figure 11-3. Share of Total Family Allowance Expenditure Going to Each Decile of the Pre-Allowance Income Distribution, Hungary, 1987

Percentage of total expenditure

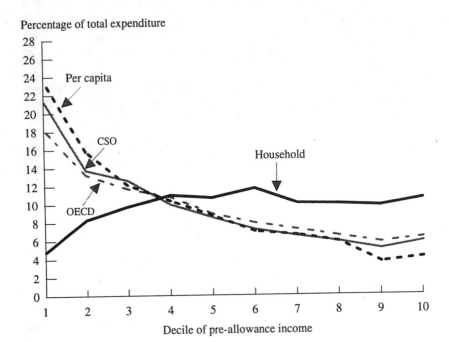

Decile of pre-allowance income

Note: The distribution in each case is the individual distribution of equivalized household income, pre–family allowance. The OECD equivalence scale is described in the text. The CSO equivalence scale is as follows:

Child under 3	0.45
Child aged 3–5	0.50
Child aged 6–10	0.60
Child aged 11–14	0.70
Child aged 15–18	0.95
Economically active person	1.00
Inactive man aged 19–59	0.90
Inactive woman aged 19–54	0.90
Inactive man aged 60+	0.80
Inactive woman aged 55+	0.80
Addition for head of household	0.20

Sources: 1988 Income Survey Microdata; see appendix 11-1. The CSO equivalence scale is from Atkinson and Micklewright 1992, table HI3.

should be treated in the distribution as an "equal citizen" (as noted by Danziger and Taussig 1979, this is consistent with individualistic welfare functions). Therefore our calculations of incidence refer to the *distribution of individuals' equivalized household pre-allowance incomes.*

The Incidence of the Family Allowance in 1987

Figure 11-3 shows the share of total family allowance expenditure recorded in the 1988 Income Survey data going to each decile of individuals in the pre-allowance income distribution.[8] The results provide evidence in support of conflicting views on the degree of targeting of family allowance in 1987. The person who wishes to argue that the benefit was quite well targeted on low-income households would point to the per capita distribution. Nearly a quarter of expenditure went to the poorest 10 percent of individuals in the population and two-fifths to the poorest 20 percent. About one-twelfth of expenditure went to the richest 20 percent of the population. The person arguing that family allowance expenditure was "wasted" on high-income households could point to the total household income distribution: the richest 20 percent of individuals captured a fifth of the expenditure—one and a half times more than was taken by the bottom 20 percent—and the bottom 10 percent got the least of all.

Neither calculation would be convincing to the person who rejects the lack of equivalizing in the total income distribution ($\alpha = 0$) but who believes that the use of a per capita scale ($\alpha = 1$) goes too far. The overall picture given by either the OECD scale or the Hungarian CSO scale is similar to that given by the per capita scale, in that the share of expenditure going to each decile of income declined as income rose. (This may reflect the fact that the values of α implied by these scales are closer to 1 than to 0.) The CSO scale gives results that are particularly close to those obtained with the per capita adjustment: more than 20 percent of expenditure still went to the bottom decile. If we look at the bottom two deciles, 40 percent of family allowance expenditure was received when the per capita scale is used, 35 percent with the CSO scale, and 32 percent with the OECD scale. One reason for the difference in results between the OECD and CSO scales may be the more sophisticated adjustment in the latter for differences in age and activity status of household members.

That these results refer to a year from the pre-reform period needs to be emphasized for at least two reasons. First, the family allowance system was not paid on a universal basis in 1987. The extension of the allowance in 1990 to persons not working in the socialized sector may have increased the share of expenditure going to low-income households and hence improved targeting on our criterion. Second, the distribution of households with children across the pre-allowance distribution may change during the transition toward a market economy. If, for a given equivalence scale, such households become more concentrated in the lower part of the distribution, then the targeting of universal family allowance—according to the criterion we have used here—would tend to increase. (It would of course fall if the opposite were true.) How the sensitivity of the results to the choice of equivalence scale would change is difficult to predict. Suppose that the inequality of pre-allowance incomes increases as a result of the transition, but that the distribution of households with children across this income distribution remains constant. Altering the equivalence scale would change the position of households with children by a smaller amount than in the pre-reform period (there will be less re-ranking). The sensitivity of the results to the choice of equivalence scale would therefore decline. The overall impact of changes in both the relative positions of households with children and pre-allowance income inequalities is not obvious.[9]

Our analysis of the incidence of family allowance demonstrates the importance of making explicit the assumptions inherent in different measures of household income and of providing results on a variety of bases. As this illustrates, the debate about targeting involves choices about measurement, and these choices will affect the conclusions drawn.

Taxing Family Allowances

In the rest of the chapter, we turn to the question of improving the targeting of the universal family allowance in Hungary by subjecting the allowance to progressive income taxation. Reducing the value of family allowance to higher-income households would indeed improve targeting using the criterion we employed in the last section: the share of total expenditure going to the lower-income deciles. This will, of course, not be true for all criteria; merely taxing family allowance will not reduce poverty and could indeed increase poverty.

Our choice to consider the option of taxation, rather than a more direct income link via a means test, reflects our view that family allowance *should* continue to be paid on a universal basis since, we believe, that the arguments for this are strong. First, there are the arguments that can be made in any society. The payment of universal family allowance recognizes the private costs of raising children with a view to equalizing consumption across households of different sizes. A universal allowance free of an income test provides support with little or no problems of take-up at low administrative cost. It provides protection against income instability arising from unemployment (if payments continue without interruption in the event of job loss) or, if the allowance is paid to the parent caring for the children, in the event of marital breakdown.

Second, there are the arguments based on the history of the allowance in Hungary. The increasing coverage in the communist period, culminating in the introduction of the universal principle in 1990, suggests that to abandon the universal nature of the allowance could be a politically destabilizing act. This might prejudice the economic reforms that are taking place. Of course, the transition from communism to a market economy requires a change in the attitudes of the population in many aspects of economic and social life. But we do not feel that a universal allowance is an unnatural feature of Hungarian social policy, and we remind the reader of the widespread occurrence of universal family allowance in the market economies of the West.

At first sight, the inclusion of family allowance within the base of the personal income tax introduced in Hungary in 1988 would be an obvious step if the worry is that excessive expenditure is going to high-income households. The personal income tax (PIT) in Hungary has a progressive rate structure. Subjecting family allowance to taxation would reduce its value to higher-income parents while leaving the full value available to those with lower incomes. The International Monetary Fund report, *Social Security Reform in Hungary*, recommended such a move (Kopits and others 1990). However, a number of issues need to be considered. These suggest that targeting via the tax system is neither as easy nor as desirable as one might first think. First, there is the unit of assessment for the PIT as compared to that appropriate to the consideration of household welfare. Second, and related to this, we need to consider the existence of any provisions in the PIT giving preferential treatment to persons with children. Does the PIT provide any support to children that may become illogical if family allowance is subject to tax? Third, there are the administrative problems of taxing family allowance to be considered. Fourth, we need to consider the effective progression of the PIT and the changes over time. We address these points in turn.

Unit of Assessment

The unit of assessment for the PIT is the individual. Each member of a household is taxed independently, and there are no additional tax allowances for marriage. Tax liability depends solely on *individual* income. Family allowance, on the other hand, is, as the name indicates, a benefit paid to *families*. Our discussion of targeting related to the incomes of the still wider unit of the *household*. If our interest in targeting is due to concern over living standards of families or households (on the assumption that income is pooled at these levels), then the distinction between these units, on the one hand, and the individual, on the other, is an important one.

In practice, we understand that the family allowance can be paid to either husband or wife. Although this may be of considerable importance to the financial arrangements made within individual marriages, it has no implications at the present time for other parts of the tax and social security system. If family allowance is brought into the PIT base, it would become necessary to indicate the parent for whom the allowance would be treated as taxable income. This raises the question of equity between parents, and it implies that considerations of vertical equity between families (or households) may not be fully taken into account. Assume that there is freedom of choice or that the allowance is treated as the mother's income. If the labor force participation rate of married women in Hungary is related negatively to the income of their husbands, then the tax paid on family allowance may actually fall with increasing family (or household) income. More generally, the degree to which taxation of the allowance under the PIT, improves its targeting according to family or household incomes depends on the joint distribution of incomes of married couples, an empirical question we have yet to establish.

Tax Treatment of the Family

As has been noted by Héthy (1991, p. 8), "Critics have looked upon the Hungarian personal income taxation as 'antisocial' or punitive to individuals with families and children." Although the PIT embodies independent treatment of husband and wife, from the outset in 1988 a small recognition of the family was introduced in the form of a tax allowance for three or more children (two or more children for single parents). The allowance goes to the parent with the highest income (Ministry of Finance 1987, sec. 17). The allowance is quite small, just Ft1,000 per month during 1988–91, which may be compared with an average monthly (gross) earnings in 1988 of Ft8,817 (*Statistical Yearbook* 1989, p. 19; Hungary's currency is the forint). Its presence has not been sufficient to assuage the critics of the PIT, noted by Héthy. Throughout the history of the PIT, there has been pressure to extend this allowance, to which the democratic government elected in 1990 has proved sympathetic. For example, in September 1990 Prime Minister Josef Antall stressed the need "to relieve [from income tax] the social strata on subsistence level and families with children of their extra burden" (quoted in the *East European Reporter* 1990, p. 18). In January 1992, the tax allowance for the third child was increased from Ft12,000 to Ft15,600 per year and, more significantly, extended to *all* children, irrespective of family size.

The child tax allowance may be set against tax liability at the individ- ual's highest marginal rate. It is worth nothing to persons not liable to tax and worth most (in absolute terms) to persons facing the maximum marginal rate. It would therefore make little sense to retain this tax allowance and yet subject the family allowance to progressive taxation. The conversion of the tax allowance into an addition to the family allowance for large families would in our view be a prerequisite for bringing family allowance into the PIT base. In extending the availability of the child tax allowance (a step we think most regrettable), the govern- ment has done little to bolster any argument for bringing the family allowance into the PIT base.

Administrative Issues

The administrative problems that would arise from taxing family allow- ance may be illustrated by considering two possible methods of taxing the allowance. First, the tax due on the family allowance may be deducted at the source, that is, by the agent responsible for the payment of the benefit. This requires that the agent know the correct marginal tax rate of the recipient on each occasion that a payment is made, taking into account other sources of income. While the family allowance continues to be paid with the wage packet through state sector employ- ers (as is the case for many recipients at present), this does not present a problem for a large section of the work force. This form of delivering family allowance is not particularly desirable and may well not be retained.

A second option is to pay each family the full benefit gross of tax. At the end of the tax year, the appropriate parent files a tax return including a declaration of the amount of family allowance received, something that may be verified by the tax authorities by reference to central records on family allowance payments. Any tax due on the allowance is then paid. This system would correspond to that used to claim the child tax allowances, that is, an end-of-year adjustment of liability. However, there is a critical distinction. Whereas the claiming of the child tax allowance leads to a tax rebate, the declaration of family allowance would lead to additional tax being due. Families who find themselves in financial difficulties when the tax must be paid (caused, for example, by unexpected unemployment or family breakup) might be unable to pay, and given the value of the family allowance, even the family in "normal" circumstances might be obliged to save during the year merely to pay the tax. This does not seem desirable.

In both cases, a larger amount of additional information must be given to the appropriate authority than is required in the administration of family allowance free of tax. Furthermore, the extension of the tax base could create even greater incentives for tax evasion in the form

Table 11-5. Estimates of the Distribution of Marginal Tax Rates on First Economy Earnings, Hungary, 1988 and 1990

Year and tax bracket (forints per month)	Marginal tax rate (percentage)	Percentage of employees paying this rate		
		All	Men	Women
1988				
Up to 5,000	0	15.3	7.8	24.3
5,000–6,833	20	23.2	17.5	29.6
6,834–8,500	25	19.8	20.5	18.8
8,501–11,000	30	19.9	24.1	14.7
11,001–13,500	35	10.0	13.1	6.8
13,501–16,000	39	5.0	6.9	2.8
16,001–21,000	44	4.1	5.8	2.0
21,001–31,000	48	2.0	3.0	0.7
31,001–51,000	52	0.5	1.0	0.1
More than 51,000	56–60	0.2	0.2	0.1
1990				
Up to 5,583	0	4.0	2.9	5.1
5,583–8,500	15	22.6	15.3	30.4
8,501–26,000	30	67.1	73.1	60.8
26,001–42,667	40	4.9	6.7	2.9
More than 42,667	50	1.4	2.0	0.7

Note: Pareto interpolation within ranges from grouped data using the INEQ package written by F. Cowell, London School of Economics. The Ft12,000 annual tax allowance for all employees is included in the calculations (the tax brackets therefore refer to total earnings rather than just taxable earnings). No account has been taken of the third-child tax allowance.

Source: Authors' own calculations using grouped data from September earnings censuses in 1988 (*Statistical Yearbook* 1988, table 4.9, p. 70) and 1990 (information provided by CSO).

of nondisclosure of income if the inclusion of family allowance in the tax base would push a taxpayer into a higher tax bracket.

Progression in the PIT

When introduced in 1988, the PIT had ten positive marginal rates, ranging from 20 percent to a top rate of 60 percent. The tax system has since been progressively simplified with a large reduction in the number of marginal rates of tax and a substantial reduction in the top rate. As of 1992, there were only three positive rates: 25, 35, and 40 percent (Economist Intelligence Unit 1992, p. 12). If the aim is to target family allowance via the tax system, then progression is an essential feature; the simplification of the tax system can be expected to have substantially reduced its usefulness in this respect.

In practice, what matters is the *effective* progression. What is important is the actual distribution of marginal tax rates rather than the tabulated rates. In table 11-5 we show our estimates of the distribution of marginal tax rates on first economy earnings for September 1988 and September 1990 (the most recent earnings distribution data available to us). The estimates are based on our application of the tax schedule to grouped data on the distribution of earnings, something made possible by the independent treatment of husband and wife in the PIT, described above (we have to ignore the third-child tax allowance in these calculations; the data source is described in Atkinson and Micklewright 1992, sources and methods). These estimates give only part of the story. There are other sources of income to consider—an aspect we stressed in the context of the importance of family allowance to household income—which may mean that the actual marginal rate at which the family allowance would be taxed could be higher.

Looking first at 1990, the table shows that an estimated two-thirds of individuals paid the same marginal rate (30 percent) on first economy earnings in that year. By contrast, the modal tax bracket in 1988 (20 percent) contained less than a quarter of employees. We also see that the revenue generated from taxing family allowance would probably be notably lower if the allowance were treated as the income of the mother: the tax rates at the margin on first economy earnings for women appear significantly lower on average. The message from the table seems clear. The reforms to the PIT introduced by the incoming democratic government in 1990 appear to have significantly weakened the potential of the PIT for enhancing the targeting of family allowance. The further simplification to just three positive rates in 1992 is unlikely to have improved matters.

In this section, we have considered the problems with bringing family allowance into the base of the progressive PIT as a means of reducing its value to persons with higher incomes. We believe that there is little to merit such a move. The unit of assessment for taxation is inappropriate for the targeting of family allowance, the administrative problems are not insignificant, and the degree of progression in the PIT may be insufficient to target the allowance effectively. We also note with regret the extension in 1992 of the system of child tax allowances.

Conclusions

Family allowances are an important part of social policy in Hungary. In this chapter, we have documented the postwar development of the scheme, analyzed the incidence of family allowance using household survey data, and considered the taxation of the allowance as a way of reducing expenditure going to higher-income households.

The reader who is looking for firm conclusions about the degree of targeting of family allowance in Hungary will be disappointed. We have stressed that the picture of targeting will depend in part on the method of measurement used. We have used just one criterion of targeting—the incidence across the income distribution—but even here a number of choices concerning measurement must be made, notably the choice of equivalence scale. As we have demonstrated, this makes a substantial difference to the results.

Our conclusions regarding the desirability of taxing family allowance are more clear-cut. We do not believe that this would be a good policy change, although more detailed use of household survey data than we have made here would throw more light on this issue. The unit of assessment and the degree of progression in the Hungarian income tax system are poorly suited to the use of taxation as a targeting mechanism.

Without changing the fundamental criteria for receipt of family allowance, there are changes to the administration of the scheme that could help improve targeting but that we have not considered in detail in this chapter. Payment to the mother (except where the father has custody) could be expected to be the most effective way of ensuring that the children get the full benefit of the allowance. Payment of the allowance through an agency unrelated to the workplace (for example, post offices) would ensure uninterrupted payment in the event of job loss.

As regards more significant changes, we have not considered a number of alternatives to the taxation of the allowance. One would be to target more effectively by demographic characteristics. Payments of family allowance in Hungary in the 1950s and 1960s were much more differentiated by family size and composition than at present. Such a system of family support may be more attractive than a policy of child tax allowances, which are inconsistent with any view that family support in Hungary needs better targeting.

Appendix 11-1. Share of Total Family Allowance Expenditure Going to Each Decile of the Pre-Allowance Net Income Distribution, Hungary, 1987

Type of distribution and decile	Per capita	Equivalence scale		
		CSO	OECD	Household
Individual distribution of pre-family allowance income				
1	23.5	21.3	18.3	5.3
2	16.0	14.0	13.5	8.7
3	12.4	12.9	12.0	10.1
4	10.7	10.3	11.1	11.3
5	9.1	8.9	9.3	11.0
6	7.4	7.6	8.3	12.0
7	7.0	6.9	7.6	10.4
8	5.3	6.3	6.9	10.3
9	4.1	5.5	6.2	10.1
10	4.6	6.3	6.7	10.9
Household distribution of pre-family allowance income				
1	25.8	21.7	16.0	2.0
2	15.8	13.9	12.3	5.1
3	12.5	12.8	12.1	7.4
4	10.7	10.2	11.4	9.1
5	8.4	9.2	10.1	11.9
6	7.2	7.5	9.1	11.9
7	6.6	6.8	8.3	13.6
8	4.8	6.0	7.4	12.7
9	4.0	5.6	6.4	12.9
10	4.2	6.1	6.9	13.4

Note: In the individual distribution, each household is weighted by its number of members. In the household distribution, each household receives a weight equal to 1. The figures for the individual distribution are illustrated in figure 11-3.
Source: Income Survey microdata.

Notes

1. There is no age restriction on eligibility for family allowance if the child concerned is a permanent invalid and is looked after by the parents. In this case, the allowance acts as a carer's benefit rather than as a family allowance.

2. We do not know if the rule concerning the number of days of work in the month, described by Vaszkó, changed over time or whether it was the same throughout the postwar period. Members of agricultural cooperatives had to demonstrate 120 days of work (80 days for women) in the preceding year (Vaszkó 1973, p. 499).

3. We use the original microdata from the 1987 income survey, not the data base formed for the incidence study of Kupa and Fajth (1990) from this survey and the 1989 budget survey.

4. In calculating this number, we exclude 640 households with one child aged over six who had a small payment recorded as "family allowance" despite the rules in 1987 excluding them from this benefit. We understand from the Hungarian CSO that the figures reflect a coding of a state transfer that was not family allowance, and we do not treat it as part of family allowance in our use of the data below.

5. In calculating this range for α for the CSO scale from the information in the notes to figure 11-3, we have treated the first adult as having a value 1.0 and the second adult and children as having the values given divided by 1.2. This allows for the additional fixed-cost element of 0.2 for the head of household, which is separately identified in the Hungarian CSO scale.

6. A review of Hungarian research based on longitudinal data into the effect of cash transfer programs on fertility is given in International Labour Office (1989, p. 87). This research concluded that the programs considered had at most altered the timing of births, but not their number.

7. In their discussion of the theoretical basis for equivalence scales, Deaton and Muellbauer (1980, p. 211) address this point explicitly in the context of income maintenance policy for families with children. See also Coulter, Cowell, and Jenkins (1992, p. 90), who note that the decision to have children is irreversible and may be based on expectations that are not realized.

8. The data on which figure 11-3 is based are given in appendix 11-1, where we also show (for purposes of comparison) results for the household distribution of pre-allowance income.

9. The decile ratio and Gini coefficient of the individual distribution of household per capita post-allowance income in the income survey data for 1987 were 2.81 and 0.244, respectively. These may be compared with figures for the distribution in 1985 defined on the same basis in the United Kingdom (which is not necessarily a representative Western yardstick) of 3.79 and 0.297 (figures for both countries are taken from Atkinson and Micklewright 1992, table 5.5).

References

Adamik, Maria. 1991. "Women and Welfare State in Hungary: The Last Forty Years and a Short Look Ahead into the Future." Mimeo.

Atkinson, Anthony B., and John Micklewright. 1992. *Economic Transformation in Eastern Europe and the Distribution of Income.* Cambridge, Eng.: Cambridge University Press.

Buhmann, Brigitte, Lee Rainwater, Gunther Schmaus, and Timothy M. Smeeding. 1988. "Equivalence Scales, Well-Being, Inequality, and Poverty." *Review of Income and Wealth* 34: 115–42.

Coulter, Fiona, Frank A. Cowell, and Stephen P. Jenkins. 1992. "Differences in Needs and Assessment of Income Distributions." *Bulletin of Economic Research* 44 (2): 77–124.

Danziger, Sheldon, and Michael K. Taussig. 1979. "The Income Unit and Anatomy of Income Distribution." *Review of Income and Wealth* 25 (4): 365–75.

Deaton, Angus, and John Muellbauer. 1980. *Economics and Consumer Behaviour.* Cambridge, Eng.: Cambridge University Press.

East European Reporter. 1990. 4 (autumn/winter): 18.

Economist Intelligence Unit. 1992. *Country Report on Hungary* 1: 12.

Ferge, Zsuzsa. 1991a. "The Social Safety Net in Hungary: A Brief Survey." In Shirley Williams, Robert P. Beschel, and Kerry S. McNamara, eds., *Social Safety Nets in East/Central Europe: A Report on Poland, Hungary, and the Czech and Slovak Republics.* Prepared for the Ford Foundation. Cambridge, Mass.: Harvard University Press.

———. 1991b. "Social Security Systems in the New Democracies of Central and Eastern Europe: Past Legacies and Possible Futures." In Giovanni A. Cornia and Sánder Sipos, eds., *Children and the Transition to a Market Economy: Safety Nets and Social Policies in Central and Eastern Europe.* A study by UNICEF. Aldershot, Hants, Eng.; Brookfield, Vt.

Gordon, Margaret S. 1988. *Social Security in Industrial Countries: A Comparative Analysis.* New York: Cambridge University Press.

Héthy, Lajos. 1991. "Structural Adjustment and Changes in Income Distribution in the 1980s in Hungary." World Employment Programme Research Working Paper 32. International Labour Office, Geneva.

International Labour Office. 1989. *From Pyramid to Pillar: Population Change and Social Security in Europe.* Geneva.

Johnson, Paul, Graham Stark, and Steven Webb. 1989. "Alternative Tax and Benefit Policies for Families with Children." IFS Commentary 18. London: Institute for Fiscal Studies.

Kopits, George, Robert Holzmann, George Schieber, and Eric Sidgwick. 1990. "Social Security Reform in Hungary." International Monetary Fund, Fiscal Affairs Department, Washington, D.C.

Kupa, Mihaly, and Gaspar Fajth. 1990. "Incidence Study '90: The Hungarian Social Policy Systems and the Distributions of Incomes of Households." Central Statistical Office and Ministry of Finance, Budapest.

Ministry of Finance. 1987. *Act on the Personal Income Tax.* Public Finance in Hungary Paper 39/B. Budapest.

Nepszava lap es konyvkiad. 1986. *A Tarsadalombiztositas negy evtizede.* Budapest.

———. 1987. *A Tarsadalombiztositas fejlodese szamokban 1950–1985.* Budapest.

Parker, Hermione, and Holly Sutherland. 1991. "Child Tax Allowances? A Comparison of Child Benefit, Child Tax Reliefs, and Basic Incomes as Instruments of Family Policy." STICERD Occasional Paper 16. London School of Economics.

Statistical Yearbook. Various years. Budapest, Hungary.

Vaszkó, Eva. 1973. "Hungary: Maternity Benefits, Child-Care Benefits, and Family Allowances." *International Social Security Review* 4: 499.

World Bank. 1992. *Hungary: Reform of Social Policy and Expenditures.* World Bank Country Study. Washington, D.C.

Zám, Mária. 1991. "Economic Reforms and Safety Nets in Hungary: Limits to Protection." In Giovanni A. Cornia and Sánder Sipos, eds., *Children and the Transition to a Market Economy: Safety Nets and Social Policies in Central and Eastern Europe.* A study by UNICEF. Aldershot, Hants, Eng.; Brookfield, Vt.

12

Private Transfers and the Effectiveness of Public Income Redistribution in the Philippines

Donald Cox and Emmanuel Jimenez

Do private interhousehold income transfers act like publicly provided social insurance in mitigating income shortfalls from unemployment or raising incomes of vulnerable groups such as the poor or retired elderly? The answer to this question could prove crucial for evaluating proposals to create or expand social insurance programs such as social security or unemployment insurance. If private and public transfers are close substitutes, an expansion of public income redistribution could prompt a reduction in private transfers, diluting program effectiveness. For example, wider social security coverage might cause children to cut back private transfers to their retired parents, so that the well-being of retired elderly parents winds up being little affected by public transfers targeted to them.

Although the connection between private and public transfers could prove critical for gauging the effectiveness of public income redistribution, assessing the strength of this connection can be troublesome. In countries with well-developed public income transfer systems, such as in countries of the Organization for Economic Cooperation and Development, public transfers may have already "crowded out" private ones to a large extent, rendering private transfer incidence amounts negligible. The researcher is left wondering whether the remaining small samples are the result of a fait accompli (the crowding out has already occurred) or some other behavior. Studying the strength of private safety nets would be more informative where government alternatives to them are relatively small.

This chapter examines private transfers in the Philippines, a country with very little publicly provided social insurance.[1] We find that private

We wish to thank Jeffrey Hammer, Homi Kharas, David Lindauer, Jonathan Morduch, Kimberly Nead, and Dominique van de Walle for useful comments on an earlier draft. Homi Kharas provided us with the FIES data set. The views expressed here are the authors' own and should not be attributed to the government of the Philippines.

transfers are large and responsive to household characteristics that can be affected by government policy. For example, our estimates indicate that income shortfalls among the very poorest households prompt large increases in private transfers. And transfers are larger when the household head is not employed. These findings are important because they suggest that household behavior can greatly offset the impact of public transfers. Indeed, our policy simulations indicate that expansion of public income redistribution in the Philippines could prompt sharp cutbacks in private safety nets. These cutbacks, though substantial, are not large enough to neutralize the effects of public transfers; the poor still gain from them even after private transfer responses. However, simple analyses that do not account for private transfer responses to public income redistribution could exaggerate the effectiveness of public programs for alleviating poverty or raising the incomes of the elderly or unemployed. Our findings indicate that policymakers should pay attention to private transfers when designing income transfer programs targeted to the poor.

Public Transfers, Private Responses, and Targeting Effectiveness

Public transfers usually affect incentives faced by beneficiaries. Only rarely would we expect households to respond passively to changes in public transfers. There are a variety of margins on which households might alter their behavior in the face of changes in public transfer payments. Receipt of cash benefits might prompt the head of a poor household to work less. A boost in social security benefits could cause households to save less for retirement, since the government provides more to retirees. Government-provided social insurance might diminish incentives to purchase private insurance. And private donors might cut back their transfers to less fortunate friends and relatives who can tap increased government aid.

Of all the private behavioral responses to public transfers, the last example, the private transfer response, is likely to be the most troublesome from a targeting perspective. To see why, we examine first the targeting problems associated with the other private responses, such as labor supply. We then contrast these problems with those created by private transfers.

To fix ideas, consider a means-tested income transfer program such as Aid to Families with Dependent Children (AFDC) in the United States. The program gives recipients an income guarantee (a certain amount associated with zero income), and welfare payments are reduced as recipient income rises. Economic theory predicts a reduction in labor supply for two reasons. First, the guarantee would reduce labor supply because of the income effect. Second, the implicit tax on earnings that comes from reducing benefits as income rises can be expected to reduce labor supply because of the substitution effect. These predictions are borne out by empirical evidence. Because of the labor supply response, to increase recipient income by $1.00, the government must raise benefits by $1.60 (Moffitt 1992). For an example of the connection between public transfer payments and labor supply in a developing country, see Sahn and Alderman (chapter 14 of this volume), who find that Sri Lankan rice subsidies reduce labor supply by around two to four days per month. In chapter 15 of this volume, Ravallion and Datt also find that public transfers, in the form of rural works programs, prompt significant behavioral responses in India. And Kanbur, Keen, and Tuomala (chapter 5 of this volume) examine in detail the targeting problems posed by labor supply responses to poverty-alleviation programs.

If we gauge a program's effectiveness strictly by its impact on the distribution of income, the labor supply response dilutes measured effectiveness. However, if we care not just about income but also about the overall well-being of recipients, the increase in nonwork time (leisure, child care time) is a good thing, especially if child care increases. Indeed, as Moffitt points out, enhanced child care was one of the original goals of AFDC.

Consider next the connection between a public transfer that a household expects to get in the future (such as social security benefits targeted to the poor) and current consumption. Households would like to spread over their life cycle the benefits that are targeted to old age, so they might increase current consumption (therefore saving less) in response to an increase in social security benefits. The savings response weakens measured program effectiveness, because social security's impact on the consumption of the elderly is less than one-for-one. But individual earnings are likely to be highly correlated over the life cycle. Someone who is poor when old is likely to have been poor when young. So reducing private savings in the face of increased public transfers is not the type of private behavioral response that is likely to diminish appreciably the targeting effectiveness of the public transfer.

The same argument applies to insurance. If publicly provided insurance causes households to reduce purchases of private insurance, this private behavioral response frees up income to be spent on other things.

Responses of private transfers to public transfer programs present much more difficult targeting problems. The reason is that private transfers are likely to originate from high-income groups. Suppose a public income transfer is targeted to a low-income household that depends in part on support coming from a high-income household. Suppose further that, in response to the public transfer program, the high-income household cuts back some of its private support. Then the high-income household indirectly benefits from a program ostensibly targeted to the poor. In terms of Lampman and Smeeding (1983), the benefits of the public transfer "slide" to "secondary beneficiaries."

The problem of secondary beneficiaries can be so severe that, at least in principle, public transfers can actually widen the distribution of income. Consider the following example. Suppose an economy is composed of high-income consumer A, middle-income consumer B, and low-income consumer C. A tax and transfer program is created, which taxes A by $50 and B by $25 and distributes the proceeds to C. On the face of it, the program appears to narrow the income distribution. But suppose that before the program, A was giving $75 to C and that after the program A stopped giving the transfer. Suppose further that B neither knows nor cares about A or C. Once private transfer responses are accounted for, it turns out that A benefits from the program, B loses, and C is just as well off. The program is in effect a transfer of $25 from middle-income B to high-income A. The income distribution widens.

The example might not be as far-fetched as it looks at first sight. It mirrors, for example, actual private transfer flows, which originate with high-income households and are given to low-income ones. Becker and Tomes (1979) provide other examples of perverse distributional effects of public transfers once private transfer responses are taken into account. Of course, private transfer responses need not necessarily generate these extreme outcomes, and in some instances actual responses turn out to be quite weak. Gauging the responsiveness of private transfers to the economic status of households is an empirical matter. Before discussing our empirical findings, we turn to a review of existing evidence.

The Connection between Public and Private Transfers: Evidence from the Literature

The vast majority of empirical work on private responses to public transfer programs has been concerned with labor supply or savings. Far less has been done to investigate private transfer responses to public income redistribution. The lack of empirical work in this area is likely due to data limitations; data sets with private transfer information are scarce. But with the increased availability of data sets containing such information economists have recently turned their attention to the connection between public and private transfers.

Using fragmentary data taken from a variety of sources, Lampman and Smeeding (1983) investigate trends in private interfamily transfers and public transfers in the United States from 1935 to 1979. They find that private transfers declined with the expansion of public transfers, but the decline in private transfers as a percentage of personal income over the period was only modest.

Cox and Jakubson (1995) use U.S. survey microdata to investigate the relationship between public and private transfers. They find that the poverty rate obtained by simply subtracting public transfers is similar to a more complex procedure that attempts to take private transfer responses into account. Their estimates suggest that if public transfer programs were removed, private interhousehold transfers would not respond enough to affect poverty rates much. These results indicate that public transfers crowd out private ones, but only slightly.

Rosenzweig and Wolpin (1994) use panel data to investigate the substitutability between public and private transfers in the United States. They find evidence that public transfers crowd out private aid, especially aid given in the form of shared housing. For example, they find that the probability of private transfers in the form of shared living arrangements rises with fertility for women who are not eligible for welfare but falls for those who are. Because of child benefits, a rise in fertility causes an increase in public welfare payments among persons who are eligible for welfare, and this boost in welfare benefits apparently crowds out private transfers.

Schoeni (1992) investigates the effects of the U.S. unemployment insurance system on private transfers. He finds that a dollar of unemployment insurance benefits may crowd out private transfers by as much as 30 cents. Gale, Maritato, and Scholtz (1992) find that public transfers in the United States tend to displace private ones. The magnitude of the displacement is not large enough to affect appreciably the impact of public transfers on poverty rates, however.

Each of the studies above uses data from the United States; less information is available concerning the connection between private and public transfers in developing countries. In one such study, Cox and Jimenez (1992) investigate the effects of social security on private, interhousehold old-age support in urban Peru. They estimate that private transfers would have been 20 percent higher in the absence of social security. The 20 percent figure indicates that crowding out is appreciable, but far from complete.

Part of the reason for the low estimated crowding out for the United States might be that public transfers are already substantial. These transfers may have already crowded out private transfers to a large extent, rendering the remaining small samples of private transfer recipients uninformative. In contrast, the Philippines has almost no public welfare payments, which makes it an ideal case study for gauging the strength of private transfers. Before proceeding to the empirical work, we describe our data set and present an overview of transfer patterns.

The 1988 Family Income and Expenditures Survey

The Family Income and Expenditures Survey (FIES) of the Philippines is undertaken every three years to gather income and consumption information for a representative cross section of Filipino households.

The primary objective of the survey is to obtain information about expenditure patterns, income sources, and inequality and to obtain information for updating weights in the consumer price index.

The survey gathers information about cash and in-kind income, demographic variables such as family size, marital status, and number of children by age, and job-related information such as earnings and employment status. In addition, survey respondents report on a variety of transfers, both in kind and in cash, from domestic sources and overseas sources. The survey's definition of private transfers includes only interhousehold transfers, so that redistribution within the household is not measured. The FIES covers 18,922 households (8,863 urban households and 10,059 rural ones). The survey also has information about the household's place of residence, used for region-specific poverty lines and useful for the policy simulations presented in the final section of the chapter.

Descriptive Overview and the Effects of Transfers on Inequality

Tables 12-1 and 12-2 provide a list of household characteristics according to transfer status. Transfer status is determined by whether households were net recipients or net givers of private transfers. Table 12-1 refers to urban households, table 12-2 to rural ones. Since the difference between urban and rural standards of living is so vast, we consider the two sectors separately.

Transfers are widespread and large: 88 percent of the urban households were involved with transfers as donors, recipients, or both. For the urban sample overall, gross transfer receipts accounted for 12 percent of total household income. For the sample of urban recipients, such receipts were nearly a *fifth* of total household income.

Many more households were net recipients than donors. Part of the reason is that international remittances accounted for a large fraction of total transfer receipts. For example, for urban households, gross transfers received from abroad accounted for two-thirds of total gross transfer receipts. Another reason for the discrepancy is that households were asked more questions in the survey about receipts than gifts. Only one module in the survey was concerned with gifts, and respondents were asked only summary questions. Three modules dealt with receipts, including receipts in kind and from abroad. Unlike most surveys with information on transfer behavior, therefore, gifts are likely to be underreported relative to receipts, rather than the other way around.

Nonetheless, splitting the sample according to transfer status is informative. For example, urban recipients had the lowest average pre-transfer income, while donors had the highest. The average pre-transfer income of "others" (households whose net receipts are zero) was in

(Text continues on page 331.)

Table 12-1. Selected Mean Characteristics of Urban Households by Private Transfer Status, the Philippines

Variable	Net transfer recipients	Net transfer donors	Others[a]	All households
Income				
Total income before transfers (pesos)	46,730	123,721	81,937	59,523
Proportion with retirement income	0.063	0.078	0.066	0.065
Retirement income (pesos)	862	2,225	1,015	1,031
Total income after transfers (pesos)	56,797	122,460	81,937	67,247
Education				
Some primary or none	0.175	0.137	0.138	0.166
Primary graduate	0.200	0.144	0.180	0.191
Some secondary	0.125	0.114	0.117	0.123
Secondary graduate	0.221	0.203	0.227	0.219
Some university	0.141	0.133	0.163	0.143
University graduate	0.139	0.268	0.174	0.158
Other characteristics				
Age of household head	45.376	47.072	44.715	45.482
Married	0.824	0.833	0.861	0.830
Female-headed households	0.185	0.131	0.114	0.170
Husband and wife both work	0.291	0.385	0.312	0.304
Head not employed	0.183	0.115	0.132	0.169
Number of children aged 1 or less	0.115	0.090	0.103	0.111
Number of children aged 1 to 7	0.789	0.650	0.763	0.771
Number of children aged 8 to 15	1.071	1.018	1.003	1.057
Household size	5.270	5.425	5.390	5.302

(Table continues on the next page.)

Table 12-1 (continued)

Variable	Net transfer recipients	Net transfer donors	Others[a]	All households
Transfers				
Proportion giving net transfers	0.000	1.000	0.000	0.110
Net transfers given (pesos)	0	1,260	0	139
Proportion receiving net transfers	1.000	0.000	0.000	0.767
Net transfers received (pesos)	10,066	0	0	7,724
Proportion giving gross transfers	0.429	1.000	0.008	0.441
Gross transfers given (pesos)	194	1,512	3	316
Proportion receiving gross transfers	1.000	0.451	0.008	0.818
Gross transfers received (pesos)	10,260	252	3	7,901
Proportion receiving from abroad	0.264	0.005	0.000	0.203
Transfers received from abroad (pesos)	6,519	25	0	5,005
Number of cases	6,801	976	1,086	8,863

a. Neither a net transfer recipient nor a net transfer donor.

Table 12-2. Selected Mean Characteristics of Rural Households by Private Transfer Status, the Philippines

Variable	Net transfer recipients	Net transfer donors	Others[a]	All households
Income				
Total income before transfers (pesos)	22,899	41,539	26,793	25,098
Proportion with retirement income	0.023	0.021	0.013	0.022
Retirement income (pesos)	221	250	142	218
Total income after transfers (pesos)	26,712	40,749	26,793	28,256
Education				
Some primary or none	0.438	0.424	0.426	0.436
Primary graduate	0.276	0.230	0.253	0.269
Some secondary	0.094	0.109	0.107	0.096
Secondary graduate	0.106	0.107	0.130	0.108
Some university	0.051	0.058	0.032	0.050
University graduate	0.036	0.071	0.051	0.041
Other characteristics				
Age of household head	46.402	45.119	45.218	46.188
Married	0.849	0.907	0.862	0.856
Female-headed households	0.123	0.066	0.102	0.116
Husband and wife both work	0.271	0.270	0.259	0.271
Head not employed	0.094	0.040	0.063	0.086
Number of children aged 1 or under	0.129	0.102	0.108	0.125
Number of children aged 1 to 7	0.896	0.850	0.862	0.889
Number of children aged 8 to 15	1.249	1.237	1.192	1.244
Household size	5.290	5.390	5.211	5.295

(Table continues on the next page.)

Table 12-2 (continued)

Variable	Net transfer recipients	Net transfer donors	Others[a]	All households
Transfers				
Proportion giving net transfers	0.000	1.000	0.000	0.104
Net transfers given (pesos)	0	790	0	82
Proportion receiving net transfers	1.000	0.000	0.000	0.828
Net transfers received (pesos)	3,812	0	0	3,158
Proportion giving gross transfers	0.473	1.000	0.013	0.497
Gross transfers given (pesos)	116	1,024	3	202
Proportion receiving gross transfers	1.000	0.611	0.013	0.893
Gross transfers received (pesos)	3,928	234	3	3,278
Proportion receiving from abroad	0.126	0.009	0.000	0.105
Transfers received from abroad (pesos)	1,835	8	0	1,521
Number of cases	8,332	1,044	683	10,059

a. Neither a net transfer recipient nor a net transfer donor.

Table 12-3. Income Inequality, with and without Private Transfers, the Philippines, 1988

Type of household	Pre-transfer	Post-transfer
Urban		
Gini coefficient	0.5867	0.5592
Variance of log-income	0.9050	0.7338
Rural		
Gini coefficient	0.4088	0.3996
Variance of log-income	0.5284	0.4667
All households		
Gini coefficient	0.5584	0.5398
Variance of log-income	0.7995	0.7002

Source: Calculated from the 1988 Family Income and Expenditures Survey data.

between that of recipients and donors. So transfers flowed from high-to low-income households. The same pattern is found for rural households. And, as for urban households, transfers among rural households are frequent and large: 93 percent of rural households were involved with transfers as either recipients or donors, and transfers accounted for 12 percent of total income for the sample overall.

These simple comparisons of income by transfer status suggest that transfers might equalize the distribution of income, and they do. Table 12-3 compares pre- and post-transfer income inequality—as measured by Gini coefficients and the variance of log-income—for urban and rural households and for the entire sample.[2] Pre-transfer income is defined as per capita household income before transfers (either receipts or gifts) occur. Post-transfer income subtracts gifts and adds receipts to pre-transfer income. In each sample, transfers alter the income distribution. For example, in the urban sample, the Gini coefficient falls 2.75 points, which indicates a very large impact of transfers on inequality in per capita income.[3]

Another way to gauge the impact of transfers on inequality is to look at their impact on the distribution of income by quintile. In table 12-4 we divide up households by quintile according to their pre-transfer per capita incomes and compare pre- and post-transfer income distributions. The figures clearly indicate that transfers have a large equalizing impact on the distribution of per capita income. In percentage terms, the income share of the lowest quintile is affected the most. The effect of transfers is most dramatic for the poorest urban households, whose per capita income share increases 80 percent once transfers are taken into account (using total household income, as opposed to *per capita* income, produces almost exactly the same results).

One way to put these distributional effects in perspective is to compare them with the effects of public income transfers in the United States. Though the Filipino figures are smaller, they are nonetheless

Table 12-4. Per Capita Income Shares, by Pre-Transfer Income Quintile of Households, the Philippines, 1988

Household income quintile	Pre-transfer	Post-transfer	Percentage change
Urban			
Lowest	3.477	6.226	+79.1
Second	6.855	7.596	+10.8
Third	10.395	10.973	+5.6
Fourth	16.110	16.493	+2.4
Highest	63.177	58.725	−7.0
Rural			
Lowest	6.053	8.850	+46.2
Second	10.354	10.660	+3.0
Third	14.639	14.799	+1.1
Fourth	21.396	21.427	+0.1
Highest	47.568	44.276	−6.9
Whole sample			
Lowest	3.919	6.390	+63.1
Second	7.256	7.919	+9.1
Third	10.905	11.453	+5.0
Fourth	17.240	17.338	+0.6
Highest	60.649	56.942	−6.1

Source: Calculated from the 1988 Family Income and Expenditure Survey data.

impressive compared to this benchmark. Cash and in-kind public transfers reduce the U.S. Gini coefficient between 6 and 20 percent, depending on the definition of the household and the time period (Danziger, Haveman, and Plotnick 1981). For example, in 1950 cash and in-kind public transfers reduced the U.S. Gini coefficient for families and unrelated individuals by 6.4 percent (Reynolds and Smolensky 1977, cited in Danziger, Haveman, and Plotnick 1981). By comparison, private transfers reduced the per capita income Gini coefficient for urban Filipinos households by 4.7 percent. (When income is measured in level, as opposed to per capita, terms, the corresponding figure is 5.5 percent.) U.S. cash and in-kind transfers increased the lowest quintile's income share from around 1.5 percent to a little under 10 percent in the mid-1970s. The comparable figures for the impact of transfers on the whole Philippines sample are 4.0 and 6.4 percent, respectively (table 12-4).[4]

Another way to gauge the importance of transfers is to compare Filipino poverty rates with and without transfers. (None of these comparisons involves behavioral responses. For example, if private transfers from one source really disappeared, perhaps another donor would step in to fill the gap. We discuss private behavioral responses to changes in income in a later section.) Table 12-5 compares the poverty rates given the current pattern of private transfers with those that would occur if transfers were removed (and nothing else happened).

Table 12-5. Incidence of Poverty, with and without Private Transfers, 1988
(percent)

Index	Urban	Rural
Pre-transfer headcount index (based on total income minus net transfers)	41.71	66.19
Post-transfer headcount index	32.34	59.49

Source: Calculations from the 1988 FIES data. Poverty lines are taken from a preliminary report of National Statistics Office 1989.

The figures indicate, for example, that if private transfers ceased altogether, urban poverty rates would be nearly a third higher.

Estimates of Transfer Functions

A look at sample characteristics in addition to income in tables 12-1 and 12-2 tends to confirm what the income comparisons discussed above suggest. Transfers flow from better- to worse-off households. In both the urban and rural samples, transfer recipients also have less education than donors, and the proportions of female-headed households and households whose head is not employed are higher among recipients than among donors. In this section, we gauge the partial effects of household characteristics on transfers. Our goal is to use these estimates to simulate the transfer effects of various public income redistribution policies.

Specification

We express net transfer receipts as a function of household pre-transfer income and other characteristics. Net transfer receipts are defined as gross transfers received minus gross transfers given. To capture any possible nonlinear effects that pre-transfer income can have on transfers, we express income as a spline function (for a detailed discussion of how nonlinearities can occur in the income transfer relationship, see Cox and Jimenez 1991). The nodes of the spline are sample income quartiles: "25th" refers to the twenty-fifth percentile for income, "50th" refers to the fiftieth percentile for income, and so on. The term "income" refers to household pre-transfer income. The spline for household income is given as follows:

Income(1) = Income if Income ≤ 25th,
Income(1) = 0 otherwise.

Income(2) = Min(Income–25th, 50th–25th) if Income > 25th,
Income(2) = 0 otherwise.

Income(3) = Min(Income–50th, 75th–50th) if Income > 50th,
Income(3) = 0 otherwise.

Income(4) = Income–75th if Income > 75th,
Income(4) = 0 otherwise.[5]

In addition to pre-transfer income, we include other household characteristics in the transfer function. Education of the household head captures permanent income effects as well as the effects of past transfers received, at least to the extent that there may be large fixed effects in private transfers. Age is included because recent evidence attests to the role of liquidity constraints in determining transfer behavior (for example, see Cox 1990; Cox and Jimenez 1991). Liquidity constraints, in turn, imply that the timing of transfers is important. For example, transfers might be targeted to younger households who have yet to establish reputations with formal sources of credit. We include gender of household head because nearly all studies of private transfers indicate that they are disproportionately targeted toward women (see Lucas and Stark 1985 for Botswana; Kaufmann and Lindauer 1986 for El Salvador; Cox and Jimenez 1991 for Peru; Guiso and Jappelli 1991 for Italy; Cox 1987 for the United States). Further, in light of recent evidence concerning private transfers and income risk (Rosenzweig 1988), we include a dummy for whether the household head is employed and whether husband and wife are both employed. The latter reflects possible mitigation of variance in income if both husband and wife are employed.

Consistent with nearly all other empirical studies of private transfers, we express transfers and income in level, rather than per capita, form (we report results from alternative specifications below). We control for demographic effects by including marital status, number of children, and household size as regressors in the transfer function.

Results

Transfer function estimates for urban households are given in table 12-6. We turn our attention first to the effects of income on transfer amounts. Income exerts a large effect on transfer amounts for households in the lowest income quartile. A one-peso increase in income for these households leads to a half-peso reduction in transfer receipts. Beyond the lowest quintile, however, income increases matter little for transfer amounts; the coefficients are small and imprecisely estimated.

Large transfers appear to be targeted to households whose head is not employed. Nonemployment raises transfer amounts by over P12,000 (the Philippines' currency is the peso). And having retirement income reduces transfer amounts by nearly P3,000.

Table 12-6. Ordinary Least Squares Estimates of Transfer Functions for Urban Households, 1988
(dependent variable—net transfers received)

Variable	Coefficient	t-ratio	Variable mean
Income			
Constant	−2,188.61	−1.34	1.0000
Income: lowest quartile	−0.505	−7.83	18,219.0
Income: second quartile	0.001	0.01	8,507.3
Income: third quartile	0.011	0.37	9,239.1
Income: highest quartile	0.0002	0.16	23,557.0
Has retirement income	−2,996.82	−3.07	0.065
Retirement income	−0.035	−1.33	1,031.1
Education			
Primary graduate	1,354.45	1.94	0.191
Some secondary	1,071.30	1.35	0.123
Secondary graduate	4,639.66	6.52	0.219
Some university	7,633.95	9.58	0.143
University graduate	8,427.77	10.27	0.158
Other characteristics			
Age of household head	−62.263	−3.20	45.482
Female-headed households	18,667.2	25.00	0.170
Married	14,049.5	18.70	0.830
Number of children aged 1 or less	−1,257.06	−1.92	0.111
Number of children aged 1 to 7	−1,346.83	−5.14	0.771
Number of children aged 8 to 15	−275.231	−1.23	1.057
Household size	714.493	5.09	5.302
Husband and wife both work	−2,884.60	−6.01	0.304
Head not employed	10,791.9	16.78	0.169
Number of observations	8,863		
Dependent variable mean	7,585.55		
R-squared	0.167		
F-statistic	88.593		

Note: The dependent variable is gross transfers received minus gross transfers given.

Households whose heads are better educated receive larger transfers. This pattern is consistent with the responsiveness of transfers to liquidity constraints. Education raises permanent income, which in turn raises desired consumption. With current income constant and no access to capital markets, the household relies on loans and subsidies from other households to fill the gap between desired consumption and current income.[6] The negative age effects are also consistent with the liquidity-constraint hypothesis, except that they are rather small (experiments with higher-order polynomial age terms failed to uncover any significant nonlinear age effects in either the urban or the rural samples).

Transfers increase with household size, but for a given household size, having more children reduces transfer amounts. Part of the reason may have to do with equivalence scales. Young children are cheaper to support than adults. Alternatively, perhaps households with young children receive as many transfers as other households, except that such transfers are provided in kind (in the form of babysitting, for example) rather than in cash (the FIES does not contain information about the value of time-intensive, in-kind services that households might receive).

For a given household income, having both husband and wife employed lowers per capita income, so we might expect that the impact of dual-earner status (husband and wife both work) would be positive. But dual-earner status also might reduce income variability, and this reduction would make the household better off, causing a reduction in private transfers. Our estimates are consistent with the latter effect.

Female-headed and married households receive many more transfers than others. The gender effect is consistent with the other studies of private transfers that find disproportionate allocation of transfers to women. Evidence for marriage effects for transfers is less clear; some studies find positive effects, and others find negative ones. Before spending too much effort interpreting these coefficients, however, we explore a very simple explanation for the demographic effects.

Consider a household whose primary earner is the husband. Suppose that he travels overseas to spend a few years earning much more than he would at home. He remits to his wife and dependent children part of his earnings from work abroad (transfers from abroad are much larger on average than those from domestic sources). Then we would observe large transfers targeted toward households that are headed by women who report that they are married.

Households headed by females are indeed overrepresented in the sample of households who report receiving transfers from abroad. For example, married female household heads account for a bit less than 5 percent of the urban sample, but for 17 percent of the sample who receive transfers from abroad.

To investigate the sensitivity of our results to the inclusion of households headed by married females, we deleted them and reestimated the transfer function (see table 12-7). The estimated gender and marital effects change a lot. The gender effect on transfers is less than one-tenth of what it was in table 12-6, and the marital status effect shrinks even more.

The effects of low-quartile income, nonemployment, and retirement status, though still substantial, are each about a third less in absolute value compared to the estimates in table 12-6. Because transfers from abroad are larger than those from domestic sources, deleting households headed by married females reduces average transfer receipts from P7,586 to P5,693.

Whether table 12-6 or 12-7 is more useful for making inferences about transfer behavior is largely a matter of definition. On the one hand,

Table 12-7. *Ordinary Least Squares Estimates of Transfer Functions for Urban Households*
(dependent variable—net transfers received)[a]

Variable	Coefficient	t-ratio	Variable mean
Income			
Constant	5,693.07	4.02	1.0000
Income: lowest quartile	−0.345	−6.11	18,372.0[b]
Income: second quartile	−0.008	−0.16	8148.8
Income: third quartile	0.016	0.69	9,358.1
Income: highest quartile	0.001	1.13	24,419.0
Has retirement income	−1,947.79	−2.42	0.067
Retirement income	−0.033	−1.47	1,029.5
Education			
Primary graduate	1,836.57	3.20	0.195
Some secondary	1,317.59	2.02	0.124
Secondary graduate	3,823.94	6.49	0.219
Some university	6,157.03	9.28	0.140
University graduate	6,113.37	8.93	0.152
Other characteristics			
Age of household head	3.108	0.19	45.718
Female-headed households	1,590.84	1.79	0.127
Married	231.575	0.29	0.821
Number of children aged 1 or less	−842.671	−1.55	0.113
Number of children aged 1 to 7	−866.850	−3.99	0.771
Number of children aged 8 to 15	−298.812	−1.60	1.050
Household size	557.148	4.77	5.322
Husband and wife both work	−1,375.84	−3.50	0.320
Head not employed	8,139.59	14.65	0.155
Number of observations	8,429		
Dependent variable mean	5,692.71		
R-squared	0.067		
F-statistic	30.255		

Note: Households headed by married females are excluded.

a. Dependent variable is gross transfers received minus gross transfers given.

b. Mean income for this sample is 60,764.

for persons interested in measuring intergenerational transfers, the apparent interspousal transfers that some married female household heads receive clearly should not be counted, and estimates from table 12-7 are more relevant. On the other hand, the design of policies targeted toward female-headed households should take into account the possibility that an absent husband's transfer behavior might adjust to changes in policy. There is probably just as much reason to be concerned about what determines transfers from husband to wife as what determines those from parents to children (for examples of studies that look at allocation within the nuclear family, see Thomas 1990; Schultz 1990).

Table 12-8. Ordinary Least Squares Estimates of Transfer Functions for Rural Households
(dependent variable—net transfers received)

Variable	Coefficient	t-ratio	Variable mean
Income			
Constant	−1,466.38	−1.90	1.0000
Income: lowest quartile	−0.363	−6.87	11,002.0
Income: second quartile	0.011	0.24	4,168.3
Income: third quartile	−0.074	−2.66	4,033.8
Income: highest quartile	−0.006	−1.70	5,894.3
Has retirement income	562.019	0.66	0.022
Retirement income	−0.105	−1.72	218.21
Education			
Primary graduate	1,365.55	6.17	0.269
Some secondary	1,391.08	4.35	0.096
Secondary graduate	2,719.75	8.65	0.108
Some university	4,893.24	11.41	0.050
University graduate	5,411.23	11.07	0.041
Other characteristics			
Age of household head	12.696	1.53	46.188
Female-headed households	6,563.56	16.90	0.116
Married	4,795.61	13.04	0.856
Number of children aged 1 or less	−792.146	−2.93	0.125
Number of children aged 1 to 7	−644.242	−5.58	0.889
Number of children aged 8 to 15	−245.950	−2.41	1.24
Household size	526.836	7.27	5.295
Husband and wife both work	−963.984	−4.65	0.271
Head not employed	6,459.98	18.18	0.086
Observations	10,059		
Dependent variable mean	3,075.76		
R-squared	0.120		
F-statistic	68.548		

Note: Dependent variable is gross transfers received minus gross transfers given.

We replicated the urban estimates in tables 12-6 and 12-7 for rural households (tables 12-8 and 12-9). Rural patterns for transfers are remarkably similar to urban ones. For example, the impact of lowest-quartile income on transfers is negative and large in absolute value (table 12-8). A one-peso increase in lowest-quartile income is associated with more than a third of a peso reduction in transfers. Further, the transfer effect of joblessness of the household head is positive and large, just as in the urban sample.

Education, household size, gender of household head, dual-earner status, and number of children all produce qualitatively similar transfer effects in the rural and urban samples.

There are two differences in the urban versus the rural estimates. The first is that the effects of retirement income on transfers is much

Table 12-9. Ordinary Least Squares Estimates of Transfer Functions for Rural Households
(dependent variable—net transfers received)[a]

Variable	Coefficient	t-ratio	Variable mean
Income			
Constant	112.349	0.16	1.000
Income: lowest quartile	−0.232	−4.82	11,036.0[b]
Income: second quartile	0.002	0.05	4,193.3
Income: third quartile	−0.048	−1.94	4,052.1
Income: highest quartile	−0.006	−1.72	5,928.2
Has retirement income	1,224.28	1.62	0.022
Retirement income	−0.072	−1.32	216.78
Education			
Primary graduate	1,239.37	6.30	0.269
Some secondary	1,477.25	5.20	0.097
Secondary graduate	2,249.62	8.00	0.106
Some university	3,244.11	8.36	0.048
University graduate	4,518.08	10.20	0.039
Other characteristics			
Age of household head	42.586	5.73	46.318
Female-headed households	899.850	2.10	0.097
Married	404.577	1.07	0.853
Number of children aged 1 or less	−526.727	−2.20	0.126
Number of children aged 1 to 7	−448.653	−4.37	0.890
Number of children aged 8 to 15	−330.149	−3.63	1.24
Household size	483.026	7.46	5.31
Husband and wife both work	−567.108	−3.09	0.276
Head not employed	4,177.07	12.72	0.079
Observations	9,846		
Dependent variable mean	2,660.40		
R-squared	0.063		
F-statistic	32.832		

Note: Households headed by married females are excluded.
a. Dependent variable is gross transfers received minus gross transfers given.
b. Mean income for this sample is 25,210.

smaller in the rural sample. But very few rural households receive retirement income—2.2 percent of the rural sample versus 6.5 percent of the urban one. Second, the effect of age on transfers is negative for the full-sample urban estimates but positive for the rural estimates. Part of the reason for the sign difference may have to do with urban/rural differences in incidence of retirement pensions. Rural households may rely more on private transfers for old-age support than urban ones. Still, the effect of age on transfers is small in each sample.

We also ran all of the regressions expressing transfers and income in per capita terms and found that the qualitative results were little changed. In particular, lowest-quartile pre-transfer income is strongly inversely related to private transfer receipts, nonemployment of household head substantially boosts transfers, and demographic/educational patterns are similar to those reported in tables 12-6 to 12-9. We also investigated the robustness of the results with respect to (a) removal of transfers from abroad, (b) estimation of gross rather than net transfers, and (c) use of quintiles and halftiles in the income spline. In each case, the qualitative nature of the results is little changed. The third experiment indicates that quartiles produce a better fit than alternative spline cutoffs.

A further issue is the potential simultaneity between pre-transfer income and transfers themselves. Such simultaneity could be present if, for example, transfers affect labor supply through the income effect. Alternatively, simultaneity could work in the opposite direction if current transfers are positively related to past ones, which in turn augment earning potential. Unfortunately, the FIES data set contains no legitimate instruments for pre-transfer income. That is, there are no variables in the data set that we can be reasonably sure are correlated with pre-transfer income but not with error terms in the transfer equation. However, while the existence of transfer-related income effects on labor supply might in principle be responsible for the inverse relationship between transfers and income, it is hard to reconcile this story with the pronounced nonlinear relationship found in the estimations. Further, Wilhelm (1992) finds no evidence that transfers (in the form of inheritance) have an impact on labor supply.

Policy-Related Simulations

What are the distributional effects of policies such as the expansion of social security benefits or the creation of unemployment insurance? Usually this question is addressed by simply adding public benefits, subtracting taxes, and recalculating the distribution of income as if families would not act differently once the new policy was put in place. But as we argue above, there are many reasons to think that public income redistribution can affect private behavior. We focus on the response of private transfers to public income redistribution. These private transfer responses can be expected to mitigate the distributional effects of public income redistribution and impart bias to the simpler calculations of policy effectiveness that do not account for such responses.

We use the estimations reported above to investigate the private transfer response and overall policy effectiveness of three policies: unemployment insurance, social security, and income grants targeted to the poor. In each case we find that private transfers cause public income redistribution to be less effective than simple first-order calculations of policy effectiveness would indicate.

Unemployment Insurance

Suppose an unemployment insurance program is created that replaces half of an unemployed worker's earnings during a spell of joblessness. How would the program affect the well-being of households whose heads are out of work? To answer this question we must calculate the private transfer responses to the creation of unemployment insurance.

We focus on the sample of prime-aged, male household heads from urban areas who reported that they were not working. Since unemployment insurance is designed to replace lost earnings, we first must answer a preliminary question: How much would these men have earned if they did have jobs? We then simulate the private transfer effects of replacing half of their earnings.

To impute earnings for the nonemployed, we must overcome one difficulty. Only total household earnings are reported in the FIES, so individual earnings can be calculated only if there is a single earner in the household. Only a fraction of the urban households (3,101 out of 8,863) had just one male earner. We want to use this sample to estimate an earnings function that we will use to impute earnings for the sample of prime-aged (thirty to fifty years) males who were not employed. But in estimating this earnings function we confront selection bias. Our earnings function estimates are conditional on both being employed and being the sole earner in the household. So first we estimate an earnings function controlling for these two sources of selection bias. We express both the probability of being employed and the probability of being a sole earner as a function of age, marital status, household size, number of children in three different age categories, financial income, retirement income, and a dummy for low education (primary or less). We use the estimated probabilities to form the selection bias terms for the earnings function, which also contains schooling dummies, a cubic function in age, marital status, and regional dummies. We then use the observable variables for the nonemployed to impute their earnings.[7]

We simulate the private transfer effects of unemployment insurance by giving the 175 nonemployed workers half of their imputed earnings. We also assume that unemployment insurance coverage causes donors of private transfers to treat these households as if their head is now employed. So our simulation does two things. It boosts the incomes of the 175 nonemployed workers by half their imputed earnings, and it shuts off the dummy variable indicating "nonemployed" status.

The averages from the simulation are summarized below:

- Predicted private transfers before unemployment insurance: P16,164

- Boost in household income from unemployment insurance: P13,146

- Reduction in private transfers as a response to unemployment insurance: P11,940
- Predicted private transfers after unemployment insurance: P4,224

Unemployment insurance that replaces half of estimated forgone earnings gives the 175 households headed by nonemployed, prime-aged males an average of P13,146 of extra income. This extra income can reduce private transfers in two ways in our simulation: through the household income effects and through the nonemployment dummy. (We use the results in table 12-6 to perform the simulation). The simulation suggests that private transfers would fall from P16,164 to P4,224. Most of this P11,940 reduction in transfers is due to the effects of shutting off the dummy for "nonemployed" status.[8] The part of the reduction due to household income effects is P1,149. The reduction in private transfers is nearly as large as the boost in income that unemployment insurance gives to households: 91 percent of the increase in household income from unemployment insurance is offset by reductions in private transfers.

Our simulation indicates that creating an unemployment insurance system for Filipino households would do no good for the targeted households. Nearly all the benefits would accrue instead to the private donors, who are likely to come from high-income brackets (see table 12-1).

Retirement Benefits

Next we investigate the connection between retirement income and transfers, again using the same estimated transfer function. We ask the following question: How much higher would private transfers be if retirement income were eliminated? Again we focus on the urban sample, in which 579 households received some retirement income, and such income averaged P15,784. The predicted transfers for this sample averaged P9,573. If retirement income were eliminated, our estimates indicate that private transfers would rise to P13,127. Put another way, if retirement income did not exist, private transfers would be 37 percent [(13,127 − 9,573) / 9,573] higher. So our results suggest that expansion of social security in the Philippines would prompt substantial reductions in private transfers.

Poverty Reduction

Finally, consider a program that attempts to eliminate poverty completely by giving each household below the poverty line the difference between its poverty line income and its actual income. How do private transfers respond?

For urban households, once private transfers adjust to this public transfer program, 47.6 percent of those below the poverty line before the program would still be below the line after the program. Those still under the poverty line would have, on average, a gap of P2,622 between the poverty line and their actual household income (including private transfers). For rural households, 94 percent would still be under the poverty line after such a program, and for them the average gap between poverty line income and actual household income would be P775. Though the extent of crowding out is less in this experiment than, say, for unemployment insurance, the welfare implications could still be severe if the gap between poverty line income and actual income prevents households from obtaining adequate nutrition or other essentials.[9]

A striking feature of these simulations is that they all contain two background conditions that likely bias downward the magnitude of crowding out. First, if increased taxes to finance public income redistribution fall disproportionately on high-income groups, and donations of private transfers are income elastic, then such taxes would prompt further reductions in private transfers. Second, since we had no information about donor's income, this variable was left out of the transfer functions. We would expect that (1) donor income would enter positively in the transfer functions and (2) recipient and donor incomes would be positively correlated. As a result, the coefficients of recipient pre-transfer income in the transfer functions are likely to be biased upward. For example, the coefficient of lowest-quartile income in table 12-6, column 2, is -0.5. If we had information about donor income and used it in the estimations, we might find that this coefficient is actually even lower, resulting in stronger crowding-out effects.

Discussion and Conclusion

Private transfers respond strongly to recipient pre-transfer incomes in the Philippines. Our simulations suggest that public transfers could be far less effective than they look because of private transfer responses. The crowding out of private transfers by public ones is not complete, however. Public transfers still benefit targeted households even after private transfers adjust. Private transfers would respond very little, for example, to public transfers targeted to persons in the second quartile of the income distribution.

Further, our results should not be construed as evidence that public income redistribution is futile or that redistribution should be conducted solely in the context of private networks. There are many reasons to prefer public sector involvement in poverty alleviation. If transfers, for example, are intended to insure households against income risk, providing such insurance through the public sector expands the risk-sharing pool. If risk-sharing were left entirely to the private sector, widespread disasters such as earthquakes or floods could impoverish entire risk-sharing networks. Coping with such risks would be better left to the public sector.

A second reason to prefer public income redistribution has to do with moral hazard. Recipients of private transfers might not work hard enough, or be careful enough, if they know that donors always stand ready to make transfers. Donors might threaten to cut off support, but such threats may not be credible if recipients know the donor to be a "soft touch" (see Bruce and Waldman 1990). The government can set inflexible rules that might mitigate this problem. In contrast, family networks might be more adept at distinguishing income shortfalls caused by negligence from those caused by bad luck.

A third advantage of public transfers is that they may enable recipients to become more independent of their donors, and such autonomy might be counted as a benefit above and beyond the pecuniary benefits of public transfers. Such additional benefits may accrue if recipients must provide services to donors in exchange for monetary transfers (Cox 1987). Finally, private and public transfers are likely to differ with respect to the fixed costs of assessing recipient needs. Recipients may be less reluctant to admit their penury to a government worker than to a relative. However, family members and friends might respond more quickly than the government to certain income shortfalls.

Despite the many advantages of public income redistribution, however, our evidence does point out that public income redistribution programs must be designed very carefully in order to deliver benefits to the poorest of the poor in countries where private networks are widespread. For example, one way to target public benefits more effectively would be to single out persons who are least likely to rely on support from relatives, such as elderly persons who are childless.

Such fine-tuned targeting is likely to pose a formidable challenge to policymakers, however. Our results imply that targeting public benefits to persons living at the subsistence level is most difficult because private transfers are most responsive for this group.

Notes

1. Though private transfers can come in many forms, including private charity in addition to interhousehold transfers, we focus solely on interhousehold, private transfers between family members and friends. Further, our private transfer measures are limited to inter vivos, or nonbequest, transfers.

2. Gini coefficients range from 0 to 1, with 1 denoting maximum income inequality. The variance of log-income is an alternative, commonly used measure of income inequality.

3. An alternative measure of household welfare is lifetime wealth, which is the appropriate concept under the assumption of perfect capital markets. The impact of transfers on the distribution of lifetime wealth could, in principle,

differ from cross-section impacts. To measure this, one would need panel data over a long period, which are generally unavailable. Moreover, in developing countries, imperfect capital markets may validate cross-section measures.

4. Although it is true that our U.S.-Philippines comparison is not symmetric (the Philippine numbers count the private "tax" of transfers given, while the U.S. numbers only contain benefits), the figures are roughly comparable because transfers given have little impact on the Gini coefficients. Because transfer receipts are so much larger than transfers given, receipts are responsible for virtually all of the change in the Gini coefficients for the Philippines.

5. The income cutoffs for quartiles are as follows: for urban households, twenty-fifth = P20,179, fiftieth = P33,890, seventy-fifth = P59,709; for rural households, twenty-fifth = P12,007, fiftieth = P18,729, seventy-fifth = P29,963.

6. Education effects could also be the artifacts of fixed effects for transfers, something on which a cross-sectional data set like the FIES cannot shed much light. For example, if parents who gave a lot early on are more likely to give a lot now, we would see a positive relationship between education that was financed by early parental transfers and current transfer receipts.

7. The earnings estimates are qualitatively consistent with most applications of the Mincerian earnings function. Earnings increase monotonically with education and follow the familiar inverted U-shaped pattern with age, peaking at age thirty-seven. Sample selection effects associated with being a sole earner are positive, as one might expect, though those associated with being in the labor force are small and statistically insignificant. The earnings regression is as follows: log earnings = 7.015 + 0.253(primary graduate) + 0.355(some secondary) + 0.489(secondary graduate) + 0.635(some university) + 1.145(university graduate) + 0.142(age) − 0.003(age squared) + 0.00002(age cubed) + 0.272(married). (R-squared = 0.27.) Each coefficient is significant at the 0.01 level, and the regression also contains regional dummies and the selection terms discussed above.

8. We experimented with the effects of nonemployment on transfers by entering separate dummies for whether or not the nonemployed head was a prime-aged male. The transfer effect of nonemployment was virtually unchanged by this procedure.

9. For every peso given to impoverished urban households, private transfers decline an average of P0.106. The corresponding figure for rural households is P0.061.

References

Becker, Gary S., and Nigel Tomes. 1979. "An Equilibrium Theory of the Distribution of Income and Intergenerational Mobility." *Journal of Political Economy* 87: 1153–89.

Bruce, Neil, and Michael Waldman. 1990. "The Rotten-Kid Theorem Meets the Samaritan's Dilemma." *Quarterly Journal of Economics* 105: 155–66.

Cox, Donald. 1987. "Motives for Private Income Transfers." *Journal of Political Economy* 95: 1045–76.

————. 1990. "Intergenerational Transfers and Liquidity Constraints." *Quarterly Journal of Economics* 105: 187–217.

Cox, Donald, and George Jakubson. 1995. "The Connection between Public Transfers and Private Interfamily Transfers." *Journal of Public Economics* 57: 129–67.

Cox, Donald, and Emmanuel Jimenez. 1991. "Motives for Private Income Transfers over the Life-Cycle: An Analytical Framework and Evidence for Peru." Boston College, Boston, Mass.

_____. 1992. "Social Security and Private Transfers in Peru." *World Bank Economic Review* (January): 155–69.

Danziger, Sheldon, Robert Haveman, and Robert Plotnick. 1981. "How Income Transfers Affect Work, Savings, and Income Distribution: A Critical Review." *Journal of Economic Literature* 19 (3): 975–1028.

Gale, William G., Nancy L. Maritato, and John Karl Scholtz. 1992. "Effects of Public and Private Transfers on Income Variability and the Poverty Rate." University of Wisconsin, Madison, Wis.

Guiso, Luigi, and Tullio Jappelli. 1991. "Intergenerational Transfers and Capital Market Imperfections: Evidence from a Cross-Section of Italian Households." *European Economic Review* 35: 103–20.

Kaufmann, Daniel, and David Lindauer. 1986. "A Model of Income Transfers for the Urban Poor." *Journal of Development Economics* 22: 337–50.

Lampman, Robert J., and Timothy Smeeding. 1983. "Interfamily Transfers as Alternatives to Government Transfers to Persons." *Review of Income and Wealth* 29: 45–66.

Lucas, Robert E. B., and Oded Stark. 1985. "Motivations to Remit: Evidence from Botswana." *Journal of Political Economy* 93: 901–18.

Moffitt, Robert. 1992. "Incentive Effects of the U.S. Welfare System: A Review." *Journal of Economic Literature* 30: 1–61.

National Statistics Office, Government of the Philippines. 1989. *Monthly Bulletin of Statistics (November)*. Manila.

Reynolds, Morgan, and Eugene Smolensky. 1977. *Public Expenditures, Taxes, and the Distribution of Income: The United States, 1950, 1961, 1970*. New York: Academic Press.

Rosenzweig, Mark. 1988. "Risk, Implicit Contracts, and the Family in Rural Areas of Low-Income Countries." *Economic Journal* 98: 1148–70.

Rosenzweig, Mark, and Kenneth Wolpin. 1994. "Parental and Public Transfers to Young Women and Their Children." *American Economic Review* 84: 1195–1212.

Schoeni, Robert F. 1992. "Another Leak in the Bucket? Public Transfer Income and Private Family Support." University of Michigan, Ann Arbor, Mich.

Schultz, T. Paul. 1990. "Testing the Neo-Classical Model of Family Labor Supply and Fertility." *Journal of Human Resources* 25: 599–634.

Thomas, Duncan. 1990. "Intra-Household Resource Allocation: An Inferential Approach." *Journal of Human Resources* 25: 635–64.

Wilhelm, Mark O. 1992. "Inheritance and Labor Supply." Pennsylvania State University, College Park, Penn.

V   *Food Subsidies*

Chapters 13 and 14 focus on food subsidies, an important and politically popular category of social spending in many developing countries. Like cash transfers, food-based schemes have the potential to raise the real incomes of the poor, redistribute income, and guarantee a minimal level of consumption. Food price subsidies can also be very expensive and not particularly effective in reaching their objectives. Budget pressures have caused many governments to look for ways to revise their food subsidy programs for greater cost-effectiveness. Much of the policy discussion has concentrated on the extent to which benefits are captured by the nonpoor and how to design targeted schemes that limit such "leakage."

In chapter 13, Cornia and Stewart question this focus. Like a number of other contributors to this volume, they argue that a single-minded concern for minimizing the proportion of benefits received by the nonpoor can obscure the evaluation of alternative interventions. They explore the ramifications of an obvious, though often ignored, factor in the policy debate. A food intervention is subject to two kinds of targeting errors, both of which entail costs. As mentioned, a scheme may include some of the nontarget population (a type II error, or what Cornia and Stewart refer to as an E-mistake for excessive program coverage), resulting in leakage of budgetary resources. But a food-based intervention may also omit some of the poor and malnourished (a type I error, referred to here as an F-mistake for failure to reach all of the target population). This type of error is associated with welfare and efficiency losses: productivity gains, and hence income, are forgone when malnutrition is left unremedied. Cornia and Stewart argue that the assessment and ranking of food interventions can change once F-mistakes are incorporated.

Cornia and Stewart review the evidence on the links between adult nutrition and labor productivity and among malnutrition at an early age, growth retardation, and labor productivity in adulthood. They conclude that potential losses from F-mistakes are substantial. The authors present empirical evidence from eight developing countries on the magnitude of the two sorts of targeting mistakes for various types of food interventions. This review reinforces points made in a number of other chapters: many instruments other than means testing exist to target program benefits to the poor; program design and the policy environment interact to determine the final incidence of benefits; and the share of the needy in the total population affects the relative desirability of targeted and universal programs. Cornia and Stewart also discuss allocation decisions within the household as another potential source of targeting mistakes. A skewed intrahousehold distribution of benefits may result in serious deviations from a program's aims (Appleton and Collier also raise this issue in chapter 19).

The authors conclude that efforts to reduce errors of excess coverage—for example, by converting a universal subsidy to a targeted food stamp program—tend to increase errors of exclusion. Although circumstances sometimes permit the design of food programs that have both low E- and F-mistakes, policymakers must often choose between food interventions with high E-mistakes and ones with high F-mistakes. A third option is suggested—namely, to use the tax system to claw back leakage of public outlays to the nonpoor. In theory, this can improve cost-effectiveness without requiring finer targeting. Jarvis and Micklewright have a similar rationale for exploring the inclusion of family allowances in the personal income tax base in Hungary (chapter 11). Here, Cornia and Stewart consider the use of indirect taxes. Such a policy route would require identification of goods consumed predominantly by groups benefiting from program leakage, which generate a large share of the revenue of indirect taxation and have a low own-price elasticity of demand.

Finally, the analysis raises the important issue of how to evaluate alternative interventions. Cornia and Stewart's chosen objective is to minimize the mistargeting ratio. Elsewhere in this book, the minimization of a poverty index has been advocated for evaluating poverty-alleviation programs. And in chapter 15, Ravallion and Datt argue that the program with the lowest errors of targeting is not always the one with the greatest impact on poverty. The mistargeting criterion may be misleading. However, the key message from Cornia and Stewart is that minimization of benefit leakage to the nonpoor—ignoring coverage of the poor—may be even more misleading.

Cornia and Stewart contribute a fresh perspective to the fairly large body of literature on targeting and efficiency in food subsidy programs. In chapter 14, Sahn and Alderman empirically investigate a potential source of program inefficiency that has received much less study in developing countries: namely, labor disincentive effects. Specifically, they examine the evidence for labor supply responses to Sri Lanka's targeted rice subsidy. Thus, like a number of other studies in this volume, chapter 14 highlights the possible presence of behavioral responses and the consequences for a program's impact on poverty.

Labor disincentive effects may ultimately lower the net income benefits received through a cash or food-related income transfer. Of course, as noted by Kanbur, Keen, and Tuomala in chapter 5, how one evaluates this reduction in work effort depends on whether one takes a welfarist or nonwelfarist approach and the value one places on the poor's consumption of leisure. In practice, policymakers ignore the poor's leisure and tend to measure the success of targeted subsidies in terms of improved nutrition or reductions in income poverty.

Using regression analysis on household data for Sri Lanka, Sahn and Alderman estimate the probability of labor force participation and number of hours worked. They then simulate the impact of receiving the rice subsidy on the individual's work effort. Their results suggest a considerable impact of the subsidy on labor supply. Both men and women reduce their time in the work force. The estimates imply a difference between the transfer amount and the net increment to income of up to 33 percent of the subsidy's gross value for men and of about 20 percent less for women.

This study highlights the significance of the issues raised by Kanbur, Keen, and Tuomala (chapter 5). It also provides an interesting counterpoint to Atkinson's summary (in chapter 3) of the evidence on labor disincentives from transfer programs in high-income economies. The disincentive effects found in this study are relatively large, especially considering that unlike many targeted programs, the Sri Lankan rice subsidy scheme did not reduce the transfer as incomes rose or remove households from the rolls if their incomes surpassed a cutoff point.

Sahn and Alderman present a number of caveats on the results and their interpretation. The model ignores any positive effects the food subsidy may have on productivity. Some of the time no longer spent in the labor market may be allocated to home production and child care. Moreover, one could argue that increasing the leisure of the poor should receive some positive weight. Urban men and women continue to work around twenty-six days a month, despite the rice subsidy's disincentive effects. Finally, the ability to generalize the findings is unclear. Nevertheless, the study emphasizes the importance of considering potential labor supply responses when designing and evaluating food subsidy and other transfer programs.

13 Two Errors of Targeting

Giovanni Andrea Cornia and Frances Stewart

This scheme [noonday meals] is the outcome of my experience of extreme starvation at an age when I knew only to cry when I was hungry. But for the munificence of a woman next door who extended a bowl of rice gruel to us and saved us from the cruel hand of death, we would have departed this world long ago. Such merciful women folk, having great faith in me, elected me as Chief Minister of Tamil Nadu. To wipe the tears of these women I have taken up this project. . . . To picture lakhs and lakhs of poor children who gather to take up nutritious meals in thousands of hamlets and villages all over Tamil Nadu and blessing us in their childish prattle, will be a glorious event.

Chief Minister of Tamil Nadu
M. G. Ramachandran, on noon meals scheme
(Harriss 1992, p. 10)

This chapter considers the appropriate design of food interventions in developing countries if they are to meet their objectives effectively. The first issue is to determine *the objective*. Until one knows this, one cannot assess alternative policy instruments. In practice, food subsidies have been intended to meet a variety of objectives, including keeping urban wages low, maintaining political support, avoiding inflation, as well as the more obvious ones of reducing poverty and improving nutrition (see Pinstrup-Andersen 1988). In fact, one reason why some food subsidies have been ineffective in transferring incomes to the poor is that this was *not* their main objective. In this chapter, we assume that the overriding objective of food interventions is to transfer incomes to poor households.

We are grateful to participants at the seminar, to Stephen Coate, and to the editors of this volume for useful comments on an earlier draft.

At first, it might appear that the best way to achieve resource transfers to poor households is to design interventions to achieve minimum leakage of program benefits to the nonpoor, so that any given resource transfer will have maximum impact on poor households. A well-targeted program, then, will achieve minimum leakage. This is a common view in the literature (see, for example, Mateus 1983; Grosh 1992). But this may be incorrect for a number of reasons, including administrative and efficiency costs, political factors, and other general equilibrium effects.[1] These will be ignored or considered only briefly in this chapter. An important additional reason why the criterion of minimizing leakage may not be the right one lies in the existence of *two errors of targeting*: errors of omission of the poor from the scheme, as well as errors of inclusion of the nonpoor. These two types of error, which correspond to type I and type II errors in statistical analysis, are the main focus of this chapter.

This chapter is organized as follows. The next section defines the two errors of targeting, considers likely relationships between them, and suggests ways of measuring them. We then summarize evidence from a variety of food subsidy programs with respect to the two errors. An attempt to evaluate the two errors follows; we demonstrate that the "optimum" food intervention can change when errors of omission are also included. Finally, since the net budgetary costs of leakage to the nonpoor depend on how far the additional benefits conferred on the nonpoor can be "clawed back" through the tax system, we briefly consider the possibilities for doing so. This discussion is followed by some concluding remarks.

Two Types of Mistakes in Targeting

In terms of the efficiency of the targeting mechanism, there are two types of mistakes to which any intervention may be subject. The first is that of failing to reach the target population. We shall describe this as an *F*-mistake, that is, a failure in the prime objective of the intervention. The second type of mistake is that made when the intervention reaches the nontarget population; this we shall call an *E*-mistake (since what is involved is excessive coverage). A major criticism of nutritional schemes in general, and *a fortiori* of untargeted schemes, is that *E*-mistakes are high. For example, in a study of targeting, Mateus (1983) argues that total costs are unnecessarily high because of the high number of *E*-mistakes in a variety of interventions; he notes that in Morocco, it was estimated that 80 percent of the budgetary costs in rural areas and 70 percent in urban areas "increased the consumption of the already well-nourished" (Mateus 1983, p. 9).

In the design of targeted interventions, attention has tended to focus on mistakes brought about by excessive coverage, with much less atten-

Table 13-1. Classification Matrix: E- and F-Mistakes of Food Interventions

Population covered	Poor	Nonpoor	Total population
All covered by nutritional intervention	P^c	NP^c (E-mistakes)	N^c
All not covered by nutritional intervention	P^{nc} (F-mistakes)	NP^{nc}	N^{nc}
Total	P	NP	N

tion being paid to mistakes resulting from failures to reach the target group. Narrowly targeted interventions often show apparently favorable cost-benefit ratios (Mateus 1983; Pinstrup-Andersen 1991). This arises from the smaller size of the target group and the fact that the more the intervention is restricted to groups in extreme deprivation, the greater one would expect the improvements from the intervention to be, measured by, say, gains in weight of malnourished children. But to date, cost-benefit analyses of food interventions have not included any evaluation of F-mistakes, or the costs of failing to cover the whole target population. F-mistakes are particularly serious where the ultra-deprived are left out and are likely to be largest where malnutrition is widespread. The larger the proportion of the population that is malnourished, the higher the potential F-mistakes and the lower the potential E-mistakes. This is one reason why the controversy (see Sukhatme 1977; Dasgupta and Ray 1987) about the extent of malnutrition is so relevant to the design of nutrition interventions.

For the most part, pursuit of low E-mistakes tends to raise F-mistakes because some members of the target group tend to be eliminated from the scheme along with the nontarget population, for the following reasons. First, some members of the target group may lack information about the targeted schemes. Second, acquiring entitlements to targeted schemes entails costs. These may include costs relating to travel, registering applications, appearing at a clinic, and so forth, depending on the targeting mechanism. Qualifications for entitlement (such as residence in a poor neighborhood) almost invariably exclude some of the target group in the process of excluding the nonpoor. Finally, social stigma associated with participating in a program targeted to the poor may deter some among the target group from participating.

How are E- and F-mistakes measured? Given a population, N, composed of poor people, P (who constitute the target of the food intervention), and nonpoor people, NP, for each intervention one can observe four categories illustrated above (see table 13-1), where

(13-1) $P + NP = N^c + N^{nc} = P^c + P^{nc} + NP^c + NP^{nc} = N.$

In the ideal case, E- and F-mistakes are nil, that is, $P^c + NP^{nc} = N,$

while in the case of total mistargeting (that is, when none of the poor are covered by the intervention and all the nonpoor are), $NP^c + P^{nc} = N$.

F-mistakes consist of P^{nc} and may be measured as a proportion of the total population, N, or P^{nc} / N, or as a proportion of the target population, P^{nc} / P. The latter is the measure of F-mistakes used in this chapter. It is a good indication of how far a scheme is failing in its primary intention to reach the target group.

E-mistakes consist of NP^c and may be measured as a proportion of the total population, NP^c / N, or as a proportion of the total nontarget population, NP^c / NP. E-mistakes may also be estimated as the money cost of the excess coverage, or vNP^c, where v is the average money cost of the subsidy received by the nontarget population, and may be expressed as a proportion of the total costs of the subsidy, or vNP^c / S, where S is the total money value of the subsidy. Where the subsidy consists of a given sum, equal for each recipient (as with school meals), this ratio is equivalent to the ratio of $NP^c / (NP^c + P^c)$.

The most common measure of E-mistakes is vNP^c / S, as it gives an estimate of the financial costs of the mistake. This is shown below as E'. Where data are available, we also show the proportion of the nontarget population covered, NP^c / NP, which we describe as E''. Where the nontarget population is a small proportion of the total population, as in very poor areas, a high E'' can be associated with low E'; conversely, if the nontarget population is a high proportion of the total, a small E'' could be associated with a high E'.

The Two Errors in Practice

This section reviews evidence from eight countries showing how the two major errors vary with the type of food support scheme; the country studies illustrate that the magnitude of the errors depends not only on the design of the scheme but also on the environment in which it is introduced. The cases examined include countries from each of the three developing regions and from middle- and low-income countries.

India (Tamil Nadu)

A noonday meals scheme, providing free school meals and infant feeding, was introduced in Tamil Nadu in 1982. The noon meals scheme is politically very popular and was one factor behind the reelection of the ruling party, ADMK, in 1984. In addition, people have access to subsidized rice through the public distribution system.

NOONDAY MEALS. Preschool children registered at nurseries (age two and older) and all registered school attenders below ten are covered by the scheme. It has also been extended to old-age pensioners, ex-servicemen, and widows below a poverty line. The scheme costs 10 percent of the state budget, which is equivalent to the deficit of the state electricity board, and exceeds the state's annual investment in agriculture. It is financed out of general revenue, additional taxes on luxuries, some voluntary contributions, plus compulsory contributions from government salaries.

The most detailed evidence of leakage mistakes is provided by Harriss (1992) in a study of two villages, a "richer" and a poorer one, in North Arcot. In both villages, more than 80 percent of the children from higher-income groups attend school, but a lower proportion eat at school in the richer village; hence the richer village has a lower E-error. In the richer village, significantly fewer children among poor households attend school than in the poor village because of greater employment opportunities (56 percent compared with 77 percent in the poor village). Hence the poorer village has a lower F-error. Overall, 60 percent of dropouts are female, so that girls suffer proportionately more F-mistakes. In both villages, there is almost universal uptake of preschool meals (which can be taken home) and therefore high E- and low F-errors for this part of the program (see table 13-2).

PUBLIC DISTRIBUTION SYSTEM. In the public distribution system, the ration of subsidized rice per household has more or less universal uptake. A more general all-India investigation of the public distribution system found that it did not—as is often suggested—have an antirural or pro-rich bias but was broadly, universally accessible (Mahendra Dev and Suryanarayana 1991). This implies low F-mistakes and substantial E-mistakes, but the study did not provide data to permit calculation of E-mistakes on an all-India basis.

Jamaica

Jamaica abolished general food subsidies in 1984 and replaced them with a more targeted food stamp scheme and school feeding program. Some general food subsidies were reinstated during the period 1986–88. The general food subsidies were again phased out in 1989 and replaced by increased benefits via the targeted program, but without full replacement in value.

The targeting was to (a) all pregnant and lactating women, children under five, the elderly, and the handicapped and (b) the poor. The benefits were broadly maintained in real terms. Targeting was of two types: self-targeting (achieved through the requirement that children and mothers attend clinics or schools to get benefits) and income testing and successful registration.

As shown in table 13-3, E-mistakes were significantly reduced as a result of the switch to targeting from general subsidies, but F-mistakes

Table 13-2. E- and F-Mistakes in North Arcot
(percent)

Type of mistake	Richer village	Poorer village	Both villages
Preschool plus school			
F	36.3	20.7	
E'	32.0	37.5	
E"	53.2	88.6	
Preschool			
F	17.0		
E'	31.2		
E"	76.9		
School			
F	54.3		
E'	33.1		
E"	36.1		
Public distribution system			
F (approximately)			0
E'			37
E" (approximately)			100

Note: F = percentage of the target group (defined as the bottom 60 percent of households) not covered; E' = percentage of the subsidy going to the nontarget population (which broadly corresponds to the percentage program savings that could be realized if there were no such mistakes); and E'' = percentage of the nontarget group covered by the subsidy.

Source: Harriss 1992.

Table 13-3. E- and F-Mistakes in Jamaica
(percent)

Target	F, poorest 20 percent	E', top 60 percent	E", top 20 percent
General subsidies	Very low	66	100
Food stamps	50	43	6
Pregnant and lactating women	25	—	4
Children under five	39	—	11
The elderly	45	—	13

— Not available.
Note: Data relate to households.
Source: Grosh 1992.

were sharply increased. The *F*-mistakes occurred because not all the poor attended clinics or schools and because registration was required for the means-tested food stamps and for the elderly. The *F*-mistakes were high (about half of all households with malnourished children did not receive benefits). On the basis of the traditional approach (that is, judging only on the basis of *E*-mistakes), Grosh (1992) concludes that food stamps are much better targeted than general food subsidies.

Table 13-4. E- and F-Mistakes in Pakistan
(percent)

Type of scheme	Rural	Urban
Ration scheme		
F	65	50
E'		52[a]
		81[b]
E"	20	21
General subsidy		
F		0
E'		78[a]
E"		100

Note: Data relate to families.

a. Percentage leakage to the top two-thirds of the population, assuming no diversion.

b. Percentage leakage to the top two-thirds of the population, assuming a 60 percent diversion.

Source: Alderman 1988.

Pakistan

Pakistan had a system of subsidized rations available only from ration shops. This system was removed in 1987 and replaced by a smaller general subsidy on unlimited quantities of wheat, which was intended to be temporary. The pre-1987 subsidized rations were for an inferior brand of flour and were available much more readily in urban than in rural areas because of the lack of rural ration shops. The budget share of rationed flour was 0.056 for the poorest group and 0.006 for the richest group. There was considerable diversion because the flour subsidy went to wheat released to mills and a large proportion (an estimated 69 percent) of subsidized wheat did not reach the ration shops.

The general subsidy saved 20 percent of the costs of the ration scheme. Because of lower cost and greater coverage, the rate of subsidy was lower for each recipient. The ration shop scheme was much worse in terms of F-mistakes (table 13-4). Moreover, E-mistakes were probably only a little smaller in the targeted scheme because of the diversion problem. Administrative costs of the new general scheme were lower than the rationed scheme. The more targeted subsidy had low political support and therefore was replaced. "While the concentration of users of the ration system on low-income users achieved a degree of targeting, it also isolated users from a broader political base" (Alderman 1988, p. 251).

Egypt

Egypt has a generous system of food subsidies with two main elements: (1) a general unrestricted subsidy on coarse and refined flour and bread and (2) ration cards for other basic commodities. The schemes are very expensive (10 to 15 percent of total government expenditure in the 1970s and 1980s) and were associated with (and often blamed for, although defense expenditure at 14.4 percent of government expenditure might equally be held responsible) large budget deficits. The international financial institutions have devoted considerable efforts to persuading Egypt to move away from the general subsidies to more targeted schemes, and some plans in this direction are under consideration.

In contrast to many other countries, Egypt has a good network of rural ration shops, and rural coverage is nearly as good as urban coverage. In the urban areas, the total value of food interventions is considerably greater for the poor than for the rich (for whom they are negative because deviations from world prices, resulting from government interventions, raise the price of some commodities consumed by the rich). In the rural areas the absolute value is somewhat greater for the top income group (see table 13-5). However, food interventions are sharply progressive for both areas when expressed as a percentage of income, being (based on 1981–82 data) 13 percent of the total expenditure of the bottom quartile and -4 percent of the top in urban areas, and 18 percent of the bottom and 5 percent of the top in rural areas.

Table 13-5. E- and F-Mistakes in Egypt
(percent)

Type of mistake	Urban	Rural
F-mistakes		
Households without ration cards	6.9	8.1
People without ration cards	4.5	7.0
Nonavailability of subsidized		
Bread	21.7	74.7
Bread/flour	2.9	12.2
E-mistakes[a]		
E'—top three-quarters	55.7	75.0
E'—top one-quarter	-5.2[b]	22.9
E'—total, rural and urban		
Top three-quarters		69.5
Top one-quarter		14.9

Note: Data relate to households.

a. Data for calculation of E″-mistakes are not available, but the reasons for failure of comprehensive coverage include (a) head of household working abroad and (b) not wanting newlyweds to claim separate ration cards. Both are likely to be greater among the nonpoor so that coverage is probably greater among low-income groups, and the true F-mistakes are likely to be lower than shown above.

b. The value of the subsidy is calculated as the effect on food prices of government interventions compared with world prices. Import restrictions on luxuries lead to a negative value for urban upper-income groups.

Source: Calculated from Alderman and von Braun 1984, 1986.

Egypt has better standards of nutrition than might be expected for its per capita income. This is likely to be due to the food subsidies as calorie consumption exhibits a high income elasticity. Alderman and von Braun (1984) calculate that the consumption of poor households is 100 to 200 calories greater per day than it would be in the absence of the interventions.

There is very high take-up of rations in both rural and urban areas: well over 90 percent of households purchase subsidized food. In the rural areas, the limited number of bakeries means that the bread subsidy is often not accessible and rural consumers rely on the flour subsidy. However, the careful investigation conducted by Alderman and von Braun indicates that for around 12 percent of rural households, neither bread nor flour was available.

Egypt's food subsidies show very low F-mistakes, in both rural and urban areas (although they are slightly higher in rural areas). E-mistakes are large if all subsidies going to the top three-quarters of the income distribution are included. Naturally, they are much lower if one includes only the subsidies going to the top quarter of the population. Targeting—in terms of E-mistakes—would be improved if the subsidy on coarse flour and the basic rations were maintained, while other interventions were abolished. This would reduce the E-mistakes without raising the F-mistakes. As is well established through the bitter resistance to their removal, the food interventions have strong political support.

Sri Lanka

Before 1979, Sri Lanka had a universal rice, wheat, and sugar subsidy that provided a minimum of two pounds of rice per person per week to the whole population at highly subsidized prices. From 1977, a new, more market-oriented government reduced and then replaced the subsidies. Entitlement was means tested, and subsequently the subsidy that was administered via ration shops was replaced by food stamps issued to households according to income and number of children. Registration was frozen in 1980. A fixed nominal sum was allocated to the stamps, whose real value declined over time. Changes in June 1986 extended the number of beneficiaries from 6.8 million to 7.2 million and provided some increases in the value of stamps for children under twelve.

The universal rice subsidy was expensive, amounting to 15 percent of government expenditure in the mid-1970s, whereas by 1984 the cost of food subsidies had dropped to only 3 percent of government expenditure. As a result of the failure to index the value of food stamps, their real value fell severely (by over half per recipient by 1981–82 compared with the rice rations). The pre-1979 system ensured virtually

Table 13-6. E- and F-Mistakes in Sri Lanka

Program	Percent
Pre-1979 rice subsidies	
F-mistakes	Very low
E-mistakes	
E'—top 80 percent	82
E'—top 60 percent	62
E"	100
1981–82 food stamps	
F-mistakes	
Bottom 20 percent	29
Bottom 40 percent	30
E-mistakes	
E'—top 80 percent	64
E'—top 60 percent	31
E"—top 60 percent	34

Note: Data relate to households.
Source: Edirisinghe 1987, table 45.

complete coverage of the target population at the cost of high E-mistakes (table 13-6). In absolute amounts, per capita receipts were greater among high-income groups than among low-income groups because they could afford to buy their full ration. But as a percentage of income, the subsidies were much greater for low-income groups. (Per capita subsidies were equivalent to 25 percent of household expenditure for the bottom quintile compared to 8.7 percent of expenditure for the top quintile.) In contrast, the new program reduced E-mistakes, although not as much as had been envisaged, since a large number of households whose incomes were above the cutoff line nonetheless secured stamps. But there was a large increase in F-mistakes, so that 29 percent of the bottom quintile was not covered. These mistakes arose from the complexity of the administrative process and from the fact that from 1980 registration was frozen.

The change to the targeted food stamp scheme was also associated with a significant worsening in nutrition among the bottom 20 percent of the population, who reduced their calorie consumption by 9 percent from 1979 to 1981–82. The next quintile reduced calorie consumption per capita marginally, while all other income groups increased their consumption. This worsening is attributed by Edirisinghe (1987) to the loss in income associated with the reduced value of (and access to) food subsidies; food subsidies contributed nearly a third of the food budget of the bottom 20 percent in 1978–79; this was reduced to one-fifth in 1981–82.

Politically, there was strong support for the pre-1979 subsidies, as evidenced by organized protest against their removal on several occasions. "These subsidies continued in part because a remarkably high

Table 13-7. E-Mistakes in Tunisia
(percent)

| | | | | Commodity composition of subsidies[a] | |
Type of mistake and commodity	Urban	Rural	Total	All groups	Lower-income groups[b]
E—all subsidies					
E'—top 90 percent			96		
E'—top 65 percent			75		
E'—top half			65		
E'—by commodity[c]					
Milk	93.1	74.3	91.4	3.2	1.6
Soft wheat	87.5	60.8	81.1	29.5	21.9
Sugar	89.0	55.3	74.9	14.4	13.8
Oil	87.6	52.1	72.1	6.2	12.2
Hard wheat	83.5	52.4	64.8	32.2	44.6

Note: Data relate to households.
a. Does not add to 100 because there are also subsidies on meat, eggs, soap, and school supplies.
b. Refers to the bottom 35 percent of households.
c. Refers to the top 65 percent of households.
Source: Calculated from Yusuf 1989, table 10.

degree of active political participation by the population, particularly the organized sector of labor force, provided sufficient pressure to ensure that they did" (Edirisinghe 1987, p. 11). Once the changeover was achieved, it appears that there was much less political support for the new scheme, so that the government was able to reduce the value of the stamps without arousing much opposition (Edirisinghe 1987, 1988).

Tunisia

Tunisia is a middle-income country, and malnutrition is estimated to affect less than 10 percent of its population. Tunisia has general unrestricted food subsidies on cereals, oils, milk, and sugar, amounting to 8 percent of government expenditure. High-income groups receive three times the absolute amount per capita of low-income groups; nonetheless, subsidies represent a smaller proportion of total income for upper-income groups than for lower.

Since they are universally available and there are very few subsistence farmers, F-mistakes are nonexistent. But E-mistakes are high. E-mistakes are significantly worse for the urban population than for the rural, mainly because there are more high-income people in urban areas (Yusuf 1989). As table 13-7 shows, there is considerable variation according to commodity, with extremely high E-mistakes for milk (more than 90 percent) and much lower ones for hard wheat than for the other commodities.

Thus E-mistakes could be significantly reduced, while maintaining negligible F-mistakes, by concentrating the subsidy on hard wheat. If the rate of subsidy on hard wheat were increased 2.1 times and the remaining subsidies were abolished, the poorest 35 percent would be as well off, while the total cost of the subsidies would be reduced by half. The one doubt about this procedure, which would also save administrative costs, is whether it would be viable politically. There is strong political support for the subsidies, as indicated by the food riots in 1984, when abolition was proposed (Yusuf 1989).

Mexico

Mexico is replacing general subsidies on maize and maize flour for urban tortilla manufacturers with targeted subsidies on tortillas and milk (means tested using complex administrative procedures) for the urban poor and the establishment of rural shops to provide subsidized maize flour. As can be seen from table 13-8, all the programs, both general subsidies and targeted ones, had very high F-mistakes. In the case of the general subsidies, this arose from failure to cover the rural poor, who accounted for approximately 54 percent of total poor families, although complete coverage of the urban poor was achieved.

Table 13-8. E- and F-Mistakes in Mexico, 1988
(percent)

Type of subsidy	Urban	Rural	Combined urban and rural	Magnitude of programs U.S. dollars a year (millions)	Magnitude of programs Total U.S. dollars a year per beneficiary household
General subsidies on maize					
F—mistake	Very low	100	54	1,652	151
E'—mistake (top three deciles)	39	0	39[b]		
Targeted subsidies					
Tortilla				98	91
F—poor families[a]	73	100	88		
F—poor pregnant/lactating women; children, 0–12	75	100	90		
E'—"better-off"	40	0	40[b]		
Urban milk program				193	106
F—poor families[a]	56	99	89		
F—pregnant/lactating women; children (poor households)	52	99	83		
E'—"better-off"	40		0		
Rural community stores				51	9
F—poor families[a]	100	6	49		
F—pregnant/lactating women; children < 5 (poor)	100	7	61		
E'—nonpoor	0		46		
Food supplementation				191	190
F—poor families[a]	76	84	81		
F—pregnant/lactating women; children < 5 (poor)			60		
F—children 5–12			88		

a. Families with incomes below 1.5 times the minimum wage.
b. Rural not covered at all.
Source: World Bank 1991.

Table 13-9. E'- and F-Mistakes in the Philippines

Type of mistake	Percent
F (in villages covered after three months)	5.0
E' (persons with more than 80 percent of recommended calories)	8.8

Source: Garcia and Pinstrup-Andersen 1987.

The switch to targeting did not reduce E-mistakes, although this had been the main intention of the change. The best targeted program from the perspective of F-mistakes—the rural community stores—also had the least spent on it, and the benefit per recipient was very small (World Bank 1991).

The Philippines

In the Philippines, a subsidized food ration scheme was introduced on a pilot basis for each household in a few villages (see table 13-9). This program had very high take-up (95 percent after three months). Because most villagers were poor, both E- and F-mistakes were very low *in the villages covered*; but since the scheme was confined to only a few villages, F-mistakes outside the chosen villages were clearly very high, poverty rates in the Philippines being of the order of 50 to 60 percent during the 1980s. However, although this is to be expected with a pilot scheme, it does illustrate a common problem associated with geographic targeting: omission of the poor outside the area covered by the scheme.

Major Conclusions from the Studies

1. F-mistakes tend to be low for universal subsidies if they are unrestricted and usually if they are rationed, if every household is entitled to rations. But where they are rationed, it is essential that the ration shops be widely accessible. In some countries, lack of ration shops in the rural areas significantly raised F-mistakes, as in the Pakistan case. But in others, such as in Sri Lanka and Egypt, the ration/subsidy shops were generally accessible and F-mistakes were low.

2. The universal schemes tend to involve significant E-mistakes, varying from 78 percent (Pakistan) to 31 percent (Sri Lanka), where an E-mistake is defined as the proportion of benefits that go to persons outside the target group. The magnitude of the E-mistakes depends on four factors:

   - *The level of income.* If average incomes are low so that a high proportion of the population falls into the "target" group, the maximum level of E-mistakes associated with universal schemes is limited. This was the case in the villages in North Arcot, where the public distribution scheme showed E-mistakes of only 37 percent, and the E-mistake for school meals and preschool feeding ranged from 32 to 38 percent. In contrast, where the target population forms only a small proportion of the total, then E-mistakes can be very high, as in Tunisia.

- *Consumption patterns among different income groups.* If consumption patterns are similar among income groups, then any universal subsidy on a basic commodity is likely to benefit rich as well as poor groups, as was the case with the rice subsidy in Sri Lanka. But if "poor people's commodities" can be identified (such as hard wheat in Tunisia), then lesser E-mistakes are associated with universal subsidies.

- *How narrowly the target group is defined.* If the target group is confined to the severely malnourished, or to particular age groups, E-mistakes are higher than if the target group also includes the moderately malnourished and extends to all ages. There is a case for differentiating E-mistakes according to the income of the beneficiaries. For example, benefits that reach members of the bottom half of the income distribution who do not fall into the "target" population are less serious, given a proegalitarian utility function, than errors involving benefits going to the top half of the income distribution.

- *The nature of the subsidy.* We have used the term "universal" subsidies, distinguishing these from "targeted" subsidies. Yet all universal subsidies contain elements of implicit targeting, since their distribution depends on the commodities subsidized and the consumption patterns of different income groups. If the subsidies fall most heavily on poor people's goods, then E-mistakes are less than if they fall on "luxuries." The contrast between the Egyptian case, where the subsidies were mainly on poor people's goods, and the Tunisian case, where a high proportion fell on luxuries (milk and sugar, for example) illustrates this point: in Egypt, the top three-quarters of the urban population received 56 percent of the subsidies, while in Tunisia the top 65 percent (urban) received 88 percent.

3. Universal unrestricted subsidies can sometimes confer much larger absolute benefits on richer than on poorer groups, since the richer groups can afford to consume more. But they may be designed to avoid this. In Egypt, richer groups in the urban areas received much less than poorer groups, while for the country as a whole there was little difference. In contrast, in Tunisia, the value of the subsidies received per head by the top 10 percent of the population

was 3.7 times that received by the bottom 10 percent. But even where they appear highly regressive, as in Tunisia, they offer much greater benefits to poorer groups as a proportion of income: in Tunisia the difference in per capita income between top and bottom groups was at least 8:1. Consequently, assuming that the subsidies are financed by taxes that are proportionate to income, they should improve secondary income distribution. In countries such as Egypt where they are designed more progressively, the subsidies greatly improve secondary income distribution.

4. In a number of countries, targeted schemes have replaced universal schemes. In almost every case, as indicated in table 13-10, the result has been a major increase in F-mistakes with some reduction in E-mistakes. In Jamaica, F-mistakes rose from almost nothing to as much as 50 percent; in Sri Lanka, they rose from very low to 30 percent; and in Pakistan (where the reverse process occurred), they fell from 65 percent (rural) and 50 percent (urban) to near zero. The reduction in E-mistakes was usually substantial, but generally not as complete as had been expected, because nontarget groups managed to secure some of the targeted benefits; for example, in Sri Lanka, the share of the top four-fifths of the income distribution dropped from 82 to 64 percent and the share of the top three-fifths fell from 60 to 30 percent. And in the case of Pakistan, diversion of the targeted rations meant there was little difference in E-mistakes between the targeted and universal schemes.

5. At best, when there was a switch from a general to a targeted subsidy, the real value of the benefits to the persons who received them was unchanged, *but this was unusual*. Mostly, it seems that the switch also leads to a reduction in the real value of the subsidy over time (as in Sri Lanka). Less strong political support for the targeted schemes probably accounts for this. Sometimes, a reduction in the real value of the subsidy was intended as part of a cost-cutting exercise.

6. The one study of school meals as a mechanism of nutritional support indicates that large numbers of poor children can be excluded, if they do not attend school because they are working. School meals would tend to discourage nonattendance (see Babu and Arne Hallam 1989 for an analysis), but as Harriss (1992) shows, significant F-mistakes may still occur. Preschool feeding programs do not have this problem.

7. The above analyses generally ignore the distribution of consumption within the household, so that E- and F-errors are defined at the household level. But distribution within the household can be another source of both types of error. E-errors may occur among households containing malnourished individuals, if additional

Table 13-10. Summary of Targeting Mistakes in Selected Countries

Country and region	General subsidies			Food stamps and rations		
	F	E'	E''a	F	E'	E''
Jamaica	very low	66 (top 60 percent)	100	50	43	—
Pakistan (urban)	very low	78 (top 60 percent)	100	50	52–80	21
Egypt	7	70 (top 60 percent) 15 (top 75 percent)	100	—	—	—
Sri Lanka	very low	62 (top 25 percent)	100	30	31 (top 60 percent)	34
Tunisia	very low	75 (top 60 percent) (top 65 percent)	100	—	—	—
Mexico (urban)	very low	39 (top 30 percent)	100	tortilla: 73 rural community stores: 6	40 (better off) 46 (nonpoor)	—
Philippines (villages)	5	9 (80 percent of recommended calories)	100 100 100	—	—	—
Tamil Nadu (two villages)	very low	37	100	—	—	—
Tamil Nadu ("richer" village)	preschool feeding: 17	31	77	school meals: 54	33	36

— Not available.

a. E'' mistakes are assumed to be 100 percent and F-mistakes to be very low for the universal subsidies. In fact, some people from both rich and poor households are likely to be omitted for various reasons, so E'' may be less than 100 percent, and F may be positive but low. Precise data are not normally available.

Source: See tables 13-2 through 13-9.

food resources go to members of the household who already have enough food; and F-errors may occur if additional food fails to reach the malnourished individuals within the household.

Whether and how far intrahousehold distribution does present a further source of errors of either type depend on how the household works. According to the neoclassical model, decisions in allocation and distribution are taken with "household utility" maximization as the objective, with food being distributed according to need in relation to productivity (Rosenzweig 1986); F-errors may occur where nutritionally deprived people have low potential productivity (the very old or the very young). With bargaining models of the household, persons with weak bargaining position (women, children, the old) may get little in relation to persons with strong bargaining power (adult males), and consequently severe E- and F-errors may occur (Folbre 1986). Empirical evidence is not conclusive as to which is the correct model, although evidence is mounting in support of the bargaining model (Guyer 1980; Miller 1981; Tripp 1981; Hoddinott and Haddad 1991). With this perspective, policies would need to be designed specifically to avoid errors arising within the household. These would include policies to increase the bargaining power of the weak members (for example, through female education and employment) and the provision of subsidies directly to deprived individuals rather than to deprived households (these issues are discussed more extensively in the annex of Cornia and Stewart 1993).

8. Administrative costs are estimated to be higher for the targeted food interventions; they range from 2 to 5 percent of the total costs of these schemes (administrative costs for the Sri Lankan and Jamaican schemes are estimated to be 2 and 4 percent of total costs, respectively). Evidence for the United Kingdom and United States supports this conclusion. In seven U.K. programs, administrative costs were estimated at around 3.5 percent of total costs for the universal programs, but between 5 and 15 percent of total costs for the means-tested programs; and in the United States, administrative costs of universal programs were found to be 2.5 percent compared with 12 percent for two means-tested programs (and 95 percent for the means-tested veterans program; Kesselman 1982). The administrative costs of nonfood schemes such as employment or credit schemes tend to be significantly higher than for food subsidy schemes, but such interventions also generate other benefits.

9. The political support for general schemes that reach some of the nonpoor (that is, that have significant E-mistakes) appears to be higher than that for the more narrowly targeted schemes, according to the evidence reported here. For this reason, the value of targeted

subsidies is more likely to be eroded over time, as observed in the case of Sri Lanka.

10. Policy conclusions based on this survey about how to avoid excessive *F*- and *E*-mistakes are:

- Subsidies or other interventions must reach the rural areas. If they do not, as is quite common, then high *F*-mistakes are unavoidable.

- Universal subsidies on staple commodities are most effective in reaching the whole target population in very low-income countries and/or areas where the majority of the population is poor and malnourished. The exception is where there is a high degree of malnutrition among a subsistence population (as in Peru; see Harrell, Parillon, and Franklin 1989). Other mechanisms are needed to reach the subsistence population.

- Targeting food interventions will "save" more resources than general food subsidies in middle-income countries, where malnutrition is fairly low. But in these contexts, targeting by commodity/geography can often (as in Tunisia) greatly reduce *E*-mistakes, without increasing *F*-mistakes, whereas targeting by income tends to involve high *F*-mistakes with little reduction in *E*-mistakes.

- Even where universal food subsidies are apparently regressive, with the well-off receiving a higher share of the subsidies than their share of the population warrants, they are usually progressive compared with the distribution of original income and also confer real benefits on the poor in absolute terms. Consequently, policymakers who wish to improve income distribution and reduce poverty should not abolish food subsidies without providing substitute interventions that are at least as effective in conferring benefits on the poor taking into account potential *F*-mistakes.

Valuing the *E*- and *F*-Mistakes

Given an initial distribution of food-deficient (or poor) households, the standard theoretical approach to comparing the relative efficiency of alternative food interventions (aimed at removing such food deficiency and characterized by different delivery mechanisms and degrees of targeting) is based on the minimization of a given objective function. One of the following approaches is usually adopted (Besley and Kanbur 1987; Chaudhuri and Ravallion 1994):

(a) Minimization of the mistargeting (or misclassification) ratio; that is, minimization of the sum of the normalized value of the off-diagonal elements of the classification matrix presented in table 13-1. Thus, the food intervention selected will be that with the lowest value of this ratio.

(b) Minimization of a poverty index (by means of a given government expenditure that does not vary from one type of food intervention to another). The poverty headcount ratio, the poverty gap ratio, or a distributionally sensitive measure of the Foster-Greer-Thorbecke (FGT) class (such as the mean squared proportionate poverty gap) are the most commonly used indexes. The FGT index is, in general, superior to the first two and to that illustrated in approach a, as it reflects whether the alternative food interventions have been able to reach, on a priority basis, the poorest (or most food-deficient) households among all the poor (or food-deficient) ones.

(c) Minimization of the E-mistakes, given an acceptably low level of the F-mistake.

These (as well as other) approaches have different properties and limitations and often operate under fairly restrictive assumptions. Although the minimization of the misclassification ratio provides an intuitive, and easily computable, way of ranking alternative food interventions, such an approach is not very sensitive in situations where the extent of poverty (or food deficiency) among the poor varies considerably. Furthermore, such an approach implicitly assumes that the elements above and below the diagonal in the classification matrix (referred to in this chapter as E-mistakes and F-mistakes, or type II and type I errors in the literature in this field) must both be given weights equal to 1. In contrast, approach b, although preferable on theoretical grounds, has formidable informational requirements and assumes real-life approaches in the delivery of food interventions that are rarely, if ever, followed. Meanwhile, although more operational than approach b, approach c entails considerable arbitrariness in establishing what "an acceptably low level of the F-mistake" should be.

Even the simplest approach (approach a), however, though neither new nor controversial from a theoretical perspective, is seldom followed in applied research, as information on F-mistakes is not routinely available. For this reason, although F-mistakes are sometimes acknowledged, the most common approach adopted by the empirical analyses in this field focuses only on the minimization of E-mistakes (see, for instance, Mateus 1983; Pinstrup-Andersen 1988).

Data limitations with respect to the food interventions reviewed here do not allow us to follow approach b. In this section, therefore, we attempt to rank the efficiency of food interventions on the basis of the first approach (which entails the measurement of *both* E-mistakes and F-mistakes). The attempt to do so is subject to the usual problems facing any evaluation: an assessment of the value to be placed on the benefits

Table 13-11. *Comparison of the Efficiency of Alternative Interventions on the Basis of Alternative Measurements of the Targeting Mistakes*

Country and type of subsidy	E only (NP^c / N)	F only (P^{nc} / N)	E + F$[a = b = 1]$ $[(NP^c + P^{nc}) / N]$	E + 3F $[a = 1, b = 3]$ $[(NP^c + 3P^{nc}) / N]$
Sri Lanka[a]				
General subsidy	0.60	0.00	0.60	0.60
Food stamps	0.20	0.12	0.32	0.56
Jamaica[b]				
General subsidy	0.20	0.00	0.20	0.20
Food stamps	0.12	0.10	0.22	0.42
Pakistan[a]				
General subsidy	0.60	0.00	0.60	0.60
Food rations	0.12[c]	0.24[d]	0.36	0.84
Tamil Nadu (richer village)[e]				
General subsidy	0.39	0.00	0.39	0.39
School meals	0.14	0.32	0.46	1.10
Preschool meals	0.30	0.12	0.42	0.66

a. Poor and nonpoor: bottom 40 percent and top 60 percent of the population.
b. Poor and nonpoor: bottom 20 percent and top 20 percent of the population.
c. Estimate.
d. Assuming 40 percent of the poor are covered.
e. Poor and nonpoor: bottom three classes and top three classes.
Source: See tables 13-2, 13-3, 13-4, 13-6.

received by different groups, the choice of weights to be attributed to E-mistakes and F-mistakes, and also the counterfactual problem. Nonetheless, we believe that even this relatively simple approach is worthwhile, as it indicates how the ranking of food interventions assessed on the basis of E-mistakes can change when F-mistakes are incorporated into the evaluation.

Measuring the Total E- + F-Mistake as the Weighted Sum of All Individuals "Mistargeted"

Let the errors to be minimized consist of $(aNP^c + bP^{nc}) / N$, where a is the weight to be given to E-mistakes and b the weight given to F-mistakes. Implicit in the usual approach is the assumption that a is equal to 1, and b is equal to 0. In contrast, we believe in general $b > a$ because the failure of a nutrition intervention to reach the target population is more serious, being a failure to achieve the basic objectives of the intervention, than is leakage to the nontarget group, which raises the cost of the intervention but does not affect the achievement of its basic objective.

A critical issue, therefore, is the value of a and b. Relevant considerations in arriving at some system of weighting are (a) the costs of E-mistakes, which will be less if there is not a major budgetary problem (such as in a revenue-rich country such as Botswana or Saudi Arabia) or if the tax system can be used to claw back E-mistakes; in either of these cases, $a < 1$; and (b) the damage caused by F-mistakes, which includes both the welfare costs and the efficiency costs of not covering the target population.

At this stage, we simply illustrate how the ordering of schemes changes as valuation of the errors varies. This is shown in table 13-11, which values the errors in four ways: (a) considering E-mistakes only, (b) considering F-mistakes only, (c) giving both E- and F-mistakes equal weights of 1, and (d) assigning (arbitrarily) F-mistakes a weight three times that of E-mistakes ($b/a = 3$). General subsidies are invariably inferior to targeted schemes considering only E-mistakes (which here may have been exaggerated, as it is assumed that 100 percent of the upper-income groups are covered). If only F-mistakes are considered, then general subsidies are invariably superior to targeted schemes in the examples considered. When both are incorporated, the outcome depends on the proportion of the population who are in or outside the target group, the magnitude of the errors of omission and commission, and the relative weight given to the two types of error. For example, in Pakistan the targeted scheme is superior to the general subsidies if the two errors are given equal weight, but the general subsidies are superior when the F-mistakes are weighted at three times the E-mistakes. For Jamaica, if only the top 20 percent are regarded as causing E-mistakes, the general subsidy is superior if E- and F-errors are weighted equally (but this would change if E-mistakes are extended to a wider section of the population).

Measuring the Total E- + F-Mistake as the Sum of the Program Leakage, Welfare Cost, and Future Income Forgone due to Mistargeting

The discussion above has illustrated how the introduction of F-mistakes and the weighting of E- and F-mistakes according to given *welfare* weights could alter the ranking of food interventions. Such discussion, however, gives no justification for selecting any particular weighting of the two errors on both *welfare and efficiency* grounds. In this section we discuss considerations relevant to the evaluation of E- and F-mistakes on efficiency grounds as well.

E-mistakes are valued here in the usual way, that is, as the leakage (L) of financial resources to nontarget groups (NP^c).[2] In the valuation of F-mistakes, however, it is important to differentiate two distinct elements: the immediate welfare cost (W) and the present value of the future income forgone, Y^*, because of the failure to reach some poor households, P^{nc}, with the intervention.

In this case also, the food interventions to be selected are those that minimize the objective function (E- + F-mistakes), where E-mistakes are a function of NP^c and F-mistakes are a function of P^{nc}. Unlike the earlier approach, however, their weights are represented by monetary parameters related to the dollar value of the leakage and of the income forgone. We are thus adopting a type of cost-minimization approach, taking the objective of the food interventions as given and focusing on cost minimization interpreted in a broad sense.[3]

Estimating the Present Value of the Income Forgone as a Result of F-Mistakes (Y^*)

To assess the value of the forgone income, the discussion that follows focuses on two important relations: (a) between adult nutrition and short-term labor productivity and (b) among growth retardation at an early age, I.Q. scores, school achievements, and long-term labor productivity.[4]

ADULT NUTRITION AND LABOR PRODUCTIVITY. A fairly large body of evidence has been amassed on the relationships between calorie intake (or body mass) and labor productivity and between micronutrient deficiency and labor productivity. Our review includes two types of evidence: experimental and nonexperimental studies. The experimental studies reviewed (Borzok 1945; Kraut and Muller 1946; Keys and others

1950; Basta and others 1979; Wolgemuth and others 1982; Viteri, Torun, and Immink 1975; Strauss 1986; Deolalikar 1988; Sahn and Alderman 1988, quoted in Strauss and Thomas 1989) usually provide more accurate estimates of productivity increases, because they are better able to control for simultaneity, sample attrition, nonobserved household decisions affecting nutrition, and random assignment of the individuals included in the test. However, they may be subject to the "Hawthorne" effect (that is, taking part in an experiment can affect behavior). The results of the nonexperimental studies considered (Belavady 1966; Satyanarayana and others 1977; Immink and others 1984; see also Horton and King 1981; Scrimshaw 1986; and McGuire and Austin 1987 for a review of the literature in this field) should be interpreted more carefully because they are often affected by unknown estimation biases such as those mentioned above.

While these caveats should be borne in mind, from our review it appears that:

- Calorie intake and micronutrient supplementation (with iron, vitamin A, and iodine) are clearly correlated with the labor productivity of manual workers. These relations are mediated by improvements in muscle strength, precision of movement, and work endurance and by a decline in the risk of morbidity and absenteeism.

- Body mass is also significantly related to labor productivity. Shorter people with a history of chronic undernutrition since childhood have lower muscle mass and, *ceteris paribus*, lower aerobic capacity. The latter has been found to influence labor productivity among agricultural, construction, and other manual workers in several high- and low-income countries (McGuire and Austin 1987).

- The relation of calorie intake, micronutrient supplementation, and body mass vis-à-vis labor productivity is strongest for micronutrients and less intense (but still clear and statistically significant) for calorie intake and body mass. The effects of calorie intake and body size are often inseparable, though they reflect the influence of two different factors, the current level of nutrition and long-term stunting.

- The relation between nutrition and productivity is more pronounced for workers at low levels of intake (1,500–2,000 calories per day) or with very low levels of hemoglobin, as clearly shown by Strauss (1986) and Basta and others (1979). It is also positive and significant, but with lower elasticities, for workers who are in the 2,000–3,500 calorie range or who are mildly anemic.

- Changes in nutritional status may not affect productivity in the short term (as found by Belavady 1966), as limited and gradual declines or increases in intake might be accommodated by an adaptation of the basal metabolic rate (Scrimshaw 1986).

Table 13-12. Estimates of the Elasticity of the Nutrition-Productivity Relation

Study	Initial level (kilocalories)	Increase (kilocalories)	Productivity gains (percent)	Wages versus calories	Elasticity of Labor productivity with respect to Calories	Weight-for-height
Kraut and Muller (1946)						
Railway workers	2,400	600	47	—	1.80	—
Mineworkers	2,800	400	37	—	2.60	—
Mineworkers	3,200	400	7	—	0.56	—
Steelworkers	—	400	22	—	—	0.52
Keys and others (1950)	3,500	-2,000	-30[b]	—	—	—
Wolgemuth and others (1982)	2,000	500	12.5	—	0.50	—
Strauss (1986)	3,000	-1,500	-40	—	0.66	—
	3,000	1,500	17	—	0.34	—
	3,750	750	—	—	0.12	—
Viteri, Torun, and Immink (1975)	2,800	350	0.2[c]	—	—	—
Deolalikar (1988)						
Calorie	—	—	—	0.2	—	—
Weight/height	—	—	—	—	—	2.0
Sahn and Alderman (1988)	—	—	—	0.2	—	—
Satyanarayana and others (1977)	45[a]	10[a]	—	—	0.58	—
	45[a]	15[a]	—	—	0.81	—
Belavady (1966)	2,400	600	0	—	0	—

— Not available.

a. In kilograms.

b. Refers to muscle strength, not to labor productivity.

c. Tons of additional sugarcane cut.

Source: Compiled by the authors.

- With the exception of the Kraut and Muller (1946) and Belavady (1966) results (which found exceptionally high and exceptionally low elasticities), providing an additional calorie supplement of 800–1,000 calories per day to manual workers with low levels of intake may result in an increase in actual consumption of 500–600 calories, which is in turn likely to be associated with a productivity increase in the range of 20 to 30 percent. If the intake is equal to the supplementation provided, the increase in productivity would range in the 30 to 40 percent bracket (table 13-12).

Assuming that the yearly productivity of low-income workers in poor developing countries is in the $300–$500 per capita bracket, the gains associated with an increase in calorie intake could be roughly assessed to be in the range of $60 to $200 per capita per year. This figure compares favorably with the cost of a food subsidy program (or of similar child feeding or school lunch programs), which is estimated at around $30 per year per 1,000 calories effectively transferred per day (World Bank 1989; Kennedy and Alderman 1987)

MALNUTRITION, GROWTH RETARDATION AT AN EARLY AGE, AND LABOR PRODUCTIVITY IN ADULTHOOD. Malnutrition at an early age, caused by dietary deficiency, infection, or lack of sensory stimulation, leads to severe impairment of cognitive capacity and to stunting. There are essentially three mechanisms through which different forms of malnutrition in infancy and childhood affect labor productivity in adulthood: (a) persistent protein energy malnutrition in infancy and childhood leads to long-term stunting and lower aerobic capacity in adult life (already discussed above); (b) severe malnutrition at an early age (before five) affects I.Q., later learning ability (both directly and through the amount of schooling, which also depends on I.Q.), skill acquisition, and future productivity; and (c) undernourishment and iron deficiency in schoolchildren affect attention span, learning ability, and school achievement and, through these, skill acquisition and future productivity.

The literature in these three areas is substantial, though there are no known well-controlled, longitudinal studies to estimate the intensity of these relations. Part of the variability of the results is due to the difficulties in controlling for intervening nonobserved variables (the time of the onset of malnutrition, its severity and type, and the living conditions of the children in the control group) and in achieving adequate standardization. Despite these drawbacks, the relevant literature shows that:

- Severe protein energy malnutrition in infancy and early childhood has a negative effect on intelligence tests and school scores during school life. These findings were confirmed in ten out of the thirteen studies surveyed by Pollitt (1984).

- The extent of the cognitive deficit among school-age children is associated with the severity and duration of the nutritional deficit at an early age. In most studies, the cognitive deficit during school age was equal to 10 to 15 percent of the average of the control group, though it varied between an upper limit of 25 I.Q. points (roughly 30 percent of the mean) in the case of malnourished South African children (Galler and others 1983) and only a few points in the case of equally severely malnourished Korean children (Winnick, Meyer, and Harris 1979).

- In the absence of longitudinal studies, the loss of future income due to malnutrition in childhood can best be estimated by combining the existing evidence on the relation among child malnutrition, learning ability, and amount of schooling completed with that on the relation ,between levels of schooling and earnings. A well-known study using data on differential I.Q. scores of normal and undernourished Chilean children and differential earnings of construction workers ranked by I.Q. levels (Selowsky and Taylor 1973) showed that providing nutritional supplements during the first two years of life to the 25,000 or so children becoming malnourished in Chile every year would generate benefits equal to six times the cost of the intervention. Similarly, a reduction in the gap between the ability scores of low- and high-income children in Cali, Colombia, due to a health-nutritional program, increased the total value of their lifetime earnings by between 2.5 and 4.6 times the yearly wage of an illiterate worker (depending on the years of schooling completed) in the case of an increase in I.Q. equal to one standard deviation, and by between 5.6 and 8.9 times the yearly wage in the case of an increase in I.Q. equal to two standard deviations (Selowsky 1981).[5]

- The current nutritional intake of schoolchildren clearly affects their academic achievements. A review of five studies on Singapore, Indonesia, the United States, and the Philippines, Pollitt (1984, p. 21) concludes, "It must be recognized that most studies reviewed concur in suggesting that the nutritional status of the student is a variable that determines in part educational performance." The Indonesian study, for instance, found that anemic children had lower school scores than nonanemic children.

Adding Up the Costs of F-Mistakes and Weighing Them Together with E-Mistakes

As noted repeatedly, part of the evidence presented in this chapter suffers from various methodological problems that may bias some of the estimated coefficients. But the results of the above survey can nevertheless be used for a tentative valuation of F-mistakes. For each intervention, the value of the E-mistake ought to be weighed together with the immediate welfare cost and the discounted value of the expected gains forgone because of the failure to incorporate the needy population in the nutritional program. As noted, the discounted value is normally composed of two elements: (a) immediate labor productivity effects on adult workers and (b) the discounted value of future forgone gains.[6] On the basis of the preceding discussion one can very *tentatively* assess the value of the E- + F-mistake as:

(13-2) $E\text{- } + F\text{-mistake} = L + Y^* + W$
           $E\text{- } + F\text{-mistake} = v\,NP^c + (\alpha\,m + \beta c)\pi\,P^{nc} + W$

where

(13-3) $L = vNP^c$
                          $Y^* = \alpha\,\pi\,m\,P^{nc} + \beta\,\pi\,c\,P^{nc}$

and where

L = monetary value of the nutritional program's leakage
v = average monetary value of the subsidy received by NP^c
W = immediate welfare cost of F-mistake
π = yearly productivity of a low-income manual worker
m = share of adult manual workers in P^{nc}
c = share of children below five years of age in P^{nc}
α = percentage average loss of productivity of malnourished manual workers not reached by the nutritional program
β = multiple of present value of future forgone income of malnourished children not reached by the nutritional program expressed in terms of the current productivity of low-income manual workers.

This approach is not fundamentally different from that presented earlier and summarized in table 13-11, where the E- + F-mistake to be minimized was equal to $(aNP^c + bP^{nc}) / N$. Beyond the welfare cost, W, and the constant term, N, the two approaches coincide except for the weights adopted. In this new approach, the weights a and b are, respectively, replaced by the weights v and $(\alpha m + \beta c)\pi$. The ranking of food interventions could therefore be altered again if, in addition to considering the welfare cost, W, the ratio a/b is substantially different from the ratio $v/(\alpha m + \beta c)\pi$.

Although lack of information does not allow us to estimate the values of Y^* and W for any of the food interventions reviewed in this chapter, the value of the forgone future incomes assessed on the basis of a broad survey of the literature appears quite large in relation to the average value of the leakage of food interventions.[7] With α and β estimated to range, respectively, between 0.3–0.4 and 2.5–4.6, π at $300–$500, and *m* and *c* likely to range, respectively, between 0.2–0.3 and 0.4–0.5, it appears that the weights of *F*-mistakes can be extremely large even without attributing any value to *W*. Food interventions that reduce *E*-mistakes but increase *F*-mistakes would therefore tend to increase substantially the total *E*- + *F*-mistake.

The Potential for Claw-back of *E*-Mistakes

The earlier discussion showed that targeted schemes can be designed to involve low *E*- and *F*-errors and *a fortiori* a low *E* + *F* total. This occurs, for example, whenever all the target population has some easily verifiable characteristic (such as geographic location, age, gender, or consumption pattern) that is not shared by the nontarget population. But such a situation is rare.

In most cases, characteristics are more evenly spread across the population, so that efforts to reduce *E*-errors tend to increase *F*-errors. This means that there is a choice between two unsatisfactory situations: (a) if the *F*-mistake is to be minimized, the *E*-mistake tends to be large (and the government deficit may increase); (b) if the *E*-mistake is to be minimized and the budget constraints respected, the *F*-mistake (and the administrative cost) tends to be high.

A possible way out of this dilemma would be to claw back the leakage in situation (a) above through the tax system. Ideally, such claw-back ought to involve the recovery of the leakage from the same nontarget population covered by the food intervention. To achieve this objective, it is necessary, however, to know the value and distribution of the leakage by income level and the incidence of the main tax instruments.

The Value and Distribution of the Leakage

The evidence suggested that the percentage share of benefits accruing to the nontarget population is typically 60 to 70 percent in the case of generalized food subsidies, 30 to 40 percent for food stamp schemes, and lower values for child feeding programs. The cost of most food subsidy schemes is between 0.4 and 1.6 percent of gross domestic product (GDP), with costs in a few countries being substantially higher (3 to 6 percent of GDP), while that of child feeding schemes generally amounts to 0.1–0.6 percent of GDP (Bird and Horton 1989; World Bank 1989). The total cost of the *E*-mistakes through food subsidies and food stamp programs may thus be estimated as being typically 0.3–1.0 percent of GDP (proportionately greater in the case of the high-cost countries). A less restrictive definition of the target population (identified in most of the studies reviewed as those in the bottom 25 or 30 percent of the population, probably a "low" estimate of absolute poverty) might reduce this total somewhat to 0.2–0.7 percent of GDP. However, the cost of the leakage is considerably smaller for infant and school feeding schemes.

The distribution of the leakage by income group varies with the type of intervention adopted. In some cases, the benefit per capita is constant for all income groups (as in the case of school meals). In the case of food subsidies, it is broadly proportional to the overall consumption of the subsidized food by each income class and tends therefore to grow with household income, while for others it might take the shape of an inverted U. When expressed as a share of the income of each group, the leakage tends to decline rapidly for each successive income decile.

Tax Incidence by Income Group and by Main Tax Instrument

Knowledge of the distribution of consumption and of tax incidence by the main tax instruments is required to identify the best approach for clawing back the leakage. Ideally, the leakage ought to be clawed back through income taxes, so as to avoid inflationary pressures and distortions in consumer preferences and because of the low incidence of direct taxes in most developing countries. Equity considerations require that each income decile's additional direct taxes be broadly equivalent to the value of the leakage to each group. This would therefore require increasing tax yields from each income group by a generally declining proportion of their incomes.

Increasing tax yields can often be achieved through improving tax collection rather than through increasing tax rates. This, of course, is an important objective per se, but it gains special justification in the context of a need to claw back leakage from food interventions. Alternatively, small adjustments in tax rates could be introduced so as to avoid negative effects on savings, labor supply, and tax evasion. Writing about India, Guhan (1992) notes, for instance, that the introduction of a small income tax surcharge (equal to 4, 2.5, and 1 percent) on each of the three top income groups (corresponding, respectively, to 1.2, 2.3, and 8.7 percent of all households) would be likely to yield 0.3 of GDP. Guhan notes that the absolute value of the proposed surcharge is moderate, in view of the fact that in India the effective income tax threshold is quite high.

A similar approach to the claw-back proposed here is already followed in a number of high-income countries in the case of universal income transfers to the household sector. In Sweden, for instance, all families with children are entitled to child allowances. These are included in the tax base and are therefore taxed whenever the combined family income exceeds a certain threshold. This approach, however, is not always practicable. In Hungary, the particular characteristics of the tax system (no pooling of family incomes, child allowances accruing to women, and limited progressivity of direct taxes) substantially reduce the desirability of clawing back the leakage in this manner (see Jarvis and Micklewright, chapter 11 of this volume).

The problems encountered in clawing back leakages through direct taxation are more acute in developing countries, where income tax administration is subject to a number of well-known problems that reduce the possibility of clawing back an adequate amount of resources. In addition, because of the limited number of (mostly urban, formal sector) people subject to direct taxation, attempts at clawing back leakage might cause equity problems, as the high-income group taxed may not coincide with the groups benefiting from the leakage.

For all these reasons, the claw-back may sometimes best be effected through indirect taxes. This requires the identification of goods (a) that are consumed predominantly by the income groups who benefited from the leakage, (b) that generate a sizable proportion of the revenue of indirect taxation, and (c) that have a fairly low own-price elasticity of demand.

A few studies provide the information required for achieving claw-back through indirect taxation. Two recent studies on India (Jha and Srinivasan 1988a, 1988b) examine the effect of a hypothetical 10 percent increase in indirect taxes on tax yields, the progressivity of indirect taxation, and inflation. The simulation is carried out on the basis of a fully specified model that includes an input/output table with fifty sectors and a final consumer demand system. The two studies identify the share of indirect revenue originating from each of the fifty sectors and the distribution of the indirect tax burden between the "rich" (broadly corresponding to the top two deciles of the population) and the "nonrich" for each group of products.

While petroleum and petroleum products constitute a sizable tax base for increasing revenue, about 60 percent of the tax burden falls on "nonrich" groups. The recovery of the leakage would, therefore, better be effected by increasing indirect taxation on other goods whose tax burden is distributed more progressively. These include cotton, silk, and other textiles, rubber products and synthetic fibers, electric machinery, motor vehicles, and other manufacturing goods for which between 65 and 75 percent of taxation falls on the top 20 percent of the population (and, probably, close to 100 percent on the top 40 percent of the population). The share of indirect taxes originating from these commodities is about 30 percent.

A 10 percent increase in indirect taxes on the above sectors (and other commodities not mentioned here for reasons of space) would generate an additional 0.3–0.4 percent of GDP, a small improvement in the degree of progressivity of indirect taxation, and (assuming no wage indexation) limited effects on inflation.

Though obviously tentative, the above calculations show that there are potentially viable tax policies that would permit recovery of a considerable part of the leakage via indirect taxation even in low-income and highly rural countries such as India. The scope for such a claw-back would obviously be greater in middle-income countries. Such an approach, which relies on variable rates of indirect taxation, is also consistent with optimal tax theory (Ahmad and Stern 1991).

Conclusions

This chapter has argued that the design of targeted food interventions has focused almost exclusively on the E-mistake—that of "wasting" resources by covering some or all of the nontarget population. In so doing, it has neglected the F-mistake—that of failing to reach the whole target population.

Empirical studies show that in general as E-mistakes are reduced through targeting, F-mistakes are increased. While E-mistakes involve additional expenditure, F-mistakes have a different kind of cost, which encompasses both the immediate welfare loss and the future income forgone as a result of malnutrition among the "missed" target group. In line with mainstream theoretical approaches to the evaluation of alternative food interventions, both types of mistakes (that is, the total mistargeting error) should be considered in designing good schemes.

Indeed, the analysis presented in this chapter indicates that incorporating both types of mistakes can alter the rankings of food interventions, from those obtained with the more usual focus on E-errors alone. Although the outlined approach needs further refinement and better testing on an appropriate data set generated for the purpose, preliminary results suggest that "narrow targeting" may generate large welfare and efficiency costs. For example, empirical estimates suggest that the efficiency cost alone of F-mistakes can be substantial. Given these costs, the twin objectives of covering the highest possible number of the poor while minimizing leakage may best be achieved by clawing back some or all of the leakage from excess coverage through a variety of direct and indirect tax measures.

This chapter has considered some of the tax mechanisms through which such claw-back could be effected by illustrating possible options in a few concrete cases. Although more work is obviously needed in this area, particularly to improve the precision of the claw-back, it appears that such an approach could substantially offset the cost of E-mistakes, while largely avoiding F-mistakes.

Notes

1. In selecting interventions, one should also consider general equilibrium effects, in particular the effects of alternative food interventions on food prices.

General food subsidies are more likely than narrowly targeted schemes to affect food prices across the board. In the short run, they may therefore lower food prices, thereby generating additional benefits for poor (and other) consumers. But the long-run effects depend on how far producer prices are affected. This chapter does not explore such general equilibrium effects.

2. The efficiency cost of the leakage to the economy (in terms of reduced labor supply and incentives) could also be added, but it is not considered in this chapter.

3. Valuation of W depends on how the income of different groups is valued; the welfare costs are likely to depend on how badly off those not covered are. From this perspective, F-mistakes should be valued more when they relate to the ultra-poor, rather than the poor, and it would be desirable to have two types of F-mistakes relating to this distinction. Our present data do not allow us to pursue this. Another approach is to adopt equity weights and value F-mistakes according to society's valuation of income going to the target group as against other groups. Thus an Atkinson utility index could be adopted, where the income of a particular group is valued as

$$W(y) = \frac{1}{1-e}\, y^{1-e}.$$

However, we do not have the detailed information necessary to estimate the value of the welfare costs of F-mistakes using this approach, nor do we know the value of e.

4. The relationship among maternal malnutrition, low birth weight in female infants, and their reproductive efficiency as adults is another, often overlooked, source of forgone income costs associated with F-errors. In some studies (Hackman and others 1983), a positive relation has been found between low birth weight and poor nutrition in the mother's childhood and her later bearing of low birth weight infants or of infants with birth defects. Estimating the forgone income effect of this kind of intergenerational transmission of malnutrition is highly conjectural, however, and is not pursued here.

5. Selowsky (1981) notes that in the early mid-1970s, the wage of an illiterate worker in six developing countries varied between 40 and 95 percent of the gross domestic product (GDP) per capita. Only in one case was the wage above GDP per capita.

6. This estimate of "forgone income" is an underestimate of its actual value, as it excludes the positive effects of nutritional interventions on mortality, morbidity, and reproductive efficiency.

7. The average annual cost per beneficiary of food interventions was found to vary, for instance, between $7 and $40 for supplementary feeding programs, between $20 and $40 for integrated health care–based schemes, and between $10 and $40 for food subsidies (see World Bank 1989, tables 8 and 9; Kennedy and Alderman 1987, table 9).

References

Ahmad, Ehtisham, and Nicholas Stern. 1991. "Tax Reform in Developing Countries." Cambridge, Eng.: Cambridge University Press.

Alderman, Harold. 1988. "The Twilight of Flour Rationing in Pakistan." *Food Policy* 13 (3): 245–56.

Alderman, Harold, and Joachim von Braun. 1984. "The Effects of the Egyptian Subsidy System on Income Distribution and Consumption." *Research Report* 45 (July). International Food Policy Research Institute, Washington, D.C.

———. 1986. "Egypt's Food Subsidy Policy: Lessons and Options." *Food Policy* 11 (3): 223–37.

Babu, Suresh C., and J. Arne Hallam. 1989. "Socioeconomic Impacts of School Feeding Programs." *Food Policy* 14 (1): 58–66.

Basta, Samir, S. M. S. Soekerman, D. Karyadi, and N. S. Scrimshaw. 1979. "Iron Deficiency Anaemia and the Productivity of Adult Males in Indonesia." *American Journal of Clinical Nutrition* 32 (4): 916–25.

Belavady, B. 1966. "Nutrition and Efficiency of Agricultural Labourers." *Indian Journal of Medical Research* 54: 971–76.

Besley, Timothy, and Ravi Kanbur. 1987. "Food Subsidies and Poverty Alleviation." Applied Economics Discussion Paper 27. Institute of Economics and Statistics, University of Oxford, Oxford, U.K. June.

Bird, Richard M., and Susan Horton. 1989. *Government Policy and the Poor in Developing Countries.* Toronto: University of Toronto Press.

Borzok, H. 1945. "The Nutrition Status of Aircraft Workers in California." *Millbank Memorial Fund Quarterly* (April).

Chaudhuri, Shubham, and Martin Ravallion. 1994. "How Well Do Static Indicators Identify the Chronically Poor?" *Journal of Public Economics* 53 (3): 367–94.

Cornia, G. A., and Frances Stewart. 1993. "Two Errors of Targeting." Innocenti Occasional Paper 36. UNICEF-ICDC, Florence. March.

Dasgupta, Partha, and Debraj Ray. 1987. "Adapting to Undernutrition: The Clinical Evidence and Its Implications." Working Paper 10. World Institute for Development Economics Research, United Nations University, Helsinki. April.

Deolalikar, Anil. 1988. "Nutrition and Labor Productivity in Agriculture: Estimates for Rural South India." *Review of Economics and Statistics* 70: 406–13.

Edirisinghe, Neville. 1987. "The Food Stamp Scheme in Sri Lanka: Costs, Benefits, and Options for Modification." Research Report 58. International Food Policy Research Institute, Washington, D.C.

———. 1988. "Recent Targeting Attempts in Sri Lanka's Food Stamp Schemes." *Food Policy* 12 (4): 401–02.

Folbre, Nancy. 1986. "Hearts and Spades: Paradigms of Household Economics." *World Development* 14 (2): 245–56.

Galler, Janina R., Frank Ramsey, Giorgio Solimano, and W. E. Lowell. 1983. "The Influence of Early Malnutrition on Subsequent Behavioural Development. II: Classroom Behavior." *Journal of the American Academy of Child Psychiatry* 22 (1): 16–22.

Garcia, M. H., and Per Pinstrup-Andersen. 1987. "The Pilot Food Price Subsidy Scheme in the Philippines: Its Impact on Income and Food Consumption." Research Report 61. International Food Policy Research Institute, Washington, D.C.

Grosh, Margaret E. 1992. "The Jamaican Food Stamps Program: A Case Study in Targeting." *Food Policy* 17 (1): 23–40.

Guhan, S. 1992. "Social Security for the Unorganized Poor: A Feasible Blueprint for India." Discussion Paper. United Nations Development Program and Indira Gandhi Institute of Development Research, Bombay. January.

Guyer, Jane. 1980. "Household Budgets and Women's Incomes." Working Paper 28. African Studies Centre, Boston University, Boston, Mass.

Hackman, E., and others 1983. "Maternal Birth Weight and Subsequent Pregnancy Outcome." *Journal of the American Medical Association* 250 (15): 2016–19.

Harrell, M. W., Cutberto Parillon, and Ralph Franklin. 1989. "Nutritional Classification Study of Peru." *Food Policy* 14 (4): 313–29.

Harriss, Barbara. 1992. *Child Nutrition and Poverty in South India*. New Delhi: Concept Publishing Co.

Hoddinott, John, and Lawrence Haddad. 1991. "Household Expenditures, Child Anthropometric Status, and the Intrahousehold Division of Income: Evidence for the Côte d'Ivoire." Research Programme in Development Studies, Princeton University, Princeton, N.J. September.

Horton, Susan, and Timothy King. 1981. *Labor Productivity: Un Tour d'Horizon*. World Bank Staff Working Paper 497. Washington, D.C.

Immink, Martin, Fernando E. Viteri, R. Flores, and Benjamin Torun. 1984. "Microeconomic Consequences of Energy Efficiency in Rural Populations in Developing Countries." In Ernesto Pollitt and P. Amante, eds., *Energy Intake and Activity*. Vol. 11, *Current Topics in Nutrition and Disease*. New York: Alan R. Liss.

Jha, Shikha, and P. V. Srinivasan. 1988a. "Who Pays More? The Case of Excise Duties in India." Discussion Paper 7. Indira Gandhi Institute of Development Research, Bombay. August.

———. 1988b. "Indirect Taxes in India: An Incidence Analysis." Discussion Paper 11. Indira Gandhi Institute of Development Research, Bombay.

Kennedy, Eileen, and Harold Alderman. 1987. "Comparative Analyses of Nutritional Effectiveness of Food Subsidies and Other Food-Related Interventions." Joint World Health Organization–UNICEF Nutrition Support Programme, International Food Policy Research Institute, Washington, D.C.

Kesselman, J. R. 1982. "Taxation Behavior and the Design of a Credit Income Tax." In I. Garfinkel, ed., *Income-Tested Programs: The Case For and Against*. New York: Academic Press.

Keys, A., J. Brozek, A. Henschel, O. Mickelson, and H. L. Taylor. 1950. *The Biology of Human Starvation*, 2 vols. Minneapolis: University of Minnesota Press.

Kraut, H. A., and E. A. Muller. 1946. "Calorie Intake and Industrial Output." *Science* 104: 495–97.

McGuire, Judith, and James E. Austin. 1987. "Beyond Survival: Children's Growth for National Development." *Assignment Children*, vol. 2. New York: UNICEF.

Mahendra Dev, S., and M. H. Suryanarayana. 1991. "Is PDS Urban Biased and Pro-Rich?" *Economic and Political Weekly* 26 (41): 2357–66.

Mateus, Abel. 1983. *Targeting Food Subsidies for the Needy: The Use of Cost-Benefit Analysis and Institutional Design*. World Bank Staff Working Paper 617. Washington, D.C.

Miller, Barbara. 1981. *The Endangered Sex: Neglect of Female Children in Rural North India*. Ithaca, N.Y.: Cornell University Press.

Pinstrup-Andersen, Per. 1991. "Targeted Nutrition Interventions." *Food and Nutrition Bulletin* 13 (3): 161–69.

Pinstrup-Andersen, Per, ed. 1988. *Food Subsidies in Developing Countries: Costs, Benefits, and Policy Options*. Baltimore, Md.: Johns Hopkins University Press.

Pollitt, Ernesto. 1984. "Nutrition and Educational Achievement." Nutrition Education Series 9, 84/WS/66. United Nations Educational, Scientific, and Cultural Organization, Paris.

Rosenzweig, Mark. 1986. "Program Interventions, Intrahousehold Distribution, and the Welfare of Households: Modelling Household Behavior." *World Development* 14 (2): 233–44.

Sahn, David E., and Harold Alderman. 1988. "The Effects of Human Capital on Wages and the Determinants of Labor Supply in a Developing Country." *Journal of Development Economics* 29 (2): 157–84.

Satyanarayana, K., A. Naidu, B. Chatterjee, and B. Narasinga Rao. 1977. "Body Size and Work Output." *American Journal of Clinical Nutrition* 30: 322–25.

Scrimshaw, Nevin. 1986. "Nutritional and Health Consequences of Economic Adjustment Policies That Increase Poverty." Paper for the North-South Round Table on Development, Salzburg.

Selowsky, Marcello. 1981. "Nutrition, Health, and Education: The Economic Significance of Complementarities at Early Age." *Journal of Development Economics* 9: 331–46.

Selowsky, Marcello, and Lance Taylor. 1973. "The Economics of Malnourished Children: An Example of Disinvestment in Human Capital." *Economic Development and Cultural Change* 22 (1): 17–30.

Strauss, John. 1986. "Does Better Nutrition Raise Farm Productivity?" *Journal of Political Economy* 94 (2): 297–320.

Strauss, John, and Duncan Thomas. 1989. "The Shape of the Calorie Expenditure Curve." Department of Economics, Yale University, New Haven, Conn.

Sukhatme, P. V. 1977. "Malnutrition and Poverty." Ninth Lal Bhaduri Shastri Memorial Lecture. Indian Agricultural Research Institute, New Delhi.

Tripp, Robert. 1981. "Farmers and Traders—Some Economic Determinants of Nutritional Status in Northern Ghana." *Journal of Tropical Paediatrics* 27: 15–22.

Viteri, Fernando E., Benjamin Torun, and M. D. C. Immink. 1975. "Interaction between Nutrition and Productivity of Agricultural Labourers." Paper prepared for the fourteenth meeting of the Advisory Committee on Medical Research of the Pan-American Health Organization.

Winnick, M., K. K. Meyer, and R. C. Harris. 1979. "Malnutrition and Environmental Enrichment by Early Adoption." *Science* 190: 1173–75.

Wolgemuth, J. C., M. C. Latham, A. Hall, A. Cheser, and D. W. T. Crompton. 1982. "Worker Productivity and Nutritional Status of Kenyan Road Construction Laborers." *American Journal of Clinical Nutrition* 36: 68–78.

World Bank. 1989. "Feeding Latin America's Children." Report 7622-LAC. World Bank, Washington, D.C.

_____. 1991. "Report and Recommendation of the President of the IBRD to Executive Directors on a Proposed Agricultural Adjustment Loan II." Report P-5520-ME (May). Washington, D.C.

Yusuf, M. D. 1989. "On Reforming Tunisia's Food Subsidy Program." World Bank, Middle East and North Africa Agriculture and Operations Division, Washington, D.C.

14 Incentive Effects on Labor Supply of Sri Lanka's Rice Subsidy

David E. Sahn and Harold Alderman

The literature on targeted subsidies mainly focuses on the degree to which transfers actually reach the intended beneficiaries. The need and mechanisms for discriminating between individuals that the program is designed to serve and those that the program would ideally exclude is a subject that has been accorded considerable attention (see, for example, Alderman 1991; Pinstrup-Andersen 1988; Ravallion 1989; and Timmons, Miller, and Drake 1983). This issue of the sensitivity and selectivity of subsidies is relevant to attempts both to design new interventions and, in the context of the universal rationing schemes, to reform existing programs. Included in the latter case are the rationing schemes of South Asian countries that were born during World War II as a response to shortages. A case in point is Sri Lanka, the subject of this study. Over time, however, the Sri Lankan food distribution system has evolved from a means to ration scarce food commodities into a targeted intervention designed to provide income support for the poor.

The restructuring of Sri Lanka's ration system achieved significant efficiencies in the targeting of subsidies toward the poor (Edirisinghe 1987). There is, however, another aspect of the efficiency of the subsidy system that has been given little attention in Sri Lanka and elsewhere: the effect of the transfer on labor supply. Under the standard theory of household utility maximization over leisure as well as goods, a change in exogenous income or in the price of commodities will affect labor allocation as well as commodity choice. With the household facing a time budget constraint, in addition to a traditional budget constraint, the net impact of a food-related income transfer on consumer budget

Priorities of names are based on a rotating order of listing over a multiyear project. The authors wish to express their gratitude to Yisehac Yohannes for his excellent research assistance and to Nancy Birdsall for comments on an earlier draft.

allocations will include this impact on labor allocation. Thus, in practice, the incentive effects of the food ration on labor supply will have potentially important implications for the level of net benefits of targeted programs. This is particularly so from a "nonwelfarist" perspective (see Kanbur, Keen, and Tuomala, chapter 5 of this volume) in which the consumption of certain goods—often food—rather than total household utility is the objective of the program.

Economists have paid considerable attention to the effects of taxes on labor supply, as well as commodity demand (Atkinson and Stern 1980; Singh, Squire, and Strauss 1986). The comparable literature on the effect of transfers is more limited. Thus, Moffitt (1992) states the following in a recent review: "The lack of research on the effects of in-kind transfer programs is a serious problem in light of the critical role such transfers have played [in the United States]." This conclusion is reached with full knowledge that some relevant studies have examined the labor supply effects of programs in the United States, such as the research on the disincentive effects of Aid for Families with Dependent Children (AFDC) (Danziger, Haveman, and Plotnick 1981), food stamps (Fraker and Moffitt 1988), and Medicaid (Winkler 1991).

The paucity of studies on intervention programs in developing countries is yet more acute. In fact, we know of no studies of how food-related income transfers have affected labor supply in developing countries. Thus, the remainder of this study will use household-level data from Sri Lanka to investigate the extent to which the labor supply decision of males and females in rural and urban areas is affected by access to the rice ration. In addressing that issue, we also distinguish between the effects on the probability of labor market participation and the response in terms of the number of days worked conditional on participation. The advantage of this two-step approach is that it allows for different variables to enter into the participation and response functions, as well as for the possibility of a discontinuous response.

The Rice Subsidy and Its Beneficiaries

The Sri Lankan food ration system persisted for more than twenty-five years as a general subsidy, with no real effort made at targeting. During this period, however, many changes occurred in the allotment, the ration price; and the level of the burden to the treasury (Sahn and Edirisinghe 1993; Edirisinghe 1987; Gavan and Chandrasekera 1979). The most fundamental change followed the election of a new government in 1977 that was committed to moving toward a more market-oriented economy with a diminished role for the state. Among the major economic reforms instituted in 1978 was the initiation of means testing as a feature of the subsidy. This was motivated, in large part,

Table 14-1. Share of Households Receiving Rice Ration by Sector and Expenditure Quintile, Sri Lanka, 1978–79
(percent)

Per capita expenditure quintile	Urban	Rural
1	77.6	83.3
2	60.7	72.0
3	45.5	58.2
4	36.8	44.1
5	11.9	24.1
All	41.0	58.6

Source: Edirisinghe 1987.

by the fact that the subsidy comprised 17 percent of government expenditures and 6 percent of gross national product.

Self-reported income provided the criterion used to reduce coverage under the system by 50 percent. In the first phase of the reform program, the quantity of free or subsidized rice that eligible families received was not changed. Subsequently, the system was converted to a food stamp program, with the targeting criterion unchanged. Undoubtedly there was considerable underreporting of incomes, because the resources and means available for checking on incomes were limited. Nonetheless, the change in the distribution of the benefits delivered through the rice subsidy was substantial, and reasonably progressive, especially in light of the relatively low administrative costs of the transition. Only 12 and 24 percent of the households in the upper-expenditure quintiles in the urban and rural areas, respectively, received rations. The corresponding numbers for the lowest-expenditure quintile were 78 and 83 percent (see table 14-1).

The Sri Lankan food ration system differs from similar in-kind welfare programs in the United States in that it does not impose a "tax rate," often referred to as a "benefit-reduction rate" on the level of work performed. While welfare programs in the United States and other high-income countries involve a reduction in benefits if the recipient earns wages in the labor market, the system in Sri Lanka neither varied the level of transfer as income rose nor monitored and removed households from the program if their incomes crossed a threshold. Thus, the budget constraint was not kinked as it is in some welfare programs. One need not model the effects of an increasing marginal tax on income and can focus directly on the substitution effect of leisure for labor as income is augmented. Once a person was deemed eligible for the subsidy, changes in earnings had no effect on the amount of transfer received. This would suggest smaller labor supply effects than when the benefit-reduction rate operates.

The analysis is also assisted by the fact that the rice ration was inframarginal for virtually the entire population. Thus, one can treat the subsidy as an income transfer and avoid having to model the corner solution often implied by a dual-price regime.

For the purpose of the analysis, however, an important question is the extent to which participation in the Sri Lankan subsidy scheme can be considered endogenous. One reason often cited for the endogeneity of participation in a variety of programs focuses on the issue of knowledge of eligibility for the program. This was clearly not relevant in this case, as universal coverage for a generation prior to program changes ensured universal awareness. A second reason is the stigma effect that could induce households to self-select out of the program (see Moffitt 1983; Ranney and Cushman 1985). Once again, this was not likely to be an issue in the Sri Lanka case due to the long period of universal entitlement. Furthermore, the preponderance of evidence indicates that households made strenuous efforts to stay eligible during the change-over, even at the risk of being accused of lying on the income forms.

A third factor that could affect participation was the transaction costs of dealing with the ration shops. The ration shop system in Sri Lanka, however, was highly efficient and convenient. Moreover, even though the rice subsidy at the shops was targeted after 1979, other nonrationed universal subsidies, such as sugar, wheat flour, and bread, continued to be enjoyed by all households.

The main source of endogeneity that enters into benefiting from the subsidy is that households that were more determined and capable of deception may have proven better able to remain in the program, despite not conforming to the income criteria. Although identification of these households is difficult, one may anticipate the direction of bias. In particular, it is likely that persons who were more aggressive in dealing with the ration system may also have been more assertive in the labor market. If this is the case, the failure to model this attitude will lead to a positive bias in the relationship between subsidies and labor. We control for individual heterogeneity by substituting a predicted subsidy for the observed subsidy in one set of estimates. We also compare these results with similar estimates that use the reported, rather than the predicted, subsidy to test our prior expectation that the negative impact of transfers on labor supply would be dampened when using the uninstrumented (reported) subsidy.

Data

This empirical analysis relies on two surveys. First, the 1978–79 Consumer Finances and Socioeconomic Survey conducted by the Central Bank of Ceylon is used to derive information on the level of benefits from the food subsidy as well as to estimate the labor market participation and response functions. The nationally representative sample survey was conducted during four rounds, from October 1978 to September 1979. While the entire survey covered nearly 8,000 households, we limit our analysis to urban and rural areas. By excluding estates, the sample is reduced by nearly 2,000 households. The quality of the data is attested to by the fact that the estimated values of the rice subsidy and food expenditures derived from the survey are 97 and 95 percent, respectively, of the figures reported in the national accounts. There is evidence from comparisons with national accounts, however, that nonfood expenditures may have been underestimated by as much as 22 percent (Edirisinghe 1987). In addition to a complete compilation of information on the structure of the households, food and nonfood expenditures, and incomes, the survey collected data on labor market participation. However, the survey did not include information that would allow us to compute hourly wages. This is an obvious drawback for the chosen topic.

In order to estimate the requisite market wage, we therefore rely on a labor force survey conducted in 1980–81 by the Department of Census and Statistics. The 5,000 household sample was also nationally representative and based on the same sampling frame. It collected detailed information on hourly earnings for all household members. Wage functions are estimated using this survey. These are reported in Sahn and Alderman (1988). The coefficients from these equations are then applied to the 1978–79 data to arrive at a predicted wage that is subsequently entered exogenously in the participation and labor supply functions.

The obvious question is why not use the 1980–81 survey for the entirety of the analysis rather than alternate between two data sets. Unfortunately, the later survey does not provide detailed enough information to determine the value of the food subsidy that was received. However, the procedure of using a predicted wage to estimate supply response is a standard approach to address missing observations on wages and the possibility of a correlation of errors on reported hours and on wages.

Empirical Approach

The two key equations discussed in this study are specified as follows:

(14-1)   *Probability of labor force participation* $= 1 - F(-\beta x_{1i})$

(14-2) $D_i^s = d(x_{2i}, \hat{s}_i, \lambda_i)$ *conditional on* $d_i > 0$,

where x_{1i} and x_{2i} are vectors of regressors, $\hat{s}_i$ is the value of the rice subsidy, λ_i is the inverse of the Mill's ratio calculated from the probit estimation 14-1, and D_i^s is labor supply measured in days worked during the last month.[1] All variable definitions are given in appendix 14-1. Among the regressors in vector x_{2i} is the predicted log of wage, $\ln\hat{W}_i$. This was derived by applying the parameters on various human capital and household structure variables to the 1978–79 data, although the parameters themselves were estimated from the 1980–81 Labor Force Survey using the standard two-step approach to estimate a market wage suggested by Heckman (1974; see also Smith 1980).[2] The superscript, *s*, for sector, is used to show that we estimate separate wage and participation equations for rural and urban residents as well as for males and females.

Participation behavior, using the 1978–79 Consumer Finance Survey (equation 14-1), includes not only the derived wage variable, but more important, the value of the subsidy. It is expected that the subsidy will have a negative effect on the probability of participating. However, the decision to participate may be lagged, that is, made earlier on the basis of having access to the subsidy prior to its being targeted. To the extent that this is the case, then, the participation decision will not be as sensitive to the receipt (or loss) of the subsidy as is the conditional labor supply. That is, the amount worked by an individual is likely to adjust to changes in the household's receipt of subsidy income more rapidly and readily than to the participation decision.

Thus, in equation 14-2, we examine the effect of the subsidy on labor supply conditional on labor force participation. This includes work in own-account activities such as agriculture and nonfarm enterprises as well as wage labor (as is often the case, a variety of home production activities such as cooking and fetching fuel are not included in the data). The labor supply equations include own-wages as well as the wage of the spouse or, in the absence of a spouse, the person of the opposite gender with the highest predicted wage.[3] In addition, the rural labor supply equations include landholding size as well as an interaction between area and wages. This latter interaction term captures any difference in the response of landholders to changes in wages, as suggested by Rosenzweig (1984). We also include a series of seasonal dummy variables to capture temporal differences in labor market conditions. Separate equations are run for rural and urban areas, as well as by gender, in order to capture any differential effect of the rice subsidy on participation and labor supply among these four groups.

In order to deal with the potential bias introduced by individual heterogeneity (reflecting the simultaneity of labor and subsidy choices), we reestimate using a predicted value for the subsidy coefficient. Identifying instruments include twenty-two district dummy variables that capture the effect of regional differences in how the income declaration forms were administered and reviewed, information on the race of the household head that captures any discrimination against non-Sinhalese, and a dummy variable on whether the family had migrated during the past year that once again captures potential problems in getting enrolled in the new targeted scheme. A second group of identifying instruments includes conspicuous housing characteristics as well as possession of assets and ownership of certain conspicuous durables that make lying on the income forms more difficult. These include the size of the house, whether there is indoor plumbing, and ownership of automobiles, motor scooters, electric stoves, and refrigerators. A third group of instruments used to identify the predicted subsidy variables includes information on the occupation of the household head.[4] Once again, the expectation is that since this information was collected in the form for self-declaration of need, it would be used by program administrators to help in efforts, albeit limited, to identify persons reporting accurate and inaccurate income information.

It is thus possible to simulate the impact of the rice subsidy using the results of the maximum likelihood participation and least squares labor supply models. To this end, we use the coefficients from the participation and labor supply equations to simulate what would have been the individual's labor market activity in the absence of the subsidy.

Results

We begin with a presentation of the results of the participation models, with the probit functions shown in table 14-2. The most important feature of the urban models is that for urban women, the rice subsidy leads to a reduction of labor force participation. This is not readily apparent from the rice subsidy variable itself; in both the men's and women's equation the coefficient is positive, although in the case of the women's equation, it is only marginally significant. However, the total derivative on the subsidy equation, taking into account the interaction of the transfer with the wage variable, is negative for the entire relevant range of wages for women. For men, however, there is an inflection point for low-wage workers. This appears to be a result of not being able to employ a sufficiently flexible functional form in the model without introducing a high degree of multicollinearity (in particular, a quadratic introduced on the subsidy variable is negative, although not significant).

In rural areas, the sign on the subsidy coefficient in the men's equation is negative. However, it is only marginally significant. For women, the subsidy variable is positive and significant, although the size of the coefficient is extremely small. The fact that the subsidy does not show a major impact on the participation decision or, in the case of rural women, that it has an effect opposite of that expected on the basis of theory, may in part be a consequence of the fact that the decision of whether to work or not was made long before the targeting of the ration. Moreover, the decision of whether to work or not is most likely less responsive to transfers than is a decision to adjust the number of hours worked.

Table 14-2. Probit Analysis of Labor Market Participation Using Reported Rice Subsidy Value, Sri Lanka, 1980–81

Independent variable	Urban		Rural	
	Women	*Men*	*Women*	*Men*
Intercept	−51.73	−44.25	−68.00	−21.52
	(−15.07)	(−13.02)	(−18.97)	(−5.86)
Age	2.83	3.54	1.36	2.23
	(13.90)	(18.21)	(16.73)	(24.96)
Age^2	−0.03	−0.04	−0.02	−0.03
	(−13.72)	(−18.95)	(−14.84)	(−24.56)
Race 2	−3.35	1.40	−7.56	−0.03
	(−3.80)	(1.43)	(−10.73)	(−0.44)
Race 3	−3.70	0.45	9.52	−0.32
	(−2.20)	(0.22)	(7.61)	(−0.19)
Race 4	3.91	2.10	−14.52	−0.05
	(3.08)	(1.51)	(−15.36)	(−0.61)
Children < 6	−0.57	0.83	−0.56	0.75
	(−1.79)	(1.99)	(−2.78)	(3.15)
Children 6–14	−0.27	−0.48	0.49	0.17
	(−1.23)	(−1.83)	(3.85)	(1.22)
Males 15–65	−1.60	−0.90	−0.84	−0.69
	(−5.93)	(−3.34)	(−5.00)	(−4.49)
Females 15–65	1.25	−0.43	−0.54	−0.31
	(5.21)	(−1.41)	(−3.49)	(−1.71)
Adults > 65	1.03	−1.21	−2.07	−1.41
	(1.84)	(−1.53)	(−5.56)	(−3.37)
Subsidy (observed)	0.01	0.10	0.03	$−6.12 \times 10^{-2}$
	(1.73)	(3.53)	(9.05)	(−1.82)
Married	−3.95	8.66	−7.88	6.26
	(−5.59)	(7.36)	(−17.42)	(10.13)
Colombo	2.14	−0.04	n.a.	n.a.
	(3.77)	(−0.07)		
Round one	−3.41	−0.60	3.03	−1.02
	(−5.08)	(−0.78)	(7.71)	(−2.37)
Female wage	−7.38	n.a.	45.53	n.a.
	(−6.24)		(9.34)	
Female wage^2	n.a.	n.a.	−6.70	n.a.
			(−3.68)	
Male wage	n.a.	−9.56	n.a.	−13.08
		(−4.61)		(−2.01)
Male wage^2	n.a.	n.a.	6.62	n.a.
			(2.18)	
Spouse wage	1.28	−1.17	−2.66	−2.75
	(1.78)	(−1.00)	(−5.44)	(−4.02)
Disabled	−7.86	−18.34	n.a.	n.a.
	(−3.14)	(−8.55)		
Age*wage < 30	0.04	0.78	n.a.	n.a.
	(0.44)	(0.61)		
Wage*subsidy	−0.06	−0.09	n.a.	n.a.
	(−4.49)	(−3.30)		
Area owned	n.a.	n.a.	−2.20	1.51
			(−2.31)	(1.34)

Table 14-2 (continued)

Independent variable	Urban		Rural	
	Women	Men	Women	Men
Wage*area	n.a.	n.a.	−0.06	−0.69
			(−0.11)	(−0.70)
Nonzero observations	634	1,839	2,407	5,901
Zero observations	2,465	792	6,230	2,042
Chi-squared (19)	386.16	1,270.19	n.a.	n.a.
Chi-squared (18)	n.a.	n.a.	2,085.32	2,456.49

n.a. Not applicable.

Note: *t*-ratios are in parentheses. All coefficients × 10.

Another result that is worth commenting on is the fact that in urban areas persons with higher expected wages, both male and female, have a lower probability of working. To determine whether there is an age dimension to this unexpected finding, we include an interaction term with a dummy for persons under thirty years of age. This variable is positive, although not significant. This same finding of a negative effect of wages on the probability of working applies to men in rural areas, although this is not the case for rural women. We assume that this finding on the wage coefficient is a result of structural unemployment in the labor market, especially among higher-wage workers. However, these unexpected signs are a source of some concern.

The other variables included in the probit models generally behave as expected. For example, all age variables are positive, with a negative quadratic indicating declining participation with age. The disability variable captures the fact that persons with physical and mental handicaps are less likely to be labor force participants. Demographic effects are also as expected. For example, urban women with children below the age of six have a reduced probability of labor force participation. Conversely, the more females between the ages of fifteen and sixty-five in the household, the greater the labor market participation of any one of them. It is assumed that this is partly due to other women substituting in home production and child care activities. Women are also more likely to be working in Colombo than in other urban areas. It is also noteworthy that in both rural and urban areas, the marriage dummy is positive for men and negative for women, in all cases being highly significant. In the case of men, there are two possible explanations. One is that family responsibilities induce men to find a job or, alternatively, that women are not willing to marry a man who is not working, leading to a correlation of job status and marriage over time. As for women, marriage affords them the possibility, or gives them the responsibility, of engaging in home production rather than market activities.

Next, turning to the labor supply equations, the value of the subsidy coefficient is negative and significant across-the-board for women and men in rural and urban areas (see table 14-3). The absolute values are greater in urban than in rural areas and for men than for women. Most other variables also have the expected sign. Most important is the wage variable, which is positive and highly significant in all cases. It is noteworthy that the magnitude of the wage coefficient is 70 percent greater for men than for women in urban areas. Likewise, the wage coefficient is nearly three times higher for men than for women in rural areas. However, in the rural equation we add an interaction between wage and land, which in the case of men is negative and significant. The negative coefficient indicates that the greater the landowning, the less the net market response of the individual to a change in wages. This result is unexpected and not easily explained. Also in both the urban and rural models, the cross-wage effects for both women and men are positive and significant. This positive cross response is observed in a number of other studies of labor force participation (Killingsworth 1983). Several explanations can be posited. Among them is that an underlying criterion in selecting a spouse involves persons who place a lower value on leisure marrying each other.

Next we turn to a discussion of the same models employing the predicted, rather than the reported, subsidy variable. The instrumenting equations for the subsidy are found in appendix 14-2. To highlight some of the results, many of the identifying instruments are plausible and significant. For example, the dummy for race, taking on the value of 1 for Sinhalese, and 0 otherwise, assumes a positive and significant sign in both rural and urban areas, being higher in the latter. Most of the coefficients for durable goods are negative, although only the coefficient for radio is significant in both rural and urban areas. The high standard errors on the other durable goods variables suggest considerable multicollinearity. The significance of most of the district dummy variables suggests considerable regional differences in access to the subsidy. Also, the negative and significant coefficients on persons engaged in high-wage, formal sector occupations, such as professionals and clerical workers, conform to our prior expectations.

The subsidy coefficients in the urban probits for participation, when evaluated at the mean wage, indicate negative derivatives with a higher absolute value than the models that use the reported subsidy (see table 14-4). In contrast, the rural probits for both men and women have an unexpected positive sign when the predicted subsidy replaces the reported value. In the case of the former, the parameter estimate is extremely small and not significant at the 5 percent level. In the case of women, however, the coefficient is significant. This is also observed when reported ration system benefits are used in the model, although the magnitude of the coefficient is greater with the predicted variable.

Table 14-3. Labor Supply Equations Using Reported Rice Subsidy
Value, Sri Lanka, 1980–81
(days worked last month)

	Urban		Rural	
Independent variable	Women	Men	Women	Men
Intercept	25.41	15.64	−1.34	3.88
	(5.66)	(5.74)	(−0.20)	(1.33)
Age	−0.20	0.24	0.54	0.55
	(−0.89)	(1.65)	(3.46)	(4.13)
Age²	0.00	0.00	−0.01	−0.01
	(0.92)	(−1.88)	(−3.53)	(−4.10)
Race 2	0.11	−0.28	3.27	2.98
	(0.12)	(−0.69)	(3.00)	(9.15)
Race 3	1.82	2.10	3.57	−0.07
	(1.18)	(2.80)	(2.56)	(−0.08)
Race 4	−1.47	−0.37	−2.91	0.27
	(−1.37)	(−0.64)	(−1.65)	(0.61)
Children < 6	0.23	−0.14	−0.39	0.16
	(0.81)	(−0.89)	(−1.91)	(1.43)
Children 6–14	0.31	0.11	−0.16	0.13
	(1.55)	(0.96)	(−1.22)	(1.87)
Males 15–65	−0.10	0.05	−0.14	−0.08
	(−0.38)	(0.41)	(−0.73)	(−0.94)
Females 15–65	0.23	−0.02	0.25	0.30
	(0.98)	(−0.11)	(1.51)	(3.07)
Adults > 65	0.14	0.62	1.26	0.64
	(0.29)	(1.84)	(3.03)	(2.84)
Subsidy (observed)	−0.03	−0.03	−0.01	−0.02
	(−5.64)	(−8.71)	(−2.06)	(−12.21)
Mills ratio	1.02	0.96	1.35	2.89
	(1.07)	(0.97)	(0.88)	(2.10)
Female wage	2.47	n.a.	8.94	n.a.
	(2.64)		(3.45)	
Male wage	n.a.	4.82	n.a.	6.23
		(5.60)		(11.15)
Spouse wage	1.54	1.14	1.49	0.66
	(2.73)	(2.37)	(2.75)	(1.87)
Married	−0.25	0.08	−2.35	0.95
	(−0.38)	(0.15)	(−2.83)	(2.31)
Area owned	n.a.	n.a.	−2.34	2.26
			(−2.21)	(3.72)
Wage*area	n.a.	n.a.	0.92	−1.56
			(1.65)	(−3.04)
R-squared	0.1343	0.1183	0.1002	0.1020
N	632	1,833	2,406	5,900

n.a. Not applicable.
Note: *t*-ratios are in parentheses. All coefficients × 10.

Table 14-4. *Probit Analysis of Labor Market Participation Using Predicted Rice Subsidy Value, Sri Lanka, 1980–81*

Independent variable	Urban		Rural	
	Women	Men	Women	Men
Intercept	−64.51	−47.84	−75.33	−20.67
	(−14.51)	(−12.64)	(−18.70)	(−5.58)
Age	3.44	3.60	1.28	2.24
	(14.30)	(18.06)	(13.93)	(24.87)
Age^2	−0.04	−0.04	−0.01	−0.03
	(−13.93)	(−18.83)	(−12.10)	(−24.49)
Race 2	−4.33	1.35	−8.34	−0.04
	(−4.40)	(1.37)	(−9.96)	(−0.07)
Race 3	−3.75	−0.03	9.27	0.67
	(−2.13)	(−0.01)	(6.85)	(0.38)
Race 4	8.30	2.13	−14.93	0.14
	(5.54)	(1.51)	(−14.74)	(0.16)
Children < 6	−0.13	0.88	−1.01	0.53
	(−0.35)	(2.02)	(−4.63)	(2.16)
Children 6–14	0.15	−0.44	0.20	0.04
	(0.56)	(−1.56)	(1.38)	(0.25)
Males 15–65	−0.90	−0.95	−1.38	−0.80
	(−3.15)	(−3.49)	(−7.60)	(−4.98)
Females 15–65	1.39	−0.37	−0.63	−0.44
	(5.12)	(−1.17)	(−3.73)	(−2.38)
Adults > 65	0.95	−0.96	−1.88	−1.47
	(1.44)	(−1.19)	(−4.53)	(−3.50)
Predicted subsidy	1.4×10^{-2}	0.20	0.09	0.02
	(0.07)	(3.84)	(11.45)	(1.89)
Married	−4.49	8.90	−7.84	6.20
	(−5.66)	(7.44)	(−15.62)	(9.92)
Colombo	1.28	−0.21	n.a.	n.a.
	(2.07)	(−0.30)		
Round one	−2.61	−0.67	3.57	−0.98
	(−3.59)	(−0.88)	(8.26)	(−2.28)
Female wage	−9.35	n.a.	56.57	n.a.
	(−6.67)		(10.76)	
Female wage^2	n.a.	n.a.	−9.42	n.a.
			(−4.85)	
Male wage	n.a.	−7.98	n.a.	−16.71
		(−3.48)		(−2.51)
Male wage^2	n.a.	n.a.	n.a.	8.36
				(2.69)
Spouse wage	2.66	−1.56	−4.14	−2.26
	(1.82)	(−1.25)	(−4.41)	(−3.19)
Disabled	−9.02	−18.41	n.a.	n.a.
	(−2.92)	(−8.57)		
Age*wage < 30	1.32	1.49	n.a.	n.a.
	(1.30)	(1.13)		
Wage*sub	−1.70	−0.20	n.a.	n.a.
	(−7.56)	(−3.80)		
Area owned	n.a.	n.a.	−1.74	1.25

Table 14-4 (continued)

Independent variable	Urban		Rural	
	Women	Men	Women	Men
Wage*area	n.a.	n.a.	(−1.56) −0.42 (−0.66)	(1.06) −0.41 (−0.39)
Nonzero observations	525	1,807	2,056	5,843
Zero observations	2,245	785	5,653	2,025
Chi-squared (19)	369.91	1,258.22	n.a.	n.a.
Chi-squared (18)	n.a.	n.a.	1,933.03	2,432.82

n.a. Not applicable.
Note: t-ratios are in parentheses. All coefficients × 10.

In contrast with these somewhat difficult-to-explain results for the probits in rural areas, the labor supply equations for rural areas follow the patterns in urban areas: negative and significant coefficients on the rice subsidy (see table 14-5). In the rural labor supply equations, as with the urban probits and urban labor supply models, the absolute value of the coefficients in the predicted subsidy model is greater than the subsidy coefficients when the reported values are used. The increase in the magnitude of the subsidy variable is particularly dramatic in the labor supply equation for women in urban areas. At the same time, the value and significance of the wage variable falls. This suggests a large bias in the wage and subsidy variables due to the endogeneity of participation in the ration system and, in particular, the correlation between the subsidy and labor supply in the earlier model that includes the reported level of benefits.

As indicated above, the models serve as the basis for simulating the effects of the subsidy on labor supply. The total effect can be broken down between the probability of working and the number of hours worked conditional on participation. Focusing on the models using the predicted subsidy variable, the results indicate that the effect on the probability of working is considerably less than the issue of conditional labor supply. This is attested to by, first, the fact that simulations using the coefficients from the probit indicate that the subsidy alters the probability of working by relatively small amounts. Second, many of the coefficients in the probit equations are not statistically significant, nor are they as robust to specifications as we would like. And third, the predicted probabilities are largely driven by the interaction effects with wages in the urban areas, and it is difficult to sort out whether the total derivative is reflecting that subsidies affect participation differently at different wage levels or, conversely, that the effect of wages on participation changes with the level of subsidy received.

We calculate the labor supply effect, conditional on participation in the labor market, evaluated at the separate mean values of the subsidy

Table 14-5. Labor Supply Equations Using Predicted Rice Subsidy Value, Sri Lanka, 1980–81

Independent variable	Urban		Rural	
	Women	Men	Women	Men
Intercept	20.90	14.68	1.62	6.65
	(3.12)	(4.79)	(0.26)	(2.24)
Age	0.05	0.43	0.46	0.51
	(0.17)	(2.64)	(3.19)	(3.81)
Age^2	0.00	−0.01	−0.01	−0.01
	(−0.08)	(−2.81)	(−3.17)	(−3.82)
Race 2	1.22	0.02	2.01	2.91
	(1.22)	(0.06)	(1.63)	(8.93)
Race 3	1.08	1.40	4.05	0.52
	(0.68)	(1.83)	(2.91)	(0.66)
Race 4	−0.17	−0.16	−2.69	−0.05
	(−0.13)	(−0.27)	(−1.54)	(−0.11)
Children < 6	0.94	0.20	−0.17	0.49
	(2.84)	(1.18)	(−0.76)	(4.26)
Children 6–14	0.55	0.34	0.24	0.42
	(2.32)	(2.79)	(1.68)	(5.62)
Males 15–65	0.20	0.24	0.33	0.21
	(0.72)	(1.83)	(1.52)	(2.27)
Females 15–65	0.18	0.19	0.66	0.56
	(0.69)	(1.31)	(3.73)	(5.52)
Adults > 65	0.46	0.68	1.09	0.80
	(0.82)	(1.95)	(2.55)	(3.56)
Predicted subsidy	−0.09	−0.07	−0.07	−0.06
	(−6.01)	(−9.60)	(−5.90)	(−15.25)
Mills ratio	1.55	1.81	2.29	2.68
	(1.24)	(1.68)	(1.67)	(1.93)
Female wage	0.87	n.a.	7.40	n.a.
	(0.68)		(2.78)	
Male wage	n.a.	2.60	n.a.	5.41
		(2.76)		(9.60)
Spouse wage	1.26	0.42	0.98	−0.04
	(1.09)	(0.83)	(0.98)	(−0.12)
Married	−0.38	0.53	−1.41	1.09
	(−0.51)	(0.97)	(−1.78)	(2.63)
Area owned	n.a.	n.a.	−3.66	2.25
			(−2.64)	(3.72)
Wage*area	n.a.	n.a.	1.65	−1.54
			(2.07)	(3.02)
R-squared	0.1773	0.1385	0.1299	0.1182
N	524	1,806	2,055	5,842

n.a. Not applicable.

Note: t-ratios are in parentheses. All coefficients × 10.

Table 14-6. *Actual Days Worked and Reduction in the Days Worked per Month as a Consequence of Receiving the Rice Subsidy, Sri Lanka, 1980–81*

Geographic location	Actual	Reduction in days worked	
and gender	days worked	Reported subsidy	Predicted subsidy
Urban			
Men	25.6	1.0	2.3
Women	26.0	1.0	2.9
Rural			
Men	23.4	0.8	2.5
Women	21.1	0.5	2.8

Note: Days are defined as eight hours. Calculated for recipients only.

received by households of men in the sample and by households of women in the sample. The results using the reported subsidy variable indicate that men will work 1.0 and 0.8 fewer days per month in urban and rural areas, respectively (see table 14-6). For women, the comparable figures are 1.0 and 0.5. When we employ the predicted subsidy value, the effect on labor market participation is even greater. Men in urban areas work 2.3 fewer days per month, and in rural areas they work 2.5 fewer days. For women, the comparable numbers are 2.9 and 2.8.

Putting this decline in labor market activity in some perspective, consider that the average daily wage of males in households that receive the rice ration is around Rs14 (Sri Lanka's currency is the rupee). The average monthly value of the transfer to these households is Rs86 in urban areas and Rs91 in rural areas. Combining these figures with the simulated labor response suggests that if men reduce their labor supply by 2.3 days, as implied by the models with the fitted subsidy variable, the difference between the net transfer and net increment in expenditures is just over 33 percent of its gross value. Using the reported subsidy variable, the disincentive effect is on the order of 16 percent. The wage for women engaged in comparable types of agricultural activities such as harvesting is generally about 20 percent less than that for men, and the predicted decline in days worked is approximately the same as that for men. This implies that the difference between the net transfer and the income decline owing to the disincentive effect is about 20 percent lower for women than for men. If the male household head and the spouse work, and both their labor supplies decline, the disincentive effect is additive. In any event, the range of the disincentive effect is high, although it does not depart greatly from that reported by Moffitt (1992) for AFDC recipients in the United States.

Reviewers and editors often request authors not to express surprise at the results reported, as if researchers do not have strong prior expectations. Nevertheless, the magnitude of the disincentive effect must be termed surprising, especially as the system in Sri Lanka did not impose an increasing marginal tax on earnings. The results indicate a high marginal propensity to demand leisure. These results, however, conform to those derived from a different method for measuring the demand for leisure also using data from Sri Lanka, although from a later year (Alderman and Sahn 1993).[5] Therefore, these results are unlikely to be artifacts of either a variable definition or a modeling technique.

Conclusions

In this study we have examined the effect of receiving a rice ration on labor supply. It is found that in rural and urban areas there is a substantial reduction in the level of work effort in response to receiving the rice ration. The large magnitude of the disincentive to work has major implications for targeted interventions in developing countries. In fact, the results of this study suggest that although researchers and policy-makers have devoted considerable time and attention to errors of inclusion and, to a lesser extent, of exclusion of transfer programs, a potentially even more important departure from stated policy goals has gone unrecognized or unheeded. This is not surprising, given the data and analytic requirements for modeling the disincentives to work.

On a related issue, the results of this study indicate that the difference between net transfers and net increment in expenditures, measured in money metric terms, will be greater the higher the wage of the persons in the household. This is simply a consequence of the income loss associated with a comparable reduction in days worked being greater for someone with higher earnings per unit of time. This implies that the errors of including high-wage, and thus high-income, households in targeted programs are compounded by the greater labor supply–mediated income losses of these individuals.

However, it would be premature to assume that the reduction of net benefits due to the change of work incentives is a deadweight loss. The model ignores whatever productivity effects may follow from the food subsidy increasing intake. It has been shown that higher calorie intakes do raise wages and, by inference, productivity in Sri Lanka (Sahn and Alderman 1988). Thus, it is reasonable to expect that whatever increase in food intake occurs from the subsidy, it will have some positive productivity effect. It is also possible, although unknown, that there may be positive effects of labor supply from the subsidy, which are indirectly due to the higher wages, that in part counter the disincentive effects.

Moreover, some of the reduced time in the labor market is likely going into home production activities. But even to the extent that there is a large labor supply response that results in increased leisure, the fact remains that in a strict welfare sense, the utility of the household is increased. The increase in utility, however, may in practice not result in an increase in the consumption bundle that corresponds to the objective function of the designer or evaluator of the subsidy scheme. For such planners, the consumption of goods, and particularly food, may be paramount (see Kanbur, Keen, and Tuomala in chapter 5 of this volume), while the consumption of leisure is viewed as wasteful or indulgent. This, of course, reflects a lack of appreciation for the disutility of labor, especially for low-income households engaged in heavy manual work, and would result in an intervention appearing ineffectual, despite its utility-raising benefits. Thus, there is a need for caution in ascribing a negative connotation to the large difference between net transfers and net increment in expenditures (for example, as implied by the word "leakage").

Finally, in interpreting the results of the Sri Lanka case, considerable care is required before generalizing the findings to a range of developing countries. For example, the response of workers in a country without the extensive and subsidized social infrastructure found in Sri Lanka may be different. There may be a different labor supply response in cases where a subsidy is introduced and viewed as a transitory income shock, in contrast to Sri Lanka where the subsidy system has an institutional history going back almost forty years. Moreover, the current study captures the effect of a subsidy on labor supply in a situation where benefits have been newly eliminated rather than newly provided. It is not at all clear that these effects would be symmetrical.

Even within a single country, the labor supply effects may also differ according to the form of the subsidy, the nature of the delivery system, and labor market conditions. For example, Sri Lanka converted its subsidy program to one that delivers food stamps and is now in the process of replacing that program with one that stresses credit and asset formation (through the Janasaviya Trust). The relative impacts of these programs on leisure and commodity demand have not been fully studied. This, in combination with the absence of comparable studies from other countries, makes the need for more research in this area compelling.

(Appendix tables start on next page.)

Appendix 14-1. Definitions of Variables

Variable	Definition
RACE 1	Equals 1 if the individual's race is Sinhalese and 0 otherwise and is omitted
RACE 2	Equals 1 if the individual's race is Ceylon Tamil and 0 otherwise
RACE 3	Equals 1 if the individual's race is Indian Tamil and 0 otherwise
RACE 4	Equals 1 if the individual's race is Moslem, Burghur, white, and others and 0 otherwise
CHILDREN < 6	The number of children under six years of age
CHILDREN 6–14	The number of children older than or equal to six and younger or equal to fourteen years of age
MALES 15–65	The number of other males older or equal to fifteen years old and younger or equal to sixty-five years of age
FEMALES 15–65	The number of other females older or equal to fifteen years old and younger or equal to sixty-five years of age
ADULTS > 65	The number of household members over sixty-five years of age
SUBSIDY (OBSERVED)	Value of rice subsidy
PREDICTED SUBSIDY	Predicted value of rice subsidy
MARRIED	Equals 1 if the individual is married and 0 otherwise
FEMALE WAGE	Predicted wage of women
FEMALE WAGE^2	PWAGEW * PWAGEW
MALE WAGE	Predicted wage of men
MALE WAGE^2	PWAGEM * PWAGEM
SPOUSE WAGE	Predicted wage of the woman/man who has highest potential earnings
DISABLED	Equals 1 if the individual is disabled and 0 otherwise
AGE*WAGE < 30	AGE * PREDICTED WAGE if the individual is under thirty years old
WAGE*SUB	PWAGEW/M * RICESUB
AREAACR	Total land area owned
WAGE*AREA	PWAGEW/M * TOTAREA
COOKDUM	Equals 1 if the household has a gas or electric cooker and 0 otherwise
REFRDUM	Equals 1 if the household has a refrigerator and 0 otherwise
SCOOTDUM	Equals 1 if the household has a scooter or motorcycle and 0 otherwise
CARDUM	Equals 1 if the household has a car and 0 otherwise
RADIODUM	Equals 1 if the household has a radio and 0 otherwise
WATERDUM	Equals 1 if the household has piped water and 0 otherwise
NEDUC1	Number of persons in the household who have not attended primary school
NEDUC2	Number of persons in the household who have attended primary school only

Appendix 14-1 (continued)

Variable	Definition
NEDUC3	Number of persons in the household who have completed between grades six and ten and have not passed the General Certificate Exam
NEDUC4	Number of persons in the household who have passed the General Certificate Exam but have not gone to university
NEDUC5	Number of persons in the household who have gone to university or done postgraduate training
DIST1–22	Dummy variables for districts
AGEMX	The oldest person in the household
AGEMX^2	AGEMX * AGEMX
MIGDUM	Equals 1 if the household head is a migrant and 0 otherwise
HHSIZE	Household size
RACEDUM	Equals 1 if the household head is other than a Sinhalese and 0 otherwise
OCCUPATIONAL DUMMIES	(PROFESSIONAL, CLERICAL, SALES, SERVICE, FARMERS, AG LABOR I, AG LABOR II, PRODUCTION, MISC)
ROUND ONE	Seasonal dummy variable

Appendix 14-2. Rice Subsidy Equations

Independent variable	Urban	Rural
INTERCEPT	23.62	−8.35
	(2.02)	(−1.11)
COOKDUM	−3.21	−7.20
	(−0.57)	(−0.79)
REFRDUM	4.13	−7.21
	(0.78)	(−0.78)
SCOOTDUM	−3.57	−3.77
	(−0.45)	(−0.47)
CARDUM	−4.53	−1.14
	(−0.73)	(−0.19)
RADIODUM	−17.13	−13.57
	(−7.05)	(−9.58)
WATERDUM	−13.72	3.75
	(−4.07)	(0.83)
NEDUC1	3.56	3.28
	(1.97)	(3.31)
NEDUC2	3.33	2.51
	(2.41)	(3.29)
NEDUC3	−0.91	0.04
	(−0.89)	(0.05)
NEDUC4	−6.48	−6.00
	(−4.97)	(−6.91)
NEDUC5	1.21	−9.23
	(0.25)	(−2.49)
DIST2	−4.19	13.21
	(−0.82)	(4.27)

Appendix 14-2 (continued)

Independent variable	Urban	Rural
DIST3	11.84	23.06
	(2.53)	(7.48)
DIST4	17.42	24.15
	(2.65)	(7.46)
DIST5	8.33	18.33
	(1.06)	(4.42)
DIST6	n.a.	26.80
		(5.21)
DIST7	− 56.27	− 35.21
	(− 3.96)	(− 4.38)
DIST8	n.a.	− 28.30
		(− 4.56)
DIST9	− 8.35	− 21.98
	(− 1.01)	(− 5.69)
DIST10	13.05	4.48
	(1.96)	(1.19)
DIST11	18.92	27.17
	(3.73)	(6.26)
DIST12	10.96	19.62
	(0.82)	(2.39)
DIST13	− 8.53	− 6.39
	(− 0.89)	(− 0.86)
DIST14	− 15.40	− 10.84
	(− 1.97)	(− 1.88)
DIST15	− 34.55	− 33.64
	(− 2.40)	(− 3.64)
DIST16	− 5.77	2.42
	(− 1.14)	(0.85)
DIST17	− 5.20	10.10
	(− 0.62)	(2.21)
DIST18	4.14	− 9.33
	(0.52)	(− 2.06)
DIST19	− 3.83	− 9.83
	(− 0.36)	(− 2.74)
DIST20	13.40	38.50
	(1.72)	(11.75)
DIST21	6.35	6.50
	(0.75)	(2.10)
DIST22	− 15.47	− 6.69
	(− 1.67)	(− 2.46)
AGEMX	− 0.69	0.53
	(− 1.13)	(1.47)
$AGEMX^2$	0.01	− 0.01
	(1.46)	(− 1.73)
MIGDUM	− 2.55	− 6.68
	(− 0.28)	(− 0.80)
HHSIZE	5.17	6.09
	(7.96)	(15.98)
AREAACR	− 0.96	− 0.33
	(− 1.04)	(− 0.43)
RACEDUM	5.07	8.41
	(1.81)	(2.90)

Appendix 14-2 *(continued)*

Independent variable	Urban	Rural
DISABLED	2.52	5.44
	(0.31)	(1.17)
PROFESSIONAL	−12.07	−14.45
	(−2.17)	(−3.98)
CLERICAL	−13.95	−20.59
	(−2.49)	(−4.98)
SALES	2.31	−7.80
	(0.46)	(−2.58)
SERVICE	−12.42	−6.68
	(−2.24)	(−1.72)
FARMERS	−3.33	−2.32
	(−0.44)	(−0.90)
AG LABOR I	4.36	3.32
	(0.53)	(1.05)
AG LABOR II	3.00	3.28
	(0.41)	(0.81)
PRODUCTION	−1.22	−2.89
	(−0.26)	(−1.10)
MISC	−5.98	0.60
	(−1.00)	(0.16)
R^2	0.2970	0.2629
N	1,475	4,556

n.a. Not applicable.

Note: *t*-ratios are in parentheses.

Notes

1. The Mill's ratio is the sample selection correcting variable derived from the participation equation. It is necessary to correct for any correlation between the error term of the uncorrected wage equation and the selection rule derived from the participation equation.

2. In particular, the predicted wage is estimated based on the 1980–81 Labor Force Survey with ordinary least squares. Consistent and unbiased estimates of human capital and household structure parameters that predict wages are obtained by including the sample selection correcting variable, λ, that is derived from the reduced-form estimate of the participation equation. The human capital variables that determine wages include education and job experience (which is proxied by age minus years of schooling). In addition, landholding variables as well as a series of seasonal dummy variables are included. See Sahn and Alderman (1988) for a more detailed discussion of the wage equation.

3. There is a potential sample truncation issue that enters the analysis insofar as the small share of households without two persons between the ages of fifteen and sixty-five are left out of the analysis.

4. The inclusion of occupation in the instrumenting equation is justified since it is largely a lagged endogenous variable that predates the implementation of the targeted subsidy. Results are not sensitive to its inclusion, however. The second block of variables can also be considered lagged; they are not conventionally included in labor supply estimation.

5. The authors estimated a complete demand system, including leisure as a good. The results showed that the marginal propensity to consume leisure was high.

References

Alderman, Harold. 1991. "Food Subsidies and the Poor." In George Psacharopoulos, ed., *Essays on Poverty, Equity, and Growth*. Oxford, Eng.: Pergamon Press.

Alderman, Harold, and David E. Sahn. 1993. "Substitution between Goods and Leisure in a Developing Country." *American Journal of Agricultural Economics* 75 (4): 875–83.

Atkinson, Anthony, and Nicholas Stern. 1980. "On the Switch from Direct to Indirect Taxation." *Journal of Public Economics* 14: 195–224.

Danziger, Sheldon, Robert Haveman, and Robert Plotnick. 1981. "How Income Transfers Affect Work, Savings, and Income Distribution: A Critical Review." *Journal of Economic Literature* 19 (3): 975–1028.

Edirisinghe, Neville. 1987. "The Food Stamp Program in Sri Lanka: Costs, Benefits, and Policy Implications." Research Report 58. International Food Policy Research Institute, Washington, D.C.

Fraker, Thomas, and Robert Moffitt. 1988. "The Effect of Food Stamps on Labor Supply: A Bivariate Selection Model." *Journal of Public Economics* 35 (1): 25–56.

Gavan, James, and Indrani Chandrasekera. 1979. "The Impact of Public Foodgrain Distribution on Food Consumption and Welfare in Sri Lanka." Research Report 13. International Food Policy Research Institute, Washington, D.C.

Heckman, James J. 1974. "Shadow Prices, Market Wages and Labor Supply." *Econometrica* 41 (4): 679–94.

Killingsworth, Mark. 1983. *Labor Supply*. Cambridge, Eng.: Cambridge University Press.

Moffitt, Robert. 1983. "An Economic Model of Welfare Stigma." *American Economic Review* 73 (5): 1023–35.

————. 1992. "Incentive Effects of the U.S. Welfare System: A Review." *Journal of Economic Literature* 30 (1): 1–61.

Pinstrup-Andersen, Per. 1988. *Consumer-Oriented Food Subsidies: Cost, Benefits, and Policy Options for Developing Countries*. Baltimore, Md.: Johns Hopkins University Press.

Ranney, Christine, and John Cushman. 1985. "Cash Equivalent, Welfare Stigma, and Food Stamps." *Southern Economic Journal* 13 (April): 1011–27.

Ravallion, Martin. 1989. "Land Contingent Poverty Alleviation Schemes." *World Development* 17 (8): 1223–37.

Rosenzweig, Mark. 1984. "Determinants of Wage Rates and Labor Supply Behavior in the Rural Sector of a Developing Country." In Hans Binswanger and Mark Rosenzweig, eds., *Contractual Arrangements, Employment, and Wages in Rural Labor Markets in Asia*. New Haven, Conn.: Yale University Press.

Sahn, David E., and Harold Alderman. 1988. "The Effects of Human Capital on Wages and the Determinants of Labor Supply in a Developing Country." *Journal of Development Economics* 29 (2): 157–83.

Sahn, David E., and Neville Edirisinghe. 1993. "The Politics of Food Policy in Sri Lanka: From Basic Human Needs to Increased Market Orientation." In Per Pinstrup-Andersen, ed., *The Political Economy of Food and Nutrition Policies.* Baltimore, Md.: Johns Hopkins University Press.

Singh, Inderjit, Lyn Squire, and John Strauss, eds. 1986. *Agricultural Household Models.* Baltimore, Md.: Johns Hopkins University Press for the World Bank.

Smith, James P., ed. 1980. *Female Labor Supply: Theory and Estimation.* Princeton, N.J.: Princeton University Press.

Timmons, Robert J., Roy I. Miller, and William D. Drake. 1983. "Targeting: A Means to Better Intervention." Report submitted to the U.S. Agency for International Development. Community Systems Foundation, Ann Arbor, Mich.

Winkler, Anne. 1991. "The Incentive Effects of Medicaid on Women's Labor Supply." *Journal of Human Resources* 26 (2): 308–37.

VI Public Employment Schemes

Given the potentially high administrative, incentive, political economy, and other costs of many targeted programs, policy interventions that foster self-selection have considerable appeal. Public employment or workfare schemes, in which individuals must provide labor in exchange for benefits, are one category of self-targeted programs that has generated a great deal of enthusiasm. Such programs offer low wages for unskilled, manual labor. It is argued that only the poor will find it in their interest to participate in such schemes, so that few of the direct program benefits "leak" to the nonpoor.

In chapter 15, Ravallion and Datt argue that even when such schemes achieve a high degree of targeting, whether they are more efficient in reducing poverty than less targeted alternatives will depend on the scale of the participation and other costs associated with the scheme. While most targeted programs exact a price of some kind from participants (for example, time and travel costs incurred in obtaining benefits or social stigma), the costs of participation may be particularly significant in employment schemes, since activities, including income-generating activities, must be abandoned in order to benefit. Moreover, together with other schemes, workfare schemes entail certain administrative and other nonwage costs.

Ravallion and Datt empirically investigate the efficiency of a public employment program in reducing poverty using household data for two villages in rural India. While earlier chapters have promoted the minimization of a poverty index for a given budget as the basis for program evaluation, Ravallion and Datt put the approach into practice and show its potential usefulness for informed policy choice. Their careful analysis, juxtaposing the impact of a workfare program relative to that of an untargeted transfer of the same budget, provides a model for the evaluation of poverty-alleviation programs. Data constraints may hinder an equally rigorous assessment in many policy settings, however.

The authors econometrically estimate the impact of a household's participation in Maharashtra's Employment Guarantee Scheme (EGS) on the amount of time allocated to wage labor, on- and off-farm self-employment, leisure and domestic work, and unemployment. Thus they are able to estimate the incomes forgone in participating in the scheme, and—with information on the wages received from EGS employment—to determine the EGS's net impact on poverty in two villages. This outcome is compared with the poverty reduction that could be achieved with a uniform transfer of the same budget to all households. The approach contrasts with that taken by, among others, Cornia and Stewart (chapter 13), who focus on minimizing the value of targeting mistakes rather than on maximizing the impact on poverty.

The analysis in chapter 15 underscores the importance of evaluating poverty-alleviation programs against a relevant counterfactual—both in terms of an alternative use of the same budget and in terms of what beneficiaries would have done in the absence of the program. Ravallion and Datt find that the costs to the poor of participating in the EGS are relatively low. Moreover, targeting is clearly better in the EGS than it would be under a uniform cash handout. But, once both nonwage costs and participation costs are factored in, a uniform transfer of the same budget is found to achieve either the same or a slightly better poverty outcome than the EGS. This is true whatever poverty line or poverty measure is chosen.

However, as the authors note, they have assumed minimal administrative and incentive costs in deriving the counterfactual. Empirical evidence of labor supply responses to food transfers, such as is presented in chapter 14 (Sahn and Alderman), raises the possibility of incentive effects even in untargeted programs. Moreover, Ravallion and Datt consider only the direct net transfer benefits to the poor; this does not include any indirect benefits or second-round income effects that the public works program is likely to have. Indeed, the authors argue that even a very modest gain to the poor from the assets created would be enough to tilt the balance in favor of the public employment scheme.

15 Is Targeting through a Work Requirement Efficient? Some Evidence for Rural India

Martin Ravallion and Gaurav Datt

Reforms to antipoverty schemes have typically aimed for cost-effectiveness, either by achieving gains to the poor without extra budgetary cost or by reducing the cost of a given impact on poverty. In recent times, a popular solution has been "better targeting," meaning that more of the poor and/or fewer of the nonpoor participate. However, participation in a targeted scheme is rarely costless to the poor, and it may often be far more costly than participation in an untargeted scheme. If the costs of participation are high enough, better targeting will *diminish* cost-effectiveness in reducing poverty.

Some antipoverty schemes insist that participants must work to gain benefits; a common term for such a scheme is "workfare." Forgone leisure is rarely valued highly by advocates of such schemes, who are typically more concerned with the income gains to participants. But, even then, participants would almost certainly not have been entirely idle had the scheme not existed. Once the costs of participation are considered, it may well be that even a very well-targeted scheme is less efficient at reducing income poverty than an alternative policy.

So how efficiently can a workfare scheme deliver resources to the poor? This chapter outlines the issues relevant to answering this question and offers an answer for two villages in rural India for which

The staff of the International Crops Research Institute for the Semi-Arid Tropics, India, provided the raw data used here and have helped us greatly in our work on those data. Residents of the village of Shirapur in Maharashtra were generous with their time during fieldwork, as were various participants and staff in the Employment Guarantee Scheme of the government of Maharashtra. For their comments on this chapter, we are grateful to Dominique van de Walle, Kim Nead, Harold Alderman, Lyn Squire, Jere Behrman, Tom Walker, and conference participants. Financial support from the World Bank's Research Committee (RPO 675-96) and the Poverty and Human Resources and Public Economics Divisions, Policy Research Department, is also gratefully acknowledged. These are the views of the authors and should not be attributed to the World Bank.

a workfare scheme is in place *and* for which we have access to suitable data. The following two sections discuss the evaluation of direct poverty-alleviation schemes; we first discuss our overall approach, including its limitations, and then look at the potential for "self-targeting," recognizing the incentive and related information problems that routinely confound attempts to reach the poor through nondistortionary lump-sum transfers. Next we briefly survey existing evidence of relevance to assessing the direct transfer benefits of rural public employment schemes in the state of Maharashtra in India (primarily through that state's famous Employment Guarantee Scheme). The following section presents the results of our analysis using longitudinal survey data for two villages in Maharashtra. We then offer an overall assessment of the cost-effectiveness of workfare in the two villages. A discussion of some important qualifications to our results follows the presentation of our findings. The final section presents our main conclusions.

Some Issues in Assessing Workfare Schemes

The first question we must address is: What is the objective of such policies? The main motivation for a workfare scheme is clearly not to produce something; there are other (and possibly better) ways of doing that. The novel feature of these schemes is their mandate to reduce poverty among participating workers. We shall assume that the alleviation of income poverty, and within a short period of time, is the central concern.

This is a common assumption in policy discussions. However, it is contentious. A number of remarks can be made:

First, this assumption ignores the preferences of the poor concerning leisure or, more generally, time allocation. A previously idle person who takes up employment on rural public works may be only slightly better off in terms of utility (allowing for the loss of leisure), but much better off in terms of income. One should not assume that this is always so; given that unemployment can be quite stigmatizing, having work may raise utility even when it has little or no effect on income. Nonetheless, this is an area of public policy where welfarist perspectives appear to carry little weight with policymakers. (On the distinction between welfarist and nonwelfarist approaches, see Sen 1979.)

Second, although we may agree on an index of poverty, in practice our ability to measure living standards for the purpose of policy evaluation (let alone targeting) is imperfect. There may be sources of real deprivation that we would like an antipoverty scheme to alleviate, but that are not picked up by even an unusually careful household survey. For example, one member of the household may suddenly lose the support of others in the household, even though household income as a whole is no lower (the plight of many widows in parts of India is an example).

Third, some discussions of targeting have focused on "errors of targeting" rather than on the impacts on poverty per se. For example, one can distinguish a scheme's ability to *exclude* the nonpoor from its ability to *include* the poor. These are sometimes referred to as type I errors (incorrectly classifying a person as not poor) versus type II errors (incorrectly classifying a person as poor); see, for example, chapter 13 by Cornia and Stewart. We shall not make an explicit distinction of this sort here, as we would argue that the concern with these two types of targeting errors arises from the fact that an appropriate measure of poverty has not fallen as much as it could have. It would then seem more appropriate to focus directly on the poverty outcome. It should also be remarked that there can be no presumption that the policy that will be most cost-effective in reducing poverty will be the one that has the lowest "errors of targeting." Given that there may be significant costs of targeting, the deliberate introduction of leakage or imperfect coverage (allowing a reduction in those costs) may well allow a greater total impact on poverty for a given budgetary outlay. Thus the ability of a policy to concentrate benefits on the poor should not be confused with its impact on poverty; the former is only one determinant of the latter.

All three points concern the importance of certain poverty measurement issues in policy analysis; the choice of an indicator of individual well-being, or the choice of a measure that aggregates information on that indicator, may well determine the final policy choice. We shall not be able to offer a convincing resolution of all these issues here, though we will try to take account of some key aspects.

The next question we must address is: What is the relevant counterfactual in assessing impacts on poverty? It is not uncommon to find that before-and-after comparisons of a program's impact are not revenue-neutral; the "after" case has a higher mean income due to the fact that no accounting is made of how the expenditures were financed. The more valuable comparison for policy purposes is between alternative allocations of the same gross budget. To illustrate the point, consider the simulations given in Ravallion (1993) of the effects of geographic targeting among the provinces of Indonesia. There it is shown that an optimally targeted set of (non-negative) transfers equivalent in aggregate cost to a doubling of existing transfers to the provinces would be able to reduce the chosen poverty index by 44 percent when compared to its initial value.[1] However, the more relevant counterfactual for assessing targeting performance is the untargeted allocation of the same gross disbursement. This would reduce the poverty index by 31 percent; the gain from (optimal) targeting would be a more modest 19 percent over that from an untargeted allocation of the same budget.

Here we will also treat the uniform allocation of the same gross disbursement as the benchmark for evaluating the performance of targeting through public works schemes. This is a natural benchmark, but it is hypothetical; it might well be argued that, without any attempt at targeting, the outcome will be worse than uniform provisioning from the point of view of the poor. Ideally, we should compare the workfare scheme to some feasible alternative, such as a credit subsidy (as available in these villages through India's Integrated Rural Development Program; for a survey of the range of interventions that have been used to fight rural poverty, see Lipton and Ravallion 1995). Unfortunately, we do not have the data needed for this comparison. We will, however, consider one (stylized) alternative to uniform transfers as the benchmark for evaluating the targeted allocation.

The Cost-Effectiveness of Workfare

The *minimum* cost of eliminating poverty with perfect information is the transfer payment needed to bring everyone up to the poverty line.[2] That cost can be readily calculated. Letting z denote the poverty line, the aggregate poverty gap is simply the sum of the differences between z and actual income or consumption for all households who are poor. This is the minimum cost of eliminating poverty with perfect information. However, the *maximum* cost (with no information) is given by the product of z and the population size; if nothing were known about who is poor and who is not, giving z to all persons would clearly eliminate poverty, but at a high cost. The ratio of the minimum cost of eliminating poverty to the maximum cost is given by the poverty gap index (Ravallion 1994; poverty measures are discussed further below). For the latest data available for India (from the 1990–91 National Sample Survey) and using the Planning Commission's poverty line, we estimate that the poverty gap index is 8.6 percent.[3] Thus the *potential* gain from targeting in India is large; indeed, the cost of eliminating poverty with perfect information is about one-twelfth of the cost with no information.

However, in practice, realizing the potential gains from targeting is a different matter. As soon as one allows for imperfect information and the incentives facing the poor, the costs of targeting can increase quickly. The set of individual specific transfers needed to fill exactly all poverty gaps implies marginal tax rates on the poor of 100 percent; for every increment in their pre-transfer income, their transfer receipts fall by the same amount, leaving final income the same, at least up to the poverty line (Besley and Kanbur 1993). If all income is derived from work, and leisure is desirable, then pre-transfer incomes fall to zero, as nobody has any incentive to work (at least from the point of view of the net income gain, which is all we are considering here). The cost of the policy could then be very much higher than the poverty gap. Indeed, under such incentive effects, the ratio of the cost of eliminating poverty with targeting based on currently observed incomes (rather than pre-intervention incomes) to the maximum cost without targeting would not be given by the poverty gap index but rather by the headcount index of poverty (given by the proportion of the population deemed to be poor). For the aforementioned poverty line, our estimate of the headcount index for India in 1990–91 is 35 percent, so the cost would be more than four times higher than when incentive effects are ignored.

In such circumstances, it is known that optimal redistributive policy interventions may entail costs that are imposed on would-be participants—costs that would be deadweight losses in a "first-best world" of perfect information and unrestricted policy instruments (see, for example, Nichols and Zeckhauser 1982; Roberts 1984; Besley and Coate 1992; for an overview of various approaches to targeting, see Besley and Kanbur 1993). The general idea of targeting through self-selection schemes such as workfare is that the policymaker can impose a cost on recipients that varies implicitly as some increasing function of their (unobserved) standard of living (which we will simply call income). This can be termed the cost-of-participation function (Ravallion 1991). The gross benefit level to participants, in contrast, is independent of income (since the policymaker cannot know incomes in this setting). Thus, persons with incomes above some critical level (which may vary with other personal characteristics) will not want to participate; those below that level will.

However, this does not mean that such a scheme will be more cost-effective than an alternative, untargeted, scheme. The key point is that we should be concerned not about the gross benefits to the poor but rather about the benefits net of the participation costs. It is not difficult to envisage an outcome in which a perfectly self-targeting scheme (that is, one in which only the poor, and all of the poor, participate) is less cost-effective than universal provision in which (although there may be sizable leakages to the nonpoor) there are no deadweight losses in participating.

To illustrate the point, consider the following example. The government is choosing between a targeted scheme and a universal scheme and will pick the one that has the greatest impact on the poverty gap for a given budgetary outlay. The cost of participation in the scheme is a strictly increasing function of income x. Only people with an income less than some number z, say, will participate, and all those will participate. As before, call z the poverty line (or, equivalently, assume that the budget is adequate to reach the poverty line). Let us make the following simplifying assumptions: (a) the cost of participation is linear in income and vanishes at zero income, (b) administrative costs of both targeted and untargeted policies are negligible, and (c) all incomes are equally likely (so that, with appropriate normalization, income x can also measure the proportion of the population with income less than x). The cost per head of the population for a targeted scheme providing a benefit level b is then $b \cdot z$ (the benefit level times the proportion of the population participating, that is, those with a cost of participation less than b). The net benefit to the poor as a whole will be half of $b \cdot z$.[4] By contrast, out of the same budget, the poor will receive $b \cdot z^2$ under uniform provisioning, being the budgetary outlay $(b \cdot z)$ times the proportion who are poor (z). By comparing the two, it is evident that targeting will be more cost-effective in reducing the poverty gap only if the headcount index of poverty is less than 50 percent; at any higher number, a uniform allocation will do better.

Things get more complicated if we relax the three assumptions above. All one can say in general is that the necessary and sufficient condition for targeting to be more cost-effective than uniform provisioning in reducing the aggregate poverty gap is that the aggregate cost of participation as a proportion of gross benefits received under targeting does not exceed the proportionate gross gain in individual benefit level under targeting relative to uniform provisioning.[5]

Nonetheless, this example adequately illustrates the key point: once participation costs are considered, even a scheme that is very successful in screening the poor need not be more efficient in reducing poverty than even very poorly targeted alternatives. Whether it is or not is an empirical question.

Evidence on Transfer Benefits from Maharashtra's Employment Guarantee Scheme

Rural public works schemes have been used or advocated for alleviating both chronic and transient poverty in India for centuries; for example, the Indian famine relief codes of the nineteenth century recommended this form of relief, and it was often implemented.[6] Such schemes have returned to the fore recently in the context of proposals to make the right to work a fundamental right in India. An ambitious national employment guarantee scheme has been proposed as a way of doing so.

The model often advocated for such policies is Maharashtra's famous Employment Guarantee Scheme (EGS). This provides unskilled manual labor on small-scale, rural public works projects such as roads, irrigation facilities, and reforestation. EGS was introduced as a statutory program in the mid-1970s and expanded rapidly to reach average annual attendances of about 100 million person-days in recent years. It is financed almost entirely out of taxes on the urban sector of the state of Maharashtra, including an income tax levy.

Figure 15-1. Self-Selection in Public Works versus Means-Tested Credit, Maharashtra, 1987–88

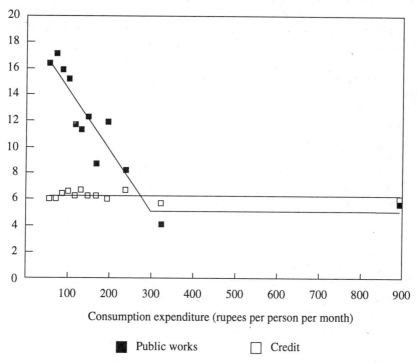

Percentage of households participating

Consumption expenditure (rupees per person per month)

■ Public works   □ Credit

One test of the performance of a rural public works scheme in screening the poor is to use survey data on incomes of participants and nonparticipants. There are well-known difficulties in assessing incomes in this context. However, from past surveys of participants in the scheme, it appears that EGS is quite well targeted; very few of the rich typically want to participate, and many of the poor do (Ravallion 1991 surveys the limited evidence available).

New evidence on the scheme's performance in reaching the rural poor is available from the National Sample Survey for 1987–88 (Government of India 1992). The survey asked whether or not anyone in the household had participated in a rural public works project (mainly, but not solely, EGS) for sixty days or more in the last year. Figure 15-1 reproduces the results for Maharashtra; participation in public works is plotted against consumption per person, along with the corresponding results for a similar question on participation (over the last five years) in the Integrated Rural Development Program, a scheme of subsidized credit targeted to the poor on the basis of an income means test.

There are a number of reasons to be cautious in interpreting these data. As we have emphasized, the fact of participation tells us nothing per se about net benefits to the participant (except that they are positive); that applies equally well to the credit scheme. Ideally, we would want to look at net gains plotted against pre-transfer living standards. We will take up these issues further below. But, nonetheless, the results in figure 15-1 are consistent with past evidence suggesting that participation in rural public works in Maharashtra tends to be greatest for the poor. They also suggest that the nonpoor are just as likely as the poor to participate in the subsidized credit scheme even though it is means tested.

Recognizing the potential errors in such assessments, and in measuring well-being generally (even on a narrow, nonwelfarist, income dimension), one can approach the targeting issue in another way. That entails looking carefully at the design and implementation of the anti-poverty scheme and asking two key questions. Are there any reasons why someone who is not poor would have any incentive to participate in such a scheme? Are there any impediments to participation by someone who is poor? If the answer is no to both, then the scheme must be well targeted.

Since its inception, the ideals behind the design of EGS have been broadly consistent with an answer "no" to both questions. It is implausible that the type of work (equivalent to the most basic agricultural labor) and the wages offered (historically on a par with those for casual agricultural labor) would be attractive to persons who are not poor by any reasonable local standard. And the scheme has aimed to provide work to anyone who wants it, at least within the district of residence (typically within a few kilometers of home). However, there have been recent signs that the practice may deviate significantly from these ideals; in mid-1988 wages rose sharply in accordance with statutory minimum wage rates (though without subsequent indexation), and there are indications of rationing of employment in the year following that wage increase (Ravallion, Datt, and Chaudhuri 1993).

The net income gains to participating households are even more difficult to measure than the scheme's targeting performance. Forgone income is the main cost involved (the monetary cost of transport to the site is probably negligible). This is likely to be highly seasonal and also to vary from year to year and across households and genders. In casual discussions with a number of groups of EGS workers in Pune district during a slack agricultural season (May 1990), we raised the question: "If you did not have this EGS work, could you obtain any other work?" Many answered that little or no work was available, but on further probing it became clear that many would have searched and, in time, found something. The women were more pessimistic than men about their prospects. Nonetheless, even in a slack season, it should not be assumed that forgone income is zero.

Unfortunately, past surveys have thrown little light on the extent of forgone incomes among EGS participants. In one of the few exceptions, Acharya and Panwalkar (1988) study two samples of 100 households each, one of which comprised households with EGS participants spread over ten villages, while the other sample was drawn from the same classes of landless and marginal farmers as the EGS households, but from ten villages where the scheme did not operate (though they give no explanation as to why the scheme was not active in the latter group of villages). Though they do not address the forgone income question, from their reported results one can calculate that the difference between the two samples in their mean incomes represented 53 percent of the mean (gross) income from EGS participation. This suggests that average forgone income accounts for about half of the average wages received (Ravallion 1991).

Self-selection into the scheme would probably lead to some overestimation of forgone income in the above calculation. The control sample of nonparticipants may be unrepresentative of (and better off than) the sample of participants. A better approach, though far more demanding in terms of both data and econometric technology, is to model econometrically the income generation process with and without the scheme. This is the methodology we have used in this chapter to address the relevant counterfactual question: What would participants be doing if the scheme did not exist?

New Evidence for Two Maharashtra Villages

We shall base our estimates of net transfer benefits to the poor on an econometric model of time allocation estimated on longitudinal household data for two Maharashtra villages. The data were collected by the International Crops Research Institute of the Semi-Arid Tropics (ICRISAT) and are described in Walker and Ryan (1990). The econometric model is consistent with the existence of involuntary unemployment of labor (insofar as the household attributes and other factors explaining time allocation can also be interpreted as the determinants of the rationing scheme for a particular activity). Thus we do not follow some recent literature in applied labor economics that assumes that *any* time allocation consistent with the overall time endowment is feasible. We believe that one cannot dismiss either the casual evidence or that from the ICRISAT survey data suggesting that quantity constraints on time allocation are common in this setting. For example, Walker and Ryan (1990) quote estimates of the rate of involuntary unemployment in the ICRISAT villages in 1975–76 of 19 percent for men and 23 percent for women (these are on a daily basis, giving the number of days in which work was desired but not obtained as a proportion of the total number of days of work desired). This aggregate figure hides a good deal of variation; for example, the rate of unemployment in slack periods was far higher, being 39 percent for men and 50 percent for women. Insufficient wage employment is clearly the main factor here. But a number of constraints on time allocation (both internal and external to the household) appear to underlie such figures. For example, there appear to be quite binding constraints on what sort of farm work different genders can do, as a result of which men are often idle in one season, while women are clearly overworked. Our model should be consistent with a potentially quite complex web of constraints on time allocation.

Our approach involves modeling intrahousehold time allocation across various activities in longitudinal data for sixty-six households in two Maharashtra villages—Shirapur and Kanzara—over six years (1979–80 to 1984–85). In essence, the model predicts the amount of time devoted to a given activity (wage labor, own-farm work and self-employment, leisure and domestic work, and unemployment) as a function of a vector of exogenous variables *and* the amount of time spent on rural public works schemes (mainly the EGS). The model allows different effects across genders and substitution effects between men and women. (So, for example, the woman may do extra work on the farm to compensate for the man joining the public works project). However, because of the negligible participation in these projects by women in Kanzara (unlike in Shirapur), a gender breakdown is not feasible in that village. Nor is it feasible to separate domestic labor from leisure; for women, a large share of the time recorded under this heading is undoubtedly domestic labor, including certain farm-related tasks. Appendix 15-1 provides further details.

Our time-allocation model can be interpreted as the solution to a household utility maximization problem in which employment on the public works projects is rationed; the relevant explanatory variables are then all fixed factors in the household production function, taste parameters, time and wealth endowments, and employment on public works. Assuming that public works employment is rationed would be consistent with the various tests reported in Ravallion, Datt, and Chaudhuri (1993), based on aggregate time-series data for the EGS. However, by including employment on public works on the right-hand side of the model for time allocated to other activities, we do not have to assume that public works employment is rationed. We can equally well derive a model with this same basic structure in which any (non-negative) allocation to public works projects is feasible, though then we must treat this variable as endogenous in the econometric estimation. Similarly, the model is also consistent with quantity constraints in other activities.

In Datt and Ravallion (1994a), we derive an appropriate consistent estimator for simultaneous Tobit models in which both the left-hand-side and some right-hand-side variables are censored and endogenous; the estimator is a generalization of that proposed by Smith and Blundell (1986) for Tobit models with uncensored endogenous right-hand-side variables. When exogeneity is rejected, we treat public works employment as endogenous. The nonlinearity of the Tobit predictions allows identification (though we experiment with some alternative specifications). The econometric specification is outlined in appendix 15-1; more complete discussions of the estimated equations can be found in Datt and Ravallion (1994b) and in the working paper version, which provides greater detail on the properties of the econometric model (Datt and Ravallion 1994a).

This model can then be used to simulate the time allocation, and hence incomes, that would be expected in the counterfactual case in which public works employment is not available. The displaced wage labor time is valued at the household- and gender-specific average daily wage rates for any given year. For the valuation of time displaced in own-farm and other self-employed activities, we use the normalized quadratic profit function estimated for these villages by Datt (1989). This profit function is used to derive an estimate of the marginal profit per acre with respect to family labor, which is then assumed to apply to both own-farm and other self-employment activities. The important point here is to use a *marginal* and not an *average* valuation. The prevailing agricultural wage rates may also grossly overstate the value of marginal time displaced in own-farm and self-employment activities. Time displaced from unemployment and leisure/domestic work is assumed to entail zero forgone income (by contrast, a welfarist approach would value these in terms of lost utility).

Thus one can predict what incomes would have been generated by each household in the absence of the public employment scheme and compare this to the incomes actually reported. The difference is the income gain attributable to the scheme, that is, wage earnings from the scheme less the forgone income associated with the displaced activities.

For participating households, public works employment on average accounted for about 22 percent of the total days worked in a year in Shirapur and about 15 percent in Kanzara. Table 15-1 gives our estimates of the average number of days in the various activities displaced by public works employment and the value of the corresponding income losses (the mean is formed over all household-years reporting positive adult participation in public works). For example, in Shirapur we estimate that the combined effect of male and female public works employment was to displace, on average, 15.6 days of male wage labor and 5.3 days of female wage labor, for a typical participating household that allocated 58.2 days of male and 48.4 days of female labor time to public works. For Shirapur (where we can identify gender differences), the main activity displaced was unemployment for males and leisure/

Table 15-1. *Average Number of Days Displaced and Average Forgone Incomes Attributed to Public Works Employment, Maharashtra, India*

| | Shirapur | | | | | | Kanzara, total[a] | |
| | Male adults | | Female adults | | Total[a] | | | |
Activity	Days	Value	Days	Value	Days	Value	Days	Value
Wage labor	15.55	127.96	5.30	22.85	20.85	150.82	32.96	182.31
Own-farm/other activities	−1.62	1.29	0	0	−1.62	1.29	23.04	2.01
Unemployment	36.28	0	0.19	0	36.47	0	11.70	0
Leisure/domestic work	7.94	0	42.87	0	50.81	0	11.51	0
All activities	58.15	129.25	48.36	22.85	112.86	152.11	84.39	184.32
Public works	58.15	454.23	48.36	233.82	112.86	717.95	84.39	571.97

Note: Values are in 1983–84 rupees; all figures are annual, averaged over participating households.

a. Totals for "all activities" and "public works" include days and values for children.

domestic work (which, unfortunately, cannot be split from the survey data) for females. The forgone income represented 28 percent of male wage earnings and 10 percent for women. In the aggregate, 43 percent of the time spent on public works sites came out of leisure/domestic work in Shirapur, while 34 percent came out of unemployment. Only 18 percent involved a sacrifice of other wage labor time. The pattern is rather different in Kanzara, where nearly 39 percent came out of other wage labor time and 27 percent was from own-farm activities. The overall level of public works employment was lower in Kanzara, though (given the pattern of displacement) its pecuniary opportunity cost was higher. This difference between the two villages probably reflects the relatively tighter labor market conditions in Kanzara.

An Assessment of Transfer Efficiency

These results do not indicate high forgone incomes. The income lost due to labor displacement was equal to about one-quarter of the gross wage earnings from public employment. Aggregating the results from the two villages, we find that the bulk of the time going into participation in the scheme came out of unemployment, leisure, or domestic work, with negligible pecuniary opportunity cost.

Though this is a study of only two villages, it is the only credible estimate of forgone incomes that we know about. And it suggests that the rough "back of the envelope" calculations of forgone income discussed in the last section are too high.

As mentioned previously, a useful benchmark for assessing the cost-effectiveness of public employment as a poverty-alleviation policy is to compare it with the reduction in poverty achievable through an untargeted (uniform) allocation of the same gross budget. Cost-effectiveness, in this comparative sense, will depend on the ability of public employment to screen the poor from the nonpoor households and also on the level and distribution of forgone incomes associated with participation in public works. It will also be determined by the share of the wage bill in total costs. For EGS, this is constrained to be at least 60 percent (though a few exceptions are allowed). The wage bill for EGS has typically represented 70 percent of the government's total outlays on the scheme, though this has declined somewhat over recent years. We assume that the wage bill represents two-thirds of the gross disbursement (Ravallion, Datt, and Chaudhuri 1993).

We also need to know what administrative cost would be incurred with uniform provision. This will depend in part on whether the transfer is uniform across households or people; the latter allocation will be more administratively costly, as it requires counting the number of persons within every household. We focus here solely on an untargeted allocation that is uniform across households and both villages (so every

Table 15-2. *Pre-Intervention and Post-Intervention Poverty Measures with and without Targeting through Public Works, Maharashtra, India*
(percent)

Location and intervention	Headcount index		Poverty gap index		Squared poverty gap index	
	Lower poverty line	Higher poverty line	Lower poverty line	Higher poverty line	Lower poverty line	Higher poverty line
Shirapur						
Pre-intervention	42.2	54.3	13.5	19.2	5.0	8.4
Post-intervention						
Public works	39.5	51.1	10.4	16.1	3.3	6.4
Uniform transfer of same budget	39.5	47.9	9.2	14.8	2.6	5.5
Equi-proportional allocation	42.2	47.9	11.4	16.7	3.8	7.0
Kanzara						
Pre-intervention	56.2	65.5	10.7	18.7	2.8	6.5
Post-intervention						
Public works	50.4	65.5	9.1	17.2	2.2	5.9
Uniform transfer of same budget	41.4	58.1	6.9	14.4	1.6	4.4
Equi-proportional allocation	45.8	58.1	7.6	15.7	1.9	5.0

Note: The headcount index is the percentage of the population living below the poverty line. The poverty gap index is the population's mean proportionate poverty gap, as given by the distance below the poverty line (zero for the nonpoor) expressed as a percentage of the poverty line. The squared poverty gap index is the population mean of the squared proportionate poverty gaps (zero for the nonpoor) multiplied by 100.

household in both villages receives the same amount). Furthermore, we assume that this can be done with negligible administrative cost, though we ask how sensitive our results are to that assumption in the next section.

We measure poverty using the distribution of mean income per person of each household, where the mean is formed over six years' income data. Two poverty lines are considered: the lower one is a long-established poverty line for rural India, namely Rs15 per month per person at 1973–74 prices, while the higher line is arbitrarily set 20 percent higher. Three poverty measures are considered, two of which we have mentioned already: the *headcount index*, given by the percentage of the population with mean income below the poverty line, and the *poverty gap index*, given by the mean poverty gap as a percentage of the poverty line (with the mean formed over all households, where the nonpoor have zero poverty gap). We shall also consider the *squared poverty gap*, given by the mean squared proportionate poverty gap (Foster, Greer, and Thorbecke 1984). This is a strictly convex measure in that it penalizes inequitable distribution among the poor.[7]

Table 15-2 gives our results for each of the three poverty measures and the two poverty lines. For each village, the first row gives the estimated poverty measure prior to intervention (based on the distribution of estimated incomes with zero participation), while the remaining rows give three sets of post-intervention poverty measures: (a) with public works participation (that is, based on the distribution of income actually observed in the data), (b) with a uniform transfer of the same gross budget, and (c) with an equi-proportional transfer, whereby the same gross budget is allocated in proportion to pre-intervention incomes (discussed in the next section).

For all three poverty measures and both villages, the poverty outcome is better, or at least no worse, with uniform transfers of the same budget, once the nonwage costs and forgone incomes of participants (even though seemingly modest) are factored into the calculation. But are these differences statistically significant? Table 15-3 gives the *t*-ratios for testing the null hypothesis that the poverty measures are the same.[8] The differences in the headcount index with public works and with uniform transfers are not statistically significant; nor for that matter is there a significant difference in this measure of poverty after uniform transfers (with the lone exception of uniform transfers in Kanzara for the lower poverty line). When compared with the pre-intervention situation, neither the transfer benefits from public works nor uniform transfers of the same budget have a significant impact on the number of people who are poor.

However, the positive impacts *below* the poverty line are larger *and* statistically significant (tables 15-2 and 15-3). In Shirapur and Kanzara, both net earnings from public works and uniform transfers of the same

Table 15-3. *Significance Tests for the Impacts on Poverty, Maharashtra, India*
(*t*-ratios for testing the null hypothesis that the poverty measures are equal)

Location and intervention	Headcount index		Poverty gap index		Squared poverty gap index	
	Lower poverty line	Higher poverty line	Lower poverty line	Higher poverty line	Lower poverty line	Higher poverty line
Shirapur						
Pre-intervention vs. public works	0.90	0.96	3.43	4.17	3.16	3.47
Pre-intervention vs. uniform transfer	0.90	1.39	4.41	5.51	3.81	4.29
Public works vs. uniform transfer	0.00	0.97	2.03	2.42	2.19	2.19
Kanzara						
Pre-intervention vs. public works	1.21	0.00	2.43	2.69	1.73	2.16
Pre-intervention vs. uniform transfer	2.05	1.39	4.46	5.15	3.15	4.55
Public works vs. uniform transfer	1.55	1.39	3.10	3.87	2.39	3.45

Note: The estimated standard errors for the differences in poverty measures allow for the fact that the pre- and post-intervention poverty measures are based on the same sample and also for differential weighting of the sample points reflecting differences in both household size and in ICRISAT's sampling rates (which differed between labor and cultivator households). See appendix 15-2 for details.

Figure 15-2. *Poverty-Incidence Curves with and without Net Earnings from Public Works, Maharashtra*

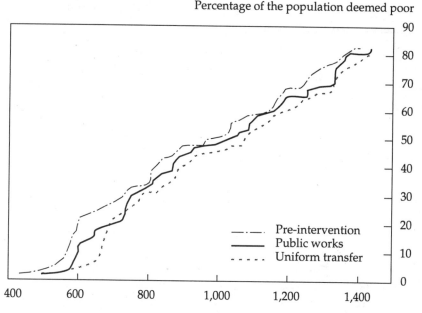

Percentage of the population deemed poor

Pre-intervention
Public works
Uniform transfer

Poverty line (six-year mean income; rupees per person per year)

budget entail a significant reduction in the poverty gap and squared poverty gap indexes; this holds for both poverty lines. Furthermore, the extra impact of uniform transfers over public works is significant for these higher-order measures (table 15-3).

Recognizing the various uncertainties that pervade poverty comparisons such as those in table 15-2, figure 15-2 gives the *poverty-incidence curves*, giving the cumulative distributions of income (per person, averaged over six years) with and without net earnings from public works, aggregated over both villages.[9] First-order dominance holds.[10] Thus, regardless of the choice of poverty line, *any* well-behaved measure of poverty will show a decrease as a result of earnings from public works (this is an application of the theory of stochastic dominance; see Atkinson 1987; for a nontechnical exposition, see Ravallion 1994). It is also notable that the greatest impact of public works earnings on the distribution of income is in the range of 10–30 percent; these are clearly not the poorest households, though they are well below conventional poverty lines in this setting.

The figure also gives the distribution implied by a uniform transfer across all households of the gross budget for public works (again assuming that this can be done with negligible administrative cost).

Figure 15-3. Poverty Deficit Curves with and without Net Earnings and from Public Works, Maharashtra

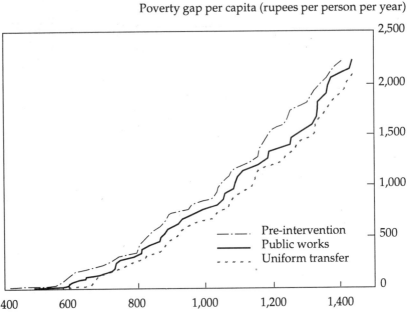

Poverty gap per capita (rupees per person per year)

Pre-intervention
Public works
Uniform transfer

Poverty line (six-year mean income; rupees per person per year)

By definition, this must first-order dominate the pre-intervention distribution. It does not first-order dominate the distribution after net earnings from public works, though it comes close to doing so. The *poverty deficit curves* (giving the aggregate poverty gap per head of the population as a function of the poverty line) are in figure 15-3; these are simply the areas under the corresponding poverty-incidence curves. The deficit curve for uniform transfers is nowhere above that for public works earnings (implying second-order dominance). Following Atkinson (1987), this implies greater poverty reduction from uniform transfers for all weakly convex additive measures that are strictly decreasing in incomes of the poor.

It is of interest to inquire further into why the public works employment appears to be generally less cost-effective than untargeted transfers. In principle, it may be either weak targeting or the extra costs associated with forgone incomes and nonwage administrative and other costs. An obvious way to measure targeting performance is with a *concentration curve*, giving the cumulative shares of benefits received by the poorest *x* percent of the population. An equal transfer to all individuals means that the concentration curve is a 45-degree line

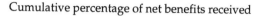

Figure 15-4. Concentration Curves for Net Benefits from Public Works and from Uniform Transfers, Maharashtra

Cumulative percentage of net benefits received

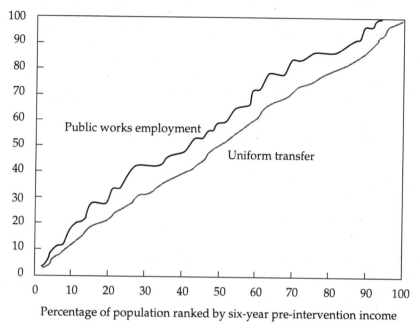

Percentage of population ranked by six-year pre-intervention income

through the origin. In figure 15-4 we plot the concentration curves for net benefits from public works employment and for uniform transfers across all households (which differ from the 45-degree line according to the variation in household size). It can be seen that the targeting performance of public works is clearly better than that of uniform transfers. It should also be noted that this is targeting performance *within* two poor villages; reaching such villages at all is already an indication of good targeting. Ipso facto, the transfer inefficiency of public works must be due in no small measure to the extra costs incurred, relative to uniform transfers.

What is the relative importance of the two sources of this extra cost, namely forgone income versus nonwage costs? Aggregated over the whole population, the total sum received under uniform transfers (equal to the total cost of public works) is almost exactly twice (2.01 times) the aggregate net earnings gain from public works. If forgone incomes were zero, the aggregate uniform transfer would only be 50 percent higher than the amount transferred via public works. Of the proportionate increase in aggregate transfer benefits due to a switch from targeting through public works employment to uniform transfers, about 40 percent is attributable to forgone incomes.

Caveats and Extensions

There are a number of important caveats on these results. We list them below and offer some observations on their likely importance, drawing on both our empirical work and more casual observations.

We have assumed that the administrative cost and incentive effects of uniform transfers are negligible. Yet even a uniform transfer can influence work effort through the income effect on demand for leisure, and the effect may not be negligible (see Sahn and Alderman, chapter 14 of this volume). To test the sensitivity of our results to this assumption, we can also ask: How high would the extra cost of uniform transfers (beyond the transfers themselves) need to be for one to be indifferent between targeting through work requirements and uniform provisioning? This can be calculated numerically. For the squared poverty gap index at our lower poverty line (the answer is very similar for the other poverty line and the poverty gap index), we estimate that the extra cost of uniform transfers would need to be 39 percent of the gross disbursement to equalize the poverty impact of the two schemes. This seems high—indeed, as high as the nonwage share of cost in the public works scheme. We do not know how high the administrative and incentive effects of uniform transfers are, but it appears that they would need to be quite sizable to overturn our conclusion that uniform transfers would be more cost-effective.

Another caveat was mentioned earlier, namely that the feasible policy alternatives to targeting through public works may well be inferior to even a uniform transfer. We do not have the data to evaluate this conjecture on a consistent basis with our evaluation of targeting through public works. However, we can offer one potentially interesting benchmark. Table 15-2 gives the poverty measures obtained when the same gross budget is allocated in proportion to pre-intervention incomes (so that relative inequalities are unaltered). When compared to this allocation rule, targeting through public works generally has a greater impact on the poverty measures in Shirapur, though not in Kanzara.

As we also noted previously, there are dimensions to poverty that could motivate participation in such schemes, but that our data on incomes could not hope to capture convincingly. Possibly the (already good) targeting performance is actually much better than our results suggest—so much so that the scheme really does better than uniform transfers. To see if this might be true, let us suppose instead that *all* participants are in fact poor and that all the poor live in participating households. The share of the gross disbursement going to the poor under uniform transfers would then be the proportion of households who participate in public works. For our data, that is 71 percent over all years. On factoring in the forgone incomes, the aggregate net transfer benefit to the poor from public works employment is 75 percent of the gross wages received. With wages accounting for two-thirds of the cost, the share of the gross disbursement going to the poor under the public works scheme is then 50 percent. It is clear then that even if one measures poverty by participation in public works schemes, the net transfer benefit going to the poor would still be higher under universal transfers.

In addition to the direct transfer benefit, one must also consider any indirect benefits (arising through the assets created or effects on markets) and risk benefits to the poor. These issues take us beyond the scope of this chapter, though they do merit closer investigation.[11] How large would the indirect benefits need to be for workfare to dominate the untargeted transfers? If the indirect benefits are uniform, then (by the same numerical method used above in assessing sensitivity to omitted administrative costs) we estimate that the present value of those benefits would only need to cover 40 percent of the scheme's current cost to equalize the poverty gap index with and without targeting. If, instead, the indirect benefits are directly proportionate to pre-intervention income (so the poor receive absolutely less), then those benefits would need to be able to cover 76 percent of the scheme's cost (representing an aggregate gain of 5.1 percent of pre-intervention income). In conventional cost-benefit accounting, benefit-to-cost ratios appreciably less than unity would be sufficient to justify targeting through workfare as the more cost-effective instrument for poverty alleviation.

Although our empirical work does not allow us to estimate these second-round income effects, we did talk about them in our fieldwork, both with EGS administrators and participants. There was clearly widespread concern that the assets created were not as valuable as they could have been, and there was also a perception among many observers of the scheme that the poor shared little in whatever future benefits were generated by the assets. However, this does not appear to be an intrinsic feature of the scheme, as exceptions are identifiable (such as new roads that clearly benefit the poor). There are also possibilities for redesigning the scheme in ways that can enhance the second-round benefits, such as by avoiding restrictions that require a minimum labor intensity for individual projects, but rather aiming to achieve a reasonably high labor intensity in the aggregate (see Ravallion 1991 for further discussion).

The importance of second-round income effects from the scheme was noted by participants in Shirapur, during fieldwork there in mid-1991. A number of persons interviewed remarked that the schemes were associated with an increase in *aggregate* employment in the village;

even if one worker left a wage labor job to join the scheme, another worker would take his place. Thus our partial equilibrium calculations could significantly overstate aggregate forgone income.[12] There are also other income effects that we have omitted; for example, a milk vendor reported that there had been a noticeable increase in demand for milk, which he attributed to rural public works activity.

Nor have we said anything about the positive role that the utility loss associated with work requirements may play in reducing dependence on welfare support. When compared to untargeted transfers, the disutility of a work requirement may leave sufficient incentive for workfare participants to take other actions that will allow them to escape poverty in the future; this is the essence of the "deterrent argument" for workfare (Besley and Coate 1992). To illustrate, consider someone employed on a public works project who is offered a preferred job, earning more with the same effort, which she takes of course. Would she do so if (instead of public works) an untargeted transfer scheme was in place, giving the same income as the workfare scheme, but not requiring work? Not necessarily; that would depend on the income gain from the new job and her leisure preferences. Nothing more can be said, in general. But there is one interesting anecdote we can offer here. In a field trip to Shirapur, a man who used to participate often in public works told one of the authors that he had saved enough from his earnings to purchase two fine milking cows from which he derived new income, permitting him to opt out of public works employment. One observation such as this does not make a test, but it does indicate that these schemes are capable of preserving adequate incentives for participants to take actions that will allow them to escape poverty by other means in the future.

Conclusions

Workfare schemes try to improve targeting performance by creating incentives that encourage self-selection by the poor and discourage participation by the nonpoor. However, the behavioral responses to those incentives may entail sizable costs of participation. Even a perfectly targeted scheme may be less effective at reducing poverty with given resources than untargeted alternatives once those costs of participation are considered. That is an empirical question.

Few of the many empirical studies of these schemes have permitted a convincing assessment of their cost-effectiveness. It appears that targeting performance is generally quite good, but surprisingly little evidence from the existing literature allows us to measure properly the forgone incomes of participants. The new estimates summarized here using household data for two villages in Maharashtra suggest that the immediate *net* income gain from rural public works employment was a large proportion of the gross wage earnings from the scheme. The opportunity cost of participation by the poor was typically quite low, at about one-quarter of wage earnings, though it was appreciably higher in one of the villages (where participation was also lower), and it was higher among men than women.

The net transfer benefits to the poor from such a scheme also depend on the unskilled wage bill as a proportion of gross disbursements. This is typically high for these schemes. Even so, the proportion of poor in the rural populations served by these schemes is also high.

Combining these calculations, our results for two Maharashtra villages suggest that net earnings from public works employment did achieve a significant reduction in the poverty gap and squared poverty gap indexes, though the gains in the percentage of people who are poor were not significant. Thus the scheme did reach persons *below* the poverty line, even if few people actually escaped poverty as a result. However, the direct impact on poverty incidence arising from employment on public works schemes was no greater than could have been achieved with a uniform (untargeted) allocation of the same gross budget across all households. And the impacts on the poverty gap indexes would actually have been significantly greater with uniform transfers as with the counterfactual. Indeed, the income distribution achieved by net earnings from public works was second-order dominated by that resulting from the untargeted disbursement of the same gross budget outlay. This was not due to targeting weaker than that implied by universal transfers; the transfer benefits from public works were better targeted. The more important factor was the loss to the poor associated with forgone incomes, administration, supervision, and other nonwage costs generated by the workfare scheme.

From a methodological perspective, our results also illustrate how deceptive the widely used concentration curve (giving the cumulative share of benefits going to the poorest fraction of the population) can be in evaluating targeted interventions. The policy that is better at targeting the poor, and (hence) has the better concentration curve, need not be the one that has greater impact on poverty for a given cost. We have illustrated the use of better analytic tools for this purpose, drawing on recent applications of stochastic dominance tests to poverty comparisons.

There are a number of caveats on our results. There are reasons to suspect that our assessment may be biased somewhat against poverty alleviation using work requirements. For one thing, a uniform transfer is a hypothetical benchmark, and it may not be attainable by feasible policy alternatives. To come close to uniform transfers in this setting might well be considered a success. Uniform transfers may also entail hidden costs (due to administration or incentive effects), though our estimates suggest that such costs would need to be quite sizable to reverse our conclusion. Also, our assessment makes no allowance for other benefits to the poor, such as through enhanced insurance against monsoon failures, second-round effects on rural wages, and improved rural infrastructure. These may well be enough to tip the scales in favor of these schemes over untargeted cash transfers. We estimate that this would take only a modest indirect benefit level, sufficient to cover about 40 percent of project cost, assuming the benefits are uniformly distributed.

Workfare schemes are often criticized for producing assets of little value. That does not mean they are an inefficient antipoverty policy, given the informational constraints on policy, particularly in poorly developed rural economies. It is theoretically possible that a workfare scheme dominates alternatives, even if the assets created or other indirect effects have no value. This case study indicates that this theoretical possibility is no more than that; the indirect effects of the scheme *will* need to have some value to the poor (or yield a recoverable benefit to the nonpoor) if it is to be judged a more efficient instrument against rural poverty than a wholly untargeted allocation of the same budget.

Appendix 15-1: The Econometric Model of Time Allocation

The results reported in this chapter are derived from a conditional time-allocation model estimated for the two Maharashtra villages. This appendix gives further details on the model and its estimation. A complete description of the model, the estimator, and its properties can be found in Datt and Ravallion (1994a).

The model is estimated on household data for thirty-three households in each of two Maharashtra villages, Shirapur and Kanzara, over the six years from 1979–80 to 1984–85. The villages differ in a number of respects. Kanzara is a richer village, is better irrigated, and has less participation in the EGS. The villages also differ in terms of the cropping pattern, the occupational structure, and the distribution of landholdings. These differences have potentially important implications for their household time-allocation patterns.

The data allow us to distinguish the time allocation of each person across five household activities: (1) wage labor other than on the EGS projects (mainly agricultural labor), (2) own-farm labor and labor on handicrafts/trade activities, (3) unemployment (number of days in which work was sought but could not be found), (4) leisure/domestic work, and (5) wage labor on EGS. These categories are self-explanatory, though we would make two observations.

First, the data do not allow leisure to be differentiated from domestic work. For women, a large proportion is probably domestic labor, which may also include some farm activities. The time allocated to leisure or domestic work is determined residually. Since the days worked on any of these activities are censored at the minimum value of zero, the resulting time allocation functions are nonlinear, and there is no obvious way of imposing additivity in the form of cross-equation parameter restrictions (Pudney 1989).

Second, the fact that positive unemployment is reported by households suggests that one or more activities must be rationed. It also indicates that the EGS is falling short of its aim of providing work to whoever wants it. But this inference is clouded a little by the possibility that involuntary unemployment may be measured with some error.

For Shirapur, we estimate the conditional time-allocation model separately for males and females, allowing for gender differences in time allocation, with cross-effects across genders. A gender disaggregation is not feasible for Kanzara owing to the very limited participation of women in the EGS there, resulting in very few nonlimit observations. This makes both the parameter estimates of the female public employment equation and its residuals sensitive to minor changes in the specification. We therefore opt for aggregating male and female time allocations for Kanzara. For similar reasons, the model is not separately estimated for children. Given their extremely low participation in the labor force and still lower participation in the projects, we assume that their workfare employment comes entirely out of the time they were not in the labor force.

The general (gender-differentiated) empirical conditional time-allocation model is as follows. Let L_{kit}^j denote time allocation to activity k by persons of gender $j = m, f$ in household i in time period t. The equations for time allocation across all other activities are (for males and females, respectively)

(15A-1) $\quad L_{kit}^{m*} = \beta_k^{m'} x_{it} + \gamma_k^{mm} L_{nit}^m + \gamma_k^{mf} L_{nit}^f + u_{kit}^m$

(15A-2) $\quad L_{kit}^{f*} = \beta_k^f x_{it} + \gamma_k^{fm} L_{nit}^m + \gamma_k^{ff} L_{nit}^f + u_{kit}^f$

$$(\text{for } k = 1,...,n-1; \; i = 1,...H; \; t = 1,...T),$$

where x_{kit} is a vector of explanatory variables to be described below, βs and γs are parameters to be estimated, and

$$L_{kit}^j = L_{kit}^{j*} \text{ if } L_{kit}^{j*} > 0,$$
$$L_{kit}^j = 0 \text{ otherwise}$$

for $j = m, f$. The dependent variables are, of course, censored at the lower bound of zero. The equations for EGS employment are

(15A-3)
$$L_{nit}^{m*} = \pi^{m'} x_{it} + v_{nit}^m$$
$$L_{nit}^{f*} = \pi^f x_{it} + v_{nit}^f,$$
$$\text{where } L_{nit}^j = L_{nit}^{j*} \text{ if } L_{nit}^{j*} > 0,$$
$$L_{nit}^j = 0 \quad \text{otherwise.}$$

A consistent limited information estimator for this problem is discussed in Datt and Ravallion (1994b). The estimator is a generalization of that proposed by Smith and Blundell (1986), who allow only continuous endogenous variables in the structural limited dependent variable model. This generalization of the Smith-Blundell estimator (and the exogeneity test) is, however, limited in scope. Specifically, the generalized estimator is consistent for a simultaneous Tobit model with censored endogenous variables and a triangular matrix of structural coefficients. Although that is appropriate for the present problem, it would not be so for the general simultaneous Tobit model where no restrictions are placed on the structural coefficients.

The basic estimation strategy involves rewriting the model 15A-1 and 15A-2 conditional on error processes v_{nit}^m and v_{nit}^f as

$$(15A\text{-}4) \quad L_{kit}^{m*} = \beta_k^{m'} x_{it} + \gamma_k^{mm} L_{nit}^m + \gamma_k^{mf} L_{nit}^f + \alpha_k^{mm} v_{nit}^m + \alpha_k^{mf} v_{nit}^f + \epsilon_{kit}^m$$

$$(15A\text{-}5) \quad L_{kit}^{f*} = \beta_k^f x_{it} + \gamma_k^{fm} L_{nit}^m + \gamma_k^{ff} L_{nit}^f + \alpha_k^{fm} v_{nit}^m + \alpha_k^{ff} v_{nit}^f + \epsilon_{kit}^f.$$

The expanded model 15A-4 and 15A-5 is estimated by the Tobit maximum likelihood estimator after replacing v_{nit}^m and v_{nit}^f by their consistent estimates; the latter are obtained as Tobit residuals from equations 15A-3 for male and female employment on EGS, respectively. The resultant estimator is shown to be consistent in Datt and Ravallion (1994a), where its asymptotic covariance matrix is also derived. It is shown that under the null hypothesis of exogeneity, this covariance matrix collapses to the covariance matrix of the Tobit maximum likelihood estimator of model 15A-1 and 15A-2. Standard t-ratios for α from a maximum likelihood estimate of model 15A-4 and 15A-5 can thus be used to test for the exogeneity of the censored regressor L_{nt}. Even when exogeneity is rejected, the maximum likelihood estimator of model 15A-4 and 15A-5 is consistent.

For any time-allocation equation, exogeneity is tested sequentially for male and female public employment, beginning with the α parameter with the lower t-ratio. If the hypothesis of exogeneity of male or female employment on the public works projects is found to be statistically acceptable (we use a significance level of 10 percent), then the time-allocation model is reestimated assuming exogeneity. If both male and female public employment variables are found to be exogenous, we are left with the standard Tobit model. In this case, we further prune the model to exclude either of the public employment variables if they turn out to be highly insignificant (with t-ratios less than unity).

Next, the time displaced in any activity k due to male and female participation in workfare (denoted D_{kit}^m and D_{kit}^f) is estimated as the difference between the expected days of work in activity k with no participation in workfare and the expected days of work in that activity conditional on the household's current level of participation. Thus

(15A-6) $D_{kit}^j = E[L_{kit}^j | x_{it}, L_{nit}^m = 0, L_{nit}^f = 0, \hat{v}_{nit}^m = 0, \hat{v}_{nit}^f = 0]$

$- E[L_{kit}^j | x_{it}, L_{nit}^m, L_{nit}^f, \hat{v}_{nit}^m, \hat{v}_{nit}^f]$ (for $j = m, f$).

The model is estimated using longitudinal data of six years' duration for the two villages with thirty-three households each. Despite the panel structure of the data set, we are unable to exploit it for estimating a fixed (or random) effects time-allocation model because of the censored nature of the dependent variables. Apart from the inconsistency of a fixed effects Tobit estimator for a short panel, to estimate a fixed effects Tobit model we would have to exclude all households with zero participation in any activity for all six years in the panel (Heckman and McCurdy 1980). For our data set, this would mean throwing out more than half the observations in many cases. A further potential problem is that the effective sample would vary enormously across activities and gender. However, we do make a partial attempt at capturing household-specific effects on time allocation by including in the set of regressors variables that are invariant over time for a household, for example, the caste ranking of the household and a six-year average of real assets of the household.

The x_{it} vector of explanatory variables in the time-allocation model includes year dummies and five sets of variables relating to (a) household size and composition, (b) value and composition of household assets, (c) caste and educational status, (d) incidence of work disability, and (e) total available time (days per year) for adult males and females. The last set of variables allows for the overall time constraint and is constructed as the total reporting days (the number of days for which the respondent provided time-allocation information) *minus* days of sickness or nonresidence in the village. The wage rates for both public and private work are deliberately excluded because of their potential endogeneity. EGS employment is remunerated on a piece-rate basis, and thus the time wage rate is not independent of the level of employment. The wage rate for private employment also has an endogeneity problem since the average wage received by a household member is an employment-weighted average of wage rates for different agricultural and nonagricultural operations performed by him or her over the year.

We also estimate the model where the x_{it} vector in the public employment equations has two additional variables: quadratic terms in caste and years of schooling of the household head. The results are very similar to those obtained using an identical set of exogenous variables (but excluding the quadratic terms) in the public employment and conditional time-allocation equations. For Shirapur, the estimates of time displaced by EGS employment in all activities except unemployment are identical in the two cases; for Kanzara too, estimates of displaced time are quite similar in the two cases.

Appendix 15-2: Testing the Statistical Significance of the Policy's Impact on Poverty

Exploiting the additivity property of many poverty measures, Kakwani (1993) has derived tests for the null hypothesis that two poverty measures are equal. However, Kakwani's tests assume that the two samples are independent. This does not hold here, since both the pre-and post-intervention poverty measures are estimated from the same sample. A covariance correction is needed. A correction is also needed for the weighting of sample points required for unbiased estimates.

Consider the (broad) class of additive measures whereby the aggregate poverty measure P is simply the sample estimate of $E(p)$, the expected value of an individual poverty measure p (for examples of this class of measures, see Atkinson 1987). The aggregate poverty measure can then be written as

$$(15A\text{-}7) \qquad\qquad P = \sum_{i=1}^{n} w_i p_i / n,$$

where p_i is the poverty measure for the ith household (zero for the nonpoor), w_i is the appropriate weight on household i to assure an unbiased estimate of the mean, and $n = \Sigma_i w_i$ is the sample size.

We have pre- and post-intervention estimates of P, namely P_A and P_B, from the same sample. The variance of the difference in poverty measures $P_A - P_B$ is

$$(15A\text{-}8) \qquad s^2 = var(P_A) + var(P_B) - 2cov(P_A, P_B),$$

where $var(P_A)$ and $var(P_B)$ are the variances of the poverty measures and $cov(P_A, P_B)$ is their covariance. Formulas for the variances of a range of poverty measures in unweighted random samples can be found in Kakwani (1993). Assuming that the weights are exogenous, the Kakwani variances need only be scaled up by a factor of $1 + var(w)$, where $var(w)$ is the variance of the weights. But what about the covariances? These can be consistently estimated by

$$(15A\text{-}9) \qquad cov(P_A, P_B) = [1 + var(w)](P_{AB} - P_A P_B)/n,$$

where the term P_{AB} denotes the sample estimate of $E(p^A p^B)$ and is given by

$$(15A\text{-}10) \qquad\qquad P_{AB} = \sum_{i=1}^{n} w_i p_i^A p_i^B / n.$$

(For the headcount index, this is simply the joint probability of being poor in both distributions.) When all weights are the same [$var(w)=0$] and the distributions are independent ($P_{AB} = P_A \cdot P_B$), equation 15A-8 collapses to the formula in Kakwani (1993). The test statistic for the null hypothesis of no significant impact of the intervention is the usual t-ratio

(15A-11) $t = (P_A - P_B)/s,$

which is asymptotically standard normal.

Notes

1. The chosen poverty index is the Foster-Greer-Thorbecke (1984) P_2 measure (also discussed later in this chapter), and an optimal allocation is one that minimizes the aggregate value of this index subject to the available budget and the non-negativity constraint on regional disbursements. (Without the latter constraint, the solution will equalize the P_1 poverty index across all regions; see Kanbur 1987.) The solution method for this problem is outlined in Ravallion and Chao (1989), and a user-friendly computer program is available for implementing that method.

2. The information requirement is quite stringent. Since incomes can (in general) be altered by potential recipients, it will not be sufficient to know only current incomes, as previously nonpoor persons may have sacrificed income to become recipients. The policymaker must know incomes in the absence of any actual or contemplated policy intervention.

3. The poverty lines are given by a per capita monthly expenditure of Rs49 in rural areas and Rs57 in urban areas at 1973–74 prices (India's currency is the rupee). The consumer price index for agricultural laborers and the consumer price index for industrial workers are used as deflators for rural and urban areas, respectively.

4. This follows from the fact that the cost of participation is assumed to be linear in income and to vanish at zero income; thus, when all incomes are equally likely, the aggregate cost of participation will be exactly half of the gross benefit.

5. This follows from the fact that the aggregate gain to the poor from the targeted scheme will be $b \cdot F(z) - C(z)$ where $F(z)$ is the proportion of the population who participate, and $C(z)$ is their aggregate cost of participation. The aggregate gain to the poor under universal provisioning is simply $B \cdot F(z)$, where B is the budget per capita.

6. There is a large literature on public employment schemes in India and elsewhere; contributions include Dandekar (1983); Acharya and Panwalkar (1988); Drèze (1990); Drèze and Sen (1989); von Braun, Teklu, and Webb (1992). For a recent survey of the theory and evidence, and a fuller set of references, see Ravallion (1991). Work or training requirements are sometimes also imposed on welfare programs in high-income countries; for example, on the U.S. experience, see Gueron (1990).

7. The poverty gap index, by contrast, is only weakly convex, being neutral to changes in inequality among the poor. All three are additive measures, such that aggregate poverty is simply the population weighted mean of subgroup poverty measures. For references and further discussion of the properties of these measures and alternatives, see Ravallion (1994).

8. The test statistic is asymptotically standard normal. The test allows for the nonindependence of the distributions and for differences in household size and in the sampling rates used by ICRISAT. Appendix 15-2 gives the formula for the test statistic under these conditions.

9. For clarity in the figure, we have cut off the top 10 percent, though our results are valid over the whole range of incomes. On poverty-incidence curves and their uses in policy evaluation, see Ravallion (1994).

10. First-order dominance means that the poverty-incidence curves do not cross each other at any interior point. That is not a tautology here, since forgone incomes have been factored in, and they could (in theory) exceed gross earnings. This could happen if public works participation is motivated by nonpecuniary factors, such as easier or lightly supervised work.

11. Elsewhere, one of the authors has studied the arguments and evidence on these issues and concluded that both the second-round effects and the risk benefits from rural public works schemes in the subcontinent are far from negligible; see Ravallion (1990).

12. Though notice that, even if aggregate forgone income for the poor is zero, and targeting is perfect, the net transfer benefit to the poor as a proportion of the budget disbursement would still be less than the proportion of the population participating (following the same basic reasoning as in our third caveat; it would still be true that the poverty gap would fall more with untargeted transfers, because workfare schemes entail higher nonwage and administrative costs than uniform cash transfer programs.

References

Acharya, Sarthi, and V. G. Panwalkar. 1988. "The Maharashtra Employment Guarantee Scheme: Impacts on Male and Female Labour." Paper prepared for the Population Council, New York.

Atkinson, Anthony B. 1987. "On the Measurement of Poverty." *Econometrica* 55: 749–64.

Besley, Timothy, and Stephen Coate. 1992. "Workfare vs. Welfare: Incentive Arguments for Work Requirements in Poverty Alleviation Programs." *American Economic Review* 82: 249–61.

Besley, Timothy, and Ravi Kanbur. 1993. "Principles of Targeting." In Michael Lipton and Jacques van der Gaag, eds., *Including the Poor*. Washington D.C.: World Bank.

Dandekar, Kumudini. 1983. *Employment Guarantee Scheme: An Employment Opportunity for Women*. Bombay: Orient Longman.

Datt, Gaurav. 1989. "Wage and Employment Determination in Agricultural Labour Markets in India." Ph.D. diss., Australian National University.

Datt, Gaurav, and Martin Ravallion. 1994a. "Income Gains to the Poor from Public Works Employment: Evidence from Two Indian Villages." Living Standards Measurement Study Working Paper 100. World Bank, Washington, D.C.

_____. 1994b. "Transfer Benefits from Public Works Employment: Evidence for Rural India." *Economic Journal* 104: 1346–69.

Drèze, Jean. 1990. "Famine Prevention in India." In Jean Drèze and Amartya Sen, eds., *The Political Economy of Hunger*, vol. 2. Oxford, Eng.: Oxford University Press.

Drèze, Jean, and Amartya Sen. 1989. *Hunger and Public Action*. Oxford, Eng.: Oxford University Press.

Foster, James, Joel Greer, and Eric Thorbecke. 1984. "A Class of Decomposable Poverty Measures." *Econometrica* 52: 761–65.

Government of India. 1992. "Report of the Fourth Quinquennial Survey on Consumer Expenditure: Impact of Selected Poverty Alleviation Programs on the Rural Population." Report 385. National Sample Survey Organization, New Delhi.

Gueron, Judith M. 1990. "Work and Welfare: Lessons on Employment Programs." *Journal of Economic Perspectives* 4: 79–98.

Heckman, James J., and Thomas E. McCurdy. 1980. "A Life Cycle Model of Female Labor Supply." *Review of Economic Studies* 47: 47–74.

Kakwani, Nanak. 1993. "Testing for the Significance of Poverty Differences with Application to Côte d'Ivoire." In Michael Lipton and Jacques van der Gaag, eds., *Including the Poor*. Washington, D.C.: World Bank.

Kanbur, Ravi. 1987. "Measurement and Alleviation of Poverty." IMF *Staff Papers* 34: 60–85.

Lipton, Michael, and Martin Ravallion. 1995. "Poverty and Policy." In Jere Behrman and T. N. Srinivasan, eds., *Handbook of Development Economics*, vol. 3. Amsterdam: North-Holland.

Nichols, Albert L., and Richard J. Zeckhauser. 1982. "Targeting Transfers through Restrictions on Recipients." *American Economic Review (Papers and Proceedings)* 72: 372–77.

Pudney, Stephen. 1989. *Modelling Individual Choice: The Econometrics of Corners, Kinks, and Holes*. Oxford, Eng.: Blackwell.

Ravallion, Martin. 1990. "Market Responses to Anti-Hunger Policies: Wages, Prices, and Employment." In Jean Drèze and Amartya Sen, eds., *The Political Economy of Hunger*, vol. 2. Oxford, Eng.: Oxford University Press.

———. 1991. "Reaching the Rural Poor through Public Employment: Arguments, Evidence, and Lessons from South Asia." *World Bank Research Observer* 6: 153–75.

———. 1993. "Poverty Alleviation through Regional Targeting: A Case Study for Indonesia." In Avishay Braverman, Karla R. Hoff, and Joseph E. Stiglitz, eds., *The Economics of Rural Organization*. Oxford, Eng.: Oxford University Press.

———. 1994. *Poverty Comparisons*. Fundamentals in Pure and Applied Economics, vol. 56. Chur, Switzerland: Harwood Academic Press.

Ravallion, Martin, and Kalvin Chao. 1989. "Targeted Policies for Poverty Alleviation under Imperfect Information: Algorithms and Applications." *Journal of Policy Modeling* 11: 213–24.

Ravallion, Martin, Gaurav Datt, and Shubham Chaudhuri. 1993. "Does Maharashtra's 'Employment Guarantee Scheme' Guarantee Employment?" *Economic Development and Cultural Change* 41: 251–76.

Roberts, Kevin. 1984. "The Theoretical Limits to Redistribution." *Review of Economic Studies* 51: 177–95.

Sen, Amartya. 1979. "Personal Utilities and Public Judgements: Or What's Wrong with Welfare Economics?" *Economic Journal* 89: 537–58.

Smith, Richard J., and Richard W. Blundell. 1986. "An Exogeneity Test for a Simultaneous Equation Tobit Model with Application to Labor Supply." *Econometrica* 54: 679–86.

von Braun, Joachim, Tesfaye Teklu, and Patrick Webb. 1992. "Labour-Intensive Public Works for Food Security in Africa: Past Experience and Future Potential." *International Labour Review* 131: 19–34.

Walker, T. S., and J. G. Ryan. 1990. *Village and Household Economies in India's Semi-Arid Tropics*. Baltimore, Md.: Johns Hopkins University Press.

VII Comparing Instruments

The chapters in part VII present analyses that emphasize comparisons across a number of dimensions. In chapter 16 Grosh compares the administrative costs and incidence of a large number of targeted programs in Latin America, examining the variations and similarities between programs, relying on different targeting instruments. Next, Milanovic analyzes the distributional impact of public transfers, both in cash and in kind, in five East European countries and in Russia and contrasts results with those obtained for Western high-income economies. Hammer, Nabi, and Cercone analyze distributional aspects of public transfers in Malaysia, comparing health and education spending and using regression analysis to complement their incidence work (chapter 18). And in chapter 19, Appleton and Collier evaluate the arguments for gender targeting of public spending and consider the relative advantages and disadvantages of targeting cash versus in-kind transfers to females.

Several chapters in this volume have emphasized the costs of finely targeting public programs, particularly through means testing (see, for example, chapters 2, 3, and 13). Indeed, a view common to much of the targeting literature is that as efforts to increase the accuracy of targeting are deployed, certain costs (relating to administration, incentive effects, costs of participation to the poor, and political economy effects) tend to escalate. Grosh tests the validity of this assumption by examining the correlations between a program's targeting mechanism, administrative costs, and targeting accuracy (chapter 16). Having amassed an impressive amount of empirical evidence on thirty social sector programs in Latin America, she attempts to ascertain which targeting mechanisms provide the best results in terms of concentrating benefits on the poor and what administrative costs are associated with these mechanisms.

The study provides a good example of a popular approach to evaluation. Similar to Cornia and Stewart (chapter 13), Grosh is concerned with targeting outcomes. Ideally, these are defined to include both effective exclusion of the nonpoor and adequate coverage of the needy population. However, data limitations mean that Grosh is unable to focus on the latter (type I errors). In her analysis, targeting outcomes are judged solely on the basis of the share of poor households in the beneficiary group. The message (made elsewhere in this book) that concentration of benefits on the poor does not ensure the greatest impact on poverty should be kept in mind.

Grosh's empirical results are intriguing and at odds with much of the literature, although the latter is primarily theoretical. Her review of Latin American experience uncovers little correlation between a program's administrative costs and its incidence. Her analysis also suggests that generalizations about the targeting accuracy and administrative burdens associated with various types of targeting mechanisms may not always hold, despite their intuitive logic. For instance, the means-tested programs reviewed here neither achieve substantially greater concentration of benefits on the poor nor entail higher administrative costs relative to the programs using geographic or self-targeting. The chapter highlights the rich possibilities for combining targeting mechanisms and for adapting a single mechanism to the particular features of the policy environment.

The programs reviewed vary in important respects, including their scale, the type and level of benefit provided, the quality of program management, and the policy setting. This study examines key questions of interest and contains more information than has previously been available on targeted programs in Latin America. However, difficulties in calculating the administrative and targeting costs with accuracy, and identically across programs, may introduce a degree of imprecision into the analysis. We may have to wait for more controlled experiments for a final word on these issues.

Chapter 17 by Milanovic also incorporates calculations made by other researchers and compares transfer programs and distributional consequences across countries. The focus here is on Eastern Europe and Russia. The programs analyzed are generally universal rather than explicitly targeted, and the distributional information is presented in the form of a single summary statistic—the concentration coefficient— rather than in the standard benefit incidence format. The analysis centers on cross-country comparisons.

Milanovic examines the social transfer systems in Eastern Europe and Russia during the period just before the start of the economic transition. He describes and compares the magnitude and distribution of various kinds of cash transfers, as well as that of health and education spending. His analysis suggests that in the aggregate, cash transfers are distributed almost equally per capita. Transfers through public health care also have a fairly flat distribution, while those from education tend to have a more pro-poor incidence.

The chapter underscores the differences between market and socialist economies in the role and structure of social transfers; in the former, cash transfers tend to be much more directed to the poor, and health spending tends to be more pro-poor than education spending. Moreover, some categories of public transfers prominent in market economies, such as unemployment benefits and social assistance, in general did not exist in Eastern Europe and Russia prior to the transition. The critical role played by the underlying policy environment in determining the appropriate characteristics of social transfer systems is highlighted.

Milanovic's use of concentration coefficients to capture the degree of progressivity in public programs differentiates his study from others we have discussed. Concentration coefficients provide a convenient snapshot of the distribution of program benefits and a way to facilitate cross-country comparisons. However, a single number also implies a loss of the richer description of benefit distribution found in an incidence table.

In chapter 18, Hammer and his coauthors closely analyze Malaysia's tremendous achievements in the health and education sectors and how the distribution of the sectors' benefits has evolved over time. Recourse to Meerman's study of public spending incidence in 1974 allows them to compare the effects of the government's New Economic Policy (NEP) at early and advanced stages of the policy's implementation. Introduced in the early 1970s, the NEP deliberately targeted resources to the economically disadvantaged Malays. The authors speculate that, over time, the policy's performance must have declined as a result of its very success: the remaining poor may be too hard to reach, and racially targeted policies work only as long as the target race remains disadvantaged.

An interesting feature of this study is its use of both incidence and regression analysis to examine the distribution of public expenditures. For example, using regression analysis, Hammer, Nabi, and Cercone determine that, even when controlling for race, location, and state, poor regions receive a larger share of public transfers to primary education than better-off regions and the poor within each region capture the lion's share of those benefits. The distribution of public spending is also illuminated by an analysis of state-level data that shows how allocations to health and education, and immunization and safe water coverage, vary according to the state's per capita income.

The study is also distinguished by its dual emphasis on the distribution of public expenditures and their impact on outcomes. The effect of NEP policies on health and education outcomes is examined using regression analysis with state-level panel data. The chapter reminds us of the importance of focusing government spending on those services where the government has an advantage over the private sector in provision. It also underlines the significance of the interplay between public and private sector options for the progressivity of spending on health and education, as this determines the extent to which the better-off opt out of public provision.

Contrary to the authors' expectations, we learn that the incidence of public health and education spending became more pro-poor over the period. Still, the study's incidence results are broadly consistent with those for other developing countries.

In part VII's final chapter, Appleton and Collier evaluate the case for targeting government transfers to females. They argue that targeting transfers on the basis of an underlying cause of disadvantage rather than on low income has some appeal, especially in developing countries. In this regard, the views expressed here are rather congruent with those espoused by Sen in chapter 2.

Appleton and Collier must first establish whether female gender is a significant source of disadvantage in developing countries. A useful and extensive survey of existing evidence leads them to conclude that in terms of food consumption and health indicators the evidence is fairly strong that females in South Asia are handicapped, although this bias is not apparent in other regions. However, with regard to educational opportunities and attainment, a widespread pattern of female disadvantage is evident across the developing world. This is consistent with the empirical studies on education presented in chapters 7 and 8, which suggest that girls in Peru and Pakistan have fewer educational opportunities and receive a smaller proportion of government spending on education than do boys.

The authors argue that there may also be a second, equally compelling reason for gender targeting. If positive externalities flow from the focus of public transfers on women, then such indirect benefits may be sufficient to justify gender targeting. The considerable body of evidence that suggests that significant externalities are associated with women's better health and education is reviewed.

Appleton and Collier then consider whether cash or in-kind transfers —specifically educational subsidies—are the better vehicle for gender targeting. Citing a variety of reasons, including the more limited scope for other household members to appropriate in-kind benefits, the chapter emphasizes the superiority of targeting education services rather than cash transfers to females. Thus in another important respect, chapter 19 converges with Sen's analysis, which also underlines the limited fungibility of benefits from publicly provided health care and education programs relative to cash transfers. Despite having established a clear case of female deprivation and opportunities for remedying the situation, Appleton and Collier conclude their chapter by noting that gender alone is likely to be a rather blunt policy tool for targeting the disadvantaged. Combining gender with other correlates of poverty, even when targeting in-kind transfers, can help to focus benefits more directly on the most disadvantaged.

16

Toward Quantifying the Trade-off: Administrative Costs and Incidence in Targeted Programs in Latin America

Margaret E. Grosh

Whether, how, and how much to target social services or subsidies to the poor depend on balancing the benefits and costs in a given set of circumstances. The benefit of targeting is that it can concentrate expenditures allocated to poverty-alleviation or social programs on the persons who need them most. In theory, this can save money and improve program efficiency. Potential costs consist of the administrative costs of identifying beneficiaries, economic losses due to disincentive effects, costs to the poor of participating, and loss of political support for the program. It is often assumed that, as the accuracy of targeting and hence the benefits increase, the associated costs increase as well (see Besley and Kanbur 1993 for a clear exposition of the issues).

This study is an attempt to quantify the tradeoff between the administrative costs of targeting and the targeting outcomes based on an empirical review of program experience in Latin America. It asks two questions: Which targeting mechanisms provide the best targeting outcomes? What are their administrative costs?

Before going further, it is important to establish what is meant in this chapter by targeting. Targeting means delivering a good or service only to a select group of individuals. In economics, we are most often concerned with delivering a subsidy (either in cash or in kind) to the

This chapter is drawn from Grosh (1994), which also includes detailed consideration of the design options, managerial requirements, and implementation experience of the programs reviewed here. In addition to the many who contributed to the larger study from which this article was drawn, I would like to thank Judy Baker, Timothy Besley, Kimberly Nead, and Dominique van de Walle for their helpful suggestions and discussion. Maria Eugenia Quintero and Barbara Diallo did the document processing and layout. Fiona Mackintosh served as editor. The findings, interpretations, and conclusions expressed in this chapter are entirely those of the author. They do not necessarily represent the views of the World Bank, its executive directors, or the countries they represent.

poor. In health, we may target persons who are ill or who are at risk of becoming ill. Targeting carries with it the idea that some group of individuals should be excluded from receiving the program benefit.

The choice and identification of persons in the target group can be thought of separately from the actual delivery of the service to them. Consider a targeted school lunch program. The targeting aspect of the program is choosing which individuals should receive the free lunch and which should be excluded. The service delivery aspect of the program includes decisions about how many calories to provide in each lunch, what food to buy, and how to hire cooks. Conceptually, the distinction is fairly clear, though, in practice, decisions about one aspect often have implications for another. Since targeting is only one aspect of a social program, judging the success or failure of targeting is not equivalent to making judgments about the program as a whole. A school lunch program may choose the right children to feed, but if it serves them expensive foods or too few calories, it will not be cost-effective.

The organization of this chapter is as follows. The first section describes the taxonomy of targeting mechanisms used in the study, followed by a section describing the study's information sources and methods. The subsequent two sections report the incidence and administrative cost results. The next section explores the relationship between the two. And finally, the conclusion contains a more qualitative discussion of the results and their implications.

An Administrative Taxonomy of Targeting Mechanisms

There is a wide variety of ways to target social services to the poor. In order to streamline the discussion, we group them here according to the basic administrative requirement of each mechanism:

(a) *Individual assessment mechanisms* require program managers to decide whether or not to accept individual applicants on the basis of various criteria, such as means tests, gender of the household head, or nutritional status of the applicant.

(b) *Group (or geographic) targeting mechanisms* grant eligibility to groups of candidates who share some easily identifiable characteristic. In practice, many such programs use some form of geographic characteristic. School lunch programs that operate only in schools in poor areas and programs that allot benefits to states, municipalities, or neighborhoods based on their average level of welfare are examples.

(c) *Self-targeting mechanisms* rely on the individual decision of a potential candidate to participate or not. The service or program is theoretically available to all but is designed in such a way as to discour-

Table 16-1. A Taxonomy of Targeting Mechanisms

Individual assessment	Group characteristic	Self-targeted
Means test	Students in uniform	Weaning food vs. milk
Social worker	Armed forces	Employment programs
evaluation	Geographic area, by	Time contribution
Proxy means test	school, by state, by	Use of public health
Gender of household	municipality, by	services
head	neighborhood	
Nutritional status		
Nutritional risk		

age the nonpoor from using it. Time costs, work requirements, stigma, or a low-quality service or product are the principal devices used to encourage self-targeting.

Within each category in the taxonomy of targeting mechanisms, there are several options. The most common are listed in table 16-1.

Sometimes policymakers decide not to target, but rather to provide services to all (examples include general food subsidies, primary education, and health care). Such services are often called universal. Primary education, for example, is usually intended to benefit all children. Since features that cause a service to be self-targeting may exist independently of any explicit design decision, the line between self-targeted services and universal services can sometimes be fuzzy. Public health care, for example, is often intended to be universal, but because it may lack quality or amenities, the nonpoor often opt to use private health care. Thus, an argument could be made that public health care is a self-targeted rather than a universal service, even though the low quality of public health services is rarely intentional or intended to induce self-targeting. Instead, it results from low budgets, inappropriate policies, or inadequate management. In this chapter, we consider public health and education to be "universal" services.

There are, of course, other ways of grouping targeting mechanisms. Besley and Kanbur (1993), for example, contrast an unrealized ideal of perfect targeting with indicator targeting and self-targeting (Besley 1989 uses the term "statistical targeting" rather than indicator targeting). Their indicator targeting class is based on the aim of finding an indicator that is less costly to identify than income but that is correlated with it. They use a household's region or the age distribution of its members as examples. Conceptually, the methods classified here under individual and group assessment fit under the rubric of indicator targeting.[1] In this chapter, it is appropriate to subdivide the indicator class of targeting mechanisms according to the administrative implications of how the various indicators would be used, since the topic of the chapter is the administrative costs of targeting schemes in practice.

Regardless of what taxonomy one chooses to use, there are two complications in categorizing real-life programs: many programs explicitly use more than one targeting mechanism, and all programs implicitly use more than one targeting mechanism. The Honduran Bono Madre Jefe de Familia program illustrates several explicit mechanisms. It is targeted to children in grades one to three (group) in selected poor areas (geographic) from female-headed households (individual assessment) that pass a means test (individual assessment).

The final incidence of every program depends on two implicit factors—the nature of the benefit and the decision of each individual about whether or not to participate—in addition to the effects of any explicit targeting mechanisms. For example, since university students tend to be drawn largely from the upper and middle classes, the potential beneficiaries of programs that are linked to university attendance are likely to be wealthy, whereas users of public primary education services are usually poorer than average. Thus programs associated with universities tend to have regressive incidence, while programs associated with primary schools tend to have more progressive incidence. Furthermore, almost all programs require beneficiaries to take some action to apply for or to collect the benefits. Some eligible persons will choose not to do so, judging the probable costs of participation to exceed the probable benefit. Therefore, it is necessary to take into account the effects that the nature of the benefit and individuals' decisions for or against participating have in determining who is in the applicant pool for a program before evaluating the additional effect that a formal screening mechanism will have in sorting the poor from the nonpoor.

The Case Studies

This chapter draws on information about thirty social sector programs in eleven countries in Latin America. Of these programs, eight deliver food commodities or subsidies, three deliver school lunches, five deliver food stamps, three deliver free or reduced-cost health services or health insurance, three deliver student loans or fee waivers, three deliver cash, two provide jobs, two provide day care, and one provides mortgages. Most have national coverage, and most are government programs, though a few are run by nongovernmental organizations. About half have either just been established or have been substantially reformed in the last five years. Several of the new programs were specifically motivated by increases in poverty in the 1980s or by the need to mitigate the social costs of macroeconomic adjustment programs. Seventeen of the programs use individual assessment mechanisms, seven use group or geographic mechanisms, and six are self-targeted. Table 16-2 provides a brief guide to the programs included.

The programs were selected for study on the basis of three criteria. First, programs that represent a mix of targeting mechanisms and benefit types were sought. Second, programs for which incidence information is available were given priority, and third, programs for which a case study could be produced at low cost were preferred. While the resulting mix of case studies is neither scientific nor exhaustive, it is certainly useful. To our knowledge, this is the most complete compilation of comparable quantitative information that is currently available.

The Methodology

An assumption underlying this work is that targeting a food supplement program is much the same as targeting a cash transfer program or an education program. All of these interventions have an element of income transfer that should be directed to the poor. All of these programs are more effective if their benefits are concentrated on the persons who need them most. All must balance improvements in targeting outcomes against the costs of targeting. And regardless of the sector in which the intervention is made, the available targeting options are similar.

There are, of course, ways in which targeting differs depending on the type of intervention. Perhaps most important, the target group itself may differ. A basic health intervention may have as the target group individuals who are sick. A safety net program may aim to reach individuals who are poor. A program with hybrid objectives may aim to reach individuals among the poor who are sick. In evaluating programs, for maximum accuracy, it is important to distinguish clearly whether they are aimed at the sick, the vulnerable poor, or the vulnerable poor who are sick (with obvious parallels for nutrition and education).

This study assumes that all the programs are aimed generally at the poor. Although not completely accurate, this assumption is plausible because poor nutrition, poor health, and low education are often correlated with poverty. Moreover, persons who are wealthy and sick have recourse to private health care providers. Given governments' limited financial and managerial capacity, serving the needs of the wealthy is not the highest priority for the public sector.

Quantifying Administrative Costs

This chapter distinguishes two levels of administrative costs that have a bearing on the targeting of services. An attempt is made in the case studies to separate them out. Total administrative costs are defined to

Table 16-2. Inventory of Programs

Country and program name	Type of program benefit	Number of beneficiaries per year	Scope	Total annual cost per beneficiary (U.S. dollars)	Targeting mechanism
Belize					
Belize hospital fee waivers	Hospital fee waivers	—	National	—	Social worker evaluation
Bolivia					
Bolivia Emergency Social Fund (ESF)	Employment	48,000 person-months per year	National	—	Self-selection (by employment)
Chile					
Pensiones Asistenciales (CAS-PASIS; pension assistance program)	Cash transfer	292,000	National	32	Proxy means test
Programa de Alimentación Escolar (PAE; school feeding program)	School lunch	570,000	National	75	Geographic (by school)
Programas Especiales de Empleo (PEM and POIH; special employment programs)	Employment	117,000	National	170–380	Self-selection (by employment)
Programa Nacional de Alimentación Complementaria (PNAC; national food supplement program)	Food supplement	1,240,000	National	40	Self-selection (by use of health services)
Subsidio Único Familiar (CAS-SUF; unified family subsidy)	Cash transfer	887,000	National	39	Proxy means test
Viviendas-Básicas (CAS; basic housing program)	Cash transfer (mortgage)	20,500	National	4,100	Proxy means test
Colombia					
Colombia Institute of Credit and Training/Abroad (ICETEX)	Student loan	48,000	National	700	Means test

(Table continues on the following page.)

Table 16-2 (continued)

Country and program name	Type of program benefit	Number of beneficiaries per year	Scope	Total annual cost per beneficiary (U.S. dollars)	Targeting mechanism
Costa Rica					
Becas Universidad de Costa Rica (scholarships at the University of Costa Rica)	University tuition waivers	25,000	University of Costa Rica	88	Proxy means test
Centros de Nutrición (CEN/CENAI; food nutrition centers)	Day care, food supplement	58,000	National	265	Nutritional risk
Comedores Escolares (school lunch program)	School lunch	450,000	National	22	Geographic (by school)
Pensiones no Contributivas (noncontributory pensions)	Cash transfer	74,000	National	350	Social worker evaluation
Programa de Asegurados por Cuenta del Estado (state-sponsored health insurance)	Free health insurance	299,000	National	132	Social worker evaluation
Dominican Republic					
Hospital fee waivers	Hospital fee waivers	—	Selected hospitals	—	Social worker evaluation
Proyecto Materno-Infantil (PROMI; mother-child project)	Maternal and child health	36,000	3 rural regions	61	Nutritional risk
Honduras					
Bono de Madre Jefe de Familia (BMJF; food stamps for female-headed households)	Food stamps	125,000	9 states	40	Means test
Bono Materno-Infantil (BMI; food stamps for mothers and infants)	Food stamps	60,000	3 health regions	50	Self-selection (by use of health services)

Jamaica					
Food stamp program (means tested)	Food stamps	200,000	National	55	Means test
Food stamp program (health services)	Food stamps	200,000	National	40	Self-selection (by use of health services)
Student loan program	Student loan	2,520	National	784	Means test
Nutribun program	School feeding	153,000	National	37	Geographic (by school)
Mexico					
Leche Industrializada Compañía Nacional de Subsistencias Populares (LICONSA; national subsidized milk program)	Subsidized milk ration	10,000,000	National (urban)	20	Means test and nutritional risk
Tortivales	Free tortilla ration	13,500,000	National (urban)	26	Means test
Peru					
Comedores Populares (soup kitchens)	Communal soup kitchen	2,450,000	National (urban)	23	Geographic (by neighborhood)
Programa de Alimentación y Nutrición para Familias de Alto Riesgo (PANFAR; nutrition and feeding program for high-risk families)	Food supplement	513,000		17	Nutritional risk
Vaso de Leche (Glass of Milk program)	Food supplement	2,900,000	National	9	Geographic (by neighborhood)
Venezuela					
Programa Beca Alimentaria (food scholarship program)	Food stamp	2,300,000	National	175	Geographic (by school)
Programa Hogares de Cuidado Diario (day care program)	Day care	106,000	National	565	Geographic (by neighborhood)
Programa Alimentario Materno Infantil (PAMI; maternal child feeding program)	Food supplement	500,000	National	180	Self-selection (by use of health services)

include all costs necessary to *deliver* the targeted benefit. Only part of these, which we call targeting costs, are incurred during the screening process that determines *who* benefits. Consider, for example, a means-tested welfare program. The time that a social worker spends interviewing the client to determine whether she or he is eligible is the cost of targeting. The time and equipment needed to keep track of the beneficiaries once enrolled, to write checks for them, and to distribute the checks are part of the general administration of the program and are not strictly related to its targeting.

Targeting Outcomes

To determine the extent to which a program succeeds in avoiding giving benefits to persons who are not needy, we calculate incidence from household survey data by counting the frequency with which beneficiary households fall in each quintile of the welfare distribution.[2] In the tradition of Meerman (1979) and Selowsky (1979), we assume that the full value of the benefit remains with the person who receives it.[3] In some of the case studies, the incidence numbers are the result of original calculations by the case study authors, and, in others, the numbers are taken from published materials. In most of the case studies, household-based quintiles are used, with households ranked on the basis of household per capita income (or consumption). The exceptions are noted in table 16-3. The incidence estimates come from nationally representative household surveys. The welfare variable is usually labor income. The rankings are post-intervention.[4]

In the following discussion, the bottom two quintiles as seen in table 16-3 are used as an approximate shorthand for the poor. Generally, our results would be the same if only the poorest quintile were used. To determine whether a program satisfactorily reaches the needy (avoids errors of exclusion), we originally intended to use participation rates, but we decided against doing so for two reasons. First, they were available only for a very few programs so that it was not possible to determine any general trends. Second, it was apparent in several of the cases for which participation rates were available that they did not measure the success or failure of the targeting mechanism in reaching the target group per se. Rather they tended to be complicated by administrative idiosyncrasies peculiar to each program and would have provided misleading conclusions about the risks of the targeting mechanism in general. The inability to study errors of exclusion was the major disappointment in this research.

Let us illustrate this problem for programs in which all pregnant/lactating women and children under the age of five who use public health services are eligible. In such programs, the most serious errors of exclusion may result if the poorest or most malnourished do not

Table 16-3. Administrative Costs and Incidence Outcome, by Targeting Mechanism

	Administrative costs				Incidence[a] (percentage of beneficiary households, by quintile)				
	Total		Targeting costs only						
Targeting mechanism	Percentage of total costs	Dollars per beneficiary per year	Percentage of total costs	Dollars per beneficiary per year	Poor 1	2	3	4	Rich 5
Individual assessment									
Means test									
Colombia—student loan[b]	21	148	—	—		48		23	29
Honduras—BMIF	12	4.50	—	—	15	31	17	23	14
Jamaica—student loan[c]	30	332	3.6	40	47	29	15	6	3
Jamaica—food stamps	10[d]	4	—	—	—	—	—	—	—
Mexico—LICONSA	28.5	5.75	—	—	—	—	—	—	—
Mexico—Tortivales	12	3.12	—	—		64[e]		36	
Social worker evaluation									
Belize—hospital fee waivers	0.4	0.57	—	—	—	—	—	—	—
Costa Rica—health insurance	5.0	6.50	1.0	1.30	55	19	13	9	5
Costa Rica—pension	3.5	12.50	0.4	1.36	39	20	15	15	11
Dominican Republic—hospital fee waivers	3.6	0.39	3.2	0.35	—	—	—	—	—
Proxy means test									
Chile—CAS, basic housing	—	—	0.1	5	28	22	20	18	12
Chile—CAS-PASIS, pension assistance	—	—	1.4	5	50	23	17	7	3
Chile—CAS-SUF, unified family subsidies	—	—	1.6	5	57	26	12	4	2
Costa Rica—university tuition waivers	16	14	8	7	—	—	—	—	—
Nutritional risk									
Costa Rica—CEN/CENAI, day care	9	23.16	1.6	4.17	44	26	16	12	3
Costa Rica—CEN/CENAI, food packets	—	—	—	—	—	—	—	—	—
Dominican Republic—PROMI, food supplements	12.3	7.50	—	—	56	23	14	8	0
Peru—PANFAR, food supplements	22	3.62	4.2	0.72	—	100			—

(Table continues on the following page.)

Table 16-3 (continued)

| | Administrative costs | | | | Incidence[a] (percentage of beneficiary households, by quintile) | | | | |
| | Total | | Targeting costs only | | | | | | |
Targeting mechanism	Percentage of total costs	Dollars per beneficiary per year	Percentage of total costs	Dollars per beneficiary per year	Poor 1	2	3	4	Rich 5
Geographic area									
By neighborhood									
Peru—Glass of Milk	4.2	0.38	1.0	0.09	42	30	20	6	3
Peru—Soup kitchens									
Comedores—CARITAS	8.9	1.95	1.0	0.23	—	—	—	—	—
Comedores—PRODIA	13.6	3.82	0.7	0.19	—	—	—	—	—
Comedores—CARITAS and Comedores—PRODIA					37[f]	←——— 56 ———→		←— 7	—
Venezuela—day care centers	16.1	86.00	2.1	11.2	—	—	—	—	—
By school									
Chile—school feeding	5	3.70	0.0	0.01	53	26	12	6	3
Costa Rica—school lunch	—	—	0.4	0.08	33	29	20	12	6
Jamaica—Nutribuns	6.8	2.50	—	—	44	28	16	9	3
Venezuela—food scholarship	4.0	6.92	—	—	—	—	—	—	—

460

Self-selection

Employment programs—work requirements

Bolivia—ESF[g]	3.5	8.50	—	—	—	31	46	19	4	0
Chile—special employment programs	—	—	—	—	—	51[h]	20	13	9	3
Use of health services										
Chile—PNAC, food supplement	6[i]	7.60	—	—	41	28	18	10	3	
Honduras—maternal-child health, food stamps	6[i]	6.92	—	—	—	—	—	—		
Jamaica—maternal-child health, food stamps	10[d]	4	—	—	—	—	—	—		
Venezuela—food supplement	3[j]	5.35	—	—	44	31	18	5	2	

— Not available.

a. Unless otherwise noted, the quintiles are for households, using post-intervention per capita household income (or consumption) as the welfare measure.

b. Quintiles are based on the individual incomes of persons in the working population.

c. Quintiles are for total household consumption.

d. Administrative costs for the means tested and the maternal-child health parts of the program are not separable.

e. Figures are for the poor, who make up one-third of households. Here, this has been approximated by the bottom two deciles.

f. 37 percent of benefits go to the extremely poor (bottom 22 percent of the population); 93 percent of benefits go to the critically poor (bottom 54 percent of the population). By subtraction, about 56 percent of benefits go to the second and third quintiles.

g. Quintiles are based on the individual primary earnings of employed males in urban areas.

h. The CASEN survey provides figures for all employment programs aggregated. About half the workers were in the POJH, about 30 percent in the PEM, and the rest in the many smaller programs.

i. Does not include time of medical staff involved in growth monitoring (Chile, Honduras) and paperwork (Honduras). If medical time is valued, administrative costs would be 19 percent in Chile and 15 percent in Honduras.

j. Does not include medical time; does include time of the distribution clerk.

use the preventive health care system. This could be said to be an "inherent" problem in targeting food or income supplements through health systems. How the program registers beneficiaries and distributes the benefits among individuals who do come to clinics also affects the participation rates, since this affects how potential beneficiaries judge whether or not the benefit outweighs the costs of participating in the program. These administrative features can be altered relatively easily so that these errors of exclusion are less inherent and are less likely to lead to the systematic exclusion of the neediest candidates than in the case of errors caused by lack of access to clinics.

The Jamaican maternal-child food stamp program is a case where low participation rates stem from administrative problems rather than from problems in the coverage of the health care system.[5] Malnourished children not receiving food stamps have about the same level of contact with the public health system as do all children under the age of five in Jamaica.[6] Administrative problems in the registration of maternal-child clients and distribution of food stamps to them occur from time to time, however, with noticeable effects on participation rates (see Anderson 1993 for discussion). Since the particular difficulties arising from the program's administration in Jamaica are not necessarily present in other countries where food rations or stamps are also targeted through maternal-child clinics, drawing general inferences about errors of exclusion from this program might be misleading.[7]

Methodological Limitations

Although this study provides much more information on the magnitude of the administrative costs and the incidence obtained in targeting social programs than was previously available, the data set has limitations. These must be borne in mind when assessing the policy implications of the findings. In any future work, it will be important to overcome some of the drawbacks that we have faced.

The biggest problem is *the imprecision with which we are able to calculate administrative costs*. This results largely from the fact that complete, separate budget information is not available for many programs.[8] A second problem is that it is often difficult to separate out the costs of screening potential beneficiaries (the targeting costs) from general administrative costs. Furthermore, it is sometimes not conceptually clear whether specific actions are costs of targeting or whether they are costs of service provision. Despite the care and diligence of the case study authors, the cost figures are only approximate. Where a cost of $5 is shown, another analyst with different informants or judgments might easily come up with an estimate of $3 or $8.[9] Nevertheless, the estimate that costs are in the order of $5, rather than $50 or $100, is probably accurate.

Let us illustrate the sensitivity of our results to these choices in the case of food supplement or food coupon programs that are self-targeted through the use of health services. These programs often require the participants to get regular physical checkups. Should we count the time spent by the medical staff on these checkups as part of the cost of the food program or as part of the underlying health service? In the case of the Chilean PNAC (Programa Nacional de Alimentación Complementaria), it is probably fair not to count it as a cost of the targeted food program, as the medical staff spend most of their time with participants just providing medical care, while other staff undertake the program paperwork and commodity distribution. In the case of the Honduran BMI (Bono Materno-Infantil), however, the nurses probably spend at least as much of their time with participants on paperwork related to food stamps as on medical care. In Jamaica and Venezuela, the program duties are divided up in a way that makes it easier to exclude medical time. If the time costs of medical staff are counted in the Chilean and Honduran programs, the mean share of administrative costs as a percentage of total program costs is 10 percent for programs that are self-targeted through the use of the health care system.[10] If medical time is not included in either case, administrative costs average 6 percent for this category. If they are included for Honduras but not Chile, the mean is 7.5 percent. We have chosen not to include the costs of medical staff time in our results, though the decision is clearly debatable.

The next issue is that, in the interest of getting a broad overview of targeting experience, *we have compared many programs of different scales, providing a wide variety of kinds and levels of benefits and from countries with different poverty levels and institutional capacities.* Holding all these factors approximately constant and making allowances for varying local prices would give a more precise estimate of the effect of differences among the targeting mechanisms themselves. It is not feasible, however, to hold so many features approximately constant and get results that could be generalized to apply to a wide variety of settings. In this study, we therefore stress breadth of coverage rather than limit ourselves to fewer, more similar cases.

If the confounding factors such as scale, type, and level of benefit are not correlated with the main variables of interest—administrative costs, targeting outcomes, and targeting mechanisms—then our conclusions regarding the latter factors are valid. We bore this in mind in selecting the case studies, and we believe we have been largely successful in avoiding confounding correlations.

A further issue is that *many programs explicitly use more than one targeting mechanism.* In such cases, the programs were placed in the category that seemed likely to have the most influence on the targeting outcome and administrative costs. These decisions were often based on qualitative information and thus a degree of subjectivity could not be avoided. To consider all the permutations found would have fragmented the analysis into too many groups to be useful in exposition here (in Grosh 1994, the book from which this chapter is drawn, more detailed comparisons are done in smaller subsets).

For example, all children under the age of five who use public health services are eligible for the Chilean PNAC food supplements. In practice, their mothers must enroll them, bring them in for regular checkups, and queue for the ration. In the sense that individuals who are eligible can choose whether or not to participate, the program is self-targeted. All public clinics participate in the program, but as more public clinics are located in poor areas than in nonpoor areas, the clinics themselves and the PNAC that relies on them are, to that extent, geographically targeted. Moreover, the level of benefit is differentiated according to nutritional risk, which is an individual assessment mechanism. We have classified the PNAC as a self-targeted program, because that seems to be the program's key targeting mechanism.

A last issue concerns *the variation in how the incidence results are calculated*. Most of the results reported here are taken from literature that is not sufficiently explicit about how the calculations were done. Most appear to be comparable, but there may be hidden surprises. We also made a conscious decision to compare some numbers that were calculated using slightly varying methods, as noted in table 16-3.

We feel confident that our findings on the ranges for the incidence and the administrative costs of the targeted programs are robust despite the shortcomings in the data. The correlation between the screening costs and the incidence outcomes may, however, be sensitive to these shortcomings. Our confidence in the robustness of the conclusions is based on having reworked the details within many of the case studies with alternate assumptions or methods and on having recalculated the medians and ranges presented numerous times as the number of case studies covered, the numbers they contained, and their classification by targeting mechanism evolved during the course of the study.

Incidence

Table 16-3 contains the comparative information for each program in detail. Because the table is somewhat unwieldy, subsets of the information it contains are drawn out in medians and ranges and are shown in graphs in the following section. The medians are calculated by ranking the programs by each criterion discussed and then taking the middle program. This avoids giving outliers undue influence. Readers who are dissatisfied with the summary comparison may refer to table 16-3, using appendix 16-1 as a guide to which programs are included in each graph.

Figure 16-1. Share of Benefits Accruing to Poorest 40 Percent, by Sector

Percent

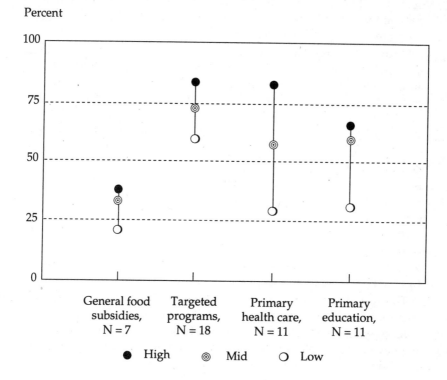

General food subsidies, N = 7   Targeted programs, N = 18   Primary health care, N = 11   Primary education, N = 11

● High   ◎ Mid   ○ Low

Three of the programs reviewed in the text have design features that constrain their ability to reach the poor: two are student loan programs (in Colombia and Jamaica) and one is a housing program with a down payment requirement (in Chile). Because these features put them in a different class of program from the others reviewed here, they are excluded from the general summary comparisons in the text. Instead, they are briefly examined separately following the discussion of the bulk of the case studies.

Targeted versus Untargeted Interventions

We begin by comparing the benefit incidence of the targeted programs with that of several types of untargeted interventions—food subsidies, primary health care, and primary education.[11] As can be seen from figure 16-1, targeted programs have much more progressive incidence than general food price subsidies. The share of the benefits of the least regressive food price subsidy accruing to the poorest 40 percent of households is 37 percent. For the least progressive of the targeted programs, 59 percent of the benefits accrue to this group. The medians, of course, diverge even more. On average, 33 percent of the benefits of general food subsidies go to the poorest two quintiles. For the targeted programs, the figure is 72 percent.

On average, targeted programs also have more progressive incidence than public primary health and public primary education services, although there is a good deal of overlap in the ranges. The most progressive of the targeted programs gives 83 percent of benefits to the poorest two quintiles. For public primary health services, in the most progressive case, 82 percent of benefits accrue to that group. For public primary education, in the most progressive case, 65 percent of services are delivered to the poorest quintiles. For the median results, the ranking is clearer. The median share of benefits going to the poorest two quintiles is 72 percent for targeted programs. For public primary health care, it is 57 percent, and for public primary education, it is 59 percent. In the least progressive cases, the ranking is even clearer. In the case of the targeted programs, 59 percent of the benefits go to the poorest 40 percent of the population; in the case of public health services, the figure is 29 percent; and in public primary education, it is 31 percent.

The fact that targeted programs have more progressive incidence than universal services is confirmed in country-by-country comparisons (see figure 16-2). In every one of the five countries for which we have comparable information, the median incidence for targeted programs is more progressive than that for primary health and primary education programs.

Many of the targeted programs that we studied are food, food stamp, or cash transfer programs that have broadly the same goals (income transfer, food security, or improvements in nutrition) as the general food subsidies but much better incidence. Thus, a targeted program may be a viable option for replacing a general price subsidy, though of course this depends on an assessment of its other important characteristics, such as its administrative costs, potential political economy effects, and any behavioral changes it may induce. The fact that the targeted programs have more progressive incidence than public primary health or education programs does not imply that targeted transfer programs should replace basic health or education services, since the goals of each are clearly different. A sensible social sector strategy must obviously include strong health and education programs.

Although public primary health and education programs have different goals than many of the targeted programs and are therefore more appropriately judged by different standards, they may also provide a natural minimum benchmark for the incidence that should be expected of targeted programs. Most of the targeted programs we reviewed attain at least that minimum standard.

Figure 16-2. Share of Benefits Accruing to Poorest 40 Percent, by Country and Sector

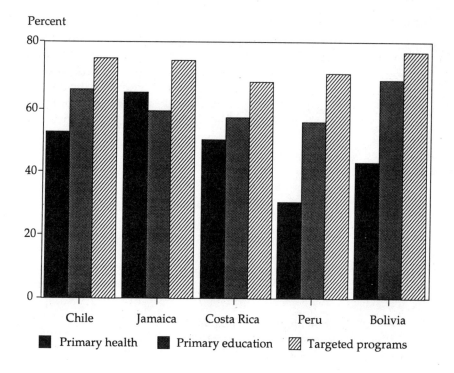

Note: An average is shown for targeted programs, and Chile, N = 5; Jamaica, N = 3; Costa Rica, N = 5; Peru, N = 2; Bolivia, N = 1.

Incidence by Targeting Mechanism

Overall, a broad spectrum of incidence is apparent across the targeted programs that we studied. The share of benefits accruing to the poorest two quintiles ranges from 59 to 83 percent (see figure 16-3).

There is little difference in incidence outcomes among classes of targeting mechanism. The incidence outcomes from a single mechanism as applied in different countries or programs are more diverse than the differences in outcomes among different mechanisms, on average. This is clear in figure 16-3. The range of outcomes for the individual assessment mechanisms is much wider than for the other mechanisms, with 59 to 83 percent of benefits going to the poorest two quintiles. The median is 73 percent. For geographic targeting mechanisms, the range is from 62 to 79 percent of benefits going to the poorest two quintiles; the median is 72 percent. For self-targeting mechanisms, the

Figure 16-3. Share of Benefits Accruing to the Poorest 40 Percent, by Targeting Mechanism

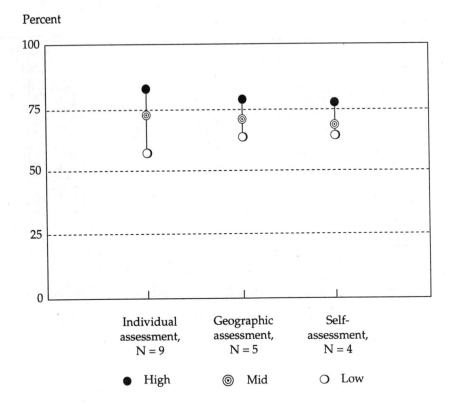

range is from 69 to 77 percent of benefits accruing to the poorest two quintiles; the median is 71 percent.

Correlations of Incidence and Country

The incidence achieved by the targeted programs differs little by country. In all five of the countries shown in figure 16-2, the median share of benefits accruing to the poorest two quintiles is about 75 percent for the targeted programs. Although the distribution of benefits across the welfare distribution is similar across countries, the prevalence of poverty is not. In Chile, the programs explicitly aim to help the poorest three deciles (Sancho 1991). In Jamaica, one-third of the population is considered to have been poor at the time of this survey (Gordon 1989). In Peru, poverty is much more common, with 54 percent of the population considered to be poor (World Bank 1992).

Figure 16-4. Total Administrative Costs as a Share of Total Costs, by Targeting Mechanism

Percent

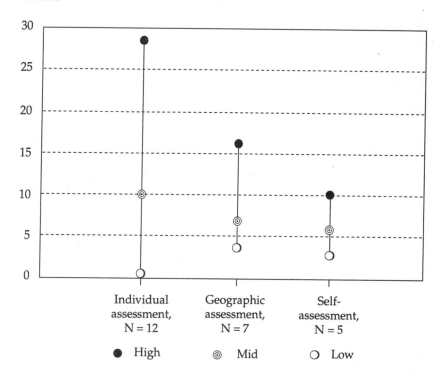

Administrative Costs

The range of total administrative costs (including the costs of screening potential beneficiaries and of delivering program benefits to them) is from 0.4 to 29 percent of total program costs (see figure 16-4). In the case of individual assessment mechanisms, the range of total administrative costs as a share of program costs is the greatest, from 0.4 to 29 percent. For geographic targeting, the range is from 4.0 to 16 percent. For self-targeting mechanisms, the range is from 3 to 10 percent. The median total administrative costs as a share of total program costs are 9 percent for individual assessment, 7 percent for geographic targeting, and 6 percent for self-targeting.

In absolute terms, the total administrative costs of the targeted programs in our case studies are below $25 per recipient per year, with one exception. The median cost is about $5 per beneficiary per year (except for student loan programs, as explained earlier). Three-quarters of the programs targeted by individual assessment have total adminis-

Figure 16-5. Targeting Costs as a Share of Total Costs, by Targeting Mechanism

Percent

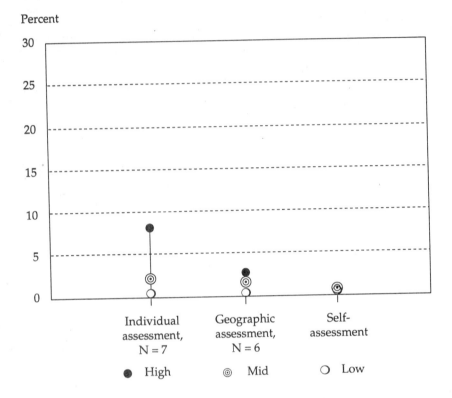

trative costs below $10 per beneficiary per year. Group targeted programs have administrative costs from $0.38 to $6.92 per beneficiary per year, with one exceptional outlier at $86 per year (the day care program in Venezuela). Self-targeted programs have administrative costs from $4.00 to $8.50 per beneficiary per year.

Only a part of total administrative costs is, strictly speaking, due to targeting (or to the screening of potential beneficiaries). In the few cases where it is possible to separate them out, targeting costs account for only a small part of total administrative costs.[12] Targeting (screening) costs run from 0.4 to 8 percent of total program costs (see figure 16-5). In dollar terms, the highest targeting cost is $11 per beneficiary per year. The median targeting cost is only $1.36 per beneficiary per year.

Concern over high administrative costs is perhaps the reason that is most commonly given for not adopting targeted programs. It is also commonly given as the reason to choose some mechanism other than those requiring individual assessment. These numbers show that the concern about administrative costs is likely to be greatly overstated.

Figure 16-6. Administrative Costs as a Share of Total Costs, by Type of Program

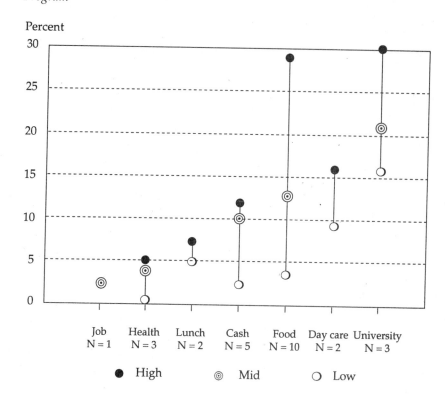

Percent

	Job	Health	Lunch	Cash	Food	Day care	University
	N = 1	N = 3	N = 2	N = 5	N = 10	N = 2	N = 3

● High   ◎ Mid   ○ Low

In fact, a wide variety of programs have found targeting mechanisms that produce moderately good incidence and that cost very little when measured as a proportion of overall program costs.

The conclusion that total administrative costs are low must be somewhat tempered, however. In several of the programs, it appears that low administrative budgets have led to deficient program management. Spending more on administration within a given program framework might lead to better service quality and/or incidence. The general level of administrative deficiency, however, seems no worse in the targeted programs than in most public social sector programs, including basic health and education programs.

The assumption that individual assessment mechanisms are much more expensive to administer than other options is not borne out by these data. The cost range for individual assessments is much wider than for the other mechanisms, but simple individual assessment targeting mechanisms are no more costly than other options.

Administrative costs vary greatly by program type, incidence less so (see figure 16-6). The costs of the health fee waiver programs are

Figure 16-7. Share of Benefits Accruing to Poorest 40 Percent, by Type of Program

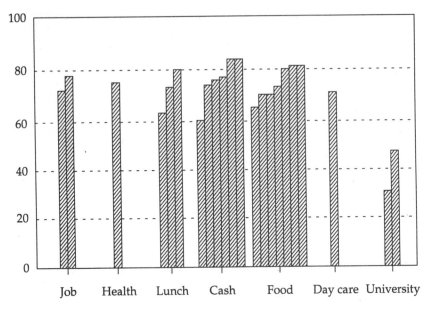

Note: Each bar indicates an individual program within the intervention category.

more tightly clustered and are much lower than most of the other interventions (0.4 to 5.0 percent). The administrative cost shares of the school lunch programs are similarly tightly clustered and fairly low (from 5 to 7 percent). For day care programs, the spread and average costs are a bit higher (9 and 16 percent). The administrative costs of the cash transfer programs range from 3.5 to 12 percent. The only job program for which we have administrative cost data shows costs of 3.5 percent. The spread is widest for the food distribution programs, where the shares range from 4.2 to 28.5 percent.

In terms of incidence, correlation by program type is less marked. For all programs, between about 60 and 80 percent of the benefits accrue to the poorest 40 percent of households. There is a heavy concentration around the center of the range (see figure 16-7).

Linking Administrative Costs and Incidence

There is no apparent correlation between incidence and shares of total administrative costs, as is clear from figure 16-8. This seems to contradict the usual hypothesis that better incidence requires burdensome administrative expenditures. The reason for this somewhat surprising

Figure 16-8. *Administrative Costs as a Share of Total Costs and Benefits Accruing to Poorest 40 Percent*

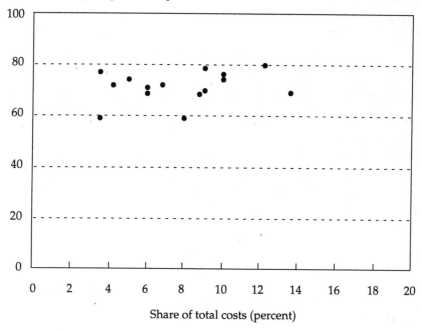

Share of benefits to poorest 40 percent

Share of total costs (percent)

result is that the screening costs of the (imperfectly) targeted programs that we studied constitute only a small share of overall administrative costs. Even programs that use very simple geographic or self-targeting methods need administrative mechanisms capable of delivering the program benefit, so their overall costs are not lowered much by having no explicit targeting costs. In addition, the programs vary a great deal in their scale, type, benefit level, and adequacy of management. These factors are also important determinants of the share of administrative costs for which we do not control in this comparison.

When isolating targeting costs, the correlation between higher screening costs and more progressive incidence becomes evident (see figure 16-9). Both have been quantified for eleven programs. The programs with targeting costs of about 1.5 percent of total program costs deliver about 80 percent of their benefits to the poorest 40 percent of households, while the programs with targeting costs of 0.5 percent of total program costs deliver about 60 percent of program benefits to the poor. This accords with the commonly held hypothesis that higher targeting costs should yield better targeting outcomes. The small number of programs and the imprecise measurement of the targeting costs, how-

Figure 16-9. Targeting Costs as a Share of Total Costs and Benefits Accruing to Poorest 40 Percent

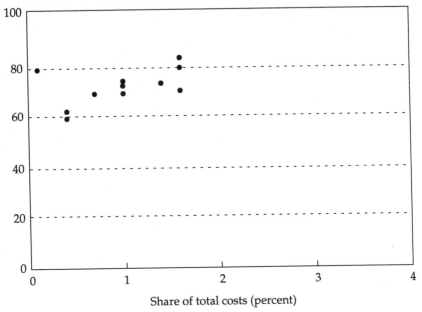

Share of benefits to poorest 40 percent

Share of total costs (percent)

ever, demand caution in drawing inferences about whether increasing screening costs further would provide similar improvements in incidence. But in these particular programs, the higher targeting costs are clearly offset by improvements in program incidence.

The share of each dollar that benefits the poor after discounting for administrative costs is a simple way of combining the incidence and administrative cost information. First, the administrative costs are subtracted from the budget. Then, the percentage of the remainder that goes to the poor is calculated. For example, Mexico's LICONSA program has administrative costs amounting to 28.5 percent of total costs. So, for each dollar spent, only 72 cents are available to be spent on the beneficiaries. Of that, 64 percent (or 46 cents) goes to the poorest two quintiles. So the share of total program *expenditures* going to the poorest two quintiles is 46 percent (this is different from the share of program *benefits* accruing to the poorest two quintiles, which is 64 percent; see the incidence calculations presented earlier).

The median of the range of program expenditures benefiting the poorest two quintiles is nearly identical for the three categories of targeting mechanisms. For individual assessment targeting, it is 68 percent; for geographic targeting, 67 percent; and for self-targeting, 67

Figure 16-10. Share of Expenditures Benefiting Poorest 40 Percent, by Targeting Mechanism

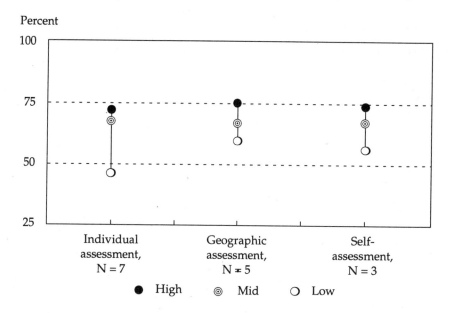

Percent

percent. The range for the individual assessment mechanisms is broader than the ranges for the other two mechanisms, but there is considerable overlap (figure 16-10).

The median of the range of program expenditures benefiting the poorest two quintiles does not differ greatly by program type (see figure 16-11). The fact that the results by share of program expenditure and by share of benefits that accrue to the poor are similar is not surprising. The incidence is similar, and the administrative cost shares are low; hence, although they vary by the type of program, they do not have much effect on the ranking of targeting mechanisms in terms of the proportion of total program expenditures that reaches the poorest.

For this sample of programs, the share of benefits and the share of program expenditures that go to the poor differ little. Indeed, Spearman's rank-order correlation for the programs on each of the two criteria is 0.93. The insensitivity of the ranking to the criteria is the result of two factors: total administrative costs are fairly low, and they are not correlated to incidence outcomes.

Figure 16-11. Share of Expenditures Benefiting Poorest 40 Percent, by Type of Program

Percent

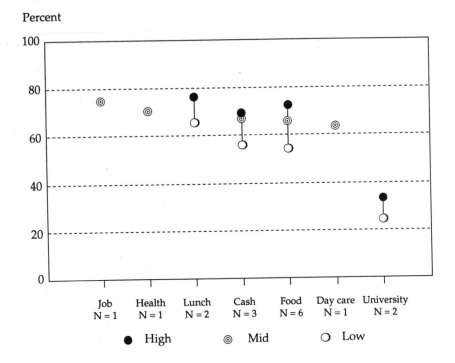

	Job	Health	Lunch	Cash	Food	Day care	University
	N = 1	N = 1	N = 2	N = 3	N = 6	N = 1	N = 2

● High   ◉ Mid   ○ Low

Outlier Programs

As was mentioned in the incidence and administrative costs section of the chapter, three programs (the Colombian and Jamaican university student loan programs and a Chilean housing program with a mortgage down payment requirement) were excluded from those summaries on the grounds that they have design features that constrain their ability to reach the poor. This makes them qualitatively different from the main body of programs reviewed, even though their targeting mechanisms are similar.

Although the three "outlier" programs do have significantly worse incidence than the others, this is not necessarily an indictment of their means-testing mechanisms per se. In Chile, for example, the same proxy means test is used both for the basic housing mortgage subsidies (Viviendas-Básicas) and for the cash transfer program (Subsidio Unico Familiar: SUF). The basic housing program has the second worst incidence of all the targeted programs we reviewed (with 50 percent of benefits accruing to the poorest two quintiles), while the SUF has the best incidence of any program reviewed (with 83 percent of benefits accruing to the poorest two quintiles). The difference in outcome apparently lies in the down payment requirement for the mortgage subsidy. Since the poor have difficulty finding the money for a down payment, they cannot participate even if they qualify under the means test. The contrast illustrates how important the kind of program benefit, and hence the composition of the pool of potential beneficiaries, can be in determining targeting outcomes.

In the case of the student loan programs, 46 percent of the benefits accrue to the poorest two quintiles in Jamaica, and only 48 percent of the benefits reach the poorest *three* quintiles in Colombia. The student loan programs also have very high total administrative costs compared to the other programs—$332 per loan for Jamaica and $148 for Colombia. Although the value of the targeted benefits is also very high, the shares of the administrative costs are still at the upper end of the spectrum (accounting for 20 to 30 percent of program costs). Those costs entail keeping track of students and their loans throughout all the years of school and repayment, in contrast to other programs whose administrative expenses only include keeping track of the beneficiary for one year of benefit at a time. This presumably explains much of the high total administrative cost. In Jamaica, the cost of processing a loan application is taken as a proxy for the cost of targeting. It comes to $40 per loan, or 3.6 percent of program costs. This is among the most costly screening processes of all the programs, although it is also among the most sophisticated.

Variations in Implementation of Targeting Mechanisms

Our case studies illustrate the enormous number of ways in which targeting mechanisms can be put into practice depending on what institutional capacity is available, what political factors have to be taken into account, and what the goals of the program might be (Grosh 1992, chaps. 5–7, provides much more detail on these issues). Let us look at three specific illustrations of this diversity: the implementation of means tests in the Jamaican and Honduran food stamp programs; the use of school-level geographic targeting in Chile, Costa Rica, and Jamaica; and the variety of mechanisms used in food programs appended to maternal-child health programs. The first two examples show how a single method may be implemented differently, while the third example shows how different methods may be used in a single type of program.

In the means-tested portion of the Jamaican food stamp program, social workers from the Ministry of Labour, Welfare, and Sport visit the candidate household to fill in a short form with the candidate's address, family information, and income. The visit to the house allows the social worker to verify whether visible living conditions are in accordance or are grossly at odds with the level of income that the family reports that it receives, but the characteristics of the dwelling or the ownership of durable goods are not formally used in the evaluation of eligibility. The program is administered by about 150 full-time field-workers. They work on a two-month cycle, with the first month devoted to identifying beneficiaries and the second month devoted to distributing the food stamps. The program has about 300,000 beneficiaries overall, of whom half are in the means-tested part of the program and half in the maternal-child health part of the program, which is not means tested.

In contrast to the Jamaican food stamp program, the Honduran Bono de Madre Jefe de Familia (BMJF) program relies on teachers to conduct simple means tests. At the beginning of the school year, primary school-teachers in participating states are required to identify which of their students are from households that are headed by females and have incomes below a set level. In order to do so, the teachers ask the students' mothers what their income level is. The teachers sometimes visit the house and sometimes interview the mother at the school. The teachers spend about three days at the beginning of the school year identifying the beneficiaries for the program. About 13,000 teachers have been involved in the seven departments where the program has operated. The program benefits about 125,000 students a year.

The use of a part-time army of teachers in Honduras provides an interesting contrast to the small cadre of full-time social workers used by the Jamaican food stamp program. In terms of the amount of staff time needed per beneficiary, some very rough calculations show that the requirements are in the same order of magnitude. The difference in costs is also slight. Total administrative costs consist of about 10 percent of program costs, or $4, per year for the Jamaican food stamp program, while for the Honduran BMJF, they are about 12 percent, or $4.50, per beneficiary per year.

Each approach has advantages. Jamaica's small cadre approach means that training can be more thorough and the standardization of operation among social workers can be greater. In Honduras, the teachers are believed to be able to carry out means tests reliably not because they have special training but because it is harder to fool a teacher who lives in the village than a social worker who visits occasionally. In Jamaica, since far fewer people handle food stamps than in Honduras, resources for ensuring program security can focus on providing protection to, and checks on, a few people handling large quantities of stamps. The costs of theft or fraud in any one case, however, would be higher.

One of the reasons that Jamaica chose to use a small number of social workers is that the country already had two welfare programs operating in a similar way. When the food stamps program was first set up, it was able to rely on existing systems and personnel to a large degree. In contrast, Honduras had no network of social workers who knew how to conduct means tests, so they used the schoolteachers who were already in place. In both countries, the food stamp programs were set up very quickly as emergency measures accompanying structural adjustment programs, so it was especially important to build on existing institutions wherever possible.

The second interesting example of the different ways in which a single targeting mechanism can be implemented occurs in school feeding programs. In Costa Rica, for many years, all schools were included in the school lunch program, and 62 percent of the benefits went to the poorest two quintiles of households. Recently, three levels of benefits have been specified, and the extent of the lunch subsidy per child that a school receives is determined by the size of the school and the poverty rating of the area that the school serves, in accord with the Planning Ministry's poverty map. As yet, no new incidence figures are available for the different levels of subsidy.

In contrast, the Nutribun program in Jamaica is meant to serve schools in poor areas. The selection of schools is based on the Ministry of Education's knowledge of which schools are located in poor areas. The program involves the daily delivery of food products from central factories, so the schools in this program must have good access to road transport, which, of course, tends to exclude schools in remote rural areas where poverty is usually most prevalent. Even with this constraint and the informal criteria for selecting schools, the program's incidence is more progressive than Costa Rica's previous universal provision—72 percent of Nutribun benefits go to the poorest two quintiles.

Chile has a much more formal system for choosing which schools will participate in its school feeding program. From a census of first graders conducted each year, the individual school reports the values of five variables that are assigned a fixed weight in a school selection algorithm.[13] This is used by the central planners to select both the schools that will receive lunches and the number of lunches each school will receive. Then, within each school, the teachers specify which children are most in need of the school's allotment of lunches. Because the meals are meant to be served outside of school hours, any issues of stigma or jealousy should be minimized. There are, however, anecdotal reports that teachers divide the rations rather than exclude some children from lunch, indicating that the individual-level targeting mechanism is overridden in at least some schools. Nevertheless, the incidence for the Chilean program is the best of the school-targeted programs in our sample—79 percent of benefits go to the poorest two quintiles of households.

A large number of food supplement programs intended to benefit pregnant/lactating women and young children are linked to the use of public preventive health care services. Whether and which additional mechanisms are used vary from program to program. The Venezuelan Programa Alimentario Materno Infantil (PAMI) is typical of the simplest case, in that no other requirements are imposed and the rations are uniform. The Honduran BMI uses geographic targeting in conjunction with self-targeting by use of services. First, the program operates only in the poorest states. Second, where the number of women and children eligible to be served by a single clinic is greater than the number that the clinic is deemed able to handle given the number of its staff, then certain villages within the clinic's catchment area are given high-priority status based on the Ministry of Health's poverty map. Thus, all women from those villages receive benefits, while women from the other villages in the clinic's catchment area receive none. The Dominican Republic's Proyecto Materno-Infantil (PROMI) program uses indicators of nutritional risk such as fertility history, age, and current anthropometric indicators to admit beneficiaries to the program. Peru's Programa de Alimentación y Nutrición para Familias de Alto Riesgo (PANFAR) uses similar biomedical risk factors, as well as socioeconomic factors, to admit children. In the Chilean PNAC, all children are eligible, but the size of the ration is larger for children who experience faltering growth than for others.

How General Are the Results Reported Here?

The programs reviewed here all tend to produce broadly similar outcomes. In terms of incidence, about 60 to 80 percent of expenditures accrue to the poorest 40 percent of households across all of the programs. Total administrative costs cluster between about 5 and 15 percent of program expenditures, with screening costs clustering between about 0.5 and 1.5 percent of program expenditures. This leads to the conclusion that, for programs with moderately good incidence, administrative expenses are not prohibitive. It is not possible, however, to infer from these data the extent to which administrative expenses would have to increase to achieve a dramatic improvement in incidence. Given the evidence of administrative inadequacy in the case studies, it seems reasonable to think that moderate increases in administrative expenses might help to achieve moderately better targeting and/or service delivery. But the fact that none of the programs comes close to perfect targeting probably means that much higher administrative expenses would be required to achieve radically lower leakage.

There are probably also limits to how general the results are in terms of concluding that the targeting mechanisms that have worked well for one kind of program would do equally well for others. For example, the geographic mechanisms common in school lunch programs seem fairly satisfactory in that application. But one would probably not want to use a solely geographic mechanism to target a large cash benefit or a student loan. Likewise, the self-targeting with repeated queuing found in several of the food stamp/food supplement programs seems to work well for those programs (and the requirement of showing adequate use of preventive health services creates another health benefit, too). One would not, however, give away a radically larger benefit and expect such progressive incidence unless a concomitantly higher cost of participation or ancillary screening mechanism were introduced.

Since poverty is often concentrated in rural areas, it is worth considering whether the results would differ between rural and urban areas. Although we cannot present hard numbers, we can comment more qualitatively about the special issues applicable in rural areas. The figures presented here are for the programs as they operate. Most of the programs studied operate nationally, though many have built-in problems of undercoverage in rural areas, since the infrastructure (health or education) to which they are tied does not completely cover rural areas. Moreover, programs with an individual assessment mechanism may have higher costs per beneficiary, since the density of beneficiaries is lower in rural areas (see Grosh 1994, chap. 8, for information on how total administrative costs for various universal services differ between rural and urban areas). In terms of administrative challenges, the programs have some degree or another of the expected problems of getting staff, goods, or information to or from the administrative centers to the rural areas. However, often the identification of beneficiaries and management of the distribution of benefits are easier in rural areas due to the greater knowledge of or cooperation from the community.

How applicable are these findings to countries that are substantially poorer, such as those in Sub-Saharan Africa? There is considerable debate about whether very poor countries should try to target their social programs. Those who question the value of doing so point out that leakage, defined as benefits given to the nonpoor, is bound to be low even with untargeted programs if a large proportion of the population falls below the poverty line. Furthermore, the institutional capacity in very poor countries tends to be quite limited, making targeting mechanisms even more difficult to administer.

That programs in poor countries such as Bolivia and Peru manage to produce targeting outcomes equivalent to those of Chile and Costa Rica's programs suggests that targeting can still be useful in moderately poor countries with weak administrative capacities. It may even suggest that the incidence that can be expected from the targeted programs may have little to do with how poor a country is. For countries with institutional systems greatly different from those in Latin America, however, it may be extrapolating out of the range where valid inference is possible to expect the same results to be achievable. This is an empirical question that cannot be answered with certainty until similar studies are done that evaluate targeted programs in other settings.

In pondering subjectively how relevant the Latin American experience is to Africa, however, it does seem that the benefits of targeting in very poor countries are not qualitatively so different from those that accrue in the countries studied here. Regardless of how large a proportion of the population is poor, some people are poorer than others. Given limited resources, it is presumably more desirable to reach those in the poorest quintile than those in the middle quintile of the welfare distribution, even if those in the middle quintile are poor according to an absolute standard.

The availability of suitable targeting options may, however, be scarcer in Africa than in Latin America. Targeted programs require service delivery capacity even if very simple targeting methods are used. Many of the simple mechanisms involve using the facilities of existing institutions or programs, especially in the health and education sectors. While improving the service delivery capacity in these sectors is clearly a high priority for its own sake, this may also make the implementation of targeted programs linked to the use of health and education services more feasible. Meanwhile, if administrative problems are substantially greater in Sub-Saharan Africa than in Latin America, the choices about targeting can reasonably be expected to be different as well.

Finally, it is interesting to compare the Latin American programs to some in the high-income world. Information on five of the largest means-tested welfare programs in the United States is shown in table 16-4. These programs account for nearly two-thirds of all means-tested public expenditures. The administrative costs of these programs as a proportion of total costs are roughly similar to those for the Latin American programs, from 4 to 14 percent.[14] Targeting accuracy, however, appears to be much better in the U.S. programs. Error rates are calculated by periodically sampling beneficiaries and recalculating their eligibility and benefit levels. On the whole, errors are quite low. Overpayments or payments to ineligibles run from 3.3 to 16.1 percent. Underpayments run from 0.6 to 4.9 percent. This greater targeting accuracy is presumably due to the fact that means testing is comparatively easier in the United States than in Latin America. In the United States, workers are employed largely in formal sector jobs with salaries that are regularly reported to the Internal Revenue Service. Verification is thus comparatively easy, though, admittedly, off-the-books earnings do occur and are likely to be more common among the poor than among other workers. Since the U.S. economy is much more monetized, there is less need to value in-kind income. Finally, the use of computerized information systems, mail and telephone inquiries for verification, and other sophisticated information technologies is much more widespread and is comparatively cheaper in the United States.

Table 16-4. Administrative Costs and Error Rates in U.S. Welfare Programs, 1985
(percent)

| | | Error rate | |
Program	Administrative costs	For overpayment and payments to the ineligible	For underpayment
Aid to Families with Dependent Children	10.7	6.2	0.6[a]
Supplemental social security	8.0	3.3	1.0
Food stamp program	13.5	8.6	2.3
Medicaid	4.8	2.7	—
Pell Grants (to university students)	—	16.1	4.9

— Not available.

a. Fiscal 1984.

Sources: Compiled from Interagency Low Income Opportunity Advisory Board 1987 (AFDC, vol. 2, pp. 9, 56; supplemental social security, vol. 2, pp. 65, 107; food stamp program, vol. 2, pp. 3, 19; Medicaid, vol. 3, pp. 3, 19); and from U.S. Department of Education 1987, pp. 3–1.

Summary and Conclusions

Briefly stated, our review of administrative costs and targeting outcomes in thirty Latin American social programs has led to three main conclusions:

(a) Targeted programs have much more progressive incidence than general food price subsidies. They even have somewhat more progressive incidence than basic public health and education services.

(b) The administrative costs of programs with moderately good incidence need not be excessively high.

(c) It is not possible to rank targeting mechanisms a priori. There are no broad correlations between the targeting mechanisms and targeting outcomes, and there appears to be only a weak correlation with administrative costs.

Appendix 16-1: Data Sources for the Figures

The graphs in the body of the paper portray information from table 16-3, except for figures 16-1 and 16-2, which have ancillary sources as described below. The individual programs included in each bar of each graph are as follows. The acronyms can be found in tables 16-2 and 16-3.

Figure 16-1: In addition to information from table 16-3, this figure relies on tables 8.1–8.3 of Grosh (1992). The programs used to compile those tables are given here. *General food subsidies*: Algeria: separate figures for flour, pasteurized milk, semolina, powdered milk; Jamaica: average for powdered milk, cornmeal, wheat; Sri Lanka: sugar, average for wheat and bread. *Targeted programs*: Bolivia: ESF; Chile: CAS-PASIS, CAS-SUF, PAE, PNAC, POJH/PEM; Costa Rica: CEN/CENAI day care, CEN/CENAI food packets, health insurance, school lunches, pensions; Dominican Republic: PROMI; Jamaica: FSP-MCH, FSP (means tested), Nutribuns; Mexico: LICONSA; Peru: Comedores, Glass of Milk. *Public primary health care*: Argentina: 1980; Chile: 1983; Colombia: 1974; Costa Rica: 1984, 1986; Dominican Republic: 1980, 1989; Jamaica: 1989; Peru: 1985; Uruguay: 1983, 1989. *Public primary education*: Argentina: 1980; Chile: 1983; Colombia, 1974; Costa Rica: 1984, 1986; Dominican Republic: 1980, 1989; Jamaica: 1989; Peru: 1985; Uruguay: 1983, 1989.

Figure 16-2: Bolivia: ESF. Chile: CAS-PASIS, CAS-SUF, PAE, PNAC, POJH/PEM. Costa Rica: CEN/CENAI food packets, CEN/CENAI day care, health insurance, pensions, school lunches. Jamaica: FSP-MCH, FSP (means tested), Nutribuns. Peru: Comedores, Glass of Milk.

Figure 16-3: *Individual assessment*: Chile: CAS-PASIS, CAS-SUF; Costa Rica: CEN/CENAI day care, CEN/CENAI food packets, health insurance, pensions; Dominican Republic: PROMI; Jamaica: FSP (means tested); Mexico: LICONSA. *Geographic assessment*: Chile: PAE; Costa Rica: school lunches; Jamaica: Nutribuns; Peru: Comedores, Glass of Milk. *Self-assessment*: Bolivia: ESF; Chile: PNAC, POJH/PEM; Jamaica: FSP-MCH.

Figure 16-4: *Individual assessment*: Belize: hospital fee waivers; Costa Rica: CEN/CENAI, health insurance, pensions, University of Costa Rica tuition waivers; Dominican Republic: hospital fee waivers, PROMI; Honduras: BMJF; Jamaica: FSP; Mexico: LICONSA, Tortivales; Peru: PANFAR. *Geographic assessment*: Chile: PAE; Jamaica: Nutribuns; Peru: Comedores-CARITAS, Comedores-PRODIA, Glass of Milk; Venezuela: Beca Alimentaria, day care centers. *Self-assessment*: Bolivia: ESF; Honduras: BMI; Jamaica: FSP; Peru: PNAC; Venezuela: PAMI.

Figure 16-5: *Individual assessment*: Chile: CAS-PASIS, CAS-SUF; Costa Rica: CEN/CENAI, health insurance, pensions; Dominican Republic: hospital fee waivers; Peru: PANFAR. *Geographic assessment*: Chile: PAE; Costa Rica: school lunches; Peru: Comedores-CARITAS, Comedores-PRODIA, Glass of Milk; Venezuela: day care program.

Figure 16-6: *Jobs*: Bolivia: ESF. *Health*: Belize: hospital fee waivers; Costa Rica: insurance; Dominican Republic: hospital fee waivers. *Lunch*: Chile: PAE; Jamaica: Nutribuns. *Cash/food stamps*: Costa Rica: pensions; Honduras: BMI, BMJF; Jamaica: FSP; Venezuela: Beca Alimentaria. *Food*: Chile: PNAC; Costa Rica: CEN/CENAI; Dominican Republic: PROMI; Mexico: LICONSA, Tortivales; Peru: Comedores-CARITAS, Comedores-PRODIA, Glass of Milk, PANFAR; Venezuela: PAMI. *Day care*: Costa Rica: CEN/CENAI;

Venezuela: day care centers. *University*: Colombia: ICETEX; Costa Rica: University of Costa Rica tuition waivers; Jamaica: SLB.

Figure 16-7: Jobs: Bolivia: ESF; Chile: PEM/POJH. *Health*: Costa Rica: health insurance. *Lunch*: Chile: PAE; Costa Rica: school lunches; Jamaica: Nutribuns. *Cash/food stamps*: Chile: CAS-PASIS, CAS-SUF; Costa Rica: pensions; Jamaica: FSP-MCH, FSP (means tested). *Food*: Chile: PNAC; Costa Rica: CEN/CENAI; Dominican Republic: PROMI; Mexico: LICONSA; Peru: Comedores, Glass of Milk. *Day care*: Costa Rica: CEN/CENAI. *University*: Colombia: ICETEX; Jamaica: SLB.

Figure 16-8: Bolivia: ESF; Chile: PAE, PNAC; Costa Rica: CEN/CENAI, health insurance, pensions; Dominican Republic: PROMI; Jamaica: FSP-MCH, Nutribuns; Peru: Comedores-CARITAS, Glass of Milk.

Figure 16-9: Chile: CAS-PASIS, CAS-SUF, PAE; Costa Rica: CEN/CENAI day care, health insurance, CEN/CENAI food packets, pensions, school lunches; Peru: Comedores-CARITAS, Comedores-PRODIA, Glass of Milk.

Figure 16-10: Individual assessment: Costa Rica: CEN/CENAI day care, CEN/CENAI food packets, insurance, pensions; Dominican Republic: PROMI; Jamaica: FSP (means tested); Mexico: LICONSA. *Geographic assessment*: Chile: PAE; Jamaica: Nutribuns; Peru: Comedores-CARITAS, Comedores-PRODIA, Glass of Milk. *Self-assessment*: Bolivia: ESF; Chile: PNAC; Jamaica: FSP-MCH.

Figure 16-11: Jobs: Bolivia: ESF. *Health*: Costa Rica: insurance. *Lunch*: Chile: PAE; Jamaica: Nutribuns. *Cash/food stamps*: Costa Rica: pensions; Jamaica: FSP-MCH, FSP (means tested). *Food*: Chile: PNAC; Costa Rica: CEN/CENAI food packets; Dominican Republic: PROMI; Peru: Comedores-CARITAS, Comedores-PRODIA, Glass of Milk. *Day care*: Costa Rica: CEN/CENAI. *University*: Colombia: ICETEX; Jamaica: SLB.

Notes

1. A possible exception may be means tests, as these try to measure income directly rather than its correlates. However, since the means tests reviewed here are so simplistic in their definitions of income and are based on uncertain information, it may be more plausible to think of the resulting figure as a correlate or predictor of true, full income similar to other indicators than to think of these simple, imperfect means tests as the ideal.

2. Errors of inclusion are an impractical means of measuring targeting accuracy in this study for two reasons. First, calculating errors of exclusion and inclusion requires a precisely defined target group. Many programs never define their target group precisely, which does not necessarily hinder them in delivering services, but which does make it difficult to assess their targeting accuracy. Second, errors of exclusion and inclusion can be misleading in cross-program comparisons if one program defines its target population much more narrowly than another. The program with the smaller target group may appear to have higher errors when, in fact, it just sets itself a higher standard.

3. If receiving the subsidy causes the behavior of the recipient or of any other individual to change in ways that alter net welfare, this will not be captured here. Cox and Jimenez (1992) provide an example of the possible

importance of behavioral change in a program similar to those studied here. They predict that, in Peru, private intrafamily transfers may fall by as much as 20 percent when elderly members of a family receive social security. The social security program, thus, provides an indirect benefit to the younger generation who reduce their support to their elders and improves the older generation's welfare by less than the amount of the social security payment. McLure (1975) is a basic reference from the tax literature on these issues. Selden and Wasylenko (1992) and Gill, Jimenez, and Shalizi (1990) discuss the effects of behavioral change for government expenditure programs.

4. Since we do not have information either on the costs of participation or on any behavioral changes induced by participation in the program, it is not possible to compute the distribution of net benefits.

5. For households with children under five years of age, the participation rate has ranged from 38 percent in 1988 to a low of 17 percent in 1990 (Anderson 1993). In interpreting these figures, it is important to remember that they pertain to all households. If the program is meant to be self-targeting in that the nonpoor choose not to participate, then the ideal nationwide participation rate will be substantially less than 100 percent.

6. The 1989 Survey of Living Conditions shows that 92 percent of both groups had contact at some time in their lives, 17 percent of malnourished nonrecipients had preventive contact within the six months prior to the survey (as opposed to 16 percent for all children), and 5 percent of each group had contact for curative care in the four weeks preceding the survey (STATIN 1989).

7. For example, the program is run by social workers from the Ministry of Labour, Welfare, and Sport, who occasionally visit health clinics, rather than staff of the Ministry of Health. This has led to chronically insufficient contact with the clinics, a situation that was exacerbated during the period in question by the transfer of most social workers from the Ministry of Labour, Welfare, and Sport to the Ministry of Local Government and by their withdrawal from the food stamp program. The occasional suspension of the program to allow for reregistration of beneficiaries has also caused errors of exclusion. These factors are not necessarily present in other programs. The general fiscal constraints on the administrative budget are, of course, more common.

8. Assigning costs to different programs that are run under the same budget or agency raises both a practical and a theoretical problem. The practical problem is that no rigorous account may be kept of how much of overhead or jointly shared staff, equipment, and supplies should be charged to which program. The theoretical issue goes deeper. In at least some cases, it may be cheaper to run the programs together than to run them separately, not just to minimize any problem of underused capacity in the overhead, but because the programs are synergistic (or have joint products). In these cases, the division of costs among the two programs will result in one or both being assigned a cost that is lower than it would be if the program stood alone.

9. All dollars are U.S. dollars.

10. In the rest of the chapter, we use medians rather than means, partly to avoid giving undue weight to outliers. In this paragraph, we use the mean, with each program given a weight of 1 because there are no serious outliers in this category and because discussing the median of a group of four is somewhat clumsy.

11. The benefit-incidence information for general food subsidies, primary health care, and primary education, presented in this section and in figures 16-1 and 16-2 for comparison with the targeted interventions, is presented in more detail in Grosh (1992, tables 8.1, 8.2, and 8.3).

12. The fact that targeting-only costs are available for only a subset of all programs raises the possibility that there may be some sort of systematic bias in the subsample for which information is available. While this must be acknowledged, it is our best guess that this is probably not a big problem in this study. Targeting-only costs are available for a range of programs by type of targeting mechanism, type of program, and country. Moreover, we do not have a sense that the programs that do and do not have targeting-only costs differ greatly in general efficiency or quality.

13. These are as follows: incidence of low height-for-age (0.233), average number of years of mothers' education (0.226), percentage of students that the teachers rate as being very urgently or urgently in need of subsidized lunches (0.192), repetition rates (19.0), and the percentage of children with high ages for grade (0.159).

14. The costs shown divide total administrative costs of the program by the value of benefits awarded. In our study, we have divided total administrative costs by the sum of the value of the benefits and the administrative costs. If the method used in this study were applied to the U.S. programs, the share of administrative costs shown would decrease by about a tenth. It is also difficult to tell from the source whether the concepts included under administrative costs are precisely similar, but they seem roughly comparable.

References

Anderson, Patricia. 1993. "The Incorporation of Mothers and Children into the Jamaican Food Stamp Programme." Jamaican Poverty Line Project Working Paper 6. Planning Institute of Jamaica, Kingston.

Besley, Timothy. 1989. "Targeting Taxes and Transfers: Administrative Costs and Policy Design in Developing Economies." Research Program in Development Studies Working Paper 146. Princeton University, Woodrow Wilson School, Princeton, N.J.

Besley, Timothy, and Ravi Kanbur. 1993. "Principles of Targeting." In Michael Lipton and Jacques van der Gaag, eds., *Including the Poor*. Washington, D.C.: World Bank.

Cox, Donald, and Emmanuel Jimenez. 1992. "Social Security and Private Transfers in Developing Countries: The Case of Peru." *World Bank Economic Review* 6 (1): 155–70.

Gill, Indermit, Emmanuel Jimenez, and Zmarak Shalizi. 1990. "Targeting Consumer Subsidies for Poverty Alleviation: A Survey and a Primer of Basic Theory." World Bank, Public Economics Division, Washington, D.C.

Gordon, Derek. 1989. "Identifying the Poor: Developing a Poverty Line for Jamaica." Jamaican Poverty Line Project Working Paper 3. Planning Institute of Jamaica, Kingston.

Grosh, Margaret. 1992. "From Platitudes to Practice: Targeting Social Programs in Latin America." Regional Studies Program Working Paper 21. World Bank, Latin American Technical Department, Washington, D.C.

_____. 1994. *Administering Targeted Social Programs in Latin America: From Platitudes to Practice*. Washington, D.C.: World Bank.

Interagency Low Income Opportunity Advisory Board. 1987. *Up from Dependency: A New National Public Assistance Strategy*, supplement 1, vols. 2 and 3. Washington, D.C.: Executive Office of the President.

McLure, Charles E., Jr. 1975. "General Equilibrium Analysis: The Harberger Model after Ten Years." *Journal of Public Economics* 4: 125–62.

Meerman, Jacob. 1979. *Public Expenditure in Malaysia: Who Benefits and Why.* New York: Oxford University Press.

Sancho, Antonio. 1991. "Participación del sector privado en la prestación de servicios sociales." Inter-American Development Bank, Washington, D.C.

Selden, Thomas M., and Michael J. Wasylenko. 1992. "Benefit Incidence Analysis in Developing Countries." Policy Research Working Paper WPS 1015. World Bank, Public Economics Division, Washington, D.C.

Selowsky, Marcelo. 1979. *Who Benefits from Government Expenditures? A Case Study of Colombia.* New York: Oxford University Press.

STATIN (Statistical Institute of Jamaica and Planning Institute of Jamaica). 1989. "Preliminary Report: Survey of Living Conditions, July 1989." Kingston.

U.S. Department of Education. 1987. *Title IV Quality Control Project: Stage Two Final Report, Executive Summary.* Contract 300-84-0020. Washington, D.C.

World Bank. 1992. "Peru: Poverty Assessment and Social Policies and Programs for the Poor." Report 1191-PE. Washington, D.C.

17 The Distributional Impact of Cash and In-Kind Transfers in Eastern Europe and Russia

Branko Milanovic

The move from socialism to capitalism requires fundamental changes in the role and structure of government. In many cases, the necessary reforms involve reducing the scope of public action—essentially getting the government out of the economy's way. However, in other instances, this transition may create a need to change and even expand what the government does. For example, as Russia and the countries of Eastern Europe evolve into more market-based economies, they may need to restructure and possibly extend their social transfer systems to address the emergence of new sources of vulnerability and increased income inequality. It is therefore important to know, as the systems of social transfers begin their slow adjustment to the market system, who are the main beneficiaries of the current programs. What social and income groups do the current systems explicitly or implicitly target? Some work in this area has been undertaken recently, mostly by the World Bank (under the research project sponsored by the Socialist Economies Unit; see papers by Topińska 1991; Dlouhý 1991; Vukotić-Cotič 1991; and Kupa and Fajth 1990). This chapter builds on some of these efforts and analyzes the distributional incidence of cash (pensions, family allowances, and maternity and sickness benefits) and in-kind (education and health) social transfers in Eastern Europe and Russia.

Using data from Bulgaria, Czechoslovakia, Hungary, Poland, Russia, and Yugoslavia, concentration coefficients are calculated for the various kinds of social transfers. These calculations serve as the basis for the transfer program and intercountry comparisons. The coefficients provide an index of transfer progressivity; they indicate how the share of benefits captured by poorer households compares to the share of benefits captured by the better-off under various social transfer programs. In order to situate the results for Eastern Europe and Russia in context, I compare them to data for OECD (Organization for Economic Cooperation and Development) countries, when the latter are available and methodologically similar. In several instances, I also use Chile as a comparator; Chile has a fairly sophisticated system of social assistance and a level of income close to that of the East European countries.

The data used in this analysis come from household surveys conducted in 1988 and 1989. These household surveys have broadly similar designs. For example, individuals are ranked by their household per capita income, and the key income concept used is gross income. The surveys differ, however, in how representative they are of the population as a whole. In addition, some of the surveys are more comprehensive in their inclusion of the various sources of income. Nevertheless, the similarity of the surveys, reflecting to some extent the similarity in the underlying economic systems, by far outweighs the differences; a comparison between these countries seems reasonably justified and meaningful (a more detailed description of the surveys is presented in appendix 17-1).

The chapter's structure is as follows. The first section discusses the use of concentration coefficients as a measure of the distribution of social transfers and methodological issues that may vitiate intercountry comparisons of transfer progressivity. Specifically, sometimes the information available for analyzing the distributional impact of transfers is presented in different forms; this can make comparisons between countries tricky. The following two sections present the main results on the distributional incidence of cash and in-kind social transfers in Eastern Europe and Russia. Comparisons with OECD countries and Chile are made when available. The next section argues that the distributional impact of cash social transfers in socialism is sufficiently different from that which occurs in capitalist countries that one can speak of a specific "world of welfare socialism." Finally, the chapter concludes with a look at how the social transfer systems in Eastern Europe and Russia may change as a result of the transition to capitalism.

The Distribution of Social Transfers: Measurement Issues

The concentration coefficient provides an index of transfer progressivity. It shows the concentration (cumulative percentage) of one variable (for example, social transfers) when recipients are ranked by amounts of a different variable (for example, gross income). The concentration coefficient ranges from -1 (the poorest recipient receives all transfers) through 0 (all recipients receive the same amount of transfer) to $+1$ (the richest recipient receives all transfers). For a transfer s, it can be written as $C_s = 2\text{cov}(s,r_y) / \bar{s}N$, where $\bar{s}$ equals mean amount of the transfer, N equals sample size, and $\text{cov}(s,r_y)$ equals covariance between s and the ranking of recipients according to income.

There are alternatives to this measure. For example, one alternative is $C - G$ where G equals the Gini coefficient of overall income.[1] When we compare two countries, C is a better indicator of the targeting of

Figure 17-1. Distribution of Income and Social Transfers

Cumulative percentage of income/transfers

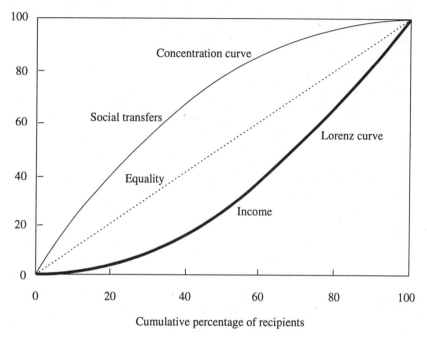

Cumulative percentage of recipients

transfers than $C-G$ because its value is independent of G. (In figure 17-1, C is equal to twice the area between the concentration curve and line of equality; $C-G$ is equal to twice the area between the concentration curve and the Lorenz curve.) Thus, in a very inegalitarian country, transfers may appear fairly progressive even if they are less focused than in an egalitarian country. For example, equal per capita transfers in Brazil ($C = 0$) would appear very progressive because Brazil's Gini coefficient is very high (about 50): then $C-G = 0-50 = -50$. Much more focused transfers in Sweden ($C = -20$) would appear less progressive because Sweden's Gini coefficient is low (about 20); then $C-G = -20-20 = -40$. If we are interested in the impact of transfers on inequality, there may be some justification in using $C-G$ or Dalton's progressivity measure (the difference between the pre- and post-transfer inequality). If, however, we are interested, as we are here, in *targeting*, the concentration coefficient is a better measure.

Although considerable detail is lost with concentration coefficients, their use has certain advantages for benefit-incidence analysis. Concentration coefficients provide an overall picture of the distributional incidence of social transfers and make it easy to see the bottom line on the distributional impact of a government program.

In comparing the distribution of total income or of social transfers for more than one country, methodological differences between data sources often hinder the task. If one has access to unit record data from household surveys, then one can usually be methodologically consistent across the countries being compared. Unfortunately, this is not always the case. Sometimes, as in this study, one is limited to using and comparing measures calculated from the unit record data by the Central Statistical Office or other researchers, or is in some other manner dependent on survey data already aggregated.[2] The variations that can limit comparability fall into three categories: (1) the concept of income used, (2) the definition of the recipient, and (3) the choice of ranking criterion. Income distribution analyses use various concepts of income: original, gross, disposable, or some variant of these. The definition of the recipient also varies: for example, the unit used in the analysis may be the individual or the household. Finally, the ranking criterion can differ. In some studies, households are ranked by total household income; in others, households or persons are ranked by household per capita income; finally, some data show households or persons ranked by household equivalent income (where household income is adjusted for the consumption needs of different household members).

In the country comparisons, I use data that are methodologically as similar as possible. Most often, this is the distribution of persons, p, according to household per capita gross income, y_p, abbreviated as $p|y_p$. It is explicitly indicated when other types of data are used. The choice is determined by the type of data generated by East European statistical offices, which have typically ranked households or persons according to gross per capita income.[3]

It is difficult to predict what biases might arise from the variations in data presentation. Attempts at making some conjectures about the impact of these differences were stymied by the numerous exceptions that were identified. There is little guidance from theory in this area. An important future research agenda will be to build up the data base for incidence analysis in these countries on a more comparable basis, along lines similar to what the Luxembourg Income Study has undertaken. But for now, I survey what is known from available sources.

Distributional Incidence of Cash Social Transfers in Eastern Europe and Russia

The following analysis of cash social transfers in Eastern Europe and Russia is based on household surveys conducted in Bulgaria, the Czech and Slovak Federal Republic (CSFR, the former Czechoslovakia), Hungary, Poland, Russia, and the former Yugoslavia. The year of analysis is 1988 for Russia and Yugoslavia and 1989 for the other four countries. The household surveys include information on the following categories of cash social transfers: pensions (all pension schemes are provided by the state), various family allowances, sickness benefits, scholarships, and other social transfers.[4] Appendix 17-1 describes the household surveys and discusses some methodological issues related to them.

The magnitude of cash transfers as a percentage of household gross income and their concentration coefficients are shown in table 17-1. The size and distribution of cash transfers are remarkably similar in the three Central European countries (CSFR, Hungary, and Poland) and Bulgaria. They account for between 21 and 25 percent of household gross income there. Social transfers in cash are a less significant source of household income in Russia and in the former Yugoslavia, where they account for less than 15 and 12 percent of household gross income, respectively.

Table 17-1 also reveals that total cash transfers are distributed almost equally per capita in Bulgaria, CSFR, and Hungary. Concentration coefficients are very small and are not statistically significantly different from zero. (A zero concentration coefficient indicates complete per capita equality in the distribution of transfers.) This almost flat per capita distribution of cash transfers in the aggregate reflects the opposing influences of strongly pro-poor, but relatively small, family allowance systems and relatively large, pro-rich or distribution-neutral pension systems.

Unlike in the other East European countries, the distribution of social transfers in the former Yugoslavia approximates the distribution of gross income (table 17-1). This is due to the "republicanization"—the absence of a centralized system—of pension and social welfare funds. Republicanization is responsible for the existence of significant differences in average pension levels (reflecting differences in wages) between richer and poorer republics; hence, the distribution of pensions is extremely pro-rich ($C = 29.9$). Moreover, pensions account for 90 percent of all cash transfers in the former Yugoslavia. So although family allowances and other social transfers are pro-poor, they have little effect on the overall progressivity of cash transfers.

Russia and, to a lesser extent, Poland are the only countries whose cash social transfers (in the aggregate) are focused on the poor (the concentration coefficient is statistically significant and negative). In Russia, this is essentially due to pensions, which, unlike in the other countries, are pro-poor in absolute terms.[5]

The practically flat distribution of cash transfers across the population in the three Central European countries is in sharp contrast to the situation in market economies, where cash transfers tend to be focused on the poorer segments of the population (see figure 17-2; a flat line in figure 17-2 means that transfers depend not on income, but only on household size).[6] The concentration coefficients of cash transfers in the OECD economies in our sample range from -16 to -44, indicating considerable focus on the poor (see table 17-2).

Table 17-1. Structure and Distribution of Cash Social Transfers

Type of transfer	Bulgaria	CSFR	Hungary	Poland	Russia	Yugoslavia[a]
Percentage of gross income						
Pensions	16.6	16.5	13.4	15.2	8.0	10.7
Family allowances	2.3	5.6	6.0	5.5	1.2	0.4
Sickness benefits	—	3.0	2.0	—	1.4	0.4
Scholarships	2.3	—	0.2	—	0.3	0.2
Other social transfers[b]	—	0.4	0.8	1.4	3.8	0.2
Total cash transfers	21.2	25.4	22.4	22.1	14.6	11.9
State sector wages	55.9	62.8	48.6	57.2	73.8	51.2
Concentration coefficient						
Pensions	10.9	8.1	9.5	−2.6	−19.6	29.9
Family allowances	−17.2	−28.4	−21.9	−12.3	−18.2	−19.9
Sickness benefits	—	13.3	22.1	—	17.1	31.0
Scholarships	5.3	—	9.3	—	19.8	50.1
Other social transfers	—	−19.5	−11.7	14.2	12.1	−24.6
Total cash transfers	7.2	0.3	1.4	−3.9	−6.8	27.5
t-ratio[c]	1.8	0.2	1.5	2.4*	3.4**	4.4**
State sector wages	20.4	26.4	24.4	30.5	28.1	37.4
Gross income[d]	21.7	19.5	24.8	26.1	21.9	36.2

—Not available.

* Significant at 5 percent.

**Significant at 1 percent.

a. Calculated from Vukotić-Cotič 1991, p. 11.

b. Other social transfers include enterprise-provided benefits and a flat-rate maternity grant in CSFR; unemployment benefits plus other benefits in Hungary; birth and funeral allowances, scholarships, trade union and enterprise benefits, imputed value of free transportation, vacation and subsidized drugs in Poland (see Topińska 1991, p. 12); unspecified other transfers plus allowance for poor families with children plus food grants in Russia; social relief and unemployment benefits in Yugoslavia.

c. Standard errors of concentration coefficients for all transfers are calculated using the jackknife technique suggested by Sandstrom, Wretman, and Walden 1988, p. 116.

d. Gross income (after payroll taxes) for all countries except Hungary, where gross income is before taxes, and Yugoslavia, where it is gross revenues.

Source: Household surveys: Yugoslavia 1989 and Czechoslovakia 1990 (both cover the year 1988); for other countries figures are reported for 1989. See appendix 17-1.

Figure 17-2. *Cash Transfers, by Income Decile*

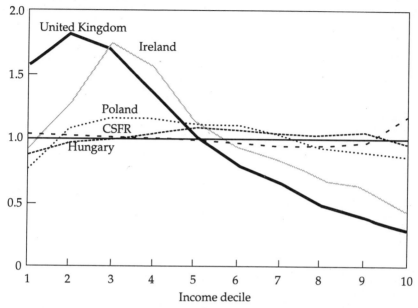

Decile share/mean share

Note: Equal per capita distribution = 1. The years and income concepts reported for the various countries are as follows: Ireland: 1987, households ranked according to household gross income. United Kingdom: 1989, households ranked according to equivalent disposable income. Hungary: 1989, individuals ranked according to household per capita disposable income. Poland: 1989, individuals ranked according to household per capita gross income. CSFR: 1988, individuals ranked according to household per capita money gross income.

Sources: Ireland: Ireland Central Statistical Office (1989). United Kingdom: U.K. Central Statistical Office (1992, table 4, appendix 1, p. 142). Poland, Hungary, and Czechoslovakia: household survey data (see appendix 17-1).

For comparability purposes, table 17-2 presents data only for those market economies where households are ranked according to gross income.[7] The more frequently available data, where households are ranked according to original income, would tend to show a different degree of progressivity.

Pensions

Pensions are the most significant cash social transfer; in every case, they constitute a larger share of household gross income than all other categories of cash transfers combined. In general, pensions' share in household gross income is contained within a very narrow range, with the share fluctuating between 11 and 17 percent. In Russia, exceptionally, the share of pensions is only 8 percent. Russian pensions, as a percentage of average wages, are low (see table 17-3). This helps to

Table 17-2. Concentration Coefficients of Cash Social Transfers

Country	Concentration coefficient
Norway	−44.0
Germany	−35.9
Canada	−34.7
United States	−30.9
Israel	−23.6
Sweden	−19.8
United Kingdom	−19.7
Ireland	−16.4
Russia	−6.8
Poland	−3.9
Czechoslovakia	0.3
Hungary	1.4
Bulgaria	7.2
Yugoslavia	27.5
Chile	32.2

Note: For all countries except Hungary, the ranking of individuals or households is according to gross income; for Hungary, the ranking is according to disposable income. The data for the market economies are of the form ($H|y_H$), households by total household income, while the data for the socialist economies and Chile are of the form ($p|y_p$), persons by household per capita income. This can be expected to influence the comparison of the degree of progressivity between these economies.

Sources: Data for high-income market economies are calculated for 1979–82 from O'Higgins, Schmaus, and Stephenson 1989, table 4; except for Ireland, which is calculated for 1987 from Ireland Central Statistical Office 1989. Data for socialist economies are from table 17-1. Data for Chile include state-mandated pensions; they are for the year 1987 and are calculated from Haindl, Budinich, and Irarrazaval 1989, table 1.10–1.12, pp. 47–49.

Table 17-3. Pensions as a Percentage of Average State Sector Wages

Country and year	Percentage
Bulgaria, 1988	47.3
CSFR, 1988	48.7
Hungary, 1989	66.9
Poland, 1989	45.4
Russia, 1988	35.6
Yugoslavia, 1988	68.6

Sources: Countries' statistical yearbooks.

explain Russia's good targeting of pensions. Because pensions are low and households that receive them have few other sources of income, pensioners are more often poor in Russia than in the East European countries. Pensions are consequently (by default) more targeted on the poor, and their concentration coefficient is strongly negative in Russia (−20), while it is close to zero in Poland (−3), mildly positive in Bulgaria, CSFR, and Hungary (between 8 and 11), and strongly positive in the former Yugoslavia (30; see table 17-1).

Family Allowances

Family allowances play a very important role in CSFR, Hungary, and Poland. For these countries, family allowances are, after pensions, the most important cash transfer, with a share in household gross income of 5 to 6 percent (see table 17-4). This contrasts with an average family allowance share of 1 to 1.5 percent in the West European market economies (calculated from O'Higgins, Schmaus, and Stephenson 1989, p. 116). Family allowances are less important in Bulgaria, where pensions constitute a much larger share of household gross income (17 versus 2 percent for family allowances). In the former Yugoslavia, family allowances are income tested ($C = -20$) and fairly small in size compared with those of the other socialist countries (0.4 percent of household gross income). Family allowances are also relatively insignificant in Russia, where although they are strongly pro-poor ($C = -18$), they make up a smaller share of household gross income than pensions, sickness benefits, and other social transfers.

Family allowances in CSFR and Hungary are paid, respectively, to children or nonworking spouses; hence, in these two countries, workers' and farmers' households benefit similarly from family allowances. In contrast, family allowances are not paid to private farmers in Poland and Yugoslavia, and thus their share in household income differs substantially between farmers and workers.

Family allowances are strongly pro-poor in absolute terms in all five East European countries and in Russia, as indicated by the concentration coefficients given in table 17-4. This means that poor households receive more not only in relative terms (as a share of income) but also in absolute amounts. For example, in CSFR, Hungary, and Poland, the poorest decile receives between three and seven times more in family allowance benefits than the richest decile (see figure 17-3).

In all the sample countries except Yugoslavia, family allowances achieve a significant reduction in inequality, lowering the overall Gini coefficient by approximately 3 percentage points in CSFR and Hungary and by about half a point in Bulgaria, Poland, and Russia (table 17-4). Family allowances are the only cash transfers in the East European countries that are both significant in size and strongly focused on the poor.

Sickness Benefits

Sickness benefits (excluding maternity benefits, which are considered part of family allowances) account for 2 and 3 percent of household gross income in Hungary and CSFR, 1.4 percent in Russia, and 0.4 percent in Yugoslavia. (Data for other countries are not available.) The share of sickness benefits in wages is 4 to 5 percent in Hungary and

Table 17-4. Size and Distributional Impact of Family Allowances

Indicator	Bulgaria 1989	CSFR 1988	Hungary 1989	Poland 1989	Russia 1989	Yugoslavia 1988
Size of family allowance[a]						
Workers	2.5	5.4	6.3	7.2	—	0.5
Farmers	1.2	6.4	7.4	0.5	—	0.1
All households	2.3	5.6	6.0	5.5	1.2	0.4
Distributional impact						
(1) Gini coefficient for gross income (minus family allowance)	22.1	22.4	27.8	26.7	22.3	36.3
(2) Gini coefficient for gross income	21.7	19.5	24.8	26.1	21.9	36.2
(2) – (1)	–0.4	–2.9	–3.0	–0.6	–0.4	–0.1
Family allowance concentration coefficient	–17.2	–28.4	–21.9	–12.3	–18.2	–19.9

—Not available.

a. Individuals are ranked by gross per capita income. The size of the family allowance is given as a percentage of that income.

Source: Same as for table 17-1. See appendix 17-1.

Figure 17-3. Family Allowances, by Income Decile

Decile share/mean share

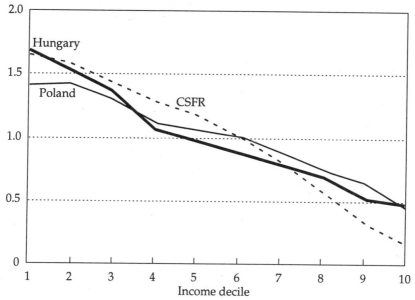

Note: Worker households for Poland. Equal per capita distribution = 1.

the former Czechoslovakia, 2 percent in Russia, and 1 percent in Yugoslavia. In contrast, in the United Kingdom sickness benefits are equal to only 0.5 percent of wages.

As expected, sickness benefits are distributed broadly in proportion to state sector wages (compare their concentration coefficients in table 17-1). For all four countries for which we have data, these transfers are pro-rich in absolute amounts. However, sickness benefits are distributed more equally than household income and thus decrease income inequality.

Scholarships

Scholarships are small in size in Hungary, Russia, and the former Yugoslavia (between 0.2 and 0.3 percent of gross incomes); they are rather significant in Bulgaria (2.3 percent), where they equal family benefits in importance (table 17-1). In Bulgaria and Hungary, they are pro-poor in relative terms; in Russia, they are proportional to gross income; while in Yugoslavia, they are very skewed toward rich households ($C = 50$). The high concentration of benefits on the rich in the former Yugoslavia appears, at first sight, to run contrary to the stated intention of scholarships, which is to provide financial aid to poorer students. This is so, however, only if one considers the Yugoslavia of

1988 as a single entity. If one looks at specific republics, where scholarships were administered and allocated, the picture changes. Richer republics (most notably, Slovenia) had a well-developed system of scholarships. In Slovenia, they were granted to the middle-income and poorer households. In contrast, poorer republics and provinces (for example, Bosnia, Kosovo, or Montenegro) granted few scholarships (see Posarac 1993, p. 97). The fact that middle-income and poor households in Slovenia were often, by Yugoslavia-wide standards, relatively well off helps to explain the high, positive value for the concentration coefficient.

Social Assistance

Social assistance (including unemployment benefits) does not have the importance in socialist economies that it has in market economies, either in its size or in its concentration on the indigent. This is due to the nature of the economic system, where social support is built in at the enterprise level. If full employment is guaranteed, the minimum wage is sufficient to support a modest standard of living, family allowances are relatively high, labor participation rates are high, and pensions are linked to previous earnings, then poverty can only be an accidental phenomenon, and unemployment assistance need not exist. An explicit state policy toward poverty was therefore not necessary in Eastern Europe and Russia and, indeed, did not exist. Antipoverty policy dealt only with "excess" cases such as that of alcoholics and the handicapped and was either undertaken half-heartedly by local authorities or by charitable organizations (in countries, such as Poland, where church involvement was politically acceptable).

Thus, it is not surprising that social assistance makes up a very small share of household gross income. In Yugoslavia, CSFR, and Hungary, respectively, social assistance accounts for 0.2, 0.4, and 0.8 percent of household gross income (see table 17-5); in Russia, social assistance is negligible (0.13 percent of household gross income). A part of social assistance in Russia (aid to poor families with children) and in Yugoslavia (social relief) appears to be extremely well targeted (with concentration coefficients of, respectively, −31 and −70). Another more important part in Russia (food grants) is distributed in proportion to gross income and is thus distribution neutral. The data for other socialist countries are not available. This reflects the minor importance of social assistance. By contrast, social assistance and unemployment benefits in France and the United Kingdom amount to between 1.3 and 3.2 percent of household gross income and are fairly well targeted.

Despite the much smaller size of social assistance in Eastern Europe and Russia, the concentration coefficients for the four socialist economies are closer to zero than the concentration coefficients for France

Table 17-5. Social Assistance Indicators

	Eastern Europe				Chile 1987	France 1984	United Kingdom 1989
Indicator	CSFR 1988	Hungary 1989	Russia 1989	Yugoslavia 1988			
Size of social assistance[a]							
All households	0.4	0.8	0.13	0.2	0.7	1.3	3.2
Concentration coefficients							
Unemployment benefits					−62.2		
Welfare	—	−15.8	—	40.6	−54.9	—	−21.3
Employment programs	—	—	−70.3	−31.2	−49.8	—	−53.1
Other transfers	−19.5	−11.5	28.4	—	—	−46.7	−36.6
All assistance	−19.5	−11.7	5.6	−31.1	−53.5	−46.7	−35.5

—Not available.

a. The size of social assistance is presented as a percentage of household income. Social assistance is defined in Eastern Europe as follows: CSFR, enterprise-provided benefits and flat-rate maternity grant; Hungary, unemployment and other benefits; Russia, allowance for poor families with children (welfare) plus food grants; Yugoslavia, social relief and unemployment benefits. It is defined in other countries as follows: Chile, unemployment compensation plus payments from state employment programs plus direct family allowance (Subsidio Unico Familiar); France, other allowances; United Kingdom, all noncontributory benefits minus child benefits and housing benefits, plus unemployment compensations. The U.K. distribution is of the type (H/y^f), where y^f = equivalent disposable income. The Chilean, East European, and Russian distributions are of the type (p/y_h), where y = gross income. The French distribution is of the type (p/y_h), where y = gross income.

Sources: Data for France are calculated from Canceill 1989. Data for the United Kingdom are calculated from U.K. Central Statistical Office 1992, table 4, app. 1, p. 142. The source for Chile is as given in table 17-2. The sources for the Eastern European countries and Russia are as given in table 17-1.

and the United Kingdom. Social assistance in socialist countries is thus not only smaller in size but also less focused on the poor (though this could be due largely to different definitions across countries).

Chile is a useful comparator because it has a level of per capita income similar to that of Eastern Europe. Chile also has a long history of social assistance and, since the Pinochet regime, has implemented a variety of fairly narrowly targeted programs often based on categorical testing. Table 17-5 includes three such programs: (1) public employment programs operating through self-targeting, (2) welfare programs targeted on children under fifteen years of age as well as on pregnant women and single mothers who are ineligible for family allowances, and (3) unemployment compensation, mostly focused on the young. They are all well targeted (the concentration coefficients range between −50 and −62). It is noteworthy that none of these social assistance programs is based on explicit means testing. The results are potentially encouraging for the countries in transition, which are likely to have to avoid means testing because of difficulties in assessing incomes with any degree of accuracy (due to the size of the informal economy, the lack of personal taxation, underreporting of official incomes, and so forth) and lack of the administrative capacity to implement reasonable income tests.

Distributional Incidence of Social Transfers in Kind in Eastern Europe and Russia

This section explores the relative importance and distributional incidence of social transfers in kind (education and health care benefits). Tables 17-6 and 17-7 show the size of, and concentration coefficients for, transfers in kind in CSFR, Hungary, Poland, and the former Yugoslavia (information on social transfers in kind is not available for Bulgaria and Russia).

Together, education and health benefits contribute between 12 and 16 percent of household gross income in the East European countries. Although this is not an insignificant contribution, with the exception of the former Yugoslavia, benefits in kind constitute a smaller share of household income than cash benefits. By way of comparison, in the United Kingdom benefits in kind and in cash are of about the same importance; in Chile, in-kind benefits are twice the size of cash benefits.

The overall distributional impact of social transfers in kind is mildly to moderately pro-poor in absolute amounts for all four East European countries: the concentration coefficients range from −4 in Hungary to −11 in former Yugoslavia (see table 17-7). In contrast, the concentration coefficient for *cash* transfers is 1 in Hungary and 28 in former Yugoslavia (table 17-1).

Table 17-6. Transfers in Kind as a Percentage of Household Gross Income

	Eastern Europe				Chile 1987	United Kingdom 1989
Indicator	CSFR 1988	Hungary 1989	Poland 1989	Yugoslavia 1988		
Education						
Kindergarten	1.0	0.9	—	—	0.3	—
Primary	3.0	3.3	3.4	—	2.0	—
Secondary and vocational	2.3[a]	1.7	1.4	—	0.8	—
University	—	0.9	0.6	—	1.0	—
Other training	—	0.3	—	—	—	—
All levels	6.3	7.1	5.5	6.3	4.3	5.4
Health care						
Medical consultations	—	—	1.5	—	—	—
Clinical	—	3.2	2.5	—	—	—
Other	—	1.8	5.2	—	—	—
All services	9.3	5.0	9.2	7.8	1.4	6.8
Total education and health	15.6	12.2	14.7	14.0	5.7	12.2
Cash transfers	25.4	22.4	22.1	11.9	2.5	13.1
Transfers in kind as a percentage of all transfers	38.0	35.3	40.0	54.0	69.5	48.2

—Not available.

Note: Education expenditures include subsidized school meals. Cash transfers as defined in table 17-1. For Chile, cash transfers include all monetary transfers including those from the Social Fund; for the United Kingdom, they include all contributory and noncontributory transfers.

a. This percentage also includes university-level schooling in CSFR.

Sources: For Czechoslovakia, calculated from Dlouhý 1991; for Hungary, calculated from Kupa and Fajth 1990; for Poland, calculated from Topińska 1991, table 16, annex 2; for Yugoslavia, calculated from Vukotić-Cotič 1991, table 1; the source for Chile is given in table 17-2, and for the United Kingdom, in table 17-5.

Table 17-7. Concentration Coefficients of Transfers in Kind

Indicator	Eastern Europe				Chile 1987	United Kingdom 1989
	CSFR 1988	Hungary 1989	Poland 1989	Yugoslavia 1988		
Education						
Kindergarten	-34.3	-24.7	—	—	-25.9	—
Primary	-21.3	-20.1	-12.6	—	-27.0	—
Secondary and vocational	-0.4[a]	-7.2	1.7	—	-13.4	—
University	—	13.0	21.6	—	42.9	—
Other training	—	20.0	—	—	—	—
All levels	-15.7	-12.0	-4.8	-22.0	-10.0	-10.1
t-ratio[b]	-3.1**	-5.5**	-1.5	-5.0**	-4.3**	-1.5
Health care						
Medical consultations	—	—	0.6	—	—	—
Clinical	—	4.0	-1.8	—	—	—
Others	—	3.9	-8.9	—	—	-9.0
All services	1.8	4.0	-5.4	-2.4	-36.0	—
t-ratio[b]	1.9	3.6**	-2.2	-2.3*	-9.0**	-5.0**
Total education and health	-5.2	-4.3	-5.2	-11.4	-16.3	-9.5
Gross income Gini	19.5	24.8	26.1	36.2	47.9	35.1

—Not available.

* Significant at 5 percent.

**Significant at 1 percent.

Note: Individuals are ranked by gross household income per capita, except for the United Kingdom, where households are ranked by equivalent disposable income. Education expenditures include subsidized school meals.

a. This figure also includes university-level schooling in CSFR.

b. Standard errors of concentration coefficients for all transfers are calculated using the jackknife technique suggested by Sandstrom, Wretman, and Walden 1988, p. 116.

Sources: For Czechoslovakia, Dlouhý 1991, pp. 13–14; for Hungary, Kupa and Fajth 1990; for Poland, Topińska 1991, pp. 29–31; for Yugoslavia, Vukotić-Cotič 1991, p. 11. The source for Chile is given in table 17-2, and for the United Kingdom, in table 17-5.

Education Benefits

The imputed value of education benefits is approximately 6 to 7 percent of household gross income. More than 60 percent of these benefits are accrued at the kindergarten and primary school levels. The degree of progressivity of benefits declines with the level of education. Most targeted are kindergarten benefits (the concentration coefficient is −34 for CSFR and −25 for Hungary), followed by primary education (the concentration coefficients are around −20 for both CSFR and Hungary). Secondary education benefits are markedly less focused on the poor: their concentration coefficients hover close to zero, indicating a practically flat distribution for these benefits. Poland follows this general pattern, although education benefits are less pro-poor at all levels in Poland than in CSFR and Hungary.

Finally, university education benefits are positively correlated with the level of income, although they are still pro-poor in that they are *less unequally* distributed than gross income. The data for Hungary and Poland (the only countries for which data are available) indicate, however, that only a little more than 10 percent of all education benefits are received at the university level (since benefits are estimated on the basis of costs, 10 percent of costs are incurred at that level). In consequence, total education benefits are pro-poor in absolute terms in all four countries, although in the case of Poland the concentration coefficient is not statistically significant.

For comparison, tables 17-6 and 17-7 also present the results for Chile and the United Kingdom. As figure 17-4 also shows, targeting in the area of education is very similar to that in Eastern Europe. Education benefits overall are pro-poor in absolute terms, and their progressivity decreases with the level of education. Chile, however, differs from Eastern Europe in that the correlation between university benefits and the level of income is much stronger: education benefits at that level are almost as skewed as income. This implies that relatively few students belong to families that are (at that point in time, at least) not well off. The size of education benefits expressed in relation to gross income appears to be less in Chile and the United Kingdom than in Eastern Europe, because private expenditures play a role in the former but not in the latter.

It is sometimes argued that the finding that education benefits become less progressive with the level of education simply reflects life cycle effects—namely, that young parents with relatively low income and still climbing up their earnings curve have young children who go to kindergarten or primary school (Birdsall and James 1993). As parents age, their income increases, reaching perhaps the peak at the time when children attend university. The life cycle effect, however, applies equally to all facets of income distribution, not only to the

Figure 17-4. Public Education Benefits

Cumulative percentage of benefits

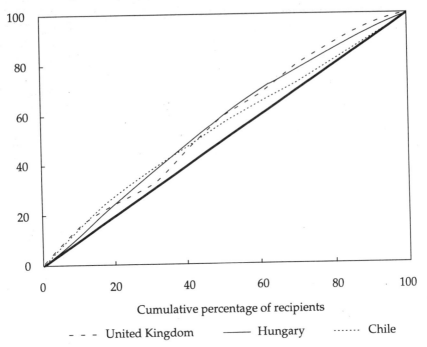

Cumulative percentage of recipients

--- United Kingdom   —— Hungary   ······· Chile

distribution of education benefits. Paglin (1975) tried to take this into account by deducting from under the standard Lorenz curve the area showing age inequality (to account for the age-income profile; although Paglin's approach was later found to be incorrect—see Danziger, Haveman, and Smolensky 1977—the idea is sound). Accounting for the life cycle effect, however, makes sense only in cross-country comparisons when (1) one country (say, socialist) displays a flat age-income profile and another (capitalist) displays a very steep one or (2) two countries have vastly different demographic profiles. Conventional measures of inequality based on annual data would, in case (1), be biased in favor of a socialist country, where calculated inequality will be less. When age-income profiles do not differ, as is indeed the case in our sample of socialist economies, Paglin's approach is redundant, because our question is not, What is life cycle ("true") inequality? but, more modestly, What is the distribution of benefits between the poor and the rich at a given moment? Persons who are now poor may later become rich and vice versa. The point is still that *today's* poor would be better off *today* if they received more benefits.

Figure 17-5. Public Health Care Benefits

Cumulative percentage of benefits

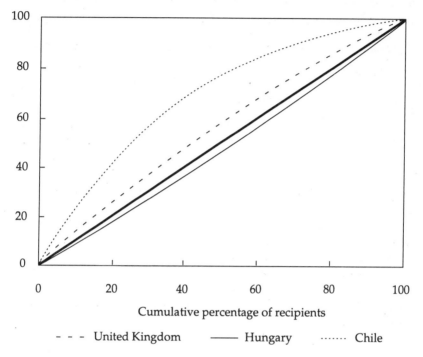

Cumulative percentage of recipients

- - - United Kingdom   ——— Hungary   ⋯⋯ Chile

Health Care Benefits

Health care benefits are, except in Hungary, larger than education benefits. They amount to more than 9 percent of household gross income in CSFR and Poland, almost 8 percent in the former Yugoslavia, and 5 percent in Hungary. Health benefits are, by and large, distributed uniformly per capita: concentration coefficients in CSFR, Poland, and the former Yugoslavia are not statistically different from zero. Hungary's concentration coefficient for health benefits is positive and statistically significant; however, the coefficient is very low (4.0). No marked difference in progressivity is detectable between various types of health benefits in countries where the breakdown is available.

The results for the United Kingdom and, particularly, for Chile indicate much greater progressivity in health benefits than that found in Eastern Europe (figure 17-5). The concentration coefficients for Chile and the United Kingdom are highly negative and significantly different from zero. This greater progressivity is due to the facts that public expenditures for health coexist with private expenditures and that recipients of the former are disproportionately poor households. In socialist economies, where health is entirely socialized, benefits cannot be focused on the poor unless the poor happen to fall sick (1) more often, (2) for longer periods, or (3) from diseases more expensive to cure. Although it is not unreasonable to assume that at least one of the three conditions does hold, it is also true that even in a fully socialized health service, the poor often receive lower quality of health care than the rich. This occurs because the rich can more easily bribe doctors or provide counterfavors (see, for example, Pataki 1992). The practice is quite common in Eastern Europe. Elements (1)–(3) are therefore offset or possibly even overwhelmed by the easier access of the rich. Health benefits are therefore unlikely to be focused on the poor in a fully socialized health system: an equal per capita distribution is the best that can be expected, and this is the result obtained for CSFR, Poland, and Yugoslavia (the concentration coefficient is not statistically significantly different from zero), while for Hungary the concentration coefficient is positive.

We can draw the following conclusions. In countries with a largely socialized education and health care system, education benefits are more focused on the poor than health benefits, which are approximately equal per capita. In countries with a relatively large private health care system, the reverse is true, because the rich tend to opt out from socialized health care. In effect, the rich opt out of socialized health care more than out of socialized education: by default, health benefits become more focused on the poor.

The World of Welfare Socialism

This chapter has explored the role, structure, and distributional impact of the social transfer systems in place in Eastern Europe and Russia as of the late 1980s. I now briefly consider the characteristics typical of social transfer systems in market economies and compare them to those found under socialism. Esping-Andersen (1990) defines three worlds (archetypes) of welfare capitalism. They are the liberal world of residual social welfare, where transfers are limited and generally means tested; the conservative and corporatist world of sizable yet mostly earnings-related transfers; and the sociodemocratic world of large social transfers, where welfare is treated as a "universal right." In terms of countries, the liberal world is confined to Anglo-Saxon countries, Japan, and Switzerland; the conservative world, to continental Europe; and the sociodemocratic world, to the Netherlands and Scandinavia.

Figure 17-6 illustrates how Russia and the Eastern European countries compare with high-income capitalist countries in terms of the targeting and size of their cash transfer systems.[8] The socialist welfare system differs from the three capitalist worlds in its almost total absence of transfer targeting. In terms of the size of transfers, it stands between

Figure 17-6. Size of Cash Transfers and Targeting

Concentration coefficient of transfers

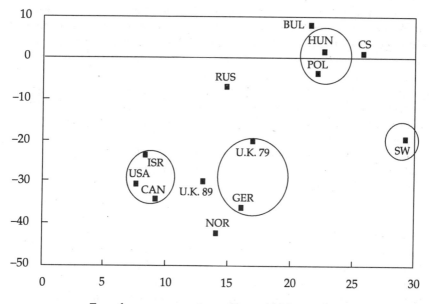

Transfers as a percentage of household gross income

Note: Market economies in 1979–82, socialist economies in 1988–89. CS, Czechoslovakia; ISR, Israel; SW, Sweden.

the conservative and sociodemocratic systems.[9] And finally, it shares with the sociodemocratic system an emphasis on universalism and a reliance on state-run pensions and health insurance schemes.

Conclusions: Lessons for the Transition

Cash transfers in socialist economies in the years immediately preceding the collapse of socialism accounted for about a fifth of population gross income, a percentage comparable to that in high-income welfare economies. They were generally unrelated to income levels and were paid with respect to demographic characteristics. To the extent that some of these characteristics were correlated with income (for example, the number of children per household was negatively correlated with per capita household income), some transfers—notably, family allowances—played a redistributive function. Overall, however, cash transfers were distributed almost equally per capita (except in Yugoslavia, where social transfers actually favored the rich in absolute amounts). This is in marked contrast to the situation in market economies, where transfers are much more focused on low-income households. Moreover, certain types of social assistance that are significant in high-income capitalist economies—for example, unemployment insurance—either did not exist or were insignificant under socialism. The analysis presented earlier in the chapter also showed that social transfers in kind (education and health benefits) were mildly to moderately pro-poor in Eastern Europe and that the percentage of household gross income accounted for by transfers in these countries was broadly similar to that for the United Kingdom.

The social transfer systems in place in Eastern Europe and Russia at the end of the 1980s were a legacy of their socialist history; they reflected the needs and structure of socialist societies. Will these transfer systems satisfy new needs under capitalism?

The relationship between income and wage distributions, on the one hand, and cash social transfers, on the other, will be an important issue during the transition. Currently, wages and cash transfers account for about 80 percent of household gross income in countries in transition. The distribution of both will change. Wages are likely to become more unequal. To counteract an increase in income disparities, social transfers must become more focused on the poor.

The relationship between increased wage disparity and better provision of social support is not novel. During the transition from feudalism to capitalism, the labor market supplanted personalized and paternalistic relationships and weakened a number of social buffers (guilds, the family). It has been argued that the transition to capitalism resulted in an increase in the number of the poor (see Polak and Williamson 1991, p. 41). This necessitated that the state take the role of provider of last resort. The situation in countries in transition from socialism to capitalism is similar. In socialism, social support was built into the system at the enterprise level. In the move to capitalism, this structure, where social protection was implicit, is being replaced by an economic system in which employment and wages play the key role. Persons who cannot earn a sufficient wage must now be supported by the state.

However paradoxical it may seem at first sight, the state in Eastern Europe is ill-prepared for this task. Although the role of the state was pervasive in socialism, as we have seen, these governments have little or no experience in identifying the needy and in administering and delivering targeted support. Yet the state will have to take on itself such a role as transition to a market system occurs.

It seems likely that the social transfer systems in Eastern Europe and Russia will evolve toward one of the three models of welfare capitalism in the wake of the transition. The question is, toward which system will they gravitate? In my view, the most probable evolution of the Central European countries is toward the corporatist model of continental Europe. The countries of continental Europe have large social transfer systems; however, these transfers have a limited redistributive role because of their relation to previous earnings. These systems are thus more akin to social insurance than to social assistance. High trade union density and Catholic corporatism are also features of this model (see Esping-Andersen 1990). It would seem that the three Central European countries (the former Czechoslovakia, Hungary, and Poland) and the new countries of Croatia and Slovenia fit that mold. Neither the size nor the main principles of transfer determination would need to be altered significantly for Central European countries to resemble their capitalist neighbors.[10]

Because transfers such as pensions will be linked to past earnings records, when most people were employed and wages were compressed, or will be based on categorical characteristics (such as number of children), poverty is likely to be highest among persons who fall between the cracks. These might include the newly unemployed with little or no previous job history; low-wage, single-parent households; or, as in Poland, the rural poor, who receive disproportionately few social transfers under the existing system. The current system will therefore have to be complemented by the introduction of several targeted mechanisms designed especially to help these groups.

The future evolution of the welfare systems in the more agricultural Balkan countries and the Slavic republics of the former Soviet Union is more difficult to predict. Some elements that characterize corporatist European systems are, however, present in these countries as well. According to Esping-Andersen (1990), corporatism is closely related to etatism, manifested (among other things) in a more exalted position enjoyed by civil servants. The number of distinct occupational pension schemes and the size of pension payments to former government employees are thus two key variables correlated with continental corporatism. Such features existed and still exist in the Balkans and Russia. In these countries, there was historically a marked split between the bureaucracy and the rest of the populace. The legacy of socialism has probably reinforced the strong pro-etatist bias.

Whether the social transfer systems in Eastern Europe and Russia evolve toward the conservative world of welfare capitalism or toward some other model, one thing is clear: these countries will need to revise their transfer systems to match their new, more capitalistic economic structures. In the world of welfare socialism, social transfers in the aggregate were generally untargeted by income, either directly or indirectly. Eastern Europe and Russia will most likely need to target their transfers more on the poor if they are to address the expected increases in vulnerability among their population. Targeting social transfers to the needy may become particularly important when the size of the government budget relative to gross domestic product shrinks under a more market-based economic structure.

Appendix 17-1: Characteristics of Surveys and Adequacy of Data

The analysis presented in this chapter is based on household survey data collected by the Central Statistical Office in each of the study countries. The measures of transfer size and progressivity are calculated from summary statistics prepared by the Central Statistical Office or other researchers, not directly from the unit record data. For three countries—CSFR, Poland, and the former Yugoslavia—I use household survey data published by the Central Statistical Office: for Czechoslovakia, the data are published in *Mikrocensus 1989:1.dil*; for Poland, *Budżety Gospodarstw Domowych w 1989*; for Yugoslavia, *Anketa o potrošnji domaćinstava u 1988: Raspoloživa i upotrebljena sredstva: Proseci po članu domaćinstva*. In the analysis for Poland, I also use the unpublished decile data supplied by the Central Statistical Office. Data for Hungary and Bulgaria are from the countries' central statistical offices and are available on computer spreadsheets from the author on request. As noted in the tables and figures, in some cases measures are also calculated from data presented in Dlouhý (1991), Kupa and Fajth (1990), Topińska (1991), Večernik (1991), and Vukotić-Cotič (1991). The Russian data are taken from Popkin (1992). They are derived from the Consumer Budget Survey for 1989 combined with the Survey of Incomes conducted by the Russian State Statistical Bureau in 1989 on a sample of 1 million persons.

The Bulgarian, Polish, and Yugoslav surveys are conducted annually. In 1988–89, they covered, respectively, 2,720, 28,285, and 18,650 households (representing approximately 0.09, 0.25, and 0.3 percent of all households). The Polish and Yugoslav surveys have been frequently used by researchers. They are considered fairly representative and reliable, even if not entirely free of problems (for example, the definition of income in the Yugoslav survey is incorrect, since the concept used is more akin to revenues). In Poland, the surveys represent about 90 percent of the population, leaving out the nonagricultural private sector, army, and police personnel. The Bulgarian and Russian surveys follow the so-called "branch principle," which means that households are selected at the place of work. This provides for a good check of wage data but biases the results, since some household incomes are unreported (the survey relies only on recollections of one member of the household), and some groups are underrepresented (private sector workers). Also, pensioner households are not included as an integral part of the survey but are added on from a special subsurvey of pensioners.

The Czechoslovak survey is a periodic survey. The last survey prior to the one in 1988 was conducted in 1985. The 1988 survey includes about 1.9 percent of all households. The Hungarian data originate from two separate sources. The first is the 1987 Income Survey done on about

Table 17A-1. Type of Distribution and Income Concepts Used in Surveys, by Country

Country	Type of distribution	Number of income groups	Income concept for ranking
Bulgaria	$(p \mid y_p)$	10	Gross income
CSFR	$(p \mid y_p)$	25	Gross money income
Hungary	$(p \mid y_p)$	14	Disposable income
Poland	$(p \mid y_p)$	10	Gross income
Russia	$(p \mid y_p)$	10	Gross income
Yugoslavia	$(p \mid y_p)$	10	Gross revenue

22,000 households (0.55 percent of all households). Income surveys are conducted every five years. The second is the 1989 Household Budget Survey. Budget surveys are done every two years on about 12,000 households. Using microsimulations, the Central Statistical Office updated earnings/incomes from the 1987 Income Survey to obtain income estimates for 1989, to be used along with the budget expenditures data. In the same manner, the Central Statistical Office also accounted for the impact of the introduction of personal income taxation in 1988. A statistical reweighting was then undertaken to reconcile the updated income survey and the budget survey and to produce a single data set.

Ranking of Recipients

The Polish and Russian surveys rank individuals into ten income groups (not necessarily deciles) according to gross income per household member. The Hungarian surveys rank individuals into fourteen income groups (the four lowest and four highest income classes, containing 5 percent of persons each, and six decile classes) according to household per capita disposable income. The Bulgarian, Czechoslovak, and Yugoslav surveys rank households and, since the data on average household size are provided, also individuals, into ten (Bulgaria and Yugoslavia) and twenty-five (CSFR) income groups according to gross money income (CSFR), gross revenue (Yugoslavia), and gross income (Bulgaria) per household member. These points are summarized in table 17A-1.

The Definition of Income

In addition to the usual difficulties, such as the treatment of capital gains and the distinction between nominal and real returns on assets, the problem of what constitutes income is compounded in this study by (1) less than full inclusion of income earned in the second (underground) economy, (2) unsatisfactory survey design (for example, the mixing of household income with revenues such as those derived from the sale of assets), and (3) the exclusion of other implicit sources of income (general subsidies, enterprise-provided benefits in kind) except for consumption in kind.

The first problem is satisfactorily dealt with only in Hungary. The other countries do not attempt to measure tips or "black incomes" or to account for possible underestimation of income by the households. The second problem—bad survey design—is present in Yugoslavia. The Yugoslav survey includes personal borrowing, withdrawals from savings accounts, and revenues from lease or sale of property as part of income. The first two items are not typically considered part of income. The last item represents a mixture of reduction in the value of property and income (leasing). A related problem is the absence of coverage of property incomes and, in particular, of income from financial assets in almost all of the surveys. Only the Hungarian survey includes the latter. Other surveys provide information (withdrawals from saving accounts) that can, after making some assumptions about the relationship between the average stock of deposits, withdrawals, and interest received, be used to estimate the value of real interest received. However, since in 1988 and 1989 the real interest rate on household deposits was negative or at best zero in all the countries, it is not necessary to make the adjustment (even if, strictly speaking, income should be reduced when real interest is negative). None of the surveys attempts to measure net returns on foreign exchange, which, in the absence of other financial instruments, was often the preferred hedge against inflation.

The third, and a more fundamental, problem is the questionable suitability of using money income alone (adjusted or unadjusted for illicit incomes) to measure inequality in the presence of rationing, subsidization, and widespread payments in kind. To quote Bergson (1984, p. 1058), "With prices below clearing levels, money income ceases to be the sole determinant of capacity to acquire goods; to a degree, fortitude in searching out supplies and standing in queues, and plain luck, become consequential." On the one hand, under socialism, households receive implicit income from consumer subsidies (holding prices below equilibrium levels), below-market rents, negative interest rates charged on consumer loans, "collective consumption" (enterprise-financed health care, cafeterias, vacations, and so forth), or special, often in-kind, bonuses and premia (enterprise-provided benefits in kind are, however, included in Polish surveys). On the other hand, household income is implicitly reduced through financial repression (the payment of negative interest rates on savings deposits) and the inflation tax on money.

Subsidies paid out by the state to cover the difference between costs of production and the retail prices of consumer goods (inclusive of

Table 17A-2. Explicit (Paid-out) Consumer Subsidies, by Country
(percent)

Country and year	GDP	Household gross income
Bulgaria, 1990	3.2	6[a]
CSFR, 1988	5.8	12.9
Hungary, 1989	6.7	12.4
Poland, 1989	6.7	13.8

Note: Excludes agricultural subsidies to producers and subsidies to loss-makers.
a. Estimate.

Sources: For Bulgaria, consumer subsidies for "essential" products (from World Bank 1991a, p. 38); for CSFR, negative turnover tax (consumer subsidies) plus subsidies for housing, residential heating, and urban transport; for Hungary, consumer and housing loan subsidies (from OECD 1991, table 10, p. 64); for Poland, food, transport and housing subsidies.

housing subsidies) give an indication of the size of implicit income. Because equilibrium prices of some subsidized products and services are greater than their costs of production (as is the case, for example, for housing or electricity, where explicit subsidies cover only operating costs), explicit subsidies represent a lower limit of actual transfers.

As table 17A-2 shows, subsidies in CSFR, Hungary, and Poland range, in terms of GDP, between 6 and 7 percent; in terms of households' gross incomes, they amount to twice that percentage. This is about half the magnitude of explicit cash transfers in these countries. Subsidies are negligible only in the former Yugoslavia (not shown in table).

The pervasiveness of the system—subsidized vacations for workers, special shops stocked with unavailable consumer durables for miners, and so forth—does not allow one to assert, as is sometimes done, that inclusion of implicit incomes would necessarily increase income disparity.[11] On the contrary, there is strong evidence that consumer subsidies, easily the largest chunk of implicit income, have an opposite effect that is likely to offset that of the nomenklatura perks.

Using estimates by Matthews (1978) and various data on nomenklatura perks in Poland, Morrisson (1984) estimates an alternative income distribution in Eastern Europe that includes the monetized value of fringe benefits appropriated by the nomenklatura. Morrisson's results (1984, table 2) suggest that the Gini coefficient increases by 3 to 4 points. However, consumer subsidies are pro-poor in relative terms and, due to their size, exert a significant impact on income distribution. For example, a study of Poland's subsidies in 1987 (World Bank 1989) finds that inclusion of consumer subsidies reduces income inequality, measured by the Gini coefficient, from 21.8 to 20.0. Kupa and Fajth (1990, p. 37) similarly calculate that the Gini coefficient for Hungary is reduced from 23.1 (for disposable income) to 22.0 (for disposable income plus subsidies). Some preliminary evidence for CSFR also points to the same conclusion: the negative turnover tax (a type of consumer subsidy) represents 7.1 percent of household expenditures in the lowest and 4.4 percent in the highest income decile (World Bank 1991b, p. 59). And on the basis of household expenditure surveys, Večernik (1991, p. 17) calculates that the lowest quartile of households in Czecho-slovakia receives per capita 7.5 percent more food subsidies than the average, while the top quartile receives 6.1 percent less than the aver-age.[12] Similar results are obtained for Algeria (Stanovnik 1991, p. 41).

The inclusion of consumer subsidies in addition to the nomenklatura in-kind benefits would thus probably bring the Gini coefficient close to its value recorded in the household surveys. It can then be argued that the use of the survey data yields an accurate picture of income inequality even in socialist economies. Moreover, as far as international comparisons are concerned, similar adjustments for in-kind benefits could easily increase the measured inequality in market economies. In some countries (for example, Japan), the fringe benefits of upper management often exceed their salaries, while offsetting effects (on income distribution) of consumer subsidies are negligible (social trans-fers to the poor are largely monetized and already included in money income).

Notes

1. Progressivity compares the distribution of an income source (transfer) or a tax with the distribution of, say, gross income. In the case of taxation, when the share of taxes in gross income increases with the level of income, we say that taxes are progressive. Conversely, for transfers, when the share of transfers in gross income *decreases* with the level of income, we say that transfers are progressive.

2. Grouped or aggregated data also introduce another problem. When one has only, say, a dozen data points rather than individual data for several thousand households, income distribution statistics are then approximations. However, several studies have shown that approximations can be very accurate (Davies and Shorrocks 1989; Jenkins 1988). Moreover, the bounds within which the "true" values of different statistics lie can be calculated.

3. Original or market income is income (wages plus net self-employment income plus property income plus other income like private transfers) before personal taxes and government transfers. Gross income is equal to original income plus social cash transfers. Gross income is the central income concept used here. Disposable income is equal to gross income minus direct personal taxes. It should be noted, however, that in Eastern Europe "gross income" is somewhat different from gross income as defined in the West. East European gross income is income after the deduction of payroll taxes (deducted at source). Since payroll taxes account for almost all of direct taxes, East European gross income is fairly close to disposable income. Only Hungary is an exception to this rule, because by 1989 its taxation system was already overhauled in accordance with that existing in market economies.

4. Family allowances vary slightly among the countries. Poland's surveys distinguish between universal family allowances (paid for each dependent child or spouse), child care benefits (paid if a dependent child requires pro-

longed medical treatment), and maternity allowances (to compensate for earnings lost during maternity leave). Czechoslovak surveys include child care benefits and maternity allowances. Hungarian data include child care benefits and family allowances. Bulgarian data combine all the above family allowances. Russian data include maternity allowances and grants paid with respect to children. Finally, Yugoslav data include only income-tested family allowances. In some countries, such as Bulgaria and Poland, sickness benefits are entirely borne by enterprises and thus are not shown as government (social) transfers.

5. Pro-poor in absolute terms means that poor households receive more of a given transfer in absolute terms (the concentration curve lies above the 45 degree line); pro-poor in relative terms means that the share of a transfer in gross income is greater for poor than for rich households, while in absolute terms, the poor receive less than the rich (the concentration coefficient lies between the 45 degree line and the Lorenz curve); finally, pro-rich transfers are such that their share in gross income increases with gross income (the concentration curve lies below the Lorenz curve).

6. The increase in transfers between the first and the second or third decile in Ireland and the United Kingdom occurs because individuals in the second and third income decile receive most of the transfers in the form of relatively higher pensions, while those in the lowest decile receive them as lower noncontributory benefits (welfare).

7. Another problem that affects the comparison between socialist and market economies is the share of pensions that are state provided or state mandated in market economies. If most or all pensions are paid by the state (as in Germany, Norway, and Sweden), the comparison is meaningful. If, however, a sizable portion of pensions either is provided by enterprise pension plans or is fully voluntary through individual savings (such as Individual Retirement Accounts, or IRAS), the comparison is biased. This is because pensions, due to their positive correlations with earnings, are less progressive than other social transfers. The result is that social transfers, which by definition exclude occupational or IRA-type pension schemes, then appear less progressive than in the countries where only state pension plans exist. Among the market economies in table 17-2, almost all pensions are state administered or state mandated: in Sweden, 94 percent of total pension expenditures are state administered or state mandated; similarly, in Germany, Norway, and the United Kingdom, the comparable figures are 89, 92, and 89 percent, respectively. Only in Canada and the United States do social security and public sector pensions account for, respectively, 62 and 79 percent of pension outlays (data for 1980, from Esping-Andersen 1990, p. 85). The comparison is therefore warranted.

8. Figure 17-7 broadly accords with Esping-Andersen's classification, except for the rather unique position of the Swedish system, whose key characteristics are not shared, as he argues, by Norway. Canada, Israel, and the United States have well-targeted systems. This is probably made necessary by the relative parsimony of their systems. The United Kingdom and Sweden have the least-targeted systems among the market economies. However, the U.K. situation had somewhat changed by the late 1980s, with a decrease in the size of transfers accompanied by increased targeting. Based on Mitchell's data (1991, app. C, p. 221), the concentration coefficient of cash transfers in the United Kingdom was -26 in 1979; in 1987, the concentration coefficient was -35 (calculated from U.K. Central Statistical Office, 1990, app. 4, table 1, p. 117). In both cases, households are ranked according to original income. The size of transfers was 20 percent of gross income in 1979 and 14 percent in 1987.

9. Social transfers, expressed in terms of total household income, are often greater in socialist than in market economies, while the reverse is true when transfers are expressed in terms of gross domestic product (GDP). Thus for the 1980s, Rutkowska (1991) finds that cash social transfers in Czechoslovakia, Hungary, Poland, and Yugoslavia averaged about 10 percent of GDP versus 12 percent for the OECD as a whole and 16 percent for social-welfare OECD countries. In terms of household income, the difference is smaller or even in favor of socialist countries. This is because households receive a smaller portion of GDP in socialism than in capitalism; for example, under socialism almost none of corporate savings and investment is mediated through personal (household) income.

10. The position of Poland is more ambiguous. Strong Catholicism with an accent on the role of the family as the main social buffer (rather than the state) and a belief in the overcoming of class divisions through corporatism seem to suggest that the Polish case might more closely resemble the rest of Catholic Europe (Austria is the best example). Recently, a liberal Polish social scientist, Janusz Korwin-Mikke (1992), wrote that he fears the rise of "Christian socialism." The same view is echoed by Lash (1991, p. 106): "Any pervasive presence of confessional politics [in Poland], such as in Germany and Holland, makes it very difficult to pursue a neo-liberal route. A strong church usually makes for social cohesion and strong 'social' element to any market economy." In contrast, Esping-Andersen (1990, p. 30) in discussing the rise of the sociodemocratic welfare state in Sweden, puts the emphasis on the emergence of a "red-green" alliance between strong workers' trade unions and farmers. Such an alliance traded a generous welfare system for workers with subsidies for farmers. An incipient alliance of that kind is evident in Poland. This alliance may tilt the system toward a more universalist stance, closer to the sociodemocratic model.

11. An exaggerated perception of the nomenklatura fringe benefits is common in Eastern Europe due to the often secretive nature in which these benefits were distributed. This led people to ascribe them greater importance than they had in reality.

12. The implicit assumption is that households with different incomes pay the same average price for the subsidized good. In other words, the percentages of consumption at subsidized and free market prices are independent of the level of income.

References

Bergson, Abram. 1984. "Inequality under Soviet Socialism." *Journal of Economic Literature* 22 (September): 1052–99.

Birdsall, Nancy, and Estelle James. 1993. "Efficiency and Equity in Social Spending: How and Why Governments Misbehave." In Michael Lipton and Jacques van der Gaag, eds., *Including the Poor.* Washington, D.C.: World Bank.

Canceill, Genevieve. 1989. "Les revenus fiscaux des ménages en 1984." Les Collections de l'INSEE, Paris.

Czechoslovakia, Federal Statistical Office. 1990. *Mikrocensus 1989:1.dil.* Prague.

Danziger, Sheldon, Robert H. Haveman, and Eugene Smolensky. 1977. "The Measurement and Trend of Inequality: Comment." *American Economic Review* 67 (3): 505–12.

Davies, James B., and A. F. Shorrocks. 1989. "Optimal Grouping of Income and Wealth Data." *Journal of Econometrics* 42 (1): 97–108.

Dlouhý, Jiri. 1991. "The Impact of Social Transfers on Income Distribution in the Czech and Slovak Federal Republic." Research Project on Social Expenditures and Their Distributional Impact in Eastern Europe, Paper 4. World Bank, Socialist Economies Reform Unit, Country Economics Department, Washington, D.C.

Esping-Andersen, Gosta. 1990. *The Three Worlds of Welfare Capitalism*. Cambridge, Eng.: Polity Press.

Haindl, Erik R., Ema Budinich, and Ignacio Irarrazaval. 1989. *Gasto social efectivo*. Santiago de Chile: Oficina de Planificación Nacional y Universidad de Chile, Facultad de Ciencias Económicas y Administrativas.

Ireland, Central Statistical Office. 1989. *Household Budget Survey*, vol. 1. Dublin. December.

Jenkins, Stephen. 1988. "Reranking and the Analysis of Income Redistribution." *Scottish Journal of Political Economy* 35 (1): 65–76.

Korwin-Mikke, Janusz. 1992. *Zycie Gospodarcze*, January 6, p. 14.

Kupa, Mihaly, and Gaspar Fajth. 1990. "Hungarian Social Policy Systems and Distribution of Incomes of Households." Budapest.

Lash, Scott. 1991. "Disorganizing Socialism?" In Jerzy Hauser, Bob Jessop, and Klaus Nielsen, eds., *Markets Politics and the Negotiated Economy: Scandinavian and Post Socialist Perspectives*. Cracow: Cracow Academy of Economics.

Matthews, Marvyn. 1978. *Privilege in the Soviet Union*. London: Allen and Unwin.

Mitchell, Deborah. 1991. *Income Transfers in Ten Welfare States*. Brookfield, Vt.: Avebery.

Morrisson, Christian. 1984. "Income Distribution in East European and Western Countries." *Journal of Comparative Economics* 8: 121–38.

OECD (Organization for Economic Cooperation and Development). 1991. *Hungary 1991*. OECD Economic Surveys. Paris.

O'Higgins, Michael, Guenther Schmaus, and Geoffrey Stephenson. 1989. "Income Distribution and Redistribution: A Microdata Analysis for Seven Countries." *Review of Income and Wealth* 35: 107–31.

Paglin, Morton. 1975. "The Measurement and Trend of Inequality: A Basic Revision." *American Economic Review* 65 (4): 598–609.

Pataki, Judith. 1992. "Reform of the Hungarian Health Care System." *Radio Free Europe/Radio Liberty Research Report* 1 (6): 59–62.

Polak, Ben, and Jeffrey G. Williamson. 1991. "Poverty, Policy, and Industrialization: Lessons from the Distant Past." Policy Research Working Paper 645. World Bank, Country Economics Department, Washington, D.C.

Poland, Central Statistical Office. 1990. *Budżety Gospodarstw Domowych w 1989*. Roku, Warsaw.

Popkin, Barry M. 1992. "Poverty in the Russian Federation: Demographics and Coverage by Current Support Systems." University of North Carolina at Chapel Hill. January 29.

Posarac, Aleksandra. 1993. "Social Transfers in the Former Yugoslavia, 1978–1989." Research Project on Social Expenditures and Their Distributional Impact in Eastern Europe, Paper 5. World Bank, Socialist Economies Reform Unit, Country Economics Department, Washington, D.C.

Rutkowska, Izabela. 1991. "Public Transfers in Socialist and Market Economies." Research Project on Social Expenditures and Their Distributional Impact in Eastern Europe, Paper 7. World Bank, Socialist Economies Reform Unit, Country Economics Department, Washington, D.C.

Sandstrom, Arne, Jan H. Wretman, and Bertil Walden. 1988. "Variance Estimators of the Gini-Coefficients—Probability Sampling." *Journal of Business and Economic Statistics* (January): 113–19.

Stanovnik, Tine. 1991. *Consumer Subsidization in Algeria*. Ljubljana: Institut za Ekonomska Raziskovanja.

Topińska, Irena. 1991. "The Impact of Social Transfers on Income Distribution: Poland." Research Project on Social Expenditures and Their Distributional Impact in Eastern Europe, Paper 2. World Bank, Socialist Economies Reform Unit, Country Economics Department, Washington, D.C.

U.K., Central Statistical Office. 1990. "The Effects of Taxes and Benefits on Household Income, 1987." *Economic Trends* 439 (May): 84–118.

———. 1992. "The Effects of Taxes and Benefits on Household Income, 1989." *Economic Trends* 459 (January): 127–65.

Večernik, Jiři. 1991. "Income Distribution in Czechoslovakia." BIRG Bulletin 13: 14.

Vukotić-Cotič, Gordana. 1991. "Social Transfers and Income Inequality in the Ante-Bellum Yugoslavia, 1988." Research Project on Social Expenditures and Their Distributional Impact in Eastern Europe, Paper 6. World Bank, Socialist Economies Reform Unit, Country Economics Department, Washington, D.C.

World Bank. 1989. *Poland: Subsidies and Income Distribution*. World Bank Report 7776-POL. Washington, D.C.

———. 1991a. *Bulgaria: Crisis and Transition to a Market Economy*, vol. 1. Washington, D.C.

———. 1991b. *Czechoslovakia: Transition to a Market Economy*. World Bank Country Study. Washington, D.C.

Yugoslavia, Federal Office of Statistics. 1989. *Anketa o potrošnji domaćinstava u 1988: Raspoloživa i upotrebljena sredstva: Proseci po članu domaćinstva*. Statistical Bulletin 1788. Belgrade.

18 Distributional Effects of Social Sector Expenditures in Malaysia, 1974–89

Jeffrey S. Hammer, Ijaz Nabi, and James A. Cercone

Social services, particularly in health and education, have been an important part of Malaysia's strategy for reducing poverty and economic disparities among ethnic groups. Investments in human capital are often highlighted as major contributors to the increased productivity of this rapidly growing country. It is now an opportune time to evaluate the contribution these services have made to the goal of promoting growth and equity for two reasons. First, the guiding policy framework of the past two decades, the New Economic Policy, has come to an end, offering a natural point for reevaluation. Second, as the government of Malaysia is currently reevaluating the relative roles of the government and the private sector in providing a wide range of infrastructure and social services, it is useful to document trends in the contribution made thus far by this set of public expenditures.

This chapter examines the impact of government spending and policy in the social sectors from the early 1970s through the late 1980s in Malaysia. It addresses the following questions. Who are the primary recipients of social sector expenditures? Has the pattern of expenditure incidence changed over time, and does that suggest the need to alter targeting practices? In addition to transferring income, social sector expenditures should also affect the health status and educational attainment of the population. In the second part of the chapter, we present evidence showing the effectiveness of government expenditures on health and education indicators.

The chapter is organized as follows. The next section provides some historical context for the subsequent analysis and describes the Malaysian government's social sector policies during the period from 1973 to 1989. The following section discusses the data and methodology

The authors wish to thank Lawrence Haddad, Bill McGreevey, Homi Kharas, Martin Ravallion, Dominique van de Walle, and Kim Nead for valuable comments and suggestions.

used in the study. Based on household survey data from 1974 to 1989, we then present findings on who receives social expenditures and how that has changed over time. These expenditures are examined as a share of total government expenditure and as a share of family income. Next, based on a panel of statewide aggregate data from 1986 to 1990, we review the relationship between public expenditures to the social sectors and overall improvements in health and education outcome measures. The conclusion collects the main findings and presents some final remarks on the policy implications of our analysis.

Background

At the time of Malaysian independence from the United Kingdom in 1957, the indigenous Malay population was disadvantaged economically with respect to the other two major ethnic groups, the Chinese and the Indians.[1] Even after independence in 1957, progress in implementing policies to restore equality among ethnic groups was extremely gradual, and rising tensions between the racial groups led to race riots in 1969. After the riots, the Malaysian government designed and implemented the New Economic Policy (NEP) to ameliorate poverty among the Malays and to reduce ethnic income disparities in the country. The policies of the NEP spanned two decades (1970–90) and maintained two basic goals: (a) the eradication of poverty by raising income levels and increasing opportunities for all Malaysians, irrespective of race, and (b) the rapid reordering of society to correct economic imbalance, so as to reduce the identification of race with economic function (Government of Malaysia 1970).

During this period, the Malaysian government channeled public resources to rural Malays through health and education services. Federal government allocations to health and education were high, averaging around 20 percent of central government expenditure, and appear to have been well designed: rural health programs were aggressively expanded, and more than 50 percent of public spending on education was directed to primary education programs. Measured in terms of indicators such as infant mortality and gross enrollment rates, these interventions also appear to have been remarkably successful. For example, immunization rates and safe water coverage expanded significantly, and the infant mortality rate declined from 39.4 per 1,000 in 1970 to 22.0 per 1,000 in 1990.

Improvements in education statistics during this time were also impressive. Between 1970 and 1985, primary enrollment rates increased from 87 to 99 percent, and the average years of schooling for all Malaysians increased from 3.2 to 5.7 years. These improvements appear to reflect both the government's heavy investment in primary education and the impact of redistributive policies to eliminate disparities between ethnic groups. A 1988 study of educational policies in Malaysia (De Tray 1988) found that Chinese and Indian children between the ages of twelve and eighteen were less likely to attend secondary school in 1976–77 than Malay children, controlling for household and socio-economic characteristics.

Despite the impressive progress made over the past twenty years, there are at least two reasons to suspect that the success of the early period of the NEP in targeting public expenditures would not have been sustained throughout the 1980s. First, due to the success of Malaysia's antipoverty efforts, it may have been more difficult to target expenditure to the very poor simply because they were harder to find. Second, to the extent that race has indeed become less identified with economic function, racially targeted policies may no longer have been an efficient means of targeting poverty groups. Although this was the original working hypothesis, it turned out not to be true.

Data and Methodological Issues

In order to evaluate the impact of government expenditures on household welfare, a comparison should ideally be made between the household's situation in the presence of public expenditures and the situation in the absence of any government expenditure. Models of incidence analysis separate the total incidence of public spending into three components: the burden of the tax used to finance the government program, the benefits accruing to the household from the use of the public services, and the redistribution of income resulting from the consumption of publicly subsidized services. According to Musgrave's theory of expenditure incidence, the analysis should simultaneously consider the determination of the entire tax and expenditure system, employing the government's aggregate subsidy on health and education as one of the parameters of the system. Unfortunately, the data available for Malaysia do not enable us to carry out an analysis according to these theoretical constructs; hence, this study considers the redistributive effect of government spending in a partial equilibrium framework.

We analyze the distribution of Malaysia's public spending in the social sectors by determining, based on household use rates, the share of government subsidies on health and education services received by quintiles of households ranked by their per capita household income.[2] The methodology used to calculate per unit subsidies, to rank households, and to distribute the subsidies across households is conceptually the same as that used in the study of Malaysia's social sectors in 1973–74 by Meerman (1979), permitting us to make comparisons over time. Thus, using the results reported in Meerman and data from the latest Malaysia Household Income Survey (Government of Malaysia 1984,

1989), we are able to compare the effect of NEP policies over a fifteen-year period, 1974 to 1989.

Determining the incidence across households of government spending on health and education involves several steps. First, we calculate the cost to the government of providing various health and education services. To account for the varying amounts of government spending across the states, the unit cost to government of providing a service is calculated separately for each state on the basis of its operating and development budget allocations and the number of service units provided (number of outpatient visits to public health centers, number of children enrolled in primary school, and so forth). In addition, unit costs are calculated by level of service provision: primary, secondary, and higher education; and public inpatient and outpatient care.[3]

In order to include the annual user cost of capital, capital expenses are calculated by constructing a capital stock series from development budgets. Capital costs are then imputed using the weighted averages of lagged development expenditures, also by state, level of education, and type of health service.[4] The results derived from this calculation are robust under different assumptions concerning depreciation.

Next, we obtain an estimate of each household's use of publicly provided services. As before, household use rates are determined separately for the three levels of education and for inpatient versus outpatient visits to public health facilities. For education, service use is measured as the number of household members attending a public primary, secondary, or higher-level institution. Similarly in health, use is represented by the household's number of health care visits to a public health facility during the year, on an inpatient and outpatient basis.[5]

Arriving at the subsidy received by each household through its use of public facilities requires that the fees collected from users be subtracted from the unit cost to the government of providing the services.[6] Corrections for this are most important for education. Finally, subsidies are aggregated across households to get each expenditure quintile's share of per capita government subsidies.

The household-level data used here are from the 1984 and 1989 rounds of the Malaysia Household Income Survey (MHIS), an individual-level household survey collected by the Malaysian Department of Statistics. The MHIS is a representative sample containing detailed household information on more than 45,000 households. The survey includes information on household characteristics, various sources of income, expenditures on both public and private goods (including health and education), and use rates for public and private health and education services. As noted above, the results for 1974 are taken from Jacob Meerman's study on the distributional incidence of public expenditures in Malaysia (Meerman 1979). Meerman's data come from a specially designed survey of 1,400 households conducted from 1973 to 1974. As with the MHIS data, the earlier survey collected a wide variety of household-level information on the expenditure and use of both public and private goods.

While the information contained in Meerman's data set is generally comparable to the MHIS data, a few differences and limitations should be illuminated. First, although data on health care use are available for 1989, due to data limitations, they could not be matched with data on household income for the same year. As a result, references to 1989 for health care refer either exclusively to use data or to data drawn from statewide averages. All distributional analysis for health therefore relies on the results from the 1984 survey. Second, the large sample size of the MHIS data set minimizes the sampling error that was inherent in Meerman's small sample of 1,400 households; furthermore, the MHIS data are representative of the entire country rather than the exclusively peninsular Malaysia data collected in Meerman's 1974 sample. We extend our analysis of social sector spending in Malaysia beyond Meerman's work by means of regression analysis that corrects for the relative effects of ethnicity and other household characteristics on the demand for health care and education. We examine a model based on statewide data to assess the impact of public expenditures on outcomes relevant to the sector. To do this, we construct a panel consisting of a time series of state-level data from 1986 to 1990 on (1) gross domestic product (GDP) per capita, (2) public expenditures on health and education, (3) infant and maternal mortality rates, (4) schooling transition rates, (5) immunization rates, (6) proportion of the population having access to safe water, (7) number of public and private doctors per capita, and (8) agriculture's share in state income. Our data sources include epidemiological surveillance data collected by the Ministry of Health, education data collected by the Ministry of Education, and statewide government spending data from the regional accounts system of the Ministry of Finance. The methodology used to analyze these data and a more detailed description of the variables included are contained in the section on outcomes and efficiency.

The Subsidy Incidence in Health

Due to the progress in raising living standards achieved by government programs in the 1960s and early 1970s, it was anticipated that the targeting performance of government programs in the social sectors would show a deterioration over the period of the NEP. Using the number of inpatient and outpatient visits per capita to public health facilities in 1984 as an indicator of the consumption of government-provided health services, we are able to calculate the distributional incidence of public spending on health in Malaysia. The analysis in this section is organized into four parts. Part one examines how the use of public health facilities per income group in 1984 differs from Meerman's results for 1974. Part two uses a simple regression to examine how use varies by ethnic group, controlling for various household characteristics. Part three looks at the size of the government subsidies in relation to the annual income of the household and the impact of these subsidies on the distribution of income. And part four uses statewide data to verify whether government spending on public goods such as immunizations and safe water is allocated progressively.

Table 18-1 presents the share of outpatient and inpatient visits to public health facilities by income quintile in 1974 and 1984. When use figures are compared for the richest and the poorest quintiles, there appears to have been an improvement in the targeting performance of public expenditures on health care rather than the suspected deterioration. In 1974, 19 percent of total government expenditures on inpatient services was received by the poorest 20 percent of the population, and 20 percent was captured by the richest 20 percent. In 1984, these figures were 25 and 16 percent, respectively, indicating that from nearly equal use of facilities in 1974, the poor increased their use of public facilities relative to the rich. For outpatient visits, the figures were 22 and 16 percent, respectively, for the lowest and highest quintiles in 1974 and remained virtually unchanged at 24 and 15 percent in 1984. For the net overall health subsidy (inpatient and outpatient visits combined), the 1974 figures were 22 and 17 percent; in 1984, the poorest and richest 20 percent received, respectively, 25 and 16 percent of the subsidy.

The decline in the use of public inpatient facilities by the wealthy relative to the poor is mirrored in the shares of visits to private facilities. The richest quintile accounted for 30 percent of private outpatient visits in 1974, and their share rose to 34 percent in 1984. More dramatically, this group accounted for 46 percent of inpatient stays in private facilities, up from 12 percent in 1974 (the second highest quintile accounted for 67 percent of private inpatient visits).

Table 18-1. Share of Total Inpatient Days and Outpatient Visits to Public Facilities, by Quintile of Household per Capita Income, Malaysia, 1974 and 1984
(percent)

Quintile	1974		1984	
	Inpatient	*Outpatient*	*Inpatient*	*Outpatient*
1	19	22	25	24
2	27	20	21	23
3	10	23	19	21
4	24	18	20	18
5	20	16	16	15

Sources: Meerman 1979; Government of Malaysia 1984.

Figure 18-1. Distribution of Outpatient Expenditures as a Share of Government Subsidy, Malaysia, 1974 and 1984

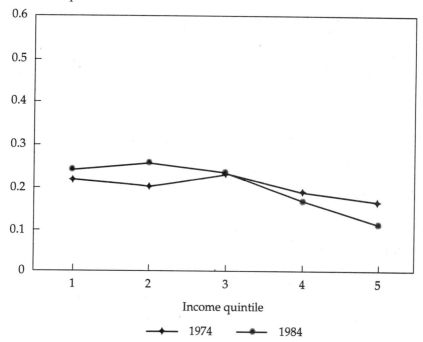

Share of expenditures

Income quintile

1974   1984

Figures 18-1 to 18-3, respectively, show the proportion of expenditure for outpatient care, inpatient care, and total health care that accrued to each quintile of the income distribution as a share of public expenditure for that category of service in 1974 and 1984. Since the functions in figure 18-3 cross each other three times, it is hard to say that one pattern is unambiguously more equitable than the other.[7] However, since the shares decreased for the richest two quintiles and increased for the poorest, a wide variety of inequality measures would conclude that government expenditures on health were better targeted in 1984 than in 1974. This is due to the much slower increase in the use of public facilities among the rich than among the poor (per capita visits increased for all groups in this period) and the disproportionate increases in the use of the private sector by the rich relative to the poor. The data set does not allow the estimation of the demand for health care. However, the demand for quality of care, defined to include amenities and savings in time, is likely to be quite income elastic. The rapid growth of income over the period would increase demand for private sector care more than for public sector care with no change in quality in either sector.

Figure 18-2. Distribution of Inpatient Expenditures as a Share of Government Subsidy, Malaysia, 1974 and 1984

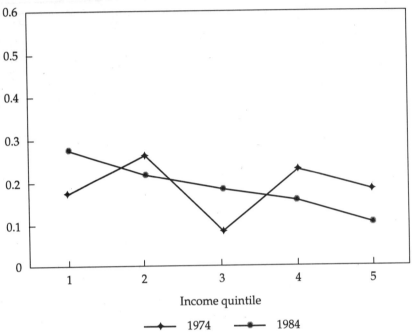

Share of expenditures

Income quintile

—◆— 1974   —✳— 1984

Are poorer people in each area or in each ethnic group using public health facilities more, thereby reflecting redistribution by income, or does the use pattern appear redistributive, because generally poorer regions or groups are favored? Regression analysis of the 1984 data allows us to evaluate the targeting performance of public expenditures in terms of income, holding region, race, and urban/rural location constant (see appendix 18-1 for regression results). Controlling for these other determinants reveals how use varies with income, *ceteris paribus.* Figure 18-4 shows relatively high use of public inpatient services by lower-income and upper middle–income groups. The regression results, which control for race, region, state, and income level, do reinforce the conclusion that the use of private health facilities generally increases with household per capita income.

We also analyze the use patterns of inpatient and outpatient facilities by ethnic group. Table 18-2 presents the use of facilities by race for 1974, 1984, and 1989. It shows that average health care use by Chinese has steadily declined over the period of the NEP from a high of 5.1 outpatient visits per year in 1974 to only 2.0 in 1989; overall, health

Figure 18-3. Distribution of All Health Expenditures as a Share of Government Subsidy, Malaysia, 1974 and 1984

Share of expenditures

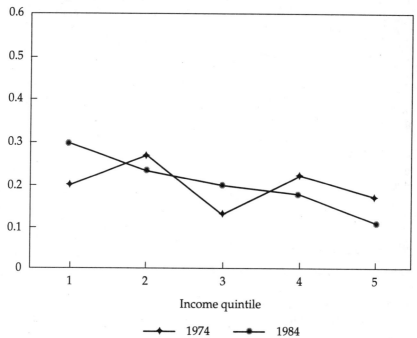

Income quintile

━━━ 1974   ━━━ 1984

care use in both public inpatient and outpatient facilities is lower than for the other ethnic groups. The regression results presented in appendix 18-1 provide additional evidence of differences among the races in the use of health facilities. Our regression of medical care use on income, region, state, and race clearly indicates that, controlling for socioeconomic characteristics, the Chinese are less likely to consume public health care services than either Malays or Indians.

The results confirm an interesting result that also appeared in Meerman (1979): modern medical facilities seem to be disproportionately used by Indians, irrespective of region, state, or income. A possible explanation is that Indians have a revealed preference for the consumption of health care. One result that has changed from the earlier study is the statewide pattern of use. In 1974, people in Selangor used facilities at much lower rates than people in other regions. For 1984 and 1989, however, there were no such dramatic differences. When the states are ordered in terms of mean per capita income, no pattern of use is found, though there is a slight indication of lower use by the poor states in peninsular Malaysia.

Figure 18-4. Use of Inpatient Medical Care, Malaysia, 1984

Days per year per capita

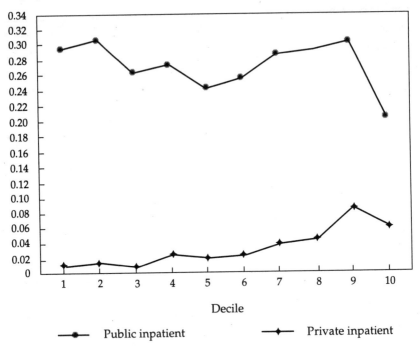

Decile

⎯●⎯ Public inpatient   ⎯◆⎯ Private inpatient

Table 18-2. Number of Inpatient Days and Outpatient Visits to Public Facilities per Household per Year, by Race, Malaysia, 1974, 1984, 1989

	1974		1984		1989	
Group	Inpatient	Outpatient	Inpatient	Outpatient	Inpatient	Outpatient
Chinese	1.90	5.12	0.78	3.08	0.41	2.00
Indian	7.21	5.92	2.92	7.23	1.48	6.74
Malay	2.08	4.24	1.38	6.06	1.05	6.80

Sources: Meerman 1979; Government of Malaysia 1984, 1989.

Figure 18-5 shows the per capita allocation of health expenditures by state, in an ascending order of average per capita income.[8] The ambiguous slope of the line indicates that there is no clear relation between the average income of the state and the size of the health budget. If Kuala Lumpur is ignored, there is a slight tendency to use budgets as a redistributive device (allocating fewer dollars to the wealthiest states), but this might simply reflect a more obvious bias toward the states of East Malaysia. Except for the higher budgets in

Figure 18-5. Per Capita Health Expenditures, by State, Ranked from Poor to Rich, Malaysia, 1990

Public expenditures (ringgit)

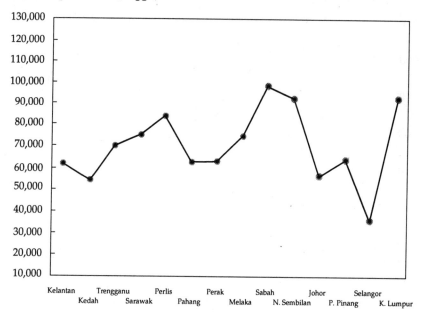

the capital and the East, it is not possible to explain the expenditure pattern. A simple regression confirms that neither income nor progress (or lack thereof) on health indicators is a determinant of budgeting decisions.

Additional information on the targeting of public health spending can be gleaned by examining the provision of public goods across the states ranked according to GDP per capita. Figure 18-6 shows the percentage of each state's population that has been immunized with a third shot of DPT (diphtheria, pertussis, and tetanus); figure 18-7 displays the percentage of the population in each state with access to public, safe water sources. In both figures, states are ranked by income per capita from poorest to richest.

Figure 18-6 illustrates the impressive progress made between 1985 and 1989 in DPT immunization coverage. The immunization rates do not correlate well with income, though private demand for immunizations probably does, thus reinforcing the impression that health expenditures were progressively allocated during the period of the NEP.

As shown in figure 18-7, the pattern for safe water is the reverse. Coverage of safe water is positively correlated with income, in that 90 percent of the people in the wealthiest states have access to safe water,

Figure 18-6. DPT Immunization Coverage, by State, Ranked from Poor to Rich, Malaysia, 1985 and 1989

Immunization rate

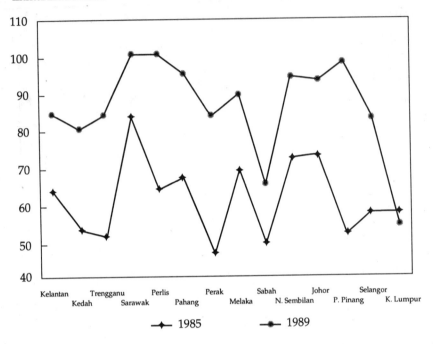

while less than 70 percent of the people in the poorest states have access. However, this should not be used to argue against the expansion of the service. While on *average*, the richer states currently receive more publicly provided safe water, the high rates of coverage imply that the *marginal* recipient from any expansion of the service would have to be from among the poor. The rich have already made sure that they receive the public services, thus there is little room for improved coverage in the rich states. The increase in coverage would therefore benefit either the poor currently without coverage in the wealthier states or the poor residing in the poorest states.

In summary, health expenditures during the period of the NEP were progressive in that disproportionately more was spent on the poor than on the rich, this relation becoming stronger over time. A primary explanation is that the increased use of private practitioners by the relatively well-off left government expenditures better targeted.

The Subsidy Incidence in Education

Malaysia continues to make great strides in the provision of basic educational services to its people. Aggressive policies to ensure univer-

Figure 18-7. Safe Water Coverage, by State, Ranked from Poor to Rich, Malaysia, 1985 and 1989

Percentage of population covered

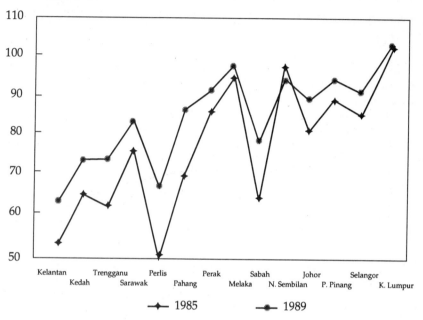

sal primary education and the expansion of secondary-level programs have benefited all Malaysians by increasing primary and secondary school participation rates and by raising educational attainment at all levels of the education system. In order to achieve this progress, Malaysia allocated more than 16 percent of government spending to education programs over the period of the NEP; based on the magnitude of this investment, it is important that this spending continue to fulfill the two principal objectives of the NEP, by not only reducing ethnic disparities but also raising the income and opportunities of all Malaysians, irrespective of race. Using the benefit-incidence methodology presented earlier, this section examines the impact of Malaysian education policies in terms of the distributional incidence of the benefits and then in terms of the government outlays to education by state.

Figures 18-8 to 18-10 show the proportion of expenditure at the different levels of education that went to each quintile of the income distribution in 1974 and 1989. As in the analysis for health, the 1974 data come from Meerman (1979); the 1989 data are from the Malaysia Household Income and Expenditure Survey.

These figures clearly illustrate that educational expenditures at all three levels became more equitably distributed over time. In 1974,

Figure 18-8. Distribution of Primary Education Benefits, Malaysia, 1974 and 1989

Share of expenditures

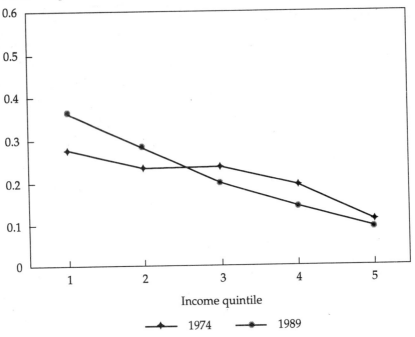

Income quintile

━━━▲━━━ 1974   ━━━✳━━━ 1989

28, 19, and 3 percent of primary, secondary, and higher education expenditures, respectively, were received by the poorest fifth of the population. In 1989, the figures were 36, 32, and 10 percent. The main reason for this improvement is the relative increase in the participation rates of the poor. During this period, primary education became virtually universal, whereas in the early 1970s, only 85 percent of poor children attended primary school. Even in 1974, expenditures on primary education were progressive, since poorer families were more likely to have larger families and hence, more school-age children. By 1989, they still had more children than richer families, but they also had all of their children in school. For secondary education, the story is similar. Expenditures were progressive both in 1974 and in 1989, largely due to the numbers of children in poor families (being equivalent essentially to a per capita subsidy). It is rare to find policies this equitable. In fact, participation rates increased continually over the period, the increases being much greater among low-income children (high-income children had been attending school all along).

For higher education, the trend is in the same direction, in that the share of expenditures going to the poorest 20 percent increased from

Figure 18-9. Distribution of Secondary Education Benefits, Malaysia, 1974 and 1989

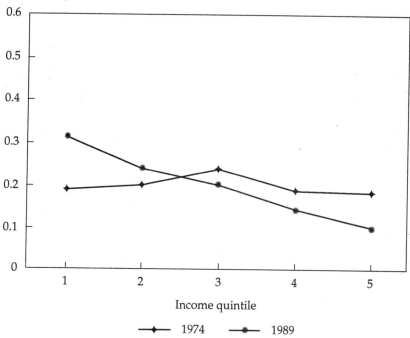

Share of expenditures

Income quintile

———◆——— 1974   ———✳——— 1989

3 to 10 percent. There was something of an acceleration of the improvement judging by the progress made from 1974 to 1984 relative to that made from 1984 to 1989. This may be attributable to the residential secondary school program, which targeted lower-income, primarily rural children, for more intensive academic preparation. However, in both periods, these figures reflect substantial subsidies to the higher-income groups.

When the net effects of subsidies are calculated for the education system as a whole, the correlation with income is very weak (see figure 18-11). Even though primary and secondary expenditures are highly progressive, the size of the higher education budget and its regressivity make the net effect of educational expenditure very flat with respect to income.

It is possible to look more carefully into the pattern of service use, and thus the pattern of subsidization, by means of multivariate analysis that explains enrollment rates by income, region, race, and urban/ rural location. The results in figure 18-12 and appendix 18-2 show the enrollment rate by income decile for primary, secondary, and higher

Figure 18-10. Distribution of Higher Education Benefits, Malaysia, 1974 and 1989

Share of expenditures

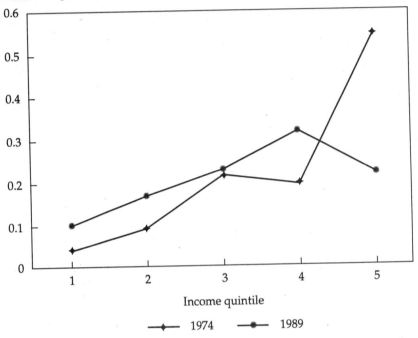

Income quintile

———◆——— 1974   ———✳——— 1989

education in 1984, controlling for race, urban/rural location, and state. The results confirm that a majority of the subsidies for primary education accrue to the lower- and middle-income groups even when controlling for these other factors. That is, it is not simply that primary education benefits are targeted to poor areas but that poor people within each area receive a larger share of the benefits of educational services.

However, while the number of children enrolled per family in public secondary schools falls with increasing income, so that government subsidies to secondary education are distributed progressively (see figure 18-9), the regression results indicate that age-specific enrollment rates at the secondary level rise steadily with household income, holding all else constant (see figure 18-12). Secondary education subsidies are pro-poor, because poor households tend to have more secondary school-age children, not because poor children are more likely to be enrolled in public secondary schools. Controlling for the right-hand-side variables held at their sample means, there is little explanatory power in any variable other than income and race as far as secondary school enrollment is concerned. Furthermore, neither urban/rural sta-

Figure 18-11. Distribution of All Education Benefits, Malaysia, 1974 and 1989

Share of expenditures

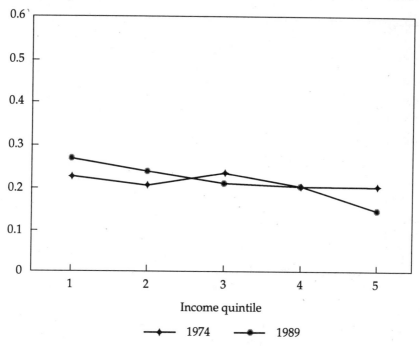

Income quintile

—◆— 1974   —✳— 1989

tus nor state variations have any explanatory power with respect to age-specific enrollment rates.

The success of the NEP policies is evident in the coefficients for race and income. Calculations based on appendix 18-2 show that Malay children attend school at significantly higher rates than Indians and other races, but that these higher rates are not due to direct discrimination on the basis of race. Malay children attend about 25 percent more frequently; that is, around 78 percent of Malay children are enrolled in school as compared to 61 percent for other races (Indonesians and tribal people) and 64 percent for Indian children. For Chinese children, the figure is 69 percent (though it is not significantly different from either Malay or other children in a statistical sense). However, the pattern of coefficients on race directly is ambiguous as to overall tendencies to attend school. The differences in the average rates of attendance are attributable to differences in location and income between the groups rather than from the coefficient on race itself.

For university enrollment, a similar story holds. Income levels and race are the main determinants of university enrollment. For given

Figure 18-12. Educational Enrollment, by Decile, Ranked from Poor to Rich, Malaysia, 1984

Enrollment rate per family

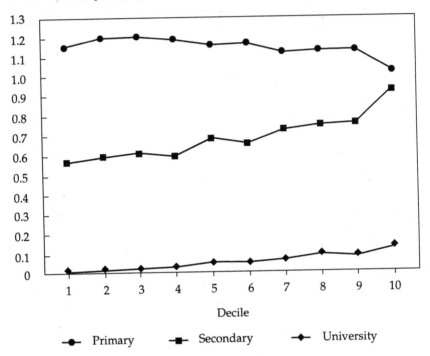

Decile

—●— Primary   —■— Secondary   —◆— University

levels of income, Malay children are more likely to attend a university than either Chinese or Indian children. At the level of the second highest decile, for example, an urban Malay from Johor has a university enrollment rate of 12 percent. In contrast, a Chinese child with the same socioeconomic characteristics has only a 5 percent probability of enrolling in the university.

Examining the allocation of government expenditures on education by state is another means to evaluate the investment strategies followed by the Malaysian government. The overarching objective of the NEP was to redistribute income and human capital to the Malay population, who were disproportionately located in the poorer areas. This pattern in the distribution of government spending across states is visible in the per student allocations by state, shown in figure 18-13. With states arranged in order of mean income per capita, the per student allocation for primary and secondary education shows a general tendency for the government to spend more in the poorer states.

Over time, the progressive allocation of funds at the lower levels of the education system has helped to ensure that the poor have equal

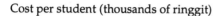

Figure 18-13. Government Expenditures per Student, by State, Ranked from Poor to Rich, Malaysia

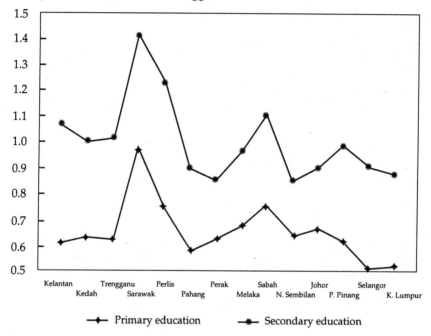

access to public services. The allocation at higher levels is not so guided, however. For higher education, the richest 40 percent of the population still captures more than 50 percent of all education expenditures. Given that the lower levels of schooling produce higher social returns, potential improvements can be made by reallocating government subsidies to the primary and secondary levels of education.

Income Transfers from Social Sector Expenditures

The analysis in the preceding sections demonstrated that, overall, the poorest households in Malaysia capture the largest share of the benefits of public expenditures on health and education services. Apart from strengthening the human capital of the poor, an important objective of Malaysia's development strategy was to improve the distribution of income. The overall distribution of private income did not change dramatically, however, as the income share of the lowest quintile remained unchanged at almost 5 percent of total income and the share of the richest 40 percent fell only slightly, from 77 to 74 percent. It appears that the rapid growth the country experienced over the period of the NEP was fairly evenly distributed, as the average income of the lowest quintile increased by 120 percent, while the income of the highest quintile increased by just over 100 percent. Thus, while the policies of the NEP were relatively successful at getting public expenditures to the disadvantaged populations, they had only a minor impact on the overall distribution of income in Malaysia.[9]

The previous section demonstrated that the largest share of the benefits from publicly financed programs in health and education is distributed to the poor, when analyzed in terms of the share of government expenditure received per household. Although this type of analysis provides an overall picture of the targeting characteristics of government policies, it is also interesting to examine government spending as a share of personal income.[10]

In 1974, the public subsidy for health and education represented 17 percent of household income (see Meerman 1979). Rapidly growing personal incomes over the period of the NEP reduced the subsidy to 13 percent of household income by 1984, but the benefits still accounted for nearly 45 percent of the lowest quintile's household income, a substantial transfer to the poor as a share of their household income. In figures 18-14 to 18-16, the progressive nature of public outlays to health and education is evident for all expenditures except higher education, where there is less variation in the distribution of the subsidy as a share of household income across all quintiles.

Comparing 1974 to 1989, we find that the subsidy for primary and secondary education decreased as a proportion of household income, reflecting faster growth of personal incomes than of the education budget. With the personal incomes of the poor increasing more rapidly than the incomes of the higher-income groups, the overall trend in public expenditure shows that public subsidies became a smaller part of the household budget. For higher education, the share of government subsidies in personal incomes increased over the period of the NEP, and this increase was greatest for the bottom 40 percent of the population (figure 18-15). It appears that higher education is highly income elastic, with rising private incomes increasing the demand for higher education, and this demand was successfully translated into public budgets.[11]

Over the period of the NEP, the demand for health care kept pace with the growing private incomes, and public expenditures to the sector increased to meet this demand. The progressive nature of government spending is again highlighted in figure 18-16, which shows that public expenditure for health care, as a share of household income, increased for the poorest quintile. As the rich opted out of the public system for private services, the poor continued to capture a larger share of the benefits as a fraction both of the government budget and of their own.

Overall, education and health expenditures helped to alleviate poverty and to improve the distribution of income. Although public outlays

Figure 18-14. Outlays for Primary and Secondary School as a Share of Household Income, Malaysia, 1974 and 1989

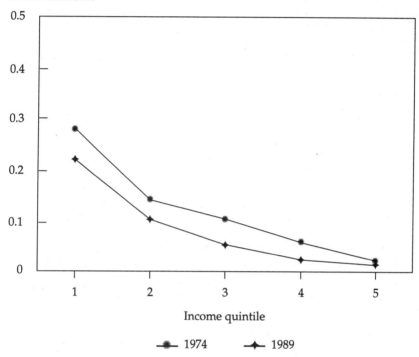

Share of income

Income quintile

—✳— 1974   —◆— 1989

are generally progressively distributed, the higher-income classes receive a disproportionate share of the subsidy for higher education. Given rising costs, the continued provision of subsidies to the rich imposes a heavy burden on the budget and thus affects the efficiency objectives as well. To lower public costs (in terms of financial as well as labor resources), it is now essential to eliminate subsidies received by upper-income groups and to use facilities more efficiently. One way to lower costs and eliminate subsidies is to encourage the private sector to participate in the provision of higher education. By responding to market signals, the private sector will also help to meet the growing private sector demand for skilled labor.

Outcomes and Efficiency

Expenditures on health and education accomplish more than a mere transfer of income. They are productive investments in the human capital of the economy. As the previous sections have documented, the poor's access to services and, more important, health and education

Figure 18-15. Public Outlays for Higher Education as a Share of Household Income, Malaysia, 1974 and 1989

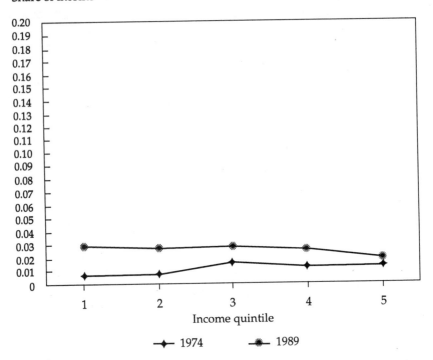

Share of income

Income quintile

◆— 1974   ✳— 1989

status dramatically improved over the past twenty years. A natural question to ask is, How much of this improvement is due to government policy, and how much merely reflects income growth over the period? Given the resource constraints that face policymakers in the social sectors, it is critical that government spending be allocated to programs that maximize the impact on health and educational status per dollar spent. Recent studies have shown that outcome measures can be evaluated as a function of government expenditure and specific government programs (Pitt, Rosenzweig, and Gibbons, chapter 6 of this volume; Hammer, Cercone, and Nabi 1994). In order to examine the relationship between public outlays to the social sectors and improvements in health and education outcome measures, this section examines trends in government expenditure in order to decompose the changes in outcome measures into their constituent parts.

Health

In order to sort out the relative effects of the determinants of health improvement, a simple regression is performed using a panel of state-

Figure 18-16. Public Outlays for Health Care as a Share of Household Income, Malaysia, 1974 and 1984

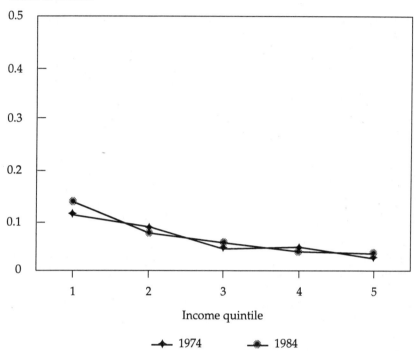

Share of income

Income quintile

—▲— 1974   —✳— 1984

level data for the years 1986–89 (or, four observations on each of the fourteen states). The basic idea is to attribute the improvement in health indicators to three types of determinants: (1) income growth, (2) public provision of services that are either public goods or goods with strong external effects, and (3) public provision of medical services, which are basically private goods. The working hypothesis is that policy instruments that engender substitution away from the private sector will be less effective than those that address a serious market failure. The measures of health status are infant and maternal mortality rates, and the explanatory variables are (1) average state income; (2) for the provision of "public" goods, complete immunization against DPT; (3) the proportion of the population with safe water; and (4) for the public provision of private goods, the number of doctors per capita who are publicly assigned (an alternative regression is also included that uses the total number of physicians per capita for comparison). Given the panel structure of the data, estimation is done using ordinary least squares, a fixed effects (over states) model of the error term, and a generalized least squares or random effects model. Details of the estimation procedure and construction of the income variable are presented in Hammer, Cercone, and Nabi (1994). The basic results are summarized below, while table 18-3 shows the full regression results.

1. Immunization rates particularly and water supply have the strongest and most robust effects on health status.

2. Although not a robust result, there is evidence that the greater the number of doctors per capita in a state, the better the health status. However, greater numbers of *publicly employed* doctors do not necessarily improve health status, and it is the publicly assigned doctor who is under the control of policymakers. The difference in the results can be interpreted to indicate that public and private medical services substitute for one another such that increases in publicly assigned doctors are partially offset by decreases in the number of doctors in private practice.

3. Income, per se, has little effect on health status. However, it is an important determinant of demand for private medical care that does affect status.

The first two results indicate the value of concentrating government resources on those activities in which the public sector has a distinct advantage in provision. If the safety of water is not guaranteed by the government, the population has few alternatives, as the private sector is unlikely to invest in such guarantees of water supply and in optional sanitation services. Even though our earlier analysis showed that the rates of safe water and immunization coverage appear relatively regressive, expansion on the margin may still be pro-poor, since any increase in coverage will be in poorer areas or at least will expand service to the poorest groups in the wealthier states. High-income groups already have safe water (through collective pressure on government) and typically ensure that their children are immunized; investments to expand coverage of these services will therefore be targeted to the poor. Further, since the poor suffer disproportionately more than the rich from infectious diseases, prevention of these diseases through population-based measures (rather than clinical services) will likely benefit the poor disproportionately as well.

Education

The allocation of resources by state to primary and secondary education is used as a redistributive device to the poorer areas (see figure 18-13). The impact of government spending, however, must be measured in terms other than program intensity or dollars spent per capita. To assess the impact of government spending effectively, it is important to use performance or outcome measures. In general, data on the perfor-

Table 18-3. Estimated Effect of Health Interventions on Infant and Maternal Mortality, Malaysia, 1986–89

Intervention	Dependent variable = infant mortality				Dependent variable = infant mortality			Dependent variable = maternal mortality		
	OLS[a]	Random effects	Fixed effects	Fixed effects[b]	OLS[a]	Fixed effects	Random effects	OLS[a]	Fixed effects	Random effects
Log income	−1.53 (1.39)	−1.03 (4.48)	−0.86 (1.82)	−1.06 (0.97)	−0.34 (1.56)	−0.622 (5.26)	0.45 (2.13)	−0.203 (0.103)	0.43 (0.14)	0.075 (0.050)
Safe water	−0.12 (0.38)	−0.112 (0.07)	−0.127 (0.05)	−0.147 (0.05)	−0.107 (0.038)	−0.102 (0.072)	−0.116 (0.05)	−0.0018 (0.0025)	−0.000 (0.003)	−0.003 (0.002)
DPT3	−0.128 (0.024)	−0.062 (0.026)	−0.071 (0.018)	−0.113 (0.04)	−0.133 (0.024)	−0.063 (0.03)	−0.075 (0.02)	−0.0047 (0.0017)	−0.0055 (0.0018)	−0.0042 (0.0024)
Population per doctor	n.a.	n.a.	n.a.	n.a.	2.07 (0.872)	2.52 (4.44)	2.07 (1.35)	n.a.	n.a.	n.a.
Population per public doctors	1.14 (0.53)	0.293 (2.40)	1.00 (0.82)	1.03 (0.79)	n.a.	n.a.	n.a.	−0.019 (0.045)	−0.071 (0.072)	0.032 (0.057)
Adjusted R^2	0.63	0.88	0.60	0.55	0.65	0.88	0.62	0.33	0.47	0.34

n.a. Not applicable.
Note: Standard errors are in parenthesis. $N = 56$.
a. Ordinary least squares regression.
b. Regression with instrumental variables.

mance of the facilities receiving public money are difficult to obtain. A common alternative is to use outcome indicators such as transition or repetition rates. These indicators are preferable to enrollment rates, because they reflect successful completion of the relevant level conditional on the number of students having entered the level. Enrollment rates both confound demographic changes over the period as well as count repeating students as a credit rather than as a problem. In this section, we use statewide, time-series data on the transition rates from primary to secondary school and from lower to upper secondary school for the years 1985 to 1990 to measure the impact of government spending per student on educational progress. In one regression, the dependent variable measures the proportion of students in the last year of primary education who continue on to the lowest grade of secondary school; in the other regression, it represents the proportion of students in the last year of lower secondary education who continue on to the lowest grade of upper secondary school. These levels are chosen simply for reasons of data availability. While participation rates for primary school show little variation across states now that primary education is virtually universal, substantial differences remain among states in terms of the probability of continuing on to secondary school.

The regression also includes the percentage of state income accounted for by agricultural production as a proxy for the opportunity cost of children's time and, to the extent of capturing expected occupational choice, the expected value of education as well. The results are presented in table 18-4.

The results reveal that public expenditure on primary education is a significant factor in stimulating higher transition rates, though it is not as important as income. The higher resources per state in the poorer areas genuinely compensate for the direct effect of lower incomes, thereby making the total effect of income nil. This is more evidence of the progressive nature of public spending on primary education.

Secondary education is harder to characterize this way and appears to require more complicated explanations than these data can support. The transition from lower to upper secondary school appears to be negatively related to the transition from primary to secondary school. Perhaps some of the less well qualified students from the high-transition states fail to make the next level. Thus, variables in one equation tend to take on the opposite sign in the other. Furthermore, variation in the individual demand for education appears to be more important at secondary school levels than at the primary level. For example, in more heavily agricultural states, the transition rates in secondary school are significantly lower than in nonagricultural states. This dependence on production structure does not appear at the primary school level. Both on equity grounds and in terms of educational performance, expenditure at the primary school level appears well justified.

Table 18-4. Regression Results for Education Transition Data, Malaysia, 1985–90
(dependent variable = transition rate)

Dependent variable	Constant	Log income	Log expenditures per student	Average share of state income	Adjusted R^2
Primary to low secondary	−155	16.66 (5.11)	15.92 (7.66)	0.03 (0.12)	0.572
Low secondary to upper secondary	181	−5.94 (2.22)	−9.68 (3.09)	−0.153 (0.054)	0.625

Note: Standard errors are in parentheses. $N = 14$.

Conclusions

The improvement of health status and the expansion of basic education are two of the most outstanding achievements of Malaysia's economic policy over the past fifteen years. In order to eliminate the vast differentials that existed between rich and poor, Malay and non-Malay, government spending in the social sectors was allocated to preferential programs in education and to the targeted expansion of access to the health care system. This chapter has examined the changes that occurred in the distributional impact of these public outlays between 1974 and 1989, using household-level data on the use of public services. In addition, state-level data were analyzed to provide further insights on the targeting and effectiveness of public spending on health and education in the 1980s.

There are a few areas of crosscutting interest, common problems, and noticeable contrasts between the health and education sectors in Malaysia. In both of the sectors, the targeting performance of government expenditures improved over the period of the NEP. Except for higher education, social service expenditures were progressive and became more so after 1974, as the poor captured the largest share of the benefits of social expenditures. Interestingly, the reasons for this common improvement are essentially opposite to one another. For education, primary-level enrollment is now virtually universal, and enrollment rates are higher due to the increased participation of the Malays. Expansion of the education system came as a result of an ethnically based targeting policy that reached lower and lower income groups. In contrast, the improved targeting of health care came predominantly as a result of the richer income groups opting out of the public system to use private practitioners. And while this raises questions of the efficiency of the sector as a whole, on equity grounds this improved the ability of the public health system to further the public interest.

The two opposing reasons for improved targeting have quite different implications for potential problems and policy issues in the two sectors. In health, there is clearly an unfinished agenda in the provision of public goods, or goods with substantial externalities; at the same time, a large, basically unregulated, private sector has emerged. On the one hand, a rapidly growing private sector could be a welcome change, as more of the publicly provided services can be concentrated on the poor if the rich opt for private care. On the other hand, this growth has taken place with little or no regulation of fees, modes of payment, or financing arrangements by the Ministry of Health. Left unregulated, the impact on health status of the private sector is ambiguous; an exodus of higher-income people to seek care in the private sector may exacerbate problems in the private markets for health care and lead to serious efficiency problems in the market.

The challenge facing government in the coming years is to maintain a clear definition of its responsibility for promoting efficient and equitable resource allocation in the health sector. This entails promoting two very different activities: first, maintaining and extending the provision of basic public health services such as safe water, sanitation, and immunization; and second, shifting focus from being the sole, or even principal, provider of health services to being a regulator of both the public and private health systems to mitigate market failures and to ensure the efficient and equitable functioning of the sector.

In education, the problem lies in the opposite direction. As a result of the policies of the NEP, Malaysia has more than completely covered its obligations to provide services with substantial external effects (primary education) and has even proceeded to provide essentially private goods (higher education) in order to restore ethnic balance. While the provision of primary and secondary schooling is pro-poor, the higher education system is regressively subsidized, and a false equilibrium is maintained through a public monopoly on the granting of higher degrees. As a result, the net distributional effect of overall education spending is flat with respect to income, and higher education enrollment rates in Malaysia are lower in comparison with other countries with similar levels of income and growth prospects (Tan and Mingat 1991). This presents something of a policy dilemma. On the one hand, the demand for highly educated people is likely to grow substantially, and Malaysia's current attainments are already lagging behind those of its competitors. On the other hand, the costs of providing education services, for higher education particularly, are relatively high, and the subsidy for higher education goes disproportionately to the rich. Although there is no clear-cut solution, policy options should focus on the public interest and on remedying market failures.

A defensible policy response to these problems is quite similar across the two sectors, though each originates from a different place. In each case, the relevant ministry might consider a shift in emphasis from the direct provision of certain services (beyond those with compelling public interest reasons for intervention) to regulation of the private sector. In health, this would entail the establishment of a regulatory structure in the public sector with authority over the private medical market. In education, this would entail allowing private institutions to develop for the provision of higher education and ensuring that the credit market is functioning so that loans can be extended to university students. A second response might be to change the pricing policy for public services. Tax and pricing policies that aim to recover costs, in both the health and education sectors, may present an opportunity to mobilize resources that can be used to expand basic services, to improve quality, and to improve the overall efficiency of the social sectors.

This chapter has shown that government policies in Malaysia that sought to target the economically disadvantaged groups of the population with public sector spending have been successful. Public policies have eroded the vast differentials in health status and educational attainment that existed at the beginning of the NEP in 1970, and through generous government subsidies, have transferred crucial resources to the poorest households. This analysis of the redistributive effect of these policies between 1974 and 1989 suggests that social sector expenditures have served Malaysia well since independence.

Appendix 18-1. Regression Results for Use of Medical Care, Malaysia, 1984

Variable	Public outpatient		Private outpatient		Public inpatient		Private inpatient	
Intercept	1.06	(7.05)	2.53	(15.05)	0.40	(2.06)	0.09	(1.8)
Region								
Rural (relative to urban)	0.19	(3.37)	−0.30	(−4.66)	0.06	(0.80)	−0.02	(−1.22)
State								
Kedah	0.39	(3.56)	0.24	(1.96)	0.15	(1.04)	−0.01	(−0.22)
Kelantan	0.02	(0.15)	−0.45	(−3.53)	−0.29	(−1.95)	−0.02	(−0.52)
Kuala Lumpur	−0.30	(−3.18)	−0.34	(−3.27)	−0.25	(−2.07)	−0.01	(−0.28)
Malacca	1.32	(8.91)	0.71	(4.25)	1.22	(6.39)	0.06	(1.33)
Negri Sembilan	0.46	(3.67)	0.25	(1.78)	0.04	(0.22)	−0.05	(−1.22)
Pahang	0.81	(7.27)	−0.17	(−1.36)	−0.04	(−0.27)	−0.03	(−0.72)
Penang	0.19	(1.82)	−0.58	(−4.94)	0.21	(1.51)	0.07	(2.19)
Perak	0.54	(5.98)	0.56	(5.61)	0.43	(3.77)	0.08	(3.04)
Perlis	0.81	(3.57)	0.06	(0.25)	−0.13	(−0.46)	−0.03	(−0.37)
Selangor	0.01	(0.11)	0.82	(8.01)	−0.13	(−1.08)	0.05	(1.82)
Trengganu	0.73	(5.75)	−0.26	(−1.86)	0.05	(0.32)	0.03	(0.73)
Race								
Chinese	−0.78	(−5.78)	0.95	(6.27)	−0.25	(−1.4)	0.13	(3.03)
Indian	0.65	(4.35)	1.23	(7.37)	1.36	(7.07)	0.15	(3.30)
Malay	−0.01	(−0.07)	0.34	(2.34)	0.05	(0.3)	0.02	(0.47)
Decile (relative to top decile)								
1	1.60	(14.01)	−1.68	(−13.14)	1.07	(7.29)	−0.10	(−2.76)
2	1.65	(14.92)	−1.19	(−9.57)	0.98	(6.80)	−0.07	(−2.05)
3	1.55	(14.26)	−0.81	(−6.61)	0.67	(4.79)	−0.13	(−3.74)
4	1.32	(12.32)	−0.51	(−4.25)	0.81	(5.82)	−0.04	(−1.23)
5	1.26	(11.89)	−0.30	(−2.55)	0.63	(4.59)	−0.09	(−2.80)
6	1.16	(10.87)	0.02	(0.14)	0.56	(4.10)	−0.07	(−2.18)
7	0.85	(8.00)	0.08	(0.66)	0.45	(3.3)	−0.07	(−1.06)
8	0.52	(4.96)	0.10	(0.81)	0.50	(3.64)	−0.03	(−1.06)
9	0.25	(2.33)	0.07	(0.62)	0.41	(3.01)	−0.001	(−0.02)
							0.05	(1.49)

Note: *t*-ratios are presented in parentheses. *N* = 40,744. Dependent variable is the number of visits per family per year to each of the listed providers.

Appendix 18-2. Regression Results for Enrollments, by Education Level, Malaysia, 1984

Variable	Primary		Secondary		University		Vocational	
Intercept	0.90	(12.97)	0.94	(9.56)	0.16	(3.94)	0.09	(1.8)
Region								
Rural (relative to urban)	−0.02	(−1.04)	−0.03	(1.60)	−0.01	(−1.34)	−0.02	(−1.0)
State								
Kedah	−0.03	(−0.92)	0.01	(0.09)	−0.01	(−0.26)	−0.01	(−0.2)
Kelantan	0.01	(0.10)	0.04	(1.08)	−0.03	(−1.54)	−0.02	(−0.5)
Kuala Lumpur	−0.02	(−0.73)	0.02	(0.55)	0.01	(0.13)	−0.01	(−0.2)
Malacca	0.05	(1.13)	−0.04	(−0.69)	0.01	(0.08)	0.06	(1.3)
Negri Sembilan	−0.04	(−0.91)	0.02	(0.36)	0.03	(1.30)	−0.05	(−1.0)
Pahang	−0.04	(−1.17)	−0.08	(−1.96)	−0.02	(−1.26)	−0.03	(−0.7)
Penang	−0.01	(−0.28)	−0.05	(−1.02)	−0.02	(−0.83)	0.07	(2.1)
Perak	−0.01	(−0.24)	−0.01	(−0.09)	0.03	(1.95)	0.08	(3.0)
Perlis	0.03	(0.41)	0.03	(0.31)	0.04	(0.82)	−0.03	(−0.3)
Selangor	−0.01	(−0.47)	−0.02	(−0.66)	0.02	(1.35)	0.05	(1.8)
Trengganu	0.00	(0.03)	−0.03	(−0.81)	0.04	(2.21)	0.03	(0.73)
Race								
Chinese	0.21	(4.50)	0.09	(1.44)	−0.07	(−2.71)	0.13	(3.0)
Indian	0.07	(1.32)	0.02	(0.25)	−0.08	(−2.78)	0.15	(3.3)
Malay	0.07	(1.62)	0.17	(3.12)	0.00	(0.06)	0.02	(0.47)
Decile (relative to top decile)								
1	0.15	(2.57)	−0.35	(−4.82)	−0.11	(−3.44)	−0.10	(−2.0)
2	0.18	(3.26)	−0.33	(−4.65)	−0.10	(−3.02)	−0.07	(−2.0)
3	0.19	(3.34)	−0.31	(−4.35)	−0.09	(−2.63)	−0.13	(−3.0)
4	0.17	(3.10)	−0.33	(−4.69)	−0.09	(−2.65)	−0.04	(−1.0)
5	0.14	(2.53)	−0.24	(−3.40)	−0.06	(−1.76)	−0.09	(−2.0)
6	0.15	(2.66)	−0.27	(−3.83)	−0.06	(−1.87)	−0.07	(−2.0)
7	0.10	(1.67)	−0.20	(−2.7)	−0.05	(−1.48)	−0.03	(−1.0)
8	0.11	(1.76)	−0.18	(−2.27)	−0.03	(−0.78)	−0.001	(−0.0)
9	0.11	(1.54)	−0.17	(−1.88)	−0.04	(−0.90)	0.05	(1.49)

Note: t-ratios are presented in parentheses. N = 2,198. Dependent variable is the number of children enrolled at each level.

Notes

1. Although the Chinese and Indian immigrants are now Malaysian nationals, and should therefore be called Chinese Malaysian or Indian Malaysian, for the sake of clarity, we refer to the three ethnic groups as Malay, Chinese, Indian, and other, which includes all other races.

2. Although it is generally acknowledged that household expenditures provide a better indication of living standards than household income, in order to ensure consistency with the methodology used in Meerman (1979) and due to data limitations in the 1984 and 1989 data sets, this study uses per capita income of the household at survey time and use of publicly provided health and education services as its measures of the economic state of a household.

3. It is not possible to disaggregate health expenditures for statewide data to the level of specific interventions available from the survey data. Thus any systematic bias in the cost of services within the aggregate of inpatient and outpatient services is present in the results.

4. The basic formula for generating a stock of physical capital and a capital stock is $K_t = \sum_{\tau=1}^{T} \delta^\tau I_{t-\tau} + \delta^t K_T$. Where I_t is capital expenditure in period t, T is the earliest year of the capital series, K_T is the (assumed) level of capital stock in that year, and δ is 1 minus the depreciation rate of capital. Capital services are equal to rK_t, where r is the user cost of capital. This procedure essentially gives a means of smoothing development expenditures in order to avoid attributing unrealistic fluctuations by year to users.

5. The inpatient variable refers to inpatient days at public health facilities, including national government hospitals, general hospitals (state level), and district hospitals. Public outpatient visits consist of consultations at any of the aforementioned public hospitals plus visits to public health centers, government rural clinics, traveling dispensaries, and native/traditional treatments.

6. The fees paid per household for education represent household expenses incurred for room and board in addition to transport, supplies, uniforms, and tuition fees. For health, the fees represent the amount paid at public clinics per inpatient or outpatient consultation.

7. There is always the possibility that the results are due, partly, to differences in sample size. The 1974 study was quite a bit smaller than the more recent surveys, and the more jagged pattern may reflect more variability from the small sample.

8. The states are ranked according to the GDP per capita *net* of income from mining and quarrying. In order to represent household income per capita more accurately, we subtract the share of GDP originating from these industries from the state total, because many of the profits from these industries are highly concentrated and often accrue to residents of other states (particularly the metropolitan areas) or, in some cases, to foreign investors.

9. It is also noteworthy that the educational burden on household income of out-of-pocket costs declined for the poorest 20 percent over the period of the NEP. The distribution was even more equitable in 1989 than it was in 1974, as the educational burden as a share of income had nearly doubled for the richest 20 percent of the population:

Quintile	1974	1989
1	0.14	0.10
2	0.08	0.07
3	0.07	0.05
4	0.05	0.03
5	0.02	0.04

10. The comparisons made in this section are based on 1974 and 1989 data for education; however, data limitations preclude the use of the year 1989 for health. As a result, the distributional results for health are derived from 1984 data.

11. Although it is clear that public expenditures for higher education grew more rapidly than personal incomes over the past twenty years, higher public expenditures are not necessarily indicative of increasing demand for public service output. That is, higher expenditures may simply reflect constantly increasing (real) prices for higher education. Baumol and Oates (1975) have argued that public services do not experience much productivity growth over time, at least not relative to the private sector. As a result, the relative costs of public services will rise geometrically at a rate equal to the difference between private and public sector productivity growth. According to their analysis, only 14 percent of the increase in public expenditure growth in the United States can be attributed to an increase in public sector outputs, while the remaining 86 percent finances relative price increases for public services.

References

Baumol, William J., and Wallace E. Oates. 1975. *The Theory of Environmental Policy.* Englewood Cliffs, N.J.: Prentice-Hall.

De Tray, Dennis. 1988. "Government Policy, Household Behavior, and the Distribution of Schooling: A Case Study of Malaysia." *Research in Population Economics* 6: 303–36.

Government of Malaysia. 1970. "Second Malaysia Plan, 1971–75." Kuala Lumpur.

————. 1984. "Malaysia Household Income Survey." Kuala Lumpur.

————. 1989. "Malaysia Household Income Survey." Kuala Lumpur.

Hammer, Jeffrey, James Cercone, and Ijaz Nabi. 1994. "Determinants of Health and Educational Status in Malaysia: Public Goods and Private Substitutes." World Bank, Policy Research Department, Washington, D.C.

Meerman, Jacob. 1979. *Public Expenditure in Malaysia: Who Benefits and Why.* New York: Oxford University Press.

Tan, Jee-Peng, and Alain Mingat. 1991. "Educational Development in Asia: A Comparative Study Focusing on Cost and Financing Issues." Asia Regional Series, Internal Discussion Paper 151. World Bank, Washington, D.C.

19 On Gender Targeting of Public Transfers

Simon Appleton and Paul Collier

Should public policy differentiate by gender? That is to say, should the transfers and services that the state provides to individuals vary according to the gender of the recipient? Gender targeting in favor of women can be advocated on two different grounds. A simple direct argument is that one gender, typically women, is often disadvantaged and thus on equity grounds should benefit from state assistance. A more indirect case can be built around the idea that targeting one gender, quite aside from raising the welfare of its members, is desirable because of added benefits to others.

Considering the former type of argument, even if it is established that one gender tends to be economically disadvantaged, it does not necessarily follow that gender targeting is appropriate. If disadvantage is unidimensional (say, income), if that dimension is readily observable, and if there are no problems of moral hazard, then it is more efficient to target transfers on the outcome (that is, on persons with low income) than on persons with characteristics likely to cause disadvantage (such as gender). The case for gender targeting in developing countries as a redistributive device relies on the fact that none of these three conditions is normally met. Disadvantage is more multidimensional, including poor health, reduced autonomy within the community, and reduced leisure. These are difficult to observe, to quantify, and to aggregate. Even household incomes are hard to measure because of considerable reliance on self-employment, and many developing countries have been unwilling to bear the cost of administering an efficient income tax system. Trying to assess intrahousehold income or consumption is

This chapter includes some findings from a World Bank–supported project, Women and Public Services in Africa. We wish to acknowledge the contribution of our colleagues on that project, namely David Bevan, Kase Burger, Jan Gunning, Lawrence Haddad, and John Hoddinott. We are also grateful to Kim Nead and Dominique van de Walle for helpful comments.

even more problematic. Moral hazard may be substantial and have a corrosive effect on the very principle of poverty alleviation, a principle much less firmly rooted in many low-income countries than in most high-income countries.

As a result of these difficulties, transfers made according to outcome-based criteria such as consumption or income are often likely to be infeasible. Fewer problems may be encountered by targeting on an alternative set of criteria based on the causes of disadvantage, of which gender may be a pertinent criterion. Indeed, it is quite possible that the errors made by targeting on well-observed causal characteristics, such as assets and gender, may be less substantial than the errors made by targeting on a partial and badly observed outcome.

Gender targeting is likely to be more feasible than many other forms of targeting for two reasons. First, it should be easier to identify the gender of the recipient than it is to identify other target groups. A problem with many targeting schemes is the design of delivery systems that can identify the targeted group. For example, Glewwe (1990) discusses the difficulties of targeting the poor when one cannot observe their incomes. By contrast, gender identification is straightforward. A second advantage of gender targeting over other forms of targeting is that it avoids a number of common problems of moral hazard. One difficulty with targeting is that people may change their behavior so as to fall into the targeted group. For example, they may deliberately neglect income-generating opportunities so as to obtain benefits targeted to the poor. With gender targeting, this simple form of incentive problem does not arise.

In the next section, we consider whether the premise of gender-caused disadvantage is empirically supported. The following section examines the advantages and limitations of using generalized transfers to offset any gender inequalities that may exist. We then discuss the role of in-kind gender transfers, with a particular focus on education. Finally, the chapter concludes with a few remarks on the potential for and limitations of gender targeting.

Evidence on Gender Differences in Welfare

We now survey the evidence on gender differences in welfare using a variety of quantitative indicators: estimated "equivalence scales," food consumption, mortality, health care, morbidity, education, and leisure.

Perhaps the most commonly used empirical measure of economic welfare is consumption (Glewwe 1991). However, using this as the basis for assessments of gender differences in welfare is problematic because data are lacking on the intrahousehold allocation of goods and services. In part, there is a shortage of information on personal consumption because of the difficulties of measurement.[1] Numerous items of expenditure such as housing and consumer durables are consumed jointly by the household. Although not all household members benefit equally from such "household public goods," allocating differential benefits is problematic. Consequently, attention is usually focused on a subset of consumption goods. One approach is to focus on individual differences in the consumption of food, a private good. This approach is informationally demanding, and an alternative method is to analyze total household consumption of "child" and/or "adult" goods. In particular, if such items can be isolated, it is possible to use the outlay equivalent method to make inferences about the intrahousehold allocation of these goods. For example, if an extra girl in the household is associated with a lower fall in the consumption of adults within the household than is an extra boy, this would seem to indicate lower household allocation of resources to girls than to boys (Schultz 1989 criticizes this method for assuming the exogeneity of household demographic composition to consumption). An interesting application of this method is by Deaton (1989) using the 1985 Côte d'Ivoire Living Standards Survey. No evidence is found to suggest boy-girl discrimination.[2] However, among adults, there is a marked gender (and age) hierarchy. In particular, prime-age men appear to be most favored within households, followed by old men, then prime-age women, and finally old women. Such findings may be culturally specific. For example, a parallel exercise for Thailand does find evidence that boys receive more resources than girls.

The adult equivalent method is rather indirect. Moreover, because it covers only goods that can be allocated exclusively to adults or children, it may span only a small share of total expenditures. By contrast, food consumption is typically a large share of household spending in developing countries. Consequently, where the data are available, it may be preferable to rely on direct observation of individual food consumption. This is difficult because food is usually purchased collectively and cooked within a household. Indeed, many surveys identify households around such "cooking pots." Hence, data on food consumption cannot be reliably obtained by simply asking how much was spent on a particular individual's diet. Instead, one method is to ask household members to recall what they ate over a short period of time (often twenty-four hours). Alternatively, mealtimes can be directly observed, which may be intrusive and alter behavior. Evidence of gender inequalities in food consumption tends to focus on India, where there is considerable evidence that girls receive less food than boys (see Agarwal 1986; Bannerjee 1983; Bardhan 1974; Behrman 1988a, 1988b; Cassen 1978; Chen, Huq, and D'Souza 1981; Sen 1984; Sen and Sengupta 1983; Taylor, Faruque, and Kielman 1983; however, Behrman 1988b finds evidence of gender discrimination in calorie intake only in the lean season). What is true for India may also be true for much of South Asia (see Hassan and Ahmad 1984 for Bangladesh). However, the evidence on South Asia is not uniform (for contrary findings, see Basu 1987; Behrman and Deolalikar 1990b; Das Gupta 1987; Harriss 1990, for example, argues that regional variations in gender discrimination are substantial).

Outside of South Asia, there is less evidence of gender inequalities in food consumption. For example, for the Philippines, Haddad and Kanbur (1990) find that neither sex is overrepresented among persons with inadequate calorie intake, although the extent of undernourishment tends to be slightly higher among females. Conversely, in deprived areas of the Philippines, Senauer and Garcia (1991) find that boys have a more adequate calorie intake than girls. Such studies using standard age-gender calorie requirements should be regarded with caution, since the inferences to be drawn vary considerably with other individual variables. In particular, nutritional requirements vary with a number of factors such as the degree of physical activity and whether a woman is pregnant or lactating. One example of the pitfalls is demonstrated by the work of Pitt, Rosenzweig, and Hassan (1990) on calorie consumption in Indonesia. This finds that an apparent pro-male bias in consumption is reversed when controls for energy exerted at work are included.

A related body of evidence concerns gender differences in child anthropometric status. Age-standardized measures of child weight and height partly reflect food consumption. Once more, studies outside of South Asia have tended to find little evidence that boys enjoy superior anthropometric status (see Thomas, Strauss, and Henriques 1990 and Thomas 1990 for Brazil; von Braun 1988 for rural Gambia; Deolalikar 1991 for Indonesia; Kennedy and Cogill 1987 for Kenya; Blau 1984 for Nicaragua; Senauer, Garcia, and Jacinto 1988 and Senauer and Garcia 1991 for the Philippines; Senauer, Sahn, and Alderman 1986 for Sri Lanka; Thomas 1991 for Brazil, Ghana, and the United States). Svedberg (1990, p. 482) summarizes the results of fifty studies in Sub-Saharan Africa and concludes:

> The main finding is that females, whatever their age, are not at a disadvantage vis-à-vis males in anthropometric status. This may not be true in each and every part of the continent, but it is true in the great majority of the Sub-Saharan countries.

This conclusion receives some support from subsequent analyses of the Living Standards Surveys collected in the second half of the 1980s in Côte d'Ivoire and Ghana (see Haddad and Hoddinott 1994, Sahn 1990, Strauss 1990 for the Côte d'Ivoire; Alderman 1990, Thomas 1991, Haddad 1990 for Ghana). However, a potentially serious limitation to this conclusion concerns the problem of the appropriate age standardization. Various researchers have found girls' anthropometric status to be significantly higher than that of boys and have questioned whether the age standardizations used are appropriate (see Appleton 1993; Thomas 1991; Senauer and Garcia 1991).[3] Following World Health Organization guidelines, a reference population from the United States is conventionally used to standardize for age (WHO 1979). This is defended on the grounds that racial differences in anthropometric characteristics within affluent societies are not large. However, this view may have to be revised, given evidence such as that cited previously. For example, in a sample of final-year students in Kenyan primary schools, Appleton finds 12 percent of the boys to be stunted compared with only 2 percent of the girls and 33 percent of the boys to have low weight-for-age compared with only 9 percent of the girls.[4] It seems implausible to attribute this effect to a pro-girl bias in food consumption; rather, it is tempting to attribute it to racial differences in the relative anthropometric characteristics of males and females.

Food consumption and anthropometric status have a special interest as welfare indicators because of their ability to predict child mortality. Gender differences in child mortality vary markedly between societies. In South Asia, female child mortality appears particularly high relative to that for males. In 1989, of those countries with populations of more than 1 million, only Bangladesh, Bhutan, India, Nepal, and Pakistan had higher rates of child mortality for girls than for boys (data from World Bank 1991). Similarly, Sen (1990) argues on the basis of cross-country variations in "sex ratios" (the proportion of women in the population) that more than 100 million women are missing. That is to say, if gender differences in mortality in Asia and North Africa mirrored those in the West, there would be 100 million more women in Asia and North Africa than presently exist.

In themselves, these figures are evidence that outcomes of interest from a welfare point of view differ markedly by gender. However, they also suggest two other points of interest. First, there is wide variation among countries. For example, much of Sub-Saharan Africa is just as impoverished as parts of South Asia but exhibits no comparable gender inequalities in mortality. This implies caution in making cross-country generalizations about the position of women. Second, gender differences in mortality rates across countries presumably reflect in large part intrahousehold inequalities in food consumption, medical care, and other "health inputs." As such, the "100 million missing women" may be only the most extreme manifestation of an underlying pattern of social disadvantage for women.

More generally, females tend to have a naturally longer life span than males (if policy is partly aimed at equalizing lifetime welfare, greater female life expectancy would provide one rationale for targeting state benefits to men). However, reproduction places gender-specific pressures on women's health, including maternal death during labor. Developing countries may have much room for improvement in this respect, since as Schultz (1989, p. 80) notes, "Death due to bearing a child is twenty times higher in South and West Asia and North and Sub-Saharan Africa than in developed countries."

Evidence on gender differences in one important health input—food consumption—has already been discussed. Sen (1987) claims that there is more agreement that females are disadvantaged in another key health input—medical care—than there is about food. However, the relevant literature on gender differences in health care in developing countries broadly mirrors that on gender differences in food consumption. For South Asia, there is evidence that boys are more likely than girls to be sent for treatment (see Chen, Huq, and D'Souza 1981 on Bangladesh; Kynch and Sen 1983, Taylor, Faruque, and Kielman 1983, Das Gupta 1987, Miller 1981, Wyon and Gordon 1971 on India; Alderman and Gertler 1988, 1989 on Pakistan). However, elsewhere, there is little evidence that boys are favored. For example, Deolalikar (1991) finds gender differences in child health care in Indonesia to be small and, if anything, to favor girls. Analyzing rural clusters in the 1985 Living Standards Survey of Côte d'Ivoire, Gertler and van der Gaag (1990) also find insignificant gender differences in child health care. Likewise, Appleton and others (1991) uncover no significant gender differences in the proportions of persons reported sick who are sent for treatment in rural Kenya and Tanzania and in Côte d'Ivoire.

Medical care and food consumption are important in reducing morbidity as well as mortality. Morbidity data have seldom been analyzed in the economics literature, although what few studies there have been are again consistent with the pattern of results discussed above for mortality, anthropometric status, food consumption, and medical care. Using nonclinically reported data, Appleton and others (1991) find no significant gender differences in either the proportions falling ill in a specified period or in the length of illness in Côte d'Ivoire, rural Kenya, and rural Tanzania. Likewise, Deolalikar (1991) finds no evidence of higher female morbidity in Indonesia. However, the one study of morbidity in South Asia to have come to our attention—that by Chen, Huq, and D'Souza (1981) in Bangladesh—does find evidence of higher female morbidity.

Aside from consumption and health-related measures of welfare, two other individual-specific variables commonly reported in socioeconomic studies may also be important indicators of welfare. One of these is education (Birdsall 1982). Although Mincer's (1974) equilibrium theory of educational investment implies that schooling should not be associated with welfare differences, in practice there are several reasons why this may not be true. For example, schooling is commonly both subsidized and rationed by the state, while the demand for schooling is often restricted by capital market failure and imperfect parental altruism. For these reasons, higher adult education within a household is often associated with higher household welfare.[5] Whether the intra-household allocation of education affects the intrahousehold distribution of welfare is less well established. However, as is discussed later in the chapter, there are several a priori reasons for supposing this to be true. Data on educational attainment in developing countries suggest fairly widespread pro-male inequalities. Unlike much of the evidence discussed above, these inequalities are not limited to South Asia, but extend to West Asia and Africa, where women receive between half and three-quarters of the years of schooling that men receive (see Herz and others 1991, table 5). By contrast, in East Asia, Latin America, and high-income countries, there is near equality in schooling attainment between the sexes, although this was not always the case.

The final measure of welfare that can be used to provide evidence on gender inequalities is leisure. Measures of consumption—often used to proxy economic welfare—typically exclude leisure. Nonetheless, leisure may be a large component of "full income" and is claimed by Schultz (1989) to be one of the most clearly private of all goods in its benefits. In developing countries, it may be difficult to measure accurately time allocation, particularly of women. For individuals without permanent, full-time, formal employment, time allocation may vary by season and from day to day, making it hard to recall in one-shot surveys. Individuals may differ in which activities they label work and leisure: child-minding, cleaning, and cooking are not universally viewed as "work." Furthermore, such activities may be hard to record accurately, with intermittent periods of leisure being interrupted by the demands of children or by small tasks that need completing. Nonetheless, data on time allocation, however imperfect, may be particularly revealing about gender differences in welfare. For example, surveys of rural Kenya and Tanzania reveal that women work significantly longer hours, even excluding time spent on child care: in Central Province, Kenya, females report an average of 42 percent more time spent working each year than men (Bevan, Collier, and Gunning 1989). This pattern may be true of many other countries where there is no evidence of corresponding gender inequalities in food consumption or health.

To summarize, it is difficult to make an overall assessment of gender differences in welfare. In part, this is inevitable because of the problem of generalizing across countries and because of the many imperfect measures of individual welfare. However, it also reflects a lack of research addressing the issue. Nonetheless, we offer three tentative conclusions. First, there is evidence of significant female disadvantage in South Asia in terms of food consumption and related health indicators (one must be wary of generalizing at such a high level of aggregation: Sri Lanka, although part of South Asia, appears to be a fairly gender-equitable society). There is no widespread evidence of similar inequalities in other regions. Second, in many developing countries throughout the world, the level of female education is significantly lower than that of men. Third, it may well be that women often receive less leisure and perhaps other goods, but the existence and extent of such disadvantage have not been widely investigated.

Gender Targeting of Generalized Transfers

We have shown that gender may be a significant determinant of disadvantage. Whether it is depends both on the particular society concerned and on the welfare indicator of interest. Where there are marked gender differences in welfare, policymakers concerned with an equitable distribution would ideally seek to offset these inequalities. We have suggested that an outcome-based system of generalized transfers is unlikely to be a practical corrective to such inequalities. Would generalized transfers targeted to women be a desirable alternative? The case for such transfers is either that they benefit women or that they benefit others, such as children.

It might be thought that generalized transfers to women would necessarily raise their welfare. However, the government may have little power to prevent the appropriation of a woman's transfer by men within the household. Within a household, property rights, particularly of weaker members, may not be well defined. Indeed, to the extent that households pool resources, any benefits targeted to women may be distributed just as any other source of household income. As Schultz (1989, p. 2) notes, "Families can compensate for most government transfers, readjusting the allocation of private resources within the family until the distribution of total resources among persons again reflects the incentives and values of the family." Such readjustments may be particularly likely in those societies where women have little power; that is to say, precisely those societies where women are most disadvantaged. This objection should not, however, be overstated. Evidence suggests that most individuals keep at least some income in "purses" separate from those of other household members (Pahl 1983). Furthermore, targeted transfers may increase the intended recipient's bargaining power over pooled household income. For example, Sen (1983, 1984) suggests that an individual's independent sources of income may affect intrahousehold bargaining by enhancing their "fallback" position, by increasing their perceived contribution to the household, by providing them with a threat in negotiations, and by affecting their sense of individuality.

Recent results of Hoddinott and Haddad (1995) and Thomas, Strauss, and Henriques (1990) are consistent with this view. Hoddinott and Haddad use household survey data for Côte d'Ivoire to attribute the cash income of the household by gender. The proportion of household income generated by women is then used as an explanatory variable for the pattern of expenditure (controlling for possible endogeneity). They find that the higher the proportion of income generated by women, the greater is the propensity to purchase goods for which women might be expected to have a preference.[6] This suggests both that preferences differ between the genders and that bargaining power is increased by earning power. Similarly, Thomas, Strauss, and Henriques find that, in Brazil, unearned female income has a greater effect than unearned male income on food consumption. Gender-targeted benefits might therefore enhance women's consumption indirectly, through increasing their bargaining power, despite fungibility. However, even though the fungibility of benefits may not pose an insuperable problem to targeted transfers, we argue later that in-kind transfers may be less fungible than generalized (that is, monetized) transfers.

Targeting female-headed households may partially avoid the problem of males appropriating benefits intended for females. A further attraction to such targeting is that female-headed households are often relatively poor, commonly lacking an adult male earner. However, targeting female-headed households reaches only some women. Moreover, there are clear moral hazard problems. In particular, both falsely reported and actual changes in the gender of household heads might be expected to occur in order to capture such benefits. These changes may be undesirable; for example, increased household dissolution may hinder child development.

The second argument for generalized gender-based transfers is that they may increase the welfare of others, such as children. Blumberg (1987) surveys evidence that women spend more than men on goods for household consumption, especially child goods, and less on items of personal expenditure. Such patterns may be due to what Blumberg terms "maternal altruism," the assumption that, compared with men, women tend to give higher priority to the welfare of other members of the household, particularly children. This argument again depends on women being able to retain control over income targeted to them but receives some support from the recent work by Hoddinott and Haddad (1995) and by Thomas, Strauss, and Henriques (1990). For Côte d'Ivoire, Hoddinott and Haddad discover that food expenditures rise with women's share of household income. For Brazil, Thomas, Strauss, and Henriques find that unearned female income raises food consumption, child survival, and anthropometric status by more than unearned male income.

In summary, there is some evidence that females are at a disadvantage and that increasing female income may partially offset this, as well as having added benefits. However, quantifying these effects is crucial for policy purposes. How significant is female disadvantage?

How much control would women retain over income targeted to them? How much would the added benefits be? Research on these questions is not sufficiently developed to warrant strong policy implications, and findings are likely to vary substantially across countries. However, two problems with generalized gender targeting are clear and common to most countries.

First, gender targeting of generalized transfers, like most forms of gender targeting, is very indiscriminate. The recipients include women in affluent households who are likely to enjoy higher welfare than men in impoverished households. Gender-targeted transfers thus involve a lot of type I and type II errors.[7] This makes them a costly means of raising the welfare of the most disadvantaged. Of course, such transfers could be supplemented with transfers targeted on other observable causes of disadvantage such as low asset holdings (for example, land-owning status). This would alleviate the problem of type I errors. Furthermore, gender might be made a qualifying characteristic for transfers only in combination with these other characteristics. This would reduce the number of type II errors.

Second, generalized transfers may be a second-best remedy for female disadvantage. They may be appropriate if the sources of female disadvantage cannot be eliminated. However, the large cross-country variation in gender differences in welfare suggests that these are not inevitable consequences of human biology. Consequently, focusing on why females are disadvantaged in particular societies may suggest more fundamental policy interventions that remove the causes of such gender inequalities rather than merely offset them. This objection extends the cause-based approach by acknowledging that in itself female gender is unlikely to be the reason for female disadvantage. For example, discrimination by employers may be one reason why women receive lower earnings than men. In such a case, legislation outlawing such behavior may be appropriate. Alternatively, if child-rearing responsibilities impose a large burden on women, then state subsidies for child care might be warranted.

However, these two causes of gender inequalities, although familiar in the setting of high-income countries, may be less relevant to some low-income countries. For example, for Côte d'Ivoire, Appleton, Collier, and Horsnell (1990) find no evidence of wage discrimination against female employees or that female formal labor market participation is hindered by having children. Instead, low education is found to be responsible for much of the gender difference in both formal labor market participation and wages. In such a case, changes in educational policy may be superior to generalized transfers. Outside of formal employment, women in developing countries may also be economically disadvantaged through ill-defined and discriminatory property rights.[8] Legal reforms to correct this situation would be preferable to palliative transfers. Given these arguments, generalized gender targeting may be less attractive than more specific policy responses. Many of these alternatives may involve gender targeting of particular government services, and it is to these that we now turn, starting with the case of education.

Gender Targeting of Education

Gender targeting of generalized transfers is not on the agenda of policymakers in developing countries. By contrast, gender targeting of education has been adopted by some developing countries and is receiving favorable attention in some external aid agencies (see Summers 1992; Herz and others 1991). Perhaps the most striking example is in Bangladesh, where secondary school scholarships for girls were introduced in 1977 and where secondary schooling was recently made free for girls (Herz and others 1991). Such policies are in many ways more attractive than gender targeting of generalized transfers. As with generalized transfers, they might be expected to increase welfare for women and to improve child health. Moreover, these benefits, both direct and indirect, may be larger for investments in female education than for generalized transfers. Furthermore, targeting education directly addresses one widely observed source of female disadvantage: lower educational attainment. Finally, there are several reasons why privately chosen levels of female education may be suboptimal and several arguments for intervention to induce a substitution toward it. Thus, the standard argument that generalized transfers are superior to in-kind transfers may not hold in the case of gender targeting of education.

Women might be expected to benefit from investments in their education since, as has previously been noted, education is likely to raise personal income. In developing countries, women's formal sector wages typically rise with education to the same extent as men's (see the literature surveys by Psacharopoulos 1985; Schultz 1993; for additional evidence, see Appleton, Collier, and Horsnell 1990 for Côte d'Ivoire; Appleton and others 1991 for Kenya and Tanzania; Behrman and Deolalikar 1990a for Indonesia; Birdsall and Sabot 1991, Khandker 1990 for Peru). Women's education also has significant returns in self-employment (see Moock 1976; Herz and Khandker 1991; Khandker 1990). Even where wage rate changes have no effect on women's earnings, they may increase women's intrahousehold bargaining power by strengthening their fallback position. To the extent that education does increase female earnings, one might expect women's control over this increase to be greater than their control over an equivalent gender-targeted generalized transfer.

There are other reasons why targeting education benefits to females may raise their welfare by more than an equivalent cash transfer. Unlike cash benefits, education given to girls cannot be directly appropriated by other members of the household. Although the household may try to offset the effects of these interventions by reallocating other goods and services among its members, such compensating behavior is likely to be less complete than if the benefits are pure lump-sum transfers. For example, if a girl receives state-subsidized secondary schooling, the household has some incentive to reduce her domestic duties and to increase her consumption of some education-related goods (perhaps including food) so as to enhance her school performance. Furthermore, education is likely to raise the recipient's bargaining power within a household when she matures. Consider two of Sen's hypothesized determinants of intrahousehold bargaining power: perceived contribution to the household and own sense of autonomy. Both are likely to rise by more if a woman's income increases due to employment (made possible after education) than if she merely enjoys state handouts (these arguments also imply that state support for female training should focus on activities whereby women can earn their own cash income rather than on household activities). Education may also improve a woman's sense of self-worth regardless of whether she works outside of the household, by making her more articulate and self-confident and by exposing her to modern values that may be more gender-equitable than traditional ones.

Female education is likely to benefit other persons as well as its recipient. A substantial body of evidence exists on the effects of maternal education on child health, family size, and child cognitive development.[9] As discussed below, these effects are often found to be greater than corresponding effects of paternal education. This may partly reflect maternal altruism and the consequences of increased female income. However, it may also reflect direct efficiency effects of education in activities for which women typically have responsibility. These direct effects may make female education more effective than generalized transfers to women.

Perhaps the most important of these effects is on child health. Evidence that female education has a greater effect than male education on child mortality is provided by cross-country studies by Cochrane, Leslie, and O'Hara (1980, 1982) and also by a time-series analysis of fifteen countries performed by Mensch, Lentzner, and Preston (1986). Some have questioned whether these effects actually represent the workings of female education or merely the operation of omitted third factors, such as parental background (Behrman 1990). However, maternal education may improve child health through a number of mechanisms. It may lead to a greater use of "health inputs" such as food, health care, and sanitation, either because of income effects or because of the effect of education on parents' knowledge, attitudes, and values. It may also increase the effectiveness with which these inputs are used (for example, preventing the incorrect dosage of drugs). To the extent that the health benefits of parental education are informational or attitudinal, they may be larger for mothers, who commonly have responsibility for tasks related to child health, such as food preparation and taking children for medical treatment. For example, Appleton and others (1991) find that, in Côte d'Ivoire and Kenya, the probability of sending a sick child for medical treatment varies significantly with maternal education, but not with paternal education. The size of these effects is large, with simulations predicting that full maternal primary schooling would induce larger rises in the take-up of medical treatment for sick children than would the provision of a health clinic in every village. There are also direct biological links between maternal (but not paternal) health and child health during pregnancy.

Another effect of female education that may be judged important is its role in reducing fertility. Such effects have been found in a large number of countries (Demographic and Health Surveys 1990). Evidence that female education has a greater inhibiting effect on fertility than male education is provided in World Bank (1980, 1986) and Schultz (1993). This is to be expected on standard neoclassical economic theories of fertility, which assume that children are more intensive in women's time and that the value of women's time rises with their education. There may also be indirect effects on fertility because education raises women's age at marriage. This may be both because attending school is incompatible with child rearing and because, on some theories, the gains to marriage decrease with female wages (and increase with male wages). Furthermore, any effects of education on fertility via increased contraceptive efficiency may be more pronounced for women if prevalent forms of contraception rely on the woman for use. For example, Rosenzweig and Schultz (1985, 1989) find that, in the United States, the wife's education is more important in determining contraceptive effectiveness than the husband's education. The fertility-reducing effect of female education may have private benefits to the extent that it arises from greater control of fertility. It may also improve maternal and child health.

A case can therefore be made for gender targeting of education due to its positive effects on women and its added benefits to others. These effects may be greater than the corresponding benefits from generalized gender targeting, both because education may be less fungible and because education may have direct effects on fertility and child health. The added benefits in terms of such direct effects may be particularly sizable. For example, Summers (1992) argues that female education is more cost-effective than either investments in health facilities or family planning. In practice, however, some care should be taken to separate the case for targeting primary education from that for targeting secondary education. The returns may differ in the two cases: for example, benefits for child health are more usually associated with maternal primary schooling, while, conversely, fertility reductions tend to be strongest in the case of female secondary schooling.

A simple objection to gender targeting of education is the standard argument for generalized transfers over in-kind transfers, namely that welfare will be higher if recipients are free to use transfers to consume whatever goods they like. A number of rejoinders may be made to this argument.

First, it must be set against the benefits discussed above of the reduced fungibility of education compared to general transfers. Allowing the household to allocate its resources freely may be undesirable on equity grounds if household decisionmakers are biased against females. Such bias may be extreme, with parents giving higher priority to increases in the welfare of sons than of daughters. This might be true in societies such as India, of which one official statement claims, "In a culture that idolizes sons and dreads the birth of a daughter, to be born female comes perilously close to being born less than human" (Government of India 1990, cited in Herz and others 1991, p. 31). Another form of pro-male bias might be prejudiced parental opinions of females' capabilities or restrictive views of their appropriate roles. These may limit female schooling both directly by causing parents to oppose girls' school attendance and indirectly by restricting girls' confidence, expectations, and aspirations.

Second, imperfect parental information may justify policies promoting education in general and female education in particular. Uneducated parents may be ignorant of the benefits of education. This seems particularly plausible in the case of nonmarket returns, such as improvements in child health and in fertility control. Observing the wage premium to education in the labor market is a relatively straightforward exercise, likely to be well understood by parents. However, for an uneducated parent to realize that educating his child will make her a better farmer, entrepreneur, or parent is rather more demanding, both informationally and psychologically. Such beneficial effects of education are often of a subtle form, working through increased knowledge (which the uneducated parent does not have and therefore may not fully appreciate) and through changed values. Consequently, it seems unlikely that the health benefits of maternal schooling influence the schooling decisions of uneducated parents. Indeed, until recently, standard rate-of-return calculations by labor economists assumed that there were no benefits to education beyond increased wages (Schultz 1993). Since men are more likely to obtain wage employment, corresponding parental neglect of the nonwage returns to education would lead to a markedly lower valuation of female education. For example, a study of Andra Pradesh, India, in 1977 finds that the returns to female primary education falls from 12 percent to zero if the estimated wage premia are adjusted to allow for low participation in the formal labor market; for men, the corresponding fall is from 9 to 7 percent. The wage returns to secondary education exhibit a similar pattern (Tilak 1987, table 6.8).

A further reason for promoting female education is that some of its benefits may be external to those individuals (typically parents) making choices about child schooling. Parental altruism may serve to internalize much of these returns within the household. Consequently, under full information, altruistic parents might be expected to take into account the beneficial effects of schooling their daughters on the health of their future grandchildren. However some gains to female education may accrue outside the household. For example, improvements in child health may have public health benefits, while reductions in fertility reduce congestion. Increased female education may increase the status of women in society in general, rather than just that of those who are well educated. In some cases, highly educated women may act as role models and encourage others. Moreover, even when benefits are limited to household members, externalities may arise if parents are incompletely altruistic and value more highly those returns to education that they receive. In the absence of state intervention, this tends to lead to underprovision of education in general and, in some societies, of female education in particular. This is because social customs in many developing countries tend to lead to sons having closer economic links with their parents, providing more remittances and greater old age support. Particularly important are what Meillassoux (1981) terms patrilocal customs, whereby young married couples reside with the grooms' kin. Related to this is the role of inheritance customs. For example, Goody (1976) notes that Africa is characterized by homogeneous (as opposed to diverging) patterns of inheritance that favor males. Hence, parents may expect to receive more of the pecuniary benefits from child schooling in the case of sons than in the case of daughters, both because sons remain part of their household for longer and because sons can expect to be rewarded with a parental bequest.[10] Consequently, imperfect parental altruism may lead to a pro-male bias in schooling.

Last, it should not be assumed that existing education levels are purely the result of parental choice. Some of the observed gender inequalities are attributable to government policies that operate to the benefit of boys. To the extent that this is true, an increase in educational investments targeted to girls may merely offset a preexisting allocation of public resources in favor of boys. This is most apparent in single-sex education systems, within which girls' schools may be underprovided. For example, Alderman and others (forthcoming, and chapter 8 of this volume) attribute most of the gender gap in educational attainment in rural Pakistan to the absence of local primary schools for girls.

However, in some countries, use of meritocratic systems for rationing state schooling unintentionally favors boys. In particular, in many developing countries, secondary schooling is subsidized by the government, and admission is granted only to students who perform well on primary leaving exams. Girls often do less well on average in these exams and thus have lower eligibility for further schooling. This rationing may account for a considerable degree of gender inequality.[11] Why girls tend to underperform in developing-country schools is thus an important question, but one that has received little attention from economists (for exceptions, see Alderman and others, forthcoming; Appleton 1993; Appleton and others 1991). In part, the answer may lead back to the household, with low parental demand for girls' schooling adversely affecting their performance by a variety of routes, both psychological and material.[12] However, other factors are also likely to be important.[13]

In summary, the relatively low levels of female education in much of the developing world are likely to be undesirable on both equity and efficiency grounds. The lower demand for female education may both reflect and perpetuate intrahousehold inequality. And because of parental ignorance of the wider benefits of education, the external nature of some of these benefits, and pro-male biases in some existing educational policies, these low levels of female education are unlikely to be efficient. Consequently, the fact that gender targeting of education leads to more female education than households would choose under generalized transfers may not represent the conventional welfare-reducing distortion of in-kind transfers. Instead, it may be a desirable corrective. Indeed, if, as seems likely, low education is one major proximate cause of female disadvantage, gender targeting of education is the obvious remedy.

However, gender targeting education does not avoid the type I and type II errors noted in the case of generalized transfers. Giving all girls educational subsidies would be costly, and able boys from impoverished families may be thought to be more appropriate recipients of assistance than some girls. Type II errors may be more severe as the level of education to be targeted increases. In many developing countries where there is substantial but not universal primary schooling, measures specifically designed to encourage female enrollment may mainly affect girls from poorer families. Conversely, if secondary schooling is still the preserve of the minority, then the "marginal" girls who might be induced to enroll by gender targeting may be from relatively advantaged backgrounds. As with generalized targeting, type I and type II errors imply the need to use other criteria in addition to gender when targeting. Regional criteria are one possibility, so that educational investments for females could be restricted to areas where female enrollment is particularly low.

Gender Targeting of Other Services

There may also be a case for targeting other government services by gender. For example, it may be efficient to target family planning services on women if the contraceptive technology involved depends primarily on women to implement. There may be an argument on similar grounds for targeting health and nutrition interventions on women. Leslie, Lycette, and Buvinic (1988) note that primary health care is markedly more cost-effective than curative hospital care.[14] They also argue that to be effective, primary health care must be participatory and that, since women are responsible for most related activities, this means in practice that primary health care interventions depend largely on women.

Such arguments for targeting are instrumental ones, relying on the premise that women may have more responsibility for household activities of interest. A different case for targeting services would be to try to ensure that females receive a larger share of the benefits of these interventions (these two forms of targeting may conflict: making women informal "health workers" may actually enhance gender inequalities by increasing the obligations on women's time). One perhaps accepted form of this is programs focused on maternal health. In addition, targeting more general health services to women may be attractive in those areas where, as discussed above, there are marked gender inequalities in nutrition, health care, and health outcomes. Indeed, household investments in the health of girls may be inefficiently low for reasons similar to those given for why too little female schooling is demanded.[15] However, directly redressing these inequalities may lead to some of the practical problems noted with general transfers. Directly altering the intrahousehold allocation of food is likely to be more difficult than directly affecting the intrahousehold allocation of schooling. For example, many researchers (including Chernichovsky and Zangwill 1988) note that, with school feeding programs, families reduce the amount of food they allocate to children who are provided with school meals. Countering low take-up of medical services for females may be more feasible, using measures similar to those mentioned for increasing female school attainment. Moreover, as with schooling, general measures to increase take-up may be particularly effective with girls. For example, Alderman and Gertler (1989) find that the demand for health care in Pakistan is more price elastic for girls than for boys.

Gender targeting may be appropriate in some government services outside the social sector. One important case may be agricultural extension services. Poor female access to these services has been widely noted (see Baxter 1986; Saito and Spurling 1991; Saito and Weidemann 1990). Sometimes this gender bias is intentional, with the assumption being that men make agricultural decisions and pass on whatever information is necessary to their wives. However, the biases may exist for other reasons. Extension agents tend to be men and usually prefer to talk to men, even where women are farmers or even heads of household. More generally, as Schultz (1989, p. 84) states, "Priority is often given to supporting cash crops, which are often managed by males, because of the commercial and governmental interests in these potential export crops that provide tax revenue."

These biases may have equity and efficiency costs, particularly in economies (such as many in Sub-Saharan Africa) where women run "own-account farms" distinct from the household farms managed by men. Work by Spring, Smith, and Kayuni (1983) in Malawi is suggestive. Female-headed households and wives are found to receive fewer extension visits than men, but women attribute more of the agricultural innovations they make to extension services. More recently, Bindlish and Evenson (1993) find in Kenya that female frontline extension workers have a powerful additional impact on the productivity of farms run by female household heads.

Recent work on agricultural innovation in Kenya has found that information variables are important and that there are substantial gender differences in information channels. Investigating the adoption of coffee, Burger, Collier, and Gunning (1993) find a powerful copying effect: households imitate the decisions of their neighbors. This by itself is not surprising, being entirely consistent with welfare maximization once it is recognized that information is costly. However, this pattern of imitation is found to be gender-specific: male decisionmakers copy only other male decisionmakers, female decisionmakers copy only other female decisionmakers. Again, there is nothing particularly puzzling about such behavior. If the function of copying the decisions of others is to free ride on their investments in information, it is advisable to copy persons whose characteristics appear to be as similar as possible to one's own. Evidently, gender is seen to be a pertinent characteristic, indicating that female decisionmakers are perceived to face distinctive constraints. This is indeed consistent with the result that the gender of the decisionmaker is the most powerful and significant of all the explanatory variables in coffee adoption. Female decisionmakers are markedly less likely to innovate, even controlling for access to information and endowments of land and labor.

The gender specificity of copying is of importance for public policy because the current endowment of role models is so different for the two genders. Male-headed households have plenty of innovators from whom to copy, female-headed households have few. The public information channels of extension and education need, therefore, to be gender targeted so as to offset a bias in private externalities. In the case of Kenyan coffee adoption, education of the decisionmaker is found to be significant in inducing innovation only for females. Education appears to be functioning as a substitute for the dearth of female role models.

There may be similar arguments for gender targeting in other areas of policy. For example, female farmers are often disadvantaged in access to credit, because inheritance practices and control of property within marriage inhibit their ability to own land (Davison 1988; Moock 1986).

Conclusions

Gender appears to be one of the dimensions of disadvantage. In developing countries, there are large gender differences in the choice of economic activity. For a variety of reasons, a consequence of these choices is that in the aggregate, women have fewer role models among the economically successful. If role models play an important part in determining activity choice, this tends to perpetuate the concentration of women in less productive activities. Education is both an example of this difference in activity choice and potentially a mechanism for offsetting it. At present, girls are less likely to be sent to school, are more likely to drop out, and tend to perform less well in examinations (contrary to their peers in high-income countries). Arguably, part of the reason for this is that parents are less aware of, or stand to benefit less from, the returns to educating a daughter than the returns to educating a son. Parents may be less able to capture the monetized returns to the education of daughters, and they may not recognize the nonpecuniary private benefits, such as the improved health of their grandchildren. Finally, they do not take into account any externalities that arise if the education of women substitutes for a dearth of role models as agricultural innovators or wage earners.

Although we have emphasized educational targeting as preferable to generalized transfers, other types of targeted intervention may also be highly cost-effective. There may be a role for the government in reforming the content of education as well as the composition of its recipients.[16] Legal reforms to strengthen female property rights may also be important in attaining both gender equity and efficiency.

Finally, we should stress a major limitation with gender targeting: in targeting half the population, it is very indiscriminate. There are also often large differentials in the takeup of specific services, with more advantaged individuals tending to take a larger share. For example, Vaughan (1987) suggests that women who take up government interventions are likely to be richer (and older) than those who do not. This suggests that even for in-kind transfers, gender is more appropriately used only in conjunction with other criteria.

Notes

1. One method of trying to circumvent the difficulties in observing personal consumption is to use personal income as a measure of welfare. Attributing the source of income to particular household members is often easier than determining the intrahousehold allocation of consumption. However, this is unlikely to be a preferable approach if the household performs a significant redistributional function. In particular, one would want to take into account intrahousehold transfers of income, and this often entails the same exercise as identifying the pattern of intrahousehold consumption, since such transfers are often in kind.

2. These results have been corroborated using the 1986 Côte d'Ivoire Living Standards Survey by Haddad and Hoddinott (1994). However, disaggregation by age and relation to the household head does suggest some pro-male bias in resources allocated to young (under seven years) nonoffspring of the household head.

3. Similarly, Sahn (1990) finds that height-for-age is significantly lower for boys than for girls in urban Côte d'Ivoire, as do Senauer and Garcia (1991) for the Philippines. Von Braun (1988) also reports higher anthropometric status for girls than for boys in rural Gambia.

4. Stunting is defined as having a height-for-age more than two standard deviations below the U.S. median. Similarly, a "low" weight is defined as a weight-for-age more than two standard deviations below the U.S. median.

5. This generalization may not always be valid: access to off-farm employment and other factors may affect the returns to education. For example, Glewwe (1991) finds that adult education is associated with higher consumption per capita in urban but not rural Côte d'Ivoire, while Appleton (1992, app. 1) finds that adult education increases household income per capita in rural Kenya, but not in rural Tanzania.

6. The results imply that doubling women's share of household income would reduce the share of alcohol and tobacco in total expenditures by 25 and 15 percent, respectively. The increase in the food share would be more modest, at 2 percent. However, the authors argue that even the effect on food spending is substantial. As an illustration, they calculate that the fall in gross domestic product in Côte d'Ivoire in the 1980s (averaging 0.6 percent per year) would not have reduced food spending if all incomes had been redistributed to women.

7. In the terminology of statistics, type I errors are rejecting something that is true, and type II errors are accepting something that is false. Thus in this context, type I errors would be denying services or transfers to men who are poor, while type II errors would be giving assistance to women who are not poor.

8. Particularly important are women's rights to property within and after marriage. One example of the former is in Zaire, where the Civil Code presumes that the wife's goods are managed by her husband, with the consequence that there is a substantial black economy of female traders (MacGaffey 1986). An instance of the latter again occurs in Africa, where women often have only usufructuary land rights, so that, after divorce or bereavement, they can no longer work family land unless supported by male relatives of the husband (Bryceson 1985).

9. Evidence for the last of these three effects is less well documented by economists. Lavy (1992) finds that maternal education in Ghana leads to greater child schooling than paternal education. However, Appleton and others (1991) find no similar pattern in Côte d'Ivoire, rural Kenya, or rural Tanzania.

10. Hoddinott (1994) finds a positive relationship between land and remittances in rural Kenya. He interprets this as the promise of a bequest of land acting as a lever by which parents may obtain transfers from their children. A logical extension of this argument is that if parents are more confident of securing remittances, they may be willing to invest more in their children's education. This extension is as yet unsubstantiated by empirical evidence.

11. For example, in Côte d'Ivoire in 1986, this state rationing, rather than low demand, was the proximate cause of lower female continuation rates from primary to secondary school. In Kenya in the mid-1980s, continuation rates were roughly equal between genders, but poorer performance by girls in the primary leaving exam led to girls being skewed into what is perceived as the lower-quality private sector (Appleton and others 1991).

12. One example of this is provided by the analysis of Appleton and others (1991) for Côte d'Ivoire. There, according to the 1986 Living Standards Survey, gender differences in performance in the primary leaving exam diminish with household consumption. This may be because poor households use girls' labor at the expense of their studies. Support is found for this in the fact that, among the poorest quartile of students, girls in the final year of school spend an average of eight hours a week less than boys in school. This pattern is not observed in other quartiles. Furthermore, multivariate analysis reveals that hours in school are significantly positively correlated with subsequent exam performance.

13. Grisay (1984) provides an interesting discussion of Côte d'Ivoire. Among the hypotheses she suggests for the inferior performance of girls in primary school are the inhibiting effect on classroom participation of cultural values, a shortage of female teachers, the use of French as a medium of instruction, and the younger ages of girls on enrollment into school.

14. They define primary health care as having eight components: (1) health education, (2) nutrition and food (purchase and preparation), (3) maternal and child health care (including family planning), (4) water and sanitation, (5) immunization, (6) disease control and prevention, (7) essential drugs, and (8) treatment of common diseases and injuries.

15. See also Rosenzweig and Schultz (1982) and Bardhan (1982, 1984), who attribute gender differences in child mortality in India to differential returns to male and female labor. Such explanations are challenged, however, by Das Gupta (1987) and Folbre (1984).

16. One relevant example of the former concerns the role of women as presented in school. For example, in school textbooks in Zambia, women rarely appeared and, when they did, were "primarily in domestic roles and were characterized as passive, stupid, and ignorant" (Tembo 1984, quoted in Hyde 1989, p. 34). Efforts to remove sexual stereotyping from textbooks have taken place or are under way in Bangladesh, Costa Rica, the Gambia, Guatemala, Mexico, and Zimbabwe (Herz and others 1991).

References

Agarwal, Bina. 1986. "Women, Poverty, and Agricultural Growth in India." *Journal of Peasant Studies* 13 (4): 165–220.

Alderman, Harold. 1990. "Nutritional Status in Ghana and Its Determinants." Social Dimensions of Adjustment in Sub-Saharan Africa Working Paper 3. World Bank, Washington, D.C.

Alderman, Harold, Jere R. Behrman, David R. Ross, and Richard Sabot. Forthcoming. "Decomposing the Gap in Cognitive Skills in a Poor Rural Economy." *Journal of Human Resources.*

Alderman, Harold, and Paul Gertler. 1988. "The Substitutability of Public and Private Health Care for the Treatment of Children in Pakistan." Living Standards Measurement Study Working Paper 57. World Bank, Washington, D.C.

———. 1989. "Family Resources and Gender Differences in Human Capital." International Food Policy Research Institute, Washington, D.C.

Appleton, Simon M. 1992. "Socio-economic Determinants of Education, Health, and Fertility in Africa." Ph.d. diss. University of Oxford, Oxford, Eng.

———. 1993. "Why Do Girls Under-perform in Kenyan Primary Schools?" McNamara Fellowship Report. World Bank, Washington, D.C.

Appleton, Simon M., D. L. Bevan, Kees Burger, Paul Collier, J. W. Gunning, Lawrence Haddad, and John Hoddinott. 1991. "Public Services and Household Allocation in Africa: Does Gender Matter?" Centre for the Study of African Economies, Oxford, Eng.

Appleton, Simon M., Paul Collier, and Paul Horsnell. 1990. "Gender, Education, and Employment in Côte d'Ivoire." Social Dimensions of Adjustment Working Paper 8. World Bank, Washington, D.C.

Bannerjee, Nirmala. 1983. "Women and Poverty: Report on a Workshop." *Economic and Political Weekly* 18: 1693–98.

Bardhan, P. K. 1974. "On Life and Death Questions." *Economic and Political Weekly* 9 (32–34): 1293–1304.

———. 1982. "Little Girls and Death in India." *Economic and Political Weekly* 17 (36): 1448–50.

———. 1984. *Land, Labor, and Rural Poverty: Essays in Development Economics.* New Delhi: Oxford University Press.

Basu, A. M. 1987. "Is Discrimination in Food Really Necessary for Explaining Sex Differentials in Childhood Mortality." National Council of Applied Economic Research, New Delhi.

Baxter, Michael. 1986. "New Developments in Agricultural Extension." World Bank, Washington, D.C.

Behrman, Jere R. 1988a. "Intrahousehold Allocation of Nutrients in Rural India: Are Boys Favoured? Do Households Exhibit Inequality Aversion?" *Oxford Economic Papers* 40 (1): 55–73.

———. 1988b. "Nutrition, Health, Birth Order, and Seasonality: Intrahousehold Allocation among Children in Rural India." *Journal of Development Economics* 28: 43–62.

———. 1990. "Women's Schooling and Non-Market Productivity: A Survey and a Reappraisal." University of Pennsylvania, Philadelphia, Penn.

Behrman, Jere R., and Anil B. Deolalikar. 1990a. "Are There Differential Returns to Schooling by Gender? The Case of Indonesian Labor Markets." University of Pennsylvania, Philadelphia, Penn.

———. 1990b. "The Intrahousehold Demand for Nutrients in Rural South India: Individual Estimates, Fixed Effects, and Permanent Income." *Journal of Human Resources* 2: 665–90.

Bevan, David, Paul Collier, and Jan W. Gunning. 1989. *Peasants and Governments*. Oxford, Eng.: Clarendon Press.

Bindlish, Vishva, and Robert Evenson. 1993. *Evaluation of the Performance of T&V Extension in Kenya*. World Bank Technical Paper 208. Washington, D.C.

Birdsall, Nancy. 1982. "Child Schooling and the Measurement of Living Standards." Living Standards Measurement Study Working Paper 14. World Bank, Washington, D.C.

Birdsall, Nancy, and Richard Sabot, eds. 1991. *Unfair Advantage: Labor Market Discrimination in Developing Countries*. Washington D.C.: World Bank.

Blau, David. 1984. "A Model of Child Nutrition, Fertility, and Women's Time Allocation: The Case of Nicaragua." In T. Paul Schultz and Kenneth Wolpin, eds., *Research in Population Economics*, vol. 5. Greenwich, Conn.: JAI Press.

Blumberg, Rae Lesser. 1987. "Income under Female vs. Male Control: Differential Spending Patterns and Consequences When Women Lose Control of Returns to Labor." World Bank, Washington, D.C.

Bryceson, Deborah. 1985. "Women's Proletarianisation and the Family in Tanzania." In H. Afshar, ed., *Women, Work, and Ideology in the Third World*. London: Tavistock.

Burger, Kase, Paul Collier, and Jan W. Gunning. 1993. "Learning by Observing: Theory and an Application to Agricultural Innovation in Kenya." Centre for the Study of African Economies, Oxford, Eng.

Cassen, R. H. 1978. *India: Population, Economy, and Society*. New York: Macmillan Press.

Chen, L. C., Emdadul Huq, and Stan D'Souza. 1981. "Sex Bias in the Family Allocation of Food and Health Care in Bangladesh." *Population and Development Review* 7 (1): 55–70.

Chernichovsky, Dov, and Linda Zangwill. 1988. "Microeconomic Theory of the Household and Nutrition Programs." Population and Human Resource Department Working Paper 82. World Bank, Washington, D.C.

Cochrane, Susan H., Joanne Leslie, and Donald J. O'Hara. 1980. *The Effects of Education on Health*. World Bank Staff Working Paper 405. Washington, D.C.

———. 1982. "Parental Education and Child Health." *Health Policy and Education* 2: 213–50.

Das Gupta, Monica. 1987. "Selective Discrimination against Female Children in Rural Punjab, India." *Population and Development Review* 13 (1): 77–100.

Davison, Jean. 1988. *Agriculture, Women, and the Land: The African Experience*. Boulder, Colo.: Westview Press.

Deaton, Angus. 1989. "Looking for Boy-Girl Discrimination in Household Expenditure Data." *World Bank Economic Review* 3 (1): 1–16.

Demographic and Health Surveys. 1990. "Women's Education: Findings from Demographic and Health Surveys." Paper presented at the World Conference on Education for All, Bangkok, Thailand.

Deolalikar, Anil B. 1991. "Intrahousehold Allocation of Health Inputs and Distribution of Health Outcomes among Indonesian Children." In *Robert S. McNamara Fellowships Program: 10th Anniversary Publication*. Washington, D.C.: World Bank, Economic Development Institute.

Folbre, Nancy. 1984. "Market Opportunities, Genetic Endowments, and Intra-family Resources Distribution: Comment." *American Economic Review* 74: 518–20.

Gertler, Paul, and Jacques van der Gaag. 1990. *The Willingness to Pay for Medical Care: Evidence from Two Developing Countries.* Baltimore, Md.: Johns Hopkins University Press.

Glewwe, Paul. 1990. "Efficient Allocation of Transfers to the Poor." Living Standards Measurement Survey Working Paper 70. World Bank, Washington, D.C.

———. 1991. "Investigating the Determinants of Household Welfare in Côte d'Ivoire." *Journal of Development Economics* 35: 307–37.

Goody, Jack. 1976. *Production and Reproduction.* Cambridge, Eng.: Cambridge University Press.

Government of India. 1990. *The Lesser Child.* Cited in Barbara Herz, K. Subbarao, and Laura Raney. *Letting Girls Learn: Promising Approaches in Primary and Secondary Education.* World Bank Discussion Paper 133. Washington, D.C., 1991.

Grisay, Alette. 1984. "Analyse des inégaliteés de rendement lieés au sexe de l'élève dans l'enseignement primaire ivorien." *International Review of Education* 30: 25–39.

Haddad, Lawrence. 1990. "Gender and Poverty in Ghana: A Descriptive Analysis." University of Warwick, Economics Department, Coventry, U.K.

Haddad, Lawrence, and John Hoddinott. 1994. "Women's Income and Boy-Girl Anthropometric Status in the Côte d'Ivoire." *World Development* 22: 543–53.

Haddad, Lawrence, and Ravi Kanbur. 1990. "How Serious Is the Neglect of Intra-household Inequality?" *Economic Journal* 100 (402): 866–81.

Harriss, Barbara. 1990. "The Intrafamily Distribution of Hunger in South Asia." In Jean Drèze and Amartya Sen, eds., *The Political Economy of Hunger*, vol. 1. Oxford, Eng.: Clarendon Press.

Hassan, Nazmul, and Kamuluddin Ahmad. 1984. "Intra-familial Distribution of Food in Rural Bangladesh." *Food and Nutrition Bulletin* 6 (4): 34–42.

Herz, Barbara K., and Shahidur R. Khandker, eds. 1991. *Women's Work, Education, and Family Welfare in Peru.* World Bank Discussion Paper 116. Washington, D.C.

Herz, Barbara, K. Subbarao, and Laura Raney. 1991. *Letting Girls Learn: Promising Approaches in Primary and Secondary Education.* World Bank Discussion Paper 133. Washington, D.C.

Hoddinott, John. 1994. "A Model of Migration and Remittances Applied to Western Kenya." *Oxford Economic Papers* 46: 459–76.

Hoddinott, John, and Lawrence Haddad. 1995. "Does Female Income Share Influence Household Expenditures? Evidence from Côte d'Ivoire." *Oxford Bulletin of Economics and Statistics* 57: 77–96.

Hyde, Karin. 1989. "Improving Women's Education in Sub-Saharan Africa: A Review of the Literature." PHREE/89/15. World Bank, Washington, D.C.

Kennedy, Eileen, and Bruce Cogill. 1987. "Income and Nutritional Effects of the Commercialisation of Agriculture in South-Western Kenya." Research Report 63. International Food Policy Research Institute, Washington, D.C.

Khandker, Shahidur R. 1990. "Labor Market Participation, Returns to Education, and Male-Female Wage Differences in Peru." Policy Research Working Paper 461. World Bank, Washington, D.C.

Kynch, Jocelyn, and A. K. Sen. 1983. "Indian Women: Well-being and Survival." *Cambridge Journal of Economics* 7 (3–4): 363–80.

Lavy, Victor. 1992. *Investment in Human Capital: Schooling Supply Constraints in Rural Ghana.* Living Standards Measurement Survey Working Paper 93. World Bank, Washington, D.C.

Leslie, Joanne, Margaret Lycette, and Mayra Buvinic. 1988. "Weathering Economic Crises: The Crucial Role of Women in Health." In David Bell and Michael Reich, eds., *Health, Nutrition, and Economic Crises: Approaches to Policy in the Third World.* Dover, Mass.: Auburn House.

MacGaffey, Janet. 1986. "Women and Class Formation in a Dependent Economy: Kisangani Entrepreneurs." In Claire C. Robertson and Iris Berger, eds., *Women and Class in Africa.* New York: Africana Publishing Company.

Meillassoux, Claude. 1981. *Maidens, Meals, and Money.* Cambridge, Eng.: Cambridge University Press.

Mensch, Barbara, Harold Lentzner, and Samuel Preston. 1986. *Socio-economic Differentials in Child Mortality in Developing Countries.* New York: United Nations.

Miller, B. D. 1981. *The Endangered Sex.* Ithaca, N.Y.: Cornell University Press.

Mincer, Jacob. 1974. *Schooling, Experience, and Earnings.* New York: Columbia University Press.

Moock, J. L. 1986. *Understanding Africa's Rural Households and Farming Systems.* Boulder, Colo.: Westview Press.

Moock, Peter. 1976. "The Efficiency of Women as Farm Managers: Kenya." *American Journal of Agricultural Economics* 58 (5): 831–35.

Pahl, J. 1983. "The Allocation of Money and the Structuring of Inequality within Marriage." *Sociology Review* 31 (2): 237–62.

Pitt, Mark M., Mark R. Rosenzweig, and M. D. Hassan. 1990. "Productivity, Health, and Inequality in the Intra-household Distribution of Food in Low Income Households." *American Economic Review* 80 (5): 1139–56.

Psacharopoulos, George. 1985. "Returns to Education: A Further International Update and Implications." *Journal of Human Resources* 20: 583–97.

Rosenzweig, Mark R., and T. P. Schultz. 1982. "Market Opportunities, Genetic Endowments, and Intrafamily Resource Distribution." *American Economic Review* 72 (4): 803–15.

———. 1985. "The Demand and Supply of Births: Fertility and Its Life Cycle Consequences." *American Economic Review* 75 (5): 992–1015.

———. 1989. "Schooling, Information, and Non-Market Productivity: Contraceptive Use and Its Effectiveness." *International Economic Review* 30 (2): 457–77.

Sahn, David. 1990. "Malnutrition in Côte d'Ivoire." Social Dimensions of Adjustment Working Paper 4. World Bank, Washington, D.C.

Saito, Katrine A., and Daphne Spurling. 1991. "Agricultural Extension and Research for Women Farmers." World Bank, Washington, D.C.

Saito, Katrine A., and C. Jean Weidemann. 1990. *Agricultural Extension for Women Farmers*. World Bank Discussion Paper 103. Washington, D.C.

Schultz, T. Paul. 1989. "Women and Development: Objectives, Frameworks, and Policy." Working Paper WPS 200. World Bank, Women in Development Division, Population and Human Resources Department, Washington, D.C.

_____. 1993. "Returns to Women's Education." In E. M. King and M. A. Hill, eds., *Women's Education in Developing Countries*. Baltimore, Md.: Johns Hopkins University Press.

Sen, Amartya K. 1983. "Economics and the Family." *Asian Development Review* 1 (2): 14–26.

_____. 1984. "Family and Food: Sex Bias in Poverty." In A. K. Sen, ed., *Resources, Values, and Development*. Cambridge, Mass.: Harvard University Press.

_____. 1987. "Africa and India: What Do We Have to Learn from One Another?" All Souls College, Oxford, Eng.

_____. 1990. "More than 100 Million Women Are Missing." *New York Review of Books* 37 (2): 61–66.

Sen, A. K., and S. Sengupta. 1983. "Malnutrition of Rural Children and the Sex Bias." *Economic and Political Weekly* 18: 855–64.

Senauer, Benjamin, and Marito Garcia. 1991. "Determinants of the Nutrition and Health Status of Pre-school Children: An Analysis with Longitudinal Data." *Economic Development and Cultural Change* 39 (2): 371–89.

Senauer, Benjamin, Marito Garcia, and Elizabeth Jacinto. 1988. "Determinants of the Intrahousehold Allocation of Food in the Rural Philippines." *American Journal of Agricultural Economics* 70 (1): 170–80.

Senauer, Benjamin, David Sahn, and Harold Alderman. 1986. "Effects of the Value of Time on Food Consumption Patterns in Developing Countries: Evidence from Sri Lanka." *American Journal of Agricultural Economics* 68 (4): 920–27.

Spring, Anita, C. Smith, and F. Kayuni. 1983. "Women Farmers in Malawi: Their Contribution to Agriculture and Participation in Development Projects." U.S. Agency for International Development, Office of Women in Development, Washington, D.C.

Strauss, John. 1990. "Households, Communities, and Preschool Children's Nutrition Outcomes: Evidence from Rural Côte d'Ivoire." *Economic Development and Cultural Change* 38 (2): 231–62.

Summers, Lawrence H. 1992. "Investing in All the People." Policy Research Working Paper 905. World Bank, Washington, D.C.

Svedberg, Peter. 1990. "Undernutrition in Sub-Saharan Africa: Is There a Gender Bias?" *Journal of Development Studies* 26 (3): 469–86.

Taylor, Carl E., Ahmed Faruque, and Arnfield A. Kielman. 1983. *Child and Maternal Health Services in Rural India*. Baltimore, Md.: Johns Hopkins University Press.

Tembo, L. P. 1984. *Men and Women in School Textbooks*. Paris: UNESCO.

Thomas, Duncan. 1990. "Intrahousehold Resource Allocation: An Inferential Approach." *Journal of Human Resources* 25 (4): 635–64.

———. 1991. *Like Father, Like Son: Gender Differences in Household Resource Allocations*. New Haven, Conn.: Yale University.

Thomas, Duncan, John Strauss, and Maria Helena Henriques. 1990. "Child Survival, Height-for-Age, and Household Characteristics in Brazil." *Journal of Development Economics* 33: 197–234.

Tilak, J. B. G. 1987. *The Economics of Inequality in Education*. New Delhi: Sage Publishers.

Vaughan, Megan. 1987. "Targeting Women." Queen Elizabeth House, Oxford University, Oxford, Eng.

von Braun, Joachim. 1988. "Effects of Technological Change in Agriculture on Food Consumption and Nutrition: Rice in a West Africa Setting." *World Development* 16: 1083–98.

WHO (World Health Organization). 1979. "Measurement of Nutritional Impact." Document FAP/79.1. Geneva, Switzerland.

World Bank. 1980. *World Development Report 1980: Poverty*. New York: Oxford University Press.

———. 1986. *World Development Report 1986: Agriculture*. New York: Oxford University Press.

———. 1991. *World Development Report 1991: The Challenge of Development*. New York: Oxford University Press.

Wyon, J. B., and J. E. Gordon. 1971. *The Khana Study*. Cambridge, Mass.: Harvard University Press.

VIII Toward a Synthesis

20 Incidence and Targeting: An Overview of Implications for Research and Policy

Dominique van de Walle

This concluding chapter critically reviews and synthesizes the book's implications for policy and research on public spending and poverty. It focuses on three key questions: (a) What is the welfare objective? (b) How are the benefits of public expenditures currently distributed? and (c) How can that distribution be improved?

What Is the Welfare Objective?

We must first define clearly the welfare objective against which outcomes are judged. This book has been primarily concerned with impacts of public spending on poverty. But, as Atkinson persuasively argues in chapter 3, even that may not be straightforward. Too often, "It is tacitly assumed that the sole objective of policy is to reduce poverty, whereas the typical social security program in Western countries has a multiplicity of objectives. Even if the alleviation of poverty were the overriding concern, the relative efficiency of different policies would depend on the precise way in which poverty is measured and on the sharpness with which the poverty objective is defined" (Atkinson, chapter 3).

The way poverty is measured—including the choice of the living standards indicator, the poverty cutoff point, and the poverty index used to aggregate—is closely intertwined with the policy objective (see, for example, Ravallion 1994). However, the delineation of objectives is not always so clear. At least three dimensions of poverty have been the focus of concern: (a) utility, (b) income, and (c) capabilities. The first is associated with an important strand of the literature on modern public economics, where the idea of utility is taken to be not only a

I am very grateful to Shanta Devarajan, Jennie Litvack, Kim Nead, and Martin Ravallion for their useful comments and advice on this chapter. All mistakes remain my own.

representation of individual preferences but also the basic objective of policy, such that only individual preferences carry any weight. This is often termed "welfarism" following Sen (1979). The income dimension is sometimes interpreted as a money metric of the utility approach and sometimes as a distinct, nonwelfarist alternative. So, for example, in the former interpretation, leisure that matters to utility would be valued and added to income to obtain a measure of "full" income. This can also be adjusted for differences in household characteristics and the prices faced. By contrast, policymakers often (it seems) espouse explicitly nonwelfarist objectives. For example, raising income—narrowly defined as command over commodities, but typically ignoring leisure—is often viewed as an objective in its own right, such as by persons who emphasize economic growth as the metric of development. Finally, the capabilities framework rejects both welfarist utility and certain nonwelfarist income-based approaches and argues instead that poverty is the lack of certain basic capabilities such as avoiding hunger and illiteracy (Sen 1985).

In chapter 2 of this volume, Sen reminds us of the many dimensions to poverty and deprivation. He defines the welfare objective in terms of the adequacy of capabilities to do things rather than the adequacy of income. Posing the question in this way gives rise to a long series of further considerations. How are adequate capabilities, such as good health for an active life, generated? What is the role of public spending on health care, education, and other services? Or is growth of household income most efficient at raising health levels? Chapters 6, 8, and 10 (by Pitt, Rosenzweig, and Gibbons; Alderman and others; and Deolalikar) empirically address some of these issues in the context of both health and education outcomes interpretable as indicators of specific capabilities.

Even if one takes a quite narrow view of the policy objective—namely, to reduce income poverty—differences in conceptualizing and implementing the objective remain. For example, concerns about errors of targeting (leakage to the nonpoor and failure to reach all of the poor) often arise in this context, and some argue that a policy's success should be judged by its ability to concentrate benefits on the poor (as in chapters 13 and 16, by Cornia and Stewart and by Grosh). In the context of the policy they examine, Ravallion and Datt (chapter 15) are concerned with the same basic objective—maximizing the impact on income poverty for a given outlay—yet argue that a focus on errors of targeting in implementing that objective is misplaced: the policy that has the greatest impact on poverty is not necessarily the one with the lowest errors of targeting.

Focusing on a specific target group may reflect either the *direct* importance of the specific policy objective or its *instrumental* importance for another end. Appleton and Collier examine the case for allocating benefits by gender (chapter 19). They argue that such a case must rest on gender being a clear dimension of disadvantage or on the existence of positive externalities accruing to others as a result of targeting benefits to women. They also share with Sen and others the view that using a group identifier such as gender has the advantages of being easy to identify and hard to manipulate. However, such broad characteristics can be highly imperfect correlates of poverty, possibly allowing only a modest impact for a given outlay (for evaluations of the poverty impact of targeting correlates of poverty, see Ravallion 1993; Ravallion and Sen 1994; Datt and Ravallion 1993). Appleton and Collier's chapter brings out well the reality that multiple objectives and constraints on instruments underlie our choice of policies.

A recurrent issue concerns the weight that should be given to the preferences of the poor. Should the welfare objective be denominated in terms of utility or income? Should we be concerned with how hard the poor must work? In short, should the adopted framework be welfarist or nonwelfarist when the main objective is poverty reduction? Kanbur, Keen, and Tuomala illustrate the consequences of this decision for targeting and evaluation rules (chapter 5). For example, they show that if the policy objective is to minimize an income-based poverty index and given labor supply responses, accepted rules-of-thumb based on the welfarist utility framework—namely, that marginal tax rates on the poor should be low—are overturned. Under the alternative nonwelfarist policy goal, simulated optimal marginal tax rates tend to exceed 60 percent (given minimal revenue requirements). Consider, further, Sahn and Alderman's empirical study (chapter 14) of the effects of Sri Lanka's targeted food stamp scheme on labor supply. They find strong disincentive effects: men and women reduce the total hours worked as a result of the transfer. Is this a good or bad outcome? If one is judging this case within a welfarist context in which leisure is accorded a high weight, the policy may then be considered a success.[1] However, from the point of view of the policymaker trying to achieve the greatest dent in income poverty for a given budget, such behavioral responses may be important costs of the scheme. The same impact may have been achieved at lower cost, and so the policy is judged a relative failure.

Consensus has clearly not been reached on these choices. Different authors have different views, and the issues often revolve around normative considerations that may never be properly resolved. Past efforts by economists to capture all welfare objectives of policy in a single well-defined monetary measure have clearly been too ambitious. A more eclectic approach is justified, recognizing that there are multiple dimensions of well-being and that they cannot be easily aggregated. In some settings, a single, somewhat narrowly defined objective, such as reducing income poverty, may be entirely defensible, while in others it must be supplemented by other information. The message that under-lying assumptions about welfare and poverty measurement influence the evaluation of public spending programs is one to keep firmly in mind. This speaks to the need for being clear about those assumptions and for recognizing how sensitive policy conclusions can be to changes in those assumptions.

How Are the Benefits of Public Spending Currently Distributed?

The measurement and valuation of the benefits of publicly provided goods have vexed economists for a long time. It can be very difficult to price such goods, since markets often do not exist for them or they are available at a cost that may not be related to their marginal valuations by consumers. As discussed by Cornes in chapter 4, complications in valuation can be attributed primarily to the existence of two factors: (a) prices and other individual or household characteristics may vary across individuals so that a given total expenditure implies different standards of living for different individuals, and the same quantity of a publicly provided good can yield different welfare gains; (b) there are quantity constraints, such that even if the correct prices are known and everywhere are the same for identical individuals, it is difficult to value benefits, since individuals are forced to consume more or less than they would like. A simple example of the first point is that a school is worth much more to a family with young children than to one without them. But there are many other examples. A supplementary feeding program benefits a household in a region or period in which food prices are high more than it does a household facing low food prices. The second factor is less obvious but may be just as important. When goods are supplied in fixed quantities by ration shops, the avail-able quantity is unlikely to equal the desired quantity, so the price paid may not reflect the true value to the consumer. The same can happen with public goods that are intrinsically lumpy—a road cannot be supplied only on the day of the week in which you happen to want to use it; it is there all the time.

Measurement of Benefits

Two general approaches to measurement can be identified. Neither is ultimately able to resolve adequately the twin difficulties of variable individual and household characteristics and quantity constraints. The first approach is found in benefit-incidence studies and assumes that the value of the benefits of a public service to the individual equals the unit cost of providing the service. The second approach attempts to value benefits using various measures related to the notion of consumer surplus, in the attempt to arrive at behaviorally consistent measures. I discuss these in turn.

BENEFIT INCIDENCE. Benefit-incidence studies, such as those found in this book, typically proceed by ranking individuals (or more typically households) by some indicator of welfare (most commonly per capita household income or expenditures). In order to make valid distributional comparisons, it is clearly important that the welfare indicator be suitably normalized for cost-of-living differentials and household demographics. Next the unit costs of providing a public service are attributed across subgroups according to information on each household's use of the public service. This exercise reveals how the government's outlay for the particular service varies across the relevant welfare indicator (the best-known standard benefit-incidence studies for developing countries are the early ones by Meerman 1979 for Malaysia and Selowsky 1979 for Colombia; Selden and Wasylenko 1992 review the literature). Though this approach has its definite uses, it also has drawbacks. These are becoming well recognized (see Selden and Wasylenko 1992), and many of them are discussed in detail throughout the book. I shall now try to bring together the main points.

In evaluating the distribution of the benefits, individuals are ranked by an often imperfect welfare indicator. It may not adequately capture the true distribution of living standards due, for example, to measurement problems. But it may also be a misleading representation of the welfare distribution in the absence of government spending. The principal aim of incidence studies is to see how the initial "pre-intervention" position of individuals is altered as a result of public spending. Hence, an approximation of the pre-intervention position is required. This is typically estimated by a welfare indicator such as income or consumption that does not include the monetary value of the benefits secured from publicly provided goods. This may be a poor approximation, since the level and composition of public spending affect incomes and expenditures: individuals often spend their incomes in ways that reflect the level of provision of public goods and services. There may also be some shifting of benefits, such as if wealthier households reduce their transfers to poorer ones as a result of the latter benefiting from a public program, as Cox and Jimenez argue in chapter 12. Similarly, behavioral responses through time allocation can mean that income net of earnings from workfare employment generally underestimates income in the absence of access to such employment, as Ravallion and Datt emphasize (chapter 15). These are all instances of the general problem of specifying the counterfactual.

Another limitation of this approach is that costs may be a poor proxy for individual benefits received. The cost represented by a nurse's administration of a polio and DPT vaccine cannot possibly reflect the value to a child of a lifetime free of polio, diphtheria, pertussis, and tetanus. Moreover, social benefits are not captured. The impact of a mother's prenatal and postnatal good health on a newborn's current and future health cannot be approximated well by the cost of a few prenatal and postnatal visits. Unit costs may also be very hard to calculate exactly. For example, unit costs of inpatient hospital visits will differ widely according to the illness being treated. They will also be badly estimated if there is rent-seeking, including, for example, the funneling of benefits away from households. Finally, the approach assumes that publicly provided services are homogeneous across all consumers. Yet, quality may vary enormously and imply higher benefits to certain households and lower ones to others.

With expanding access to improved and more detailed data sets, some of these problems are being tackled. Various chapters (including 7, 9, 11, and 18) demonstrate some of the corrections and innovations that can be made to improve the benefit-incidence approach. Many of its deficiencies have more to do with data inadequacies than with limitations intrinsic to the approach and are thus shared with other methodologies. For example, nothing in the traditional benefit-incidence methodology prevents the incorporation of quality differentials. As elsewhere, the major impediment stems from the deficiencies of available data.

What policy conclusions can we draw from such exercises? Although the methodology is far from ideal, and so precise magnitudes may not be correct, it is generally assumed that the broad qualitative conclusions are indicative of reality. We still know rather little about how much difference behavioral responses can make to key policy conclusions. Nonetheless, even a crude but careful incidence study can be valuable to governments, which often have little or no awareness of the possible distributional implications of their policies, and to policymakers generally. The issue of how public spending benefits are distributed is an important one, and incidence analysis appears to provide a useful first approximation. I shall later summarize some of the results to have emerged.

BEHAVIORAL APPROACHES. As already noted, a general problem underlying evaluations of policy impacts, including public spending changes, is the lack of the relevant counterfactual. Ideally, we would like to compare situations with and without a change in spending policy. What would have happened had the policy not been implemented or the public good not provided? But we are rarely able to observe such a baseline. Many facets of the economic behavior of beneficiaries and nonbeneficiaries alike—including labor supply, consumption, saving, and investment decisions—may be affected by public policies. It is difficult to trace responses and their full general-equilibrium effects accurately. Yet these responses have potentially important implications for a policy's final impact. This issue has come up repeatedly in this volume, and a number of the studies can be interpreted as attempts to resolve the problem by modeling behavioral responses.

Various estimation-based techniques have been developed that attempt to capture key behavioral responses. The general approach has consisted of trying to measure the program beneficiary's own valuation of the benefit received. The latter is deemed sufficient for—or at least relevant to—attributing benefits from public services. (Alternative nonwelfarist approaches, which are discussed earlier and in Sen's chapter, tend to downplay the relevance of such subjectivist evaluations, though not dissimilar problems emerge in these approaches, as I discuss later.) The conventional welfarist measures allow for behavioral responses to price and income changes. They are generalizations of the old notion of consumer surplus—the monetary value of a change in welfare due to a change in prices. In the simplest version, this is measured by the area under the Marshallian demand curve. As such, it can be interpreted as the sum of incremental benefits from each additional consumption unit valued at marginal willingness to pay.

As is well known, the fundamental problem with consumer surplus is that it ignores the income effects of price changes. This has led theorists and some practitioners to turn to the Hicksian measures derived from the compensated demand function along which utility is held constant. Provided one knows—or can infer—preferences, these new measures represent exact analogs to consumer surplus (see, for example, McKenzie 1983; King 1983; Cornes 1992, chapter 4 of this volume). Under certain identifying assumptions and provided demand functions satisfy the theoretical conditions of utility maximization, information about utility functions can be retrieved from observed demand behavior. This then enables the calculation of better welfare measures based on the monetary amount that would make beneficiaries as well off without the transfer as they are with it.

The same methods have also been used in attempting to make behaviorally consistent comparisons of well-being across individuals facing different circumstances. Prices and household characteristics, which are in general household specific, must be controlled for. This is required to make the empirical welfare measures interpersonally comparable. Various measures, including the behaviorally consistent measures discussed above, aim to provide an exact money measure of an individual's welfare. For example, money metric or "equivalent income" measures fix a population-wide reference price vector and household type as the basis for comparing welfare levels (Cornes, chapter 4 of this volume; King 1983). The equivalent income is then the money income that would be required by each household to maintain its present standard of living at reference prices and reference household characteristics. It can be calculated to establish a ranking of households in the initial pre-policy position as well as to establish welfare-level rankings following proposed or implemented changes in economic policy.

A special case of this idea is an equivalence scale, which gives the welfare equivalence between households at different compositions and sizes (Deaton and Muellbauer 1986; Browning 1992). Equivalence scales often incorporate both potential scale economies and social judgments about the needs of preferential groups such as the elderly or children. When data are not available or there are problems of inferring unique scales from behavior (a general problem I will return to), a decision must be made on which equivalence scale to use. The choice can matter to policy. This message is strongly emphasized by Atkinson and by Jarvis and Micklewright in the volume. The latter (chapter 11) convincingly show that one's view of how well targeted to the poor the Hungarian family allowance scheme has been depends in part on the weights attached to household size and composition in the welfare indicator. Indeed, they make a convincing case that the incidence of family allowances could be used to defend a wide gamut of policy reforms, depending on the underlying assumption about the equivalence scale (see chapter 3; van de Walle, Ravallion, and Gautam 1994, also in the context of Hungary).

The behaviorally consistent welfare measures have their limitations even within the confines of a purely welfarist approach. Unfortunately, these are particularly worrisome in the present context of public and publicly provided private goods. Severe problems arise in identifying preferences from behavior for the purposes of calibrating utility-consistent welfare measures, such as real income per equivalent adult, and equivalent and compensating variations. Conventional demand models do not capture effects on utility that are separable from the consumption of market goods; if the private benefits derived from children or from public goods do not alter marginal utilities derived from market goods, then those benefits will not be evident in observed demand for market goods. In practice, we identify the parameters of conditional preferences from demand models—conditional on certain nonmarket goods—while welfare is about unconditional preferences (Pollak 1991). No doubt, it will always be highly problematic to infer the utility derived from public goods (for which no markets exist and households are quantity constrained) by looking solely at demand for private market goods (Cornes, chapter 4 of this volume).

More recently, one strand of the subject has directly studied revealed demand for publicly provided social services. In one approach, loosely referred to as willingness to pay, demand functions for publicly provided services are estimated to calculate service- or facility-specific price and income elasticities for diverse income and other subgroups (Gertler, Locay, and Sanderson 1987; Gertler and van der Gaag 1990;

Gertler and Glewwe 1989). The elasticities are then used to calculate behavioral welfare measures of the willingness to pay (the compensating variation) of different groups for a change in provision. To get around the obstacle of missing markets, prices are proxied by measures of the full costs of public service use, including fees, travel, and waiting costs. Hence, an exploration of the nonprice allocative mechanisms that determine consumption is used to calculate willingness to pay for the nonmarketed good and for changes in its provision. Applications have analyzed the distributional consequences of introducing user fees and earmarking them for improvements in access and quality of facilities (for a review of results and a critique, see Litvack and Bodart 1993). The method is discussed by Selden and Wasylenko and contrasted with a nonbehavioral approach in chapter 7.

Another strand of the literature has focused more on health and educational outcomes that implicitly have welfare significance. Although the practitioners of this approach (as represented by chapters 6, 10, and 18) do not explicitly define capabilities as their objective function, one presumes that an empirical formulation of Sen's (1985) capabilities approach would in some ways resemble this one. The idea is to estimate econometrically a reduced-form relationship (representing a potentially quite complex household model, usually encompassing both demand and production functions, preferences, and budget constraints). This links a particular outcome (such as educational attainment or health status)—often as proxied by an indicator of that outcome (such as enrollment rates or infant mortality rates)—to a wide set of inputs, including socioeconomic characteristics, incomes, prices, use of public services, availability of private services, and other complementary public services and government spending.

Deolalikar's study presents one example of this approach. In chapter 10, he strives to isolate the marginal impact of provincial-level government expenditures on the health outcomes (and facility use) of different income groups by controlling for a multitude of other factors and inputs that may influence that relationship. The method throws light on the incremental, or marginal, incidence of benefits. It can be used to examine how changes in government spending are distributed, but not how inframarginal spending is distributed across groups.

In the same spirit, econometric techniques have been used to control for behavioral responses and for simultaneity when attempting to assign causality to public expenditures (see chapters 6, 8, 10, and 18). The study by Pitt, Rosenzweig, and Gibbons (chapter 6) is concerned with purging estimates of the impact of public services on social indicators of the repercussions of endogenous factors in their placement. The fact that public programs are often geographically located as a result of unobservables (whose effects are then difficult to sort out from those of the programs) has long put a damper on evaluations of the impact of public investments in infrastructure (see Binswanger, Khandker, and Rosenzweig 1993; Rosenzweig and Wolpin 1986). Pitt, Rosenzweig, and Gibbons implement a methodology for dealing with the nonrandomness of program placement and demonstrate how important doing so is for estimating the kinds of reduced-form relationships discussed above. Estimations of both the magnitude and direction of the impact on outcomes are found to be influenced. To give just one example, cross-sectional estimation, typically used in evaluation work, suggests that family planning facilities in Indonesia increase fertility. By contrast, the estimation procedure that allows for program placement effects does not.

Despite their interesting methodological and empirical insights and contribution, studies such as those by Deolalikar and by Pitt, Rosenzweig, and Gibbons have somewhat unclear welfare and policy interpretations. They eschew a welfare framework that would allow a valuation of the benefits from an improved outcome or a public investment and a rule for judging them against other spending. For example, both a health outcome and an education outcome may be strongly influenced by public spending in the respective sectors. How do we decide relative tradeoffs between them?

The study by Alderman and others (chapter 8) adopts a similar approach to the issues but is couched within a potentially broader framework. The authors estimate the impact of both the quantity and quality of schooling on cognitive achievement outcomes. They then estimate the impact of cognitive achievements (and implicitly of public spending) on earnings. Next, gains in earnings can be linked up to estimates of the costs of schooling improvements and conclusions drawn about targeted public spending based on social rates of return. A utility function defined over earnings (or income) therefore underlies the analysis, supplying a method for aggregation of social costs and benefits. This provides a way in which to valuate benefits from the publicly provided inputs, something other studies have been unable to do. The methodology in chapter 8 could be further generalized to include multiple outcomes—cognitive achievements and discipline, for example—and the tradeoffs in concentrating public investments on either outcome could also be assessed. However, this approach is confined to measuring the income gains from public services; direct welfare gains (independent of income) are not identified.

All these methods are handicapped by measurement problems. Outcomes, in particular, are hard to measure accurately. Like the traditional benefit-incidence approach, the econometric approaches, including the study by Alderman and others, are limited in their ability to capture the effects of externalities. They therefore tend to underestimate impacts when positive external benefits exist. For example, the kinds of external benefits discussed at length by Appleton and Collier in the context of targeting women—the effects of maternal education on child health, for example—remain difficult to measure and account for in a systematic way. Finding ways in which satisfactorily to approximate the size and importance of externalities and to account for them in measuring impacts of public spending is an important area for further empirical research.

The welfare-economic underpinnings of the various "partial" approaches to welfare measurement are not always clear. A key question concerns *aggregation* in the absence of an explicit evaluation function. What tradeoffs are admitted against the health outcome, for example (Deolalikar, chapter 10)? Aggregation across sectors is one issue. Another pertains to the aggregation across individuals and the policy implications and operationalization of the measures. Take the case of willingness-to-pay approaches. Most applications tie fees to willingness to pay, but whose willingness to pay? If a flat fee is charged, there are often distributional implications. For example, if willingness to pay for schools is an increasing function of income, as one would expect, and a flat fee is introduced, wealthier students need to be undercharged so as not to lose poorer ones. But, the policy then transfers rents from poor to rich households; there is no impact on poverty in utility space, and inequality increases. Differentiating fees across income levels can, in principle, get around such problems, but they have their own disadvantages, a point to which I will return. A further issue is that imperfect information and endogenous preferences may result in tensions between individual (based on estimated willingness to pay) and social objectives, and it is unclear how one would go about resolving such potential conflicts. The literature gives us little guidance on these issues.

So far, the discussion has implicitly focused largely on utility, in the welfarist context. Things may not be much easier if we focus on capabilities instead. Like "utility," we do not typically observe "capabilities" as such, but rather certain "achievements"—for example, we directly observe illiteracy, not the capability of being literate—and behavioral assumptions are needed to close the gap (Anand and Ravallion 1993). However, little work has been done yet on the identification problem in capabilities-based empirical approaches or on how different capabilities should be aggregated. As utility-based conceptualizations come into question, marked differences may arise in the properties of more practical welfare measures. For example, for equivalence scales, Lanjouw and Ravallion (1995) show that scales calibrated by conventional utility-based demand approaches have attributes very different from scales based on approaches that rely on information about achievements of certain basic capabilities of individuals. The move toward broader concepts of well-being in the economic assessment of policy choices will need further empirical research to help inform those choices.

INCORPORATING BEHAVIORAL RESPONSES IN INCIDENCE STUDIES. Behavioral approaches contain important lessons for benefit-incidence studies. All incidence studies are essentially comparisons of pre- and post-intervention distributions. The contribution of behavioral approaches in this context is to obtain a better measure of the distribution of welfare than would have been observed without intervention—the counterfactual. By measuring benefits net of behavioral responses, the approaches thus try to work out the real impact of policy. Economic analyses, such as some of those discussed above, often try to do this in the aggregate for some "representative household." The next step is to determine impacts at the household level and to assign those impacts correctly in the distribution of welfare. The studies reported in chapters 12, 14, and 15 provide interesting empirical examples of such an approach (see also van de Walle, Ravallion, and Gautam 1994). They illustrate how econometrically estimated parameters and simulation techniques allow what are basically benefit-incidence studies to be modified so as to incorporate incentive effects and thereby attain a more precise estimation of the distribution of a policy's net benefits across households.

In order to assess the real impact of a public employment scheme on poverty, Ravallion and Datt (chapter 15) argue that the forgone incomes of participants must be netted out of the distribution of transfer benefits. Their task is to estimate the cumulative distribution of incomes that would have existed had the workfare option not been available and then to compare that distribution with the one observed with the policy. To begin, they econometrically model individual time allocation across all potential activities (including self- and wage employment, leisure, domestic work, and unemployment). Next, they use the results to simulate time use and incomes in the absence of public employment and to draw conclusions about the intervention's net welfare outcome.

In the same spirit, Sahn and Alderman (chapter 14) examine how labor supply disincentive effects of food-based income transfers result in a divergence between net public expenditure increments and net transfers to households. They proceed by modeling labor supply conditional on labor market participation. They then use the resulting parameters to simulate the counterfactual of what individuals' labor market effort, and hence incomes, would have been in the absence of the Sri Lankan food stamp scheme.

In chapter 12, Cox and Jimenez turn the issue on its head and look at how the behavioral responses of some key *non*beneficiaries may also have bearing on a policy's net impact. Their concern is with the responsiveness of interhousehold charity to the introduction of public redistributive programs. Cox and Jimenez econometrically estimate the determinants of net transfers received in the absence of government intervention using household-level data for the Philippines; they use the predicted parameters to simulate the likely private transfer response to the introduction of unemployment benefits, lump-sum transfers to persons below the poverty line, and retirement benefits.

Simulation techniques are often used, here and elsewhere, to draw out behavioral implications from empirical models. It is worth noting that simulations may often require additional assumptions, which may in turn be important in drawing policy conclusions. To illustrate the point, let us examine more closely the interesting findings of Cox and Jimenez in chapter 12. The unemployment insurance simulation—which indicates a dramatic displacement effect of 74 percent of private transfers—assumes that unemployed male household heads are provided with cash transfers equal to half of their imputed earnings *and* that this causes donors to treat these households as if their head is now employed. As the authors point out, the bulk (more than 90 percent) of the displacement is driven by the shutting off of the "household head not employed" dummy variable in their econometric model. The state of being unemployed is a strong attractor of transfers independent of income.

The analysis provides us with an upper- and lower-bound estimate of private transfer displacement and flags how critically the results depend on an assumption that is itself difficult to test. Given our limited knowledge of how donors view unemployed people receiving unemployment compensation, it is important to be aware of this assumption. It might be argued, for example, that it is equally plausible that donors continue to view the household head as unemployed even if he receives unemployment compensation from the government, since he is in fact still jobless and receiving only half of his normal earnings. Possibly donors will ultimately look at people's consumption—what the recipient household can afford relative to what it is accustomed to afford. The interpretation of the (highly significant) positive coefficient on the unemployment dummy—controlling for income—in the regression model clearly matters to the policy conclusions. The dummy variable could be proxying for a fall in income connected with unemployment, or it could indicate sensitivity of the donor to the increased risks faced by the unemployed or to the real drop in income since the previous period.

The lesson here is how crucial the interpretation of the empirical model can be to the policy implications. Underlying theoretical assumptions must be examined carefully, and one should probe the sensitivity of simulation results to those assumptions.

More and better data and methods will yield added scope for incorporating behavioral responses into incidence assessments. This is to be welcomed in that it allows us to relax some of the assumptions of standard incidence analysis. However, this development can be a mixed blessing. As I have tried to illustrate, new assumptions have to be made, and these may, in and of themselves, largely determine the conclusions. More empirical work is needed to test those assumptions. An important but often neglected role for research is that of comparing policy applications under alternative sets of assumptions. For example, case studies comparing policy conclusions from simple nonbehavioral rule-of-thumb methods with more complex, theoretically correct ones would be very useful. In chapter 7, Selden and Wasylenko provide one example. There is also a need to understand *when* ignoring behavioral responses will matter most. Sensitivity analysis will help to clarify the generality and applicability of findings. This also involves understanding underlying theoretical reasons. For example, it should be clear from past theory and evidence that poor people are more responsive to price changes than are rich people. Yet, in early discussions of the effects of cost recovery, a constant elasticity was assumed, and the likely curvature of the Slutsky matrix conveniently was ignored. In sum, we should not automatically assume that more complicated models will produce better or fundamentally different policy advice. However, more research is needed to determine whether they do or not.

DATA AND POLICY. Our knowledge about the poor in developing countries—their location, their sources of livelihood, their links to the economy—has greatly expanded with the availability of more and better-quality household-level data sets (Lipton and Ravallion 1995 review recent evidence). Yet it remains that methodologies, results, and policy implications are in many ways molded by severe informational constraints. As I have pointed out in various instances, general data inadequacies add to the impediments of correctly measuring the distributional impacts of public spending. Let me elaborate here on a few additional data-related points to emerge from this volume.

We are ultimately interested in the impacts on *individual* welfare. Since data are most often available at the household rather than at the individual level, assumptions must be made about the distribution of resources within the household. Common practice is to assume equitable repartition and to rely on per capita (or some other equivalization) measures of individual consumptions. Most authors in this volume have (implicitly or otherwise) made such an assumption. Yet, there is some evidence that the intrahousehold distribution of resources may not always be equal and that public policy–induced changes in household consumption may not affect the welfare of each household member identically (see Haddad and Kanbur 1990, 1993); in chapter 13, Cornia and Stewart discuss the implications of this for efforts to target food interventions. This measurement issue has vexed the question of whether women are "poorer," or in some sense more deprived, than men, as discussed by Appleton and Collier in chapter 19. Behavioral responses within households can also alter assessments of policy impacts at the household level; for example, in chapter 15 Ravallion and Datt show how cross-gender effects in time allocation *within* the household have bearing on the net benefits from workfare.

Our understanding of certain dynamic issues in the incidence of public spending has also been greatly constrained by data limitations. The analysis of the impact of government programs has been for the most part static. Yet, in developing countries (particularly in rural settings) and in transition economies, a key concern pertains to the variability in living standards to which the poor, in particular, are prone. The performance of public spending programs in providing effective safety nets that lower risk and income variability, protecting households from uninsurable risks and shocks for which insurance markets do not exist, is clearly of considerable importance. Evaluations based on a single cross section may not be very informative about impacts on living standards. As shown in chapters 9 and 18, analysis of two cross sections or more reveals how marginal changes in public expenditures are distributed ignoring all behavioral incentive effects. Panel data, which follow households over time, present a promising new avenue for combining determination of both dynamic and behavioral effects. As yet, few studies have applied this approach to examining the distributional performance of public programs over time. One exception uses a Hungarian panel to examine how well the social safety net performed both in protecting families from falling into poverty and in promoting the poor out of poverty during a period of the early transition (van de Walle, Ravallion, and Gautam 1994; Ravallion, van de Walle, and Gautam 1995). The collection and setting up of panels are becoming more common, which should make the exploration of dynamic issues easier. This is a ripe area for future research.

Finally, economists doing research in this area have tended to focus exclusively on household decisionmaking, while taking government outlays as given and simply ignoring other factors, such as the macroeconomic, political economy, and institutional environments. As shown by Pitt, Rosenzweig, and Gibbons in chapter 6, an understanding of government budget allocation and program placement rules may be fundamental to coming to grips with public spending impacts. This will require that effort be invested in the collection of new sorts of data, such as time series of the stock of spatially available infrastructure and of the "history" of government investments. Such new data need to be accompanied by imaginative ways of getting at, and incorporating into measurement methodologies, the context within which households and governments make their decisions.

The overall macroeconomic environment clearly has bearing on the effectiveness and sustainability of specific poverty-alleviation strategy and spending decisions. Public expenditure plans are made within the context of general policies and the state of the economy. For example, the capacity to tax is pertinent to public spending objectives and outcomes. A growing economy that is generating broad-based employment provides a very different context for discussing public spending decisions than one that is in recession. Governments also worry about the political consequences of their policies. Political economy considerations are critical to understanding motivations, constraints, and outcomes of public spending policy. Details on institutional and service delivery capacity—of which there has also been a lack of consideration—are likewise relevant to explaining the distribution of public spending. Household survey data and government budgetary data throw little light on these relevant features. The above information will be important in determining how to improve incidence but also in assessing why benefits are distributed in the way that they are. For example, there may exist bounds to how progressive public spending benefits can be, due to political economy, macroeconomic, and institutional factors, which too often are ignored. Incorporating information on such constraints may provide us with more realistic benchmarks against which to judge distributional outcomes.

Assessing incidence and determining how best to improve distributional outcomes are the vital first steps. But, the follow-up—reform implementation—begs a further understanding of the political economy of reform. Why and when is reform undertaken? Why and when is it successful? Economists are often at a loss when such issues come to the fore, but they should make no mistake about their relevance.

Results

Provided one is aware of their deficiencies, much of the data and methods commonly used in practice can be useful and informative. The (few) studies that have attempted to compare results on incidence have found that the methodologies are broadly in agreement (Selden and Wasylenko discuss this issue in chapter 7). Still, the results should be taken as indicative of likely directions of benefit incidence rather than as precise magnitudes. Subject to the caveats discussed above, some reasonably clear patterns can be discerned from studies of the distribution of benefits from public spending in developing countries. They are briefly summarized here (Selden and Wasylenko 1992 summarize incidence results for high-income countries).

LESSONS FROM BENEFIT-INCIDENCE STUDIES. Only a few benefit-incidence studies have examined the totality of public spending (Selden and Wasylenko 1992 provide a review). Studies more commonly focus on one or two sectors, as do the case studies in this book. I will follow suit here.

A distinction should always be made between the distribution of benefits in monetary amounts and that of benefits expressed as a percentage of the welfare indicator (typically per capita consumption or income). Investigations of the education, health, social transfers, and nutrition sectors commonly find that in the aggregate subsidies are at least mildly progressive in that they are higher for the poor as a percentage of initial income or expenditure. In contrast, absolute benefit levels often increase with the welfare indicator; the poor get less in absolute amounts than the rich, though inequality is still reduced. Finally, an implicit urban bias is common in that public spending amounts are often found to be higher in more urbanized areas.

However, study after study highlights the importance of looking at within-sector components. For example, in the education sector, benefit-incidence analyses typically find that primary, and often secondary, schooling is pro-poor both in absolute levels and percentage terms. This is a consequence of the fact that in most developing countries poorer families (at least as measured on a per capita income basis) tend to have more and younger children and that poorer children are more likely to attend school at the primary than at other education levels. Tertiary education, in contrast, is invariably pro-rich. The overall progressivity often depends on the composition of education spending. For example, as only a small share of the education budget is devoted to university training in the economies of Eastern Europe, the overall distribution of education expenditures is pro-poor (chapter 17). In comparison, high university subsidies imply a flat overall distribution of education benefits for Malaysia, despite the unusually strong progressivity of both primary and secondary spending (chapter 18). Generally, the more educationally advanced a country, and the more developed its private sector, the more public spending on higher levels of education reaches poor children.

These general patterns are supported by Selden and Wasylenko's investigation of the education sector in Peru (chapter 7) and the Hammer, Nabi, and Cercone study of Malaysia (chapter 18). The former also find that spending levels are higher in urban areas and that, as beneficiaries of education subsidies, girls are deprived relative to boys. Milanovic (chapter 17) finds that in the East European economies too, the distribution of education benefits is progressive, though decreasingly so the higher the education level. Kindergarten benefits exhibit the best pro-poor targeting, while university benefits are the least well targeted.

Health sector expenditures also vary in their incidence according to the level of service. In particular, primary health care centers dispensing preventive and curative care are usually more pro-poor than hospital services. Van de Walle (chapter 9) determines that although the health subsidy in Indonesia is progressive, an untargeted uniform lump-sum transfer would be more so. Hammer, Nabi, and Cercone (chapter 18) find that in Malaysia the poor garner a disproportionate amount of the subsidy on health care. This is attributed in great part to the fact that wealthier households opt for the private sector for their medical care. In the East European economies, total as well as specific health sector components are found to be equally distributed across individuals. Milanovic (chapter 17) argues that this results from the combination of free socialized medicine and the nonexistence of a private alternative.

The story concerning general food subsidies is similar. Universal food subsidies tend to be quite progressive when expressed as a proportion of income, while absolute amounts tend to be lower for the poor (see chapters 13 and 16). However, food schemes are heterogeneous and are more often targeted and implemented under a multitude of guises, including food stamp and ration schemes, infant feeding, school meals, and so forth. Their incidence varies according to the food commodity (incidence is more progressive for goods that the poor favor more than the rich) and the degree of targeting generally. Grosh (chapter 16) shows that benefits are better concentrated on the poor under targeted schemes than under universal food subsidies in the Latin American programs she reviews. However, as I will discuss shortly, targeting brings about its own costs, which should be netted out in determining the incidence of benefits. Cornia and Stewart also argue that there are important costs to excluding some of the target group, a common result of narrowly targeting food programs (chapter 13).

Social cash transfers, comprising pensions, family allowances, sick pay, scholarships, and other transfers, represent a significant source of income for households in the former communist economies of Eastern Europe and in most economies of the Organization for Economic Cooperation and Development (OECD). Although there are variations among the former, Milanovic argues that, at the start of transition, the total cash transfer distribution was more or less uniformly distributed across income groups. This reflects the fact that the most substantive of the transfers—pensions and family allowances—had opposing incidence patterns. Pensions showed a tendency to be pro-rich (Russia provides one exception), while family allowances were generally quite pro-poor (in percentage and absolute terms), for reasons not dissimilar to why primary education is pro-poor in developing countries. However, Jarvis and Micklewright (chapter 11) caution that, at least with respect to Hungary in the pre-reform period (pre-1990), this result hinges on the equivalence scale used in ranking households in the pre-intervention state (see also van de Walle, Ravallion, and Gautam 1994).

Two studies in the book explore incidence changes over time using the benefit-incidence methodology for two points in time. To my knowledge, no other studies have done this. A comparison of incidence at two or more dates enables a determination of how spending changes were distributed across different groups. It is sometimes argued that if the rich already gain from public services, marginal spending must perforce reach the poor. Yet, additional scenarios can be ventured. For example, spending increases may be devoted to quality improvements for current beneficiaries. Political economy considerations may buttress this prospect. So, the issue provides an interesting empirical question. The results indicate that distributional improvements occurred for Indonesia's public health sector outlays (chapter 9) and for Malaysia's health and education expenditures (chapter 18). In both countries, the poor's participation rates increased markedly over the period. The benefit-incidence methodology is unable to account fully for the factors underlying incidence patterns. In the Indonesian case, it is not clear to what degree government policy as opposed to income growth was responsible for increased equity in public expenditure incidence during the period, though both factors were undoubtedly instrumental. What is clear is that much of the distributional gain was captured by the urban poor. Chapter 18 attempts to understand causality by supplementing the incidence analysis with regression analysis. Malaysia's policy of ethnic targeting is credited with the success in the education sector, while pro-poor improvements in the health sector are attributed to the private sector's increasing ability to attract wealthier households. The latter also appears to have been a factor in pro-poor changes in urban Indonesia.

LESSONS FROM BEHAVIORAL APPROACHES. There is less to say here, as the literature concerned with allowing for behavioral responses remains at an early stage and has yet to develop proven patterns in its empirical results. Heavy data requirements (such as on prices) and methodological pitfalls (simultaneity, endogeneity, and self-selection biases) have made progress slow. The research, which has focused on estimating the effects of price changes on behavior and welfare, has for the most part found that in the aggregate the demand for public services tends to be price inelastic. More important from an equity viewpoint, however, the studies also find that elasticities vary across income groups and that the poor are invariably more price responsive (Gertler and van der Gaag 1990).

Attempts to measure the impact of public spending investments on outcomes (such as those by Pitt, Rosenzweig, and Gibbons; Deolalikar; and Alderman and others in this volume) find that this can be a noisy relationship and arduous to isolate. Deolalikar's results indicate that marginal changes in Indonesia's provincial health spending have a positive effect on children's use of facilities and on their health outcomes, though both results apply to a greater degree for children of well-off households. This leads him to conclude that Indonesia's public health care services are poorly targeted. Alderman and others establish that girls and children in a poor region are relatively disadvantaged with respect to public schooling benefits in rural Pakistan. The situation could be improved with little cost to productivity by targeting improvements in schooling quantity and quality to the disadvantaged groups. The Pitt, Rosenzweig, and Gibbons investigation emphasizes the difficulties in econometrically establishing ex post the impact of public expenditures. Once the authors have controlled for fixed effects and the nonrandomness of program placement (again for Indonesia), with one or two exceptions, few programs are evidenced to have much direct impact on health and education outcome variables. The Alderman and others study highlights some of the severe difficulties that make the estimation of public investment impacts so elusive.

LESSONS FROM INCORPORATING BEHAVIORAL RESPONSES IN INCIDENCE STUDIES. The key lessons here are already evident from the behavioral approaches discussed above. Behavioral responses can be of consequence to conclusions about the distributional impacts of policy interventions. In a number of the empirical case studies included in this volume, efforts at reproducing the relevant counterfactual have been used to inform policy evaluations. Accounting for forgone incomes in assessing the poverty impact of public employment schemes is found to be of importance in chapter 15; Ravallion and Datt's study estimates that forgone incomes in two villages participating in the Employment Guarantee Scheme (EGS) of India's Maharashtra State account for about one-quarter of total wage earnings on the scheme. Labor market participation responses to the rice subsidy discussed in chapter 14 have marked repercussions for the scheme's net transfer benefits. Sri Lanka's targeted food stamp scheme is estimated to have resulted in a fall in labor market participation of as much as 2.5 days per month for males and 2.9 days for females. Finally, the public provision of social security is estimated to result in substantial displacement of the private moral economy that exists between households in the Philippines (chapter 12).

How Can the Distribution of Public Spending Be Improved?

A good benefit-incidence study can directly inform proposals for spending policy reforms aimed at improving the distribution of benefits. The preceding discussion has emphasized our still limited knowledge and continuing uncertainty about how to measure benefits and, hence, judge the distributional impact of public spending. Several areas where further investigation may pay off were identified. Still, specific country case studies (including ones in this book) do contain some clear and consonant implications for improving the distribution of public expenditures. First, governments should invest and reallocate budgets toward basic services. The provision of such services often fails to attract private sector interest and thus accords with the principle that governments should be responsible for valuable goods that would otherwise be underprovided. But, above all, services such as primary education and basic health care are found to be among the best ways to reach the poor. Of course, care should always be taken that marginal spending increases are not being squandered on better quality for existing services consumed by the better off. Among other categories of public spending, including food subsidy schemes, social security, and cash transfers, there have been both successes and failures. Many programs that claim to reduce poverty do not.

The most commonly heard proposal for achieving a more pro-poor benefit distribution is "improved targeting." That is the main focus of this section. Several chapters of this volume throw light on this policy issue, both at the level of methodology and in substantive policy conclusions. Reform proposals also often raise new issues, such as administrative feasibility and political economy considerations. In many developing economies, the middle classes are currently the primary beneficiaries of public social spending. Many of the poor are left out, while the rich have alternatives—namely, the private sector at home or abroad. Redirecting or "targeting" spending toward the poor will hurt the middle classes who, in the worst-case scenario, may no longer be able to afford the services. Households in this group are often the most vocal and politically important constituency for the government (Nelson 1992). This political economy reality has considerable bearing on final reform outcomes and is a key issue to which I will return.

Targeting: Issues and Options

Targeting is here defined as a deliberate attempt to shift the benefits of public expenditures to the poor by means that aim to screen them as the direct beneficiaries. This is by no means a universally accepted definition. The word is used to mean various things. Indeed, the research literature and policy documents are littered with different uses. To give one example, it is not unusual to come across the word targeting being used synonymously with means (or income) testing. This is a rather restrictive use of the concept and fosters a narrow interpretation of the policy instruments at a policymaker's disposal. Although the aim is ultimately to reach individuals with unacceptably low living standards—often proxied by income—means testing is only one of many methods by which to identify the poor.

Targeting has its critics. The antitargeting view argues that finely targeted programs have usually failed either in fully covering the poor or in avoiding leakage to the nonpoor. They are bad for morale and create dependency. They are not sustainable because they lack political support. "Programs for the poor are poor programs" is a frequent criticism. Furthermore, if governments effectively promote economic growth and invest in basic social services for all—through broad targeting of budgetary allocations—there should be no need for more finely targeted programs.

By contrast, for many, targeting is unquestionably the solution to the poverty problem. Why spread money around when, with targeting, gains to the poor come at lower cost? For some, the choice between "targeting" and "universal provision" is now viewed as one of ideology. One commentator writes:

> An implicit objective of those who argue against targeting and in favor of universal welfare states is distributivist. This is not surprising as they are by and large socialists who subscribe to the common end of egalitarianism. [Lal 1994, p. 1]

It is surprising to hear that "socialists" prefer that less of a given budget should go to the poor and that "egalitarianism" entails equal benefits to all rather than larger benefits to poorer people. Views such as these suggest that there may be scope for greater conceptual clarity on this policy issue.

Without any attempt at targeting, a development path in which both participation in economic growth and access to basic social services are broad—including both poor and nonpoor—can be an effective route to improving the living standards of the poor (World Bank 1990; Lipton and Ravallion 1995). Yet, country experience (in both high- and low-income countries) also shows us that circumstances often require supplementary, more finely targeted, public action. There are many examples. Undernourished children should not be made to wait for long-term solutions such as education and jobs if we can relieve their suffering now at modest cost—or even positive benefit—to long-term welfare. In the midst of an extended drought, broad-based solutions may offer little to famine victims. An effective transfer program providing food for work, for example, can mean the difference between life and death and also prevent damaging responses, such as asset sales, that inhibit long-term poverty reduction. And, even in the best of times, some among the elderly and the disabled, for instance, will require public assistance in order to meet their most basic needs. Without a concerted targeting effort, some disadvantaged groups, such as girls severely disadvantaged in terms of education in rural Pakistan (see chapter 8), may never catch up to men. The vast majority of societies would no doubt agree with these principles.

Policies that attempt to identify the poor and target benefits to them can serve important redistributive and safety net roles in a market economy (World Bank 1990; Lipton and Ravallion 1995). The risk is when targeted programs are seen as the main instrument for poverty reduction. Although a well-designed scheme can provide an important *complement* to a longer-term poverty-reduction strategy founded on equitable growth and pro-poor broad targeting of public spending, it is an imperfect substitute. Decisions on targeted schemes must always be made contingent on the general economic and social sector policy environment. Moreover, in each specific case, the choice about whether and how finely to target should be decided on economic grounds, starting from the (political) value judgment that the economic value of targeting to the poor is what matters most. The key questions for policy become, How much targeting is needed? and, What form should it take?

Choices and Tradeoffs

In theory, targeting can lessen the social cost of reducing poverty. However, in practice, the ability of a policy to concentrate benefits on the poor and to reduce poverty, albeit often confused, are not equivalent. The most perfectly targeted policy may not be the one with the greatest impact on poverty. Whether it is depends on how costly it is to identify the poor and target benefits to them, as well as on the size of the disincentive effects and participation costs incurred as a result of targeting. The benefits from better targeting can be large, but they can never be achieved costlessly. This point comes up repeatedly in the book's chapters. Chapters 2 and 3 provide a detailed description and analysis of the costs associated with targeting benefits.

THE COSTS OF TARGETING. The costs of administering a program can rise substantially when discrimination between beneficiaries is required. There is a widespread perception that the more finely a scheme attempts to target, the higher the administrative costs it will have, largely as a consequence of imperfect information (see Atkinson, chapter 3 of this volume; Besley and Kanbur 1993 for a theoretical exposition). There is some evidence for this view. For example, a comparison of means-tested programs (in which recipients are screened by their level of income) and universal programs (in which access is open to all) in the United States found that administrative costs varied from 12 percent of total costs for the former to 2.5 percent for the latter (Kesselman 1982). In chapter 16, Grosh disputes this view. Based on her analysis of a large set of targeted and universal programs in Latin America, Grosh concludes that the administrative costs of targeting have tended to be overestimated. Indeed, her research suggests that they do not systematically vary in any significant way across the diverse targeting mechanisms examined: the costs of administering individual assessment techniques (generally assumed to be the highest) do not appear to vary much from that of less-intensive methods such as geographic and self-targeting. Grosh finds the median administrative costs for these respective targeting mechanisms to be 9, 7, and 6 percent of total program costs.

Still, the debate is unlikely to end here. Grosh's definition of the administrative costs of targeting is somewhat narrow, as it relates only to initial screening costs. Yet, once the target group has been identified, it is still necessary to incur costs associated with delivery of the benefit to that group to the exclusion of others. Her study also highlights the considerable difficulties faced in accurately and comparably quantifying administrative costs across programs. What can be said for sure is that administrative costs are likely to vary according to administrative and political contexts. Indeed, they could be prohibitive in areas where service delivery systems and institutional and infrastructural capacities are not sufficiently developed. This is an area where a lot more research is needed.

Targeted transfer schemes (like other public interventions) may also cause individuals to change their behavior. Such behavioral responses can intervene between a program's stated objectives and its actual outcomes. We have already seen how important behavioral responses can be in welfare measurement and benefit incidence. In the specific case of targeted interventions, behavioral responses can entail additional costs and benefits, which can have bearing on outcomes. Their magnitude will vary across schemes and can also be influenced by design and implementation choices. Several of the empirical chapters examine behavioral responses from diverse perspectives with relevance to assessments of the costs of targeting.

For example, the results of Cox and Jimenez (chapter 12) suggest that the introduction of public transfer programs, such as unemployment insurance, often causes the well-off to cut back on their private transfers. They find evidence of that for the Philippines and, elsewhere, for Peru (Cox and Jimenez 1992). Sahn and Alderman explore the much heralded issue of the effects of a targeted subsidy on labor supply incentives (chapter 14; see also chapter 3, by Atkinson). They estimate the food stamp scheme in Sri Lanka to have produced on average a two- to three-day monthly reduction in labor market participation, which translates into roughly 33 percent of the value of the subsidy benefits. Such behavioral responses may alter the distribution of the costs and benefits expected by policymakers (subject to the underlying welfare objective, as discussed earlier). Public employment schemes are another example. Participants must provide labor in exchange for a cash or food transfer. In so doing, they must forgo other work and the incomes they would have earned had the scheme not been available. This is a cost to participants that should be netted out in order to measure actual gains from the scheme. As we have seen, Ravallion and Datt find that earnings in two villages in the absence of the EGS would have been equal to around one-quarter of that earned on the public works projects. As a result of these costs, and the additional nonwage costs, the scheme entails a net transfer of about half of its budget to the poor.

As always, one should be careful in drawing lessons for policy from all such empirical results. They do not imply that public intervention is unnecessary or that it should be discouraged. In general, displacement—of private transfers by public ones or of private employment by public employment, for example—is *partial* (many recipients are still better off), and conclusions also depend on differences in *coverage*, such as that between private and public transfers. There may also be reasons to prefer government programs. For example, private transfers may not be able to deal with widespread crises where income shocks are covariate (as in a recession or drought). Public transfers may also have important advantages over private transfers in terms of their reliability or insurance benefits. It also seems plausible that private transfers impose higher costs on recipients—accepting money from the government does not make the recipient beholden to the donor in the same way that accepting money from a relative, patron, or friend does. Even if public transfers crowd out private transfers entirely (that is, the recipient ends up with exactly the same amount of money), the recipient is likely to perceive herself as better off for receiving the cash transfer from the government. Still other indirect benefits may tilt the balance in favor of the targeted intervention. Even a modest gain to the poor from the assets created through public works schemes (a good deal less than cost) would be sufficient to make this policy more cost-effective than many poorly targeted alternatives.

One important, though often disregarded, message here is that private behavior responds to public intervention, whether targeted or untargeted. The problem may be more pronounced under targeted interventions, particularly due to adverse work incentives. Effective marginal tax rates of or exceeding 100 percent are not uncommon and lead to poverty traps. Potential recipients (for example, individuals above but close to the poverty line) will face an incentive to falsify their situation. Fortunately, design features can usually be found that can reduce such distortions. The second important message is that it is important to allow for behavioral responses both in assessing policy effectiveness and in devising effective policy interventions.

Other costs are associated with participation. Atkinson discusses the widespread phenomenon of low take-up—the nonclaiming of benefits by eligible parties (chapter 3). Lack of information about programs partly explains incomplete take-up. But additional reasons include the time costs, stigma, and other costs perceived by potential beneficiaries. Again, a scheme's benefits should be calculated net of such costs (see also Besley 1990).

A further cost often associated with targeted programs is their perceived failure to achieve political support, because they help but a fraction of the population, and one typically lacking political clout. Indeed, an incidence of public spending biased against the poor is professed to reflect the reality that governments "misbehave" precisely to please powerful elites and hold on to power (Birdsall and James 1993). It is also often argued that universally available public spending schemes are successful and sustainable due to the fact that a wide spectrum of the community maintains a stake in them and perceives them as a nonstigmatizing right (chapter 2; Skocpol 1991). Some programs may require a socially and economically mixed group of participants for their success. For example, in the United States, this argument has been invoked as grounds for not limiting public housing project units to the very neediest.

There are country examples for which these explanations are persuasive. Yet, some targeted schemes—usually ones with important indirect benefits—are known to have achieved quite widespread support, well beyond direct participants. The popularity and sustainability of Maharashtra's EGS is often explained by the scheme's indirect benefits: well-off urban dwellers, whose taxes finance the EGS, support it because it helps to stem rural migration to Bombay; the rural elite derive benefits from the assets built and the fact that the scheme keeps their labor force in the area through the lean seasons (Echeverri-Gent 1988); finally, in an environment prone to drought and other sources of severe vulnerability, the scheme's promise of a job in times of need provides a form of insurance, or safety net, and hence achieves support from many rural inhabitants who do not participate in normal times (Ravallion 1991). Others argue, as Jarvis and Micklewright do in chapter 11, that the historical evolution of policies is an important factor influencing both the attitudes of the public and of reformers and the political economy of targeted policies.

Clearly, the fact that a program is well targeted does not ensure that it is a cost-effective way to reduce poverty, since the extra costs incurred by targeting and the political economy responses may actually worsen the final distribution of living standards when compared to untargeted programs. There can be no *general* supposition in favor of targeting; the choice must be made on a case-by-case basis. How should that choice be made?

EVALUATING A TARGETED SCHEME. In stylized form, the policy problem is as follows. The goal is to reduce poverty, but to do so in the most efficient way—"efficient" in that it would not be possible to have a greater impact on the living standards of the poor with the available resources. The impact on poverty depends on the benefits that the poor realize from the scheme less any costs they incur in participating. The resources include the budgetary cost, and in some cases they may also include certain costs incurred by the nonpoor and not properly accounted for in the budgetary cost. A convincing evaluation should compare a scheme's impact on poverty with the impact that could have been achieved through realistic alternative uses of the same resources. It is sometimes unclear what the policy options are, but we can always compare a targeted policy's impact with that attainable through a universal (untargeted) handout of the same budget. Ravallion and Datt discuss and illustrate the use of this approach, and variations on the approach, for assessing the targeting effectiveness of Maharashtra's EGS (chapter 15).

The appraisal of a targeted scheme's impact on poverty (compared to what could have been done otherwise) is not always easy. As I have emphasized, perhaps the greatest difficulty is in assessing the relevant counterfactual: what would happen without the scheme? I have already discussed the important efforts of chapters 12, 14, and 15 on this front. Of these, only Ravallion and Datt (chapter 15) use their estimation of the counterfactual to go the further step and see how the policy's actual poverty impact compares to that achievable through a hypothetical alternative use of the same budget. Their results are sobering. Once all the costs associated with the public works scheme have been weighed, the same outlay uniformly transferred to all households— rich and poor—appears to make no less of a dent in income poverty. The authors offer certain caveats and reasons for why they may have underestimated the benefits from the employment scheme—they have ignored externalities arising from the infrastructure the schemes build, for example. Either way, their results should give policymakers and advisers committed to reducing poverty reason to pause.

The studies included in the book notwithstanding, there are in fact very few examples of good evaluations in the development context. This may be due in part to the high cost of properly evaluating such programs. But there also seems to be a systematic neglect of evaluation; only a tiny fraction of resources used go into seeing if they are properly used. In addition to expanding research efforts in the direction of incorporating behavioral responses into benefit-incidence studies, we also need to introduce—ex ante—careful monitoring and experimental methods on a selective basis to understand better what works and what does not.

In the meantime, there are ways to take a first stab at such assessments. One should begin by listing all the different social costs that a scheme is likely to entail: administration, costs of participation (such as forgone incomes through displaced labor or displaced transfers from rich patrons), and any indirect costs incurred by the nonpoor (such as the loss to previous beneficiaries from an untargeted scheme). Some of these costs may be weighted differently than others; for example, assessments often attach low or zero weight to small losses to the rich. Some are also less important than others, depending on the specific circumstances faced (forgone incomes in a rural public works scheme will naturally be low during a drought, for example).

Next, one should take stock and make a judgment about whether these costs are high relative to the benefits to the poor. In general, benefits will be dispersed widely among the poor, and so there will be an issue of how gains at different levels should be weighted; the most widely accepted judgment is that gains to the poorest should receive highest weight (chapter 3 discusses this issue). Some commonly used measuring rods do not do this (such as the mean monetary transfer or the change in the number of the poor). Without imposing an explicit formula for aggregation, much can be learned by forming a simple tabulation—a quick and dirty incidence of benefits table—of what the likely monetary gains will be for each broad subgroup of the poor— ultra-poor, poor, near-poor. The ability to make clear quantitative assessments will vary greatly, depending on the availability of data. However, a reasonably well-researched qualitative picture may often be informative.

One should also look closely at how benefits can be enhanced, and costs reduced, such as through taking more care in designing and implementing targeted schemes.

DESIGN AND IMPLEMENTATION CAN HELP TO REDUCE TARGETING COSTS. A key lesson from experience and many of the chapters in the book is that the costs and benefits from fine targeting depend critically on program design (chapters 3, 11, 13, 15, 16, and 19). Subsidizing a food staple heavily consumed by the rich, or setting the wage rate too high in a public works scheme, can destroy targeting performance. Under ideal circumstances, the policymaker would know incomes and distribute transfers to eliminate poverty accordingly. All of the poor and none of the nonpoor would be covered, and the cost of bringing everyone to the poverty line would exactly equal the poverty gap. In practice, the most extreme form of targeting, means testing, is difficult and costly to do well in developing countries. Incomes are particularly hard to measure in poor agricultural settings, where they are also often subject to extreme variability from one season to the next. Effective means testing would require collection of detailed and comprehensive information coupled with continual updating and verification. This is well beyond the capabilities of most administrative agencies. Reliance on local agents with intimate local knowledge has been found to work well sometimes and to flounder sometimes in nepotism and corruption. Chapter 15 provides evidence on the feeble connection between living standards and benefits received from the Integrated Rural Development Programme credit scheme in one Indian state—a supposedly means-tested program. Atkinson elaborates on the severe difficulties experienced with means testing even in high-income countries (chapter 3).

Hence, we often search for identifying characteristics, or indicators, that are highly correlated with low incomes. In targeting on the basis of indicators—what Atkinson here terms categorical transfers—it will always be better to use correlates that are easily observed and difficult to manipulate. Employment or nutritional status are easier to manipulate than gender and old age, for example. Female headship is claimed to be highly correlated with low living standards in some countries. Yet, use of such an identifier has also been found to result in severe moral hazard problems conspiring against the formation of stable adult family relationships. Possible further impacts on children's emotional development may cause the deleterious effects to go well beyond the misrepresentation of who heads the household (chapter 19). Such negative consequences of choosing an indicator should be carefully avoided.

Combining several indicators has often worked well to achieve a fairly high level of targeting without resorting to costly means testing. In chapter 3, Atkinson details the vast array of categorical conditions Western social security systems have used to fine-tune the targeting of family benefits—family size, age and activity of children, work profile of parents, and so forth. Appleton and Collier argue for using gender in combination with other indicators (chapter 19). For example, Bangladesh's well-respected Grameen Bank credit scheme screens on the basis of female gender, landlessness, and rural residence.

However, the correlation between popular indicators and poverty is often far from exact. It is important to be aware of the limits of much indicator targeting. Where research efforts have tried to gauge possible impacts on poverty, results call for qualified optimism at best (Ravallion 1993; Ravallion and Sen 1994; Datt and Ravallion 1993). Geographical location and landlessness are two indicators that are typically associated with deprivation. Ravallion (1993) and Datt and Ravallion (1993) turn their attention to the evaluation of geographical targeting through redistributive public transfers to Indonesia's poorest regions and India's poorest states, respectively. When the targeting instrument cannot be sharpened further (as in targeting more finely within regions), the potential poverty impact of even an optimal, administratively costless, allocation of a set budget is found to be very small for both countries. In a similar vein, Ravallion and Sen (1994) simulate the effects of targeting transfers to the landless in Bangladesh with and without effects on productivity. The results indicate that, due to the indicator's bluntness, too many nonpoor would benefit, while many of the poor would be excluded from such a scheme. Poverty would be alleviated, but the maximum impact—even under seemingly ideal conditions—is likely to be small from such indicators.

In some cases, letting the poor select themselves both minimizes targeting costs and results in well-targeted benefit incidence (chapters

13, 15, and 16). Self-targeting schemes are designed such that the poor, and only the poor, wish to participate. They achieve this by imposing a cost of participation that only the poor are willing to incur, as for example, a work requirement in return for low wages. Only individuals who cannot command a better wage will turn up for the scheme. Another example is given by subsidies on lower-quality (real or perceived) goods, which wealthier groups will tend to shun. Although the administrative costs of identifying the poor are avoided, the costs of participation should not be ignored. But there are ways to ensure that they are minimized. A public employment scheme can reduce participation costs by being implemented in an area or time period particularly hard hit by unemployment. Inferior quality should not also mean unnutritional or indigestible.

In general, tacking on a targeted scheme to existing social welfare infrastructure can also minimize administrative costs. Many of the transfer programs reviewed by Grosh in chapter 16 follow this principle. Public health clinics that the rich bypass can be used to provide additional benefits such as food stamps to the persons attending. School lunch and supplementary feeding programs in disadvantaged regions are another example. Attempts at targeting the poor through the public primary education or health care system tend to be more effective when well-developed private systems already serve the rich. This last point is brought out forcefully in the Malaysian health sector case, where, while public sector reforms aimed toward investments in public goods and improvements in equity, the private sector grew both in quality and importance (chapter 18). Design can also improve political sustainability: for example, by promising insurance to a wide set of people and by exploiting the external benefits to the nonpoor from reducing poverty, as in the Maharashtra EGS situation discussed above.

Finally, some schemes successfully blend various design features, including reliance on a combination of targeting mechanisms, to enhance performance. For example, a food stamp program in Honduras bases eligibility on village of residence and being a child under age five or a pregnant/lactating woman (indicator targeting) and use of health services (self-targeting). The scheme piggybacks on existing service delivery infrastructure (health posts) and provides an incentive for vulnerable groups to use primary health care. Some additional interesting examples are presented in chapter 3 in the context of existing and past practice with respect to targeting family benefits in Western high-income economies.

In Conclusion

The case for government spending as a redistributive instrument will depend at least partly on what other instruments are available for this purpose. Although developing countries tend to have quite limited opportunities for redistributive direct taxation, even when a country can implement an optimal nonlinear income tax, there can still be an important redistributive role for public spending (Boadway and Marchand 1995).

Public spending is a potentially powerful instrument for fighting poverty. How well does it perform in this capacity? How can it have greater impact on poverty? These are the broad questions with which this book has been concerned.

We must first be clear on how performance is to be judged. Disparate assumptions about policy objectives are often at the root of disagreements and controversies in program assessments and recommendations. Agreeing on the relevance of the welfare objective is easier than reaching consensus on what precisely it should be—the gulf between welfarists and nonwelfarists and the camps within each paradigm may never be fully bridged. That need not derail assessments of public spending programs and efforts at reform. But it should alert us to the need for clarity in the underlying assumptions and attentiveness to how these may influence policy conclusions.

Evaluating a policy's impact requires assessing how different the situation would have been in its absence. However, the counterfactual of no intervention is tricky to quantify precisely. One approach—known as benefit incidence—ignores behavioral responses and second-round effects and simply uses the cost of provision as a proxy for benefits received. Other methods focus entirely on the individual's valuation of the policy benefits allowing for responses to changes in the individual's budget set. Recent studies attempt to incorporate behavioral responses into incidence assessments. However, allowing for behavioral responses in policy analysis often requires that other assumptions be introduced. It would be premature at this time to assume that more complicated methodologies necessarily result in better and/or essentially different policy advice.

The search for answers is also constrained by less than ideal data. In several areas known to be potentially critical to policy conclusions—such as dynamic issues in public spending incidence and intrahousehold distribution—adequate data are only now starting to be collected. Economists have also tended to give scant attention to the macroeconomic, political economy, and institutional environments. There is ample evidence that these influence spending decisions and outcomes.

Some reasonably robust conclusions have emerged from studies of public spending incidence, including some in this volume. Spending on *basic* services—notably primary and secondary education and basic health care—is found to reach the poor almost universally. The case for "broad targeting" by expanding the share of public spending on these services is well substantiated. Yet even here, care is required in monitoring that marginal investments are not lavished on increased quality for the better-off. Certain food subsidy and distribution schemes, social cash transfers (such as are common in the former U.S.S.R. countries and Eastern Europe), public employment schemes, and other targeted transfer schemes have at times been quite pro-poor. However, many programs whose stated rationale is to reduce poverty have instead been dismal and expensive failures. A popular reaction has been to clamor for reforms of public spending toward finer targeting of benefits to the poor.

Most public spending programs are to some degree "targeted." The key question is, What *degree* of targeting is optimal? Other things being equal, the more ways one discriminates between beneficiaries, the greater the impact of targeting on poverty. However, other things are not equal. Fine targeting sometimes comes at a cost to the poor. Administrative costs may escalate, political support may vanish, and behavioral responses may create extra costs to targeted interventions. There is no simple answer to how much targeting is desirable, but there are some clear principles to guide choice and some suggestive empirical evidence from past experience, including many of the studies in this volume.

The optimal mix of targeted and universal programs in fighting poverty depends on a number of factors, including the characteristics of the poor (who the poor are, how many there are, and why they are poor) and country-specific circumstances (initial conditions, infrastructure development, and administrative capabilities). When poverty is widespread and administrative capacities are low, broad targeting is particularly desirable, and results from incidence of public spending studies should help to guide sectoral and intrasectoral allocations. In general, what is needed is a combination of universalism in certain categories of spending and finer targeting in others, such as in providing safety nets. Such a two-pronged approach is a sound starting point for policy design. In implementing it, one should, however, never confuse the ends and the means of policy. Targeting should be seen as a potential instrument, never as an objective in its own right.

Note

1. From Sahn and Alderman's study, it is not clear how the released work time is allocated. One would first have to ascertain whether leisure has indeed increased. Whether the poor's leisure increases more than the rich's would also be germane. Other issues arise. Parents may be devoting more time to their children, in which case there may also be important externalities to take into account.

References

Anand, Sudhir, and Martin Ravallion. 1993. "Human Development in Poor Countries: On the Role of Private Incomes and Public Services." *Journal of Economic Perspectives* 7: 133–50.

Besley, Timothy. 1990. "Means Testing Versus Universal Provision in Poverty Alleviation." *Economica* 57: 119–29.

Besley, Timothy, and Ravi Kanbur. 1993. "Principles of Targeting." In Michael Lipton and Jacques van der Gaag, eds., *Including the Poor*. Washington, D.C.: World Bank.

Binswanger, Hans, Shahidur Khandker, and Mark Rosenzweig. 1993. "How Infrastructure and Financial Institutions Affect Agricultural Output and Investment in India." *Journal of Development Economics* 41: 337–66.

Birdsall, Nancy, and Estelle James. 1993. "Efficiency and Equity in Social Spending: How and Why Governments Misbehave." In Michael Lipton and Jacques van der Gaag, eds., *Including the Poor*. Washington, D.C.: World Bank.

Boadway, Robin, and Maurice Marchand. 1995. "The Use of Public Expenditures for Redistributive Purposes." *Oxford Economic Papers* 47: 45–59.

Browning, Martin. 1992. "Children and Household Behavior." *Journal of Economic Literature* 30: 1434–75.

Cornes, Richard. 1992. *Duality and Modern Economics*. New York: Cambridge University Press.

Cox, Donald, and Emmanuel Jimenez. 1992. "Social Security and Private Transfers in Peru." *World Bank Economic Review* 6 (1): 155–69.

Datt, Gaurav, and Martin Ravallion. 1993. "Regional Disparities, Targeting, and Poverty in India." In Michael Lipton and Jacques van der Gaag, eds., *Including the Poor*. Washington, D.C.: World Bank.

Deaton, Angus, and John Muellbauer. 1986. "On Measuring Child Costs: With Application to Poor Countries." *Journal of Political Economy* 94: 720–44.

Echeverri-Gent, John. 1988. "Guaranteed Employment in an Indian State: The Maharashtra Experience." *Asian Survey* 28: 1294–310.

Gertler, Paul, and Paul Glewwe. 1989. "The Willingness to Pay for Education in Developing Countries." Living Standards Measurement Study Working Paper 54. World Bank, Washington, D.C.

Gertler, Paul, Luis Locay, and Warren Sanderson. 1987. "Are User Fees Regressive? The Welfare Implications of Health Care Financing Proposals in Peru." *Journal of Econometrics* 33: 67–88.

Gertler, Paul, and Jacques van der Gaag. 1990. *The Willingness to Pay for Medical Care: Evidence from Two Developing Countries*. Baltimore, Md.: Johns Hopkins University Press for the World Bank.

Haddad, Lawrence, and Ravi Kanbur. 1990. "How Serious Is the Neglect of Intra-Household Inequality?" *Economic Journal* 100: 866–81.

———. 1993. "Is There an Intra-Household Kuznets Curve? Some Evidence for the Philippines." *Public Finance* 47 (supplement): 77–93.

Kesselman, J. R. 1982. "Taxation Behavior and the Design of a Credit Income Tax." In I. Garfinkel, ed., *Income-Tested Programs: The Case For and Against*. New York: Academic Press.

King, Mervyn. 1983. "Welfare Analysis of Tax Reforms Using Household Level Data." *Journal of Public Economics* 21: 183–214.

Lal, Deepak. 1994. "Labor Market Insurance and Social Safety Nets." HROWP 41. World Bank, Human Resources Development and Operations Policy Department, Washington, D.C.

Lanjouw, Peter, and Martin Ravallion. 1995. "Poverty and Household Size." *Economic Journal* 105 (November).

Lipton, Michael, and Martin Ravallion. 1995. "Poverty and Policy." In Jere R. Behrman and T. N. Srinivasan, eds., *Handbook of Development Economics*, vol. 3. Amsterdam: North-Holland.

Litvack, Jennie, and Claude Bodart. 1993. "User Fees Plus Quality Equals Improved Access to Health Care: Results of a Field Experiment in Cameroon." *Social Science and Medicine* 37 (3): 369–83.

McKenzie, George W. 1983. *Measuring Economic Welfare: New Methods.* Cambridge, Eng.: Cambridge University Press.

Meerman, Jacob. 1979. *Public Expenditure in Malaysia: Who Benefits and Why.* New York: Oxford University Press.

Nelson, Joan. 1992. "Poverty, Equity, and the Politics of Adjustment." In Stephan Haggard and Robert Kaufman, eds., *The Politics of Economic Adjustment: International Constraints, Distributive Conflicts, and the State.* Princeton, N.J.: Princeton University Press.

Pollak, Robert A. 1991. "Welfare Comparisons and Situation Comparisons." *Journal of Econometrics* 50: 31–48.

Ravallion, Martin. 1991. "Reaching the Rural Poor through Public Employment: Arguments, Experience, and Lessons from South Asia." *World Bank Research Observer* 6: 153–75.

———. 1993. "Poverty Alleviation through Regional Targeting: A Case Study for Indonesia." In Karla Hoff, Avishay Braverman, and Joseph Stiglitz, eds., *The Economics of Rural Organization: Theory, Practice and Policy.* New York: Oxford University Press for the World Bank.

———. 1994. *Poverty Comparisons.* Fundamentals of Pure and Applied Economics, vol. 56. Chur, Switzerland: Harwood Academic Publishers.

Ravallion, Martin, and Binayek Sen. 1994. "Impacts of Land-Based Targeting on Rural Poverty." *World Development* 22 (6): 823–38.

Ravallion, Martin, Dominique van de Walle, and Madhur Gautam. 1995. "Testing a Social Safety Net." *Journal of Public Economics* 57 (2): 175–99.

Rosenzweig, Mark, and Kenneth Wolpin. 1986. "Evaluating the Effects of Optimally Distributed Public Programs: Child Health and Family Planning Interventions." *American Economic Review* 76: 470–82.

Selden, Thomas, and Michael Wasylenko. 1992. "Benefit Incidence Analysis in Developing Countries." WPS 1015. World Bank, Country Economics Department, Washington, D.C.

Selowsky, Marcello. 1979. *Who Benefits from Government Expenditures? A Case Study of Colombia.* New York: Oxford University Press.

Sen, Amartya. 1979. "Personal Utilities and Public Judgements: Or What's Wrong with Welfare Economics?" *Economic Journal* 89: 537–58.

————. 1985. *Commodities and Capabilities*. Amsterdam: North-Holland.

Skocpol, Theda. 1991. *Protecting Soldiers and Mothers: The Politics of Social Provision in the United States, 1870–1920*. Cambridge, Mass.: Harvard University Press.

van de Walle, Dominique, Martin Ravallion, and Madhur Gautam. 1994. *How Well Does the Social Safety Net Work? The Incidence of Cash Benefits in Hungary 1987–89*. Living Standards Measurement Study Working Paper 102. Washington, D.C.: World Bank.

World Bank. 1990. *World Development Report 1990: Poverty*. New York: Oxford University Press.